STUDENT VALUE EDITION

DAVID M. KROENKE

Using MIS

2014

3D Printing

The Cloud

BigData

BYOD

SOA / Web Services

BPM

7E

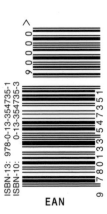

ISBN-13: 978-0-13-354735-1
ISBN-10: 0-13-354735-3

EAN

Before purchasing this text, please be sure this is the correct book for your course. Once this package has been opened, you may not be able to return it to your bookstore.

ALWAYS LEARNING

PEARSON

Dear Student,

You are about to embark on the study of one of the most important subjects in your college career. In fact, Chapter 1 argues that it is the most important course you will take. Why? Because in modern business, knowledge of information systems is key to obtaining and succeeding in interesting and rewarding professional jobs.

Like all college students, you have many claims on your time: friends, family, sports, hobbies, love life, whatever, but you owe it to your future to seriously consider how you want to spend the bulk of your waking hours for the next 30 to 40 years. You want a job that you find so satisfying that you can hardly wait to get to work in the morning. Believe it or not, there are such jobs, and there is one for you. But that kind of job won't be handed to you at graduation. You have to prepare for it, find it, and obtain it in an intensely competitive job market; then you have to know enough to be able to thrive in that job.

This course is key to that endeavor because information systems are the major influence on the modern economy, and that influence has not been beneficial for everyone. Bank lobbies were once filled with bookkeepers, accountants, and accounting managers. Those jobs disappeared with computer systems. Half-asleep, mediocre business school graduates once managed rooms full of typists and clerical workers. Those jobs disappeared as attorneys, auditors, and other business professionals began conducting their own correspondence using email, text, and videoconferencing.

The trick to turning information systems to your advantage is getting ahead of their effect. During your career, you will find many opportunities for the innovative application of information systems in business and government, but only if you know how to look for them. Once found, those opportunities become your opportunities when you—as a skilled, non-routine problem solver—apply emerging technology to facilitate your organization's strategy. This is true whether your job is in marketing, operations, sales, accounting, finance, entrepreneurship, or another discipline.

Congratulations on your decisions so far. Congratulations on deciding to go to college, and congratulations on deciding to study business. Now, double down on those good decisions and use this course to help you obtain and then thrive in an interesting and rewarding career. Start in Chapter 1 by learning how Jennifer lost her job and what you can do to ensure that you are never in her shoes! After that, learn more than just the MIS terminology; understand the ways information systems are transforming business and the many, many ways you can participate in that transformation.

In this endeavor, I wish you, a future business professional, the very best success!

David Kroenke
Whidbey Island, WA

Why This Seventh Edition?

The changes in this seventh edition are listed in Table 1. Chapters 1 through 6 begin with a new discussion of AllRoad Parts, an online vendor of off-road parts that is considering 3D printing and ultimately rejects that idea because of the effect it would have on business processes and IS. Instead, the company offers 3D printing designs as a product as revealed in Chapters 1 through 6. Because of the importance of mobility and the cloud, Chapters 7 through 12 continue to be introduced with PRIDE, an information system that uses cloud technology and a wide array of mobile devices to integrate patient exercise data with healthcare providers, health clubs, insurance agencies, and employers. In addition to motivating the chapter material, both case scenarios provide numerous opportunities for students to practice one of Chapter 1's key skills: "Assess, evaluate, and apply emerging technology to business."

A second broad change in this seventh edition concerns the teaching of ethics. In this edition, every Ethics Guide asks students to apply Immanuel Kant's categorical imperative, utilitarianism, or both to the business situation described in the guide. I hope you find the ethical considerations richer and deeper with these exercises. The categorical imperative is introduced in the Ethics Guide in Chapter 1 (pages 20–21) and utilitarianism is introduced in the Ethics Guide in Chapter 2 (pages 56–57).

As shown in Table 1, some sort of change was made to every chapter. Major changes include using the collaboration IS from Chapter 2 to make the notion of IS more personal to students. Chapter 4 includes recent developments in operating systems and a reduced emphasis on Microsoft. See in particular Chapter 4's 2024 discussion (page 144).

The biggest change has been the major rewrite of Chapter 6 to focus entirely on the cloud. Data communications technology is presented only in its role as supporting the cloud. I've increased coverage of SOA and provided more material on Web services that is used in subsequent chapters.

Numerous changes are made throughout the chapters in an attempt to keep them up to date. Events move fast, and to keep the text current, we check every sentence and industry reference for obsolescence. For example, the sixth edition's glorification of Apple's success in Chapter 4 needed to be softened given Apple's recent experience. The excitement about Microsoft Surface that was prevalent when I wrote the sixth edition had to be placed into context of Surface's mediocre success. Meanwhile, 3D printing is hot, and I wanted to give students an opportunity to consider its effect on processes and IS in the AllRoad scenarios.

TABLE 1 CHANGES IN THE SEVENTH EDITION

Chapter	Change
1–6	New AllRoad Parts case vignettes introduce chapters and are integrated throughout.
all	Categorical imperative and utilitarianism used in Ethics Guides.
1	New employment data; update job requirements from MIT study.
2	Update terms, especially Microsoft's new definition of *Office 365*.
2	Reduce Microsoft emphasis. Illustrate use of Google Drive. Incorporate product changes since sixth edition. Introduce LibreOffice and thin-client Office alternatives.
2	Sharpen the discussion to use collaboration IS to enforce IS concepts (Q4 and Q8). New collaboration case to enable students to practice creating a collaboration IS.
3	Work AllRoad Parts into competitive strategy. Adjust Yikes! Bikes! Ethics Guide. Adapt Case 3 for AllRoad Parts.
3	Add new theme to 2024 discussion.
4	Work AllRoad Parts into hardware/software discussion. Reduce Microsoft presence. Discuss flop of Win 8 RT, problems in Win 8 and Surface Pro.
4	New Ethics Guide replaces Churn and Burn.
4	Update and adapt InClass Exercise.
4	Emphasize importance of JavaScript and recognize it as an object-oriented language.
4	Rewrite 2024? to consider the death of the PC; pick Amazon as the ultimate winner.
5	Use AllRoad Parts to set up the need for database knowledge.
5	New Ethics Guide addresses corporate social responsibility.
5	Replace Q4 with a more modern thin-client database application. Introduce Node.js and other server-side concepts used in new Chapter 6.
5	Update 2024? to use term *nonrelational DBMS;* introduce MongoDB as well as NoSQL products.
6	Entirely rewritten to focus on the cloud. Incorporate AllRoad Parts' use of the cloud.
6	Rewrite data communications technology as support for the cloud.
6	Enlarge discussion of SOA and Web services.
6	Discuss how organizations, including AllRoad, can use the cloud and cloud services like SaaS, PaaS, IaaS, and CDN.
6	New Ethics Guide on a partnership's use of excess profits.
6	New end-of-chapter case addresses FinQloud.
7	New InClass Exercise; former exercise moved to Chapter 12.
7	Update chapter to take advantage of SOA and related new content in Chapter 6.
8	New InClass Exercise on Salesforce.com's Chatter. GE jet engines as social network participants?
8	New Guide discusses use of social media for developing a personal brand.
8	Update discussion of Web revenue to remove fear of revenue loss due to use of mobile devices.
9	New examples in Q1.
9	Change illustrative case to use the simpler, easier-to-teach AllRoad business model (Q2).
9	New Ethics Guide concerning data aggregators.
10	Move sixth edition Chapter 7 InClass Exercise to Chapter 10 where it is a better fit.
10	Update Ethics Guide.
11	Update Ethics Guide.
12	Update computer crime statistics.
12	New collaboration exercise to investigate the cost of computer crime.
12	New case introduces FIDO as a replacement for current use of passwords.
International Dimension	Include Ghemawat's "Why the World Isn't Flat" data. Modernize discussion of hardware and distributed databases to utilize cloud terms.

The Guides

Each chapter includes three unique **guides** that focus on current issues in information systems. In each chapter, one of the guides focuses on an ethical issue in business, and the second focuses on security. The third guide addresses the application of the chapter's contents to some other dimension of business. The content of each guide is designed to stimulate thought, discussion, and active participation in order to help *you* develop your problem-solving skills and become a better business professional.

Learning Aids for Students

We have structured this book so you can maximize the benefit from the time you spend reading it. As shown in the following table, each chapter includes various learning aids to help you succeed in this course.

Resource	Description	Benefit	Example
Guides	Each chapter includes three guides that focus on current issues in information systems. One addresses ethics, one addresses security, and the third addresses other business topics.	Stimulate thought and discussion. Address ethics and security once per chapter. Help develop your problem-solving skills.	"Social Recruiting," p. 314
Chapter Introduction Business Example	Each chapter begins with a description of a business situation that motivates the need for the chapter's contents. We focus on two different businesses over the course of the text: AllRoad Parts, an online vendor of off-road vehicle parts, and PRIDE, a cloud-based, healthcare start-up opportunity.	Understand the relevance of the chapter's content by applying it to a business situation.	Chapter 1, "Fired?," p. 3; Chapter 7, "Every morning I get a report about the exercise your mother's getting so I can see how she's doing," p. 242
Query-Based Chapter Format	Each chapter starts with a list of questions, and each major heading is a question. The Active Review contains tasks for you to perform in order to demonstrate your ability to answer the questions.	Use the questions to manage your time, guide your study, and review for exams.	Chapter 6, starting on p. 199 with "Q1 Why Is the Cloud the Future for Most Organizations?"
Using MIS InClass	Each chapter of this text includes an exercise called "Using MIS InClass." This feature contains exercises, projects, and questions for you and a group of your fellow students to perform in class. Some of these exercises can be done in a single class period; others span several class sections with out-of-class activities in between.	Understand how the material in the chapter applies to everyday situations.	Using MIS InClass 4, "Place Your Bets Now" on the tablet marketing race, p. 124
2024?	Each chapter concludes with a discussion of how the concepts, technology, and systems described in that chapter might change by 2024.	Learn to anticipate changes in technology and recognize how those changes may impact the future business environment.	Chapter 4, "The PC Is Dead, So What?," p. 144; Chapter 7, "Mobile Devices Meet SAP," p. 269

Resource	Description	Benefit	Example
Active Review	This review provides a set of activities for you to perform in order to demonstrate your ability to answer the primary questions addressed by the chapter.	After reading the chapter, use the Active Review to check your comprehension. Use for class and exam preparation.	Chapter 2, Active Review, p. 72
Using Your Knowledge	These exercises ask you to take your new knowledge one step further by applying it to a practice problem.	Test your critical-thinking skills.	Chapter 3, Questions 3-1 through 3-3, p. 105
Collaboration Exercises	These exercises and cases ask you to collaborate with a group of fellow students, using collaboration tools introduced in Chapter 2.	Practice working with colleagues toward a stated goal.	Chapter 2, Construct a collaboration IS, p. 74
Case Studies	Each chapter includes a case study at the end.	Apply newly acquired knowledge to real-world situations.	Case Study 3, "Fulfillment by Amazon (FBA)," p. 106; Case Study 9, "Hadoop the Cookie Cutter," p. 369
Application Exercises	These exercises ask you to solve situations using spreadsheet (Excel) or database (Access) applications.	Develop your computer skills.	Exercise 1-1, p. 506; Exercise 7-1, p. 515
International Dimension	Module at the end of the text that discusses international aspects of MIS. Includes the importance of international IS, the localization of system components, the roles of functional and cross-functional systems, international applications, supply chain management, and challenges of international systems development.	Understand the international implications and applications of the chapters' content.	p. 489

Using MIS

David M. Kroenke

SEVENTH EDITION

PEARSON

Boston   Columbus   Indianapolis   New York   San Francisco   Upper Saddle River
Amsterdam   Cape Town   Dubai   London   Madrid   Milan   Munich   Paris   Montréal   Toronto
Delhi   Mexico City   São Paulo   Sydney   Hong Kong   Seoul   Singapore   Taipei   Tokyo

Dedicated to CJ, Carter, and Charlotte

Editor-in-Chief: Stephanie Wall
Executive Editor: Bob Horan
Development Editor: Laura Town
Program Manager Team Lead: Ashley Santora
Program Manager: Denise Vaughn
Editorial Assistant: Kaylee Rotella
Director of Marketing: Maggie Moylan
Executive Marketing Manager: Anne Fahlgren
Project Manager Team Lead: Judy Leale
Project Manager: Jane Bonnell
Operations Specialist: Michelle Klein
Creative Director: Blair Brown
Senior Art Director: Janet Slowik
Interior and Cover Designer: Karen Quigley

Interior Illustrations: Simon Alicea
Cover Photos: Elegant wave: Zeed/Shutterstock; sprocket: Lori Druzhynets/Photos.com
VP, Director of Digital Strategy & Assessment: Paul Gentile
Digital Editor: Brian Surette
Digital Development Manager: Robin Lazrus
Senior Digital Project Manager: Alana Coles
MyLab Product Manager: Joan Waxman
Digital Production Project Manager: Lisa Rinaldi
Full-Service Project Management and Composition: Integra
Printer/Binder: Courier/Kendallville
Cover Printer: Lehigh-Phoenix Color/Hagerstown
Text Font: 9.5/13 Utopia

Credits and acknowledgments borrowed from other sources and reproduced, with permission, in this textbook appear on the appropriate page within text.

Many of the designations by manufacturers and sellers to distinguish their products are claimed as trademarks. Where those designations appear in this book, and the publisher was aware of a trademark claim, the designations have been printed in initial caps or all caps.

Library of Congress Cataloging-in-Publication Data

Kroenke, David M.
    Using MIS / David M. Kroenke.—Seventh edition.
       pages cm
    Includes index.
    ISBN 978-0-13-354643-9
    1. Management information systems.   I. Title.
    HD30.213.K76 2015
    658.4'038011—dc23
                          2013035311

10 9 8 7 6 5 4 3 2
V011

ISBN 10:   0-13-354643-8
ISBN 13: 978-0-13-354643-9

Brief Contents

Describes how this course teaches four key skills for business professionals. Defines *MIS, information systems,* and *information.*

Describes characteristics, criteria for success, and the primary purposes of collaboration.

Discusses components of collaboration IS and describes collaboration for communication and content sharing. Illustrates use of Google Drive, SharePoint, and other collaboration tools.

Describes reasons why organizations create and use information systems: to gain competitive advantage, to solve problems, and to support decisions.

Describes the manager's essentials of hardware and software technology. Discusses mobile device operating systems, mobile USX, and BYOD policies.

Explores database fundamentals, applications, modeling, and design. Discusses the entity-relationship model. Explains the role of Access and enterprise DBMS products. Defines BigData and describes nonrelational and NoSQL databases.

Explains why the cloud is the future. Describes basic network technology that underlies the cloud, how the cloud works, and how organizations, including AllRoad Parts, can use the cloud. Explains SOA and summarizes fundamental Web services standards.

Discusses workgroup, enterprise, and inter-enterprise IS. Describes problems of information silos and cross-organizational solutions. Presents CRM, ERP, and EAI. Discusses ERP vendors and implementation challenges.

Describes components of social media IS (SMIS) and explains how SMIS can contribute to organizational strategy. Discusses the theory of social capital and the role of SMIS in the hyper-social organization. Explains the ways organizations manage the risks of SMIS.

Describes business intelligence and knowledge management, including reporting systems, data mining, and social media–based knowledge management systems.

Discusses the need for BPM and the BPM process. Introduces BPMN. Differentiates between processes and information systems. Presents SDLC stages. Describes agile technologies and scrum and discusses their advantages over the SDLC.

Describes the role, structure, and function of the IS department; the role of the CIO and CTO; outsourcing; and related topics.

Describes organizational response to information security: security threats, policy, and safeguards.

CONTENTS

2: COLLABORATION INFORMATION SYSTEMS   35

3: STRATEGY AND INFORMATION SYSTEMS   81

Part 2: Information Technology   109

4: HARDWARE, SOFTWARE, AND MOBILE SYSTEMS   111

5: DATABASE PROCESSING   157

6: THE CLOUD   197

Part 3: Using IS for Competitive Advantage   239

7: PROCESSES, ORGANIZATIONS, AND INFORMATION SYSTEMS   241

Part 4: Information Systems Management 373

10: DEVELOPMENT PROCESSES 375

11: INFORMATION SYSTEMS MANAGEMENT 423

12: INFORMATION SECURITY MANAGEMENT 451

David Kroenke has many years of teaching experience at Colorado State University, Seattle University, and the University of Washington. He has led dozens of seminars for college professors on the teaching of information systems and technology; in 1991, the International Association of Information Systems named him Computer Educator of the Year. In 2009, David was named Educator of the Year by the Association of Information Technology Professionals-Education Special Interest Group (AITP-EDSIG).

David worked for the U.S. Air Force and Boeing Computer Services. He was a principal in the startup of three companies, serving as the vice president of product marketing and development for the Microrim Corporation and as chief of database technologies for Wall Data, Inc. He is the father of the semantic object data model. David's consulting clients have included IBM, Microsoft, and Computer Sciences Corporations, as well as numerous smaller companies. Recently, David has focused on using information systems for teaching collaboration and teamwork.

His text *Database Processing* was first published in 1977 and is now in its 13th edition. He has authored and coauthored many other textbooks, including *Database Concepts*, 6th ed. (2013), *Experiencing MIS*, 5th ed. (2015), *MIS Essentials*, 4th ed. (2015), *SharePoint for Students* (2012), *Office 365 in Business* (2012), and *Processes, Systems, and Information: An Introduction to MIS*, 2nd ed. (2015). David lives on Whidbey Island, Washington, and has two children and three grandchildren. He enjoys woodworking, making both furniture and small sailboats.

PART 1

Why MIS?

AllRoad Parts is a 10-year-old, privately owned company that sells parts for adventure vehicles. Its products include specialized brakes and suspension systems for mountain bikes and suspensions and off-road gear for dirt bikes (motorcycles designed for use in rough terrain), and it has recently started selling bumpers, doors, and soft tops for Jeeps and other off-road, 4-wheel-drive vehicles. Two-thirds of the company's sales are to small businesses like bike shops, motorcycle specialty stores, and off-road customization businesses. The other third are direct sales to consumers.

Jason Green is AllRoad's founder and CEO. Jason has always had a strong interest in off-road vehicles; as a teenager he rebuilt a Volkswagen in his parents' garage for off-road use. In college, he started mountain biking and competitively raced cross-country, winning several regional contests and finishing near the top in the world championships in Purgatory, Colorado. He knew that a big part of his success was his innovative, high-quality equipment. In his senior year of college, he started a part-time, profitable eBay business buying and selling hard-to-find mountain bike parts.

Jason was a strong believer in (and customer of) Fox mountain bike racing parts (*www.RideFox.com*), and through contacts made at one of the championship events, he obtained a marketing job at Fox. Part of his job was road testing new equipment, a task he loved. Jason worked at Fox for five years, gaining marketing and management experience. However, he never forgot the success he had selling parts himself on eBay and was convinced he could start a parts business on his own. In 2003, he left Fox to start AllRoad Parts.

Today, AllRoad sells nearly $20 million in bike, motorcycle, and 4-wheel parts for adventure riding. Jason no longer uses eBay, but true to his vision, the bulk of AllRoad's revenue is earned via online sales.

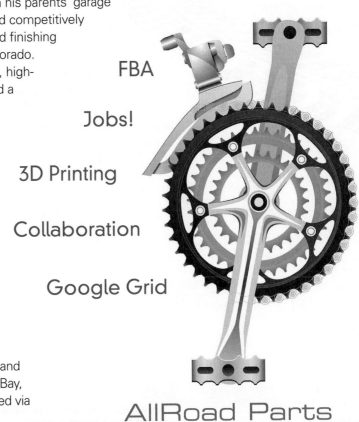

FBA

Jobs!

3D Printing

Collaboration

Google Grid

AllRoad Parts

In addition to selling high-end, expensive parts obtained from Fox and other manufacturers, AllRoad also sells a line of specialized, hard-to-find repair parts. These parts have high margins, but those margins are reduced by the cost of the large inventory AllRoad must carry. Jason knows his inventory is expensive, but he views having a large selection of repair parts as key to AllRoad's competitive success. "People know they will find that rare, 10 mm stainless steel Nylex cap on our site. Sure, it sells for maybe a dollar, but once we get people on our site, we have a chance to sell them a $2,000 suspension system as well. We don't sell one every day, but it does happen. Our huge parts selection is strong bait to our customers, and I'm not going to cut back on it."

At a recent manufacturer's trade show, Jason saw a demonstration of 3D printing, which is the process of creating three-dimensional objects by fusing two-dimensional layers of plastic, metal, and other substances on top of one another. Because 3D printing has very small machine setup costs, it can be used to economically produce single-unit quantities. It also enables anyone who can afford a 3D printer to become a manufacturer.[1]

AllRoad hasn't used 3D printing yet, and Jason's not sure that it makes sense for the company. Still, he knows that if AllRoad could manufacture very small quantities, even single units, of some of the more specialized parts, it could substantially reduce inventory costs. But he has so many questions: Is 3D printing technology real? Does it produce quality products? How can past sales be analyzed to determine how much the company might save? Which parts should AllRoad manufacture and which should it continue to buy? How much will it cost for equipment and information systems to support 3D printing? How can AllRoad integrate in-house manufacturing into its existing purchasing and sales information systems?

Jason doesn't know the answers to these questions, but he doesn't want to wait for AllRoad's competition to show him the way. So, he forms a project team to investigate. He asks Kelly Summers, AllRoad's CFO, to lead a team to assess the opportunity. Kelly asks Lucas Massey, the director of IT services, Drew Mills, the Operations Manager, and Addison Lee, head of Purchasing, to participate. Kelly also includes Jennifer Cooper, a relatively new employee about whom she's received a number of complaints. "I'll work closely with her to learn what she can do," Kelly says to herself.

---

[1] **3D printing**, also known as **additive manufacturing**, is fascinating. If you haven't yet seen it in action, search the Internet for *3D printing examples*.

The Importance of MIS

"Fired? You're firing me?"

"Well, *fired* is a harsh word, but…well, AllRoad has no further need for your services."

"But, Kelly, I don't get it. I really don't. I worked hard, and I did everything you told me to do."

"Jennifer, that's just it. You did everything *I* told you to do."

"I put in so many hours. How could you fire me?"

"Your job was to find ways to reduce our inventory costs using 3D printing."

"Right! And I did that."

"No, you didn't. You followed up on ideas *that I gave you*. But we don't need someone who can follow up on my plans. We need someone who can figure out what we need to do, create her own plans, and bring them back to me…and others."

"How could you expect me to do that? I've only been here 6 months!"

"It's called teamwork. Sure, you're just learning our business, but I made sure all of our senior staff would be available to you…"

"I didn't want to bother them."

"Well, you succeeded. I asked Drew what he thought of the plans you're working on. 'Who's Jennifer?' he asked."

"But doesn't he work down at the warehouse?"

"Right. He's the operations manager…and it would seem to be worth talking to him."

"I'll go do that!"

"Jennifer, do you see what just happened? I gave you an idea, and you said you'd do it. That's not what I need. I need you to find solutions on your own."

"I worked really hard. I put in a lot of hours. I've got all these reports written."

"Has anyone seen them?"

"I talked to you about some of them. But I was waiting until I was satisfied with them."

"Right. That's not how we do things here. We develop ideas and then kick them around with each other. Nobody has all the smarts. Our plans get better when we comment and rework them…I think I told you that."

"But today, they're not enough."

"Maybe you did. But I'm just not comfortable with that."

"Well, it's a key skill here."

"I know I can do this job."

"Jennifer, you've been here almost 6 months; you have a degree in business. Several weeks ago, I asked you to conceptualize a way to determine the products for 3D printing. When I asked you how you were doing, do you remember what you said?"

"Yes, I wasn't sure how to proceed. I didn't want to just throw something out that might not work."

"But how would you find out if it would work?"

"I don't want to waste money..."

"No, you don't. So, when you didn't get very far with that task, I backed up and asked you to send me a diagram of our supply chain...how we select the vendors, how we negotiate with them, how we order, receive the goods in our inventory, track sales, and reorder, and so on. Not details, just the overview."

"Yes, I sent you that diagram."

"Jennifer, it made no sense. Your diagram had us placing goods in inventory before we'd even ordered them."

"I know that process, I just couldn't put it down on paper. But I'll try again!"

"Well, I appreciate that attitude, but we're a small company—really, still a startup. Everyone needs to pull more than their own weight here. Maybe if we were a bigger company, I'd be able to find for a spot for you, see if we could bring you along. But we can't afford to do that now."

"What about my references?"

"I'll be happy to tell anyone that you're reliable, that you work 40 to 45 hours a week, and that you're honest and have integrity."

"Those are important!"

"Yes, they are. But today, they're not enough."

STUDY QUESTIONS

Q1 Why is Introduction to MIS the most important class in the business school?

Q2 What is MIS?

Q3 How can you use the five-component model?

Q4 Why is the difference between information technology and information systems important?

Q5 What is information?

Q6 What are necessary data characteristics?

Q7 2024?

"But today, they're not enough."

Do you find that statement sobering? And if hard work isn't enough, what is? We'll begin this book by discussing the key skills that Jennifer (and you) need and explaining why this course is the single best course in all of the business school for teaching you those key skills.

You may find that last statement surprising. If you are like most students, you have no clear idea of what your MIS class will be about. If someone were to ask you, "What do you study in that class?" you might respond that the class has something to do with computers and maybe computer programming. Beyond that, you might be hard-pressed to say more. You might add, "Well, it has something to do with computers in business," or maybe, "We are going to learn to solve business problems with computers using spreadsheets and other programs." So, how could this course be the most important one in the business school?

We begin with that question. After you understand how important this class will be to your career, we will discuss fundamental concepts. We'll wrap up with some practice on one of the key skills you need to learn.

Q1 Why Is Introduction to MIS the Most Important Class in the Business School?

Introduction to MIS is the most important class in the business school. That statement was not true in 2005, and it may not be true in 2020. But it is true in 2014.

Why?

The ultimate reason lies in a principle known as **Moore's Law**. In 1965, Gordon Moore, cofounder of Intel Corporation, stated that because of technology improvements in electronic chip design and manufacturing, "The number of transistors per square inch on an integrated chip doubles every 18 months." His statement has been commonly misunderstood to be, "The speed of a computer doubles every 18 months," which is incorrect but captures the sense of his principle.

Because of Moore's Law, the ratio of price to performance of computers has fallen from something like $4,000 for a standard computing device to a fraction of a penny for that same computing device.[2] See Figure 1-1.

As a future business professional, however, you needn't care how fast of a computer your company can buy for $100. That's not the point. Here's the point:

> **Because of Moore's Law, the cost of data processing, communications, and storage is essentially zero.**

---

[2]These figures represent the cost of 100,000 transistors, which can roughly be translated into a unit of a computing device. If you doubt any of this, just look at your $199 Kindle Fire and realize that you pay nothing for its wireless access. Geoff Colvin claims the cost of 125,000 transistors is less than the cost of a grain of rice. See: *http://chowtimes.com/2010/09/11/food-for-though/food-for-thought/*.

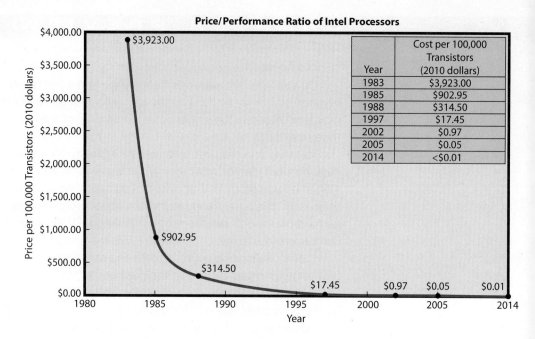

Figure 1-1
Computer Price/Performance
Ratio Decreases

Think about that statement before you hurry to the next paragraph. What happens when those costs are essentially zero? Here are some consequences:

- YouTube
- Facebook
- Pandora
- LinkedIn
- Pinterest
- Woot
- Twitter
- Foursquare

None of these companies was prominent in 2005, and, in fact, most didn't exist in 2005.

What Are Cost-Effective Business Applications of Facebook or Twitter, or Whatever Else Will Soon Appear?

Social networking is the rage. Go to any Web page and you'll find the Facebook "Like" and the Twitter "Follow" buttons. The question is, are these applications cost-effective? Do they generate revenue worth the time and expense of running them? Someone needs to be examining that question, and that person works in marketing…not in a technical field. We'll examine this question in more depth in Chapter 8. For now, think about the first businesses that saw the potential of Facebook and Twitter. They gained a competitive advantage by being ahead of the crowd in adopting these new technologies.

It's not over. Facebook and Twitter are not the end. Right now, AllRoad Parts and PRIDE (an application you'll study in Chapters 7–12) are employing new processing capabilities called *the cloud* in innovative ways…using technology and techniques that have never been seen before. All of this leads us to the first reason Introduction to MIS is the most important course in the business school today:

> **Future business professionals need to be able to assess, evaluate, and apply emerging information technology to business.**

You need the knowledge of this course to attain that skill.

How Can I Attain Job Security?

Many years ago I had a wise and experienced mentor. One day I asked him about job security, and he told me that the only job security that exists is "a marketable skill and the courage to use it." He continued, "There is no security in our company, there is no security in any government program, there is no security in your investments, and there is no security in Social Security." Alas, how right he turned out to be.

So what is a marketable skill? It used to be that one could name particular skills, such as computer programming, tax accounting, or marketing. But today, because of Moore's Law, because the cost of data processing, storage, and communications is essentially zero, any routine skill can and will be outsourced to the lowest bidder. And if you live in the United States, Canada, Australia, Europe, or another advanced economy, that is unlikely to be you.

Numerous organizations and experts have studied the question of what skills will be marketable during your career. Consider two of them. First, the RAND Corporation, a think tank located in Santa Monica, California, has published innovative and groundbreaking ideas for more than 60 years, including the initial design for the Internet. In 2004, RAND published a description of the skills that workers in the 21st century will need:

> Rapid technological change and increased international competition place the spotlight on the skills and preparation of the workforce, particularly the ability to adapt to changing technology and shifting demand. Shifts in the nature of organizations...favor strong nonroutine cognitive skills.[3]

Whether you're majoring in accounting, marketing, finance, or information systems, you need to develop strong nonroutine cognitive skills.

What are such skills? Robert Reich, former Secretary of Labor, enumerates four:[4]

- Abstract reasoning
- Systems thinking
- Collaboration
- Ability to experiment

Figure 1-2 shows an example of each. Reread the AllRoad Parts case that started this chapter, and you'll see that Jennifer lost her job because of her inability to practice these key skills.

Skill	Example	Jennifer's Problem at AllRoad Parts
Abstract reasoning	Construct a model or representation.	Hesitancy and uncertainty when conceptualizing a method for identifying parts for 3D printing.
Systems thinking	Model system components and show how components' inputs and outputs relate to one another.	Inability to model AllRoad Parts' supply chain.
Collaboration	Develop ideas and plans with others. Provide and receive critical feedback.	Unwilling to work with others on work-in-progress.
Ability to experiment	Create and test promising new alternatives, consistent with available resources.	Fear of failure prohibited discussion of new ideas.

Figure 1-2
Examples of Critical Skills for Nonroutine Cognition

---

[3]Lynn A. Kaoly and Constantijn W. A. Panis, *The 21st Century at Work* (Santa Monica, CA: RAND Corporation, 2004), p. xiv.
[4]Robert B. Reich, *The Work of Nations* (New York: Alfred A. Knopf, 1991), p. 229.

How Can Intro to MIS Help You Learn Nonroutine Skills?

Introduction to MIS is the best course in the business school for learning these four key skills because every topic will require you to apply and practice them. Here's how.

Abstract Reasoning

Abstract reasoning is the ability to make and manipulate models. You will work with one or more models in every course topic and book chapter. For example, later in this chapter you will learn about a *model* of the five components of an information system. This chapter will describe how to use this model to assess the scope of any new information system project; other chapters will build upon this model.

In this course, you will not just manipulate models that your instructor or I have developed, you will also be asked to construct models of your own. In Chapter 5, for example, you'll learn how to create data models, and in Chapter 10 you'll learn to make process models.

Systems Thinking

Can you go down to a grocery store, look at a can of green beans, and connect that can to U.S. immigration policy? Can you watch tractors dig up a forest of pulpwood trees and connect that woody trash to Moore's Law? Do you know why Cisco Systems is one of the major beneficiaries of YouTube? Answers to all of these questions require systems thinking. **Systems thinking** is the ability to model the components of the system, to connect the inputs and outputs among those components into a sensible whole that reflects the structure and dynamics of the phenomenon observed.

As you are about to learn, this class is about information *systems*. We will discuss and illustrate systems; you will be asked to critique systems; you will be asked to compare alternative systems; you will be asked to apply different systems to different situations. All of those tasks will prepare you for systems thinking as a professional.

Collaboration

Collaboration is the activity of two or more people working together to achieve a common goal, result, or work product. Chapter 2 will teach you collaboration skills and illustrate several sample collaboration information systems. Every chapter of this book includes collaboration exercises that you may be assigned in class or as homework.

Here's a fact that surprises many students: Effective collaboration isn't about being nice. In fact, surveys indicate the single most important skill for effective collaboration is to give and receive critical feedback. Advance a proposal in business that challenges the cherished program of the VP of marketing, and you'll quickly learn that effective collaboration skills differ from party manners at the neighborhood barbeque. So, how do you advance your idea in the face of the VP's resistance? And without losing your job? In this course, you can learn both skills and information systems for such collaboration. Even better, you will have many opportunities to practice them.

Ability to Experiment

"I've never done this before."
"I don't know how to do it."
"But will it work?"
"Is it too weird for the market?"

Fear of failure: the fear that paralyzes so many good people and so many good ideas. In the days when business was stable, when new ideas were just different verses of the same song, professionals could allow themselves to be limited by fear of failure.

Let's take an example of the application of social networking to the oil change business. Is there a legitimate application of social networking there? If so, has anyone ever done it? Is there anyone in the world who can tell you what to do? How to proceed? No. As Reich says, professionals in the 21st century need to be able to experiment.

Successful experimentation is not throwing buckets of money at every crazy idea that enters your head. Instead, **experimentation** is making a reasoned analysis of an opportunity, envisioning potential solutions, evaluating those possibilities, and developing the most promising ones, consistent with the resources you have.

In this course, you will be asked to use products with which you have no familiarity. Those products might be Microsoft Excel or Access, or they might be features and functions of Blackboard that you've not used. Or you may be asked to collaborate using Office 365 or SharePoint or Google Drive. Will your instructor explain and show every feature of those products that you'll need? You should hope not. You should hope your instructor will leave it up to you to experiment, to envision new possibilities on your own, and to experiment with those possibilities, consistent with the time you have available.

Jobs

Employment is the third factor that makes the Introduction to MIS course vitally important to you. During most of 2013, the U.S. unemployment rate averaged 7.5 percent over all ages and job categories, but according to the U.S. Bureau of Labor Statistics, unemployment of those ages 20 to 24 averaged over 13 percent.[5] Employment was better for college graduates than for those without degrees, but even college grads had a high rate of unemployment. Hope Yen, writing for the Associated Press, said in April 2012 that one in two college graduates is either unemployed or underemployed.[6] But this is not the case in job categories that are related to information systems.

Spence and Hlatshwayo studied employment in the United States from 1990 to 2008.[7] They defined a *tradable job* as one that was not dependent on a particular location; this distinction is important because such jobs can be outsourced overseas. As shown in Figure 1-3, Computer Systems Design and Related Services had the strongest growth of any job type in that category. The number of jobs dipped substantially after the dot-com bust in 2000; since 2003, however, job growth has not only recovered, but accelerated dramatically. While this category includes technical positions such as computer programmer and database administrator, it includes nontechnical sales, support, and business management jobs as well. By the way, because Figure 1-3 shows tradable jobs, it puts an end to the myth that all the good computer jobs have gone overseas. According to their data analysis, sourced from the U.S. Bureau of Labor Statistics, that simply has not happened.

However, information systems and computer technology provide job and wage benefits beyond just IS professionals. Acemoglu and Autor published an impressive empirical study of jobs and wages in the United States and parts of Europe from the 1960s to 2010. They found that early in this period, education and industry were the strongest determinants of employment and salary. However, since 1990, the most significant determinant of employment and salary is the nature of work performed. In short, as the price of computer technology plummets, the value of jobs that benefit from it increases dramatically.[8] For example, plentiful, high-paying jobs are available to business professionals who know how to use information systems to improve business process quality, or those who know how to interpret data mining results for improved marketing, or those who know how to use emerging technology like 3D printing to create new products and address new markets. See the Guide on pages 26–27 for more thoughts on how you might consider an IS-related job.

---

[5]Bureau of Labor Statistics, "Labor Force Statistics from the Current Population Survey," United States Department of Labor, last modified July 5, 2013, *http://www.bls.gov/web/empsit/cpseea10.htm*.
[6]*http://news.yahoo.com/1-2-graduates-jobless-underemployed-140300522.html*.
[7]Michael Spence and Sandile Hlatshwayo, *The Evolving Structure of the American Economy and the Employment Challenge* (New York: Council on Foreign Relations, 2011).
[8]Daron Acemoglu and David Autor, "Skills, Tasks, and Technologies: Implications for Employment and Earnings" (working paper, National Bureau of Economic Research, June 2010), *http://www.nber.org/papers/w16082*.

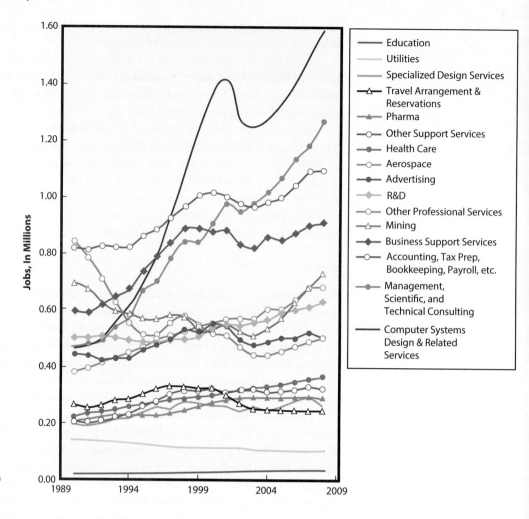

Figure 1-3

**Growth of Jobs by Sector
from 1989 to 2009**

Source: From *The Evolving Structure
of the American Economy* and the
Employment Challenge by Michael
Spence and Sandile Hlatshwayo.
Copyright © 2011 by The Council on
Foreign Relations Press. Reprinted with
permission.

What Is the Bottom Line?

The bottom line? This course is the most important course in the business school because:

1. It will give you the background you need to assess, evaluate, and apply emerging information systems technology to business.
2. It can give you the ultimate in job security—marketable skills—by helping you learn abstraction, systems thinking, collaboration, and experimentation.
3. Many MIS-related jobs are available.

With that introduction, let's get started!

 What Is MIS?

We've used the term *MIS* several times, and you may be wondering exactly what it is. **MIS** stands for **management information systems**, which we define as *the management and use of information systems that help organizations achieve their strategies*. This definition has three key elements: *management and use, information systems,* and *strategies*. Let's consider each, starting first with information systems and their components.

Components of an Information System

A **system** is a group of components that interact to achieve some purpose. As you might guess, an **information system (IS)** is a group of components that interact to produce information. That sentence, although true, raises another question: What are these components that interact to produce information?

Figure 1-4 shows the **five-component framework**—a model of the components of an information system: **computer hardware**, **software**, **data**, **procedures**, and **people**. These five components are present in every information system, from the simplest to the most complex. For example, when you use a computer to write a class report, you are using hardware (the computer, storage disk, keyboard, and monitor), software (Word, WordPerfect, or some other word-processing program), data (the words, sentences, and paragraphs in your report), procedures (the methods you use to start the program, enter your report, print it, and save and back up your file), and people (you).

Consider a more complex example, say an airline reservation system. It, too, consists of these five components, even though each one is far more complicated. The hardware consists of dozens or more computers linked together by data communications hardware. Hundreds of different programs coordinate communications among the computers, and still other programs perform the reservations and related services. Additionally, the system must store millions upon millions of characters of data about flights, customers, reservations, and other facts. Hundreds of different procedures are followed by airline personnel, travel agents, and customers. Finally, the information system includes people, not only the users of the system, but also those who operate and service the computers, those who maintain the data, and those who support the networks of computers.

The important point here is that the five components in Figure 1-4 are common to all information systems, from the smallest to the largest. As you think about any information system, including a new one like social networking, learn to look for these five components. Realize, too, that an information system is not just a computer and a program, but rather an assembly of computers, programs, data, procedures, and people.

As we will discuss later in this chapter, these five components also mean that many different skills are required besides those of hardware technicians or computer programmers when building or using an information system. See the Guide starting on page 26 for more.

Before we move forward, note that we have defined an information system to include a computer. Some people would say that such a system is a **computer-based information system**. They would note that there are information systems that do not include computers, such as a calendar hanging on the wall outside of a conference room that is used to schedule the room's use. Such systems have been used by businesses for centuries. Although this point is true, in this book we focus on computer-based information systems. To simplify and shorten the book, we will use the term *information system* as a synonym for *computer-based information system*.

Management and Use of Information Systems

The next element in our definition of MIS is the *management and use* of information systems. Here we define management to mean develop, maintain, and adapt. Information systems do not pop up like mushrooms after a hard rain; they must be developed. They must also be maintained, and because business is dynamic, they must be adapted to new requirements.

You may be saying, "Wait a minute, I'm a finance (or accounting or management) major, not an information systems major. I don't need to know how to manage information

Figure 1-4

Five Components of an
Information System

Five-Component Framework

Hardware	Software	Data	Procedures	People

systems." If you are saying that, you are like a lamb headed for shearing. Throughout your career, in whatever field you choose, information systems will be built for your use, and sometimes under your direction. To create an information system that meets your needs, you need to take an *active role* in that system's development. Even if you are not a programmer or a database designer or some other IS professional, you must take an active role in specifying the system's requirements and in managing the system's development project. Without active involvement on your part, it will only be good luck that causes the new system to meet your needs.

As a business professional, you are the person who understands business needs and requirements. If you want to apply social networking to your products, you are the one who knows how best to obtain customer responses. The technical people who build networks, the database designers who create the database, the IT people who configure the computers—none of these people know what is needed and whether the system you have is sufficient or whether it needs to be adapted to new requirements. You do!

In addition to management tasks, you will also have important roles to play in the *use* of information systems. Of course, you will need to learn how to employ the system to accomplish your job tasks. But you will also have important ancillary functions as well. For example, when using an information system, you will have responsibilities for protecting the security of the system and its data. You may also have tasks for backing up data. When the system fails (most do, at some point), you will have tasks to perform while the system is down as well as tasks to accomplish to help recover the system correctly and quickly.

Security is critically important when using information systems today. You'll learn much more about it in Chapter 12. But you need to know about strong passwords and their use now, before you get to that chapter. Read and follow the Security Guide on pages 24-25.

Achieving Strategies

The last part of the definition of MIS is that information systems exist to help organizations *achieve their strategies*. First, realize that this statement hides an important fact: Organizations themselves do not "do" anything. An organization is not alive, and it cannot act. It is the people within a business who sell, buy, design, produce, finance, market, account, and manage. So, information systems exist to help people who work in an organization to achieve the strategies of that business.

Information systems are not created for the sheer joy of exploring technology. They are not created so the company can be "modern" or so the company can show it has a social networking presence on the Web. They are not created because the information systems department thinks it needs to be created or because the company is "falling behind the technology curve."

This point may seem so obvious that you might wonder why we mention it. Every day, however, some business somewhere is developing an information system for the wrong reasons. Right now, somewhere in the world, a company is deciding to create a Facebook presence for the sole reason that "every other business has one." This company is not asking questions such as:

- "What is the purpose of our Facebook page?"
- "What is it going to do for us?"
- "What is our policy for employees' contributions?"
- "What should we do about critical customer reviews?"
- "Are the costs of maintaining the page sufficiently offset by the benefits?"

For more information on how an understanding of MIS can broaden your career options, see the Guide on pages 26-27.

But that company should ask those questions! Chapter 3 addresses the relationship between information systems and strategy in more depth. Chapter 8 addresses social media and strategy specifically.

Again, MIS is the development and use of information systems that help businesses achieve their strategies. Already you should be realizing that there is much more to this class than buying a computer, working with a spreadsheet, or creating a Web page.

How Can You Use the Five-Component Model?

The five-component model in Figure 1-4 can help guide your learning and thinking about IS, both now and in the future. To understand this framework better, first note in Figure 1-5 that these five components are symmetric. The outermost components, hardware and people, are both actors; they can take actions. The software and procedure components are both sets of instructions: Software is instructions for hardware, and procedures are instructions for people. Finally, data is the bridge between the computer side on the left and the human side on the right.

Now, when we automate a business task, we take work that people are doing by following procedures and move it so that computers will do that work, following instructions in software. Thus, the process of automation is a process of moving work from the right side of Figure 1-5 to the left.

The Most Important Component—YOU

You are part of every information system that you use. When you consider the five components of an information system, the last component, people, includes you. Your mind and your thinking are not merely a component of the information systems you use; they are the most important component.

As you will learn later in this chapter, computer hardware and programs manipulate data, but no matter how much data they manipulate, it is still just data. It is only humans that produce information. When you take a set of data, say a list of customer responses to a marketing campaign, that list, no matter if it was produced using 10,000 servers and Hadoop (Chapter 9), is still just data. It does not become information until you or some other human take it into your mind and are informed by it.

Even if you have the largest computer farm (Chapter 4) in the world, and even if you are processing that data with the most sophisticated programs, if you do not know what to do with the data those programs produce, you are wasting your time and money. The quality of your thinking is what determines the quality of the information that is produced.

Substantial cognitive research has shown that although you cannot increase your basic IQ, you can dramatically increase the quality of your thinking. That is one reason we have emphasized the need for you to use and develop your abstract reasoning. The effectiveness of an IS depends on the abstract reasoning of the people who use it.

All Components Must Work

Information systems often encounter problems—despite our best efforts, they don't work right. And in these situations, blame is frequently placed on the wrong component. You will often hear people complain that the computer doesn't work, and certainly hardware or software is sometimes at fault. But with the five-component model, you can be more specific, and you have more suspects to interrogate. Sometimes the data is not in the right format, and in many cases, the procedures are not clear and the people using the system are not properly trained. By using the five-component model, you can better locate the cause of a problem and create effective solutions.

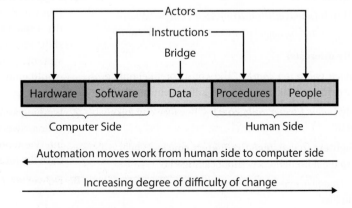

Figure 1-5
Characteristics of the Five Components

Using MIS InClass 1

Information Systems and Online Dating

"Why should I go to a bar and take the risk that nobody I'm interested in will be there during the 2 hours I'm there, when I can spend half an hour searching online for people that I am likely to be interested in? At worst, I've wasted half an hour. And at least I didn't have to blow-dry my hair."

> • **Lori Gottlieb**, in "Logging On For Love" interview by Elizabeth Wasserman, The Atlantic, February 7, 2006

Some online dating services match couples using a proprietary algorithm (method) based on a theory of relationships:

Chemistry (*www.chemistry.com*). Matches are made on the basis of a personality test developed by Dr. Helen Fisher.

eHarmony (*www.eharmony.com*). Matches are made on the basis of a test called the "Compatibility Matching System," by Dr. Neil Clark Warren.

PerfectMatch (*www.perfectmatch.com*). Matches are made on the basis of a test based on Duet, a system developed by Dr. Pepper Schwartz.

Plenty of Fish (*www.pof.com*). Matches made on the basis of a chemistry predictor of five personality factors.

Other sites match people by limiting members to particular groups or interests:

Political interests:

Conservative Dates (*www.republicanpeoplemeet.com*)— "Creating Relationships. Connecting Lives."

Liberal Hearts (*www.liberalhearts.com*)—"Uniting Democrats, Greens, animal lovers & environmentalists who are like in mind and liberal in love."

Common social/economic interests:

Good Genes (*www.goodgenes.com*)—"[Helping] Ivy Leaguers and similarly well-educated graduates and faculty find others with matching credentials."

MillionaireMatch (*www.millionairematch.com*)—"Where you can add a touch of romance to success and achievement!"

Common activity interests:

Golfmates (*www.golfmates.com*)—"The world's premier online dating service designed specifically for the golfing community."

Farmers Only (*www.farmersonly.com*)—"Because city folks just don't get it."

Single FireFighters (*www.singlefirefighters.com*)—"The ONLY place to meet firefighters without calling 911!"

Asexual Pals (*www.asexualpals.com*)—"Because there is so much more to life!"

InClass Group Exercise

1. Visit one of the proprietary method sites and one of the common interest sites.

2. Summarize the matching process that is used by each site.

3. Describe the revenue model of each site.

4. Using general terms, describe the need these sites have for:
   a. Hardware
   b. Software
   c. Data
   d. Procedures
   e. People

5. People sometimes stretch the truth, or even lie, on matching sites. Describe one innovative way that one of the two companies your team chose in step 1 could use information systems to reduce the impact of this tendency. As you prepare your team's answer, keep the availability of nearly free data communications and data storage in mind.

6. Suppose that the company in your answer to step 5 has requested your team to implement your idea on reducing the impact of lying. Explain how having strong personal skills for each of Reich's four abilities (i.e., abstract thinking, systems thinking, experimentation, and collaboration) would enable each of you to be a better contributor to that team.

7. Working as a team, prepare a 3-minute verbal description of your answers to steps 5 and 6 that all of you could use in a job interview. Structure your presentation to illustrate that you have the four skills in step 6.

8. Deliver your answer to step 7 to the rest of the class.

High-Tech Versus Low-Tech Information Systems

Information systems differ in the amount of work that is moved from the human side (people and procedures) to the computer side (hardware and programs). For example, consider two different versions of a customer support information system: A system that consists only of a file of email addresses and an email program is a very low-tech system. Only a small amount of work has been moved from the human side to the computer side. Considerable human work is required to determine when to send which emails to which customers.

In contrast, a customer support system that keeps track of the equipment that customers have and the maintenance schedules for that equipment and then automatically generates email reminders to customers is a higher-tech system. This simply means that more work has been moved from the human side to the computer side. The computer is providing more services on behalf of the humans.

Often, when considering different information systems alternatives, it will be helpful to consider the low-tech versus high-tech alternatives in light of the amount of work that is being moved from people to computers.

Understanding the Scope of New Information Systems

The Ethics Guide in each chapter of this book considers the ethics of information systems use. These guides challenge you to think deeply about ethical standards, and they provide for some interesting discussions with classmates. The Ethics Guide on pages 20–21 considers the ethics of using data that deceives the viewer.

The five-component framework can also be used when assessing the scope of new systems. When in the future some vendor pitches the need for a new technology to you, use the five components to assess how big of an investment that new technology represents. What new hardware will you need? What programs will you need to license? What databases and other data must you create? What procedures will need to be developed for both use and administration of the information system? And, finally, what will be the impact of the new technology on people? Which jobs will change? Who will need training? How will the new technology affect morale? Will you need to hire new people? Will you need to reorganize?

Components Ordered by Difficulty and Disruption

Finally, as you consider the five components, keep in mind that Figure 1-5 shows them in order of ease of change and the amount of organizational disruption. It is a simple matter to order additional hardware. Obtaining or developing new programs is more difficult. Creating new databases or changing the structure of existing databases is still more difficult. Changing procedures, requiring people to work in new ways, is even more difficult. Finally, changing personnel responsibilities and reporting relationships and hiring and terminating employees are all very difficult and very disruptive to the organization.

Why Is the Difference Between Information Technology and Information Systems Important?

Information technology and information systems are two closely related terms, but they are different. **Information technology (IT)** refers to the products, methods, inventions, and standards that are used for the purpose of producing information. IT pertains to the hardware, software, and data components. In contrast, an *information system (IS)* is an assembly of hardware, software, data, procedures, and people that produces information.

Information technology drives the development of new information systems. Advances in information technology have taken the organizations from the days of punched cards to e-commerce and social media, and such advances will continue to take the industry to the next stages and beyond.

Why does this difference matter to you? Knowing the difference between IT and IS can help you avoid a common mistake: You cannot buy an IS.

You can buy IT; you can buy or lease hardware, you can license programs and databases, and you can even obtain predesigned procedures. Ultimately, however, it is *your* people who execute those procedures to employ that new IT.

For any new system, you will always have training tasks (and costs), you will always have the need to overcome employees' resistance to change, and you will always need to manage the employees as they use the new system. Hence, you can buy IT, but you cannot buy IS.

Consider a simple example. Suppose your organization decides to develop a Facebook page. Facebook provides the hardware and programs, the database structures, and standard procedures. You, however, provide the data to fill your portion of its database, and you must extend its standard procedures with your own procedures for keeping that data current. Those procedures need to provide, for example, a means to review your page's content regularly and a means to remove content that is judged inappropriate. Furthermore, you need to train employees on how to follow those procedures and manage those employees to ensure that they do.

Managing your own Facebook page is as simple an IS as exists. Larger, more comprehensive IS that involve many, even dozens, of departments and thousands of employees require considerable work. Again, you can buy IT, but you can never buy an IS!

 # What Is Information?

Based on our earlier discussions, we can now define an information system as an assembly of hardware, software, data, procedures, and people that interact to produce information. The only term left undefined in that definition is *information*, and we turn to it next.

Definitions Vary

Information is one of those fundamental terms that we use every day but that turns out to be surprisingly difficult to define. Defining information is like defining words such as *alive* and *truth*. We know what those words mean, we use them with each other without confusion, but nonetheless, they are difficult to define.

In this text, we will avoid the technical issues of defining information and will use common, intuitive definitions instead. Probably the most common definition is that **information** is knowledge derived from data, whereas *data* is defined as recorded facts or figures. Thus, the facts that employee James Smith earns $70.00 per hour and that Mary Jones earns $50.00 per hour are *data*. The statement that the average hourly wage of all the graphic designers is $60.00 per hour is *information*. Average wage is knowledge that is derived from the data of individual wages.

Another common definition is that *information is data presented in a meaningful context.* The fact that Jeff Parks earns $30.00 per hour is data.[9] The statement that Jeff Parks earns less than half the average hourly wage of AllRoad's Web designers, however, is information. It is data presented in a meaningful context.

---

[9]Actually, the word *data* is plural; to be correct, we should use the singular form *datum* and say, "The fact that Jeff Parks earns $30 per hour is a datum." The word *datum* however, sounds pedantic and fussy, and we will avoid it in this text.

Another definition of information that you will hear is that *information is processed data,* or sometimes, *information is data processed by summing, ordering, averaging, grouping, comparing, or other similar operations.* The fundamental idea of this definition is that we do something to data to produce information.

There is yet a fourth definition of information, which was set out by the great research psychologist Gregory Bateson. He defined information as *a difference that makes a difference.*

For the purposes of this text, any of these definitions of information will do. Choose the definition of information that makes sense to you. The important point is that you discriminate between data and information. You also may find that different definitions work better in different situations.

Where Is Information?

Suppose you create a graph of Amazon.com's stock price and net income over its history, like that shown in Figure 1-6. Does that graph contain information? Well, if it shows a difference that makes a difference or if it presents data in a meaningful context, then it fits two of the definitions of information, and it's tempting to say that the graph contains information.

However, show that graph to your family dog. Does your dog find information in that graph? Well, nothing about Amazon.com, anyway. The dog might learn what you had for lunch, but it won't obtain any information about Amazon.com's stock price over time.

Reflect on this experiment and you will realize that the graph is not, itself, information. The graph is data that you and other humans perceive, and from that perception you conceive information. In short, if it's on a piece of paper or on a digital screen, it's data. If it's in the mind of a human, it's information.

Why, you're asking yourself, do I care? Well, for one, it further explains why you, as a human, are the most important part of any information system you use. The quality of your thinking, of your ability to conceive information from data, is determined by your cognitive skills. *The data is the data, the information you conceive from it is the value that you add to the information system.*

Furthermore, people have different perceptions and points of view. Not surprisingly, then, they will conceive different information from the same data. You cannot say to someone, "Look, it's right there in front of you, in the data," because it's not right there in the data. Rather, it's in your head, and in their heads, and your job is to explain what you have conceived so that others can understand it.

Finally, once you understand this, you'll understand that all kinds of common sentences make no sense. "I sent you that information," cannot be true. "I sent you the data, from which you conceived the information," is the most we can say. During your business career, this observation will save you untold frustration if you remember to apply it.

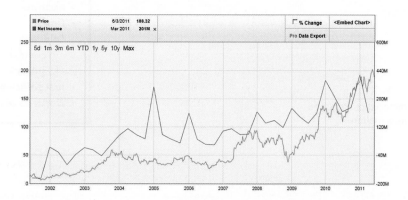

Figure 1-6

Amazon.com Stock Price and Net Income

What Are Necessary Data Characteristics?

You have just learned that humans conceive information from data. As stated, the quality of the information that you can create depends, in part, on your thinking skills. It also depends, however, on the quality of the data that you are given. Figure 1-7 summarizes critical data characteristics.

Accurate

First, good information is conceived from accurate, correct, and complete data, and it has been processed correctly as expected. Accuracy is crucial; business professionals must be able to rely on the results of their information systems. The IS function can develop a bad reputation in the organization if a system is known to produce inaccurate data. In such a case, the information system becomes a waste of time and money as users develop work-arounds to avoid the inaccurate data.

A corollary to this discussion is that you, a future user of information systems, ought not to rely on data just because it appears in the context of a Web page, a well-formatted report, or a fancy query. It is sometimes hard to be skeptical of data delivered with beautiful, active graphics. Do not be misled. When you begin to use a new information system, be skeptical. Cross-check the data you are receiving. After weeks or months of using a system, you may relax. Begin, however, with skepticism. Again, you cannot conceive accurate information from inaccurate data.

Timely

Good information requires that data be timely—available in time for its intended use. A monthly report that arrives six weeks late is most likely useless. The data arrives long after the decisions have been made that needed your information. An information system that sends you a poor customer credit report after you have shipped the goods is unhelpful and frustrating. Notice that timeliness can be measured against a calendar (6 weeks late) or against events (before we ship).

When you participate in the development of an IS, timeliness will be part of the requirements you specify. You need to give appropriate and realistic timeliness needs. In some cases, developing systems that provide data in near real time is much more difficult and expensive than producing data a few hours later. If you can get by with data that is a few hours old, say so during the requirements specification phase.

Figure 1-7
Data Characteristics Required
for Good Information

> - **Accurate**
> - **Timely**
> - **Relevant**
>   – To context
>   – To subject
> - **Just sufficient**
> - **Worth its cost**

Consider an example. Suppose you work in marketing and you need to be able to assess the effectiveness of new online ad programs. You want an information system that not only will deliver ads over the Web, but that also will enable you to determine how frequently customers click on those ads. Determining click ratios in near real time will be very expensive; saving the data in a batch and processing it some hours later will be much easier and cheaper. If you can live with data that is a day or two old, the system will be easier and cheaper to implement.

Relevant

Data should be relevant both to the context and to the subject. Considering context, you, the CEO, need data that is summarized to an appropriate level for your job. A list of the hourly wage of every employee in the company is unlikely to be useful. More likely, you need average wage information by department or division. A list of all employee wages is irrelevant in your context.

Data should also be relevant to the subject at hand. If you want data about short-term interest rates for a possible line of credit, then a report that shows 15-year mortgage interest rates is irrelevant. Similarly, a report that buries the data you need in pages and pages of results is also irrelevant to your purposes.

Just Barely Sufficient

Data needs to be sufficient for the purpose for which it is generated, but just barely so. We are inundated with data; one of the critical decisions that each of us has to make each day is what data to ignore. The higher you rise into management, the more data you will be given, and because there is only so much time, the more data you will need to ignore. So, data should be sufficient, but just barely.

Worth Its Cost

Data is not free. There are costs for developing an information system, costs of operating and maintaining that system, and costs of your time and salary for reading and processing the data the system produces. For data to be worth its cost, an appropriate relationship must exist between the cost of data and its value.

Consider an example. What is the value of a daily report of the names of the occupants of a full graveyard? Zero, unless grave robbery is a problem for the cemetery. The report is not worth the time required to read it. It is easy to see the importance of economics for this silly example. It will be more difficult, however, when someone proposes new technology to you. You need to be ready to ask, "What's the value of the information that I can conceive from this data?" "What is the cost?" "Is there an appropriate relationship between value and cost?" Information systems should be subject to the same financial analyses to which other assets are subjected.

Ethics Guide

ETHICS AND PROFESSIONAL RESPONSIBILITY

Suppose you're a young marketing professional who has just taken a new promotional campaign to market. The executive committee asks you to present a summary of the sales effect of the campaign, and you produce the graph shown in Figure 1. As shown, your campaign was just in the nick of time; sales were starting to fall the moment your campaign kicked in. After that, sales boomed.

But note the vertical axis has no quantitative labels. If you add quantities, as shown in Figure 2, the performance is less impressive. It appears that the substantial growth amounts to less than 20 units. Still the curve of the graph is impressive, and if no one does the arithmetic, your campaign will appear successful.

This impressive shape is only possible, however, because Figure 2 is not drawn to scale. If you draw it to scale, as shown in Figure 3, your campaign's success is, well, problematic, at least for you.

Which of these graphs do you present to the committee?

Each chapter of this text includes an Ethics Guide that explores ethical and responsible behavior in a variety of MIS-related contexts. In this chapter, we'll examine the ethics of data and information.

Centuries of philosophical thought have addressed the question "What is right behavior?" and we can't begin to discuss all of it here. You will learn much of it, however, in your business ethics class. For our purposes, we'll use two of the major pillars in the philosophy of ethics. We introduce the first one here and the second in Chapter 2.

The German philosopher Immanuel Kant defined the *categorical imperative* as the principle that *one should behave only in a way that one would want the behavior to be a universal law.* Stealing is not such behavior because if everyone steals, nothing can be owned. Stealing cannot be a universal law. Similarly, lying cannot be consistent with the categorical imperative because if everyone lies, words are useless.

When you ask whether a behavior is consistent with this principle, a good litmus test is "Are you willing to publish your behavior to the world? Are you willing to put it on your Facebook page? Are you willing to say what you've done to all

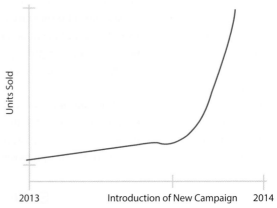

Figure 1

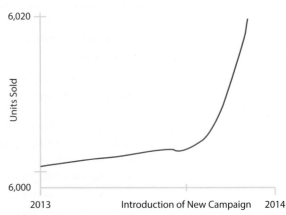

Figure 2

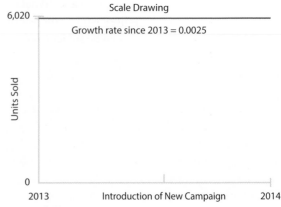

Figure 3

the players involved?" If not, your behavior is not ethical, at least not in the sense of Kant's categorical imperative.

Kant defined *duty* as the necessity to act in accordance with the categorical imperative. *Perfect duty* is behavior that must always be met. Not lying is a perfect duty. *Imperfect duty* is action that is praiseworthy, but not required according to the categorical imperative. Giving to charity is an example of an imperfect duty.

Kant used the example of cultivating one's own talent as an imperfect duty, and we can use that example as a way of defining professional responsibility. Business professionals have an imperfect duty to obtain the skills necessary to accomplish their jobs. We also have an imperfect duty to continue to develop our business skills and abilities throughout our careers.

We will apply these principles in the chapters that follow. For now, use them to assess your beliefs about Figures 1–3 by answering the following questions.

Source: .shock/Fotolia

 DISCUSSION QUESTIONS

1. Restate Kant's categorical imperative using your own words. Explain why cheating on exams is not consistent with the categorical imperative.

2. While there is some difference of opinion, most scholars believe that the Golden Rule ("Do unto others as you would have them do unto you.") is not equivalent to Kant's categorical imperative. Justify this belief.

3. Using the Bateson definition (discussed in Q5) that information is a difference that makes a difference:
   a. Explain how the features of the graph in Figure 1 influence the viewer to create information.
   b. Explain how the features of the graph in Figure 3 influence the viewer to create information.
   c. Which of these graphs is consistent with Kant's categorical imperative?

4. Suppose you created Figure 1 using Microsoft Excel. To do so, you keyed the data into Excel and clicked the Make Graph button (there is one, though it's not called that.) Voila, Excel created Figure 1 without any labels and drawn out of scale as shown. Without further consideration, you put the result into your presentation.
   a. Is your behavior consistent with Kant's categorical imperative? Why or why not?
   b. If Excel automatically produces graphs like Figure 1, is Microsoft's behavior consistent with Kant's categorical imperative? Why or why not?

5. Change roles. Assume now you are a member of the executive committee. A junior marketing professional presents Figure 1 to the committee, and you object to the lack of labels and the scale. In response, the junior marketing professional says, "Sorry, I didn't know. I just put the data into Excel and copied the resulting graph." What conclusions do you, as an executive, make about the junior marketing professional in response to this statement?

6. Is the junior marketing person's response in question 5 a violation of a perfect duty? Of any imperfect duty? Of any duty? Explain your response.

7. As the junior marketing professional, which graph do you present to the committee?

8. According to Kant, lying is not consistent with the categorical imperative. Suppose you are invited to a seasonal barbeque at the department chair's house. You are served a steak that is tough, overcooked, and so barely edible that you secretly feed it to the department chair's dog (who appears to enjoy it). The chairperson asks you, "How is your steak?" and you respond, "Excellent, thank you."
   a. Is your behavior consistent with Kant's categorical imperative?
   b. The steak seemed to be excellent to the dog. Does that fact change your answer to a?
   c. What conclusions do you draw from this example?

Q7  2024?

In Q1, we said that future businesspeople need to be able to assess, evaluate, and apply emerging technology. What technology might that be? And how might it pertain to future business?

Let's take a guess at technology in the year 2024. Of course, we won't have perfect insight and, in fact, these guesses will probably seem ludicrous to the person who finds this book for sale for a dollar at a Goodwill store in 2024. But let's exercise our minds in that direction.

One near certainty is that most computers won't look like computers. Apple's iPad, for example, does not look like a traditional desktop or laptop, but you can use it to watch videos, listen to music, read books, store photos, surf the Internet, and network online. You can also buy apps for the iPad that are educational, such as ones designed to aid toddlers in learning their ABCs and others focused on helping high school students learn the periodic table.

Amazon.com's Kindle Fire, which is advertised as a media device, is a computer. It just doesn't look like one. What happens when you turn on that Kindle? You are connected, magically as it were, to the Amazon.com store. You can buy books and magazine subscriptions, and so on, with a single click.

Furthermore, everyday items now have computers in them. Tanita offers a scale that sends an electrical pulse through your body and then provides not only your weight, but also your body fat, bone mass, metabolism, and level of hydration. You can wear a watch that counts the calories you have burned and the number of miles you have walked or run and reports them back to a Web site. You could link this data with your doctor's office so that your physician could actually prescribe exercise, just like drugs. In fact, you'll see a prototype of this very application in Chapters 7–12!

We can expect that televisions and autos and parking meters will all be computers, or at least have a computer inside. We can further imagine some middle-aged, overweight man sitting at a Pizza Hut when the 911 staff arrives to carry him away.

"Why are you here?" he'll say, "I'm fine."

"Oh, no you're not. Your pacemaker called us because you're having a heart attack."

By 2024, it's likely that desktop and portable computers as we know them today will have disappeared. They'll be replaced by mobile devices of many different types. Your employer might not even provide you a computer; you may be expected to bring your own computing device to work, or maybe all workplaces will have computing devices that you make personal by signing in. We explore these possibilities further in Chapter 4.

But let's apply systems thinking to the social implications of these changes. If everyone in the world is wearing Google Glasses or something similar by 2024, would the Boston Marathon bomber be caught in minutes? Doing so would require not just the image data, but also huge networks of computers to process the image data in real time. And, if so, what does that mean for privacy? And where are the business opportunities in all of that?[10]

---

[10]Anton Wahlman, "Could Google Glass Catch the Boston Bomber?" *TheStreet*, last updated April 18, 2013, *http://money.msn.com/technology-investment/post.aspx?post=f0d8f47e-1d83-4c0b-a9f1-c6bbf250fc3c.*

Will people still go to work? Why? Yahoo! CEO Marissa Mayer required her employees to come to work and earned the disdain of many. Is she on the wrong side of that trend? She says important work gets done in informal meetings around the coffee pot, but will this matter when meeting at the coffee pot is a virtual experience? And what about organizations? What will we need organizations for? Will employees—at least talented, symbolic workers like you will be—need organizations? Or will they band together in temporary teams, work together, and then band together in another way?

Bring this closer to home. What about classrooms?

Why go to class if you have a classroom in a box? Let's phrase this differently because the traditional classroom does have value, especially to those students who learn from comments and questions asked by more able students.[11] Put it this way: Suppose you can go to a traditional class-room for $25,000 a year or go to the classroom in a box for $3,500 per year. Either way, you earn a degree; maybe the box's degree is not as prestigious, but it is an accredited degree. Which would you choose?

We'll take a 2024 look at the end of each chapter. For now, think about it: Who are the winners and the losers in the products-that-compute era?

---

[11]Louise Nemanich, Michael Banks, and Dusya Vera, "Enhancing Knowledge Transfer in Classroom Versus OnLine Settings: The Interplay Among Instructor, Student, and Context," *Decision Sciences Journal of Innovative Education* 7, no. 1 (2009): 140.

Security Guide

PASSWORDS AND PASSWORD ETIQUETTE

All forms of computer security involve passwords. Most likely, you have a university account that you access with a user name and password. When you set up that account, you were probably advised to use a **"strong password."** That's good advice, but what is a strong password? Probably not "sesame," but what then? Microsoft, a company that has many reasons to promote effective security, provides a definition that is commonly used. Microsoft defines a strong password as one with the following characteristics:

- Has at least 10 characters; 12 is even better
- Does not contain your user name, real name, or company name
- Does not contain a complete dictionary word, in any language
- Is different from previous passwords you have used
- Contains both upper- and lowercase letters, numbers, and special characters (such as ˜ ! @; # $ % ^ &; * ( ) _ +; - =; { } | [ ] \ : " ; ' <; >;? , ./)

Examples of good passwords are:

- Qw37^T1bb?at
- 3B47qq<3>5!7b

The problem with such passwords is that they are nearly impossible to remember. And the last thing you want to do is write your password on a piece of paper and keep it near the device where you use it. Never do that!

One technique for creating memorable, strong passwords is to base them on the first letter of the words in a phrase. The phrase could be the title of a song or the first line of a poem or one based on some fact about your life. For example, you might take the phrase, "I was born in Rome, New York, before 2000." Using the first letters from that phrase and substituting the character < for the word *before*, you create the password IwbiR,NY<2000. That's an acceptable password, but it would be better if all of the numbers were not placed on the end. So, you might try the phrase, "I was born at 3:00 AM in Rome, New York." That phrase yields the password Iwba3:00AMiR,NY which is a strong password that is easily remembered.

Once you have created a strong password, you need to protect it with proper behavior. Proper password etiquette is one of the marks of a business professional. Never write down your password, and do not share it with others. Never ask someone else for his password, and never give your password to someone else.

But what if you need someone else's password? Suppose, for example, you ask someone to help you with a problem on your computer. You sign on to an information system, and for some reason, you need to enter that other person's password. In this case, say to the other person, "We need your password," and then get out of your chair, offer your keyboard to the other person, and look away while she enters the password. Among professionals working in

organizations that take security seriously, this little "do-si-do" move—one person getting out of the way so another person can enter her password—is common and accepted.

If someone asks for your password, do not give it out. Instead, get up, go over to that person's machine, and enter your own password, yourself. Stay present while your password is in use, and ensure that your account is logged out at the end of the activity. No one should mind or be offended in any way when you do this. It is the mark of a professional.

 DISCUSSION QUESTIONS

1. Here are the first two lines of a famous poem by T. S. Eliot, "Let us go then, you and I, When the evening is spread out against the sky." Explain how to use these lines to create a password. How could you add numbers and special characters to the password in a way that you will be able to remember?

2. List two different phrases that you can use to create a strong password. Show the password created by each.

3. One of the problems of life in the cyberworld is that we all are required to have multiple passwords—one for work or school, one for bank accounts, another for eBay or other auction sites, and so forth. Of course, it is better to use different passwords for each. But in that case you have to remember three or four different passwords. Think of different phrases you can use to create a memorable, strong password for each of these different accounts. Relate the phrase to the purpose of the account. Show the passwords for each.

4. Explain proper behavior when you are using your computer and you need to enter, for some valid reason, another person's password.

5. Explain proper behavior when someone else is using her computer and that person needs to enter, for some valid reason, your password.

Guide

FIVE-COMPONENT CAREERS

Some years, even some decades, students can wait until their last semester to think seriously about jobs. They can pick a major, take the required classes, and prepare to graduate, all the while assuming that job recruiters will be on campus, loaded with good jobs, sometime during their senior year. *Alas, today is not one of those periods.*

In the current employment situation, you need to be proactive and aggressive in your job search. Think about it: you will be spending one-third of your waking life in your job. One of the best things you can do for yourself is to begin to think seriously about your career prospects now. You don't want to find yourself working as a barista after four years of business school, unless, of course, you're planning on starting the next Starbucks.

So, start here. Are you interested in a career in MIS? At this point, you don't know enough to know, but Figure 1-3 should catch your attention. With job growth like that, in a category of jobs that is net of outsourcing, you should at least ponder whether there is a career for you in IS and related services.

But what does that mean? If you go to the U.S. Bureau of Labor Statistics, you can find that there are more than a million computer programmers in the United States today, and more than 600,000 systems analysts. You probably have some notion of what a programmer does, but you don't yet know what a systems analyst is. Examine the five components in Figure 1-4, however, and you can glean some idea. Programmers work primarily with the software component, while systems analysts work with the entire system, with all five

components. So, as a systems analyst, you work with system users to determine what the organizational requirements are and then with technical people (and others) to help develop that system. You work as a cultural broker: translating the culture of technology into the culture of business, and the reverse.

Fortunately for you, many interesting jobs are not captured by the bureau's data. Why fortunate? Because you can use what you're learning in this course to identify and obtain jobs that other students may not think about, or even know about. If so, you've gained a competitive advantage.

The chart on the next page provides a framework for thinking about careers in an unconventional way. As you can see, there are technical jobs in MIS, but fascinating, challenging, high-paying, nontechnical ones as well. Consider, for example, professional sales. Suppose you have the job of selling enterprise-class software to the Mayo Clinic. You will sell to intelligent, highly motivated

Source: Hurst Photo/Shutterstock

professionals, with tens of millions of dollars to spend. Or suppose you work for the Mayo Clinic, on the receiving end of that sales pitch. How will you spend your tens of millions? You will need knowledge of your business, and you will also need to understand enough technology to ask intelligent questions, and interpret the responses.

Give this some thought by answering the boxed questions, even if they aren't assigned for a grade!

	Hardware	Software	Data	Procedures	People
Sales & Marketing	Vendors (IBM, Cisco, etc.)	Vendors (Microsoft, Oracle, etc.)	Vendors (Acxiom, Google, etc.)	Vendors (SAP, Infor, Oracle)	Recruiters (Robert Half, Lucas Group)
Support	Vendors Internal MIS	Vendors Internal MIS	Database administration Security	Vendors and internal customer support	Customer support Training
Development	Computer engineering Internal MIS	Application programmer Quality test Engineer	Data modeler Database design	Business process management Process reengineering	Training Internal MIS recruiting
Management	Internal MIS	Internal MIS	Data administration	Project management	Technical management
Consulting	Project management, development, pre- and postsale support				

 DISCUSSION QUESTIONS

1. What does the phrase *in a category of jobs that is net of outsourcing* mean? Reread the discussion of Figure 1-3 if you're not certain. Why is this important to you?
2. Examine the Five-Component Careers chart and choose the row that seems most relevant to your interests and abilities. Describe a job in each component column of that row. If you are uncertain, Google the terms in the cells of that row.
3. For each job in your answer to question 2, describe what you think are the three most important skills and abilities for that job.
4. For each job in your answer to question 2, describe one innovative action that you can take this year to increase your employment prospects.

ACTIVE REVIEW

Use this Active Review to verify that you understand the ideas and concepts that answer the chapter's study questions.

Q1 Why is Introduction to MIS the most important class in the business school?

Define *Moore's Law* and explain why its consequences are important to business professionals today. State how business professionals should relate to emerging information technology. Give the text's definition of *job security* and use Reich's list to explain how this course will help you attain that security. Summarize IS-related job opportunities.

Q2 What is MIS?

Identify the three important phrases in the definition of *MIS*. Name the five components of an information system. Explain why end users need to be involved in the management of information systems. Explain why it is a misconception to say that organizations do something.

Q3 How can you use the five-component model?

Name and define each of the five components. Explain the symmetry in the five-component model. Show how automation moves work from one side of the five-component structure to the other. Name the most important component and state why it is the most important. Use the five-component model to describe the differences between high-tech and low-tech information systems. Explain how the components are ordered according to difficulty of change and disruption.

Q4 Why is the difference between information technology and information systems important?

Using the five-component model, explain the difference between IT and IS. Explain why you can buy IT, but you can never buy IS. What does that mean to you, as a potential future business manager?

Q5 What is information?

State four different definitions of information. Identify the one that is your favorite and explain why. State the difference between data and information. Explain why information can never be written on a piece of paper or shown on a display device.

Q6 What are necessary data characteristics?

Create a mnemonic device for remembering the characteristics of good data. Explain how these data characteristics relate to information quality.

Q7 2024?

What trends do you expect to see in 2024? Explain the term classrooms-in-a-box. Why is your college or university challenged by classrooms-in-a-box? Is it seriously challenged, or is this just a passing fad? If your school is publicly funded, is it more at risk? Summarize how answering these questions contributes to your skill as a nonroutine thinker.

Using Your Knowledge with AllRoad Parts

Reread the AllRoad Parts vignette at the start of this chapter. Using the knowledge you've gained from this chapter, especially that in Q1, identify five mistakes that Jennifer made. For each, explain what you would do differently. Be specific.

KEY TERMS AND CONCEPTS

3D printing (additive
   manufacturing)   8
Abstract reasoning   8
Collaboration   8
Computer hardware   11
Computer-based information
   system   11
Data   11

Experimentation   9
Five-component framework   11
Information   16
Information system (IS)   11
Information technology (IT)   15
Management information systems
   (MIS)   10
Moore's Law   5

People   11
Procedures   11
Software   11
Strong password   24
System   11
Systems thinking   8

MyMISLab

Go to **mymislab.com** to complete the problems marked with this icon .

USING YOUR KNOWLEDGE

1-1. One of life's greatest gifts is to be employed doing work that you love. Reflect for a moment on a job that you would find so exciting that you could hardly wait to get to sleep on Sunday night so that you could wake up and go to work on Monday.

  a. Describe that job. Name the industry, the type of company or organization for whom you'd like to work, the products and services they produce, and your specific job duties.

  b. Explain what it is about that job that you find so compelling.

  c. In what ways will the skills of abstraction, systems thinking, collaboration, and experimentation facilitate your success in that job?

  d. Given your answers to parts a through c, define three to five personal goals for this class. None of these goals should include anything about your GPA. Be as specific as possible. Assume that you are going to evaluate yourself on these goals at the end of the quarter or semester. The more specific you make these goals, the easier it will be to perform the evaluation. Use Figure 1-3 for guidance.

1-2. Consider costs of a system in light of the five components: costs to buy and maintain the hardware; costs to develop or acquire licenses to the software programs and costs to maintain them; costs to design databases and fill them with data; costs of developing procedures and keeping them current; and finally, human costs both to develop and use the system.

  a. Over the lifetime of a system, many experts believe that the single most expensive component is people. Does this belief seem logical to you? Explain why you agree or disagree.

  b. Consider a poorly developed system that does not meet its defined requirements. The needs of the business do not go away, but they do not conform themselves to the characteristics of the poorly built system. Therefore, something must give. Which component picks up the slack when the hardware and software programs do not work correctly? What does this say about the cost of a poorly designed system? Consider both direct money costs as well as intangible personnel costs.

  c. What implications do you, as a future business manager, take from parts a and b? What does this say about the need for your involvement in requirements and other aspects of systems development? Who eventually will pay the costs of a poorly developed system? Against which budget will those costs accrue?

1-3. Consider the four definitions of information presented in this chapter. The problem with the first definition, "knowledge derived from data," is that it merely substitutes one word we don't know the meaning of (*information*) for a second word we don't know the meaning of (*knowledge*). The problem with the second definition, "data presented in a meaningful context," is that it is too subjective. Whose context? What makes a context meaningful? The third definition, "data processed by summing, ordering, averaging, etc.," is too mechanical. It tells us what to do, but it doesn't tell us what information is. The fourth definition, "a difference that makes a difference," is vague and unhelpful.

  Also, none of these definitions helps us to quantify the amount of information we receive. What is the information content of the statement that every human being has a navel? Zero—you already know that. In contrast, the statement that someone has just deposited $50,000 into your checking account is chock-full of information. So, good information has an element of surprise.

Considering all of these points, answer the following questions:

a. What is information made of?

b. If you have more information, do you weigh more? Why or why not?

c. When you give a copy of your transcript to a prospective employer, how is information produced? What part of that information production process do you control? What, if anything, can you do to improve the quality of information that the employer conceives?

d. Give your own best definition of information.

e. Explain how you think it is possible that we have an industry called the *information technology industry,* but we have great difficulty defining the word *information.*

COLLABORATION EXERCISE 1

Collaborate with a group of fellow students to answer the following questions. For this exercise, do not meet face to face. Coordinate all of your work using email and email attachments, only. Your answers should reflect the thinking of the entire group, and not just one or two individuals.

1. Abstract reasoning.
   a. Define *abstract reasoning,* and explain why it is an important skill for business professionals.
   b. Explain how a list of items in inventory and their quantity on hand is an abstraction of a physical inventory.
   c. Give three other examples of abstractions commonly used in business.
   d. Explain how Jennifer failed to demonstrate effective abstract-reasoning skills.
   e. Can people increase their abstract-reasoning skills? If so, how? If not, why not?

2. Systems thinking.
   a. Define *systems thinking,* and explain why it is an important skill for business professionals.
   b. Explain how you would use systems thinking to explain why Moore's Law caused a farmer to dig up a field of pulpwood trees. Name each of the elements in the system, and explain their relationships to each other.
   c. Give three other examples of the use of system thinking with regard to consequences of Moore's Law.
   d. Explain how Jennifer failed to demonstrate effective systems thinking skills.
   e. Can people improve their system thinking skills? If so, how? If not, why not?

3. Collaboration.
   a. Define *collaboration,* and explain why it is an important skill for business professionals.
   b. Explain how you are using collaboration to answer these questions. Describe what is working with regard to your group's process and what is not working.

   c. Is the work product of your team better than any one of you could have done separately? If not, your collaboration is ineffective. If that is the case, explain why.
   d. Does the fact that you cannot meet face to face hamper your ability to collaborate? If so, how?
   e. Explain how Jennifer failed to demonstrate effective collaboration skills.
   f. Can people increase their collaboration skills? If so, how? If not, why not?

4. Experimentation.
   a. Define *experimentation,* and explain why it is an important skill for business professionals.
   b. Explain several creative ways you could use experimentation to answer this question.
   c. How does the fear of failure influence your willingness to engage in any of the ideas you identified in part b?
   d. Explain how Jennifer failed to demonstrate effective experimentation skills.
   e. Can people increase their willingness to take risks? If so, how? If not, why not?

5. Job security.
   a. State the text's definition of *job security.*
   b. Evaluate the text's definition of job security. Is it effective? If you think not, offer a better definition of job security.
   c. As a team, do you agree that improving your skills on the four dimensions in the Collaboration Exercise Questions will increase your job security?
   d. Do you think technical skills (accounting proficiency, financial analysis proficiency, etc.) provide job security? Why or why not? Do you think you would have answered this question differently in 1990? Why or why not?

The Amazon of Innovation

On November 26, 2012, Amazon.com customers ordered 26.5 million items worldwide, an average of 306 items per second. On its peak order-fulfillment day, Amazon shipped more than 15.6 million units, and the last unit delivered in time for Christmas was ordered on December 24 at 11:44 AM and delivered that same day, 3 hours later.[12] Such performance is only possible because of Amazon's innovative use of information systems. Some of its major innovations are listed in Figure 1-8.

You may think of Amazon as simply an online retailer, and that is indeed where the company achieved most of its success. To do this, Amazon had to build enormous supporting infrastructure—just imagine the information systems and fulfillment facilities needed to ship 15.6 million items on a single day. That infrastructure, however, is only needed during the busy holiday season. Most of the year, Amazon is left with excess infrastructure capacity. Starting in 2000, Amazon began to lease some of that capacity to other companies. In the process, it played a key role in the creation of what are termed *cloud services*, which you will learn about in Chapter 4. For now, just think of cloud services as computer resources somewhere out in the Internet that are leased on flexible terms. Today, Amazon's business lines can be grouped into three major categories:

- Online retailing
- Order fulfillment
- Cloud services

Consider each.

Amazon created the business model for online retailing. It began as an online bookstore, but every year since 1998 it has added new product categories. In 2011, the company sold goods in 29 product categories. Undoubtedly, there will be more by the time you read this.

Amazon is involved in all aspects of online retailing. It sells its own inventory. It incentivizes you, via the Associates program, to sell its inventory as well. Or it will help you sell your inventory within its product pages or via one of its consignment venues. Online auctions are the major aspect of online sales in which Amazon does not participate. It tried auctions in 1999, but it could never make inroads against eBay.[13]

Today, it's hard to remember how much of what we take for granted was pioneered by Amazon. "Customers who bought this, also bought that;" online customer reviews; customer ranking of customer reviews; books lists; Look Inside the Book; automatic free shipping for certain orders or frequent customers; and Kindle books and devices were all novel concepts when Amazon introduced them.

Amazon's retailing business operates on very thin margins. Products are usually sold at a discount from the stated retail price, and 2-day shipping is free for Amazon Prime members (who pay an annual fee of $79). How do they do it? For one, Amazon drives its employees incredibly hard. Former employees claim the hours are long, the pressure is severe, and the workload is heavy. But what else? It comes down to Moore's Law and the innovative use of nearly free data processing, storage, and communication.

In addition to online retailing, Amazon also sells order fulfillment services. You can ship your inventory to an Amazon warehouse and access Amazon's information systems just as if they were yours. Using technology known as Web services (discussed in Chapter 6), your order processing information systems can directly integrate, over the Web, with Amazon's inventory, fulfillment, and shipping applications. Your customers need not know that Amazon played any role at all. You can also sell that same inventory using Amazon's retail sales applications.

Amazon Web Services (AWS) allows organizations to lease time on computer equipment in very flexible ways. Amazon's Elastic Cloud 2 (EC2) enables organizations to expand and contract the computer resources they need within minutes. Amazon has a variety of payment plans, and it is possible to buy computer time for less than a penny an hour. Key to this capability is the ability for the leasing organization's computer programs to interface with Amazon's to automatically scale up and scale down the resources leased. For example, if a news site publishes a story that causes a rapid ramp-up of traffic, that news site can, programmatically, request, configure, and use more computing resources for an hour, a day, a month, whatever.

Finally, with the Kindle devices, Amazon has become a vendor of both tablets and, even more importantly in the long term, a vendor of online music and video. And to induce customers to buy Kindle apps, in 2013 Amazon introduced its own currency, Amazon Coins.

---

[12]"For the Eighth Consecutive Year, Amazon Ranks #1 in Customer Satisfaction During the Holiday Shopping Season," *Amazon.com*, last modified December 27, 2012, *http://phx.corporate-ir.net/phoenix.zhtml?c=176060&p=irol-newsArticle&ID=1769785&highlight=*.

[13]For a fascinating glimpse of this story from someone inside the company, see "Early Amazon: Auctions" at *http://glinden.blogspot.com/2006/04/early-amazon-auctions.html*, accessed August 2012.

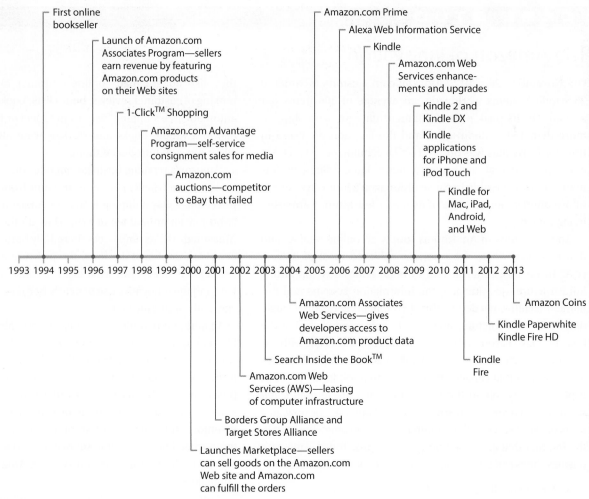

Figure 1-8
Innovation at Amazon
Source: Data from Amazon.com: *http://phx.corporate-ir.net/phoenix.zhtml?c=176060&p=irol-corporateTimeline,* accessed June 2013.

QUESTIONS

1-4. In what ways does Amazon, as a company, evidence the willingness and ability to collaborate?

1-5. In what ways does Amazon, as a company, evidence the willingness and ability to experiment? Use Amazon Coins as an example: *https://developer.amazon.com/post/Tx2EZGRG23VNQ0K/Introducing-Amazon-Coins-A-New-Virtual-Currency-for-Kindle-Fire.html.*

1-6. In what ways do you think the employees at Amazon must be able to perform systems and abstract thinking?

1-7. Describe, at a high level, the principal roles played by each of the five components of an information system that supports order fulfillment.

1-8. Choose any five of the innovations in Figure 1-8 and explain how you think Moore's Law facilitated each innovation.

1-9. Suppose you work for Amazon or a company that takes innovation as seriously as Amazon does. What do you suppose is the likely reaction to an employee who says to his or her boss, "But, I don't know how to do that!"?

1-10. Using your own words and your own experience, what skills and abilities do you think you need to have to thrive at an organization like Amazon?

MyMISLab

Go to **mymislab.com** for Auto-graded writing questions as well as the following Assisted-graded writing questions:

1-11.   The text states that data should be worth its cost. Both cost and value can be broken into tangible and intangible factors. *Tangible* factors can be directly measured; *intangible* ones arise indirectly and are difficult to measure. For example, a tangible cost is the cost of a computer monitor; an intangible cost is the lost productivity of a poorly trained employee.

   Give five important tangible and five important intangible costs of an information system. Give five important tangible and five important intangible measures of the value of an information system. If it helps to focus your thinking, use the example of the class scheduling system at your university or some other university information system. When determining whether an information system is worth its cost, how do you think the tangible and intangible factors should be considered?

1-12.   Mymislab Only – comprehensive writing assignment for this chapter.

Collaboration
Information Systems

"No, Felix! Not again! Over, and over, and over! We decide something one meeting and then go over it again the next meeting and again the next. What a waste!"

"What do you mean, Drew?" asks Felix, AllRoad's customer service manager. "I think it's important we get this right."

"Well, Felix, if that's the case, why don't you come to the meetings?"

"Well, since you added me to the team, I've just missed a couple."

"Right. Last week we met here for, oh, 2, maybe 3, hours, and we decided to analyze our sales data to identify products that we could possibly produce ourselves, using 3D printing."

"But Drew, if we can't afford a 3D printer or learn how to use it, what difference does it make if there are parts that we could produce?"

"Felix! We discussed that last week and we think we can, but we won't know for sure until *we've identified the products we might want to produce.* We can't assess 3D costs until we know what we might print, er, manufacture."

"Look, Drew, Kelly just wants something reasonable to tell Jason. If we tell her these 3D puppies cost a half a million, which I happen to think they will, Jason will cancel this project and we can get back to work...selling high-quality parts manufactured by those who know what they're doing!"

"Felix, you're driving me nuts. We discussed this *ad nauseam* last week. Let's make some progress." Drew looks imploringly at the rest of the team. "Please, somebody, help me out here! Addison, what do you think?"

"Felix, Drew is right," Addison chimes in. "We did have a long discussion on how to go about this—and we did agree to focus first on identifying products that we *might* be able to manufacture ourselves. And those for which it would be worthwhile to do so."

"Well, Addison," Felix snaps, "I think it's a mistake. Why didn't anyone tell me? I put a lot of time into getting the 3D printer cost data."

"Did you read the email?" Addison asks tentatively.

"What email?" Felix looks confused.

"The meeting summary email that I send out each week," Addison says with a sigh.

"I got the email, but I couldn't download the attachment. Something weird about a virus checker couldn't access a gizmo or something like that…" Felix trails off.

Drew can't stand that excuse, "Here, Felix, take a look at mine. I'll underline the part where we concluded that we'd focus on analyzing past sales so you can be sure to see it."

"Drew, there's no reason to get snippy about this. I thought I had a good idea," Felix says, sounding hurt.

"OK, so we're agreed—*again this week*—that we're going to process sales data to find candidate products," Drew grumbles. "Now, we've wasted enough time covering old ground. Let's get some new thinking on how we're going to do that."

"I got the email, but I couldn't download the attachment."

Felix slumps back into his chair and looks down at his cell phone.

"Oh, no, I missed a call from Mapplethorpe. Ahhhh."

"Felix, what are you talking about?" asks Drew.

"Mapplethorpe, my contact at General Sports. He wants to know why those new disk brakes are so expensive. I'm sorry, but I've got to call him. I'll be back in a few minutes."

Felix leaves the room.

Drew looks at Addison.

"Now what?" he asks. "If we go forward, we'll have to rediscuss everything when Felix comes back. Maybe we should just take a break?"

Addison shakes her head. "Drew, let's not. It's tough for all of us to get to these meetings. I wasn't even supposed to be in the office today; I drove in just for this. I've only got a couple of hours before I have to pick up Simone from day care, and we haven't done anything yet. Let's just ignore Felix."

"OK, Addison, but it isn't easy to ignore Felix."

The door opens, and Kelly walks in.

"Hi everyone! How's it going?" she asks brightly. "Is it OK if I sit in on your meeting?"

STUDY QUESTIONS

Q1   What are the two key characteristics of collaboration?

Q2   What are three criteria for successful collaboration?

Q3   What are the four primary purposes of collaboration?

Q4   What are the requirements for a collaboration information system?

Q5   How can you use collaboration tools to improve team communication?

Q6   How can you use collaboration tools to manage shared content?

Q7   How can you use collaboration tools to manage tasks?

Q8   Which collaboration IS is right for your team?

Q9   2024?

CHAPTER PREVIEW

Business is a social activity. While we often say that organizations accomplish their strategy, they don't. *People* in organizations accomplish strategy by working with other people, almost always working in groups. People do business with people.

Over the years, technology has increasingly supported group work. In your grandfather's day, communication was done using letter, phone, and office visits. Those technologies were augmented in the 1980s and 1990s with fax and email and more recently by texting, conference calls, and videoconferencing. Today, products such as Office 365 provide a wide array of tools to support collaborative work.

This chapter investigates ways that information systems can support collaboration. We begin by defining collaboration, discussing collaborative activities, and setting criteria for successful collaboration. Next, we'll address the kinds of work that collaborative teams do. Then we'll discuss requirements for collaborative information systems and illustrate important collaborative tools for improving communication and sharing content. After that, we'll bring this closer to your needs today and investigate the use of three different collaboration IS that can improve your student collaborations. Finally, we'll wrap up with a discussion of collaboration in 2024!

Q1 What Are the Two Key Characteristics of Collaboration?

To answer this question, we must first distinguish between the terms *cooperation* and *collaboration*. **Cooperation** is a group of people working together, all doing essentially the same type of work, to accomplish a job. A group of four painters, each painting a different wall in the same room, are working cooperatively. Similarly, a group of checkers at the grocery store or clerks at the post office are working cooperatively to serve customers. A cooperative group can accomplish a given task faster than an individual working alone, but the cooperative result is usually not better in quality than the result of someone working alone.

In this text, we define **collaboration** as a group of people working together to achieve a common goal *via a process of feedback and iteration*. Using feedback and iteration, one person will produce something, say the draft of a document, and a second person will review that draft and provide critical feedback. Given the feedback, the original author or someone else will then revise the first draft to produce a second. The work proceeds in a series of stages, or *iterations*, in which something is produced, members criticize it, and then another version is produced. Using iteration and feedback, the group's result can be better than what any single individual can produce alone. This is possible because different group members provide different perspectives. "Oh, I never thought of it that way" is a typical signal of collaboration success.

Many, perhaps most, student groups incorrectly use cooperation rather than collaboration. Given an assignment, a group of five students will break it up into five pieces, work to accomplish their piece independently, and then merge their independent work for grading by the professor. Such a process will enable the project to be completed more quickly, with less work by any single individual, but it will not be better than the result obtained if the students were to work alone.

In contrast, when students work collaboratively, they set forth an initial idea or work product, provide feedback to one another on those ideas or products, and then revise in accordance with feedback. Such a process can produce a result far superior to that produced by any student working alone.

Importance of Effective Critical Feedback

Given this definition, for collaboration to be successful members must provide and receive *critical* feedback. A group in which everyone is too polite to say anything critical cannot collaborate. As Darwin John, the world's first chief information officer (CIO) (see Chapter 11) once said, "If two of you have the exact same idea, then we have no need for one of you." On the other hand, a group that is so critical and negative that members come to distrust, even hate, one another cannot effectively collaborate either. For most groups, success is achieved between these extremes.

To underline this point, consider the research of Ditkoff, Allen, Moore, and Pollard. They surveyed 108 business professionals to determine the qualities, attitudes, and skills that make a good collaborator.[1] Figure 2-1 lists the most and least important characteristics reported in the survey. Most students are surprised to learn that 5 of the top 12 characteristics involve disagreement (highlighted in red in Figure 2-1). Most students believe that "we should all get

---

Twelve Most Important Characteristics for an Effective Collaborator

1. Is enthusiastic about the subject of our collaboration.

2. Is open-minded and curious.

3. Speaks his or her mind even if it's an unpopular viewpoint.

4. Gets back to me and others in a timely way.

5. Is willing to enter into difficult conversations.

6. Is a perceptive listener.

7. Is skillful at giving/receiving negative feedback.

8. Is willing to put forward unpopular ideas.

9. Is self-managing and requires "low maintenance."

10. Is known for following through on commitments.

11. Is willing to dig into the topic with zeal.

12. Thinks differently than I do/brings different perspectives.

Nine Least Important Characteristics for an Effective Collaborator

31. Is well organized.

32. Is someone I immediately liked. The chemistry is good.

33. Has already earned my trust.

34. Has experience as a collaborator.

35. Is a skilled and persuasive presenter.

36. Is gregarious and dynamic.

37. Is someone I knew beforehand.

38. Has an established reputation in field of our collaboration.

39. Is an experienced businessperson.

Figure 2-1

Important and Not Important Characteristics of a Collaborator

---

[1]Mitch Ditkoff, Tim Moore, Carolyn Allen, and Dave Pollard, "The Ideal Collaborative Team," *Idea Champions*, accessed July 5, 2013, *http://www.ideachampions.com/downloads/collaborationresults.pdf*.

along" and more or less have the same idea and opinions about team matters. Although it is important for the team to be sociable enough to work together, this research indicates that it is also important for team members to have different ideas and opinions and to express them to each other.

When we think about collaboration as an iterative process in which team members give and receive feedback, these results are not surprising. During collaboration, team members learn from each other, and it will be difficult to learn if no one is willing to express different, or even unpopular, ideas. The respondents also seem to be saying, "You can be negative, as long as you care about what we're doing." These collaboration skills do not come naturally to people who have been taught to "play well with others," but that may be why they were so highly ranked in the survey.

The characteristics rated *not relevant* are also revealing. Experience as a collaborator or in business does not seem to matter. Being popular also is not important. A big surprise, however, is that being well organized was rated 31st out of 39 characteristics. Perhaps collaboration itself is not a very well-organized process.

Guidelines for Giving and Receiving Critical Feedback

Giving and receiving critical feedback is the single most important collaboration skill. So, before we discuss the role that information systems can play for improving collaboration, study the guidelines for giving and receiving critical feedback shown in Figure 2-2.

Many students have found that when they first form a collaborative group, it's useful to begin with a discussion of critical feedback guidelines like those in Figure 2-2. Begin with this list, and then, using feedback and iteration, develop your own list. Of course, if a group member does not follow the agreed-upon guidelines, someone will have to provide critical feedback to that effect as well.

Warning!

If you are like most undergraduate business students, especially freshmen or sophomores, your life experience is keeping you from understanding the need for collaboration. So far, almost everyone you know has the same experiences as you and, more or less, thinks like you. Your friends and

Guideline	Example
Be specific.	"I was confused until I got to Section 2" rather than "The whole thing is a disorganized mess."
Offer suggestions.	"Consider moving Section 2 to the beginning of the document."
Avoid personal comments.	Never: "Only an idiot would miss that point … or write that document."
Strive for balance.	"I thought Section 2 was particularly good. What do you think about moving it to the start of the document?"
Question your emotions.	"Why do I feel so angry about the comment he just made? What's going on? Is my anger helping me?"
Do not dominate.	If there are five members of the group, unless you have special expertise, you are entitled to just 20 percent of the words/time.
Demonstrate a commitment to the group.	"I know this is painful, but if we can make these changes our result will be so much better." or "Ouch. I really didn't want to have to redo that section, but if you all think it's important, I'll do it."

Figure 2-2
Guidelines for Providing and Receiving Critical Feedback

associates have the same educational background, scored more or less the same on standardized tests, and have the same orientation toward success. So, why collaborate? Most of you think the same way, anyway: "What does the professor want and what's the easiest, fastest way to get it to her?"

So, consider this thought experiment. Your company is planning to build a new facility that is critical for the success of a new product line and will create 300 new jobs. The county government won't issue a building permit because the site is prone to landslides. Your engineers believe your design overcomes that hazard, but your chief financial officer (CFO) is concerned about possible litigation in the event there is a problem. Your corporate counsel is investigating the best way to overcome the county's objections while limiting liability. Meanwhile, a local environmental group is protesting your site because it believes the site is too close to an eagle's nest. Your public relations director is meeting with these local groups every week.

Do you proceed with the project?

To decide, you create a working team of the chief engineer, the CFO, your legal counsel, and the PR director. Each of those people has different education and expertise, different life experience, and different values. In fact, the only thing they have in common is that they are paid by your company. That team will participate collaboratively in ways that are far different from your experience so far. Keep this example in mind as you read this chapter.

Bottom line: The two key characteristics of collaboration are iteration and feedback.

What Are Three Criteria for Successful Collaboration?

J. Richard Hackman studied teamwork for many years, and his book *Leading Teams* contains many useful concepts and tips for future managers.[2] According to Hackman, there are three primary criteria for judging team success:

- Successful outcome
- Growth in team capability
- Meaningful and satisfying experience

Successful Outcome

Most students are primarily concerned with the first criterion. They want to achieve a good outcome, measured by their grade, or they want to get the project done with an acceptable grade while minimizing the effort required. For business professionals, teams need to accomplish their goals: make a decision, solve a problem, or create a work product. Whatever the objective is, the first success criterion is, "Did we do it?"

Although not as apparent in student teams, most business teams also need to ask, "Did we do it within the time and budget allowed?" Teams that produce a work product too late or far over budget are not successful, even if they did achieve their goal.

Growth in Team Capability

The other two criteria are surprising to most students, probably because most student teams are short-lived. But, in business, where teams often last months or years, it makes sense to ask, "Did the team get better?" If you're a football fan, you've undoubtedly heard your college's coach say, "We really improved as the season progressed." (Of course, for the team with 2 wins and

---

[2]J. Richard Hackman, *Leading Teams: Setting the Stage for Great Performances* (Boston: Harvard Business Press, 2002).

12 losses, you didn't hear that.) Football teams last only a season. If the team is permanent, say a team of customer support personnel, the benefits of team growth are even greater. Over time, as the team gets better, it becomes more efficient; thus, over time the team provides more service for a given cost or the same service for less cost.

How does a team get better? For one, it develops better work processes. Activities are combined or eliminated. Linkages are established so that "the left hand knows what the right hand is doing," or needs, or can provide. Teams also get better as individuals improve at their tasks. Part of that improvement is the learning curve; as someone does something over and over, he or she gets better at it. But team members also teach task skills and give knowledge to one another. Team members also provide perspectives that other team members need.

Meaningful and Satisfying Experience

The third element of Hackman's definition of team success is that team members have a meaningful and satisfying experience. Of course, the nature of team goals is a major factor in making work meaningful. But few of us have the opportunity to develop a life-saving cancer vaccine or safely land a stricken airliner in the middle of the Hudson River in winter. For most of us, it's a matter of making the product, or creating the shipment, or accounting for the payment, or finding the prospects, and so on.

So, in the more mundane world of most business professionals, what makes work meaningful? Hackman cites numerous studies in his book, and one common thread is that the work is perceived as meaningful by the team. Keeping prices up to date in the product database may not be the most exciting work, but if that task is perceived by the team as important, it will become meaningful.

Furthermore, if an individual's work is not only perceived as important, but the person doing that work is also given credit for it, then the experience will be perceived as meaningful. So, recognition for work well done is vitally important for a meaningful work experience.

Another aspect of team satisfaction is camaraderie. Business professionals, just like students, are energized when they have the feeling that they are part of a group, each person doing his or her own job, and combining efforts to achieve something worthwhile that is better than any could have done alone.

What Are the Four Primary Purposes of Collaboration?

Collaborative teams accomplish four primary purposes:

- Become informed
- Make decisions
- Solve problems
- Manage projects

These four purposes build on each other. For example, making a decision requires that team members be informed. In turn, to solve a problem, the team must have the ability to make decisions (and become informed). Finally, to conduct a project, the team must be able to solve problems (and make decisions and become informed).

Before we continue, understand you can use the hierarchy of these four purposes to build your professional skills. You cannot make good decisions if you do not have the skills to inform yourself. You cannot solve problems if you are unable to make good decisions. And you cannot manage projects if you don't know how to solve problems!

In this question, we will consider the collaborative nature of these four purposes and describe requirements for information systems that support them, starting with the most basic: becoming informed.

Becoming Informed

Informing is the first and most fundamental collaboration purpose. Recall from Chapter 1 that two individuals can receive the same data but construct different interpretations or, as stated in the terms of Chapter 1, conceive different information. The goal of the informing is to ensure, as much as possible, that team members are conceiving information in the same way.

For example, as you read in the opening scenario, the team at AllRoad has been assigned the task of investigating the 3D printing opportunity. One of the team's first tasks is to ensure that everyone understands that goal and, further, understands the basics of 3D printing technology and what is required to implement it.

Informing, and hence all of the purposes of collaboration, presents several requirements for collaborative information systems. As you would expect, team members need to be able to share data and to communicate with one another to share interpretations. Furthermore, because memories are faulty and team membership can change, it is also necessary to document the team's understanding of the information conceived. To avoid having to go "over and over and over" a topic, a repository of information, such as a wiki, is needed. We will say more about this in Q5.

Making Decisions

Collaboration is used for some types of decision making, but not all. Consequently, to understand the role for collaboration we must begin with an analysis of decision making. Decisions are made at three levels: *operational, managerial,* and *strategic.*

Operational Decisions

Operational decisions are those that support operational, day-to-day activities. Typical operational decisions are: How many widgets should we order from vendor A? Should we extend credit to vendor B? Which invoices should we pay today?

Managerial Decisions

Managerial decisions are decisions about the allocation and utilization of resources. Typical decisions are: How much should we budget for computer hardware and programs for department A next year? How many engineers should we assign to project B? How many square feet of warehouse space do we need for the coming year?

In general, if a managerial decision requires consideration of different perspectives, then it will benefit from collaboration. For example, consider the decision of whether to increase employee pay in the coming year. No single individual has the answer. The decision depends on an analysis of inflation, industry trends, the organization's profitability, the influence of unions, and other factors. Senior managers, accountants, human resources personnel, labor relationships managers, and others will each bring a different perspective to the decision. They will produce a work product for the decision, evaluate that product, and make revisions in an iterative fashion—the essence of collaboration.

Strategic Decisions

Strategic decisions are those that support broad-scope, organizational issues. Typical decisions at the strategic level are: Should we start a new product line? Should we open a centralized warehouse in Tennessee? Should we acquire company A?

Strategic decisions are almost always collaborative. Consider a decision about whether to move manufacturing operations to China. This decision affects every employee in the organization, the organization's suppliers, its customers, and its shareholders. Many factors and many perspectives on each of those factors must be considered.

The Decision Process

Information systems can be classified based on whether their decision processes are *structured* or *unstructured*. These terms refer to the method or process by which the decision is to be made, not to the nature of the underlying problem. A **structured decision** process is one for which there is an understood and accepted method for making the decision. A formula for computing the reorder quantity of an item in inventory is an example of a structured decision process. A standard method for allocating furniture and equipment to employees is another structured decision process. Structured decisions seldom require collaboration.

An **unstructured decision** process is one for which there is no agreed-on decision-making method. Predicting the future direction of the economy or the stock market is a classic example. The prediction method varies from person to person; it is neither standardized nor broadly accepted. Another example of an unstructured decision process is assessing how well suited an employee is for performing a particular job. Managers vary in the manner in which they make such assessments. Unstructured decisions are often collaborative.

The Relationship Between Decision Type and Decision Process

The decision type and decision process are loosely related. Decisions at the operational level tend to be structured, and decisions at the strategic level tend to be unstructured. Managerial decisions tend to be both structured and unstructured.

We use the words *tend to be* because there are exceptions to the relationship. Some operational decisions are unstructured (e.g., "How many taxicab drivers do we need on the night before the homecoming game?"), and some strategic decisions can be structured (e.g., "How should we assign sales quotas for a new product?"). In general, however, the relationship holds.

Decision Making and Collaboration Systems

As stated, few structured decisions involve collaboration. Deciding, for example, how much of product A to order from vendor B does not require the feedback and iteration among members that typify collaboration. Although the process of generating the order might require the coordinated work of people in purchasing, accounting, and manufacturing, there is seldom a need for one person to comment on someone else's work. In fact, involving collaboration in routine, structured decisions is expensive, wasteful, and frustrating. "Do we have to have a meeting about everything?" is a common lament.

The situation is different for unstructured decisions because feedback and iteration are crucial. Members bring different ideas and perspectives about what is to be decided, how the decision will be reached, what criteria are important, and how decision alternatives score against those criteria. The group may make tentative conclusions and discuss potential outcomes of those conclusions, and members will often revise their positions. Figure 2-3 illustrates the change in the need for collaboration as decision processes become less structured.

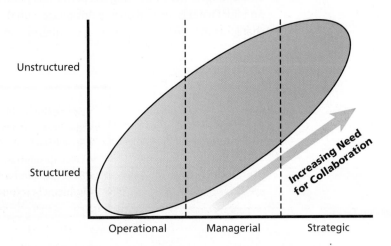

Figure 2-3
Collaboration Needs
for Decision Making

Solving Problems

Solving problems is the third primary reason for collaborating. A **problem** is a perceived difference between what is and what ought to be. Because it is a perception, different people can have different problem definitions.

Therefore, the first and arguably the most important task for a problem-solving collaborative group is defining the problem. For example, the AllRoad Parts team has been assigned the problem of determining whether manufacturing certain parts via 3D printing is a viable option. As stated as part of the informing purpose, the group needs first to ensure that the team members understand this goal and have a common understanding of what 3D printing entails.

See the Guide on pages 70–71 to learn one technique that business professionals use to obtain a common definition of a problem. That technique requires effective communication.

However, because a problem is a difference between what is and what ought to be, the statement "reduce operational expenses" does not go far enough. Is saving one dollar enough of a reduction? Is saving $100,000 enough? Does it take $1,000,000 for the reduction to be enough? A better problem definition would be to reduce operational expenses by 10 percent or by $100,000 or some other more specific statement of what is desired.

Figure 2-4 lists the principal problem-solving tasks. Because this text is about information systems and not about problem solving per se, we will not delve into those tasks here. Just note the work that needs to be done, and consider the role of feedback and iteration for each of these tasks.

Managing Projects

Managing projects is a rich and complicated subject, with many theories and methods and techniques. Here we will just touch on the collaborative aspects of four primary project phases.

Projects are formed to create or produce something. The end goal might be a marketing plan, the design of a new factory, or a new product, or it could be performing the annual audit. Because projects vary so much in nature and size, we will summarize generic project phases here. Figure 2-5 shows project management with four phases, the major tasks of each, and the kinds of data that collaborative teams need to share.

Starting Phase

The fundamental purpose of the starting phase is to set the ground rules for the project and the team. In industry, teams need to determine or understand what authority they have. Is the project given to the team? Or is part of the team's task to identify what the project is? Is the team free to determine team membership, or is membership given? Can the team devise its own methods for accomplishing the project, or is a particular method required? Student teams differ from those in industry because the team's authority and membership are set by the instructor. However, although student teams do not have the authority to define the project, they do have the authority to determine how that project will be accomplished.

Other tasks during the starting phase are to set the scope of the project and to establish an initial budget. Often this budget is preliminary and is revised after the project has been planned. An initial team is formed during this phase with the understanding that team membership may change as the project progresses. It is important to set team member expectations at the outset.

Figure 2-4
Problem-Solving Tasks

- Define the problem.
- Identify alternative solutions.
- Specify evaluation criteria.
- Evaluate alternatives.
- Select an alternative.
- Implement solution.

Phase	Tasks	Shared Data
Starting	Set team authority. Set project scope and initial budget. Form team. Establish team roles, responsibilities, and authorities. Establish team rules.	Team member personal data Start-up documents
Planning	Determine tasks and dependencies. Assign tasks. Determine schedule. Revise budget.	Project plan, budget, and other documents
Doing	Perform project tasks. Manage tasks and budget. Solve problems. Reschedule tasks, as necessary. Document and report progress.	Work in process Updated tasks Updated project schedule Updated project budget Project status documents
Finalizing	Determine completion. Prepare archival documents. Disband team.	Archival documents

Figure 2-5
Project Management Tasks and Data

What role will each team member play, and what responsibilities and authority will he or she have? Team rules are also established as discussed under decision making.

Planning Phase

The purpose of the planning phase is to determine "who will do what and by when." Work activities are defined, and resources such as personnel, budget, and equipment are assigned to them. As you'll learn when we discuss project management in Chapter 10, tasks can depend on one another. For example, you cannot evaluate alternatives until you have created a list of alternatives to evaluate. In this case, we say that there is a *task dependency* between the task *Evaluate alternatives* and the task *Create a list of alternatives.* The *Evaluate alternatives* task cannot begin until the completion of the *Create a list of alternatives* task.

Once tasks and resources have been assigned, it is possible to determine the project schedule. If the schedule is unacceptable, more resources can be added to the project or the project scope can be reduced. Risks and complications arise here, however, as will be discussed in Chapter 10. The project budget is usually revised at this point as well.

Doing Phase

Project tasks are accomplished during the doing phase. The key management challenge here is to ensure that tasks are accomplished on time and, if not, to identify schedule problems as early as possible. As work progresses, it is often necessary to add or delete tasks, change task assignments, add or remove task labor or other resources, and so forth. Another important task is to document and report project progress.

Finalizing Phase

Are we done? This question is an important and sometimes difficult one to answer. If work is not finished, the team needs to define more tasks and continue the doing phase. If the answer is yes, then the team needs to document its results, document information for future teams, close down the project, and disband the team.

Review the third column of Figure 2-5. All of this project data needs to be stored in a location accessible to the team. Furthermore, all of this data is subject to feedback and iteration. That means that there will be hundreds, perhaps thousands, of versions of data items to be managed. We will consider ways that collaborative information systems can facilitate the management of such data in Q6.

What Are the Requirements for a Collaboration Information System?

As you would expect, a **collaboration information system**, or, more simply, a **collaboration system**, is an information system that supports collaboration. In this section, we'll discuss the components of such a system and use the discussions in Q1 and Q2 to summarize the requirements for a collaboration IS.

A collaboration information system is a practical example of IS, one that you and your teammates can, and should, build. Because you are new to thinking about IS, we begin first with a summary of the five components of such a system, and then we will survey the requirements that teams, including yours, should consider when constructing a collaboration IS.

The Five Components of an IS for Collaboration

Collaboration tools provide useful capabilities, but they also present some serious security risks. The Security Guide on pages 68–69 discusses those risks and how to avoid them.

As information systems, collaboration systems have the five components of every information system: hardware, software, data, procedures, and people. Concerning hardware, every team member needs a device for participating in the group's work, either a personal computer or a mobile device like an iPad. In addition, because teams need to share data, most collaboration systems store documents and other files on a server somewhere. Google Grid and Microsoft Sky Drive provide servers that are accessed via the Internet, in what is called *the cloud*, which you will learn about in Chapter 6. For now, think of it as one or more computers that store and retrieve your files, somewhere out on the Internet.

Collaboration programs are applications like email or text messaging, Google Drive, Microsoft Web Apps, and other tools that support collaborative work. We will survey those tools in Q5 through Q7.

Regarding the data component, collaboration involves two types. **Project data** is data that is part of the collaboration's work product. For example, for a team that is designing a new product, design documents are examples of project data. A document that describes a recommended solution is project data for a problem-solving project. **Project metadata** is data that is used to manage the project. Schedules, tasks, budgets, and other managerial data are examples of project metadata. Both types of data, by the way, are subject to iteration and feedback.

Collaboration information systems procedures specify standards, policies, and techniques for conducting the team's work. An example is procedures for reviewing documents or other work products. To reduce confusion and increase control, the team might establish a procedure that specifies who will review documents and in what sequence. Rules about who can do what to which data are also codified in procedures. Procedures are usually designed by the team; sometimes they need to be adjusted because of limitations in the collaboration tools being used.

The final component of a collaboration system is, of course, people. We discussed the importance of the ability to give and receive critical feedback in Q1. In addition, team members know how and when to use collaboration applications.

Primary Functions: Communication and Content Sharing

Figure 2-6 shows requirements categorized according to Hackman's three criteria for team success (discussed in Q2). For doing the work on time and on budget, teams need support from their collaboration system to communicate, to manage many versions of content, and to

Criterion for Team Success	Requirement
Complete the work, on time, on budget	Communicate (feedback) Manage many versions of content (iteration) Manage tasks (on time, on budget)
Growth in team capability	Record lessons learned Document definitions, concepts, and other knowledge Support intra–team training
Meaningful and satisfying experience	Build team espirit Reward accomplishment Create sense of importance

Figure 2-6
Requirements for a
Collaboration IS

manage tasks. We will discuss tools that support each of those requirements in Q5 through Q7. Notice that these requirements support iteration and feedback, as you would expect for an IS that supports collaboration. Figure 2-6 also shows requirements for growth in team capability and for creating a meaningful and satisfying experience.

As you will learn, there are numerous alternatives for constructing an IS to meet those requirements. We will investigate three in Q8. You will then have the opportunity of creating an IS for your team in Collaboration Exercise 2 on pages 73–74. Doing so will be greatly beneficial because it will teach you firsthand the role of each of the five components and it will also give you a result that you can use with other teams, in other courses, and, of course, during your career.

Figure 2-7 lists the four purposes of collaboration activities discussed in Q3 and summarizes IS requirements for collaboration systems for each purpose. When you construct your own collaboration IS, first determine the type of effort you are engaged in and then use Figure 2-7 to help you determine your requirements.

Team Purpose	Requirements
Become informed	Share data Support group communication Manage project tasks Store history
Make decisions	Share decision criteria, alternative descriptions, evaluation tools, evaluation results, and implementation plan Support group communication Manage project tasks Publish decision, as needed Store analysis and results
Solve problems	Share problem definitions, solution alternatives, costs and benefits, alternative evaluations, and solution implementation plan Support group communication Manage project tasks Publish problem and solution, as needed Store problem definition, alternatives, analysis, and plan
Manage projects	Support starting, planning, doing, and finalizing project phases (Figure 2–5) Support group communication Manage project tasks

Figure 2-7
Requirements for Different
Collaboration Purposes

How Can You Use Collaboration Tools to Improve Team Communication?

Because of the need to provide feedback, team communication is essential to every collaborative project. In addition to feedback, however, communication is important to manage content, project tasks, and the other requirements shown in Figures 2-6 and 2-7. Developing an effective communication facility is the first thing your team should do, and it is arguably the most important feature of a collaboration IS.

The particular tools used depend on the ways that the team communicates, as summarized in Figure 2-8. **Synchronous communication** occurs when all team members meet at the same time, such as with conference calls or face-to-face meetings. **Asynchronous communication** occurs when team members do not meet at the same time. Employees who work different shifts at the same location or team members who work in different time zones around the world must meet asynchronously.

Most student teams attempt to meet face to face, at least at first. Arranging such meetings is always difficult, however, because student schedules and responsibilities differ. If you are going to arrange such meetings, consider creating an online group calendar in which team members post their availability, week by week. Also, use the meeting facilities in Microsoft Outlook to issue invitations and gather RSVPs. If you don't have Outlook, use an Internet site such as Evite (*www.evite.com*) for this purpose.

For most face-to-face meetings, you need little; the standard Office applications or their freeware lookalikes, such as Open Office, will suffice. However, recent research indicates that face-to-face meetings can benefit from shared, online workspaces, such as that shown in Figure 2-9.[3] With such a whiteboard, team members can type, write, and draw simultaneously, which enables more ideas to be proposed in a given period of time than when team members must wait in sequence to express ideas verbally. If you have access to such a whiteboard, try it in your face-to-face meetings to see if it works for your team.

However, *given today's communication technology, most students should forgo face-to-face meetings.* They are too difficult to arrange and seldom worth the trouble. Instead, learn to use **virtual meetings** in which participants do not meet in the same place, and possibly not at the same time.

If your virtual meeting is synchronous (all meet at the same time), you can use conference calls, multiparty text chat, screen sharing, webinars, or videoconferencing. Some students find it weird to use text chat for school projects, but why not? You can attend meetings wherever you are, without using your voice. Google Text supports multiparty text chat, as does Microsoft Lync. Google or Bing "multiparty text chat" to find other, similar products.

Screen-sharing applications enable users to view the same whiteboard, application, or other display. Figure 2-9 shows an example whiteboard for an AllRoad Parts meeting. This whiteboard,

The Ethics Guide on pages 56–57 addresses some of the ethical challenges that arise when team members have opposing viewpoints.

Synchronous		Asynchronous
Shared calendars Invitation and attendance		
Single location	Multiple locations	Single or multiple locations
Office applications such as Word and PowerPoint Shared whiteboards	Conference calls Multiparty text chat Screen sharing Webinars Videoconferencing	Email Discussion forums Team surveys

Virtual meetings

Figure 2-8
Collaboration Tools for Communication

[3]Wouter van Diggelen, *Changing Face-to-Face Communication: Collaborative Tools to Support Small-Group Discussions in the Classroom* (Groningen: University of Groningen, 2011).

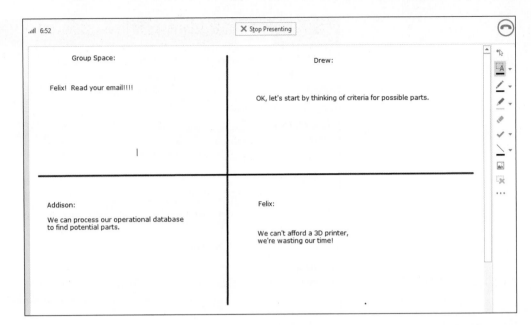

Figure 2-9
Office 365 Lync Whiteboard
Showing Simultaneous
Contributions

which is part of Office 365 Lync, allows multiple people to contribute simultaneously. To organize the simultaneous conversation, the whiteboard real estate is divided among the members of the group, as shown. Some groups save their whiteboards as minutes of the meeting.

A **webinar** is a virtual meeting in which attendees view one of the attendees' computer screens for a more formal and organized presentation. WebEx (*www.webex.com*) is a popular commercial webinar application used in virtual sales presentations.

If everyone on your team has a camera on his or her computer, you can also do **video-conferencing**, like that shown in Figure 2-10. You can use Skype, Google+, or Microsoft Lync,

Figure 2-10
Videoconferencing Example
Source: Tom Merton/Getty Images

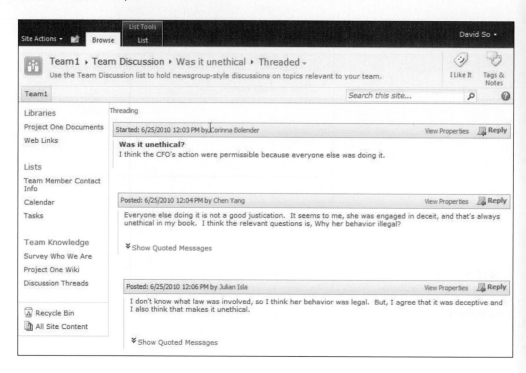

Figure 2-11
Example Discussion Forum

which we will discuss in Q8. Videoconferencing is more intrusive than text chat (you have to comb your hair), but it does have a more personal touch.

In some classes and situations, synchronous meetings, even virtual ones, are impossible to arrange. You just cannot get everyone together at the same time. In this circumstance, when the team must meet asynchronously, most students try to communicate via **email**. The problem with email is that there is too much freedom. Not everyone will participate because it is easy to hide from email. (Was Felix, in the opening scenario, really unable to open the attachment?) Email threads become disorganized and disconnected. After the fact, it is difficult to find particular emails, comments, or attachments.

Discussion forums are an alternative. Here, one group member posts an entry, perhaps an idea, a comment, or a question, and other group members respond. Figure 2-11 shows an example. Such forums are better than email because it is harder for the discussion to get off track. Still, however, it remains easy for some team members not to participate.

Team surveys are another form of communication technology. With these, one team member creates a list of questions and other team members respond. Surveys are an effective way to obtain team opinions; they are generally easy to complete, so most team members will participate. Also, it is easy to determine who has not yet responded. Figure 2-12 shows the results of one team survey. SurveyMonkey (*www.surveymonkey.com*) is one common survey application program. You can find others on the Internet. Microsoft SharePoint has a built-in survey capability, as we discuss in Q8.

Video and audio recordings are also useful for asynchronous communication. Key presentations or discussions can be recorded and played back for team members at their convenience. Such recordings are also useful for training new employees.

How Can You Use Collaboration Tools to Manage Shared Content?

Content sharing is the second major function of collaboration systems. To enable iteration and feedback, team members need to share both project data (such as documents, spreadsheets, and presentations) and work-product data, as well as project metadata (such as tasks,

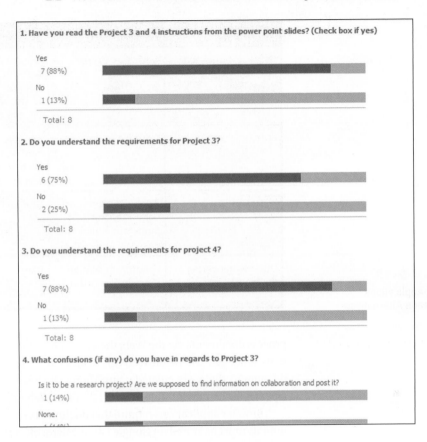

Figure 2-12
Example Survey Report

schedules, calendars, and budgets). The applications teams use and the means by which they share data depend on the type of content. Figure 2-13 provides an overview.[4]

For teams that are sharing Office documents such as Word, Excel, and PowerPoint, the gold standard of desktop applications is Microsoft Office. However, it is also the most expensive. To minimize costs, some teams use either LibreOffice (*www.libreoffice.org*) or Apache OpenOffice (*www.openoffice.org*). Both are license-free, open-source products. (You'll learn more about these terms in Chapter 4; for now, think free.) These products have a small subset of the features and functions of Microsoft Office, but they are robust for what they do and are adequate for many businesses and students. (See Using MIS InClass 2, pages 60–61, for more.)

Teams that share documents of other types need to install applications for processing those particular types. For examples, Adobe Acrobat processes PDF files, Photoshop and Google Picasa process photos, and Camtasia produces computer screen videos that are useful for teaching team members how to use computer applications.

In addition to desktop applications, teams can also process some types of content using Web applications inside their browsers (Firefox, Chrome, and so on). Both Google Docs and Microsoft Web Applications can process Word, Excel, and PowerPoint files. However, Google has its own version of these files. Consequently, if the user uploads a Word document that was created using a desktop application and then wishes to edit that document, he or she must convert it into Google Docs format by opening it with Google Docs. After editing the document, if the user wants to place the document back into Word format, he or she will need to specifically save it in Word format. This is not difficult once the user is aware of the need to do so. Of course, if the team never uses a desktop application and instead uses Google Docs to create and

---

[4]Warning: The data in this figure is changing rapidly. The features and functions of both web applications and cloud drives may have been extended from what is described here. Check the vendor's documentation for new capabilities.

Content Type	Desktop Application	Web Application	Cloud Drive
Office documents (Word, Excel, PowerPoint)	Microsoft Office LibreOffice OpenOffice	Google Docs (Import/ Export non–Google Docs) Microsoft Web Apps (Microsoft Office only)	Google Grid Microsoft SkyDrive Microsoft SharePoint
PDFs	Adobe Acrobat	Viewers in Google Grid and Microsoft Web SkyDrive and SharePoint	Google Grid Microsoft SkyDrive Microsoft SharePoint Drop Box
Photos, videos	Adobe Photoshop, Camtasia, and numerous others	Google Picasa	Google Grid Microsoft SkyDrive Microsoft SharePoint Apple iCloud Drop Box
Other (engineering drawings)	Specific application (Google SketchUp)	Rare	Google Grid Microsoft SkyDrive Microsoft SharePoint Drop Box

Figure 2-13
Content Applications and Storage Alternatives

process documents via the Web, then no conversion between the desktop and Google Docs formats is needed. Microsoft Web Apps can be used in a similar way, but Web Apps will only edit documents that were created using Microsoft Office. Documents created using LibreOffice and OpenOffice cannot be edited using Microsoft Web Apps.

Browser applications require that documents be stored on a cloud server. Google Docs documents must be stored on Google Drive; Microsoft Web Apps must be stored on either Microsoft SkyDrive or Microsoft SharePoint. We will illustrate the use of Google Docs and Google Grid when we discuss version management later in this chapter.

Documents other than Office documents can be stored (but not processed via the browser) on any cloud server. Team members store the documents on the server for other team members to access. DropBox is one common alternative, but you can use Google Grid, SkyDrive, and SharePoint as well. You can also store photos and videos on Apple's iCloud.

Figure 2-14 lists collaboration tools for three categories of content: no control, version management, and version control.

Shared Content with No Control

The most primitive way to share content is via email attachments. However, email attachments have numerous problems. For one, there is always the danger that someone does not receive an email, does not notice it in his or her inbox, or does not bother to save the attachments. Then, too, if three users obtain the same document as an email attachment, each changes it, and each sends back the changed document via email, then different, incompatible versions of that document will be floating around. So, although email is simple, easy, and readily available, it will not suffice for collaborations in which there are many document versions or for which there is a desire for content control.

Alternatives for Sharing Content		
No Control	Version Management	Version Control
Email with attachments Shared files on a server	Google Drive Windows Web Apps Microsoft Office	Microsoft SharePoint

Figure 2-14
Collaboration Tools for Sharing Content

Increasing degree of content control

Another way to share content is to place it on a shared **file server**, which is simply a computer that stores files…just like the disk in your local computer. If your team has access to a file server at your university, you can put documents on the server and others can download them, make changes, and upload them back onto the server. You can also store files on the cloud servers listed in Figure 2-13.

Storing documents on servers is better than using email attachments because documents have a single storage location. They are not scattered in different team members' email boxes, and team members have a known location for finding documents.

However, without any additional control, it is possible for team members to interfere with one another's work. For example, suppose team members A and B download a document and edit it, but without knowing about the other's edits. Person A stores his version back on the server and then person B stores her version back on the server. In this scenario, person A's changes will be lost.

Furthermore, without any version management, it will be impossible to know who changed the document and when. Neither person A nor person B will know whose version of the document is on the server. To avoid such problems, some form of version management is recommended.

Shared Content with Version Management on Google Drive

Systems that provide **version management** track changes to documents and provide features and functions to accommodate concurrent work. For office documents, you can obtain version management services from Google Drive, Microsoft SkyDrive, and Microsoft SharePoint. Here we will discuss the use of Google Drive.

Google Drive is a free service that provides a virtual drive in the cloud into which you can create folders and store files. You can upload files of any type, but only files that are processed by Google Docs receive version management. We'll restrict the rest of this discussion to files of those types.

Anyone with a gmail address automatically has a Google Drive site. Users who do not have a gmail address can either obtain such an address or can create a Google account that is affiliated with some other email address, say your university email address. To do so, and to view the form shown in Figure 2-15, go to *http://accounts.google.com/SignUp*. If you click "I prefer to use my current email address" (red arrow in Figure 2-15), you can use your current email address. Fill out the rest of the form to receive a Google Account.

Figure 2-15
Form for Creating a
Google Drive Account

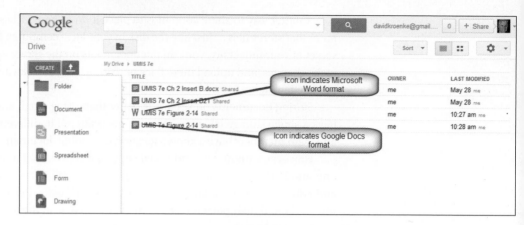

Figure 2-16
Available Types of Documents
on Google Drive

To create a Google document, go to *http://drive.google.com* (note that there is no *www* in this address). Sign in with your Google account. From that point on, you can create, upload, process, save, and download documents. Figure 2-16 shows a user in the process of creating a new document in a folder named UMIS 7e. After clicking the CREATE button, Grid displays the document types that can be created on the left-hand side. You can also save most of those documents to PDF and Microsoft Office formats, such as Word, Excel, and PowerPoint.

With Google Drive, you can make documents available to others by entering their email addresses or Google accounts. Those users are notified that the document exists and are given a link by which they can access it. If they have a Google account, they can edit the document; otherwise they can just view the document. Figure 2-16 shows that the four documents in the folder have all been shared. Clicking on the folder with the + sign displays the names of the people with whom the document is shared, as shown in Figure 2-17.

Because folders and documents are stored on a Google Grid, server users can simultaneously see and edit documents. In the background, Google Docs merges the users' activities into

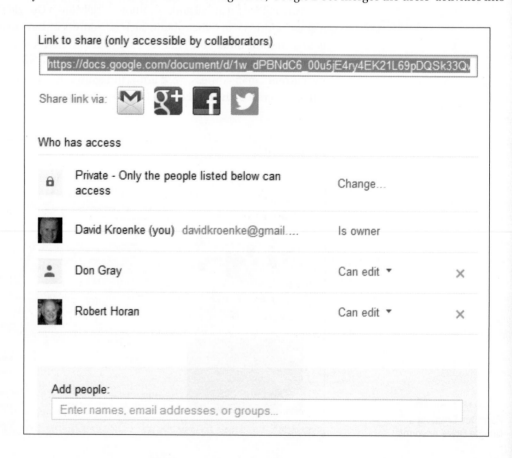

Figure 2-17
Document Sharing on Google
Drive

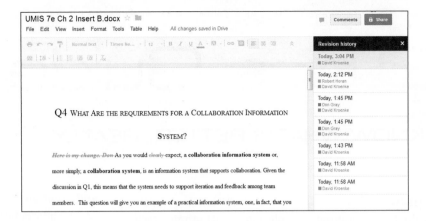

Figure 2-18
Example of Editing a Shared
Document on Google Drive

a single document. You are notified that another user is editing a document at the same time as you are, and you can refresh the document to see their latest changes. Google tracks document revisions, with brief summaries of changes made. Figure 2-18 shows a sample revision document that has been edited by three users.

You can improve your collaboration activity even more by combining Google Drive with Google+.

Google Drive is free and very easy to use. Both it and Microsoft SkyDrive are far superior to exchanging documents via email or via a file server. If you are not using one of these two products, you should. Go to *http://drive.google.com* and *www.skydrive.com* and check them out. You'll find easy-to-understand demos if you need additional instruction.

Shared Content with Version Control

Version management systems improve the tracking of shared content and potentially eliminate problems caused by concurrent document access. They do not, however, provide **version control**, the process that occurs when the collaboration tool limits, and sometimes even directs, user activity. Version control involves one or more of the following capabilities:

- User activity limited by permissions
- Document checkout
- Version histories
- Workflow control

Microsoft SharePoint is a large, complex, and very robust application for all types of collaboration. It has many features and functions, including all of those just listed. It also contains features for managing tasks, sharing non-Office documents, keeping calendars, publishing blogs, and many more capabilities. Some organizations install SharePoint on their own Windows servers; others access it over the Internet using SharePoint Online. Office 365 Professional and other versions of Office 365 include SharePoint.

SharePoint is an industrial-strength product, and if you have an opportunity to use it, by all means learn to do so. SharePoint is used by thousands of businesses, and SharePoint skills are in high demand. The latest version is SharePoint 2013, but it is not yet generally available; we will illustrate its use here with the more common SharePoint 2010 product. With that introduction to SharePoint, consider the SharePoint implementation of the four functions listed.

Permission-Limited Activity

With SharePoint (and other version control products), each team member is given an account with a set of permissions. Then shared documents are placed into shared directories, sometimes called **libraries**. For example, on a shared site with four libraries, a particular user might

Ethics Guide

I KNOW WHAT'S BETTER, REALLY

Suppose you work for a small startup company involved in the innovative application of 3D printing technology, like AllRoad Parts. Your company is 2 years old, employs 50 people, and, like many startup companies, is short of money. Even though you're relatively junior, you've impressed the company's founders, and they have asked you to take a leadership role on a number of special projects. Recently, the company has been investigating developing an information system to store 3D engineering designs and make them available to customers for purchase. You've been assigned to a committee that is developing alternative IS designs for consideration by senior management.

You and a co-worker, Leslie Johnson, have developed two different alternatives for consideration by the committee. You believe that Alternative Two is vastly preferable to Alternative One, but Leslie believes just the opposite. You think if Leslie's alternative is chosen, the result will be a major financial loss, one that your young startup company is unlikely to survive. Even if that does not occur, so much time will be lost pursuing Leslie's alternative that your company will fall behind the competition in your dynamic, developing market and will lose substantial market share to the competition as a result.

Unfortunately, Leslie is called away due to a family emergency on the day the two of you are to present your alternatives. You so strongly believe that Leslie's plan is likely to cause irreparable harm to the company that you decide to present only your plan. While you never lie outright, you lead the committee to believe that both of you strongly support your plan. The committee adopts your plan, and Leslie never learns that the committee saw only one alternative. Is your behavior ethical?

The Ethics Guide in Chapter 1 introduced Kant's categorical imperative as one way of assessing ethical conduct. This guide introduces a second way, one known as *utilitarianism*. The basis of this theory goes back to early Greek philosophers, but the founders of the modern theory are considered to be Jeremy Bentham and John Stuart Mill, as you will learn in your business ethics class.

According to utilitarianism, the morality of an act is determined by its outcome. Acts are judged to be moral if they result in the greatest good to the greatest number, or if they maximize happiness and reduce suffering. The prior sentence contains a great deal of subtlety that has led to numerous flavors of utilitarianism, flavors that are beyond the scope of this text. Here we will work with the gist of those statements.

Using utilitarianism as a guide, killing can be moral if it results in the greatest good to the greatest number. Killing Adolf Hitler would have been moral if it stopped the Holocaust. Similarly, utilitarianism can assess lying or other forms of deception as moral if the act results in the greatest good to the greatest number. Lying to someone with a fatal illness that you're certain they'll recover is moral if it increases that person's happiness and decreases his or her suffering.

Our Recommended Alternatives

Alternative One
- In-house stores 3D Diagrams
- Direct connect to e-commerce server

Alternative Two Use the Cloud
- 3D Diagrams stored on elastic cloud servers
- Use MongoDB on AWS
- SOA connections to e-commerce server

DISCUSSION QUESTIONS

1. According to Kant's categorical imperative, is your action not to present Leslie's alternative ethical?

2. According to utilitarianism, is your action not to present Leslie's alternative ethical?

3. Assume:
   a. You were right. Had the company embarked on Leslie's alternative, it would have driven the company into bankruptcy. Does this fact make your actions more ethical? Explain your answer.
   b. You were wrong. Leslie's alternative would have been far superior to yours for the company's future. Does this fact make your actions less ethical? Explain your answer.

4. In your opinion, do the intended consequences or the actual consequences have more bearing when assessing ethics from a utilitarian perspective?

5. You could postpone the meeting until Leslie is able to attend and thus allow Leslie to present the alternative to yours. Doing so, however, increases the likelihood that the committee selects Leslie's alternative, and you firmly believe that decision will be fatal to the company.

   a. According to Kant's categorical imperative, is a decision not to postpone ethical?
   b. According to utilitarianism, is a decision not to postpone ethical?

6. Suppose Leslie learns you presented only your alternative, and you two become archenemies. To the company's disadvantage, the two of you are never able to work together again. According to utilitarianism, does this outcome change the ethics of your behavior?

7. Suppose that instead of not presenting Leslie's alternative at all, you present it, but in a very negative light. You are honest when you focus the bulk of your description of it on disadvantages because that's what you believe. However, you also know that Leslie does not agree with the way you see the situation. Given your biased presentation, the committee selects your alternative.

   a. According to Kant's categorical imperative, is your behavior ethical?
   b. According to utilitarianism, is your behavior ethical?

8. What would you do in this circumstance? Justify the ethics of your decision.

be given read-only permission for library 1; read and edit permission for library 2; read, edit, and delete permission for library 3; and no permission even to see library 4.

Document Checkout

With version control applications, document directories can be set up so that users are required to check out documents before they can modify them. When a document is checked out, no other user can obtain it for the purpose of editing it. Once the document has been checked in, other users can obtain it for editing.

Figure 2-19 shows a screen for a user of Microsoft SharePoint 2010. The user, Allison Brown (shown in the upper right-hand corner of the screen), is checking out a document named Project One Assignment. Once she has it checked out, she can edit it and return it to this library. While she has the document checked out, no other user will be able to edit it, and her changes will not be visible to others.

Version History

Because collaboration involves feedback and iteration, it is inevitable that dozens, or even hundreds, of documents will be created. Imagine, for example, the number of versions of a design document for the Boeing 787. In some cases, collaboration team members attempt to keep track of versions by appending suffixes to file names. The result for a student project is a file name like *Project1_lt_kl_092911_most_ recent_draft.docx* or something similar. Not only are such names ugly and awkward, no team member can tell whether this is the most current version.

Collaboration tools that provide version control have the data to readily provide histories on behalf of the users. When a document is changed (or checked in), the collaboration tool records the name of the author and the date and time the document is stored. Users also have the option of recording notes about their version. You can see an example of a version history report produced by SharePoint 2010 later in the chapter in Figure 2-33 (page 78).

Workflow Control

Collaboration tools that provide **workflow control** manage activities in a predefined process. If, for example, a group wants documents to be reviewed and approved by team members in a particular sequence, the group would define that workflow to the tool. Then the workflow is started, and the emails to manage the process are sent as defined. For example, Figure 2-20

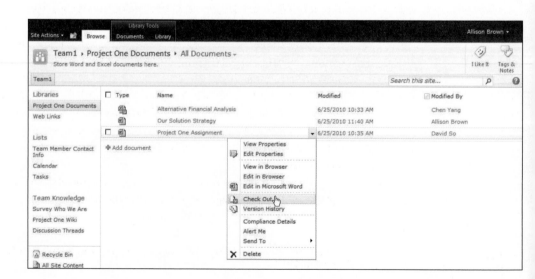

Figure 2-19
Checking Out a Document

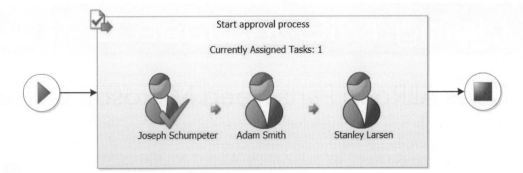

Figure 2-20
Example Workflow

shows a SharePoint workflow in which the group defined a document review process that involves a sequence of reviews by three people. Given this definition, when a document is submitted to a library, SharePoint assigns a task to the first person, Joseph Schumpeter, to approve the document and sends an email to him to that effect. Once he has completed his review (the green checkmark means that he has already done so), SharePoint assigns a task for and sends an email to Adam Smith to approve the document. When all three reviewers have completed their review, SharePoint marks the document as approved. If any of the reviewers disapprove, the document is marked accordingly and the workflow is terminated.

Workflows can be defined for complicated, multistage business processes. See *SharePoint for Students*[5] for more on how to create them.

Numerous version control applications exist. For general business use, SharePoint is the most popular. Other document control systems include MasterControl (*www.mastercontrol.com*) and Document Locator (*www.documentlocator.com*). Software development teams use applications such as CVS (*www.nongnu.org/cvs*) or Subversion (*http://subversion.apache.org*) to control versions of software code, test plans, and product documentation.

How Can You Use Collaboration Tools to Manage Tasks?

As you will learn in project management classes, one of the keys for making team progress is keeping a current task list. One senior project manager once advised me that every team meeting should end with an updated list of tasks, including who is responsible for getting each task done and the date by which he or she will get it done. We've all been to meetings in which many good ideas were discussed, even agreed upon, but nothing happened after the meeting. When teams create and manage task lists, the risks of such nonaction diminish. Managing with a task list is critical for making progress.

Task descriptions need to be specific and worded so it is possible to decide whether the task was accomplished. "Create a good requirements document" is not an effective, testable task description, unless all team members already know what is supposed to be in a good requirements document. A better task would be "Define the contents of the requirements document for the XYZ project."

In general, one person should be made responsible for accomplishing a task. That does not mean that the assigned person does the task; it means that he or she is responsible for

---

[5]Carey Cole, Steve Fox, and David Kroenke, *SharePoint for Students* (Upper Saddle River, NJ: Pearson Education, 2012), pp. 116–129.

Using MIS InClass 2

Does AllRoad Parts Need Microsoft Office? Do You?

For the past 25 years, the answer to that question was so obviously yes that no one bothered to ask it. Whether as an individual or as a business, when you purchased a new computer, you automatically purchased a license for Microsoft Office as well. The only decision might have been which version to get.

But today? The answer is not nearly as clear. You can license Office from Microsoft for as little as $10 per month. That's $120 per employee per year, which may not sound like much, but what if you have 1,000 employees? Or what if you're a startup with five employees and every dollar of that $600 license fee is needed to build your new business? Or what if you're a starving student? What if you're AllRoad Parts?

If you're a law firm, constantly receiving Microsoft Word and other Microsoft Office documents from other law firms, the courts, and so on, you have no choice. You need to see the documents exactly as they were created. LibreOffice, Apache Open Office, and Google Docs all have differences in the way they render and edit Office documents. As a law firm, you can't afford the possibility that you'll miss something. Plus, when you send documents to other law firms, they'll want them in the standard Microsoft format as well. So, if you regularly exchange Microsoft Office documents with customers, business partners and associates, or suppliers, you probably need Microsoft Office, or at least some employees in your organization do. Similarly, if you do complex financial analyses, you'll need the capabilities of Microsoft Excel.

But what about the rest of us? According to Rajen Sheth, senior product manager at Google Apps, Google didn't try to duplicate Office. Regarding Microsoft Office, he told *Computerworld*, "We think that 90% of users really only use 10% of the functionality. We put a lot of time and effort into figuring out what that 10% is that people use and how to build that into Google Docs."[6]

That begs the question: Does your organization or you need any of that missing 90 percent? If so, you'll need to pay the $10 a month for Microsoft Office, or maybe you can use LibreOffice. Or you may be just fine with Google Docs alone. How do you decide?

Suppose that Kelly at AllRoad Parts asks you whether AllRoad can get by without Microsoft Office. Form a team as directed by your professor, and complete the following activities.

1. Create a list of criteria for deciding whether AllRoad needs Microsoft Office. Cost is one criterion, but what else should AllRoad consider? Revise your answer as you work your way through these questions.

2. Suppose that Addison tells you, "Look, it's $10 a month. Our average labor cost is $35 an hour. If anyone wastes an hour of time messing around with a problem with LibreOffice or Google Docs, that equals three-and-a-half months of that person's license fee. Just pay for Microsoft Office and forget about it." Do you think her statement has merit? Explain why or why not.

3. On the other hand, suppose Lucas tells you, "The problem with any desktop product, whether it's Microsoft Office or LibreOffice, is that it has to be installed on the users' computers. You wouldn't believe how much time we waste installing and reinstalling programs for our employees. If we can get by with Google Docs, there are no installations; Docs run from the browser and all my installation problems go away." Do you think his statement has merit? Explain why or why not.

4. Divide your team into two subteams, A and B. Obtain a Google account for each of the two subteams. If team members have their own Google accounts, use those accounts if you want.
   a. Create a document as follows:
      1. For subteam A, download LibreOffice from *www.libreoffice.org/download*. Install it on the computer of one of the members of subteam A.
      2. For subteam B, use Microsoft Office. If one of the team members has Office already installed, use it. Otherwise, go to *www.office.microsoft.com/en-us/try/* and download and install the trial version of Microsoft Office.
   b. Using either Microsoft Word or LibreOffice Text Document (whichever product your subteam has), create a document containing the instructions in question 4 as sample text. Use the indentation style that you see here. Save your document using your subteam's name.

---

[6]Robert L. Mitchell, "Google Docs Strategy: Be Good Enough and Better," *Computerworld*, May 12, 2010, *http://blogs.computerworld.com/16094/google_docs_strategy_be_good_enough_and_better*.

c. Upload your document to Google Grid and convert it to Google Docs format.

d. Open and edit the other subteam's document as a Google Docs document. Remove the instruction for question 4c. Correct the paragraph numbering for items d and e. When the other team has finished its edits, reopen the documents and look for formatting oddities that have been introduced by the other team's work.

e. Using your notes, comment on inconsistencies in the way these products handle document formatting.

5. As you have just seen, there are significant differences in formatting features among these three products. If you were at AllRoad, how would you go about finding out what other differences exist? For example, as of this writing, Google Spreadsheet does not have a pivot table, but Microsoft Excel does. How would you find out about other such differences and missing features?

6. Summarize ways that you could use a sample of AllRoad employees to answer question 5.

7. Based on your experiences in this exercise, answer Kelly's question. If you do not have an answer based on your experience in this exercise, explain how you think AllRoad should proceed to answer her question.

ensuring that it gets done. Finally, no benefit will come from this list unless every task has a date by which it is to be completed. Further, team leaders need to follow up on tasks to ensure that they are done by that date. Without accountability and follow-up, there is no task management.

As you'll learn in your project management classes, you can add other data to the task list. You might want to add critical resources that are required, and you might want to specify tasks that need to be finished before a given task can be started. We will discuss such task dependencies further in Chapter 10, when we discuss the management of systems development projects.

For team members to utilize the task list effectively, they need to share it. In this question, we will consider two options: sharing a task spreadsheet on Google Grid and using the task list feature in Microsoft SharePoint. Google gmail and Calendar also have a task list feature, but as of this writing, it is impossible to share it with others, so it is not useful for collaboration.

Sharing a Task List on Google Grid

Sharing a task list on Google Grid is simple. To do so, every team member needs to obtain a Google account. Then one team member can create a team folder and share it with the rest of the team, giving everyone edit permission on documents that it contains. One of the team members then creates a task spreadsheet on that folder.

Figure 2-21 shows a sample task list containing the name of each task, the name of the person to whom it is assigned, the date it is due, the task's status, and remarks. Because every member of the team has edit permission, everyone can contribute to this task list. Google Grid will allow simultaneous edits. Because Grid tracks version history, it will be possible, if necessary, to learn who made which changes to the task list.

Setting up such a list is easy, and having such a list greatly facilitates project management. The key for success is to keep it current and to use it to hold team members accountable.

Sample Tasklist

	A	B	C	D	E
1	Task	Assigned To	Date Due	Status	Remarks
2					
3	**Get Set Up:**				
4	Determine how we will meet	Bob	Sept 15	Complete	Bob will set up the meeting and drive the discussion to conclusion.
5	Decide communication method	Don	Sept 20	Complete	Don will identify alternatives to show the team ... and get team decision
6	Identify cloud server alternatives	David	Sept 15	Complete	David will do this via email ... until we can get our cloud server up
7	Select a cloud server	Bob	Sept 22	Late	Bob will drive us to a decision and document it
8	Set up cloud server	Bob	Sept 25	In process	Set up the server for use by the team; communicate to all how to use it.
9	Determine office document alternatives	Don	Sept 25	In process	Use cloud server from here on out!
10	Select office document applications	Don	Sept 25	In process	Don will drive the team to a decision and document.
11	Specify task list contents	David	Sept 25	Complete	Done, but can't place on cloud server until Bob finishes.
12	Determine how to store task list	David	Sept 28	Not started	David will drive team to a decision here.
13	Document requirements	Don	Sept 30	Not started	Document all on the requirements document on our cloud server.

Figure 2-21
Sample Task List Using Google Grid

Sharing a Task List Using Microsoft SharePoint

SharePoint includes a built-in content type for managing task lists that provides robust and powerful features. The standard task list can be readily modified to include user-customized columns, and many different views can be constructed to show the list in different ways for different users. Like the rest of SharePoint, its task lists are industrial-strength.

Figure 2-22 shows a task list that we used for the production of this text. The first six columns are built-in columns that SharePoint provides. The last column, labeled Book, is the book for which the task was assigned. For example, UMIS stands for the book titled *Using MIS.* When one of our team members opens this site, the view of the task list shown in Figure 2-23 is displayed. The tasks in this view are sorted by Assigned To value and are filtered on the value of Status so any task that has been completed is not shown. Hence, this is a to-do list. Another view of this list, shown in Figure 2-24, includes only those tasks in which Status equals Completed. That view is a "what we've done so far" list.

Alerts are one of the most useful features in SharePoint task lists. Using alerts, team members can request SharePoint to send emails when certain events occur. Our team sets alerts so

Title	Assigned To	Status	Due Date	% Complete	Predecessors	Book
UMIS Review Summary	Kelly Loftus	Completed	2/1/2013			UMIS
Mark-up EMIS review questionnaire and return to Kelly	David Kroenke	Completed	1/7/2013			EMIS
EMIS Review Summary	Kelly Loftus	Completed	2/8/2013			EMIS
Write PSI 2e Ch 3	David Kroenke	Completed				PSI
Write PSI 2e Chapter 4	David Kroenke	Completed				PSI
Review Illustration Specs for new chapter opening scenario for Ch1-6 (in Planning documents library on this site)	Jane Bonnell	Completed	4/29/2013			UMIS
Illustration specs for new chapter opening for Ch 1-6	David Kroenke	Completed	4/29/2013			EMIS
Review New photo ideas for Chapters 1-6 Ethics Guides	Jane Bonnell	Not Started				Other
Review dk-reviewed Ch 1 & submit	Laura Town	Not Started				UMIS
Review dk-reviewed Ch 3 & Submit	Laura Town	Completed				UMIS

Figure 2-22
UMIS Production Task List in SharePoint

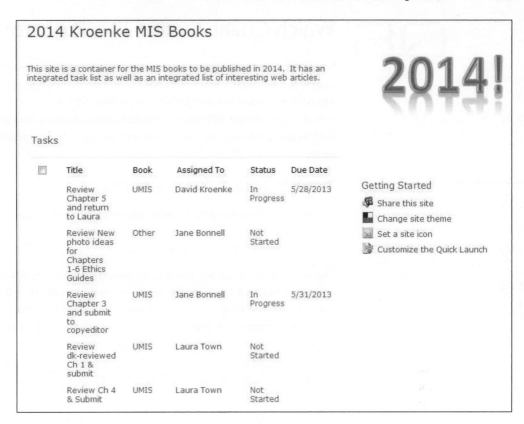

Figure 2-23
UMIS To-Do List in SharePoint

Figure 2-24
UMIS Completed Tasks in SharePoint

SharePoint sends a team member an email whenever a task is created that is assigned to him or her. Figure 2-31 (on page 77) shows the email that SharePoint sent to me when team member Laura Town assigned a new task to me. Having SharePoint send such alerts means that no team member need continually check the task list for new tasks. Team members will receive an email when a new task is created.

SharePoint task lists provide features and functions that are far superior to the Google spreadsheet shown in Figure 2-21. Again, if you can obtain access to SharePoint, you should strongly consider using it, a possibility we address in the next question.

Which Collaboration IS Is Right for Your Team?

Your MIS class will help you gain knowledge and skills that you'll use throughout your business career. But why wait? You can benefit from this knowledge right now and put it to use tonight. Most business courses involve a team project; why not use what you've learned to construct a collaboration IS that will make teamwork easier and can help your team achieve a better product? In this question, we will define and set up your evaluation of three sets of collaboration tools.

Three Sets of Collaboration Tools

Figure 2-25 summarizes three different sets of collaboration tools that you might use.

The Minimal Collaboration Tool Set

The first, the Minimal set, has the minimum possible set of tools and is shown in the second column of Figure 2-25. With this set, you should be able to collaborate with your team, though you will get little support from the software. In particular, you will need to manage concurrent access by setting up procedures and agreements to ensure that one user's work doesn't conflict with another's. Your collaboration will be with text only; you will not have access to audio or video so you cannot hear or see your collaborators. You also will not be able to view documents or whiteboards during your meeting. This set is probably close to what you're already doing.

The Good Collaboration Tool Set

The second set, the Good set, shown in the third column of Figure 2-25, shows a more sophisticated set of collaboration tools. With it, you will have the ability to conduct multiparty audio and video virtual meetings, and you will also have support for concurrent access to document, spreadsheet, and presentation files. You will not be able to support surveys, wikis, and blogs and share pictures and videos with this set. If you want any of them, you will need to search the Internet to find suitable tools.

Three Collaboration Tool Sets

	Minimal	Good	Comprehensive
Communication	Email; multiparty text chat	Google Hangouts	Microsoft Lync
Content Sharing	Email or file server	Google Drive	SharePoint
Task Management	Word or Excel files	Google Calendar	SharePoint lists integrated with email
Nice-to-Have Features		Discussion boards, surveys, wikis, blogs, share pictures/videos from third-party tools	Built-in discussion boards, surveys, wikis, blogs, picture/video sharing
Cost	Free	Free	$10/month per user or Free
Ease of Use (time to learn)	None	1 hour	3 hours
Value to Future Business Professional	None	Limited	Great
Limitations	All text, no voice or video; no tool integration	Tools not integrated, must learn to use several products	Cost, learning curve required

Figure 2-25
Three Collaboration Tool Sets

Component	Features
Lync	Multiparty text chat Audio- and videoconferencing Online content sharing Webinars with PowerPoint
SharePoint Online	Content management and control using libraries and lists Discussion forums Surveys Wikis Blogs
Exchange	Email integrated with Lync and SharePoint Online
Office 2013	Concurrent editing for Word, Excel, PowerPoint, and OneNote
Hosted integration	Infrastructure built, managed, and operated by Microsoft

Figure 2-26
Office 365 Features You Need for the Comprehensive Tool Set

The Comprehensive Collaboration Tool Set

The third set of collaboration tools, the Comprehensive set, is shown in the last column of Figure 2-25. You can obtain this tool set with certain versions of Office 365. However, Microsoft continually revises the versions and what's included in them, so you'll need to investigate which version provides the features of the comprehensive tool set. Look for a version (perhaps a free trial) that includes all the products shown in Figure 2-26. If your school has adopted Office 365 for Education, then you should be able to obtain these features for free.

This set is the best of these three because it includes content management and control, workflow control, and online meetings with sharing as just described. Furthermore, this set is integrated; SharePoint alerts can send emails via the Microsoft email server Exchange when tasks or other lists and libraries change. You can click on users' names in emails or in SharePoint, and Office 365 will automatically start a Lync text, audio, or video conversation with that user if he or she is currently available. All text messages that you send via Lync are automatically recorded and stored in your email folder.

Choosing the Set for Your Team

Which set should you choose for your team? Unless your university has already standardized on the Office 365 version you need, you will have to pay for it. You can obtain a 30-day free trial, and if your team can finish its work in that amount of time, you might choose to do so. Otherwise, your team will need to pay a minimum of $10 per month per user. So, if cost is the only factor, you can rule out the comprehensive tool set.

And even if you can afford the most comprehensive set, you may not want to use it. As noted in Figure 2-25, team members need to be willing to invest something on the order of 3 hours to begin to use the basic features. Less time, on the order of an hour, will be required to learn to use the Good tool set, and you most likely already know how to use the Minimal set.

When evaluating learning time, consider Figure 2-27. This diagram is a product **power curve**, which is a graph that shows the relationship of the power (the utility that one gains from a software product) as a function of the time using that product. A flat line means you are investing time without any increase in power. The ideal power curve starts at a positive value at time zero and has no flat spots.

The Minimal product set gives you some power at time zero because you already know how to use it. However, as you use it over time, your project will gain complexity and the problems of controlling concurrent access will actually cause power to decrease. The Good set has a short flat spot as you get to know it. However, your power then increases over time until you reach the most capability your team can do with it. The Comprehensive set has a longer flat spot in the

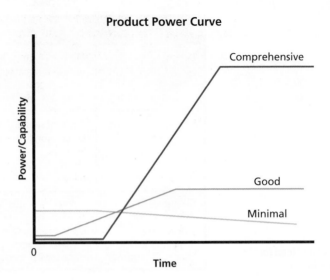

Figure 2-27
Product Power Curve

beginning because it will take longer to learn. However, because it has such a rich collaboration feature set, you will be able to gain considerable collaborative power, much more so than the Good set, and the maximum capability is much greater than the Good set.

Finally, consider the next-to-last row in Figure 2-25. The Minimal set has no value to you as a future professional and contributes nothing to your professional competitive advantage. The Good set has some limited value; as you know, there are organizations that use Google Drive and Hangouts. The Comprehensive set has the potential to give you a considerable competitive advantage, particularly because SharePoint skills are highly valued in industry. You can use knowledge of it to demonstrate the currency of your knowledge in job interviews.

So, which is the right set for your team? It's up to you. See Collaboration Exercise 2 on page 73.

Don't Forget Procedures and People!

One last and very important point: Most of this chapter focuses on collaboration tools, the software component of an information system. Regarding the other four components, you need not worry about hardware, at least not for the Good or Comprehensive sets, because those tools are hosted on hardware in the cloud. The data component is up to you; it will be your content as well as your metadata for project management and for demonstrating that your team practiced iteration and feedback.

As you evaluate alternatives, however, you need to think seriously about the procedure and people components. How are team members going to use these tools? Your team needs to have agreement on tools usage, even if you do not formally document procedures. As noted, such procedures are especially necessary for controlling concurrent access in the minimal system. You need to have agreement not only on how to use these tools, but also on what happens when teammates don't use these tools. What will you do, for example, if teammates persist in emailing documents instead of using Google Drive or SharePoint?

Additionally, how will your team train team members in the use of these tools? Will you divvy up responsibility for learning features and then teach the skills to one another? You will find a plethora of training materials on the Web.[7] But who will find them, learn them, and then teach the others?

Finally, does your team need to create any special jobs or roles? Do you want to identify, for example, someone to monitor your shared documents to ensure that deliverables are stored appropriately? Do you want someone identified to store minutes of meetings? Or to remove

---

[7]See also David Kroenke and Donald Nilson, *Office 365 in Business* (Indianapolis, IN: John Wiley & Sons, 2011).

completed tasks from a task list? Or to keep the task list in agreement with current planning? Consider these and similar needs and, if needed, appoint such a person before problems develop.

Remember this example as a future business professional: In commerce, we are never selecting just software; to put that software to use as a system, we need to create all five of the IS components!

 ## 2024?

So, how will we collaborate in 2024? Where will the current trends take us? Clearly, free data communications and data storage will make collaboration systems cheaper and easier to use. One consequence is that by 2024 face-to-face (F2F) meetings will be rare.

F2F meetings require everyone to be in the same place at the same time, and both of those *sames* can be problematic. When employees work in different locations, bringing them together is expensive in travel cost and time. Employees standing in line in airport security or waiting in their cars in traffic are hardly productive. And bringing everyone together is unfriendly to the environment.

Even when employees work at the same location, they may have schedule conflicts or they may not work at that location at the same time. And, unless employees are providing an in-person service, such as physical training, or surgery, or construction, why do they need to work in the same location?

Furthermore, what happens when you finally do get employees together? Say you bring the top managers into the home office for training. They no sooner sit down than their cell phones ring, and off they go to the lobby to handle some raging problem back home. Twenty minutes later, they're back for another 5 minutes before their phones ring again. Meanwhile, a good portion of the managers who stayed in the meeting are texting their offices throughout the training.

In 2024, employees whose services need not be provided in person will work at home, if not full time, then at least several days a week. Nearly all corporate training will be online. Most will be asynchronous.

A mining company (that chooses to remain anonymous) in Washington State provided an international example back in 2011. The company is located in the United States, close to the Canadian border, but owns several mines in Canada. For its annual audit, the company needed the services of a Canadian-chartered accounting firm from Vancouver, British Columbia. During the audit period, the border crossing was crowded, and the auditors were billing dozens of hours of expensive time while sitting unproductively in their cars at the crossing. To reduce the audit expense, the company eliminated most of this travel by storing audit data in SharePoint libraries.

But, by 2024, why be unproductive in your car? By then you should be able to use the full capabilities of whatever collaboration tools you choose on any mobile device. So, as long as you're not driving, you'll use your device in your car, or your golf cart, or your boat to get work done.

Further, as the example provided shows, by 2024 collaboration systems will greatly ease international business. If teams meet virtually most of the time, and if it doesn't matter where team members are located, then projects can involve the best, or perhaps the most affordable, workers worldwide. Further, work can follow the sun. Workers in the United States can submit documents for feedback from team members in Asia. The Asian workers can contribute their feedback during their normal workday and pass the documents along to European team members for review during *their* normal workday. All the reviewed work will be available to the U.S. workers when their next day begins.

Business travel will be a shadow of its former self. The travel industry will reorganize for mostly recreational travel. Even conventions will become, well, virtual.

Because of these trends, now is a great time for you to learn online, asynchronous collaboration skills. It's also a good time for you, as a future knowledge worker, to prepare yourself for global opportunities...and global competition. And, finally, when you're buying commercial real estate, buy that hotel in Hawaii, not the one in Paramus, New Jersey (unless, of course, it has a water slide for kids, a spa, a nearby golf course, and a casino)!

Security Guide

SECURING COLLABORATION

The collaboration tools described in this chapter do indeed facilitate collaboration: They help groups improve the quality of their work, while reducing travel and other logistical expenses and facilitating international work. They can enable people to participate in meetings asynchronously. However, they also pose security risks—possibly serious ones.

Consider Office 365. All documents are stored on Microsoft servers, which are located, well, who knows where. Does Microsoft protect those computers appropriately? If those computers are located in, say, San Francisco, will they survive an earthquake? Microsoft is a responsible, rich, and knowledgeable company that understands the need for disaster preparedness. But, as outsiders, we do not know how it protects its sites. Natural disasters are not the only threat; computer crime, the actions of disgruntled employees, and computer viruses (computer programs that replicate themselves) must be considered as well.

But chances are—even that phrase is revealing, do you really want to gamble with your data?—Microsoft knows what it is doing, and your data is more than reasonably protected. However, how does the data get to that Microsoft site? All the traffic to and from Lync and SharePoint is protected by encryption (Chapter 12), but email is not. As you will learn in Chapter 6, most wireless traffic, including email, is unprotected from wireless snoopers. Are you processing that data at a local coffee shop? Do you care that anyone in that shop can copy your data? And the situation is worse for tools that do not automatically encrypt data.

But, more likely, you pose a greater risk to data security than either Microsoft, Google, or a snooper. To see why, suppose you are the manager of a product line and you observe an odd pattern in sales for your products. That pattern might be related to differences in advertising among geographic regions, or it might have something to do with changes in consumer purchasing behavior. You decide to have a webinar with some of your staff, employees of your advertising agency, and a marketing guru who specializes in contemporary consumer behavior.

To prepare for the meeting, you access your corporate computer systems and obtain all of the sales for your products over the past 12 months. That data is highly confidential and is protected by your IS department in many ways. You can access it only because you have access authority as an employee. But, without thinking about security, you post that data in a Google Drive folder and share it with your employees, your advertising agency, and the

marketing guru. You have just violated corporate security. That confidential data is now available to the agency and the consultant. Either party can download it, and you have no way of knowing that the download was made or what was done with it.

Suppose the marketing guru makes a copy and uses it to improve her knowledge of consumer behavior. Unknown to you, she also consults for your chief rival. She has used your data to improve her knowledge and is now using that knowledge to benefit your competitor.

(This sets aside the even uglier possibility that she gives or sells your data to that competitor.)

Office 365 has extensive security features, and, except for email, as long as you stay within its bounds, it should be well protected. But, of course, SharePoint makes it easy to download data, and if you share that data with others via Google Drive or SkyDrive... well, you get the picture.

Collaboration tools have many benefits, but they do open the door to loss of critical assets. Let the collaborator beware!

 DISCUSSION QUESTIONS

1. In most circumstances, email or instant messages that you send over a wireless device are open. Anyone with some free software and a bit of knowledge can snoop on your communications. In class, your professor could read all of your email and instant messages, as could anyone else in the class. Does this knowledge change your behavior in class? Why or why not?

2. Unless you are so foolish as to reveal personal data, such as credit card numbers, a Social Security number, or a driver's license number in an email or instant message, the loss of privacy to you, as an individual, is small. Someone might learn that you were gossiping about someone else, and it might be embarrassing, but that loss is not critical. How does that situation change for business communications? Describe losses, other than those in this guide, that could occur when using email or Google Drive.

3. In addition to Google Drive, Google offers gmail, a free email service with an easy-to-use interface and that famous Google search capability. Using gmail, searching through past emails is easy, fast, and accurate. In addition, because mail is hosted on Google computers, it is easy to access one's email, contacts, and other data from any computer at any location. Many employees prefer using gmail to their corporate email system. What are the consequences to the organization of some employees doing most of their email via gmail? What are the risks?

4. Summarize the risks of using SharePoint Online in a business setting. How can organizations protect themselves from such risks? Is there any new risk here? After all, organizations have been sharing data in other formats with their business partners for years. Is this much ado about nothing? Why or why not?

5. Do you think the risks of using collaboration tools like Google Drive, SharePoint Online, or Office 365 can be so large that it makes sense for organizations to disallow their use? Why or why not? What are the costs of disallowing such use? How could an organization prevent an employee from uploading data using a corporate computer at work and then accessing that data from browsers on iPads or other mobile devices?

Guide

EGOCENTRIC VERSUS EMPATHETIC THINKING

As stated earlier, a problem is a perceived difference between what is and what ought to be. When developing information systems, it is critical for the development team to have a common definition and understanding of the problem. This common understanding can be difficult to achieve, however.

Cognitive scientists distinguish between egocentric and empathetic thinking. Egocentric thinking centers on the self; someone who engages in egocentric thinking considers his or her view as "the real view" or "what really is." In contrast, those who engage in empathetic thinking consider their view as one possible interpretation of the situation and actively work to learn what other people are thinking.

Different experts recommend empathetic thinking for different reasons. Religious leaders say that such thinking is morally superior; psychologists say that empathetic thinking leads to richer, more fulfilling relationships. In business, empathetic thinking is recommended because it is smart. Business is a social endeavor, and those who can understand others' points of view are always more effective. Even if you do not agree with others' perspectives, you will be much better able to work with them if you understand their views.

Consider an example. Suppose you say to your MIS professor, "Professor Jones, I couldn't come to class last Monday. Did we do anything important?" Such a statement is a prime example of egocentric thinking. It takes no account of your professor's point of view and implies that your professor talked about nothing important. As a professor, it is tempting to say, "No, when I noticed you weren't there, I took out all the important material."

To engage in empathetic thinking, consider this situation from the professor's point of view. Students who do not come to class cause extra work for their professors. It does not matter how valid your reason for not attending class; you may actually have been contagious with a fever of 102. But, no matter what, your not coming to class is more work for your professor. He or she must do something extra to help you recover from the lost class time.

Using empathetic thinking, you would do all you can to minimize the impact of your absence on your professor.

Source: © rnl/Fotolia

For example, you could say, "I couldn't come to class, but I got the class notes from Mary. I read through them, and I have a question about establishing alliances as competitive advantage.... Oh, by the way, I'm sorry to trouble you with my problem."

Before we go on, let's consider a corollary to this scenario: Never, ever, send an email to your boss that says, "I couldn't come to the staff meeting on Wednesday. Did we do anything important?" Avoid this for the same reasons as those for missing class. Instead, find a way to minimize the impact of your absence on your boss.

Now, what does all of this have to do with MIS? Consider the AllRoad Parts team at the start of this chapter. What is the problem? Drew thinks a big problem is that Felix doesn't come to meetings. Felix thinks the team is focused on the setup cost of 3D printing technology. Addison thinks the team should determine which parts—if any—are candidates for in-house manufacturing. Kelly, once she understands what is going on, is likely to be focused on wasted employee time and the lack of consensus among team members.

Now imagine yourself in that meeting. If everyone engages in egocentric thinking, what will happen? The meeting will be argumentative and acrimonious and likely will end with nothing accomplished.

Suppose, instead, that the attendees think empathetically. In this case, Drew may make an effort to find out why Felix is missing meetings. Felix would make an effort to understand why his behavior is a problem to the team. The team would make a concerted effort to address the different points of view, and the outcome will be much more positive—possibly a recognition that the team should be meeting virtually and asynchronously. Either way, the attendees have the same information; the difference in outcomes results from the thinking style of the attendees.

Empathetic thinking is an important skill in all business activities. Skilled negotiators always know what the other side wants; effective salespeople understand their customers' needs. Buyers who understand the problems of their vendors get better service. And students who understand the perspective of their professors get better...

DISCUSSION QUESTIONS

1. In your own words, explain how egocentric and empathetic thinking differ.
2. Suppose you miss a staff meeting. Using empathetic thinking, explain how you can get needed information about what took place in the meeting.
3. How does empathetic thinking relate to problem definition?
4. Suppose you and another person differ substantially on a problem definition. Suppose she says to you, "No, the real problem is that..." followed by her definition of the problem. How do you respond?
5. Again, suppose you and another person differ substantially on a problem definition. Assume you understand his definition. How can you make that fact clear?
6. Explain the following statement: "In business, empathetic thinking is smart." Do you agree?

ACTIVE REVIEW

Use this Active Review to verify that you understand the ideas and concepts that answer the chapter's study questions.

Q1   What are the two key characteristics of collaboration?

In your own words, explain the difference between cooperation and collaboration. Name the two key characteristics of collaboration and explain how they improve group work. Name the key component of a collaboration IS and explain why the text claims this is so. Summarize important skills for collaborators and list what you believe are the best ways to give and receive critical feedback.

Q2   What are three criteria for successful collaboration?

Name and describe three criteria for collaboration success. Summarize how these criteria differ between student and professional teams.

Q3   What are the four primary purposes of collaboration?

Name and describe four primary purposes of collaboration. Explain their relationship. Describe ways that collaboration systems can contribute to each purpose.

Q4   What are the requirements for a collaboration information system?

Name and describe the five components of a collaboration information system. Summarize the primary requirements for collaboration information systems and relate those requirements to the need for iteration and feedback as well as the three criteria for successful collaboration.

Q5   How can you use collaboration tools to improve team communication?

Explain why communication is important to collaboration. Define *synchronous* and *asynchronous communication* and explain when each is used. Name two collaboration tools that can be used to help set up synchronous meetings. Describe collaboration tools that can be used for face-to-face meetings. Describe tools that can be used for virtual, synchronous meetings. Describe tools that can be used for virtual, asynchronous meetings.

Q6   How can you use collaboration tools to manage shared content?

Summarize alternatives for processing Office documents on the desktop as well as over the Internet. Describe two ways that content is shared with no control and explain the problems that can occur. Explain the difference between version management and version control. Describe how user accounts, passwords, and libraries are used to control user activity. Explain how check-in/checkout works. Describe workflows and give an example.

Q7   How can you use collaboration tools to manage tasks?

Explain why managing tasks is important to team progress. Demonstrate how a task should be described. List the minimal content of a task list. Summarize the advantages and disadvantages of using Google Drive and Microsoft SharePoint for managing tasks.

Q8   Which collaboration IS is right for your team?

Describe the three collaboration tool sets described and indicate how each meets the minimum requirements for collaboration. Explain the differences among them. Summarize the criteria for choosing the right set for your team. Explain the meaning of the power curve and discuss the power curve for each of the three alternatives described.

Q9   2024?

Describe the impact that free data storage and data communications have on collaboration systems. Explain why F2F meetings are expensive in both cost and time. Explain why meetings such as F2F training sessions can be ineffective. Summarize the ways collaboration systems reduce the costs and difficulties of international business. Explain how collaboration systems are changing the scope of workers with whom you will compete. Describe consequences of all this to the travel industry. If you disagree with any of the conclusions in this 2024, explain how and why.

Using Your Knowledge with AllRoad Parts

Reread the AllRoad scenario at the start of this chapter. Using the knowledge you've gained from this chapter, explain how this team could use collaboration tools to be more effective. Describe how such tools can solve Felix's problems as well as result in better communication and higher quality results for the team.

KEY TERMS AND CONCEPTS

MyMISLab

Go to **mymislab.com** to complete the problems marked with this icon .

USING YOUR KNOWLEDGE

2-1. Reflect on your experience working on teams in previous classes as well as on collaborative teams in other settings, such as a campus committee. To what extent was your team collaborative? Did it involve feedback and iteration? If so, how? How did you use collaborative information systems, if at all? If you did not use collaborative information systems, describe how you think such systems might have improved your work methods and results. If you did use collaborative information systems, explain how you could improve on that use, given the knowledge you have gained from this chapter.

2-2. Using your experience working in past teams, give an example of an unhelpful statement for each of the guidelines in Figure 2-2. Correct your examples to a more productive and helpful comment.

2-3. Using a past team project from your own experience, summarize how your team conducted the four phases listed in Figure 2-5. Evaluate how your team conducted problem-solving, decision-making, and informing activities. Rate your past team on Hackman's criteria as discussed in Q2.

2-4. This exercise requires you to experiment with Microsoft SkyDrive. You will need two Office IDs to complete this exercise. The easiest way to do it is to work with a classmate. If that is not possible, set up two Office accounts using two different Hotmail addresses.

    a. Go to *www.skydrive.com* and sign in with one of your accounts. Create a memo about collaboration tools using the Word Web App. Save your memo. Share your document with the email in your second Office account. Sign out of your first account.

        (If you have access to two computers situated close to each other, use both of them for this exercise. If you have two computers, do not sign out of your Office account. Perform step b and all actions for the second account on that second computer. If you are using two computers, ignore the instructions in the following steps to sign out of the Office accounts.)

    b. Open a new window in your browser. Access *www.skydrive.com* from that second window and sign in using your second Office account. Open the document that you shared in step a.

    c. Change the memo by adding a brief description of content management. Do not save the document yet. If you are using just one computer, sign out from your second account.

    d. Sign in on your first account. Attempt to open the memo and note what occurs. Sign out of your first account and sign back in with your second account. Save the document. Now, sign out of your second account and sign back in with the first account. Now attempt to open the memo. (If you are using two computers, perform these same actions on the two different computers.)

    e. Sign in on your second account. Reopen the shared document. From the *File* menu, save the document as a Word document. Describe how SkyDrive processed the changes to your document.

In this exercise, you will first build a collaboration IS and then use that IS to answer four questions in a collaborative fashion. You might want to read the four questions (in item 4 below) before you build your IS.

Until you answer question 1, you'll have to make do with email or face-to-face meeting. Once you've answered that question, use your communication method to answer question 2. Once you've answered question 2, use your communication and your content-sharing method to answer question 3. Then use the full IS to answer question 4.

1. Build a communication method:
   a. Meet with your team and decide how you want to meet in the future. Use Figure 2-8 as a guide.
   b. From the discussion in a, list the requirements for your communication system.
   c. Select and implement a communication tool. It could be Skype, Google Hangouts, or Microsoft Lync.
   d. Write procedures for the team to use when utilizing your new communication tool.

2. Build a content-sharing method:
   a. Meet with your team and decide the types of content that you will be creating.
   b. Decide as a team whether you want to process your content using desktop applications or cloud-based applications. Choose the applications you want to use.
   c. Decide as a team the server you will use to share your content. You can use Google Grid, Microsoft SkyDrive, Microsoft SharePoint, or some other server.
   d. Implement your content-sharing server.
   e. Write procedures for the team to use when sharing content.

3. Build a task management method:
   a. Meet with your team and decide how you want to manage tasks. Determine the task data that you want to store on your task list.

   b. Decide, as a team the tool and server you will use for sharing your tasks. You can use Google Drive, Microsoft SkyDrive, Microsoft SharePoint, or some other facility.
   c. Implement the tool and server in a.
   d. Write procedures for the team to use when managing tasks.

4. Using your new collaboration information system, answer the following questions:
   a. What is collaboration? Reread Q1 in this chapter, but do not confine yourselves to that discussion. Consider your own experience working in collaborative teams, and search the Web to identify other ideas about collaboration. Dave Pollard, one of the authors of the survey on which Figure 2-1 is based, is a font of ideas on collaboration.
   b. What characteristics make for an effective team member? Review the survey of effective collaboration skills in Figure 2-1 and the guidelines for giving and receiving critical feedback, and discuss them as a group. Do you agree with them? What skills or feedback techniques would you add to this list? What conclusions can you, as a team, take from this survey? Would you change the rankings in Figure 2-1?
   c. What would you do with an ineffective team member? First, define an ineffective team member. Specify five or so characteristics of an ineffective team member. If your group has such a member, what action do you, as a group, believe should be taken?
   d. How do you know if you are collaborating well? When working with a group, how do you know whether you are working well or poorly? Specify five or so characteristics that indicate collaborative success. How can you measure those characteristics?
   e. Briefly describe the components of your new collaboration IS.
   f. Describe what your team likes and doesn't like about using your new collaboration system.

Eating Our Own Dog Food

Dogfooding is the process of using a product or idea that you develop or promote. The term arose in the 1980s in the software industry when someone observed that the company wasn't using the product it developed. Or "they weren't eating their own dog food." Wikipedia attributes the term to Brian Valentine, test manager for Microsoft LAN Manager in

1988, but I recall using the term before that date. Whatever its origin, if, of their own accord, employees choose to dogfood their own product or idea, many believe that product or idea is likely to succeed.

You may be asking, "So what?" Well, this text was developed by a collaborative team, using Office 365 Professional and many of the techniques described in this chapter. We dog-fooded the ideas and products in this chapter.

Figure 2-28 shows a diagram of the process that transforms a draft chapter in Word, PowerPoint, and PNG image format into PDF pages. You will learn more about process diagrams like this in Chapter 10. For now, just realize that each column represents the activities taken by a role, which in this case is a particular person. The process starts with the thin-lined circle in the top left and ends with the thick-lined circle near the bottom right. The dashed lines represent the flow of data from one activity to another.

As shown in Figure 2-28, the author works closely with the developmental editor, who ensures that the text is complete and complies with the market requirements, as specified by the acquisitions editor. We need not delve into this process in detail here; just observe that many different versions of chapter text and chapter art are created as people playing the various roles edit and approve and adjust edits.

Face-to-face meetings are impossible because the people fulfilling the roles in Figure 2-28 live in different geographic locations. In the past, the developmental process was conducted using the phone, email, and an ftp server. As you can imagine, considerable confusion can ensue with the hundreds of documents, art exhibits, and multiple reviewed copies of each. Furthermore, task requests that are delivered via email are easily lost. Dropped tasks and incorrect versions of documents and art are not common, but they do occur.

When we decided to begin publishing a new edition every year, we knew we needed to find some way of increasing our

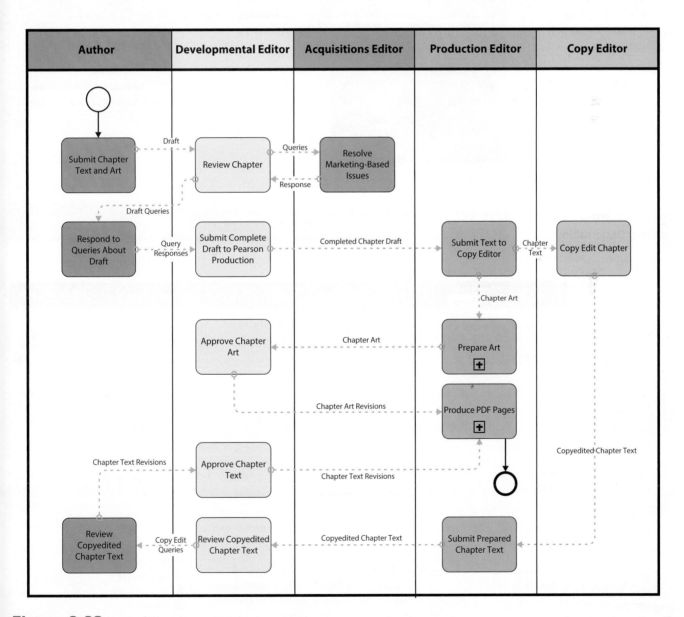

Figure 2-28
Chapter Development Process

productivity. Consequently, our development team decided to eat its own dogfood and use Office 365 Professional. During this process, the author, the developmental editor Laura Town, and the production editors Kelly Loftus and Jane Bonnell met frequently on Lync. Figure 2-29 shows a typical Lync meeting. Notice that the three actors in this process are sharing a common whiteboard. Each can write or draw on that whiteboard. At the end of the meeting, the whiteboards were saved and placed on the team's SharePoint site to be used as minutes of the meeting.

Figure 2-30 shows the team's SharePoint site. The **Quick Launch** (left-side vertical menu) has links to important content on the site. The center portion has tasks that have a value other than "Completed" for Status.

The team set up alerts so that when new tasks were created in the Tasks list, SharePoint would send an email to the person

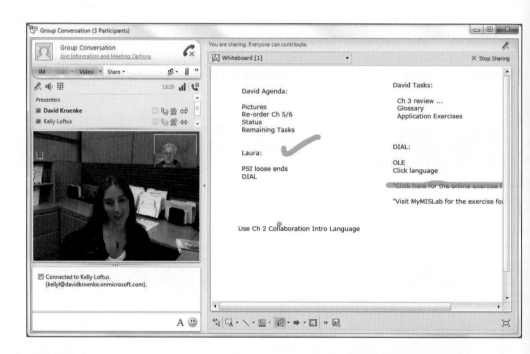

Figure 2-29
Lync Group Conversation

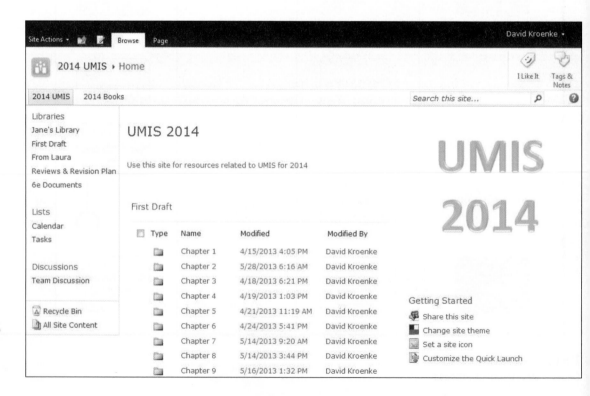

Figure 2-30
Using MIS 7th Edition SharePoint Development Site

who had been assigned that task. Figure 2-31 shows an email that was sent to David when Laura added a task to the Tasks list.

All documents and figures were stored and managed in SharePoint libraries. Figure 2-32 shows the contents of the First Draft Chapter 2 library at the time this chapter was written. The folder Chapter 2 has the text and figures for this chapter. By storing documents in SharePoint, the team took advantage of library version tracking. Figure 2-33 shows a portion of the version history of Chapter 6 of this text.

When it is completed, Laura will need to review the final chapter version, so a task should be created asking her to do so. That new task will spawn an email to her like the email in Figure 2-31. I will create that task just as soon as I finish this sentence! That's dogfooding!

QUESTIONS

2-5. In your own words, define *dogfooding*. Do you think dog-fooding is likely to predict product success? Why or why not? When would dogfooding not predict product success?

2-6. Explain how this team uses the shared whiteboard to generate minutes. What are the advantages of this technique?

2-7. Explain how this team uses alerts. Summarize the advantages to this team of using alerts.

2-8. Summarize the advantages to this team of using Lync.

2-9. Summarize the advantages to this team of using SharePoint.

2-10. Explain how you think Office 365 Professional contributes to the efficiency of the development team. How might it contribute to the quality of this text?

2-11. Which aspects of Office 365 Professional described here could have value to you when accomplishing student team projects? Explain why they add value compared to what you are currently doing.

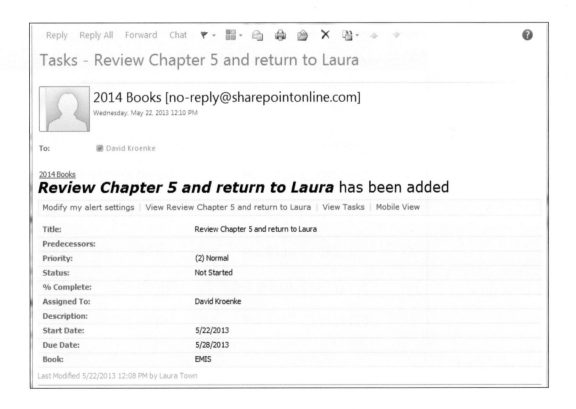

Figure 2-31
Example Email from SharePoint

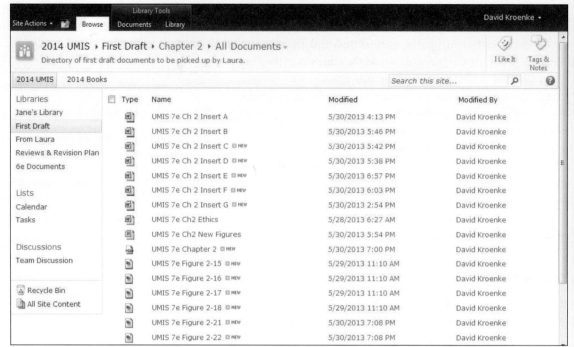

Figure 2-32
First Draft Document
Library Contents

Figure 2-33
Chapter 6 Version History

MyMISLab

Go to **mymislab.com** for Auto-graded writing questions as well as the following Assisted-graded writing questions:

2-12. Reread about 2024 in Q9. Do you agree with the conclusions? Why or why not? If F2F meetings become rare, what additional impacts do you see on the travel industry? In light of this change, describe travel industry investments that make sense and those that do not. What are promising investments in training? What are promising investments in other industries?

2-13. This exercise requires you to experiment with Google Drive. You will need two Google accounts to complete this exercise. If you have two different email addresses, then set up two Google accounts using those addresses. Otherwise, use your school email address and set up a Google gmail account. A gmail account will automatically give you a Google account.

    a. Using Microsoft Word, write a memo to yourself. In the memo, explain the nature of the communication collaboration driver. Go to *http://drive.google.com* and sign in with one of your Google accounts. Upload your memo using Google Drive. Save your uploaded document in Google Docs format and share your document with the email in your second Google account. Sign out of your first Google account.

       (If you have access to two computers situated close to each other, use both of them for this exercise. You will see more of the Google Drive functionality by using two computers. If you have two computers, do not sign out of your Google account. Perform step b and all actions for the second account on that second computer. If you are using two computers, ignore the instructions in the following steps to sign out of the Google accounts.)

    b. Open a new window in your browser. Access *http://drive.google.com* from that second window and sign in using your second Google account. Open the document that you shared in step a.

    c. Change the memo by adding a brief description of content management. Save the document from your second account. If you are using just one computer, sign out from your second account.

    d. Sign in on your first account. Open the most recent version of the memo and add a description of the role of version histories. Save the document. (If you are using two computers, notice how Google warns you that another user is editing the document at the same time. Click *Refresh* to see what happens.) If you are using just one computer, sign out from your first account.

    e. Sign in on your second account. Reopen the shared document. From the *File* menu, save the document as a Word document. Describe how Google processed the changes to your document.

2-14. Mymislab Only – comprehensive writing assignment for this chapter.

Strategy and Information Systems

"Drew, what's your hurry?" Addison Lee jumps out of the way as Drew comes barreling out of his office.

"Workload, Addison, workload. They've given me the task of setting up our new 3D printing facility. I don't know anything about it. But no one else does, either."

"Wow. So, we've decided to get into 3D printing?" Addison is so curious about this idea.

"Well, not that I know. All I know is that Jason and Kelly want me to set it up and see what it can do." Drew's not complaining, just worried.

"Well, you'll figure it out. You always do."

"Thanks, Addison, I appreciate the vote of confidence," Drew continues. "But you know what really bothers me?"

"No, what?" Addison looks closely at him and realizes that he really is exhausted.

"Who are we?"

"What do you mean?" Addison thinks she knows who they are.

"Well, as a company, who are we? We've always been the one place you can go to find just about any part for an adventure vehicle. Yeah, sure, we don't have tires for Jeeps, but you know what I mean. Any part that has to do with specialty off-road equipment, that's us."

"So…"

"So, we buy our parts from others, who really know how to make them. We've never been a manufacturer. We start manufacturing spare parts, even if it's just simple ones … well, that's a whole new business." Drew sounds very worried as he speaks.

"Sounds exciting to me."

"Yeah, and wrestling with alligators is also exciting."

"What most concerns you?"

"Where do I begin? Hmm. We don't have internal processes for manufacturing. What items do we decide to build? When? On what schedule? How do we order the raw materials? How do we set up the equipment? What information systems do we need? What personnel? How do we control for quality? Do we need new information systems there? Databases to store manufacturing and quality data? And, Addison, I'm just getting started."

"Sounds like you've got your hands full."

"Yeah, I do. And I'm still running operations."

"You think this is a bad idea?"

"Maybe. I don't know. If this is the future, then we need to get on board. On the other hand, we could waste plenty of money and ruin our reputation with our customers. And 3D printing might be just a fad."

"Hey, Drew, I've got to run. But let me know if I can help somehow."

"OK. Thanks. I just hope Jason and Kelly know one thing."

"What's that?"

"This isn't like taking on a new line of parts. It means changing the business we're in. And we've got a lot of process and systems work to do if we want to do that. It's not just the $10,000 for the machine, that's for sure."

"Well, tell 'em that."

"I will. I hope they already know it, though."

"And we've got a lot of process and systems work to do."

STUDY QUESTIONS

Q1 How does organizational strategy determine information systems structure?

Q2 What five forces determine industry structure?

Q3 How does analysis of industry structure determine competitive strategy?

Q4 How does competitive strategy determine value chain structure?

Q5 How do business processes generate value?

Q6 How does competitive strategy determine business processes and the structure of information systems?

Q7 How do information systems provide competitive advantages?

Q8 2024?

Recall from Chapter 1 that MIS is the development and use of information systems that enable organizations to achieve their strategies. In Chapter 2, you learned how information systems can help people collaborate. This chapter focuses on how information systems support competitive strategy and how IS can create competitive advantages. As you will learn in your organizational behavior classes, a body of knowledge exists to help organizations analyze their industry, select a competitive strategy, and develop business processes. In the first part of this chapter, we will survey that knowledge and show how to use it, via several steps, to structure information systems. Then, in the last section, we will discuss how companies use information systems to gain a competitive advantage.

AllRoad Parts provides a good example. Its strategy has been to differentiate itself by having the biggest inventory of adventure-vehicle spare parts, anywhere. It has systems and processes to do that. But, as Drew states, what's the company's business strategy if it wants to start manufacturing? And, if it does, the company has a lot of systems and process work ahead of it.

Q1 How Does Organizational Strategy Determine Information Systems Structure?

For a real-life example illustrating the relationship of competitive strategy, business processes, and information systems, go to the PT Sails Videos in Chapter 3 at mymislab.com.

According to the definition of MIS, information systems exist to help organizations achieve their strategies. As you will learn in your business strategy class, an organization's goals and objectives are determined by its *competitive strategy*. Thus, ultimately, competitive strategy determines the structure, features, and functions of every information system.

Figure 3-1 summarizes this situation. In short, organizations examine the structure of their industry and determine a competitive strategy. That strategy determines value chains, which, in turn, determine business processes. The structure of business processes determines the design of supporting information systems.

Michael Porter, one of the key researchers and thinkers in competitive analysis, developed three different models that can help you understand the elements of Figure 3-1. We begin with his five forces model.

Figure 3-1
Organizational Strategy
Determines Information Systems

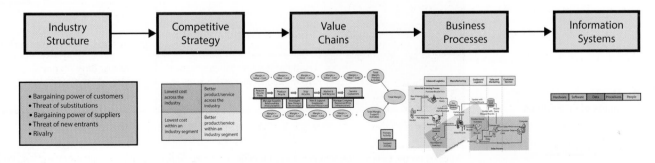

Figure 3-2

Porter's Five Forces Model of Industry Structure

Source: Based on Michael E. Porter, *Competitive Advantage: Creating and Sustaining Superior Performance* (The Free Press, a Division of Simon & Schuster Adult Publishing Group). Copyright © 1985, 1998 by Michael E. Porter.

- Bargaining power of customers
- Threat of substitutions
- Bargaining power of suppliers
- Threat of new entrants
- Rivalry

What Five Forces Determine Industry Structure?

Organizational strategy begins with an assessment of the fundamental characteristics and structure of an industry. One model used to assess an industry structure is Porter's **five forces model**,[1] summarized in Figure 3-2. According to this model, five competitive forces determine industry profitability: bargaining power of customers, threat of substitutions, bargaining power of suppliers, threat of new entrants, and rivalry among existing firms. The intensity of each of the five forces determines the characteristics of the industry, how profitable it is, and how sustainable that profitability will be.

To understand this model, consider the strong and weak examples for each of the forces in Figure 3-3. A good check on your understanding is to see if you can think of different forces of each category in Figure 3-3. Also, take a particular industry—say, auto repair—and consider how these five forces determine the competitive landscape of that industry.

Jason is concerned that 3D printing may place AllRoad Parts at a competitive disadvantage. Figure 3-4 shows the team's analysis of the new competitive landscape. The larger customers from whom the company receives two-thirds of its revenue (major bike shops, motorcycle dealers, Jeep and other customization shops) will gain considerable force power if they can make parts themselves using 3D printing. The threat of new entrants from existing, local manufacturers is also strong. The other forces are not as worrisome to AllRoad. In most cases, there aren't any substitute repair parts, and, given the reality of 3D printing, AllRoad Parts' suppliers are

Force	Example of Strong Force	Example of Weak Force
Bargaining power of customers	Toyota's purchase of auto paint (because Toyota is a huge customer that will purchase paint in large volume)	Your power over the procedures and policies of your university
Threat of substitutions	Frequent traveler's choice of auto rental	Patients using the only drug effective for their type of cancer
Bargaining power of suppliers	Students purchasing gasoline (because there are many gas stations that students can choose from)	Grain farmers in a surplus year (an oversupply makes the product less valuable and less profitable)
Threat of new entrants	Corner latte stand (because it is an easy business to replicate)	Professional football team (because it is an incredibly expensive business to replicate)
Rivalry	Used car dealers (because there are many to choose from)	Google or Bing (expensive to develop and market a search engine)

Figure 3-3

Examples of Five Forces

[1]Michael Porter, *Competitive Strategy: Techniques for Analyzing Industries and Competitors* (New York: Free Press, 1980).

Force	AllRoad Parts Example	Force Strength	AllRoad Parts' Response
Bargaining power of customers	"I'll make it myself."	Strong, if 3D printing is real	Do its own 3D printing
Threat of substitutions	"I'll buy a different part."	Very weak; in most cases, there are no substitute parts	Maintain a large inventory
Bargaining power of suppliers	"We won't sell you our 3D design files."	Medium	Sell other vendors' designs
Threat of new entrants	"A local company has started 3D printing of parts I used to buy from you."	Possibly strong	3D printing?
Rivalry	"With local 3D manufacturers, I can buy right here in town."	Weak	Evolve with rivals, if necessary

Figure 3-4
Five Forces at AllRoad Parts

likely to sell 3D designs for repair parts...to protect the sales of their gear. Jason doesn't think the threat of 3D printing from rivals is as strong because, like AllRoad Parts, they don't have manufacturing systems, processes, or expertise, either.

Like AllRoad Parts, organizations examine these five forces and determine how they intend to respond to them. That examination leads to competitive strategy.

Q3 How Does Analysis of Industry Structure Determine Competitive Strategy?

See the Ethics Guide on pages 86–87 to learn how a change in strategy can greatly affect a company's culture.

An organization responds to the structure of its industry by choosing a **competitive strategy**. Porter followed his five forces model with the model of four competitive strategies, shown in Figure 3-5.[2] According to Porter, firms engage in one of these four strategies. An organization can focus on being the cost leader, or it can focus on differentiating its products or services from those of the competition. Further, the organization can employ the cost or differentiation strategy across an industry, or it can focus its strategy on a particular industry segment.

Consider the car rental industry, for example. According to the first column of Figure 3-5, a car rental company can strive to provide the lowest-cost car rentals across the industry, or it can seek to provide the lowest-cost car rentals to an industry segment—say, U.S. domestic business travelers.

	Cost	**Differentiation**
Industry-wide	Lowest cost across the industry	Better product/service across the industry
Focus	Lowest cost within an industry segment	Better product/service within an industry segment

Figure 3-5
Porter's Four Competitive Strategies

[2]Based on Michael Porter, *Competitive Strategy* (New York: Free Press, 1985).

Ethics Guide

YIKES! BIKES

Suppose you are an operations manager for Yikes! Bikes, an AllRoad Parts customer that manufactures high-end mountain bicycles. Yikes! has been in business more than 25 years and has an annual revenue of $35 million. The founder and sole owner recently sold the business to an investment group, Major Capital. You know nothing about the sale until your boss introduces you to Andrea Parks, a partner at Major Capital, who is in charge of the acquisition. Parks explains to you that Yikes! has been sold to Major Capital and that she will be the temporary general manager. She explains that the new owners see great potential in you, and they want to enlist your cooperation during the transition. She hints that if your potential is what she thinks it is, you will be made general manager of Yikes!

Parks explains that the new owners decided there are too many players in the high-end mountain bike business, and they plan to change the competitive strategy of Yikes! from high-end differentiation to lowest-cost vendor. Accordingly, they will eliminate local manufacturing, fire most of the manufacturing department, and import bikes from China. Further, Major Capital sees a need to reduce expenses and plans a 10 percent across-the-board staff reduction and a cut of two-thirds of the customer support department. The new bikes will be of lesser quality than current Yikes! bikes, but the price will be substantially less. The new ownership group believes it will take a few years for the market to realize that Yikes! bikes are not the same quality as they were. Finally, Parks asks you to attend an all-employee meeting with the founder and her.

At the meeting, the founder explains that, due to his age and personal situation, he decided to sell Yikes!

to Major Capital and that starting today Andrea Parks is the general manager. He thanks the employees for their many years of service, wishes them well, and leaves the building. Parks introduces herself to the employees and states that Major Capital is very excited to own such a great company with a strong, quality brand. She says she will take a few weeks to orient herself to the business and its environment and plans no major changes to the company.

You are reeling from all this news when Parks calls you into her office and explains that she needs you to prepare two reports. In one, she wants a list of all the employees in the manufacturing department, sorted by their salary (or wage for hourly employees). She explains that she intends to cut the most costly employees first. "I don't want to be inflexible about this, though," she says. "If there is someone whom you think we should keep, let me know, and we can talk about it."

Source: Claudiu Paizan/Shutterstock and PSD photography/Shutterstock

She also wants a list of the employees in the customer support department, sorted by the average amount of time each support rep spends with customers. She explains, "I'm not so concerned with payroll expense in customer support. It's not how much we're paying someone, it's how much time they're wasting with customers. We're going to have a bare-bones support department, and we want to get rid of the gabby chatters first."

You are, understandably, shocked and surprised...not only at the speed with which the transition has occurred, but also because you wouldn't think the founder would do this to the employees. You call him at home and tell him what is going on.

"Look," he explains, "when I sold the company, I asked them to be sure to take care of the employees. They said they would. I'll call Andrea, but there's really nothing I can do at this point; they own the show."

In a black mood of depression, you realize you don't want to work for Yikes! anymore, but your wife is 6 months pregnant with your first child. You need medical insurance for her at least until the baby is born. But what miserable tasks are you going to be asked to do before then? And you suspect that if you balk at any task, Parks won't hesitate to fire you, too.

As you leave that night, you run into Lori, the most popular customer support representative and one of your favorite employees. "Hey," Lori asks you, "what did you think of that meeting? Do you believe Andrea? Do you think they'll let us continue to make great bikes?"

 DISCUSSION QUESTIONS

1. In your opinion, did the new owners take any illegal action? Is there evidence of a crime in this scenario?

2. Consider the ethics of the statement that Parks made to all of the employees. Using both the categorical imperative (pages 20–21) and utilitarianism (pages 54–55), assess the ethics of that statement. Were you to question her about the ethics of her statement, how do you think she would justify herself?

3. What do you think Parks will tell the founder if he calls as a result of your conversation with him? Does he have any legal recourse? Is Major Capital's behavior toward him unethical? Why or why not?

4. Parks is going to use data to perform staff cuts. What do you think about her criteria? Ethically, should she consider other factors, such as number of years of service, past employee reviews, or other criteria?

5. How do you respond to Lori? What are the consequences if you tell her what you know? What are the consequences of lying to her? What are the consequences of saying something noncommittal? Consider both the categorical imperative and utilitarianism perspectives in your response.

6. If you actually were in this situation, would you leave the company? Why or why not?

7. In business school, we talk of principles like competitive strategy as interesting academic topics. But, as you can see from the Yikes! case, competitive strategy decisions have human consequences. How do you plan to resolve conflicts between human needs and tough business decisions?

8. How do you define *job security*?

As shown in the second column, a car rental company can seek to differentiate its products from the competition. It can do so in various ways—for example, by providing a wide range of high-quality cars, by providing the best reservation system, by having the cleanest cars or the fastest check-in, or by some other means. The company can strive to provide product differentiation across the industry or within particular segments of the industry, such as U.S. domestic business travelers.

According to Porter, to be effective, the organization's goals, objectives, culture, and activities must be consistent with the organization's strategy. To those in the MIS field, this means that all information systems in the organization must reflect and facilitate the organization's competitive strategy.

AllRoad Parts has chosen the differentiation strategy of having the largest inventory of spare parts for the off-road cycling, dirt bike, and off-road vehicle markets. This strategy is threatened by 3D printing, which is why the company is investigating it.

Q4 How Does Competitive Strategy Determine Value Chain Structure?

Organizations analyze the structure of their industry, and, using that analysis, they formulate a competitive strategy. They then need to organize and structure the organization to implement that strategy. If, for example, the competitive strategy is to be *cost leader*, then business activities need to be developed to provide essential functions at the lowest possible cost.

A business that selects a *differentiation* strategy would not necessarily structure itself around least-cost activities. Instead, such a business might choose to develop more costly processes, but it would do so only if those processes provided benefits that outweighed their costs. Jason at AllRoad Parts knows his large inventory is expensive, and he judges the extra costs worthwhile. He may judge 3D printing to be worthwhile, too.

Porter defined **value** as the amount of money that a customer is willing to pay for a resource, product, or service. The difference between the value that an activity generates and the cost of the activity is called the **margin**. A business with a differentiation strategy will add cost to an activity only as long as the activity has a positive margin.

A **value chain** is a network of value-creating activities. That generic chain consists of five **primary activities** and four **support activities.**

Primary Activities in the Value Chain

To understand the essence of the value chain, consider one of AllRoad Parts' suppliers, a small manufacturer—say, a bicycle maker (see Figure 3-6). First, the manufacturer acquires raw materials using the inbound logistics activity. This activity concerns the receiving and handling of raw materials and other inputs. The accumulation of those materials adds value in the sense that even a pile of unassembled parts is worth something to some customer. A collection of the parts needed to build a bicycle is worth more than an empty space on a shelf. The value is not only the parts themselves, but also the time required to contact vendors for those parts, to maintain business relationships with those vendors, to order the parts, to receive the shipment, and so forth.

In the operations activity, the bicycle maker transforms raw materials into a finished bicycle, a process that adds more value. Next, the company uses the outbound logistics activity to deliver the finished bicycle to a customer. Of course, there is no customer to send the bicycle to without the marketing and sales value activity. Finally, the service activity provides customer support to the bicycle users.

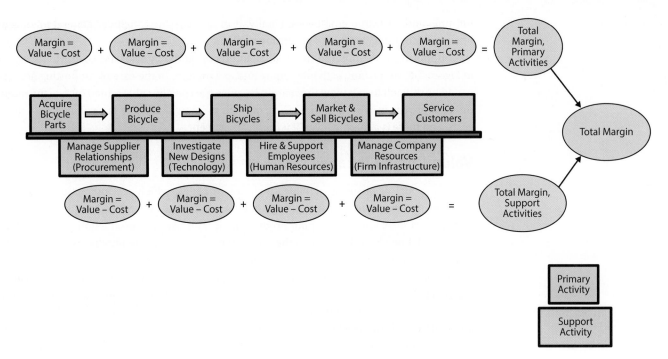

Figure 3-6
Bicycle Manufacturer's Value Chain

Each stage of this generic chain accumulates costs and adds value to the product. The net result is the total margin of the chain, which is the difference between the total value added and the total costs incurred. Figure 3-7 summarizes the primary activities of the value chain.

Support Activities in the Value Chain

The support activities in the generic value chain contribute indirectly to the production, sale, and service of the product. They include procurement, which consists of the processes of finding vendors, setting up contractual arrangements, and negotiating prices. (This differs from inbound logistics, which is concerned with ordering and receiving in accordance with agreements set up by procurement.)

Porter defined technology broadly. It includes research and development, but it also includes other activities within the firm for developing new techniques, methods, and procedures. He defined human resources as recruiting, compensation, evaluation, and training of

Figure 3-7
Task Descriptions for Primary Activities of the Value Chain

Source: Based on Michael E. Porter, *Competitive Advantage: Creating and Sustaining Superior Performance* (The Free Press, a Division of Simon & Schuster Adult Publishing Group). Copyright © 1985, 1998 by Michael E. Porter.

Primary Activity	Description
Inbound Logistics	Receiving, storing, and disseminating inputs to the products
Operations/Manufacturing	Transforming inputs into the final products
Outbound Logistics	Collecting, storing, and physically distributing the products to buyers
Sales and Marketing	Inducing buyers to purchase the products and providing a means for them to do so
Customer Service	Assisting customers' use of the products and thus maintaining and enhancing the products' value

full-time and part-time employees. Finally, firm infrastructure includes general management, finance, accounting, legal, and government affairs.

Supporting functions add value, albeit indirectly, and they also have costs. Hence, as shown in Figure 3-6, supporting activities contribute to a margin. In the case of supporting activities, it would be difficult to calculate the margin because the specific value added of, say, the manufacturer's lobbyists in Washington, D.C., is difficult to know. But there is a value added, there are costs, and there is a margin, even if it is only in concept.

Value Chain Linkages

Porter's model of business activities includes **linkages**, which are interactions across value activities. For example, manufacturing systems use linkages to reduce inventory costs. Such a system uses sales forecasts to plan production; it then uses the production plan to determine raw material needs and then uses the material needs to schedule purchases. The end result is just-in-time inventory, which reduces inventory sizes and costs.

By describing value chains and their linkages, Porter started a movement to create integrated, cross-departmental business systems. Over time, Porter's work led to the creation of a new discipline called business process design. The central idea is that organizations should not automate or improve existing functional systems. Rather, they should create new, more efficient business processes that integrate the activities of all departments involved in a value chain. You will see an example of a linkage in the next section.

Value chain analysis has a direct application to manufacturing businesses like the bicycle manufacturer. However, value chains also exist in service-oriented companies such as medical clinics. The difference is that most of the value in a service company is generated by the operations, marketing and sales, and service activities. Inbound and outbound logistics are not typically as important.

 ## How Do Business Processes Generate Value?

A **business process** is a network of activities that generate value by transforming inputs into outputs. The **cost** of the business process is the cost of the inputs plus the cost of the activities. The margin of the business process is the value of the outputs minus the cost.

A business process is a network of activities. Each **activity** is a business function that receives inputs and produces outputs. An activity can be performed by a human, by a computer system, or by both. The inputs and outputs can be physical, like bicycle parts, or they can be data, such as a purchase order. A **repository** is a collection of something; a database is a repository of data and a raw material repository is an inventory of raw materials. We will refine and extend these definitions in Chapter 7 and again in Chapter 10, but these basic terms will get us started.

Consider the three business processes for a bicycle manufacturer shown in Figure 3-8. The materials ordering process transforms cash[3] into a raw materials inventory. The manufacturing process transforms raw materials into finished goods. The sales process transforms finished goods into cash. Notice that the business processes span the value chain activities. The sales process involves sales and marketing as well as outbound logistics activities, as you would expect. Note, too, that while none of these three processes involve a customer-service activity, customer service plays a role in other business processes.

---

[3]For simplicity, the flow of cash is abbreviated in Figure 3-8. Business processes for authorizing, controlling, making payments, and receiving revenue are, of course, vital.

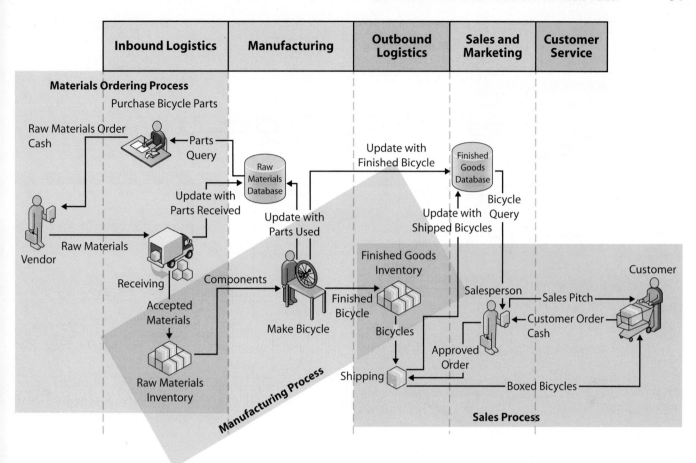

Figure 3-8

Three Examples of Business
Processes

Also notice that activities get and put data resources from and to databases. For example, the purchase-bicycle-parts activity queries the raw materials database to determine the materials to order. The receiving activity updates the raw materials database to indicate the arrival of materials. The make-bicycle activity updates the raw materials database to indicate the consumption of materials. Similar actions are taken in the sales process against the finished goods database.

Business processes vary in cost and effectiveness. In fact, the streamlining of business processes to increase margin (add value, reduce costs, or both) is key to competitive advantage. You will learn about process design when we discuss **business process management** in Chapter 10. To get a flavor of process design, however, consider Figure 3-9, which shows an alternate process for the bicycle manufacturer. Here the purchase-bicycle-parts activity not only queries the raw materials inventory database, it also queries the finished goods inventory database. Querying both databases allows the purchasing department to make decisions not just on raw materials quantities, but also on customer demand. By using this data, purchasing can reduce the size of raw materials inventory, reducing production costs and thus adding margin to the value chain. This is an example of using a linkage across business processes to improve process margin.

As you will learn, however, changing business processes is not easy to do. Most process design requires people to work in new ways and to follow different procedures, and employees often resist such change. In Figure 3-9, the employees who perform the purchase-bicycle-parts activity need to learn to adjust their ordering processes to use customer purchase patterns. Another complication is that data stored in the finished goods database likely will need to be redesigned to keep track of customer demand data. As you will learn in Chapter 10, that redesign effort will require that some application programs be changed as well.

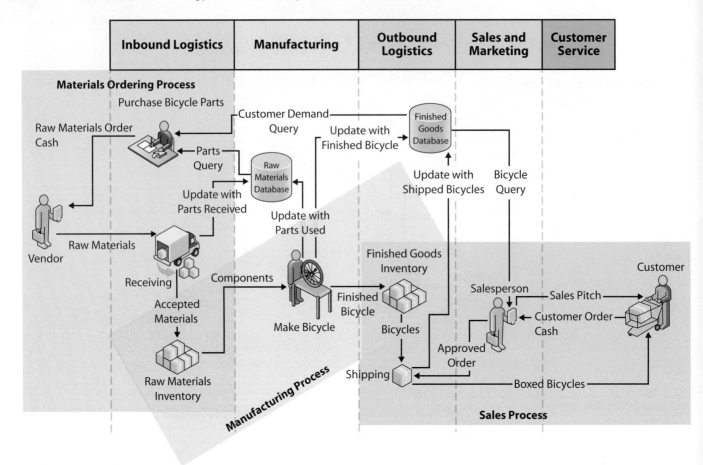

Figure 3-9
Improved Material Ordering
Process

Q6 How Does Competitive Strategy Determine Business Processes and the Structure of Information Systems?

Figure 3-10 shows a business process for renting bicycles. The value-generating activities are shown in the top of the table, and the implementation of those activities for two companies with different competitive strategies is shown in the rows below.

The first company has chosen a competitive strategy of low-cost rentals to students. Accordingly, this business implements business processes to minimize costs. The second company has chosen a differentiation strategy. It provides "best-of-breed" rentals to executives at a high-end conference resort. Notice that this business has designed its business processes to ensure superb service. To achieve a positive margin, it must ensure that the value added will exceed the costs of providing the service.

Now, consider the information systems required for these business processes. The student rental business uses a shoebox for its data facility. The only computer/software/data component in its business is the machine provided by its bank for processing credit card transactions.

The high-service business, however, makes extensive use of information systems, as shown in Figure 3-11. It has a sales tracking database that tracks past customer rental activity and an inventory database that is used to select and up-sell bicycle rentals as well as to control bicycle inventory with a minimum of fuss to its high-end customers.

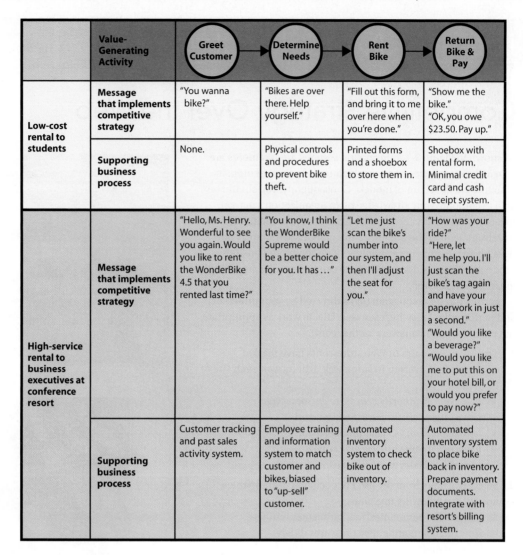

	Value-Generating Activity	**Greet Customer** →	**Determine Needs** →	**Rent Bike** →	**Return Bike & Pay**
Low-cost rental to students	**Message that implements competitive strategy**	"You wanna bike?"	"Bikes are over there. Help yourself."	"Fill out this form, and bring it to me over here when you're done."	"Show me the bike." "OK, you owe $23.50. Pay up."
	Supporting business process	None.	Physical controls and procedures to prevent bike theft.	Printed forms and a shoebox to store them in.	Shoebox with rental form. Minimal credit card and cash receipt system.
High-service rental to business executives at conference resort	**Message that implements competitive strategy**	"Hello, Ms. Henry. Wonderful to see you again. Would you like to rent the WonderBike 4.5 that you rented last time?"	"You know, I think the WonderBike Supreme would be a better choice for you. It has …"	"Let me just scan the bike's number into our system, and then I'll adjust the seat for you."	"How was your ride?" "Here, let me help you. I'll just scan the bike's tag again and have your paperwork in just a second." "Would you like a beverage?" "Would you like me to put this on your hotel bill, or would you prefer to pay now?"
	Supporting business process	Customer tracking and past sales activity system.	Employee training and information system to match customer and bikes, biased to "up-sell" customer.	Automated inventory system to check bike out of inventory.	Automated inventory system to place bike back in inventory. Prepare payment documents. Integrate with resort's billing system.

Figure 3-10
Operations Value Chains for Bicycle Rental Companies

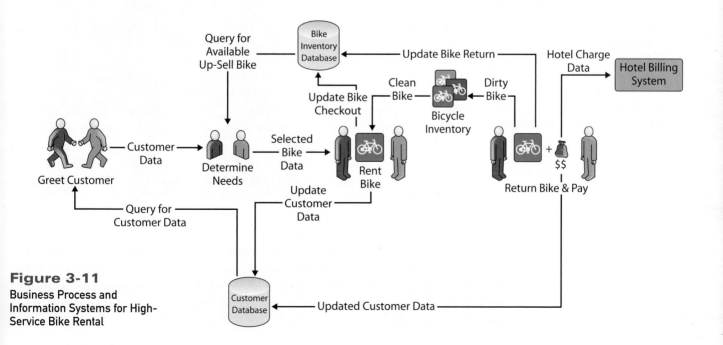

Figure 3-11
Business Process and Information Systems for High-Service Bike Rental

Using MIS InClass 3 | A GROUP EXERCISE

Competitive Strategy Over the Web

As shown in Figure 3-1, information systems' requirements are a logical consequence of an organization's analysis of industry structure via the chain of models. Consequently, you should be able to combine your knowledge of an organization's market, together with observations of the structure and content of its Web storefront, to infer the organization's competitive strategy and possibly make inferences about its value chains and business processes. The process you use here can be useful in preparing for job interviews as well.

Source: Pavel Losevsky/Fotolia

Form a three-person team (or as directed by your professor) and perform the following exercises. Divide work as appropriate, but create common answers for the team.

1. The following pairs of Web storefronts have market segments that overlap in some way. Briefly visit each site of each pair:
   - *www.sportsauthority.com* vs. *www.soccer.com*
   - *www.target.com* vs. *www.sephora.com*
   - *www.woot.com* vs. *www.amazon.com*
   - *www.petco.com* vs. *www.wag.com*
   - *www.llbean.com* vs. *www.rei.com*

2. Select two pairs from the list. For each pair of companies, answer the following questions:
   a. How do the companies' market segments differ?
   b. How do their competitive pressures differ?
   c. How do their competitive strategies differ?
   d. How is the "feel" of the content of their Web sites different?
   e. How is the "feel" of the user interface of their Web sites different?
   f. How could either company change its Web site to better accomplish its competitive strategy?
   g. Would the change you recommended in item f necessitate a change in one or more of the company's value chains? Explain.

3. Use your answers in step 2 to explain the following statement: "The structure of an organization's information system (here a Web storefront) is determined by its competitive strategy." Write your answer so that you could use it in a job interview to demonstrate your overall knowledge of business planning.

4. Present your team's answers to the rest of the class.

Source: corinaldo/Fotolia

So the bottom line is this: Organizations analyze their industry and choose a competitive strategy. Given that strategy, they design business processes that span value-generating activities. Those processes determine the scope and requirements of each organization's information systems. Given this background, we will now examine how information systems generate a competitive advantage.

Q7 How Do Information Systems Provide Competitive Advantages?

You can also apply these principles to your personal competitive advantage, as discussed in the Guide on pages 102–103.

In your business strategy class, you will study the Porter models in greater detail than we have discussed here. When you do so, you will learn numerous ways that organizations respond to the five competitive forces. For our purposes, we can distill those ways into the list of principles shown in Figure 3-12. Keep in mind that we are applying these principles in the context of the organization's competitive strategy.

Some of these competitive techniques are created via products and services, and some are created via the development of business processes. Consider each.

Competitive Advantage via Products

The first three principles in Figure 3-12 concern products or services. Organizations gain a competitive advantage by creating *new* products or services, by *enhancing* existing products or services, and by *differentiating* their products and services from those of their competitors.

Information systems create competitive advantages either as part of a product or by providing support to a product. Consider, for example, a car rental agency like Hertz or Avis. An information system that produces information about the car's location and provides driving instructions to destinations is part of the car rental, and thus is part of the product itself (see Figure 3-13a). In contrast, an information system that schedules car maintenance is not part of the product, but instead supports the product (see Figure 3-13b). Either way, information systems can help achieve the first three principles in Figure 3-12.

The remaining five principles in Figure 3-12 concern competitive advantage created by the implementation of business processes.

Competitive Advantage via Business Processes

Organizations can *lock in customers* by making it difficult or expensive for customers to switch to another product. This strategy is sometimes called establishing high **switching costs**. Organizations can *lock in suppliers* by making it difficult to switch to another organization, or, stated positively, by making it easy to connect to and work with the organization. Finally, competitive advantage can be gained by *creating entry barriers* that make it difficult and expensive for new competition to enter the market.

Another means to gain competitive advantage is to *establish alliances* with other organizations. Such alliances establish standards, promote product awareness and needs, develop market size, reduce purchasing costs, and provide other benefits. Finally, organizations can gain competitive advantage by *reducing costs*. Such reductions enable the organization to reduce prices and/or to increase profitability. Increased profitability means not just greater shareholder value, but also more cash, which can fund further infrastructure development for even greater competitive advantage.

One advantage a company can create is ensuring that it has the proper security procedures in place. For more information on security, see the Security Guide on pages 100–101.

All of these principles of competitive advantage make sense, but the question you may be asking is, "How do information systems help to create competitive advantage?" To answer that question, consider a sample information system.

Figure 3-12
Principles of Competitive Advantage

> **Product Implementations**
> 1. Create a new product or service
> 2. Enhance products or services
> 3. Differentiate products or services
>
> **Process Implementations**
> 4. Lock in customers and buyers
> 5. Lock in suppliers
> 6. Raise barriers to market entry
> 7. Establish alliances
> 8. Reduce costs

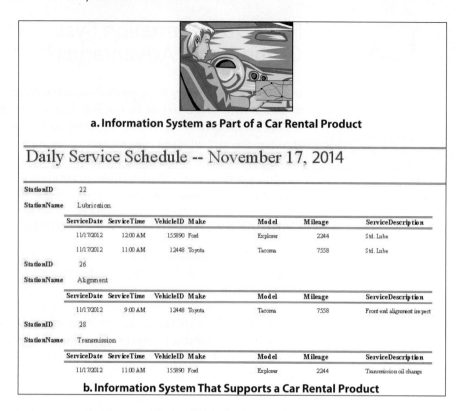

Figure 3-13
Two Roles for Information
Systems Regarding Products

How Does an Actual Company Use IS to Create Competitive Advantages?

ABC, Inc.,[4] is a worldwide shipper with sales well in excess of $1 billion. From its inception, ABC invested heavily in information technology and led the shipping industry in the application of information systems for competitive advantage. Here we consider one example of an information system that illustrates how ABC successfully uses information technology to gain competitive advantage.

ABC maintains customer account data that include not only the customer's name, address, and billing information, but also data about the people, organizations, and locations to which the customer ships. Figure 3-14 shows a Web form that an ABC customer is using to schedule a shipment. When the ABC system creates the form, it fills the Company name drop-down list with the names of companies that the customer has shipped to in the past. Here the user is selecting Pearson Education.

When the user clicks the Company name, the underlying ABC information system reads the customer's contact data from a database. The data consist of names, addresses, and phone numbers of recipients from past shipments. The user then selects a Contact name, and the system inserts that contact's address and other data into the form using data from the database, as shown in Figure 3-15. Thus, the system saves customers from having to reenter data for people to whom they have shipped in the past. Providing the data in this way also reduces data-entry errors.

Figure 3-16 (page 98) shows another feature of this system. On the right-hand side of this form, the customer can request that ABC send email messages to the sender (the customer), the recipient, and others as well. The customer can choose for ABC to send an email when the shipment is created and when it has been delivered. In Figure 3-16, the user has provided three email addresses. The customer wants all three addresses to receive delivery notification, but only the sender will receive shipment notification. The customer can add a personal message as well. By adding this capability to the shipment scheduling system, ABC has extended its product from a package-delivery service to a package- *and* information-delivery service.

---

[4]The information system described here is used by a major transportation company that did not want its name published in this textbook.

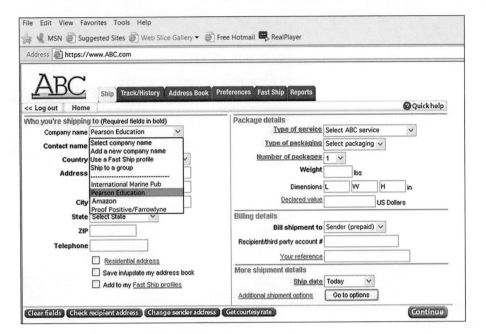

Figure 3-14

ABC, Inc., Web Page to Select a Recipient from the Customer's Records

Figure 3-17 shows one other capability of this information system. It has generated a shipping label, complete with bar code, for the user to print. By doing this, the company not only reduces errors in the preparation of shipping labels, but it also causes the customer to provide the paper and ink for document printing! Millions of such documents are printed every day, resulting in a considerable savings to the company.

How Does This System Create a Competitive Advantage?

Now consider the ABC shipping information system in light of the competitive advantage factors in Figure 3-12. This information system *enhances* an existing service because it eases the effort of creating a shipment to the customer while reducing errors. The information system also helps to *differentiate* the ABC package delivery service from competitors that do not have a similar system. Further, the generation of email messages when ABC picks up and delivers a package could be considered to be a *new* service.

Because this information system captures and stores data about recipients, it reduces the amount of customer work when scheduling a shipment. Customers will be *locked in* by this

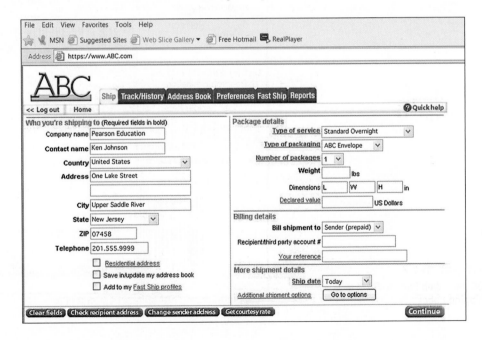

Figure 3-15

ABC, Inc., Web Page to Select a Contact from the Customer's Records

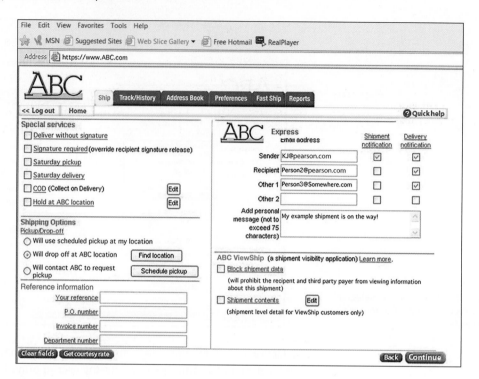

Figure 3-16
ABC, Inc., Web Page to Specify
Email Notification

system: If a customer wants to change to a different shipper, he or she will need to rekey recipient data for that new shipper. The disadvantage of rekeying data may well outweigh any advantage of switching to another shipper.

This system achieves a competitive advantage in two other ways as well. First, it raises the barriers to market entry. If another company wants to develop a shipping service, it will not only have to be able to ship packages, but it will also need to have a similar information system. In addition, the system reduces costs. It reduces errors in shipping documents, and it saves ABC paper, ink, and printing costs.

Of course, to determine if this system delivers a *net savings* in costs, the cost of developing and operating the information system will need to be offset against the gains in reduced errors

Figure 3-17
ABC, Inc., Web Page to Print a
Shipping Label

and paper, ink, and printing costs. It may be that the system costs more than the savings. Even still, it may be a sound investment if the value of intangible benefits, such as locking in customers and raising entry barriers, exceeds the net cost.

Before continuing, review Figure 3-12. Make sure that you understand each of the principles of competitive advantage and how information systems can help achieve them. In fact, the list in Figure 3-12 probably is important enough to memorize, because you can also use it for non-IS applications. You can consider any business project or initiative in light of competitive advantage.

Q8   2024?

Models of business strategy, competitive advantages, and their relationship to processes and IS are unlikely to change in the next 10 years. They may evolve, there may be some new models that rise to the surface, but those new models are likely to be extensions of existing models, within the existing paradigms.

What is likely to change, however, is pace. Because of the Internet and related technology, the speed of business is accelerating. The Web, Twitter, Facebook, and other social sites enable the rapid spread of new ideas and innovations and require businesses to be constantly on the alert for changes that may affect their strategy in short periods of time.

AllRoad Parts is an excellent example. It has had a successful, growing business supplying parts for adventure equipment for some time. But 3D printing arises, and now, as discussed in Figure 3-4, it's possible that some customers can manufacture some parts for themselves. Even more worrisome, some small manufacturers, local to AllRoad Parts' customers, may also begin to manufacture spare parts as well. Both of these possibilities threaten AllRoad Parts' differentiation strategy of having the largest parts inventory.

Many similar stories will occur in the next 10 years. How fast will Google Glass and copycat products be adopted? We don't know, but if they're as quickly adopted as, say, the iPhone or iPad, it will be fast. Businesses that depend on digital cameras, whether in phones or in other devices, need to attend to these new products. Like AllRoad Parts, they, too, need to evaluate and adapt their competitive strategies. Further, what opportunities will all that new, automatically generated image data create? What new businesses or business models become possible? We don't know, but we do know that opportunities will abound.

So, we can reasonably assume that the pace of change and the pace of integration of new technology will be fast and increasing, possibly accelerating, in the next 10 years. We can lament this fact; we can ignore it, but doing so is like standing on the shore of the Mississippi, telling it to flow elsewhere.

Instead, we, and especially *you*, need to view this increased pace as rapidly creating opportunities in which you can excel. You know it's coming; you know that, if not Google Glass, then Google Car, or Amazon TV, or some product that is today being constructed in someone's garage, maybe with 3D printing, some new technology-based products will change the competitive landscape for the company for which you will work. Knowing that, how can you take advantage of it?

When gold was discovered along the Colorado River in Arizona in the 1850s, thousands of pioneers ran to the mine fields. The odds were slim on success, and only a few struck it rich. A much surer bet was made by those who started the clothing and supply stores, or the railroads that moved the raw ore to the smelter, or the steamships that carried goods up the Colorado from the Sea of Cortez.

Maybe you want to be a modern-day prospector and use technology to create new products like 3D printing. If so, do it. But, maybe, like AllRoad Parts, you want to attend to the innovative products that others are making and create new strategies or build new businesses that take advantage of the opportunities that new products create. You can be certain that, 10 years from now, you will have even more opportunity to do so.

Security Guide

DIFFERENTIATING ON SECURITY

Information systems and nearly free data storage and data communications have created new, valuable targets for crime. Before data was centralized in computers, data theft had limited scope. When criminals target credit card data in desk drawers in homes, a thief can steal the data for perhaps eight credit cards per day. And those thefts involve considerable physical risk. But a computer criminal can break into an organization's database that holds data on millions of credit cards. Those millions of records can be downloaded to a computer in Africa and sold for $10 each from an Internet site in Uzbekistan to computer gamers in the United States, all within 24 hours. Or, even more graphically, a mugger waiting on a street corner can rob only a single person in a few hours; a computer criminal waiting on an Internet router (Chapter 6) can mug millions of people in those same few hours.

For some, such computer crime is just a problem, but others find a way to turn that problem into an opportunity to gain a competitive advantage. Namely, professionals and organizations that take steps to protect themselves and their organizations from such threats gain an advantage over those that do not. That sounds brutal, and perhaps it is, but it is also today's reality.

Consider yourself as an example. Suppose you send your Social Security number in an email. Unless your email system is secure, and very few are, that Social Security number is vulnerable to an electronic mugger. Suppose your Social Security number is

compromised, and someone gains control over your identity. Soon criminals have piled up a mountain of debt on your accounts, and your credit rating plummets. Your credit cards are useless, and you can't obtain replacements. With considerable work, agony, and expense, you will be able to undo most of this damage, eventually. But the near-term impact on your time and reputation is severe.

Now, compare your situation to that of one of your coworkers who learned not to send sensitive data in email. You are spending hours solving your credit problem while she is learning new skills, networking with

other professionals, accomplishing extra projects at work, and so forth. Thus, knowledge of security and controls gives your coworkers a substantial competitive advantage over you.

Take this line of thought to the organizational level. Organizations that create strong security programs have a competitive advantage over those that do not. In fact, some organizations go even further to make security a differentiator of their product or service. A portion of that organization's added value is strong security.

No organization, of course, is going to claim publicly, "We've never suffered a data loss due to a computer virus." That statement is unlikely to be true, and if it were, making it would serve as a juicy invitation to every hacker in the world to attempt a break-in. But an organization can develop industry-leading security policies and procedures and use those policies and standards to support a competitive strategy of differentiation.

Consider Teleperformance, a multinational $3 billion company that provides call desk support as a service.

Teleperformance employs 130,000 people in 250 data centers in 49 countries who perform customer service, technical support, telesales, and similar call desk support to their customers on a contract basis. If you visit *www.teleperformance.com*, you'll see a menu item labeled *Business Model Differentiators*. Click on that item and you'll see *Security* listed as one of their key differentiators. Click on *Security* and you'll see the certifications that Teleperformance earned for its controls and other security safeguards as well as specific measures that it takes to control fraud. Clearly, Teleperformance makes security a key part of their service offerings.

According to the value chain model, organizations add costs to activities as long as those additions generate value greater than their cost. An organization that chooses to differentiate on security will add security features as long as that improved security adds value greater than its cost. Viewed in this light, security is not just an overhead expense; it becomes a key part of the product or service. Consider viewing security the same way for yourself and make it a key part of your professional product.

 DISCUSSION QUESTIONS

1. Summarize how knowledge of security can give you a professional competitive advantage. Do you believe this is just an academic exercise, or do you think security knowledge has true value? In what ways does your answer depend on your employer's industry or products and services? To what extent does it depend on your job?

2. How can you demonstrate your security knowledge and skills to a potential employer? What courses might you take? What course projects might you do to demonstrate such knowledge? What else can you do?

3. Give five examples of business products and services that vary in the need for security. Rank your examples

   from 1 to 5, where 1 is a need for little security and 5 is a need for considerable security. Justify your rankings.

4. As a manager, how can you make security a key differentiator for you as a business professional? Use the examples in your answer to question 3 in your answer.

5. Visit *www.teleperformance.com*. Navigate to the description of their security differentiators. List the certifications that Teleperformance has earned. Search the Internet for one of those certifications and describe what it is and why it is important to Teleperformance security. To what extent does the award of that certification create a competitive advantage? Explain your answer.

Guide

YOUR PERSONAL COMPETITIVE ADVANTAGE

Consider the following possibility: You work hard, earning your degree in business, and you graduate, only to discover that you cannot find a job in your area of study. You look for 6 weeks or so, but then you run out of money. In desperation, you take a job waiting tables at a local restaurant. Two years go by, the economy picks up, and the jobs you had been looking for become available. Unfortunately, your degree is now 2 years old; you are competing with students who have just graduated with fresh degrees (and fresh knowledge). Two years of waiting tables, good as you are at it, does not appear to be good experience for the job you want. You're stuck in a nightmare—one that will be hard to get out of, and **one that you cannot allow to happen**.

Examine Figure 3-12 again, but this time consider those elements of competitive advantage as they apply to you personally. As an employee, the skills and abilities you offer are your personal product. Examine the first three items in the list and ask yourself, "How can I use my time in school—and in this MIS class, in particular—to create new skills, to enhance those I already have, and to differentiate my skills from the competition?" (By the way, you will enter a national/international market. Your competition is not just the students in your class; it's also students in classes in Ohio, California, British Columbia, Florida, New York, and every place else they're teaching MIS today.)

Suppose you are interested in professional sales. Perhaps you want to sell in the pharmaceutical industry. What skills can you learn from your MIS class that will make you more competitive as a future salesperson? Ask yourself, "How does the pharmaceutical industry use MIS to

gain competitive advantage?" Get on the Internet and find examples of the use of information systems in the pharmaceutical industry. How does Pfizer, for example, use a customer information system to sell to doctors? How can your knowledge of such systems differentiate you from your competition for a job there? How does Pfizer use a knowledge management system? How does the firm keep track of drugs that have an adverse effect on each other?

The fourth and fifth items in Figure 3-12 concern locking in customers, buyers, and suppliers. How can you interpret those elements in terms of your personal competitive advantage? Well, to lock in a relationship, you first have to have one. So do you have an internship? If not, can you get one? And once you have an internship, how can you use your knowledge of MIS to lock in your job so that you get a job offer? Does the company you are interning for have a sales tracking system (or any other information system that is important to the company)? If users are happy with

the system, what characteristics make it worthwhile? Can you lock in a job by becoming an expert user of this system? Becoming an expert user not only locks you into your job, but it also raises barriers to entry for others who might be competing for the job. Also, can you suggest ways to improve the system, thus using your knowledge of the company and the system to lock in an extension of your job?

Human resources personnel say that networking is one of the most effective ways of finding a job. How can you use this class to establish alliances with other students? Is there an email list server for the students in your class? What about Facebook? LinkedIn? Twitter? How can you use those facilities to develop job-seeking alliances with other students? Who in your class already has a job or an internship? Can any of those people provide hints or opportunities for finding a job?

Don't restrict your job search to your local area. Are there regions of your country where jobs are more plentiful? How can you find out about student organizations in those regions? Search the Web for MIS classes in other cities, and make contact with students there. Find out what the hot opportunities are in other cities.

Finally, as you study MIS, think about how the knowledge you gain can help you save costs for your employers. Even more, see if you can build a case that an employer would actually save money by hiring you. The line of reasoning might be that because of your knowledge of IS you will be able to facilitate cost savings that more than compensate for your salary.

In truth, few of the ideas that you generate for a potential employer will be feasible or pragmatically useful. The fact that you are thinking creatively, however, will indicate to a potential employer that you have initiative and are grappling with the problems that real businesses have. As this course progresses, keep thinking about competitive advantage, and strive to understand how the topics you study can help you to accomplish, personally, one or more of the principles in Figure 3-12.

 DISCUSSION QUESTIONS

1. Summarize the efforts you have taken thus far to build an employment record that will lead to job offers after graduation.
2. Considering the first three principles in Figure 3-12, describe one way in which you have a competitive advantage over your classmates. If you do not have such a competitive advantage, describe actions you can take to obtain one.
3. In order to build your network, you can use your status as a student to approach business professionals. Namely, you can contact them for help with an assignment or for career guidance. For example, suppose you

want to work in banking and you know that your local bank has a customer information system. You could call the manager of that bank and ask him or her how that system creates a competitive advantage for the bank. You also could ask to interview other employees and go armed with the list in Figure 3-12. Describe two specific ways in which you can use your status as a student and the list in Figure 3-12 to build your network in this way.
4. Describe two ways that you can use student alliances to obtain a job. How can you use information systems to build, maintain, and operate such alliances?

ACTIVE REVIEW

Use this Active Review to verify that you understand the ideas and concepts that answer the chapter's study questions.

Q1 How does organizational strategy determine information systems structure?

Diagram and explain the relationship of industry structure, competitive strategy, value chains, business processes, and information systems. Working from industry structure to IS, explain how the knowledge you've gained in these first three chapters pertains to that diagram.

Q2 What five forces determine industry structure?

Name and briefly describe the five forces. Give your own examples of both strong and weak forces of each type, similar to those in Figure 3-3.

Q3 How does analysis of industry structure determine competitive strategy?

Describe four different strategies as defined by Porter. Give an example of four different companies that have implemented each of the strategies.

Q4 How does competitive strategy determine value chain structure?

Define the terms *value*, *margin*, and *value chain*. Explain why organizations that choose a differentiation strategy can use value to determine a limit on the amount of extra cost to pay for differentiation. Name the primary and support activities in the value chain and explain the purpose of each. Explain the concept of linkages.

Q5 How do business processes generate value?

Define *business process, cost,* and *margin* as they pertain to business processes. Explain the purpose of an activity and describe types of repository. Explain the importance of business process redesign and describe the difference between the business processes in Figure 3-8 and those in Figure 3-9.

Q6 How does competitive strategy determine business processes and the structure of information systems?

In your own words, explain how competitive strategy determines the structure of business processes. Use the examples of a clothing store that caters to struggling students and a clothing store that caters to professional businesspeople in a high-end neighborhood. List the activities in the business process for the two companies and create a chart like that in Figure 3-9. Explain how the information systems' requirements differ between the two stores.

Q7 How do information systems provide competitive advantages?

List and briefly describe eight principles of competitive advantage. Consider your college bookstore. List one application of each of the eight principles. Strive to include examples that involve information systems.

Q8 2024?

Describe the ways that business strategies are likely to change in the next 10 years. Using Google Glass as an example, describe companies whose strategy is likely to be challenged. Summarize the lesson that gold mining on the Colorado River in the 1850s can teach us.

Using Your Knowledge with AllRoad Parts

Explain in your own words how AllRoad Parts' competitive strategy is threatened by 3D printing. Describe AllRoad Parts' planned response and summarize the problems that Drew perceives with that response. Recommend a course of action for AllRoad Parts. Use the example of Drew's idea for using vendor cost data as part of vendor selection to illustrate your answer.

KEY TERMS AND CONCEPTS

Activity   90
Business process   90
Business process management   91
Competitive strategy   85
Cost   90

Five forces model   84
Linkages   90
Margin   88
Primary activities   88
Repository   90

Support activities   88
Switching costs   95
Value   88
Value chain   88

MyMISLab

Go to **mymislab.com** to complete the problems marked with this icon .

USING YOUR KNOWLEDGE

3-1. Apply the value chain model to a mail-order company such as L.L.Bean (*www.llbean.com*). What is its competitive strategy? Describe the tasks L.L.Bean must accomplish for each of the primary value chain activities. How does L.L.Bean's competitive strategy and the nature of its business influence the general characteristics of its information systems?

3-2. Suppose you decide to start a business that recruits students for summer jobs. You will match available students with available jobs. You need to learn what positions are available and what students are available for filling those positions. In starting your business, you know you will be competing with local newspapers, Craigslist (*www.craigslist.org*), and your college. You will probably have other local competitors as well.

   a. Analyze the structure of this industry according to Porter's five forces model.

   b. Given your analysis in part a, recommend a competitive strategy.

   c. Describe the primary value chain activities as they apply to this business.

   d. Describe a business process for recruiting students.

   e. Describe information systems that could be used to support the business process in part d.

   f. Explain how the process you describe in part d and the system you describe in part e reflect your competitive strategy.

3-3. Consider the two different bike rental companies in Figure 3-10. Think about the bikes that they rent. Clearly, the student bikes will be just about anything that can be ridden out of the shop. The bikes for the business executives, however, must be new, shiny, clean, and in tip-top shape.

   a. Compare and contrast the operations value chains of these two businesses as they pertain to the management of bicycles.

   b. Describe a business process for maintaining bicycles for both businesses.

   c. Describe a business process for acquiring bicycles for both businesses.

   d. Describe a business process for disposing of bicycles for both businesses.

   e. What roles do you see for information systems in your answers to the earlier questions? The information systems can be those you develop within your company or they can be those developed by others, such as Craigslist.

COLLABORATION EXERCISE 3

Using the collaboration IS you built in Chapter 2 (pages 73–74), collaborate with a group of students to answer the following questions.

   Singing Valley Resort is a top-end 50-unit resort located high in the Colorado mountains. Rooms rent for $400 to $4,500 per night, depending on the season and the type of accommodations. Singing Valley's clientele are well-to-do; many are famous entertainers, sports figures, and business executives. They are accustomed to, and demand, superior service.

   Singing Valley resides in a gorgeous mountain valley and is situated a few hundred yards from a serene mountain lake. It prides itself on superior accommodations; tip-top service; delicious, healthful, organic meals; and exceptional wines. Because it has been so successful, Singing Valley is 90 percent occupied except during the "shoulder seasons" (November, after the leaves change and before the snow arrives, and late April, when winter sports are finished but the snow is still on the ground).

Singing Valley's owners want to increase revenue, but because the resort is nearly always full and because its rates are already at the top of the scale, it cannot do so via occupancy revenue. Thus, over the past several years it has focused on up-selling to its clientele activities such as fly-fishing, river rafting, cross-country skiing, snowshoeing, art lessons, yoga and other exercise classes, spa services, and the like.

To increase the sales of these optional activities, Singing Valley prepared in-room marketing materials to advertise their availability. Additionally, it trained all registration personnel on techniques of casually and appropriately suggesting such activities to guests on arrival.

The response to these promotions was only mediocre, so Singing Valley's management stepped up its promotions. The first step was to send email to its clientele advising them of the activities available during their stay. An automated system produced emails personalized with names and personal data.

Unfortunately, the automated email system backfired. Immediately upon its execution, Singing Valley management received numerous complaints. One long-term customer objected that she had been coming to Singing Valley for 7 years and asked if they had yet noticed that she was confined to a wheelchair. If they had noticed, she said, why did they send her a personalized invitation for a hiking trip? The agent of another famous client complained that the personalized email was sent to her client and her husband, when anyone who had turned on a TV in the past 6 months knew the two of them were involved in an exceedingly acrimonious divorce. Yet another customer complained that, indeed, he and his wife had vacationed at Singing Valley 3 years ago, but he had not been there since. To his knowledge, his wife had not been there, either, so he was puzzled as to why the email referred to their visit last winter. He wanted to know if, indeed, his wife had

recently been to the resort, without him. Of course, Singing Valley had no way of knowing about customers it had insulted who never complained.

During the time the automated email system was operational, sales of extra activities were up 15 percent. However, the strong customer complaints conflicted with its competitive strategy so, in spite of the extra revenue, Singing Valley stopped the automated email system, sacked the vendor who had developed it, and demoted the Singing Valley employee who had brokered the system. Singing Valley was left with the problem of how to increase its revenue.

Your team's task is to develop two innovative ideas for solving Singing Valley's problem. At the minimum, include the following in your response:

a. An analysis of the five forces of the Singing Valley market. Make and justify any necessary assumptions about their market.

b. A statement of Singing Valley's competitive strategy.

c. A statement of the problem. Recall from Chapter 2 that a problem is a perceived difference between what is and what ought to be. If the members of your group have different perceptions of the problem, all the better. Use a collaborative process to obtain the best possible problem description to which all can agree.

d. Document in a general way (like the top row of Figure 3-10) the process of up-selling an activity.

e. Develop two innovative ideas for solving the Singing Valley problem. For each idea, provide:
- A brief description of the idea
- A process diagram (like Figure 3-11) of the idea. Figure 3-11 was produced using Microsoft Visio; if you have access to that product, you'll save time and have a better result if you also use it.
- A description of the information system needed to implement the idea

f. Compare the advantages and disadvantages of your alternatives in part e and recommend one of them for implementation.

CASE STUDY 3

Fulfillment by Amazon (FBA)

As stated in Case Study 1 (page 31), Amazon has three primary product offerings: an online retail store, computing infrastructure that it leases on an elastic basis, and order fulfillment services. In this case, you'll examine whether a company like AllRoad Parts might be able to use Amazon's order fulfillment services advantageously.

To begin, what is it?

Fulfillment by Amazon (FBA) is an Amazon service by which other sellers can ship goods to Amazon warehouses for stocking, order packaging, and shipment. FBA customers pay a fee for the service as well as for inventory space. Amazon uses its own inventory management and order fulfillment business processes and information systems to fulfill the FBA customers' orders.

FBA customers can sell their goods on Amazon.com, sell them via their own sales channels, or both. If the FBA customer sells on Amazon.com, Amazon will provide customer service for order processing (handling returns, fixing erroneously packed orders, answering customer order queries, and the like).

The costs for Fulfillment by Amazon are as follows:

- Order handling per order is $0.00 through Amazon and a minimum of $1.90 if sold elsewhere.
- Pick and pack per item is $1.00 through Amazon and $.60 if sold elsewhere.
- Weight handling is a minimum of $.42 per pound if sold through Amazon and a minimum of $.45 per pound if sold elsewhere.
- Storage per cubic foot per month is a $.45 minimum, although rates vary throughout the year for products sold through Amazon. The price is the same for products sold elsewhere.

The list above summarizes the FBA fees for products like sporting goods as of May 2013. (By the way, in the past year, the price of order handling via Amazon.com has decreased from $1.00 to zero. The cost of order handling for goods sold elsewhere has decreased from a minimum of $4.75. Clearly, Amazon.com has achieved efficiencies somewhere.)[5]

If goods are sold via Amazon.com, Amazon uses its own information systems to drive the order fulfillment process. However, if the goods are sold via an FBA customer's sales channel, then the FBA customer must connect its own information systems with those at Amazon. Amazon provides a standardized interface by which this is done called Amazon Marketplace Web Service (MWS). Using Web-standard technology (see Chapter 6), FBA customers' order and payment data are directly linked to Amazon's information systems.

FBA enables companies to outsource order fulfillment to Amazon, thus avoiding the cost of developing their own processes, facilities, and information systems for this purpose. Is FBA right for AllRoad Parts?

QUESTIONS

In answering questions 3-4 through 3-10, first assume that AllRoad Parts does not use 3D printing to manufacture parts.

3-4. In your own words, summarize AllRoad Parts' competitive strategy.

3-5. Summarize the advantages and disadvantages for AllRoad Parts to sell items via Amazon.com. Would you recommend that the company do so?

3-6. For items that it sells itself, compute AllRoad Parts' cost of using FBA to process:
  a. An order of 10 sets of bicycle pedals weighing a total of 25 pounds.
  b. An order of a single set of bicycle pedals weighing 2.5 pounds.
  c. The cost of a cycling shirt weighing 10 ounces.
  d. The cost of storing 1,000 sets of bicycle pedals for 3 months (using your own assumptions).

3-7. If AllRoad Parts were to use FBA, what business processes would it not need to develop? What costs would it save?

3-8. If AllRoad Parts were to use FBA, what information systems would it not need to develop? What costs would it save?

3-9. If AllRoad Parts were to use FBA, how would it integrate its information systems with Amazon's? (To add depth to your answer, Google the term *Amazon MWS.*)

3-10. In your opinion, does it make sense for AllRoad Parts to use FBA? Justify your answer.

3-11. How, if at all, would your answers to questions 3-4 through 3-10 change if AllRoad Parts makes some of its parts using 3D printing?

---

[5]"Help Boost Your Sales with Amazon's World-Class Fulfillment," *Amazon Services,* accessed July 7, 2013, *http://services.amazon.com/fulfillment-by-amazon/pricing.htm?ld=AS.*

MyMISLab

Go to **mymislab.com** for Auto-graded writing questions as well as the following Assisted-graded writing questions:

3-12. Samantha Green owns and operates Twigs Tree Trimming Service. Samantha graduated from the forestry program of a nearby university and worked for a large landscape design firm, performing tree trimming and removal. After several years of experience, she bought her own truck, stump grinder, and other equipment and opened her own business in St. Louis, Missouri.

Although many of her jobs are one-time operations to remove a tree or stump, others are recurring, such as trimming a tree or groups of trees every year or every other year. When business is slow, she calls former clients to remind them of her services and of the need to trim their trees on a regular basis.

Samantha has never heard of Michael Porter or any of his theories. She operates her business "by the seat of her pants."

a. Explain how an analysis of the five competitive forces could help Samantha.

b. Do you think Samantha has a competitive strategy? What competitive strategy would seem to make sense for her?

c. How would knowledge of her competitive strategy help her sales and marketing efforts?

d. Describe, in general terms, the kind of information system that she needs to support sales and marketing efforts.

3-13. YourFire, Inc., is a small business owned by Curt and Julie Robards. Based in Brisbane, Australia, YourFire manufactures and sells a lightweight camping stove called the YourFire. Curt, who previously worked as an aerospace engineer, invented and patented a burning nozzle that enables the stove to stay lit in very high winds—up to 90 miles per hour. Julie, an industrial designer by training, developed an elegant folding design that is small, lightweight, easy to set up, and very stable. Curt and Julie manufacture the stove in their garage, and they sell it directly to their customers over the Internet and via phone.

a. Explain how an analysis of the five competitive forces could help YourFire.

b. What does the YourFire competitive strategy seem to be?

c. Briefly summarize how the primary value chain activities pertain to YourFire. How should the company design these value chains to conform to its competitive strategy?

d. Describe business processes that YourFire needs in order to implement its marketing and sales and also its service value chain activities.

e. Describe, in general terms, information systems to support your answer to part d.

3-14. Mymislab Only – comprehensive writing assignment for this chapter.

PART 2

Information Technology

The next three chapters address the technology that underlies information systems. You may think that such technology is unimportant to you as a business professional. However, as you will see, today's managers and business professionals work with information technology all the time as consumers, if not in a more involved way.

Chapter 4 discusses hardware, software, and mobile systems and defines basic terms and fundamental computing concepts as well as the importance of mobile systems and modern application user experience design. You will also see that AllRoad Parts has important decisions to make about a critical software development project.

Chapter 5 addresses the data component of information systems by describing database processing. You will learn essential database terminology and will be introduced to techniques for processing databases. We will also introduce data modeling because you may be required to evaluate data models for databases that others develop for you.

Chapter 6 continues the discussion of computing devices begun in Chapter 4 and describes data communications, Internet technologies, and an emerging capability known as *the cloud*. AllRoad Parts needs to make decisions about building its infrastructure for the next stage of its growth. To make those decisions, it needs to understand the advantages and disadvantages of cloud-based computing.

The purpose of these three chapters is to teach technology sufficient for you to be an effective IT consumer, like Jason, Addison, Drew, and Kelly at AllRoad Parts. You will learn basic terms, fundamental concepts, and useful frameworks so that you will have the knowledge to ask good questions and make appropriate requests of the information systems professionals who will serve you. Those concepts and frameworks will be far more useful to you than the latest technology trend, which may be outdated by the time you graduate.

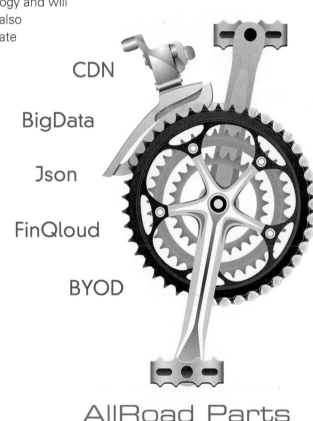

CDN

BigData

Json

FinQloud

BYOD

AllRoad Parts

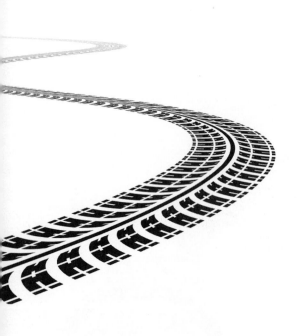

Hardware, Software, and Mobile Systems

Jason Green, CEO of AllRoad Parts, is meeting with the committee he asked to investigate the 3D printing opportunity. Committee members Kelly Summers, CFO; Lucas Massey, IT director; Drew Mills, operations manager; and Addison Lee, head of purchasing, are with him around a conference table.

Jason starts the meeting.

"First, I have to thank Drew for all the hard work he put into setting up the new printer, experimenting with it, and teaching us about the reality of 3D printing. We're not manufacturers, 3D technology won't give us the processes and IS we need, and the parts we could produce may not stand up to the rough treatment off-roading involves. So, now we know that 3D printing isn't for us...at least not right now."

There's a pause in the conversation, and then Kelly speaks up. "Well, we all agree about that, but we do think that, as a supplier, there is something related to 3D printing that we could sell to our customers."

Jason is curious; that's not what he expected Kelly to say. "OK, I'll bite," he says. "What is it?"

"Designs," she replies. "Part designs. We don't want to manufacture parts because we don't want to get into the quality issues that Drew identified, but our customers might want to manufacture parts on their own 3D printers."

"You mean sell 3D-ready part designs as a product?" Jason sounds dubious.

"Exactly," Kelly shoots back.

"Who's gonna want to print their own parts? I don't see Dad making bike parts for his kids..." Jason trails off.

"No, probably not," Drew chimes in, "but I did a quick query on past orders, and there are customers who order large quantities of particular products. They're mostly service shops. Anyway, larger customers like that could make parts for themselves. Or make them for Dad to install on his kids' bikes."

"Hmm. Seems like a stretch to me," says Jason. "First of

all, can we get the rights to sell the plans? Second, even if we can, why wouldn't our customers buy the plans directly from the manufacturer?"

"Well, they might, but we already deal with a similar problem." Drew continues, "Our customers can buy anything that we sell straight from Fox. But they don't. Like we always say, our huge inventory provides one-stop shopping for all their parts."

"...if we do a native app, we have to do iOS and an Android version and maybe a Win 8 version..."

"Besides, there's something else to consider here," Lucas speaks up. "If you call a manufacturer to order a part, what do they ask for first? The part number. When our customers call in, they say something like, 'I want the little green plastic gizmo that goes next to big black round thing that's right above the fork.' It drives the manufacturers crazy."

"Yeah, you don't have to tell me," Jason replies. "That's what makes our sales costs so high."

"So, here's what we do," says Lucas. "We create an app—maybe just a browser app, or maybe we have to do a native app, I'm not sure yet—but the app allows customers to search for the vehicles they want to service. They click on the major system for which they need parts. We know from our orders which parts each customer is most likely to order, so we highlight them. Customers click or tap on the highlighted area and keep driving down until they find the part they need. They click that part, and we offer to sell them the part if we have it in inventory or the 3D-ready file if they want to make it themselves."

This example refocuses Jason on sales costs. "Lucas, why aren't we already doing this for our in-inventory parts? It seems like a good way to reduces sales costs," he says.

"Lucas and I have been talking about this for some time," Addison retorts. "But building the app is expensive, and our margins on our in-inventory parts support high sales costs. So, we never brought it to you."

STUDY QUESTIONS

Q1 What do business professionals need to know about computer hardware?

Q2 What do business professionals need to know about software?

Q3 Is open source software a viable alternative?

Q4 What are the differences between native and thin-client applications?

Q5 Why are mobile systems increasingly important?

Q6 What characterizes quality mobile user experiences?

Q7 What are the challenges of personal mobile devices at work?

Q8 2024?

"But," Lucas picks up Addison's line of thought, "the prices we can charge for selling part designs are so low that we'll lose money if customers are calling and speaking to sales reps for help. Sales labor costs will eat up any possible margins. So, design sales need an app like this."

Jason is intrigued. "How expensive is the app?" he asks.

"That depends on whether we do a thin-client app or a native app," replies Lucas. "It also depends on how much open source we can get."

"Here we go again," Jason grumbles. "And if we do a native app, we have to do iOS and an Android version and maybe a Win 8 version…And do we do it in-house or off-shore? Yada yada. It seems like we're always having this conversation."

"Yup, it does," Lucas agrees.

"OK," Jason sighs. "Bring me a proposal, and let's see what we can do. And…good work, Kelly, to you and your team."

Jason leaves the room, muttering to himself, "Android, smandroid. Riding bikes was fun. Maybe I *could* have made it riding the professional circuit?"

CHAPTER PREVIEW

What would you do if you were Drew? Or Kelly? How hard is it to build the new application? How much should it cost? How should they proceed? Is Lucas too conservative? If you're wondering why, as a future business professional, you need to know about hardware and software, think about those questions. Those and others of greater complexity—most likely ones involving technology that will be invented between now and the time you start working—will come your way.

You don't need to be an expert. You don't need to be a hardware engineer or a computer programmer. You do need to know enough, however, to be an effective consumer. You need the knowledge and skills to ask important, relevant questions and understand the answers.

We begin with basic hardware and software concepts. Next, we will discuss open source software development and then investigate the differences between native and thin-client applications. Following that, we'll discuss the importance of mobile systems and the characteristics of quality mobile user experiences. Employees are increasingly bringing their computers to work, which creates new challenges, as you'll learn in Q7. Finally, we'll wrap up by forecasting trends in hardware and software in 2024.

Q1 What Do Business Professionals Need to Know About Computer Hardware?

Computer hardware consists of electronic components and related gadgetry that input, process, output, and store data according to instructions encoded in computer programs or software. All hardware today has more or less the same components, at least to the level that is important to us. We'll begin with those components and then we'll quickly survey basic types of computers.

Hardware Components

Over the course of your career, application software, hardware, and firmware will change, sometimes rapidly. The Guide on pages 148–149 challenges you to choose a strategy for addressing this change.

Every computer has a **central processing unit (CPU)**, which is sometimes called "the brain" of the computer. Although the design of the CPU has nothing in common with the anatomy of animal brains, this description is helpful because the CPU does have the "smarts" of the machine. The CPU selects instructions, processes them, performs arithmetic and logical comparisons, and stores results of operations in memory. Some computers have two or more CPUs. A computer with two CPUs is called a **dual-processor** computer. **Quad-processor** computers have four CPUs. Some high-end computers have 16 or more CPUs.

CPUs vary in speed, function, and cost. Hardware vendors such as Intel, Advanced Micro Devices, and National Semiconductor continually improve CPU speed and capabilities while reducing CPU costs (as discussed under Moore's Law in Chapter 1). Whether you or your department needs the latest, greatest CPU depends on the nature of your work.

The CPU works in conjunction with **main memory**. The CPU reads data and instructions from memory, and it stores results of computations in main memory. Main memory is sometimes called **RAM**, for random access memory.

All computers include **storage hardware**, which is used to save data and programs. Magnetic disks are still the most common storage device, although optical disks such as CDs and DVDs also are popular. Thumb drives are small, portable storage devices that can be used to back up data and transfer it from one computer to another.

Types of Hardware

Figure 4-1 lists the basic types of hardware. Personal computers (PCs) are classic computing devices that are used by individuals. In the past, PCs were the primary computer used in business. Today, they are gradually being supplanted by tablets and other mobile devices. The Mac Pro is an example of a modern PC. Apple brought tablets (sometimes called **slates**) to prominence with the iPad. In 2012, Microsoft announced Surface and Google announced the Nexus series, all tablets. Smartphones are cell phones with processing capability; the Motorola (now owned by Google) Droid is a good example. Today, because it's hard to find a cell phone that isn't smart, people often just call them phones.

A **server** is a computer that is designed to support processing from many remote computers and users. You can think of a server as a PC on steroids. As a business professional, you probably will not be involved in the choice of server hardware. As of 2013, a good example is the Dell PowerEdge server. Finally, a **server farm** is a collection of, typically, thousands of servers. (See Figure 4-2.) Server farms are often placed in large truck trailers that hold 5,000 servers or more. Typically a trailer has two large cables coming out of it; one is for power and the other is for data communications. The operator of the farm backs a trailer into a pre prepared slab (in a warehouse or sometimes out in the open air), plugs in the power and communications cables, and voilà, thousands of servers are up and running!

Hardware Type	Example (s)
Personal Computer (PC) *Including desktops and laptops*	Apple Mac Pro
Tablet *Including e-book readers*	iPad, Microsoft Surface, Google Nexus 7, Kindle Fire
(Smart)Phone	Motorola (Google) Droid
Server	Dell PowerEdge 12G Server
Server Farm	Racks of servers (Figure 4-2)

Figure 4-1
Basic Types of Hardware

Increasingly, server infrastructure is delivered as a service in what is termed *the cloud*. We will discuss cloud computing in Chapter 6, after you have some knowledge of data communications. PCs, tablets, and smartphones that access servers and the cloud are called **clients**.

The capacities of computer hardware are specified according to data units, which we discuss next.

Computer Data

Computers represent data using **binary digits**, called **bits**. A bit is either a zero or a one. Bits are used for computer data because they are easy to represent physically, as illustrated in Figure 4-3. A switch can be either closed or open. A computer can be designed so that an open switch represents zero and a closed switch represents one. Or the orientation of a magnetic field can represent a bit: magnetism in one direction represents a zero; magnetism in the opposite direction represents a one. Or, for optical media, small pits are burned onto the surface of the disk so that they will reflect light. In a given spot, a reflection means a one; no reflection means a zero.

Computer Data Sizes

All forms of computer data are represented by bits. The data can be numbers, characters, currency amounts, photos, recordings, or whatever. All are simply a string of bits. For reasons that

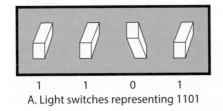

A. Light switches representing 1101

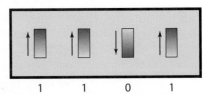

B. Direction of magnetism representing 1101

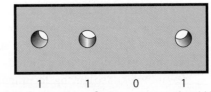

C. Reflection/no reflection representing 1101

Figu
Bits Are sent
Physica

Term	Definition	Abbr
Byte	Number of bits to represent one character	
Kilobyte	1,024 bytes	
Megabyte	1,024 K = 1,048,576 bytes	
Gigabyte	1,024 MB = 1,073,741,824 bytes	
Terabyte	1,024 GB = 1,099,511,627,776 bytes	
Petabyte	1,024 TB = 1,125,899,906,842,624 bytes	
Exabyte	1,024 PB = 1,152,921,504,606,846,976 bytes	

Figure 4-4
Important Storage-Capacity Terminology

interest many but are irrelevant for future managers, bits are grouped iks called **bytes**. For character data, such as the letters in a person's name, one ct into one byte. Thus, when you read a specification that a computing device h bytes of memory, you know that the device can hold up to 100 million character

Bytes are used to measure sizes of noncharacter data as well. Some for example, that a given picture is 100,000 bytes in size. This statement means the bit string that represents the picture is 100,000 bytes or 800,000 bits (because ther byte).

The specifications for the size of main memory, disk, and othevices are expressed in bytes. Figure 4-4 shows the set of abbreviations that aresent data storage capacity. A **kilobyte**, abbreviated **K**, is a collection of 1,024 byte, or **MB**, is 1,024 kilobytes. A **gigabyte**, or **GB**, is 1,024 megabytes; a **terabyte**, gigabytes; a **petabyte**, or **PB**, is 1,024 terabytes; and an **exabyte, or EB**, is 1,024 petimes you will see these definitions simplified as 1K equals 1,000 bytes and 1MB, etc. Such simplifications are incorrect, but they do ease the math.

Specifying Hardware with Computer Data Sizes

Buying hardware can be tricky and expensive whether you are buying for personal or company use. Consumers can now check out a new computer at a traditional brick-and-mortar store and take the hardware for a test drive and then purchase online. Is this "showrooming" ethical? Read the Ethics Guide on pages 132-133 and decide.

Computer disk capacities are specified according to the amount of datain. Thus, a 500GB disk can contain up to 500GB of data and programs. There is d, so it is not quite 500GB, but it's close enough.

You can purchase computers with CPUs of different speeds. Cxpressed in cycles called *hertz*. In 2013, a slow personal computer has a speed of. A fast personal computer has a speed of 3+ Gigahertz, with dual processors. As Moore's Law, CPU speeds continually increase.

Additionally, CPUs today are classified as 32-bit or 64-bit. Withou the particulars, a 32-bit is less capable and cheaper than a 64-bit CPU. The latts more main memory; you need a 64-bit processor to effectively use more than 4. 64-bit processors have other advantages as well, but they are more expensive tlcessors.

An employee who does only simple tasks such as word procet need a fast CPU; a 32-bit, 1.5 Gigahertz CPU will be fine. However, an employee s large, complicated spreadsheets or who manipulates large database files or cture, sound, or video files needs a fast computer like a 64-bit, dual processor wertz or more. Employees whose work requires them to use many large applicatioe time need 4 GB or more of RAM. Others can do with less.

One last comment: The cache and main memory are **volatile**, r contents are lost when power is off. Magnetic and optical disks are **nonvolati**heir contents survive when power is off. If you suddenly lose power, the contentmemory—say, documents that have been altered—will be lost. Therefore, get into thuently (every few minutes or so) saving documents or files that you are changing. uments before your roommate trips over the power cord.

Q2 What Do Business Professionals Need to Know About Software?

Operating systems can become infected with malware. Read the Security Guide on pages 146–147 to learn more.

As a future manager or business professional, you need to know the essential terminology and software concepts that will enable you to be an intelligent software consumer. To begin, consider the basic categories of software shown in Figure 4-5.

Every computer has an **operating system (OS)**, which is a program that controls that computer's resources. Some of the functions of an operating system are to read and write data, allocate main memory, perform memory swapping, start and stop programs, respond to error conditions, and facilitate backup and recovery. In addition, the operating system creates and manages the user interface, including the display, keyboard, mouse, and other devices.

Although the operating system makes the computer usable, it does little application-specific work. If you want to check the weather or access a database, you need application programs such as an iPad weather application or Oracle's customer relationship management (CRM) software.

Both client and server computers need an operating system, though they need not be the same. Further, both clients and servers can process application programs. The application's design determines whether the client, the server, or both, process it.

You need to understand two important software constraints. First, a particular version of an operating system is written for a particular type of hardware. For example, Microsoft Windows works only on processors from Intel and companies that make processors that conform to the Intel instruction set (the commands that a CPU can process). Furthermore, the 32-bit version of Windows is designed for Intel computers with 32-bit CPUs, and the 64-bit version of Windows runs only on Intel computers with 64-bit CPUs. With other operating systems, such as Linux, many versions exist for many different instruction sets and for both 32- and 64-bit computers.

Second, two types of application programs exist. **Native applications** are programs that are written to use a particular operating system. Microsoft Access, for example, will only run on the Windows operating system. Some applications come in multiple versions. For example, there are Windows and Macintosh versions of Microsoft Word. But unless you are informed otherwise, assume that a native application runs on just one operating system. Native applications are sometimes called **thick-client** applications.

A **thin-client** application is designed to run within a computer browser such as Firefox, Chrome, Opera, and Internet Explorer. Thin-client applications run within the browser and can run on any type of computer. Ideally, a thin-client application can also run within any browser, though this is not always true as you will learn.

Consider next the operating system and application program categories of software.

What Are the Major Operating Systems?

The major operating systems are listed in Figure 4-6. Consider each.

Nonmobile Client Operating Systems

Nonmobile client operating systems are used on personal computers. The most popular is **Microsoft Windows**. Some version of Windows resides on more than 85 percent of the world's desktops, and, if we consider just business users, the figure is more than 95 percent.

Figure 4-5
Categories of Computer Software

	Operating System	Application Programs
Client	Programs that control the client computer's resources	Applications that are processed on client computers
Server	Programs that control the server computer's resources	Applications that are processed on server computers

Category	Operating System	Used for	Remarks
Nonmobile Clients	Windows	Personal Computer Clients	Most widely used operating system in business. Current version is Windows 8. Includes a touch interface.
	Mac OS	Macintosh Clients	First used by graphic artists and others in arts community; now used more widely. First desktop OS to provide a touch interface. Current version is the Mac OS X Mountain Lion.
	Unix	Workstation Clients	Popular on powerful client computers used in engineering, computer-assisted design, architecture. Difficult for the nontechnical user. Almost never used by business clients.
	Linux	Just about anything	Open-source variant of Unix. Adapted to almost every type of computing device. On a PC, used with Open Office application software. Rarely used by business clients.
Mobile Clients	Symbian	Nokia, Samsung, and other phones	Popular worldwide, but less so in North America.
	Blackberry OS	Research in Motion Blackberries	Device and OS developed for use by business. Very popular in beginning, but losing market share to iOS and Android.
	iOS	iPhone, iPod Touch, iPad	Rapidly increasing installed base with success of the iPhone and iPad. Based on Mac OS X.
	Android	T-Mobile and other phones. Tablets and e-readers like the Kindle Fire	Linux-based phone/tablet operating system from Google. Rapidly increasing market share.
	Windows 8	Microsoft Surface and Microsoft Phones	Windows 8 (RT) tailored specifically for ARM devices, mostly tablets. Full Windows 8 on Surface Pro.
Servers	Windows Server	Servers	Businesses with a strong commitment to Microsoft.
	Unix	Servers	Fading from use. Replaced by Linux.
	Linux	Servers	Very popular. Aggressively pushed by IBM.

Figure 4-6
Major Operating Systems

The most recent client version of Windows is Windows 8, a major rewrite of prior versions. Windows 8 is distinguished by what Microsoft calls **modern-style applications**.[1] These applications are touch-screen oriented and provide context-sensitive, pop-up menus. They can also be used with a mouse and keyboard. Microsoft claims that modern-style applications work just as well on portable, mobile devices, such as tablet computers, as they do on desktop computers. One key feature of modern-style applications is the minimization of menu bars, status lines, and other visual overhead. Figure 4-7 shows an example of a modern-style version of searching for images in Windows Explorer.

Apple Computer, Inc., developed its own operating system for the Macintosh, **Mac OS**. The current version is Mac OS X Mountain Lion. Apple touts it as the world's most advanced desktop operating system, and until Windows 8, it was without doubt. Windows 8 now gives it a run for the money in terms of that title.

Until recently, Mac OS was used primarily by graphic artists and workers in the arts community. But for many reasons, Mac OS has made headway into the traditional Windows market. According to NetApplications, as of March 2013, all versions of Windows account for 90 percent of business applications. OS X accounts for 7 percent.[2]

---

[1]Previously called metro-style. Name change by Microsoft, reputedly because of a trademark lawsuit from Europe.
[2]"Net Applications," accessed July 15, 2013, *http://www.netapplications.com.*

Figure 4-7
Example of the Modern-Style Interface
Source: Microsoft Corporation

Mac OS was designed originally to run the line of CPU processors from Motorola, but today a Macintosh with an Intel processor is able to run both Windows and the Mac OS.

Unix is an operating system that was developed at Bell Labs in the 1970s. It has been the workhorse of the scientific and engineering communities since then. Unix is seldom used in business.

Linux is a version of Unix that was developed by the open source community (discussed on page 123). This community is a loosely coupled group of programmers who mostly volunteer their time to contribute code to develop and maintain Linux. The open source community owns Linux, and there is no fee to use it. Linux can run on client computers, but usually only when budget is of paramount concern. By far, Linux is most popular as a server OS.

Mobile Client Operating Systems

Figure 4-6 also lists the five principal mobile operating systems. **Symbian** is popular on phones in Europe and the Far East, but less so in North America. **BlackBerry OS** was one of the most successful early mobile operating systems and was used primarily by business users on BlackBerry devices. It is now losing market share to iOS, Android, and Windows 8.

iOS is the operating system used on the iPhone, iPod Touch, and iPad. When first released, it broke new ground with its ease of use and compelling display, features that are now being copied by the BlackBerry OS and Android. With the popularity of the iPhone and iPad, Apple has been increasing its market share of iOS and according to Net Applications is used on 61 percent of mobile devices.[3] The current version of iOS is iOS 7.

Android is a mobile operating system licensed by Google. Android devices have a very loyal following, especially among technical users. Recently, Android has been gaining market share over the BlackBerry OS on phones, and it received a big boost when it was selected for the Amazon Kindle Fire. Net Applications estimates Android's market share to be nearly 25 percent.

Most industry observers would agree that Apple has led the way, both with the Mac OS and the iOS, in creating easy-to-use interfaces. Certainly, many innovative ideas have first appeared in a Macintosh or iSomething and then later were added, in one form or another, to Android and Windows.

---

[3]"Net Applications," accessed July 15, 2013, *http://www.netapplications.com.*

Windows RT is a version of Windows designed for use on ARM devices. **ARM** is a computer architecture and instruction set that is designed for portable devices such as phones and tablets. Windows RT is a version of Windows 8 that is specifically designed to provide a touch-based interface for devices that use this architecture. As of May 2013, Windows RT appears to be a flop. Instead, users who wish to use Windows 8 on mobile devices seem to be choosing full Windows 8 on a Surface Pro device. Windows 8 phone sales have a miniscule market share.

The smartphone market has always been huge, but recently, e-book readers and tablets have substantially increased the market for mobile client operating systems. As of June 2013, one in three Americans owned at least one of these devices.[4]

Server Operating Systems

The last three rows of Figure 4-6 show the three most popular server operating systems. **Windows Server** is a version of Windows that has been specially designed and configured for server use. It has much more stringent and restrictive security features than other versions of Windows and is popular on servers in organizations that have made a strong commitment to Microsoft.

Unix can also be used on servers, but it is gradually being replaced by Linux.

Linux is frequently used on servers by organizations that want, for whatever reason, to avoid a server commitment to Microsoft. IBM is the primary proponent of Linux and in the past has used it as a means to better compete against Microsoft. Although IBM does not own Linux, IBM has developed many business systems solutions that use Linux. By using Linux, neither IBM nor its customers have to pay a license fee to Microsoft.

Virtualization

Virtualization is the process by which one computer hosts the appearance of many computers. One operating system, called the **host operating system**, runs one or more operating systems as applications. Those hosted operating systems are called **virtual machines (vm)**. Each virtual machine has disk space and other resources allocated to it. The host operating system controls the activities of the virtual machines it hosts to prevent them from interfering with one another. With virtualization, each vm is able to operate exactly the same as it would if it were operating in a stand-alone, nonvirtual environment.

Three types of virtualization exist:

- PC virtualization
- Server virtualization
- Desktop virtualization

With **PC virtualization**, a personal computer, such as a desktop or portable computer, hosts several different operating systems. Say a user needs, for some reason, to have both Linux and Windows 8 running on a computer. In that circumstance, the user can install a virtual host operating system and then both Linux and Windows 8 on top of it. In that way, the user can have both systems on the same hardware. VMWare Workstation is a popular PC virtualization product that runs both Windows and Linux operating systems.

With **server virtualization**, a server computer hosts one, or more, other server computers. In Figure 4-8, a Windows Server computer is hosting two virtual machines. Users can log on to either of those virtual machines, and they will appear as normal servers. Figure 4-9 shows how virtual machine VM3 appears to a user of that server. Notice that a user of VM3 is running a browser that is accessing SharePoint. In fact, this virtual machine was used to generate many of the SharePoint figures in Chapter 2. Server virtualization plays a key role for cloud vendors, as you'll learn in Chapter 6.

PC virtualization is interesting as well as quite useful, as you will learn in Chapter 6. Desktop virtualization, on the other hand, has the potential to be revolutionary. With **desktop virtualization**,

---

[4]*http://www.zdnet.com/a-third-of-american-adults-now-own-tablet-computers-7000016867/*, accessed August 2013.

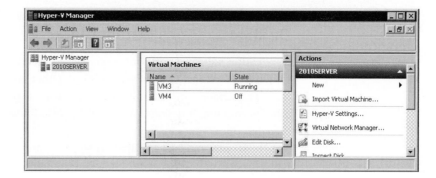

Figure 4-8
Windows Server Computer
Hosting Two Virtual Machines
Source: Microsoft Corporation

a server hosts many versions of desktop operating systems. Each of those desktops has a complete user environment and appears to the user to be just another PC. However, the desktop can be accessed from any computer to which the user has access. Thus, you could be at an airport and go to a terminal computer and access your virtualized desktop. To you, it appears as if that airport computer is your own personal computer. Later, you could do the same with a utility computer while sitting in your hotel room. Meanwhile, many other users could have accessed the computer in the airport, and each thought he or she had his or her personal computer. IBM offers PC virtualization for as low as $12 a month per PC.

Desktop virtualization is in its infancy, but it might have major impact during the early years of your career, as discussed in Q8, 2024?.

Own Versus License

When you buy a computer program, you are not actually buying that program. Instead, you are buying a **license** to use that program. For example, when you buy a Mac OS license, Apple is selling you the right to use Mac OS. Apple continues to own the Mac OS program. Large organizations do not buy a license for each computer user. Instead, they negotiate a **site license**, which is a flat fee that authorizes the company to install the product (operating system or application) on all of that company's computers or on all of the computers at a specific site.

In the case of Linux, no company can sell you a license to use it. It is owned by the open source community, which states that Linux has no license fee (with certain reasonable restrictions). Large companies such as IBM and smaller companies such as RedHat can make money by supporting Linux, but no company makes money selling Linux licenses.

Figure 4-9
Virtual Machine Example
Source: Microsoft Corporation

What Types of Applications Exist, and How Do Organizations Obtain Them?

Application software performs a service or function. Some application programs are general purpose, such as Microsoft Excel or Word. Other application programs provide specific functions. QuickBooks, for example, is an application program that provides general ledger and other accounting functions. We begin by describing categories of application programs and then describe sources for them.

Horizontal-market application software provides capabilities common across all organizations and industries. Word processors, graphics programs, spreadsheets, and presentation programs are all horizontal-market application software.

Examples of such software are Microsoft Word, Excel, and PowerPoint. Examples from other vendors are Adobe's Acrobat, Photoshop, and PageMaker and Jasc Corporation's Paint Shop Pro. These applications are used in a wide variety of businesses, across all industries. They are purchased off the shelf, and little customization of features is necessary (or possible).

Vertical-market application software serves the needs of a specific industry. Examples of such programs are those used by dental offices to schedule appointments and bill patients, those used by auto mechanics to keep track of customer data and customers' automobile repairs, and those used by parts warehouses to track inventory, purchases, and sales.

Vertical applications usually can be altered or customized. Typically, the company that sold the application software will provide such services or offer referrals to qualified consultants who can provide this service.

One-of-a-kind application software is developed for a specific, unique need. The IRS develops such software, for example, because it has needs that no other organization has.

You can acquire application software in exactly the same ways that you can buy a new suit. The quickest and least risky option is to buy your suit off the rack. With this method, you get your suit immediately, and you know exactly what it will cost. You may not, however, get a good fit. Alternately, you can buy your suit off the rack and have it altered. This will take more time, it may cost more, and there's some possibility that the alteration will result in a poor fit. Most likely, however, an altered suit will fit better than an off-the-rack one.

Finally, you can hire a tailor to make a custom suit. In this case, you will have to describe what you want, be available for multiple fittings, and be willing to pay considerably more. Although there is an excellent chance of a great fit, there is also the possibility of a disaster. Still, if you want a yellow and orange polka-dot silk suit with a hissing rattlesnake on the back, tailor-made is the only way to go. You can buy computer software in exactly the same ways: **off-the-shelf software, off-the-shelf with alterations software**, or tailor-made. Tailor-made software is called **custom-developed software**.

Organizations develop custom application software themselves or hire a development vendor. Like buying the yellow and orange polka-dot suit, such development is done in situations where the needs of the organization are so unique that no horizontal or vertical applications are available. By developing custom software, the organization can tailor its application to fit its requirements.

Custom development is difficult and risky. Staffing and managing teams of software developers is challenging. Managing software projects can be daunting. Many organizations have embarked on application development projects only to find that the projects take twice as long—or longer—to finish than planned. Cost overruns of 200 and 300 percent are not uncommon. We will discuss such risks further in Chapter 10.

In addition, every application program needs to be adapted to changing needs and changing technologies. The adaptation costs of horizontal and vertical software are amortized over all the users of that software, perhaps thousands or millions of customers. For custom-developed software, however, the using organization must pay all of the adaptation costs itself. Over time, this cost burden is heavy.

Software Source

	Off-the-shelf	Off-the-shelf and then customized	Custom-developed
Horizontal applications			
Vertical applications			
One-of-a-kind applications			

(Software Type)

Figure 4-10
Software Sources and Types

Because of the risk and expense, custom development is the last-choice alternative, used only when there is no other option. Figure 4-10 summarizes software sources and types.

What Is Firmware?

Firmware is computer software that is installed into devices such as printers, print servers, and various types of communication devices. The software is coded just like other software, but it is installed into special, read-only memory of the printer or other device. In this way, the program becomes part of the device's memory; it is as if the program's logic is designed into the device's circuitry. Therefore, users do not need to load firmware into the device's memory.

Firmware can be changed or upgraded, but this is normally a task for IS professionals. The task is easy, but it requires knowledge of special programs and techniques that most business users choose not to learn.

Is Open Source Software a Viable Alternative?

To answer this question, you first need to know something about the open source movement and process. Most computer historians would agree that Richard Matthew Stallman is the father of the movement. In 1983, he developed a set of tools called **GNU** (a self-referential acronym meaning *GNU Not Unix*) for creating a free Unix-like operating system. Stallman made many other contributions to open source, including the **GNU general public license (GPL) agreement**, one of the standard license agreements for open source software. Stallman was unable to attract enough developers to finish the free Unix system, but continued making other contributions to the open source movement.

In 1991, Linus Torvalds, working in Helsinki, began work on another version of Unix, using some of Stallman's tools. That version eventually became Linux, the high-quality and very popular operating system discussed previously.

The Internet proved to be a great asset for open source, and many open source projects became successful, including:

- Open Office (a Microsoft Office look-alike)
- Firefox (a browser)
- MySQL (a DBMS, see Chapter 5)
- Apache (a Web server, see Chapter 6)
- Ubuntu (a Windows-like desktop operating system)
- Android (a mobile-device operating system)
- Cassandra (a NoSQL DBMS, see Chapter 5)
- Hadoop (a BigData processing system, see Chapter 9)

Using MIS InClass 4

Place Your Bets Now!

In June, 2012, Microsoft announced Microsoft **Surface**, a tablet device to compete with the iPad and Kindle.

Just another hardware announcement? Not quite. For the first time in Microsoft's 37-year history, it decided to manufacture its own hardware. (Except for keyboards, mice, and the Xbox, that is.)

Microsoft has been notorious for not manufacturing hardware. In the early PC days, Microsoft expressly left hardware manufacturing to IBM, Compaq, Hewlett-Packard, Dell, and so on. It gained considerable market share over Apple because that decision enabled those powerful companies to succeed in selling Microsoft Windows on their hardware, which in turn set the stage for Microsoft Office. In the 1980s, Bill Gates famously wrote Steve Jobs telling him that he needed to give up hardware and focus on software.

But was Steve Jobs right all along? At the Surface announcement, Steve Ballmer, former Microsoft CEO, indicated there were features that Microsoft could build, or at least build better, if it controlled the hardware. Is owning manufacturing one of the keys for Apple's ability to create such beautiful, easily used, and highly functional devices? Maybe so.

Meanwhile, that same month, Google finalized its acquisition of Motorola Mobility, thus becoming a manufacturer of smartphone hardware. Is its manufacture of tablet hardware just around the corner? Or, perhaps by the time you read this, Google will have announced that it is manufacturing its own tablet. (The Nexus 10 is made by Samsung, not Google.)

But Google and Microsoft have a problem that Apple doesn't have: channel conflict. Apple is the only manufacturer of Apple hardware. But numerous companies other than Google make Android phones and tablets, and several companies other than Microsoft make Windows phones and tablets. What happens to those businesses? Have they been thrown under the technology bus?

It's a three-way race for market share: Apple far in the lead, Google following up, and Microsoft struggling for footing back in the dust. They're all strong horses; all have deep technical staff, knowledge, patents, and plenty of money. Place your bets now!

Form a group as directed by your professor and answer the following questions:

1. Update the table (on the next page) with the latest announcements and data. Go to *http://finance.yahoo.com* and update the financial data. Add new devices as appropriate. Search the Internet, using terms such as *iPhone vs. Android market share* to update the market share data.

2. According to the latest data, how has the market share of these three companies changed? Has Apple made continued inroads on Android phones? Has Surface made inroads on

the iPad? What's happened to the Kindle? And what about Microsoft's measly 2 percent of the phone market? Has Surface helped? Or has Microsoft finally given up on smartphones?

3. Unlike Apple and Google, Microsoft controls Windows Server, a server operating system. Does that provide an advantage to Microsoft in this race? There are rumors, in fact, that Apple runs Windows Server in its iCloud data center. If true, does it matter?

4. In October 2011, Microsoft purchased Skype. Does Skype contribute to Surface? Can you find announcements that indicate there is some convergence there?

5. Microsoft makes and sells the Xbox with motion-sensing Kinect. Can you envision a way for Microsoft to use either of those to help increase market share of its Surface/phone devices? If so, what?

6. Microsoft enjoys incredible success in the PC market, but it has, at least so far, never been able to succeed with a phone, and as of May 2013, Microsoft Surface does not seem very successful. Christopher Mims thinks it's time for Microsoft to give up on consumers and focus on businesses,[5] especially business back-office applications. What do you think Microsoft should do?

7. Suppose your group has $500,000 to invest in AAPL, GOOG, or MSFT. You must put all of it in one stock. Which stock do you choose and why?

---

[5]Christopher Mims, "It's Time for Microsoft to Give Up on Consumers," *Quartz*, last modified April 17, 2013, *http://qz.com/75423/ its-time-for-microsoft-to-give-up-on-the-consumer/*.

	Apple		Google		Microsoft	
Device	iPhone	iPad	Android Phones	Kindle Fire[1]	Windows Phones	Surface
Hardware Manufacturer	Apple	Apple	Google & others	Others	Others	Microsoft & others
OS	iOS	iOS	Android	Android	Windows 8 RT	Windows 8 Windows 8 RT
Market Share	30%[2]	68%	46%	13%	2%	<2%
Camera	Yes	Yes	Yes	No	Yes	No
Keyboard	Internal	Internal	Internal	Internal	Internal	Internal and External
Revenue	$169 billion		$56 billion		$78 billion	
Cash 7/31/13	$43 billion		$44 billion		$76 billion	
Market Cap 7/31/13	$411 billion		$296 billion		$265 billion	
Share Price 7/31/12	$611		$633		$29	
Share Price 7/31/13	$453		$887		$32	
Annual Price Growth	−26%		40%		0%	

[1]Device is manufactured and sold by Amazon.
[2]Meaning, 30 percent of the cell phone market

Source of Financial Data: finance.yahoo.com

Why Do Programmers Volunteer Their Services?

To a person who has never enjoyed writing computer programs, it is difficult to understand why anyone would donate his or her time and skills to contribute to open source projects. Programming is, however, an intense combination of art and logic, and designing and writing a complicated computer program can be exceedingly pleasurable (and addictive). Like many programmers, at times in my life I have gleefully devoted 16 hours a day to writing computer programs—day after day—and those days would fly by. If you have an artistic and logical mind, you ought to try it.

The first reason that people contribute to open source is that it is great fun! Additionally, some people contribute to open source because it gives them the freedom to choose the projects they work on. They may have a programming day job that is not terribly interesting—say, writing a program to manage a computer printer. Their job pays the bills, but it's not fulfilling.

In the 1950s, Hollywood studio musicians suffered as they recorded the same style of music over and over for a long string of uninteresting movies. To keep their sanity, those musicians would gather on Sundays to play jazz, and a number of high-quality jazz clubs resulted. That's what open source is to programmers: a place where they can exercise their creativity while working on projects they find interesting and fulfilling.

Another reason for contributing to open source is to exhibit one's skill, both for pride and to find a job or consulting employment. A final reason is to start a business selling services to support an open source product.

How Does Open Source Work?

The term **open source** means that the source code of the program is available to the public. **Source code** is computer code as written by humans and understandable by humans. Figure 4-11 shows a portion of the computer code that I wrote for the PRIDE project (see start of Chapter 7).

Source code is compiled into **machine code** that is processed by a computer. Machine code is, in general, not understandable by humans and cannot be modified. When a user accesses a Web site, the machine code version of the program runs on the user's computer. We do not show machine code in a figure because it would look like this:

11010010100101111110011101111001000111000001111110111101111100111…

Figure 4-11
Source Code Sample

```
/// <summary>
/// Allows the page to draw itself.
/// </summary>
private void OnDraw(object sender, GameTimerEventArgs e)
{
    SharedGraphicsDeviceManager.Current.GraphicsDevice.Clear(Color.CornflowerBlue);

    SharedGraphicsDeviceManager.Current.GraphicsDevice.Clear(Color.Black);

    // Render the Silverlight controls using the UIElementRenderer.
    elementRenderer.Render();

    // Draw the sprite
    spriteBatch.Begin();

    // Draw the rectangle in its new position
    for (int i = 0; i < 3; i++)
    {
        spriteBatch.Draw(texture[i], bikeSpritePosition[i], Color.White);
    }

    // Using the texture from the UIElementRenderer,

    // draw the Silverlight controls to the screen.
    spriteBatch.Draw(elementRenderer.Texture, Vector2.Zero, Color.White);

    spriteBatch.End();
}
```

In a **closed source** project, say Microsoft Office, the source code is highly protected and only available to trusted employees and carefully vetted contractors. The source code is protected like gold in a vault. Only those trusted programmers can make changes to a closed source project.

With open source, anyone can obtain the source code from the open source project's Web site. Programmers alter or add to this code depending on their interests and goals. In most cases, programmers can incorporate code they find into their own projects. They may be able to resell those projects depending on the type of license agreement the project uses.

Open source succeeds because of collaboration. A programmer examines the source code and identifies a need or project that seems interesting. He or she then creates a new feature, redesigns or reprograms an existing feature, or fixes a known problem. That code is then sent to others in the open source project who evaluate the quality and merits of the work and add it to the product, if appropriate.

Typically, there is a lot of give and take. Or, as described in Chapter 2, there are many cycles of iteration and feedback. Because of this iteration, a well-managed project with strong peer reviews can result in very high quality code, like that in Linux.

So, Is Open Source Viable?

The answer depends on to whom and for what. Open source has certainly become legitimate. According to *The Economist,* "It is now generally accepted that the future will involve a blend of both proprietary and open-source software."[6] During your career, open source will likely take a greater and greater role in software. However, whether open source works for a particular situation depends on the requirements and constraints of that situation. You will learn more about matching requirements and programs in Chapter 10.

In some cases, companies choose open source software because it is "free." It turns out that this advantage may be less important than you'd think because in many cases support and operational costs swamp the initial licensing fee.

What Are the Differences Between Native and Thin-client Applications?

In the chapter opening, when Lucas mentioned *thin-client app* and *native app*, Jason didn't hesitate. He knew exactly what those terms meant and the issues involved with each. And Jason is a CEO. He knows those issues, as does the AllRoad Parts team, and so should you.

To begin, as stated, applications can be categorized as native applications that run on just one operating system or thin-client applications that run in browsers. In the latter case, the browser provides a more-or-less consistent environment for the application; the peculiarities of operating systems and hardware are handled by the browser's code and hidden from the thin-client application.

Figure 4-12 contrasts native and thin-client applications on their important characteristics. Consider the Native Applications column first.

Developing Native Applications

Native applications are developed using serious, heavy-duty, professional programming languages. Mac OS and iOS applications are constructed using Objective-C, Linux (Android) applications are constructed using Java, and Windows applications are constructed using C#, VB.NET, C++, and others. All of these languages are **object-oriented**, which means they can be

---

[6]"Unlocking the Cloud," *The Economist,* May 28, 2009.

	Native Applications	**Thin-client Applications**
Development Languages	Objective-C Java C#, C++, VB.NET (object-oriented languages)	html5 css3 JavaScript (scripting language)
Developed by	Professional programmers, only	Professional programmers and technically oriented Web developers and business professionals
Skill level required	High	Low to high
Difficulty	High	Easy to hard, depending on application requirements
Developer's Degree	Computer science	Computer science Information systems Graphics design
User Experience	Can be superb, depending on programming quality	Simple to sophisticated, depending on program quality
Possible applications	Whatever you can pay for...	Some limits prohibit very sophisticated applications
Dependency	iOS, Android, Windows	Browser differences, only
Cost	High. Difficult work by highly paid employees, multiple versions required.	Low to high ... easier work by lesser-paid employees, only multiple browser files necessary. Sophisticated applications may require high skill and pay.
Application distribution	Via application stores (e.g., Apple Store)	Via Web sites
Example	Vanguard iPad application (free in Apple's iTunes store)	Seafood Web site: *www.wildrhodyseafood.com* Picozu editor: *www.picozu.com/editor*

Figure 4-12
Characteristics of Native and Thin-client Applications

used to create difficult, complex applications, and, if used properly, will result in high-performance code that is easy to alter when requirements change. The particular characteristics of object-oriented languages are beyond the scope of this text.

Object-oriented languages can only be used by professional programmers who have devoted years to learning object-oriented design and coding skills. Typically, such developers were computer science majors in college.

The benefit of such languages is that they give programmers close control over the assets of the computing device and enable the creation of sophisticated and complex user interfaces. If the programs are well written, they perform fast and use memory efficiently. The limits on native applications are usually budgetary, not technological. As a business person, you can get just about any application you can afford.

The downside of native applications is that they are, well, native. They only run on the operating system for which they are programmed. An iOS application must be completely recoded in order to run on Android and recoded again to run on Windows.[7] Thus, to reach all users, an organization will need to support and maintain three separate versions of the same application. It will also have to staff and manage three different development teams, with three different skill sets.

---

[7]Not quite true. Much of the design and possibly some of the code can be reused between native applications. But, for your planning, assume that it all must be redone. Not enough will carry over to make it worth considering.

As a general rule, the cost of native applications is high. Many organizations reduce that cost by outsourcing development to India and other countries (see the introduction to Chapter 11), but native applications are still expensive relative to thin-client applications. The standard way to distribute native applications is via a company store, such as iTunes, owned by Apple. An excellent example of a native application is Vanguard's iPad application. It is easy to use, has complex functionality, and is highly secure, as you would expect. Companies such as Vanguard must and can afford to pay for exceedingly high-quality applications.

Developing Thin-client Applications

The third column in Figure 4-12 summarizes thin-client application characteristics. Such applications run inside a browser such as Firefox, Chrome, Opera, or Internet Explorer (IE). The browser handles the idiosyncrasies of the operating system and underlying hardware. In theory, an organization should be able to develop a single application and have it run flawlessly on all browsers on all devices. Unfortunately, there are some differences in the way that browsers implement the thin-client code. The announcement in Figure 4-13 exhibits the frustration of Gethu Games' developers when trying to make their thin-client application SpiroCanvas run on Internet Explorer 9[8] (*www.GethuGames.in/SpiroCanvas/*).

As shown in the first row of Figure 4-12, thin-client development languages are html5, css3, and Javascript. html5 is the latest version of html, which you will learn about in Chapter 6. The advantages of this version are support for graphics, animation, 2D animations, and other sophisticated user experiences. css3 is used with html5 to specify the appearance of content coded in html. JavaScript is a scripting programming language that is much easier to learn than native-client languages. It is used to provide the underlying logic of the application.

Thin-client applications can be written by professional programmers, and, indeed, most are. However, it is possible for technically oriented Web developers and business professionals to develop them as well. The entry-level technical skill required is low, and simple applications are relatively easy to develop. Sophisticated user experiences, like that in SpiroCanvas, are difficult. Thin-client application developers may have degrees in computer science, information systems, or graphics design.

The user experience provided by a thin-client application varies considerably. Some are simply fancy Web-based brochures (*www.wildrhodyseafood.com*), others are quite sophisticated, such as SpiroCanvas in Figure 4-14 (*www.gethugames.in/*), or even more impressive, *www.biodigitalhuman.com* in Figure 4-15 (runs in Opera; may not work in other browsers).

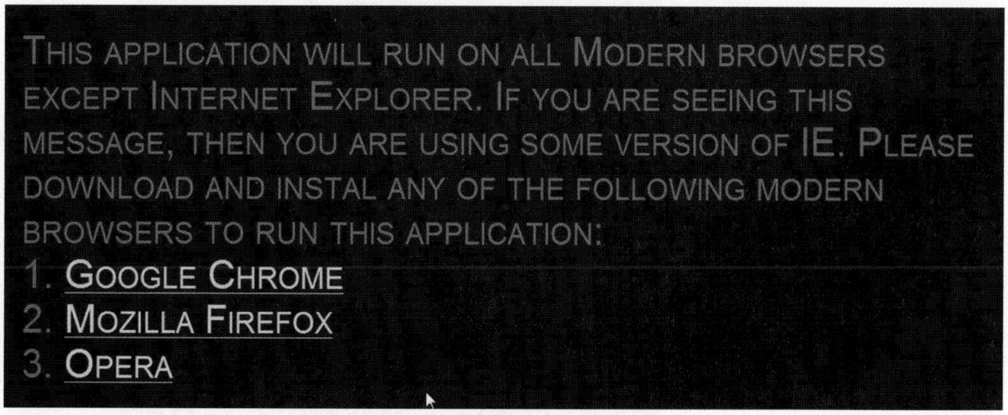

Figure 4-13
One Consequence of Browser Differences for Thin-client Applications
Source: http://www.gethugames.in/ spirocanvas/ Reprinted by permission.

THIS APPLICATION WILL RUN ON ALL MODERN BROWSERS EXCEPT INTERNET EXPLORER. IF YOU ARE SEEING THIS MESSAGE, THEN YOU ARE USING SOME VERSION OF IE. PLEASE DOWNLOAD AND INSTAL ANY OF THE FOLLOWING MODERN BROWSERS TO RUN THIS APPLICATION:
1. GOOGLE CHROME
2. MOZILLA FIREFOX
3. OPERA

---

[8]This sad saga continues beyond IE 9. As of May 2013, IE 10, the latest version of IE, will not support JavaScript for touch on the Microsoft Surface. The same JavaScript on Firefox runs just fine.

Figure 4-14
GethuGames' SpiroCanvas

Thin-client applications are limited by the capabilities of the browser. While browsers are becoming increasingly sophisticated, they cannot offer the full capabilities of the underlying operating system and hardware. Thus, thin-browser applications are unable to support very specialized and complex applications, though this becomes less true each year.

As stated, the major advantage of thin-client over native applications is that they will run on any operating system and device. As demonstrated in Figure 4-13, there are some browser differences, but these differences are very minor when compared with the differences among iOS, Android, and Windows. In general, unlike native applications, you can assume that a thin-client application has one code base and one development team.

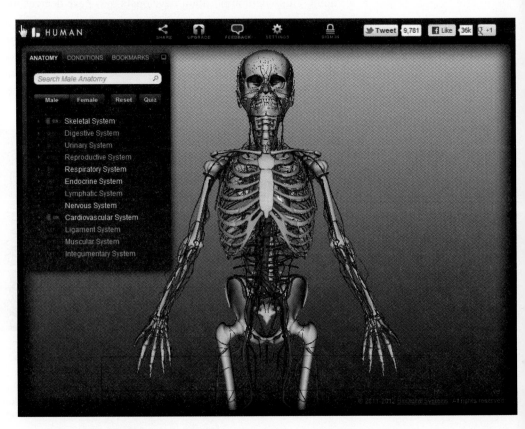

Figure 4-15
Sophisticated html5 Application

Because thin-client applications can be developed by less skilled, lesser-paid employees and because only one code base and one development team are necessary, they are considerably cheaper to develop than native applications. However, this statement assumes applications of equivalent complexity. A simple native application can be cheaper to develop than a complex thin-client application.

Users obtain thin-client applications via the Web. For example, when you go to *www .picozu.com/editor* the required html5, css3, and JavaScript files are downloaded automatically over the Web. Updates to the application are automatic and seamless. You need not install (or reinstall) anything. This difference is an advantage to the user; it makes it more difficult, however, to earn money from your application. Amazon, for example, will sell your native application and pay you a royalty. However, unless you require users to buy your thin-client application (which is possible, but rare), you'll have to give it away. To companies like AllRoad Parts, royalty revenue from their application is not important. To you, it might be.

Which Is Better?

You know the answer to that question. If it were clear-cut, we'd only be discussing one alternative. It's not. The choice depends on your strategy, your particular goals, the requirements for your application, your budget, your schedule, your tolerance for managing technical projects, your need for application revenue, and other factors. In general, thin-client applications are cheaper to develop and maintain, but they may lack the wow factor. You and your organization have to decide for yourselves!

Why Are Mobile Systems Increasingly Important?

Mobile systems are information systems that support users in motion. Mobile systems users access the system from *any place*—at home, at work, in the car, on the bus, or at the beach—using any smart device, such as smartphone, tablet, or PC. The possibilities are endless.

Mobile systems users move not only geographically, but also from device to device. The user who starts reading a book on an iPad on a bus, continues reading that book on a PC at work, and finishes it on a Kindle Fire at home is mobile both geographically and across devices.

As shown in Figure 4-16, the major elements in a mobile system are *users in motion, mobile devices, wireless connectivity*, and a *cloud-based resource*. A **mobile device** is a small, lightweight, power-conserving, computing device that is capable of wireless connectivity. Almost all mobile devices have a display and some means for data entry. Mobile devices include smartphones, tablets, personal digital assistants, and small, light laptops. Desktop computers, Xboxes, and large, heavy, power-hungry laptops are not mobile devices.

You will learn about wireless connectivity and the cloud in Chapter 6. For now, just assume that the cloud is a group of servers on the other end of a connection with a mobile device. When downloading a book for a Kindle, for example, the cloud is one or more servers on the other end that store that book and download a copy of it to your device.

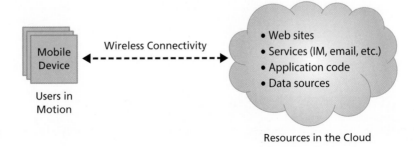

Figure 4-16
Elements of a Mobile Information System

Ethics Guide

SHOWROOMING: THE CONSEQUENCES

Showrooming occurs when someone visits a brick-and-mortar store to examine and evaluate products without the intention of them buying at that store. Rather, once the consumer has decided on the most suitable product, he or she purchases that product elsewhere, usually online. Thus, if you visit a Best Buy store, check out the Windows 8 touch computers, ask the sales personnel questions about the various alternatives, and then return home to purchase the one you like best from an online vendor, you are showrooming Best Buy computers.

In most cases, online vendors charge less than brick-and-mortar vendors because they save money on rent, employees, utilities, and other costs of operating a physical retail presence. If they choose, online vendors can pass those savings on to the purchaser, either in the form of lower prices, free shipping, or both.

Online vendors have another advantage. While all brick-and-mortar stores must pay sales tax, unless an online vendor has a physical presence in your state, that vendor need not pay. You, as the purchaser of goods from out of state, are supposed to declare and pay state tax on your purchase, but few people do. Thus, the price charged by a brick-and-mortar store can be the same as the online vendor, but it can be cheaper to buy online if the cost of shipping is less than your state's sales tax (assuming you do not declare and pay that tax).

To facilitate showrooming, Amazon.com developed a mobile, native application called *Price Check* that is available for iOS and Android devices. Using mobile devices, consumers can scan a UPC product code, take a picture of a product, or say the name of a product, and Amazon.com will respond with its price as well as prices from many other online vendors.

Source: .shock/Fotolia

DISCUSSION QUESTIONS

1. In your opinion, with regard to showrooming, are online vendors behaving unethically? Use both the categorical imperative (pages 20–21) and utilitarianism (pages 54–55) in your answer.

2. In your opinion, is Amazon.com behaving unethically by creating and disseminating the Price Check app? Use both the categorical imperative and utilitarianism in your answer.

3. In your opinion, are consumers behaving unethically when they showroom? Use both the categorical imperative and utilitarianism in your answer.

4. What are the long-term consequences of showrooming? Do they matter?

5. How would you advise senior managers of brick-and-mortar stores to respond to showrooming?

6. Consider a consumer who elects not to pay state tax on online purchases from a vendor who need not pay that tax on his or her behalf:

   a. Is there an ethical responsibility to pay state tax? Again, consider both categorical imperative and utilitarianism perspectives.

   b. Suppose a consumer says, "Look, most of the state tax money just goes to bloated retirement programs anyway. All those old people aren't entitled to my money." Does this posture change your answer to question 6a? Why or why not?

   c. Suppose a consumer says, "I'm just one of millions who are doing this in our state. My piddly $50 really doesn't matter." Does this posture change your answer to question 6a? Why or why not?

   d. Suppose a consumer says, "I will do more for society in our state with my $50 than the state government ever will." Does this posture change your answer to question 6a? Why or why not?

   e. Suppose a consumer says, "The state makes it so hard to pay this tax. I have to keep track of all my online purchases, and then I don't even know whom to contact. Plus, once they have my name and address and know that I buy online, who knows how they'll hassle me. Amazon.com makes it easy to pay; until the state does the same, they can forget about revenue from me." Does this posture change your answer to question 6a? Why or why not?

7. How would you advise your state legislature to respond to tax avoidance for online purchases?

	Hardware	Software	Data	Procedures	People
Impact of mobile systems growth	Many, many more mobile devices will be sold.	Compact interfaces; new technology for active users; application scaling.	More data, but more information? Less device real estate means fewer ads possible.	Always on, always at work. Employee lifestyle becomes hybrid of personal and professional.	Ability to thrive in a dynamic environment more important.
Industry changes	PCs less important; high demand (and requirement) for innovative devices as well as cheap copycats.	html5, css3, and JavaScript increase capability of thin-clients.	Loss of control. Ad model in danger?	Personal mobile devices at work.	More part-time employees and independent contractors.
Career opportunities	Jobs for mobile device sales, marketing, support.	New technology levels the playing field for html5. Business expertise needed for mobile requirements. New companies!	Reporting and data mining even more important. Design of effective mobile reports.	Innovative use of just-in-time data. Need for adjusting business processes gives another premium to non-routine problem solvers.	Independent contractors (and some employees) work where and when they want. What is this new social organism?

Figure 4-17
Five Components of Mobile
Change and Opportunity

The major reason for the importance of mobile systems is the size of their market. As of 2013, there are 6.8 billion wireless subscriptions.[9] According to mobiThinking (an excellent source for worldwide mobile device use), worldwide mobile subscriptions outnumber fixed lines by five to one. In some countries, like China, mobile Web usage is much greater than PC Web usage; this is expected to occur in the United States in 2015.[10]

According to a May 2012 issue of the *MIT Technology Review*, smartphones have achieved mainstream use by 40 percent of the U.S. market in four years. That's faster than any other technology except television in the early 1950s, which tied the smartphone adoption rate.[11]

Additionally, mobile use is favored by the young. According to Nielsen's measures of mobile device use, the younger the age group, the greater the percentage of people with mobile devices. Further, younger people have more devices per capita than older groups.[12] These young cohorts will further increase mobile systems use in the years to come.

Because of this vast and growing market, mobile systems are having a major impact on business and society today—impact that is forcing industry change while creating new career opportunities for mobile-IS-savvy professionals, as well as large numbers of new, interesting mobile-IS-related jobs.

Figure 4-17 summarizes the mobile-system impact for each of the five components of an information system. We will discuss each of the components in this figure, starting with hardware.

Hardware

Clearly, increasing demand for mobile systems means the sales of many more mobile devices, often at the expense of PC sales. Hewlett-Packard, a large PC manufacturer, learned this fact when it didn't respond quickly enough to the onslaught of mobile devices and was forced to

---

[9]Brahima Sanou, "ICT Facts and Figures," ITU Telecommunication Development Bureau, accessed July 15, 2013, *http://www.itu.int/en/ITU-D/Statistics/Documents/facts/ICTFactsFigures2013.pdf.*
[10]mobiThinking, "Global Mobile Statistics 2013 Part A," last modified May 2013, *http://mobithinking.com/mobile-marketing-tools/latest-mobile-stats/a#subscribers.*
[11]Michael Degusta, "Are Smart Phones Spreading Faster Than Any Other Technology in Human History?" *MIT Technology Review,* May 9, 2012, *http://www.technologyreview.com/business/40321/.*
[12]*http://blog.nielsen.com/nielsenwire/online_mobile/survey-new-u-s-smartphone-growth-by-age-and-income,* accessed May 2012.

eliminate 27,000 jobs in 2012. In the future, there will be high demand for innovative mobile devices as well as cheap copycats.

If you're reading this book, you're unlikely to be a hardware engineer, and if you're not living in Asia, you're also unlikely to be involved in hardware manufacturing. However, any market having 3.9 billion prospects is ripe with opportunities in marketing, sales, logistics, customer support, and related activities.

Software

The reduced size of mobile devices requires the invention of new, innovative interfaces, as we will discuss in Q6. The mobile user is an active user and expects an active screen experience. The premium will be for moving graphics, changing Web pages, and animation. Applications will need to scale from the very smallest to the very largest, while providing a user experience appropriate to the device's size.

Rapid technology change in mobile software continually levels the playing field. Today, for example, expert programmers in Objective-C better not relax. html5 and css3 are gaining popularity, and they will reduce the need for Objective-C expertise. Further, as you learned in Q4, while languages like Objective-C are difficult and time-consuming to learn, html5, css3, and JavaScript are less so. With the reduced barrier to entry, hordes of less experienced and less educated new entrants will appear as competitors. You might be one of them.

Not a computer programmer? Are you a business analyst? Do you want to be Drew at AllRoad Parts? If so, Jason, Kelly, and Lucas will rely on you to provide requirements for AllRoad Parts' mobile applications. The capabilities of mobile software in two years will be drastically different from those today. How do you, as Drew, respond? Maybe an html5 application is all the company needs. Maybe it need not even consider a native app. AllRoad Parts and many other organizations will need employees with the skills and abilities to assess the contribution that mobile technology can make to their strategies.

Additionally, continually evolving software means new and exciting entrepreneurial opportunities. Are you sorry that you missed the early days working at Facebook? Right now, somewhere, there is another Mark Zuckerberg starting...well, what? Because of the continually changing software environment, new opportunities abound and will continue to do so for decades.

Data

Many more mobile systems mean an incredible amount of new data, data that professionals can use to create much more information. But, as you learned in Chapter 1, more data doesn't necessarily mean more information. In fact, many business professionals believe they're drowning in data while starving for information. What can be done with all of this mobile-systems data to enable humans to conceive information of greater value to them? Data mining and better reporting are possibilities for you that are discussed in Chapter 9.

On the other hand, not all the news is good, at least not for many organizations. For one, smaller screens means less room for advertising, a factor that limited the success of the Facebook public offering in May 2012. Also, mobile systems increase the risk of organizations losing control over their data. In the past, employees used only computer equipment provided by the employer and connected only via employer-managed networks. In that situation, it is possible for the organization to control who does what with which data and where. No longer. Employees come to work with their own mobile devices. Data leakage is inevitable.

With more people switching to mobile devices and with less room for ads, online advertising revenue may be sharply reduced, possibly endangering the revenue model that supports most of the Web's free content. If this happens, dramatic change is just around the corner!

Procedures

Mobile systems are always on. They have no business hours. And people who use mobile systems are equally always on. In the mobile world, we're always open for business. It is impossible to be out of the office.

One consequence of always-on is the blending of our personal and professional lives. Such blending means, in part, that business will intrude on your personal life, and your personal life will intrude on your business. This intrusion can be distracting and stressful; on the other hand, it can lead to richer, more complex relationships. For example, with mobility, Addison may find herself discussing a problem with her daughter while talking at home to a seller at Fox. Their business relationship can become more personal and hence stronger, but it can also become awkward and weird.

As stated, employees will expect to use their mobile devices at work. But because of the loss of control, should they? In truth, who can keep them from it? If the organization blocks them from connecting to the work-related networks, they can connect over the wireless networks that they pay for themselves. In this case, the organization is entirely out of the loop. We will discuss these issues in more detail in Q8.

Mobile systems offer the potential of **just-in-time data**, which is data delivered to the user at the precise time it is needed. A pharmaceutical salesperson uses just-in-time data when she accesses a mobile system to obtain the latest literature on a new drug while waiting for the doctor to whom she will pitch it. She needn't remember the drug's characteristics any longer than it takes her to walk down the hallway and make the sale.

Furthermore, some organizations will passively wait for change to happen, while others will proactively reengineer their processes to incorporate mobile systems for higher process quality. Either way, the need for business process change creates opportunity for creative, nonroutine business problem solvers.

People

Mobile systems change the value of our thinking. For example, just-in-time data removes the premium on the ability to memorize vast quantities of product data, but creates a premium for the ability to access, query, and present that data. Mobile systems increase the speed of business, giving an advantage to those who can nimbly respond to changing conditions and succeed with the unexpected.

With the ability to be connected and always on, organizations may find they can be just as effective with part-time employees and independent contractors. The increasing regulatory complexity and cost of full-time employees will create an incentive for organizations to do just that.

As that occurs, professionals who can thrive in a dynamic environment with little need for direct supervision will find that they can work both where and when they want, at least a good part of the time. Once you're always-on and remote, it doesn't matter if you're always-on in New Jersey or at a ski area in Vermont. New lifestyle choices become possible for such workers.

Beyond individuals, what entity are we creating with this new always-on, always-connected society? Biologists say that multicellular organisms such as amoeba arose when individual cells bonded together for mutual benefit. Are mobile systems the analog of the nervous system? Is a group of continually connected people, working together in the context of inter related jobs and personal lives, something new? Is a new, always-on, part business, part personal, multi person organism being born before our eyes? And, if so, what does that mean for commerce? What an incredible time to be starting a business career!

What Characterizes Quality Mobile User Experiences?

A **user interface (UI)** is the presentation format of an application. It consists of windows, menus, icons, dialog boxes, toolbars, and so on, as well as user content. A **user experience (UX)** is a newer term that refers not only to the UI, but also to the way the application affects the user's emotions and motivation to continue to use the interface.

Apple redefined the UX for mobile applications when it introduced the iPhone with touch, gravity-sensing portrait/landscape orientation, and other innovative UX behavior. Since then Microsoft defined modern-style applications that build and (possibly) improve upon Apple's UX. Apple will likely advance UX again. Stay tuned.

Figure 4-18 lists the primary characteristics of a quality mobile user experience.[13] Consider each.

Feature Content

First, quality mobile user interfaces should place the primary emphasis on users' content, giving such content as much of the display as possible. Rather than show menus, toolbars, and heavy window borders, the content should be shown cleanly and in center stage. **Chrome** is a term that refers to the visual overhead in a computer display. It is the windows, the menus, and other apparatus that drive the application. Because mobile screen size is often limited, modern mobile applications eliminate it as much as possible. (By the way, do not confuse this use of *chrome* with Google Chrome, the popular browser.)

Figure 4-19 shows a portion of the chrome-less Start screen on a Windows Surface Pro device. The user doesn't need a toolbar (chrome) for starting a program; the user intuitively knows to click the image to start the application.

Using content to drive application behavior is called **direct interaction**. For another example, when you see blue, underlined type, you know to tap on it to navigate to that Web site. Similarly, if users want to highlight a word, they know to touch it to see what will happen.

Use Context-sensitive Chrome

Designing for direct action reduces the need for chrome, but not entirely. In an online store application, once you select the application, say a game, you'll need controls to play it. For such cases, mobile applications do provide chrome, but it is **context-sensitive chrome**, meaning it pops up in the display when appropriate. Ideally, no button or command name is ever shown in a disabled (grayed-out) state. Instead, if it's disabled, the application doesn't show it, thus simplifying the UI and reserving more of the display for the users' content.

Figure 4-18
Characteristics of Quality
Mobile UX

- Feature content and support direct interaction
- Use context-sensitive chrome when needed
- Provide animation and lively behavior
- Design to scale and share (display and data)
- Use the cloud

---

[13]See *http://msdn.microsoft.com/en-us/library/windows/apps/hh464920.aspx* for the source of much of this figure, as well as for an extended discussion of Metro-style UX, accessed May 2012.

Figure 4-19
Chrome-less Interface
Source: © Microsoft Corporation

Provide Animation and Lively Behavior

Great mobile applications are lively. They capture your attention with motion and sound. If you are not doing something, they are. For example, an icon to play a movie has the movie's preview playing inside it. An unused game displays a sample game underway. When you do act, something happens immediately. The touched word or image changes color, pops up, or does something to give you active feedback that the application is alive and running.

All of this is easy to comprehend for games and entertainment applications. How these ideas pertain to commercial applications is on the leading edge of commercial UX design. Everyone wants activity, but when you access your mobile Vanguard application, do you really want to watch the application shrink if your portfolio value has diminished? Or watch it crash to the bottom of your display if the market is down substantially? Or hear *Money, Money, Money* when the market is up? Probably not. Also, rapidly changing screen icons are hard to ignore and therefore often annoying. What is appropriate is being determined today; there is incredible opportunity for techno-savvy, marketing-oriented, graphics designers here.

Design to Scale and Share

Mobile applications appear on phones, tablets, PCs, and even large displays. Applications must be designed to scale up and down without appearing awkward or taking over the device. Note the different appearances of the application in the displays in Figure 4-20.

Modern operating systems (native applications) and browsers (thin-client applications) are designed to support such scaling. IE10, for example, allows applications to provide three sizes and versions of graphics; IE10 will choose the appropriate version for the size of the device on which it is running.

Mobile applications share their device with other mobile applications. They need to be designed to share the display effectively; applications that aggressively take over the screen are unappreciated by users and other application developers.

Mobile applications also need to be designed to share data. For example, Windows 8 introduces a feature called **charms**, which are icons that slide in from the right of the display. One of the default charms is Share; it is used to share data from one mobile application to another. IE10 allows Web pages to share thumbnails, descriptions, and links with other applications. If a user

Figure 4-20

Example of Application Scaling

Source: Scanrail/Fotolia

wants to email a page, IE10 will provide the shared thumbnail, description, and link to the mail application, as shown in Figure 4-21.

Understand the power of this functionality; in the example, the JetSetter thin-client application in the Web page has declared that it will share the thumbnail picture, the description, and the link as shown underneath the email address in Figure 4-21. Any charm that is invoked can obtain this data. The JetSetter Web page programmer has no idea where that data may go or how it will be displayed. It could be emailed, as shown here, but it could equally go to a graphics, a travel planning, a social networking, or an event planning application.

This example focuses on Windows 8 and IE10, but the concepts pertain equally to iOS, Android, and browsers other than IE as well.

Use the Cloud

Figure 4-21

Example Use of Web Page Data Declared as Shared

Source: Microsoft: *blogs.msdn.com/b/ b8/archive/2012/03/13/web-browsing-in-windows-8-consumer-preview-with-ie10.aspx*

Figure 4-22 lists the primary cloud assets that mobile applications use. Web sites and services such as IM and email are obvious. Less obvious are the use of services such as Fulfillment by Amazon (see Case Study 3 on page 106). By using that service, the developers of the mobile

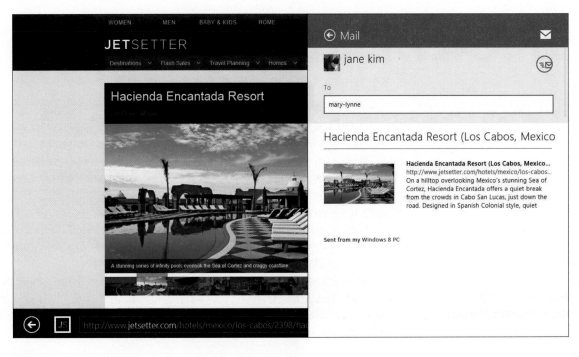

- Web sites
- Text, email, and other services
- Extend application onto servers
  - Use more powerful servers
  - Support roaming across devices (transparently)
- Data and news
  - Push
  - Pull

Figure 4-22
Mobile Systems Cloud Use

application can harness the power of Amazon's inventory and process management software with very little development work on their own.

Another use of the cloud is to extend the application itself. Mobile devices are frequently (almost always?) running on battery power; thus, minimizing power use is important. Consequently, some applications move complex code that requires substantial processing onto powered and powerful cloud servers. Doing so also improves security because data used for intermediate calculations need not be transmitted over the Internet.

Roaming occurs when users move their activities, especially long-running transactions (reading a book, for example) across devices. The best mobile applications do this transparently; the user need take no action. Figure 4-23 shows a message created by the Kindle app when a book was opened on an iPad that had previously been read on an iPhone. This tracking and informing were entirely automatic.

Roaming on reading devices is interesting, but even greater power will be achieved when mobile applications allow roaming for other long-running transactions as well; editing a document, spreadsheet, or other Office document are examples. At some point (not yet), enterprise applications such as CRM and ERP (Chapter 7) will support roaming as well.

The last cloud use in Figure 4-22 concerns data. Live, active mobile applications are designed to receive the latest application data and automatically show it to the user, perhaps in a graphically exciting *breaking news*-type banner. Such data includes industry or employee news, but it could also be SharePoint alerts, updates to orders, changes in credit ratings or banking

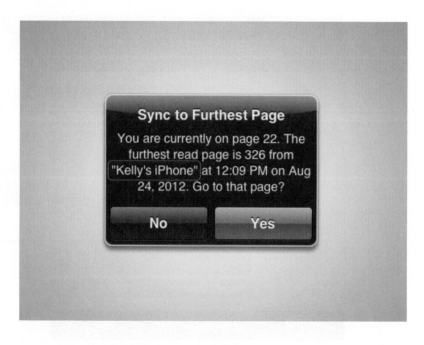

Figure 4-23
Kindle Roaming Message

accounts, and so forth. **Push data** is data that the server sends to, or pushes onto, the device. **Pull data** is data that the device requests from the server. (Notice that those terms use the server's perspective.) Of the two types, push data is more impressive to users because they need do nothing to receive data. However, excessive pushing is annoying.

Drew and the others at AllRoad Parts should use the knowledge in this section and the list in Figure 4-22 when defining the requirements for their mobile application. So should you!

What Are the Challenges of Personal Mobile Devices at Work?

So far, we've focused on mobile applications that organizations create for their customers and others to use. In this question we will address the use of mobile systems *within* organizations.

In truth, organizations today have a love/hate relationship with their employees' use of their own mobile devices at work. They love the cost-saving possibility of having employees buy their own hardware, but they hate the increased vulnerability and loss of control. The result, at least today, is a wide array of organizational attitudes. In fact, as of 2012, the majority of organizations are waffling; only 43 percent of all organizations have created an official mobile-use policy at all.[14]

Advantages and Disadvantages of Employee Use of Mobile Systems at Work

Figure 4-24 summarizes the advantages and disadvantages of employee use of mobile systems at work. Advantages include the cost savings just mentioned as well as greater employee satisfaction of using devices that they chose according to their own preferences rather than organization-supplied PCs. Because employees are already using these devices for their own purposes, they need less training and can be more productive. All of this means reduced support costs.

On the other hand, employee use of mobile devices has significant disadvantages. First, there is the real danger of lost or damaged data. When data is brought into employee-owned computing devices, the organization loses control over where it goes or what happens to it. In May 2012, IBM disallowed the use of Apple's voice searching application, Siri, on employees' mobile devices for just that reason.[15] Also, if an employee loses his or her device, the data goes with it, and when employees leave the organization, the data on their personal devices needs to be deleted somehow.

Advantages	Disadvantages
Cost savings	Data loss or damage
Greater employee satisfaction	Loss of control
Reduced need for training	Compatibility problems
Higher productivity	Risk of infection
Reduced support costs	Greater support costs

Figure 4-24
Advantages and Disadvantages of Employee Use of Mobile Systems at Work

[14]"CDH," accessed July 15, 2013, *http://www.cdh.com.*
[15]Robert McMillan, "IBM Worries iPhone's Siri Has Loose Lips," last modified May 24, 2012, *http://www.cnn.com/2012/05/23/tech/mobile/ibm-siri-ban/index.html?iphoneemail.*

Organizations also lose control over the updating of software and the applications that users employ. This control loss leads to compatibility problems; users can process data, for example edit documents, with software that is incompatible with the organization's standard software. The result to the organization is a mess of inconsistent documents.

Possibly the greatest disadvantage of employee use of their own devices is the risk of infection. The organization cannot know where the users have been with their devices nor what they've done when they've been there. The possibility of severe viruses infecting the organization's networks is both frightening and real. Finally, all of these disadvantages can also lead, ironically, to greater support costs.

Given all that, organizations cannot avoid the issue. Whatever the costs and risks, employees are bringing their own devices to work. Ignoring the issue will simply make matters worse.

Survey of Organizational BYOD Policy

A **BYOD (bring your own device) policy** is a statement concerning employees' permissions and responsibilities when they use their own device for organizational business. Figure 4-25 arranges BYOD policies according to functionality and control. Starting in the lower left-hand corner, the most primitive policy is to ignore mobile use. That posture, which provides neither functionality to the employee nor control to the organization, has no advantages and, as just stated, cannot last.

The next step up in functionality is for the organization to offer its wireless network to mobile devices, as if it were a coffee shop. The advantage to the organization of this policy is that the organization can sniff employees' mobile traffic, thus learning how employees are using their devices (and time) during work. See Question 6 of the Security Guide on page 147 for more on sniffing.

The next policy provides more functionality and somewhat more control. Here the organization creates secure application services using https (explained in Chapter 12) that require employee sign-on and can be accessed from any device, mobile or not. Such applications can be used when employees are at work or elsewhere. These services provide controlled access to some organizations' assets.

		Control				
		Low ⟵				⟶ High
High	Full VPN Access to Organizational Systems			You're responsible for damage	We'll check it out, reload software and data, and manage it remotely	If you connect it, we own it
	Organizational Services on Public Internet		We'll offer limited systems you can access from any device			
	Access to Internet	We'll be a coffee shop				
Low	None	They don't exist				

Figure 4-25
Six Common BYOD Policies

(Functionality — vertical axis label)

BYOD Policy	Description	Advantage to Organization
They don't exist	Organization looks the other way when employees bring mobile devices to work.	None
We'll be a coffee shop	You'll be able to sign in to our wireless network using your mobile device.	Packet sniffing of employee mobile device use at work.
We'll offer limited systems you can access from any device	Organization creates https applications with sign-in and offers access to noncritical business systems.	Employees gain public access from any device, not just mobile devices, without having to use VPN accounts.
You're responsible for damage	Threatening posture to discourage employee use of mobile devices at work.	Appear to be permissive without actually being so.
We'll check it out, reload software, then manage remotely	Employees can use their mobile devices just as if they were computers provided by the corporate IS department.	Employee buys the hardware (perhaps with an employer's contribution).
If you connect it, we own it	Employees are not to use mobile devices at work. If they do, they lose them. Part of employment agreement.	Ultimate in control for highly secure work situations (intelligence, military).

Figure 4-26
Advantages of Example BYOD Policies

A fourth policy is more of a gambit than a policy. The organization tells employees that they can sign on to the organization's network with their mobile devices, but the employee is financially responsible for any damage he or she does. The hope is that few employees know what their exposure is and hence decide not to do so.

A more enlightened policy is to manage the users' devices as if they were owned by the organization. With this policy, employees turn over their mobile devices to the IS department, which cleanses and reloads software and installs programs that enable the IS department to manage the device remotely. Numerous vendors license products called **mobile device management (MDM) software** that assist this process. These products install and update software, back up and restore mobile devices, wipe employer software and data from devices in the event the device is lost or the employee leaves the company, report usage, and provide other mobile device management data.

This policy benefits the organization, but some employees resist turning over the management of their own hardware to the organization. This resistance can be softened if the organization pays at least a portion of the hardware expense.

The most controlling policy is for the organization to declare that it owns any mobile device that employees connect to its network. To be enforceable, this policy must be part of the employee's contract. It is taken by organizations that manage very secure operations and environments. In some military/intelligence organizations, the policy is that any smart device that ever enters the workplace may never leave it. The advantages of these six policies are summarized in Figure 4-26.

BYOD policies are rapidly evolving, and many organizations have not yet determined what is best for them. If your employer has a committee to develop such policies, join it if you can. Doing so will provide a great way to gain exposure to the leading technology thinkers at your organization.

Q8  2024?

The writing is on the wall. The PC is dead. As stated, mobile web usage will surpass PC web usage in the United States by 2015. In China and a few other countries, it already has. By 2024, nine years after that, the PC will be as rare as typewriter erasers.

So, who will be the big winners? In 2013, the contenders are Microsoft, Apple, Google, and Amazon, though there is the possibility that some company, maybe Samsung or another that's not yet on the radar, will emerge from China or India and pass them all. For now, let's consider the prospects for the four contenders we do know.

Microsoft? Doubtful. Microsoft developed the earliest phone and tablet software and bungled every one of its many attempts to bring that software to market. Most recently, Windows RT is a sales disaster and the interface of the Surface Pro is a mucked-up mess of Windows 7 and the so-called *modern interface* of Windows 8. Context-sensitive chrome may work for buying applications in app stores, but try it in Office. Figure 4-27 shows the modern interface for OneNote; the context chrome is shown in purple at the bottom. Where do you go to find out how to capture a screenshot? Help? But just like Macavity, it isn't there.

Turns out you can do screenshots on a Surface Pro; you press the Windows key and the lower-speaker-volume button on the left side of the device. Not exactly a smooth-as-silk UI. But wait, don't push the Windows button on your $150 add-on keyboard; that one doesn't work for screenshots. Use the one at the bottom of Surface Pro screen (the one that you knock over when you press that Windows button).

The Surface Pro is a touch device, except tracking touches in JavaScript code using IE10 doesn't work. Works fine in Firefox, though. (By the way, if you're going to learn one programming language between now and 2024, learn JavaScript. Mobile applications will make it the major language by 2024.)

Will Microsoft fix these problems? Eventually, probably. But when you're so far behind the leaders (see Using MIS InClass 4, page 124), you cannot stumble this badly out of the gate.

If this were the first bungled Microsoft mobile foray, I might still believe. But not again. By 2024, Microsoft will sell and support back-office operating systems and business software. And be but a shadow of what it is today.

Figure 4-27

Modern Interface for OneNote

Apple? Alas, if only Steve Jobs were still alive. He was the Mozart of the modern computing era, and all of us suffer loss because of his early death. Can Apple thrive without him? As you can read in Case Study 4, the company floundered when it fired him in the 1990s, and without him, it will flounder again. Apparently, the stock market agrees; Apple's stock plummeted from a high of $705 in 2012 to $390 in April 2013. By 2024, without PCs, Apple will have lost its Macintosh revenue. Sadly, while Apple has been the most innovative hardware/software vendor, bar none, it has lost its innovator-in-chief. Apple stock is overpriced at half its current price.

Google? Maybe. The Nexus series, Android, Google Glass, Google Cars, Street View, Google+, Google Hangouts, Google Grid—all have innovative (free!) software that seems to anticipate what we want to do. If only Google had a revenue stream beyond ads for Google Search and YouTube.

Still, unlike Microsoft, Google gets it, and unlike Apple, it is not dependent on the leadership of a once-in-a-millennium visionary king. And ads have been with us for forever, so maybe that revenue stream isn't as suspect as it seems. Google is the next-most-likely-to-lead-in-2024 company.

The 2024 winner? Amazon. Reread Case Study 1, The Amazon of Innovation (pages 31–32). Amazon turned what appeared to be, and might have only been, an online bookstore into a technological juggernaut that crosses the business spectrum. It can do it all. It sells real things; it's an innovation leader in supply chain and logistics processes, systems, and facilities. It'll sell your stuff for you or let you sell its stuff for it. Either way, you get paid and it earns profit. It knows what customers want: Jeff Bezos, CEO, says the best customer service is none at all; at Amazon, the need for customer service is its failure.[16]

Amazon can practically give away the Kindle because it sells the content. To induce developers to build Kindle applications, Amazon invented its own currency for buying games and then flooded the market with that currency for free. (Application developers are paid royalties in real money, however.) It's producing its own TV programs. Stephen King self-publishes on the Kindle.

Ah, you say, but when it has to pay its fair share of taxes (see the Ethics Guide on showrooming, page 132), it all will come crumbling down. Not likely. In states where Amazon already has a presence, where it already pays state tax, it has placed warehouses with same-day delivery. Order by noon, and get it by 4. Local retailers beware, someone is gaining on you!

To house its employee growth, Amazon just bought a major portion of downtown Seattle real estate from Microsoft cofounder Paul Allen. That says it all.

---

[16]Here is the quote from Jeff Bezos: "Our version of a perfect customer experience is one in which our customer doesn't want to talk to us. Every time a customer contacts us, we see it as a defect. I've been saying for many, many years, people should talk to their friends, not their merchants. And so we use all of our customer service information to find the root cause of any customer contact. What went wrong? Why did that person have to call? Why aren't they spending that time talking to their family instead of talking to us? How do we fix it?" *http://www.wired.com/magazine/2011/11/ff_bezos/all/1*, accessed June 2013.

Security Guide

"BECAUSE IT'S WHERE THE MONEY IS..."
Willie Sutton, on why he robbed banks.

For years, Microsoft endured many more problems with computer viruses and other malware than Apple. Apple enthusiasts attribute that to their belief that Apple developers write higher quality code. That might be true, but the recent success of viruses for Apple products indicates there could be another reason: Hackers write code where the money is; as long as Windows had a vastly greater market share than the Mac, it was far more lucrative to write against Windows. But with the popularity of Apple's mobile devices....

To start, let's be clear about what problems exist. Malware is a broad category of software that includes viruses, spyware, and adware:

- **Viruses:** A **virus** is a computer program that replicates itself. Unchecked replication is like computer cancer; ultimately, the virus consumes the computer's resources. Furthermore, many viruses also take unwanted and harmful actions. The program code that causes the unwanted actions is called the **payload**. The payload can delete programs or data—or even worse, modify data in undetected ways. Imagine the impact of a virus that changed the credit rating of all customers. Some viruses publish data in harmful ways—for example, sending out files of credit card data to unauthorized sites.
  - **Trojan horses: Trojan horses** are viruses that masquerade as useful programs or files. The name refers to the gigantic mock-up of a horse that was filled with soldiers and moved into Troy during the Trojan War. A typical Trojan horse appears to be a computer game, an MP3 music file, or some other useful, innocuous program.

- **Worms:** A **worm** is a virus that propagates using the Internet or other computer network. Worms spread faster than other virus types because they are specifically programmed to spread. Unlike non-worm viruses, which must wait for the user to share a file with a second computer, worms actively use the network to spread. Sometimes, worms so choke a network that it becomes unstable or unusable.

- **Spyware:** **Spyware** programs are installed on the user's computer without the user's knowledge or permission. Spyware resides in the background and, unknown to the user, observes the user's actions and keystrokes, monitors computer activity, and reports the user's activities to sponsoring organizations. Some malicious spyware, called **key loggers**, captures keystrokes to obtain user names, passwords, account numbers, and other sensitive information. Other spyware supports marketing

146

analyses such as observing what users do, Web sites visited, products examined and purchased, and so forth.

- **Adware: Adware** is similar to spyware in that it is installed without the user's permission and that it resides in the background and observes user behavior. Most adware is benign in that it does not perform malicious acts or steal data. It does, however, watch user activity and produce pop-up ads. Adware can also change the user's default window or modify search results and switch the user's search engine. For the most part, it is just annoying, but see Case Study 9 (page 369) for sobering facts about where it's headed.

Because of Apple's inexperience in dealing with malware, its response to events so far has been ham-handed.

In April 2012, a Trojan horse called *Flashback* infected more than 650,000 Macs. The problem was discovered and reported by the Russian firm Dr. Web and, according to Boris Sharov, Dr. Web's CEO, "attempts to warn Apple about Flashback went unheeded." In fact, Apple asked that one of the sites Dr. Web had set up to trap the virus be shut down. Apple finally fixed the problem . . . six weeks after Microsoft had fixed it on Windows machines.[17]

With the rise in popularity of Apple products, it seems likely that Apple had better get ready for an avalanche of attacks. Willie Sutton knows why. And, alas, apparently Willie never made that statement; it's an urban legend.

 DISCUSSION QUESTIONS

1. Payloads that damage users' files and steal data for malicious purposes are clearly illegal. But what about adware and spyware that cause no damage or loss? Are they illegal? Explain your answer.

2. Do you think there is such a thing as harmless spyware? If so, define it. If not, say why not.

3. Is spyware or adware unethical? Why or why not?

4. When a vendor such as Microsoft or Apple learns of a vulnerability to malware in one of its products, how should they respond? Does it have a legal responsibility to warn users? Does it have an ethical responsibility to do so? Does your answer depend on the actions of the malware's payload? Why or why not?

5. Given the Willie Sutton principle, do you think a small company can ethically decide not to pay attention to computer security because it's small? "No one would want to sue us because we don't have assets that make it worth their while. Same for stealing our data." Do you agree with that attitude? As you answer, keep in mind that resources are always scarce at small companies. On the other hand, even though they are small, they could be storing your credit card data.

6. Suppose your professor installs spyware on the personal computers and mobile devices that you bring to class. The spyware records all of the text messages and emails that you send while in class, and it records all of the sites you visit and all of the terms for which you searched. Like all spyware, you have no idea that it has been installed on your devices. Under which, if any, of the following circumstances is your professor's action unethical?

   a. She uses the data for a research project on how today's students spend class time.

   b. She uses the data to determine which parts of her presentation are least interesting to students.

   c. She uses the data to decide how serious you are about the class and how, ultimately, to grade you.

   d. She uses the data for faculty meeting entertainment. "You won't believe what my student Jamie Anderson searched for today. Listen to this. . . ."

   e. She uses the data to blackmail you.

7. Examine your answers to question 6 and state your guideline (s) concerning the ethics of spyware.

---

[17]John Leyden, "Apple Trails Behind World and Microsoft in 'Flashback' Malware Debacle," *The Register,* last modified April 11, 2012, *http://www.theregister.co.uk/2012/04/11/apple_snubs_mac_botnet_fighter/.*

Guide

KEEPING UP TO SPEED

Have you ever been to a cafeteria where you put your lunch tray on a conveyor belt that carries the dirty dishes into the kitchen? That conveyor belt reminds me of technology. Like the conveyor, technology just moves along, and all of us run on top of the technology conveyor, trying to keep up. We hope to keep up with the relentless change of technology for an entire career without ending up in the techno-trash.

Technology change is a fact, and the only appropriate question is, "What am I going to do about it?" One strategy you can take is to bury your head in the sand: "Look, I'm not a technology person. I'll leave it to the pros. As long as I can send email and use the Internet, I'm happy. If I have a problem, I'll call someone to fix it."

That strategy is fine, as far as it goes, and many businesspeople have used it. Following that strategy won't give you a competitive advantage over anyone, and it will give someone else a competitive advantage over you, but as long as you develop your advantage elsewhere, you'll be OK—at least for yourself.

What about your department, though? If an expert says, "You should be buying your employees Windows 8 RT tablet devices," are you going to nod your head and say, "Great. Sell 'em to me!"? Or are you going to know enough to realize that it may be too early to know what the success of Windows RT will be? Or to know that maybe you'll have problems getting homegrown, in-house applications down from whatever stores Microsoft sets up?

At the other end of the spectrum are those who love technology. You'll find them everywhere—they may be accountants, marketing professionals, or production-line supervisors who not only know their field, but also enjoy information technology. Maybe they were IS majors or had double majors that combined IS with another area of expertise (e.g., IS with accounting). These people read CNET News and ZDNet most days, and they can tell you the latest on desktop virtualization or html5 or Windows 8 RT. Those people are sprinting along the technology conveyor belt; they will never end up in the techno-trash, and they will use their knowledge of IT to gain competitive advantage throughout their careers.

Many business professionals fall in between these extremes. They don't want to bury their heads, but they don't have the desire or interest to become technophiles (lovers of technology), either. What to do? There are a couple of strategies. For one, don't allow yourself to ignore technology. When you see a technology article in *The Wall Street Journal*, read it. Don't just skip it because

it's about technology. Read the technology ads, too. Many vendors invest heavily in ads that instruct without seeming to. Another option is to take a seminar or pay attention to professional events that combine your specialty with technology. For example, when you go to the bankers' convention, attend a panel or two on "Mobile Device Use at Banks." There are always sessions like that, and you might make a contact with similar problems and concerns in another company.

Probably the best option, if you have the time for it, is to get involved as a user representative on technology committees in your organization. At a company like AllRoad Parts, get involved in the specifications for the iOS app. Or, if your company is doing a review of its BYOD policy, see if you can get on the review committee. Alternatively, when there's a need for a representative from your department to discuss needs for the next-generation helpline system, sign up. Or, later in your career, become a member of the business practice technology committee or whatever they call it at your organization.

Just working with such groups will add to your knowledge of technology. Presentations made to such groups, discussions about uses of technology, and ideas about using IT for competitive advantage will all add to your IT knowledge. You'll gain important contacts and exposure to leaders in your organization as well.

It's up to you. You get to choose how you relate to technology. But be sure you choose; don't let your head get stuck in the sand without thinking about it.

 DISCUSSION QUESTIONS

1. Do you agree that the change of technology is relentless? What do you think that means to most business professionals? To most organizations?
2. Think about the three postures toward technology presented here. Which camp will you join? Why?
3. Write a two-paragraph memo to yourself justifying your choice in question 2. If you chose to ignore technology, explain how you will compensate for the loss of competitive advantage. If you're going to join one of the other two groups, explain why, and describe how you're going to accomplish your goal.
4. Given your answer to question 2, assume that you're in a job interview and the interviewer asks about your interest in and knowledge of technology. Write a three-sentence response to the interviewer's question.

ACTIVE REVIEW

Use this Active Review to verify that you understand the ideas and concepts that answer the chapter's study questions.

Q1 What do business professionals need to know about computer hardware?

List types of hardware and give an example of each. Define *bit* and *byte*. Explain why bits are used to represent computer data. Define the units of bytes used to size memory.

Q2 What do business professionals need to know about software?

Review Figure 4-6 and explain the meaning of each cell in this table. Describe three kinds of virtualization, and explain the use of each. Explain the difference between software ownership and software licenses. Explain the differences among horizontal-market, vertical-market, and one-of-a-kind applications. Describe the three ways that organizations can acquire software.

Q3 Is open source software a viable alternative?

Define *GNU* and *GPL*. Name three successful open source projects. Describe four reasons programmers contribute to open source projects. Define *open source, closed source, source code,* and *machine code.* In your own words, explain why open source is a legitimate alternative but may or may not be appropriate for a given application.

Q4 What are the differences between native and thin-client applications?

In your own words, summarize the differences between native applications and thin-client applications. In high-level terms, explain the difference between object-oriented languages and scripting languages. Explain each cell of Figure 4-12. State which is better: native or thin-client applications. Justify your answer.

Q5 Why are mobile systems increasingly important?

Define *mobile systems*. Name and describe the four elements of a mobile system. Describe the size of the mobile market and explain why there are 3.9 billion mobile prospects. Explain why the mobile market will become stronger in the future. Explain why a problem for one organization is an opportunity for another. Using the five-component model, describe particular opportunities for each component. Define *just-in-time data* and explain how it changes the value of human thinking.

Q6 What characterizes quality mobile user experiences?

Explain the difference between the terms *UI* and *UX*. Describe how each of the following can impact the UX of a mobile application: user content, context-sensitive chrome, animation and lively behavior, scaling and sharing, the cloud. Define *chrome, charms, roaming, push,* and *pull.*

Q7 What are the challenges of personal mobile devices at work?

Summarize the advantages and disadvantages of employees' using mobile systems at work. Define *BYOD* and *BYOD policy.* Name six possible policies and compare them in terms of functionality and organizational control. Summarize the advantage of each to employers.

Q8 2024?

Explain why the PC is dead. List the four companies that will contend for mobile leadership in 2024, at least according to this discussion. Summarize the author's opinion about why each will finish where predicted.

Using Your Knowledge with AllRoad Parts

Suppose you are part of this AllRoad Parts team. Briefly summarize how the knowledge in this chapter would help you contribute. Explain why AllRoad Parts decides not to manufacture with 3D printing. Summarize what they do plan to sell and the challenges of doing so.

KEY TERMS AND CONCEPTS

MyMISLab

Go to **mymislab.com** to complete the problems marked with this icon .

USING YOUR KNOWLEDGE

4-1. Microsoft offers free licenses of certain software products to students at colleges and universities that participate in its DreamSpark program (formerly known as the Microsoft Developer Network (MSDN) Academic Alliance (AA)). If your college or university participates in this program, you have the opportunity to obtain hundreds of dollars of software for free. Here is a partial list of the software you can obtain:

- Microsoft Access 2010
- OneNote 2010
- Expression Studio 4
- Windows 2008 Server
- Microsoft Project 2010
- Visual Studio Developer
- SQL Server 2008
- Visio 2010

a. Search *www.microsoft.com*, *www.google.com*, or *www.bing.com* and determine the function of each of these software products.

b. Which of these software products are operating systems and which are application programs?

c. Which of these programs are DBMS products (the subject of the next chapter)?

d. Which of these programs should you download and install tonight?

e. Either (1) download and install the programs in your answer to part d or (2) explain why you would not choose to do so.

f. Does the MSDN AA provide an unfair advantage to Microsoft? Why or why not?

⭐ **4-2.** Visit the Open Source Initiative's Web site at *www.opensource.org*. Summarize the mission of this foundation. Find the definition of *open source* on this site, and summarize that definition in your own words. Explain this foundation's role with regard to open source licenses. Summarize the process for having a license approved by the foundation. Describe the advantage of having the foundation's approval.

⭐ **4-3.** Suppose that you are Lucas at AllRoad Parts. List five criteria you would use in helping AllRoad Parts decide whether it should develop a native or a thin-client mobile application. Justify your criteria.

4-4. Describe how the class enrollment application at your university could benefit from a mobile application that uses the cloud.

4-5. Judging from your personal experience, describe the BYOD policy that appears to be in place at your university. Explain the advantages and disadvantages of the policy to you as a student and to the organization as a whole. How do you think that BYOD policy will change in the next five years? Explain your answer.

4-6. Read Q8, 2024?, if you have not already done so. Critically evaluate the opinions of the author. Do you agree with this list of four contenders? If so, say why. If not, nominate another company or companies and explain your nomination. Develop your own rank of mobile leadership in 2024 and support your ranking with your own opinions.

COLLABORATION EXERCISE 4

Using the collaboration IS you built in Chapter 2 (pages 73–74), collaborate with a group of students to answer the following questions.

In the past few years, Microsoft has been promoting **PixelSense**, a hardware–software product that enables people to interact with data on the top of a table. PixelSense initiates a new product category, and the best way to understand it is to view one of Microsoft's promotional videos at *www.microsoft.com/en-us/pixelsense/default.aspx*.

PixelSense paints the top of the 30-inch table with invisible, near-infrared light to detect the presence of objects. It can respond to up to 52 different touches at the same time. According to Microsoft, this means that four people sitting around the PixelSense table could use all 10 of their fingers to manipulate up to 12 objects, simultaneously.

PixelSense uses wireless and other communications technologies to connect to devices that are placed on it, such as cameras or cell phones. When a camera is placed on PixelSense, pictures "spill" out of it, and users can manipulate those pictures with their hands. Products can be placed on PixelSense, and their product specifications are displayed. Credit cards can be placed on PixelSense, and items to be purchased can be dragged or dropped onto the credit card.

Currently, Microsoft PixelSense is marketed and sold to large-scale commercial organizations in the financial services, healthcare, hospitality, retail, and public service business sectors. Also, smaller organizations and individuals can purchase a PixelSense unit from Samsung (*www.samsunglfd.com/solution/sur40.do*).

One of the first implementers of PixelSense was the iBar lounge at Harrah's Rio All-Suite Hotel and Casino in Las Vegas, Nevada. The subtitle for the press release announcing iBar's system read, "Harrah's Reinvents Flirting and Offers New Uninhibited Fun and Play to iBar Patrons."[18]

The potential uses for PixelSense are staggering. Maps can display local events, and consumers can purchase tickets to those events by just using their fingers. PixelSense can also be used for new computer games and gambling devices. Children

---

[18]"Harrah's Entertainment Launches Microsoft Surface at Rio iBar, Providing Guests with Innovative and Immersive New Entertainment Experiences." Microsoft Press Release, last modified June 11, 2008, *http://www.microsoft.com/presspass/press/2008/jun08/06-11HETSurfacePR.mspx*.

can paint on PixelSense with virtual paintbrushes. Numerous other applications are possible. At the product's announcement, Steve Ballmer, former CEO of Microsoft, said "We see this as a multibillion dollar category, and we envision a time when PixelSense computing technologies will be pervasive, from tabletops and counters to the hallway mirror. PixelSense is the first step in realizing that vision."[19]

As you can see at the PixelSense Web site, this product can be used for many different purposes in many different places, such as restaurants, retail kiosks, and eventually at home. Probably most of the eventual applications for PixelSense have not yet been envisioned. One clear application, however, is in the gambling and gaming industry. Imagine placing your credit card on a PixelSense gambling device and playing the night away. Every time you lose, a charge is made against your credit card. Soon, before you know it, you've run up $15,000 in debt, which you learn when PixelSense tells you you've reached the maximum credit limit on your card.

Recall the RAND study cited in Chapter 1 that stated there will be increased worldwide demand for workers who can apply new technology and products to solve business problems in innovative ways. PixelSense is an excellent example of a new technology that will be applied innovatively.

1. Consider uses for PixelSense at your university. How might PixelSense be used in architecture, chemistry, law, medicine, business, geography, political science, art, music, or any other discipline in which your team has interest? Describe one potential application for PixelSense for five different disciplines.

2. List specific features and benefits for each of the five applications you selected in question 1.

3. Describe, in general terms, the work that needs to be accomplished to create the applications you identified in question 1.

4. Until June 2012, PixelSense was called Surface. At that time, Microsoft repurposed the name to use on its tablet devices. Surface was changed to PixelSense. What conclusions do you draw from these naming decisions?

5. You will sometimes hear the expression, "Emerging technology is constantly leveling the playing field," meaning that technology eliminates competitive advantages of existing companies and enables opportunities for new companies. How does this statement pertain to PixelSense, Surface, Windows 8, Apple, and Google?

CASE STUDY 4

The Apple of Your i

A quick glance at Apple's stock history in Figure 4-28 will tell you that Apple is an incredibly successful and dramatic company, having peaks around the turn of the century, in 2007–2008, and again in 2012. At its high, it had the highest market value of any public company worldwide. Apple has been so successful that the NASDAQ stock exchange concluded Apple's price was skewing the price of the NASDAQ 100 Index and reduced Apple's weight in that index from 20 to 12 percent. But today? As of this writing, Apple stock is trading at $390, from its high of over $700. Since Steve Jobs' death, there haven't been any groundbreaking products like the iPod, iPhone, and iPad. What does the future look like for Apple and its shareholders? Bleak, especially if you consider its past history without Jobs.

Early Success and Downfall

At the dawn of the personal computer age, in the early 1980s, Apple pioneered well-engineered home computers and innovative interfaces with its Apple II PC for the home and its Macintosh computer for students and knowledge workers. At one point, Apple owned more than 20 percent of the PC market, competing against many other PC vendors, most of which are no longer relevant (or in business).

However, Apple lost its way. In 1985, Steve Jobs, Apple's chief innovator, lost a fight with the Apple board and was forced out. He founded another PC company, NeXT, which developed and sold a groundbreaking PC product that was too innovative to sell well in that era. Meanwhile, Apple employed a succession of CEOs, starting with John Sculley, who was hired away from Pepsi-Cola where he'd enjoyed considerable success. Sculley's knowledge and experience did not transfer well to the PC business, however, and the company went downhill so fast that CNBC named him the 14th worst American CEO of all time.[20] Two other CEOs followed in Sculley's footsteps.

During this period, Apple made numerous mistakes, among them not rewarding innovative engineering, creating too many products for too many market segments, and losing the respect of the retail computer stores. Apple's PC market share plummeted.

---

[19]Microsoft Press Release, May 29, 2007.
[20]"Portfolio's Worst American CEOs of All Time," *CNBC.com.*, accessed July 15, 2013, *http://www.cnbc.com/id/30502091?slide=8.*

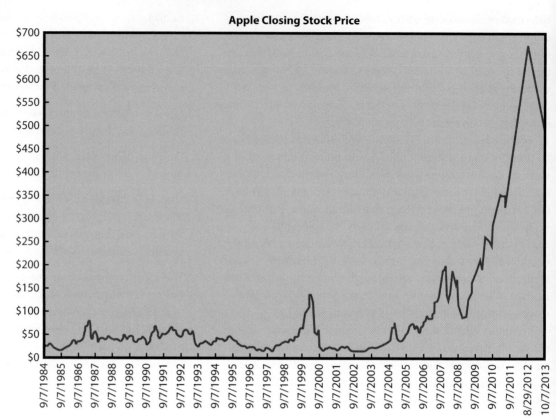

Figure 4-28
Growth in Apple Stock Price
Source: Data from Yahoo! Finance.

Steve Jobs, Second Verse

In 1996, Apple bought Jobs' NeXT computing and gained technology that became the foundation of Mac OS X, today's Macintosh operating system. The true asset it acquired, however, was Steve Jobs. Even he, however, couldn't create an overnight miracle. It is exceedingly difficult to regain lost market share and even more difficult to regain the respect of the retail channel that had come to view Apple's products with disdain. Even by 2011, Apple's PC market share was in the range of 10 to 12 percent, down from a high of 20 percent in the 1980s.

In response to these problems, Apple broke away from the PC and created new markets with its iPod, iPhone, and iPad. It also countered retailer problems by opening its own stores. In the process, it pioneered the sale of music and applications over the Internet.

iPod, iPhone, and iPad devices are a marvel of creativity and engineering. They exude not only ease of use, but also now/wow/fun coolness. By selling hot music for the iPod,

Apple established a connection with a dynamic segment of the market that was willing to spend lots of money on bright, shiny objects. The ability to turn the iPhone on its side to rotate images probably sold more iPhones than anything else. With the iPad, portable devices became readable, and the market responded by awarding Apple a 44 percent (and growing) share of the mobile market.[21] And Apple's success continues with the iPhone 5, which as of this writing, is selling well.

All of this success propelled Apple's stores not only beyond vanilla retailers like Best Buy, but also beyond the lofty heights of Tiffany & Co. In 2011, Apple stores were grossing more than $4,000 per square foot, compared to $3,000 for Tiffany and a mere $880 for Best Buy. As of 2011, Apple operates more than 300 such retail outlets and has welcomed more than a billion customer visits.[22]

Apple encourages customer visits and loyalty with its open and inviting sales floor, its Genius Bar help desk, and its incredibly well-trained and disciplined sales force. Salespeople, who are not commissioned, are taught to be consultants who

---

[21]Apple presentation at the Apple Worldwide Developers Conference, June 6, 2011.
[22]Carl Howe, "Apple Reboots Retail with Connected Experiences," Yankee Group, last modified March 23, 2011, *http://www.yankeegroup.com/ ResearchDocument.do?id=56472.*

help customers solve problems. Even some vocabulary is standardized. When an employee cannot solve a customer's problem, the word *unfortunately* is to be avoided; employees are taught to use the phrase *as it turns out,* instead.[23] Try that on your next exam!

Apple has sold 15 billion songs through its iTunes online store, 130 million books through its iBookstore, and a mere 14 billion applications through its App Store, the latter in less than 3 years. Apple is now the number one PC software channel and the only place a customer can buy the Mac X Lion, which sells for $30 instead of the $130 for the earlier OS X that sold through the software channel.[24]

To encourage the development of iPhone and iPad apps, Apple shares its revenue with application developers. That would be $2.5 billion paid to developers in less than 3 years! Developers responded by creating 445,000 iOS applications, and an army of developers are at work building thousands more while you read this.

By the way, if you want to build an iOS application, what's the first thing you need to do? Buy a Macintosh. Apple closed its development to any other development method. Adobe Flash? No way. Apple claims that Flash has too many bugs, and perhaps so. Thus, Flash developers are excluded. Microsoft Silverlight? Nope. Microsoft developers are out in the cold, too. The non-Apple development community was furious, and Apple's response was, in essence, "Fine, we'll pay our $2.5 billion to someone else."

The bottom line? Until Jobs' death, every sales success fed every other sales success. Hot music fed the iPod. The iPod fed iTunes and created a growing customer base that was ripe for the iPhone. Sales of the iPhone fed the stores, whose success fed the developer community, which fed more applications, which fed the iPhone and set the stage for the iPad, which fed the App Store, which enabled the $30 price on the OS X Lion, which led to more loyal customers, and, of course, to more developers.

Apple without Steve Jobs

It's hard to see a happy future for Apple. It floundered when Jobs was fired in the 1990s, and it most likely will flounder again. Sure, it'll be around for a long time, but the days of its incredible innovative leadership are most likely, alas, over.

QUESTIONS

4-7. Which of Porter's four competitive strategies does Apple engage in? Explain.

4-8. What do you think are the three most important factors in Apple's past success? Justify your answer.

4-9. Steve Jobs passed away in October 2011. Until his death, he had been the heart and soul of Apple's innovation. Today, 35,000 Apple employees continue onward in his absence. A huge question for many investors is whether the company can be successful without him. The current stock price would seem to indicate that the market does not. What do you think? What role did Jobs play? How can Apple respond to his loss? Would you be willing to invest in Apple without his leadership? Why or why not?

4-10. Microsoft took an early lead in the development of slate devices (like the iPad), and it had the world's leading operating system and applications for more than 20 years. Provide five reasons why Microsoft has not been able to achieve the same success that Apple has. Most industry analysts would agree that the skills and abilities of Microsoft's 88,000 employees are as good, on average, as Apple's.

4-11. Considering your answers to the four questions above, if you had a spare $5,000 in your portfolio and wanted to buy an equity stock with it, would you buy AAPL (Apple)? Why or why not?

[23]Yukari Iwatani Kane and Ian Sherr, "Secrets from Apple's Genius Bar: Full Loyalty, No Negativity," *Wall Street Journal,* last modified June 15, 2011, *http://online.wsj.com/article/SB10001424052702304563104576364071955678908.html.*
[24]Apple presentation at the Apple Worldwide Developers Conference, June 6, 2011.

MyMISLab

Go to **mymislab.com** for Auto-graded writing questions as well as the following Assisted-graded writing questions:

4-12. Examine Figure 4-17 and reflect on each component.
    a. Describe a job that you would like to have upon graduation.
    b. Describe how changes in mobile hardware will impact that job.
    c. Explain how your knowledge of the differences between native and thin-client mobile application development could help you in that job.
    d. Explain two ways that just-in-time data will impact that job.
    e. Describe two ways that mobile systems will change business processes in that job.
    f. Explain ways that mobile systems will change the premium on the skills necessary for that job.
    g. Summarize your answers to questions b-f in a two-paragraph statement that you could use in a job interview.

4-13. Choose a mobile application that you frequently use. It could be Facebook, Twitter, or some other, more vertical application. Evaluate that application according to the principles in Figure 4-18.

4-14. Mymislab Only – comprehensive writing assignment for this chapter.

Database Processing

After their last meeting, Jason Green, CEO, asked Kelly Summers and her team to investigate the possibility of selling 3D-ready part plans as a product. Kelly gave Drew Mills and Addison Lee the task of identifying parts that might be good candidates for selling as 3D printing design files. Drew and Addison know that the data in AllRoad Parts' past orders will help them, but they're not sure how. They're meeting to discuss how to proceed.

"Drew, let's start by figuring out the criteria for a candidate part."

"Makes sense. Expensive parts, maybe?"

"No, I don't think so. Expensive parts are complicated and would be hard for customers to produce."

"OK, how about popular parts?"

"Yeah, that could be. But popular because the parts are frequently ordered? Or popular because we sell large quantities of them?"

"I think because they're ordered frequently. If customers buy a lot of a part at once, they need a lot. And 3D printing will be too slow. Seems like it should be something that people frequently want, but just need one or two of."

Addison and Drew continue working in this way until they have a list of five key criteria.

"Now, Drew, are there parts like that? And if so, how often are they ordered and by which customers?"

"Well, the answer's in our sales database."

"Yup. Let's go see Lucas."

Addison and Drew walk down the hall to Lucas' office.

"Oh, oh. This looks like trouble! The two of you at once, I mean." Lucas is only partly kidding.

"Oh, come on, Lucas, you can handle us just fine," Drew responds as he sits down. "Besides, from the appearance of that Jeep top, it looks like you've already had trouble." Drew points at the Jeep top in the corner.

"Hey, on a day like this, you think I want to drive around under a roof?"

"OK, here's the deal," Addison interrupts; she doesn't have patience for this small talk. "We're trying to find candidate parts for which we could sell 3D-ready plans as a product."

"For example," Drew jumps in, "we want to find parts that are frequently ordered, in small quantities, and that meet other conditions..."

"That's seems sensible. Where do I come in?" asks Lucas.

"We need data. We don't know if there are such parts or how many of them there might be or who orders them." Addison is pleased to get to the point.

"Hmm," Lucas pauses. "I've got a few consulting dollars, maybe I can find someone who could create some queries for you. Take a couple of weeks."

"No!" Addison's strong tone surprises herself. "I mean, that's too long."

"Well, I can't do it much faster."

"Just give us an extract of our orders over the past three years. We'll write our own queries."

"But, Addison, we don't know anything about..." Drew starts to object when Addison overrides him.

"Can you put the data into Access?"

"Sure. I can do that by Monday."

"All right. What time Monday?"

"Noon?"

"OK."

After the meeting, Addison and Drew are talking quietly on their way back to Drew's office.

"Addison, what are you doing? We don't know anything about creating queries..." Drew whispers.

"No, Drew, *you* don't know anything about creating queries. This isn't hard. If he gives us the data, I can munge around in Access to make the report. It's just for us; we're not gonna post it on the Web site."

"Seems hard to me, but I'll go along. I hope that's not a mistake."

"It won't be. Just watch."

"No, Drew, you don't know anything about creating queries."

STUDY QUESTIONS

Q1 What is the purpose of a database?

Q2 What is a database?

Q3 What is a database management system (DBMS)?

Q4 How do database applications make databases more useful?

Q5 How are data models used for database development?

Q6 How is a data model transformed into a database design?

Q7 What is the users' role in the development of databases?

Q8 2024?

CHAPTER PREVIEW

Businesses of every size organize data records into collections called *databases*. At one extreme, small businesses use databases to keep track of customers; at the other extreme, huge corporations such as Boeing and Verizon use databases to support complex sales, marketing, and operations activities. In between are businesses such as AllRoad Parts that use databases as a crucial part of their operations. Such businesses have a small staff of professionals and can't always support special needs, like those of Addison and Drew at AllRoad Parts. To obtain the one-of-a-kind reports they need, Addison and Drew need to be creative and adaptable.

This chapter discusses the why, what, and how of database processing. We begin by describing the purpose of databases and then explain the important components of database systems. We then overview the process of creating a database system and summarize your role as a future user of such systems.

Users have a crucial role in the development of database applications. Specifically, the structure and content of the database depend entirely on how users view their business activity. To build the database, the developers will create a model of that view using a tool called the entity-relationship model. You need to understand how to interpret such models because the development team might ask you to validate the correctness of such a model when building a system for your use. Finally, we describe the various database administration tasks.

This chapter focuses on database technology. Here we consider the basic components of a database and the functions of database applications. You will learn how Addison used database reporting to solve the AllRoad Parts problem in Chapter 9.

Q1   What Is the Purpose of a Database?

The purpose of a database is to keep track of things. When most students learn that, they wonder why we need a special technology for such a simple task. Why not just use a list? If the list is long, put it into a spreadsheet.

In fact, many professionals do keep track of things using spreadsheets. If the structure of the list is simple enough, there is no need to use database technology. The list of student grades in Figure 5-1, for example, works perfectly well in a spreadsheet.

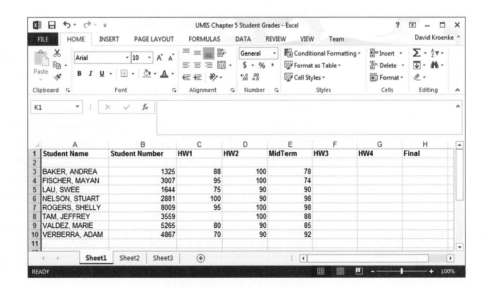

Figure 5-1
A List of Student Grades
Presented in a Spreadsheet
Source: Microsoft Excel 2013

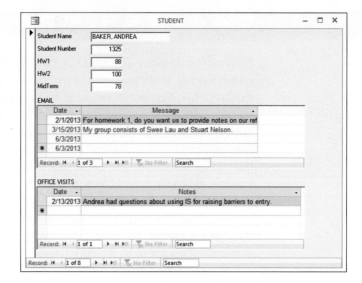

Figure 5-2
Student Data Shown in a Form
from a Database
Source: Microsoft Access 2013

Suppose, however, that the professor wants to track more than just grades. Say that the professor wants to record email messages as well. Or perhaps the professor wants to record both email messages and office visits. There is no place in Figure 5-1 to record that additional data. Of course, the professor could set up a separate spreadsheet for email messages and another one for office visits, but that awkward solution would be difficult to use because it does not provide all of the data in one place.

Instead, the professor wants a form like that in Figure 5-2. With it, the professor can record student grades, emails, and office visits all in one place. A form like the one in Figure 5-2 is difficult, if not impossible, to produce from a spreadsheet. Such a form is easily produced, however, from a database.

As you will see, databases can be more difficult to develop than spreadsheets; this difficulty causes some people to prefer to work with spreadsheets—or at least pretend to—as described in the Security Guide on pages 186–187.

The key distinction between Figures 5-1 and 5-2 is that the data in Figure 5-1 is about a single theme or concept. It is about student grades only. The data in Figure 5-2 has multiple themes; it shows student grades, student emails, and student office visits. We can make a general rule from these examples: Lists of data involving a single theme can be stored in a spreadsheet; lists that involve data with multiple themes require a database. We will say more about this general rule as this chapter proceeds.

 # What Is a Database?

A **database** is a self-describing collection of integrated records. To understand the terms in this definition, you first need to understand the terms illustrated in Figure 5-3. As you learned in Chapter 4, a **byte** is a character of data. In databases, bytes are grouped into **columns**, such as *Student Number* and *Student Name*. Columns are also called **fields**. Columns or fields, in turn, are grouped into **rows**, which are also called **records**. In Figure 5-3, the collection of data for all columns (*Student Number, Student Name, HW1, HW2,* and *MidTerm*) is called a *row* or a *record*. Finally, a group of similar rows or records is called a **table** or a **file**. From these definitions, you can see that there is a hierarchy of data elements, as shown in Figure 5-4.

It is tempting to continue this grouping process by saying that a database is a group of tables or files. This statement, although true, does not go far enough. As shown in Figure 5-5, a database is a collection of tables *plus* relationships among the rows in those tables, *plus* special data, called *metadata*, that describes the structure of the database. By the way, the cylindrical symbol labeled "database" in Figure 5-5 represents a computer disk drive. It is used like this because databases are stored on disks.

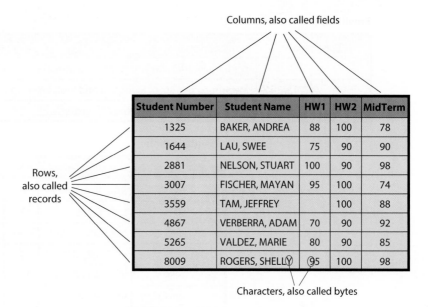

Columns, also called fields

Student Number	Student Name	HW1	HW2	MidTerm
1325	BAKER, ANDREA	88	100	78
1644	LAU, SWEE	75	90	90
2881	NELSON, STUART	100	90	98
3007	FISCHER, MAYAN	95	100	74
3559	TAM, JEFFREY		100	88
4867	VERBERRA, ADAM	70	90	92
5265	VALDEZ, MARIE	80	90	85
8009	ROGERS, SHELLY	95	100	98

Rows, also called records

Characters, also called bytes

Figure 5-3
Student Table (also called a file)

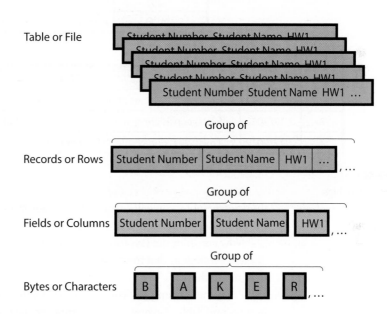

Figure 5-4
Hierarchy of Data Elements

Relationships Among Rows

Consider the terms on the left-hand side of Figure 5-5. You know what tables are. To understand what is meant by *relationships among rows in tables*, examine Figure 5-6. It shows sample data from the three tables *Email, Student,* and *Office_Visit*. Notice the column named *Student Number* in the *Email* table. That column indicates the row in *Student* to which a row of *Email* is connected. In the first row of *Email*, the *Student Number* value is 1325. This indicates that this particular email was received from the student whose *Student Number* is 1325. If you examine

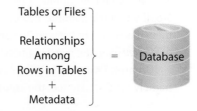

Tables or Files
+
Relationships Among Rows in Tables
+
Metadata

= Database

Figure 5-5
Components of a Database

Email Table

EmailNum	Date	Message	Student Number
1	2/1/2012	For homework 1, do you want us to provide notes on our references?	1325
2	3/15/2012	My group consists of Swee Lau and Stuart Nelson.	1325
3	3/15/2012	Could you please assign me to a group?	1644

Student Table

Student Number	Student Name	HW1	HW2	MidTerm
1325	BAKER, ANDREA	88	100	78
1644	LAU, SWEE	75	90	90
2881	NELSON, STUART	100	90	98
3007	FISCHER, MAYAN	95	100	74
3559	TAM, JEFFREY		100	88
4867	VERBERRA, ADAM	70	90	92
5265	VALDEZ, MARIE	80	90	85
8009	ROGERS, SHELLY	95	100	98

Office_Visit Table

VisitID	Date	Notes	Student Number
2	2/13/2012	Andrea had questions about using IS for raising barriers to entry.	1325
3	2/17/2012	Jeffrey is considering an IS major. Wanted to talk about career opportunities.	3559
4	2/17/2012	Will miss class Friday due to job conflict.	4867

Figure 5-6

Example of Relationships Among Rows

the *Student* table, you will see that the row for Andrea Baker has this value. Thus, the first row of the *Email* table is related to Andrea Baker.

Now consider the last row of the *Office_Visit* table at the bottom of the figure. The value of *Student Number* in that row is 4867. This value indicates that the last row in *Office_Visit* belongs to Adam Verberra.

From these examples, you can see that values in one table relate rows of that table to rows in a second table. Several special terms are used to express these ideas. A **key** (also called a **primary key**) is a column or group of columns that identifies a unique row in a table. *Student Number* is the key of the *Student* table. Given a value of *Student Number*, you can determine one and only one row in *Student*. Only one student has the number 1325, for example.

Every table must have a key. The key of the *Email* table is *EmailNum*, and the key of the *Office_Visit* table is *VisitID*. Sometimes more than one column is needed to form a unique identifier. In a table called *City*, for example, the key would consist of the combination of columns (*City, State*) because a given city name can appear in more than one state.

Student Number is not the key of the *Email* or the *Office_Visit* tables. We know that about *Email* because there are two rows in *Email* that have the *Student Number* value 1325. The value 1325 does not identify a unique row; therefore, *Student Number* cannot be the key of *Email*.

Nor is *Student Number* a key of *Office_Visit*, although you cannot tell that from the data in Figure 5-6. If you think about it, however, there is nothing to prevent a student from visiting a professor more than once. If that were to happen, there would be two rows in *Office_Visit* with the same value of *Student Number*. It just happens that no student has visited twice in the limited data in Figure 5-6.

In both *Email* and *Office_Visit*, *Student Number* is a key, but it is a key of a different table, namely *Student*. Hence, the columns that fulfill a role like that of *Student Number* in the *Email* and *Office_Visit* tables are called **foreign keys**. This term is used because such columns are keys, but they are keys of a different (foreign) table than the one in which they reside.

Before we go on, databases that carry their data in the form of tables and that represent relationships using foreign keys are called **relational databases**. (The term *relational* is used because another, more formal name for a table like those we're discussing is **relation**.) You'll learn about another kind of database, or data store, in Q8 and in Case Study 5.

Metadata

Recall the definition of database: A database is a self-describing collection of integrated records. The records are integrated because, as you just learned, rows can be tied together by their key/ foreign key relationship. Relationships among rows are represented in the database. But what does *self-describing* mean?

It means that a database contains, within itself, a description of its contents. Think of a library. A library is a self-describing collection of books and other materials. It is self-describing because the library contains a catalog that describes the library's contents. The same idea also pertains to a database. Databases are self-describing because they contain not only data, but also data about the data in the database.

Metadata is data that describes data. Figure 5-7 shows metadata for the *Email* table. The format of metadata depends on the software product that is processing the database. Figure 5-7 shows the metadata as it appears in Microsoft Access. Each row of the top part of this form describes a column of the *Email* table. The columns of these descriptions are *Field Name, Data Type*, and *Description*. *Field Name* contains the name of the column, *Data Type* shows the type of data the column may hold, and *Description* contains notes that explain the source or use of the column. As you can see, there is one row of metadata for each of the four columns of the *Email* table: *EmailNum, Date, Message*, and *Student Number*.

The bottom part of this form provides more metadata, which Access calls *Field Properties*, for each column. In Figure 5-7, the focus is on the *Date* column (note the light rectangle drawn around the *Date* row). Because the focus is on *Date* in the top pane, the details in the bottom pane pertain to the *Date* column. The Field Properties describe formats, a default value for Access to supply when a new row is created, and the constraint that a value is required for this

Figure 5-7
Sample Metadata (in Access)
Source: Microsoft Access 2013

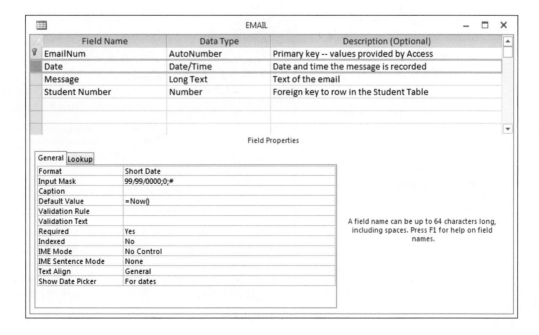

Ethics Guide

QUERYING INEQUALITY?

MaryAnn Baker works as a data analyst in human relations at a large, multinational corporation. As part of its compensation program, her company defines job categories and assigns salary ranges to each category. For example, the category M1 is used for first-line managers and is assigned the salary range of $75,000 to $95,000. Every job description is assigned to one of these categories, depending on the knowledge and skills required to do that job. Thus, the job titles Manager of Customer Support, Manager of Technical Writing, and Manager of Product Quality Assurance are all judged to involve about the same level of expertise and are all assigned to category M1.

One of MaryAnn's tasks is to analyze company salary data and determine how well actual salaries conform to established ranges. When discrepancies are noted, human relations managers meet to determine whether the discrepancy indicates a need to:

- Adjust the category's salary range;
- Move the job title to a different category;
- Define a new category; or
- Train the manager of the employee with the discrepancy on the use of salary ranges in setting employee compensation.

MaryAnn is an expert in creating database queries. Initially, she used Microsoft Access to produce reports, but much of the salary data she needs resides in the organization's Oracle database. At first she would ask the IS Department to extract certain data and move it into Access, but over time she learned that it was faster to ask IS to move all employee data from the operational Oracle database into another Oracle database created just for HR data analysis. Although Oracle provides a graphical query interface like that in Access, she found it easier to compose complex queries directly in SQL, so she learned it and, within a few months, became a SQL expert.

"I never thought I'd be doing this," she said. "But it turns out to be quite fun, like solving a puzzle, and apparently I'm good at it."

One day, after a break, MaryAnn signed into her computer and happened to glance at the results of a query that she'd left running while she was gone. "That's odd," she thought, "all the people with Hispanic surnames have lower salaries than the others." She wasn't looking for that pattern; it just happened to jump out at her as she glanced at the screen.

As she examined the data, she began to wonder if she was seeing a coincidence or if there was a discriminatory pattern within the organization. Unfortunately for MaryAnn's purposes, the organization did not track employee race in its database, so she had no easy way of identifying employees of Hispanic heritage other than reading through the list of surnames. But, as a skilled problem solver, that didn't stop MaryAnn. She realized that many employees having Hispanic origins were born in certain cities in Texas, New Mexico, Arizona, and California. Of course, this wasn't true for all employees; many non-Hispanic employees were born in those cities, too, and many Hispanic employees were born in other cities. This data was still useful, however, because MaryAnn's sample queries revealed that the proportion of employees with Hispanic surnames who were also born in those cities was very high. "OK," she thought, "I'll use those cities as a rough surrogate."

Using birth city as a query criterion, MaryAnn created queries that determined employees who were born in the selected cities earned, on average, 23 percent less than those who were not. "Well, that could be because they work in lower-pay-grade jobs." After giving it a bit of thought, MaryAnn realized that she needed to examine wages and salaries within job categories. "Where," she wondered, "do people born in those cities fall in the ranges of their job categories?" So, she constructed SQL to determine where within a job category the compensation for people born in the selected cities fell. "Wow!" she said to herself, "almost 80 percent of the employees born in those cities fall into the bottom half of their salary range."

MaryAnn scheduled an appointment with her manager for the next day.

 ## DISCUSSION QUESTIONS

When answering the following questions, suppose that you are MaryAnn:

1. Given these query results, do you have an ethical responsibility to do something? Consider both the categorical imperative (pages 20–21) and the utilitarian (pages 54–55) perspectives.
2. Given these query results, do you have a personal or social responsibility to do something?
3. What is your response if your manager says, "You don't know anything; it could be that starting salaries are lower in those cities. Forget about it."
4. What is your response if your manager says, "Don't be a troublemaker; pushing this issue will hurt your career."
5. What is your response if your manager says, "Right. We already know that. Get back to the tasks that I've assigned you."
6. Suppose your manager gives you funding to follow up with a more accurate analysis, and, indeed, there is a pattern of underpayment to people with Hispanic surnames. What should the organization do? For each choice below, indicate likely outcomes:
   a. Correct the imbalances immediately.
   b. Gradually correct the imbalances at future pay raises.
   c. Do nothing about the imbalances, but train managers not to discriminate in the future.
   d. Do nothing.
7. Suppose you hire a part-time person to help with the more accurate analysis, and that person is so outraged at the outcome that he quits and notifies newspapers in all the affected cities of the organization's discrimination.
   a. How should the organization respond?
   b. How should you respond?
8. Consider the adage, "Never ask a question for which you do not want the answer."
   a. Is following that adage ethical? Consider both the categorical imperative and utilitarian perspectives.
   b. Is following that adage socially responsible?
   c. How does that adage relate to you, as MaryAnn?
   d. How does that adage relate to you, as a future business professional?
   e. With regard to employee compensation, how does that adage relate to organizations?

column. It is not important for you to remember these details. Instead, just understand that metadata is data about data and that such metadata is always a part of a database.

The presence of metadata makes databases much more useful. Because of metadata, no one needs to guess, remember, or even record what is in the database. To find out what a database contains, we just look at the metadata inside the database.

What Is a Database Management System (DBMS)?

A **database management system (DBMS)** is a program used to create, process, and administer a database. As with operating systems, almost no organization develops its own DBMS. Instead, companies license DBMS products from vendors such as IBM, Microsoft, Oracle, and others. Popular DBMS products are **DB2** from IBM, **Access** and **SQL Server** from Microsoft, and **Oracle Database** from the Oracle Corporation. Another popular DBMS is **MySQL**, an open source DBMS product that is license-free for most applications.[1] Other DBMS products are available, but these five process the great bulk of databases today.

Note that a DBMS and a database are two different things. For some reason, the trade press and even some books confuse the two. A DBMS is a software program; a database is a collection of tables, relationships, and metadata. The two are very different concepts.

Creating the Database and Its Structures

Database developers use the DBMS to create tables, relationships, and other structures in the database. The form in Figure 5-7 can be used to define a new table or to modify an existing one. To create a new table, the developer just fills the new table's metadata into the form.

To modify an existing table—say, to add a new column—the developer opens the metadata form for that table and adds a new row of metadata. For example, in Figure 5-8 the developer has added a new column called *Response?*. This new column has the data type *Yes/No*, which means that the column can contain only one value—*Yes* or *No*. The professor will use this column to indicate whether he has responded to the student's email. A column can be removed by deleting its row in this table, though doing so will lose any existing data.

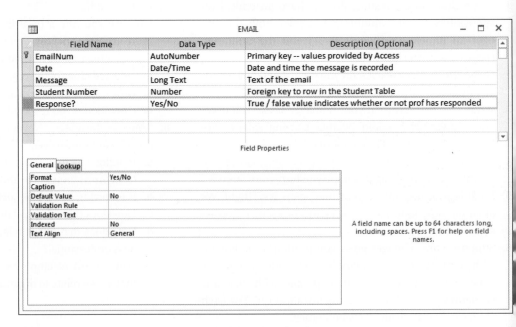

Figure 5-8
Adding a New Column to a Table
(in Access)
Source: Microsoft Access 2013

---

[1]MySQL was supported by the MySQL company. In 2008, that company was acquired by Sun Microsystems, which was, in turn, acquired by Oracle later that year. However, because MySQL is open source, Oracle does not own the source code.

Using MIS InClass 5

How Much Is a Database Worth?

The Firm, Minneapolis (*www.TheFirmMpls.com*), is a workout studio that realizes more than 15,000 person-visits per month, an average of 500 visits per day. Neil Miyamoto, one of the two business partners, believes that the database is The Firm's single most important asset. According to Neil:

> Take away anything else—the building, the equipment, the inventory—anything else, and we'd be back in business 6 months or less. Take away our customer database, however, and we'd have to start all over. It would take us another 8 years to get back where we are.[2]

Why is the database so crucial? It records everything the company's customers do. If The Firm decides to offer an early morning kickboxing class featuring a particular trainer, it can use its database to offer that class to everyone who ever took an early morning class, a kickboxing class, or a class by that trainer. Customers receive targeted solicitations for offerings they care about and, maybe equally important, they don't receive solicitations for those they don't care about. Clearly, The Firm database has value and, if it wanted to, The Firm could sell that data.

In this exercise, you and a group of your fellow students will be asked to consider the value of a database to organizations other than The Firm.

1. Many small business owners have found it financially advantageous to purchase their own building. As one owner remarked upon his retirement, "We did well with the business, but we made our real money by buying the building." Explain why this might be so.

2. To what extent does the dynamic you identified in your answer to item 1 pertain to databases? Do you think it likely that, in 2050, some small business owners will retire and make statements like, "We did well with the business, but we made our real money from the database we generated?" Why or why not? In what ways is real estate different from database data? Are these differences significant to your answer?

3. Suppose you had a national database of student data. Assume your database includes the name, email address, university, grade level, and major for each student. Name five companies that would find that data valuable, and explain how they might use it. (For example, Pizza Hut could solicit orders from students during finals week.)

4. Describe a product or service that you could develop that would induce students to provide the data in item 3.

5. Considering your answers to items 1 through 4, identify two organizations in your community that could generate a database that would potentially be more valuable than the organization itself. Consider businesses, but also think about social organizations and government offices.

   For each organization, describe the content of the database and how you could entice customers or clients to provide that data. Also, explain why the data would be valuable and who might use it.

6. Relate what you have learned in this exercise to the 3D printing discussion at AllRoad Parts.

7. Prepare a 1-minute statement of what you have learned from this exercise that you could use in a job interview to illustrate your ability to innovate the use of technology in business.

8. Present your answers to items 1–6 to the rest of the class.

---

[2]Personal conversation with the author, 2012. Reprinted by permission.

Processing the Database

The second function of the DBMS is to process the database. Such processing can be quite complex, but, fundamentally, the DBMS provides applications for four processing operations: to read, insert, modify, or delete data. These operations are requested in application calls upon the DBMS. From a form, when the user enters new or changed data, a computer program behind the form calls the DBMS to make the necessary database changes. From a Web application, a program on the client or on the server calls the DBMS directly to make the change.

Structured Query Language (SQL) is an international standard language for processing a database. All five of the DBMS products mentioned earlier accept and process SQL (pronounced "see-quell") statements. As an example, the following SQL statement inserts a new row into the *Student* table:

```
INSERT INTO Student
([Student Number], [Student Name], HW1, HW2, MidTerm)
VALUES
(1000, 'Franklin, Benjamin', 90, 95, 100);
```

As stated, statements like this one are issued "behind the scenes" by programs that process forms and reports. Alternatively, they can be issued directly to the DBMS by an application program.

You do not need to understand or remember SQL language syntax. Instead, just realize that SQL is an international standard for processing a database. SQL can also be used to create databases and database structures. You will learn more about SQL if you take a database management class.

Administering the Database

A third DBMS function is to provide tools to assist in the administration of the database. **Database administration** involves a wide variety of activities. For example, the DBMS can be used to set up a security system involving user accounts, passwords, permissions, and limits for processing the database. To provide database security, a user must sign on using a valid user account before she can process the database.

Permissions can be limited in very specific ways. In the Student database example, it is possible to limit a particular user to reading only *Student Name* from the *Student* table. A different user could be given permission to read the entire *Student* table, but limited to update only the *HW1, HW2,* and *MidTerm* columns. Other users can be given still other permissions.

In addition to security, DBMS administrative functions include backing up database data, adding structures to improve the performance of database applications, removing data that are no longer wanted or needed, and similar tasks.

For important databases, most organizations dedicate one or more employees to the role of database administration. Figure 5-9 summarizes the major responsibilities for this function. You will learn more about this topic if you take a database management course.

How Do Database Applications Make Databases More Useful?

A set of database tables, by itself, is not very useful; the tables in Figure 5-6 contain the data the professor wants, but the format is awkward at best. The data in database tables can be made more useful, or more available for the conception of information, when it is placed into forms like that in Figure 5-2 or other formats.

A **database application** is a collection of forms, reports, queries, and application programs[3] that serves as an intermediary between users and database data. Database applications reformat

---

[3]Watch out for confusion between a *database application* and a *database application program*. A database application includes forms, reports, queries, and database application programs.

Figure 5-9
Summary of Database
Administration (DBA) Tasks

Category	Database Administration Task	Description
Development	Create and staff DBA function	Size of DBA group depends on size and complexity of database. Groups range from one part-time person to small group.
	Form steering committee	Consists of representatives of all user groups. Forum for community-wide discussions and decisions.
	Specify requirements	Ensure that all appropriate user input is considered.
	Validate data model	Check data model for accuracy and completeness.
	Evaluate application situation design	Verify that all necessary forms, reports, queries, and applications are developed. Validate design and usability of application components.
Operation	Manage processing rights and responsibilities	Determine processing rights/restrictions on each table and column.
	Manage security	Add and delete users and user groups as necessary; ensure that security system works.
	Track problems and manage resolution	Develop system to record and manage resolution of problems.
	Monitor database performance	Provide expertise/solutions for performance improvements.
	Manage DBMS	Evaluate new features and functions.
Backup and Recovery	Monitor backup procedures	Verify that database backup procedures are followed.
	Conduct training	Ensure that users and operations personnel know and understand recovery procedures.
	Manage recovery	Manage recovery process.
Adaptation	Set up request tracking system	Develop system to record and prioritize requests for change.
	Manage configuration change	Manage impact of database structure changes on applications and users.

database table data to make it more informative and more easily updated. Application programs also have features that provide security, maintain data consistency, and handle special cases.

The specific purposes of the four elements of a database application are:

Forms	View data; insert new, update existing, and delete existing data
Reports	Structured presentation of data using sorting, grouping, filtering, and other operations
Queries	Search based upon data values provided by the user
Application programs	Provide security, data consistency, and special purpose processing, e.g., handle out-of-stock situations

Database applications came into prominence in the 1990s and were based on the technology that was available at that time. Many existing systems today are long-lived extensions to those applications; the ERP system SAP (discussed in Chapter 7) is a good example of this concept. You should expect to see these kinds of applications during the early years of your career.

Today, however, many database applications are based on newer technology that employs browsers, the Web, and related standards. These browser-based applications can do everything the older ones do, but they are more dynamic and better suited to today's world. To see why, consider each type.

Figure 5-10

Components of a Database
Application System

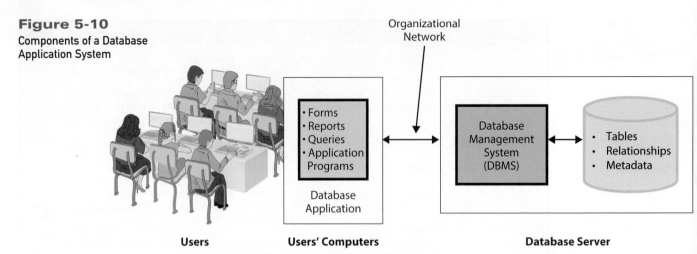

Traditional Forms, Queries, Reports, and Applications

Database technology puts unprecedented ability to conceive information into the hands of users. But what do you do with that information when you find something objectionable? See the Ethics Guide on pages 164–165 for an example case.

In most cases, a traditional database is shared among many users. In that case, the application shown in Figure 5-10 resides on the users' computers and the DBMS and database reside on a server computer. A network, in most cases *not* the Internet, is used to transmit traffic back and forth between the users' computers and the DBMS server computer.

Single-user databases like those in Microsoft Access are an exception. With such databases, the application, the DBMS, and the database all reside on the user's computer.

Traditional forms appeared in window-like displays like that in Figure 5-2. They serve their purpose; users can view, insert, modify, and delete data with them, but by today's standards, they look clunky.

Figure 5-11 shows a traditional report, which is a static display of data, placed into a format that is meaningful to the user. In this report, each of the emails for a particular student is shown

Figure 5-11

Example of a Student Report

Student Homework Progress with Emails	
Student Name	BAKER, ANDREA
Student Number	1325
HW1	88
HW2	100
Date	Message
2/1/2013	For homework 1, do you want us to provide notes on our references?
3/15/2013	My group consists of Swee Lau and Stuart Nelson.
Student Name	LAU, SWEE
Student Number	1644
HW1	75
HW2	90
Date	Message
3/15/2012	Could you please assign me to a group?

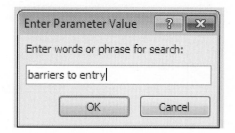

Figure 5-12a

Sample Query Form Used to
Enter Phrase for Search

Figure 5-12b

Sample Query Results of Query
Operation

Source: Microsoft Access 2013

after the student's name and grade data. Figure 5-12 shows a traditional query. The user specifies query criteria in a window-like box (Figure 5-12a), and the application responds with data that fit those criteria (Figure 5-12b).

Traditional database application programs are written in object-oriented languages such as C++ and VisualBasic (and even in earlier languages like COBOL). They are thick applications that need to be installed on users' computers. In some cases, all of the application logic is contained in a program on users' computers and the server does nothing except run the DBMS and serve up data. In other cases, some application code is placed on both the users' computers and the database server computer.

As stated, in the early years of your career, you will still see traditional applications, especially for enterprise-wide applications like ERP and CRM. Most likely, you will also be concerned, as a user if not in a more involved way, with the transition from such traditional applications into browser-based applications.

Browser Forms, Reports, Queries, and Applications

The databases in browser-based applications are nearly always shared among many users. As shown in Figure 5-13, the users' browsers connect over the Internet to a Web server computer,

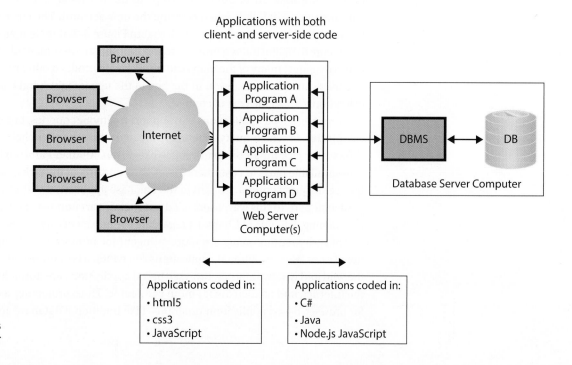

Figure 5-13

Four Application Programs
on a Web Server Computer

Figure 5-14
Account Creation Browser Form

which in turn connects to a database server computer (often many computers are involved on the server side of the Internet).

Browser applications are thin-client applications that need not be pre installed on the users' computers. In most cases, all of the code for generating and processing the application elements is shared between the users' computers and the servers. JavaScript is the standard language for user-side processing. Languages like C# and Java are used for server-side code, though JavaScript is starting to be used on the server with an open source product named Node.js (all of this is discussed further in Chapter 6).

Browser database application forms, reports, and queries are displayed and processed using html and, most recently, using html5, css3, and JavaScript as you learned in Chapter 4. Figure 5-14 shows a browser form that is used to create a new user account in Office 365. The form's content is dynamic; the user can click on the blue arrow next to *Additional Details* to see more data. Also, notice the steps in the left-hand side that outline the process that administrator will follow when creating the new account. The current step is shown in color. Compare and contrast this form with that in Figure 5-2; it is cleaner, with much less chrome.

Figure 5-15 illustrates a browser report that shows the content of a SharePoint site. The content is dynamic; many of the items can be clicked to produce other reports or take other actions. The user can select a criterion in the box in the upper-right-hand corner to filter the report to display only a specific type of content.

Browser-based applications can support traditional queries, but more exciting are **graphical queries**, in which query criteria are created when the user clicks on a graphic. Figure 5-16 shows a car jack for an off-road vehicle like a Jeep. AllRoad Parts might use a photo like this to show available parts to customers. Users click on parts of the jack and, in browser code behind the scene, query criteria are sent to the database application to display part order data for that particular part. In this way, users need not specify part numbers and so on when ordering. (See the opening dialogue of Chapter 4 regarding the impact of sales costs on that situation.)

Security requirements are more stringent for browser-based applications than for traditional ones. Most traditional applications run within a corporate network that is protected from the wild and woolly Internet. Browser-based applications are normally open to the public, over the Internet, and as such are far more vulnerable. Thus, protecting security is a major function for browser-based application programs. Like traditional database application programs, they

Figure 5-15
Browser Report

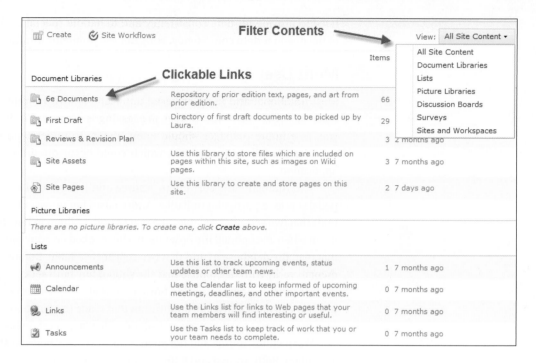

Create   Site Workflows   **Filter Contents** →   View: All Site Content ▾

		Items	All Site Content
Document Libraries	**Clickable Links** →		Document Libraries
6e Documents	Repository of prior edition text, pages, and art from prior edition.	66	Lists
First Draft	Directory of first draft documents to be picked up by Laura.	29	Picture Libraries
Reviews & Revision Plan		3 2 months ago	Discussion Boards
Site Assets	Use this library to store files which are included on pages within this site, such as images on Wiki pages.	3 7 months ago	Surveys
Site Pages	Use this library to create and store pages on this site.	2 7 days ago	Sites and Workspaces

Picture Libraries

There are no picture libraries. To create one, click Create above.

Lists

Announcements	Use this list to track upcoming events, status updates or other team news.	1 7 months ago
Calendar	Use the Calendar list to keep informed of upcoming meetings, deadlines, and other important events.	0 7 months ago
Links	Use the Links list for links to Web pages that your team members will find interesting or useful.	0 7 months ago
Tasks	Use the Tasks list to keep track of work that you or your team needs to complete.	0 7 months ago

Figure 5-16
Off-road Vehicle Jack
Source: © Willy Matheisl/age fotostock

need to provide for data consistency and to handle special conditions as well. As an example of the need for data consistency, consider the problems introduced by multi-user processing.

Multi-User Processing

Most traditional and browser-based applications involve multiple users processing the same database. While such **multi-user processing** is common, it does pose unique problems that you, as a future manager, should know about. To understand the nature of those problems, consider the following scenario, which could occur on either a traditional or browser-based application.

Two AllRoad Parts customers, Andrea and Jeffrey, are both attempting to buy the last two pedal sets for a particular trail bike. Andrea uses her browser to access the AllRoad Web site and finds that two sets are available. She places both of them in her shopping cart. She doesn't know it, but when she opened the order form, she invoked an application program on AllRoad's server that read the database to find that two sets are available. Before she checks out, she takes a moment to verify with her spouse that she should buy both sets.

Meanwhile, Jeffrey uses his browser and also finds that two sets are available because his browser activates that same application that reads the database and finds (because Andrea has not yet checked out) that two are available. He places both in his cart and checks out.

Meanwhile, Andrea and her spouse decide to buy both, so she checks out. Clearly, we have a problem. Both Andrea and Jeffrey have purchased the same two pedal sets. One of them is going to be disappointed.

This problem, known as the **lost-update problem**, exemplifies one of the special characteristics of multi-user database processing. To prevent this problem, some type of locking must be used to coordinate the activities of users who know nothing about one another. Locking brings its own set of problems, however, and those problems must be addressed as well. We will not delve further into this topic here, however.

Be aware of possible data conflicts when you manage business activities that involve multi-user processing. If you find inaccurate results that seem not to have a cause, you may be experiencing multi-user data conflicts. Contact your IS department for assistance.

 ## How Are Data Models Used for Database Development?

In Chapter 10, we will describe the process for developing information systems in detail. However, business professionals have such a critical role in the development of database applications that we need to anticipate part of that discussion here by introducing two topics—data modeling and database design.

Because the design of the database depends entirely on how users view their business environment, user involvement is critical for database development. Think about the Student database. What data should it contain? Possibilities are: *Students, Classes, Grades, Emails, Office_Visits, Majors, Advisers, Student_Organizations*—the list could go on and on. Further, how much detail should be included in each? Should the database include campus addresses? Home addresses? Billing addresses?

In fact, there are dozens of possibilities, and the database developers do not and cannot know what to include. They do know, however, that a database must include all the data necessary for the users to perform their jobs. Ideally, it contains that amount of data and no more. So, during database development the developers must rely on the users to tell them what to include in the database.

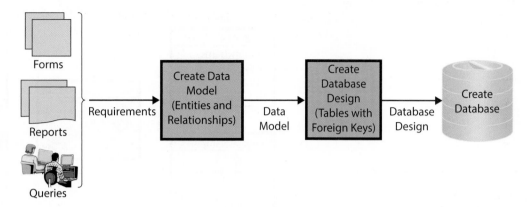

Figure 5-17
Database Development Process

Database structures can be complex, in some cases very complex. So, before building the database the developers construct a logical representation of database data called a **data model**. It describes the data and relationships that will be stored in the database. It is akin to a blueprint. Just as building architects create a blueprint before they start building, so, too, database developers create a data model before they start designing the database.

For a philosophical perspective on data models, see the Guide on pages 188–189.

Figure 5-17 summarizes the database development process. Interviews with users lead to database requirements, which are summarized in a data model. Once the users have approved (validated) the data model, it is transformed into a database design. That design is then implemented into database structures. We will consider data modeling and database design briefly in the next two sections. Again, your goal should be to learn the process so that you can be an effective user representative for a development effort.

What Is the Entity-Relationship Data Model?

The **entity-relationship (E-R) data model** is a tool for constructing data models. Developers use it to describe the content of a data model by defining the things (*entities*) that will be stored in the database and the *relationships* among those entities. A second, less popular tool for data modeling is the **Unified Modeling Language (UML)**. We will not describe that tool here. However, if you learn how to interpret E-R models, with a bit of study you will be able to understand UML models as well.

Entities

An **entity** is some thing that the users want to track. Examples of entities are *Order, Customer, Salesperson,* and *Item*. Some entities represent a physical object, such as *Item* or *Salesperson*; others represent a logical construct or transaction, such as *Order* or *Contract*. For reasons beyond this discussion, entity names are always singular. We use *Order*, not *Orders*; *Salesperson*, not *Salespersons*.

Entities have **attributes** that describe characteristics of the entity. Example attributes of *Order* are *OrderNumber, OrderDate, SubTotal, Tax, Total,* and so forth. Example attributes of *Salesperson* are *SalespersonName, Email, Phone,* and so forth.

Entities have an **identifier**, which is an attribute (or group of attributes) whose value is associated with one and only one entity instance. For example, *OrderNumber* is an identifier of *Order* because only one *Order* instance has a given value of *OrderNumber*. For the same reason, *CustomerNumber* is an identifier of *Customer*. If each member of the sales staff has a unique name, then *SalespersonName* is an identifier of *Salesperson*.

Before we continue, consider that last sentence. Is the salesperson's name unique among the sales staff? Both now and in the future? Who decides the answer to such a question? Only the users know whether this is true; the database developers cannot know. This example underlines why it is important for you to be able to interpret data models because only users like you will know for sure.

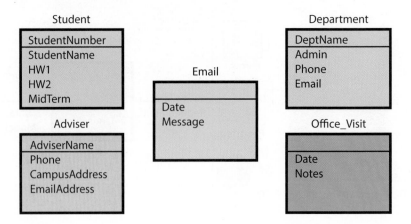

Figure 5-18
Student Data Model Entities

Figure 5-18 shows examples of entities for the Student database. Each entity is shown in a rectangle. The name of the entity is just above the rectangle, and the identifier is shown in a section at the top of the entity. Entity attributes are shown in the remainder of the rectangle. In Figure 5-18, the *Adviser* entity has an identifier called *AdviserName* and the attributes *Phone, CampusAddress,* and *EmailAddress.*

Observe that the entities *Email* and *Office_Visit* do not have an identifier. Unlike *Student* or *Adviser,* the users do not have an attribute that identifies a particular email. We *could* make one up. For example, we could say that the identifier of *Email* is *EmailNumber,* but if we do so we are not modeling how the users view their world. Instead, we are forcing something onto the users. Be aware of this possibility when you review data models about your business. Do not allow the database developers to create something in the data model that is not part of your business world.

Relationships

Entities have **relationships** to each other. An *Order,* for example, has a relationship to a *Customer* entity and also to a *Salesperson* entity. In the Student database, a *Student* has a relationship to an *Adviser,* and an *Adviser* has a relationship to a *Department.*

Figure 5-19 shows sample *Department, Adviser,* and *Student* entities and their relationships. For simplicity, this figure shows just the identifier of the entities and not the other attributes. For this sample data, *Accounting* has three professors—Jones, Wu, and Lopez—and *Finance* has two professors—Smith and Greene.

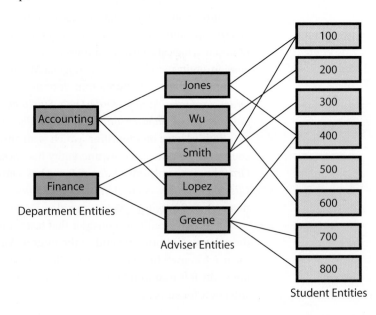

Figure 5-19

Example of Department, Adviser, and Student Entities and Relationships

Figure 5-20
Sample Relationships Version 1

The relationship between *Advisers* and *Students* is a bit more complicated because in this example an adviser is allowed to advise many students and a student is allowed to have many advisers. Perhaps this happens because students can have multiple majors. In any case, note that Professor Jones advises students 100 and 400 and that student 100 is advised by both Professors Jones and Smith.

Diagrams like the one in Figure 5-19 are too cumbersome for use in database design discussions. Instead, database designers use diagrams called **entity-relationship (E-R) diagrams**. Figure 5-20 shows an E-R diagram for the data in Figure 5-19. In this figure, all of the entities of one type are represented by a single rectangle. Thus, there are rectangles for the *Department, Adviser*, and *Student* entities. Attributes are shown as before in Figure 5-18.

Additionally, a line is used to represent a relationship between two entities. Notice the line between *Department* and *Adviser*, for example. The forked lines on the right side of that line signify that a department may have more than one adviser. The little lines, which are referred to as **crow's feet**, are shorthand for the multiple lines between *Department* and *Adviser* in Figure 5-19. Relationships like this one are called **1:N,** or **one-to-many relationships**, because one department can have many advisers, but an adviser has at most one department.

Now examine the line between *Adviser* and *Student*. Notice the short lines that appear at each end of the line. These lines are the crow's feet, and this notation signifies that an adviser can be related to many students and that a student can be related to many advisers, which is the situation in Figure 5-19. Relationships like this one are called **N:M,** or **many-to-many relationships**, because one adviser can have many students and one student can have many advisers.

Students sometimes find the notation N:M confusing. Interpret the *N* and *M* to mean that a variable number, greater than one, is allowed on each side of the relationship. Such a relationship is not written *N:N* because that notation would imply that there are the same number of entities on each side of the relationship, which is not necessarily true. *N:M* means that more than one entity is allowed on each side of the relationship and that the number of entities on each side can be different.

Figure 5-21 shows the same entities with different assumptions. Here, advisers may advise in more than one department, but a student may have only one adviser, representing a policy that students may not have multiple majors.

Which, if either, of these versions is correct? Only the users know. These alternatives illustrate the kinds of questions you will need to answer when a database designer asks you to check a data model for correctness.

Figures 5-20 and 5-21 are typical examples of an entity-relationship diagram. Unfortunately, there are several different styles of entity-relationship diagrams. This one is called, not surprisingly, a **crow's-foot diagram** version. You may learn other versions if you take a database management class.

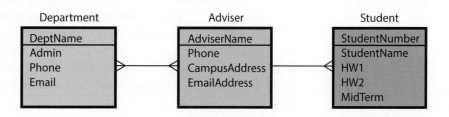

Figure 5-21
Sample Relationships Version 2

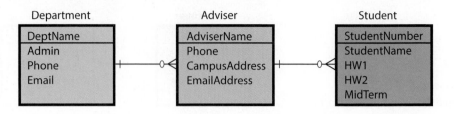

Figure 5-22
Sample Relationships Showing
Both Maximum and Minimum
Cardinalities

The crow's-foot notation shows the maximum number of entities that can be involved in a relationship. Accordingly, they are called the relationship's **maximum cardinality**. Common examples of maximum cardinality are 1:N, N:M, and 1:1 (not shown).

Another important question is, "What is the minimum number of entities required in the relationship?" Must an adviser have a student to advise, and must a student have an adviser? Constraints on minimum requirements are called **minimum cardinalities**.

Figure 5-22 presents a third version of this E-R diagram that shows both maximum and minimum cardinalities. The vertical bar on a line means that at least one entity of that type is required. The small oval means that the entity is optional; the relationship *need not* have an entity of that type.

Thus, in Figure 5-22 a department is not required to have a relationship to any adviser, but an adviser is required to belong to a department. Similarly, an adviser is not required to have a relationship to a student, but a student is required to have a relationship to an adviser. Note, also, that the maximum cardinalities in Figure 5-22 have been changed so that both are 1:N.

Is the model in Figure 5-22 a good one? It depends on the policy of the university. Again, only the users know for sure.

Q6 How Is a Data Model Transformed into a Database Design?

Database design is the process of converting a data model into tables, relationships, and data constraints. The database design team transforms entities into tables and expresses relationships by defining foreign keys. Database design is a complicated subject; as with data modeling, it occupies weeks in a database management class. In this section, however, we will introduce two important database design concepts: normalization and the representation of two kinds of relationships. The first concept is a foundation of database design, and the second will help you understand important design considerations.

Normalization

Normalization is the process of converting a poorly structured table into two or more well-structured tables. A table is such a simple construct that you may wonder how one could possibly be poorly structured. In truth, there are many ways that tables can be malformed—so many, in fact, that researchers have published hundreds of papers on this topic alone.

Consider the *Employee* table in Figure 5-23a. It lists employee names, hire dates, email addresses, and the name and number of the department in which the employee works. This table seems innocent enough. But consider what happens when the Accounting department changes its name to Accounting and Finance. Because department names are duplicated in this table, every row that has a value of "Accounting" must be changed to "Accounting and Finance."

Employee

Name	HireDate	Email	DeptNo	DeptName
Jones	Feb 1, 2010	Jones@ourcompany.com	100	Accounting
Smith	Dec 3, 2012	Smith@ourcompany.com	200	Marketing
Chau	March 7, 2012	Chau@ourcompany.com	100	Accounting
Greene	July 17, 2011	Greene@ourcompany.com	100	Accounting

(a) Table Before Update

Employee

Name	HireDate	Email	DeptNo	DeptName
Jones	Feb 1, 2010	Jones@ourcompany.com	100	Accounting and Finance
Smith	Dec 3, 2012	Smith@ourcompany.com	200	Marketing
Chau	March 7, 2012	Chau@ourcompany.com	100	Accounting and Finance
Greene	July 17, 2011	Greene@ourcompany.com	100	Accounting

(b) Table with Incomplete Update

Figure 5-23
A Poorly Designed Employee Table

Data Integrity Problems

Suppose the Accounting name change is correctly made in two rows, but not in the third. The result is shown in Figure 5-23b. This table has what is called a **data integrity problem**: Some rows indicate that the name of Department 100 is "Accounting and Finance," and another row indicates that the name of Department 100 is "Accounting."

This problem is easy to spot in this small table. But consider a table like the *Customer* table in the Amazon.com database or the eBay database. Those databases have millions of rows. Once a table that large develops serious data integrity problems, months of labor will be required to remove them.

Data integrity problems are serious. A table that has data integrity problems will produce incorrect and inconsistent results. Users will lose confidence in the data, and the system will develop a poor reputation. Information systems with poor reputations become serious burdens to the organizations that use them.

Normalizing for Data Integrity

The data integrity problem can occur only if data are duplicated. Because of this, one easy way to eliminate the problem is to eliminate the duplicated data. We can do this by transforming the table design in Figure 5-23a into two tables, as shown in Figure 5-24. Here the name of the department is stored just once; therefore, no data inconsistencies can occur.

Of course, to produce an employee report that includes the department name, the two tables in Figure 5-24 will need to be joined back together. Because such joining of tables is common, DBMS products have been programmed to perform it efficiently, but it still requires work. From this example, you can see a trade-off in database design: Normalized tables eliminate data duplication, but they can be slower to process. Dealing with such trade-offs is an important consideration in database design.

The general goal of normalization is to construct tables such that every table has a *single* topic or theme. In good writing, every paragraph should have a single theme. This is true of databases as well; every table should have a single theme. The problem with the table design in Figure 5-23 is that it has two independent themes: employees and departments. The way to correct the problem is to split the table into two tables, each with its own theme. In this case, we create an *Employee* table and a *Department* table, as shown in Figure 5-24.

Employee

Name	HireDate	Email	DeptNo
Jones	Feb 1, 2010	Jones@ourcompany.com	100
Smith	Dec 3, 2012	Smith@ourcompany.com	200
Chau	March 7, 2012	Chau@ourcompany.com	100
Greene	July 17, 2011	Greene@ourcompany.com	100

Department

DeptNo	DeptName
100	Accounting
200	Marketing
300	Information Systems

Figure 5-24
Two Normalized Tables

As mentioned, there are dozens of ways that tables can be poorly formed. Database practitioners classify tables into various **normal forms** according to the kinds of problems they have. Transforming a table into a normal form to remove duplicated data and other problems is called *normalizing* the table.[4] Thus, when you hear a database designer say, "Those tables are not normalized," she does not mean that the tables have irregular, not-normal data. Instead, she means that the tables have a format that could cause data integrity problems.

Summary of Normalization

As a future user of databases, you do not need to know the details of normalization. Instead, understand the general principle that every normalized (well-formed) table has one and only one theme. Further, tables that are not normalized are subject to data integrity problems.

Be aware, too, that normalization is just one criterion for evaluating database designs. Because normalized designs can be slower to process, database designers sometimes choose to accept non-normalized tables. The best design depends on the users' processing requirements.

Representing Relationships

Figure 5-25 shows the steps involved in transforming a data model into a relational database design. First, the database designer creates a table for each entity. The identifier of the entity becomes the key of the table. Each attribute of the entity becomes a column of the table. Next, the resulting tables are normalized so that each table has a single theme. Once that has been done, the next step is to represent relationship among those tables.

For example, consider the E-R diagram in Figure 5-26a. The *Adviser* entity has a 1:N relationship to the *Student* entity. To create the database design, we construct a table for *Adviser*

> - Represent each entity with a table
>   - Entity identifier becomes table key
>   - Entity attributes become table columns
> - Normalize tables as necessary
> - Represent relationships
>   - Use foreign keys
>   - Add additional tables for N:M relationships

Figure 5-25
Transforming a Data Model into
a Database Design

---

[4]See David Kroenke and David Auer, *Database Concepts*, 6th ed., pp. 72–82 (Upper Saddle River, NJ: Pearson Education, 2013) for more information.

Figure 5-26

Representing a 1:N Relationship

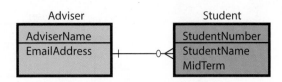

(a) 1:N Relationship Between Adviser and Student Entities

Adviser Table—Key is AdviserName

AdviserName	EmailAddress
Jones	Jones@myuniv.edu
Choi	Choi@myuniv.edu
Jackson	Jackson@myuniv.edu

Student Table—Key is StudentNumber

StudentNumber	StudentName	MidTerm
100	Lisa	90
200	Jennie	85
300	Jason	82
400	Terry	95

(b) Creating a Table for Each Entity

Adviser Table—Key is AdviserName

AdviserName	EmailAddress
Jones	Jones@myuniv.edu
Choi	Choi@myuniv.edu
Jackson	Jackson@myuniv.edu

Foreign Key
Column
Represents
Relationship

Student—Key is StudentNumber

StudentNumber	StudentName	MidTerm	AdviserName
100	Lisa	90	Jackson
200	Jennie	85	Jackson
300	Jason	82	Choi
400	Terry	95	Jackson

(c) Using the *AdviserName* Foreign Key to Represent the 1:N Relationship

and a second table for *Student*, as shown in Figure 5-26b. The key of the *Adviser* table is *AdviserName*, and the key of the *Student* table is *StudentNumber*.

Further, the *EmailAddress* attribute of the *Adviser* entity becomes the *EmailAddress* column of the *Adviser* table, and the *StudentName* and *MidTerm* attributes of the *Student* entity become the *StudentName* and *MidTerm* columns of the *Student* table.

The next task is to represent the relationship. Because we are using the relational model, we know that we must add a foreign key to one of the two tables. The possibilities are: (1) place the foreign key *StudentNumber* in the *Adviser* table or (2) place the foreign key *AdviserName* in the *Student* table.

The correct choice is to place *AdviserName* in the *Student* table, as shown in Figure 5-26c. To determine a student's adviser, we just look into the *AdviserName* column of that student's row. To determine the adviser's students, we search the *AdviserName* column in the *Student* table to determine which rows have that adviser's name. If a student changes advisers, we

Figure 5-27
Representing an N:M
Relationship

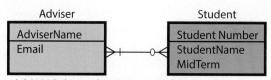

(a) N:M Relationship Between Adviser and Student

Adviser—Key is AdviserName

AdviserName	Email
Jones	Jones@myuniv.edu
Choi	Choi@myuniv.edu
Jackson	Jackson@myuniv.edu

No room to place second or third AdviserName

Student—Key is StudentNumber

StudentNumber	StudentName	MidTerm	AdviserName
100	Lisa	90	Jackson
200	Jennie	85	Jackson
300	Jason	82	Choi
400	Terry	95	Jackson

(b) Incorrect Representation of N:M Relationship

Adviser—Key is AdviserName

AdviserName	Email
Jones	Jones@myuniv.edu
Choi	Choi@myuniv.edu
Jackson	Jackson@myuniv.edu

Student—Key is StudentNumber

StudentNumber	StudentName	MidTerm
100	Lisa	90
200	Jennie	85
300	Jason	82
400	Terry	95

Adviser_Student_Intersection

AdviserName	StudentNumber
Jackson	100
Jackson	200
Choi	300
Jackson	400
Choi	100
Jones	100

Student 100 has three advisers

(c) Adviser_Student_Intersection Table Represents the N:M Relationship

simply change the value in the *AdviserName* column. Changing *Jackson* to *Jones* in the first row, for example, will assign student 100 to Professor Jones.

For this data model, placing *StudentNumber* in *Adviser* would be incorrect. If we were to do that, we could assign only one student to an adviser. There is no place to assign a second adviser.

This strategy for placing foreign keys will not work for N:M relationships, however. Consider the data model in Figure 5-27a; here advisers and students have a many-to-many relationship. An adviser may have many students, and a student may have multiple advisers (for multiple majors).

To see why the foreign key strategy we used for 1:N relationships will not work for N:M relationships, examine Figure 5-27b. If student 100 has more than one adviser, there is no place to record second or subsequent advisers.

To represent an N:M relationship, we need to create a third table, as shown in Figure 5-27c. The third table has two columns, *AdviserName* and *StudentNumber*. Each row of the table means that the given adviser advises the student with the given number.

As you can imagine, there is a great deal more to database design than we have presented here. Still, this section should give you an idea of the tasks that need to be accomplished to create a database. You should also realize that the database design is a direct consequence of decisions made in the data model. If the data model is wrong, the database design will be wrong as well.

What Is the Users' Role in the Development of Databases?

As stated, a database is a model of how the users view their business world. This means that the users are the final judges as to what data the database should contain and how the records in that database should be related to one another.

The easiest time to change the database structure is during the data modeling stage. Changing a relationship from one-to-many to many-to-many in a data model is simply a matter of changing the 1:N notation to N:M. However, once the database has been constructed and loaded with data and forms, reports, queries, and application programs have been created, changing a one-to-many relationship to many-to-many means weeks of work.

You can glean some idea of why this might be true by contrasting Figure 5-26c with Figure 5-27c. Suppose that instead of having just a few rows, each table has thousands of rows; in that case, transforming the database from one format to the other involves considerable work. Even worse, however, is that someone must change application components as well. For example, if students have at most one adviser, then a single text box can be used to enter *AdviserName*. If students can have multiple advisers, then a multiple-row table will need to be used to enter *AdviserName* and a program will need to be written to store the values of *AdviserName* into the *Adviser_Student_Intersection* table. There are dozens of other consequences, consequences that will translate into wasted labor and wasted expense.

Thus, *user review of the data model is crucial.* When a database is developed for your use, you must carefully review the data model. If you do not understand any aspect of it, you should ask for clarification until you do. *Entities must contain all of the data you and your employees need to do your jobs, and relationships must accurately reflect your view of the business.* If the data model is wrong, the database will be designed incorrectly, and the applications will be difficult to use, if not worthless. Do not proceed unless the data model is accurate.

As a corollary, when asked to review a data model, take that review seriously. Devote the time necessary to perform a thorough review. Any mistakes you miss will come back to haunt you, and by then the cost of correction may be very high with regard to both time and expense. This brief introduction to data modeling shows why databases can be more difficult to develop than spreadsheets.

 2024?

With ever cheaper data storage and data communications, we can be sure that the volume of database data will continue to grow, probably exponentially, through 2024. All that data contains patterns that can be used to conceive information to help businesses and organizations achieve their strategies, as you'll learn when you study business intelligence in Chapter 9. Furthermore, as databases become bigger and bigger, they're more attractive as targets for theft or mischief, a subject you'll consider in Chapter 12.

Setting these ideas aside, what else can we imagine for database technology by 2024? We can get a glimpse into that future by recognizing that the major principles of the relational model—the fixed-sized tables, the relationships among tables via foreign keys, and the theory of normalization—all came about because of limited storage space and limited processing speeds back in the 1960s and early 1970s.[5] At some point, maybe the mid-1990s, these limitations were removed by improved storage and processing technology, and today they do not exist. Today the relational model is not needed.

Furthermore, the relational model was never a natural fit with business documents. For example, users want to store sales orders; they do not want to break up sales orders via normalization and store the data in separate tables. It's like taking your car into a parking garage and having the attendant break it up into pieces, store the pieces in separate piles, and then reassemble it from the pieces when you come back to get it. And why? For the efficiency and convenience of the management of the parking garage.

This is not to say that relational databases will be replaced anytime soon. Organizations have created thousands of relational databases with millions of lines of application code that process SQL statements against relational data structures. There is also a strong social trend among older technologists to hang onto the relational model. But the primary reason for the relational model's existence is gone, and document piece-making via normalization is no longer necessary.

Also, organizations today want to store new types of data such as images, audios, and videos. Those files are large collections of bits, and they don't fit into relational structures. Collections of such files still need metadata; we need such data to record when, where, how, and for what purpose the files exist, but we don't need to put it into relational databases just to obtain metadata. AllRoad Parts' desire to store images for customers' image query provides an excellent example.

MongoDB is an open source document-oriented DBMS that AllRoad Parts could use to store its nonstructured data. MongoDB does not require normalized data; instead, it manages collections of documents where those documents can have a variety of structures, including large bit files for image, audio, and video data. MongoDB can also store documents like sales orders without requiring that they be normalized. It is used by companies like Craigslist and foursquare; the name *MongoDB* is a play on the adjective *humongous.*

But MongoDB is not alone. A few years ago, Amazon.com determined that relational database technology wouldn't meet its needs, and it developed a nonrelational data store called **Dynamo**.[6] Meanwhile, for many of the same reasons, Google developed a nonrelational data store called **Bigtable**.[7] Facebook took concepts from both of these systems and developed a third nonrelational data store called **Cassandra**.[8] In 2008, Facebook turned Cassandra over to the open source community, and now Apache has dubbed it a Top Level Project (TLP), which is the height of respectability among open source projects.

Such nonrelational databases have come to be called **NoSQL databases,** where NoSQL means nonrelational databases that support very high transaction rates processing relatively simple data structures, replicated on many servers in the cloud. NoSQL is not the best term; *NotRelationalDatabases* would have been better, but the die has been cast. You can learn more about the rationale for NoSQL products and some of their most intriguing features in Case Study 5, page 194.

---

[5]For a summary of this early history and an amplification of these ideas, see David Kroenke, "Beyond the Relational Model," *IEEE Computer,* June 2005.

[6]Werner Vogel, "Amazon's Dynamo," All Things Distributed blog, last modified October 2, 2007, *http://www. allthingsdistributed.com/2007/10/amazons_dynamo.html.*

[7]Fay Chang, Jeffrey Dean, Sanjay Ghemawat, Wilson C. Hsieh, Deborah A. Wallach, Mike Burrows, Tushar Chandra, Andrew Fikes, and Robert E. Gruber, "Bigtable: A Distributed Storage System for Structured Data," OSDI 2006, Seventh Symposium on Operating System Design and Implementation, Seattle, WA, last modified November 2006, *http://labs.google.com/papers/bigtable.html.*

[8]Jonathan Ellis, "Cassandra: Open Source Bigtable + Dynamo," accessed June 2011, *http://www.slideshare.net/ jbellis/cassandra-open-source-bigtable-dynamo.*

Use of these NoSQL products has led to the definition of a new type of data store. **BigData** (also spelled Big Data) is used to describe data collections that are characterized by huge *volume*, rapid *velocity*, and great *variety*. Considering volume, BigData refers to data sets that are at least a petabyte in size, and usually larger. A data set containing all Google searches in the United States on a given day is BigData in size. Additionally, BigData has high velocity, meaning that it is generated rapidly. (If you know physics, you know that *speed* would be a more accurate term, but speed doesn't start with a *v*, and the *vvv* description has become a common way to describe BigData.) The Google search data for a given day is generated, in, well, just a day. In the past, months or years would have been required to generate so much data.

Finally, BigData is varied. BigData may have structured data, but it also may have free-form text, dozens of different formats of Web server and database log files, streams of data about user responses to page content, and possibly graphics, audio, and video files.

Today some of the major challenges are finding and reporting patterns and relationships in BigData stores. NoSQL databases are used for this purpose, along with another open source product named Hadoop, which we will discuss in Chapter 9.

So, we can conclude that by 2024, many, many NoSQL databases will exist, and not just in leading-edge companies like Amazon.com, Google, and Facebook. What does that mean to you as a business professional? First, such knowledge is useful; stay abreast of developments in this area. If you were Addison and you went to a meeting today with Lucas and said something like, "Lucas, have you thought about using MongoDB for storing our 3D parts and image data?" you would gain his attention and admiration immediately. You'd likely find yourself on Lucas's key users' committee, or whatever AllRoad Parts calls it, and that would be a great career opportunity for you. Also, watch NoSQL developments from an investor's perspective. Not all such products will be open source; even if they are, there will be companies that integrate them into their product or service offerings, and those companies may well be good investment opportunities.

If you're interested in IS as a discipline or as a second major, pay attention to these products. You still need to learn the relational model and the processing of relational databases; they will be the bread-and-butter of the industry, even in 2024. But exciting new opportunities and career paths will also develop around NoSQL databases. Learn about them as well, and use that knowledge to separate you from the competition when it comes to job interviews.

Lots of interesting, promising developments are under way!

Security Guide

NO, THANKS, I'LL USE A SPREADSHEET

"I'm not buying all this stuff about databases. I've tried them and they're a pain—way too complicated to set up, and most of the time, a spreadsheet works just as well. We had one project at the car dealership that seemed pretty simple to me: We wanted to keep track of customers and the models of used cars they were interested in. Then, when we got a car on the lot, we could query the database to see who wanted a car of that type and generate a letter to them.

"It took forever to build that system, and it never did work right. We hired three different consultants, and the last one finally did get it to work. But it was so complicated to produce the letters. You had to query the data in Access to generate some kind of file, then open Word, then go through some mumbo jumbo using mail/merge to cause Word to find the letter and put all the Access data in the right spot. I once printed more than 200 letters and had the name in the address spot and the address in the name spot and no date. And it took me over an hour to do even that. I just wanted to do the query and push a button to get my letters generated. I gave up. Some of the salespeople are still trying to use it, but not me.

"Besides, think about security. I don't want to share my data with anyone. How do I know that one of the other salespeople here doesn't steal my clients? Or, worse, what if some weirdo virus gets in here and destroys my files? Without my customer list, I'd have to start all over. No, thanks!"

"My motto is, 'Keep it simple.' I use an Excel spreadsheet with four columns: Name, Phone Number, Car Interests, and Notes. When I get a new customer, I enter the name and phone number, and then I put the make and model of cars they like in the Car Interests column. Anything else that I think is important I put in the Notes column—extra phone numbers, address data if I have it, email addresses, spouse names, last time I called them, and so on. The system isn't fancy, but it works fine.

"When I want to find something, I use Excel's Data Filter. I can usually get what I need. Of course, I still can't send form letters, but it really doesn't matter. I get most of my sales using the phone, anyway."

DISCUSSION QUESTIONS

1. To what extent do you agree with the opinions presented here? To what extent are the concerns expressed here justified? To what extent might they be due to other factors?

2. What problems do you see with the way that the car salesperson stores address data? What will he have to do if he ever does want to send a letter or an email to all of his customers?

3. From his comments, how many different themes are there in his data? What does this imply about his ability to keep his data in a spreadsheet?

4. Does the concern about not sharing data relate to whether or not he uses a database?

5. Consider his security concern. Write a requirement for a feature in the database application that would address his needs. Be specific about what access both for viewing and updating the application should allow. In practical terms, after that feature is implemented, how could he tell if other salespeople are truly locked out? How can he tell if the database is appropriately protected from viruses and other threats?

6. Another possibility is that the salesman is resisting because he is stealing other salespeople's customers. If they are using the database ("some of the salespeople are still trying to use it"), he might be signing into the database and obtaining their customer data. Again, write a requirement for a feature for this database application that would prohibit this.

7. Yet another possibility is that he wants to keep his customers' data himself so that he can take his customer list with him when he goes to work for another dealer. Suppose that is so. Does putting his customer data in a database protect the dealership from this possibility? Why or why not?

8. It is also possible that his concerns have nothing to do with security. Perhaps he just doesn't like change. His posture with regard to his spreadsheet is, "It may be bad, but at least I'm used to it." Suppose you are his manager. How would you respond to his resistance?

Guide

IMMANUEL KANT, DATA MODELER

Only the users can say whether a data model accurately reflects their business environment. What happens when the users disagree among themselves? What if one user says orders have a single salesperson, but another says that sales teams produce some orders? Who is correct?

It's tempting to say, "The correct model is the one that better represents the real world." The problem with this statement is that data models do not model "the real world." A data model is simply a model of what the data modeler perceives. This very important point can be difficult to understand, but if you do understand it, you will save many hours in data model validation meetings and be a much better data modeling team member.

The German philosopher Immanuel Kant reasoned that what we perceive as reality is based on our perceptive apparatus. That which we perceive he called phenomena. Our perceptions, such as of light and sound, are processed by our brains and made meaningful. But we do not and cannot know whether the images we create from the perceptions have anything to do with what might or might not really be.

Kant used the term *noumenal world* to refer to the essence of "things in themselves"—to whatever it is out there that gives rise to our perceptions and images. He used the term *phenomenal world* to refer to what we humans perceive and construct.

It is easy to confuse the noumenal world with the phenomenal world, because we share the phenomenal world with other humans. All of us have the same mental apparatus, and we all make the same constructions. If you ask your roommate to hand you the toothpaste, she hands you the toothpaste, not a hairbrush. But the fact that we share this mutual view does not mean that the mutual view describes in any way what is truly out there. Dogs construct a world based on smells, and orca whales construct a world based on sounds. What the "real world" is to a dog, a whale, and a human are completely different. All of this means that we cannot ever justify a data model as a "better representation of the real world." Nothing that humans can do represents the real, noumenal world. A data model, therefore, is a model of a human's model of what appears to be "out there." For example, a model of a salesperson is a model of the model that humans make of salespeople.

To return to the question that we started with, what do we do when people disagree about what should be in a data model? First, realize that anyone attempting to justify

her data model as a better representation of the real world is saying, quite arrogantly, "The way I think of the world is the way that counts." Second, in times of disagreement we must ask the question, "How well does the data model fit the mental models of the people who are going to use the system?" The person who is constructing the data model may think the model under construction is a weird way of viewing the world, but that is not the point. The only valid point is whether it reflects how the users view their world. Will it enable the users to do their jobs?

 DISCUSSION QUESTIONS

1. What does a data model represent?
2. Explain why it is easy for humans to confuse the phenomenal world with the noumenal world.
3. If someone were to say to you, "My model is a better model of the real world," how would you respond?
4. In your own words, how should you proceed when two people disagree on what is to be included in a data model?

ACTIVE REVIEW

Use this Active Review to verify that you understand the ideas and concepts that answer the chapter's study questions.

Q1 What is the purpose of a database?

State the purpose of a database. Explain the circumstances in which a database is preferred to a spreadsheet. Describe the key difference between Figures 5-1 and 5-2.

Q2 What is a database?

Define the term *database*. Explain the hierarchy of data and name three elements of a database. Define *metadata*. Using the example of *Student* and *Office_Visit* tables, show how relationships among rows are represented in a database. Define the terms *primary key, foreign key*, and *relational database*.

Q3 What is a database management system (DBMS)?

Explain the acronym DBMS and name its functions. List five popular DBMS products. Explain the difference between a DBMS and a database. Summarize the functions of a DBMS. Define *SQL*. Describe the major functions of database administration.

Q4 How do database applications make databases more useful?

Explain why database tables, by themselves, are not very useful to buiness users. Name the four elements of a database application and describe the purpose of each. Explain the difference between a database application and a database application program. Describe the nature of traditional database applications. Explain why browser-based applications are better than traditional ones. Name the primary technologies used to support browser-based applications.

Q5 How are data models used for database development?

Explain why user involvement is critical during database development. Describe the function of a data model. Sketch the database development process. Define *E-R model, entity, relationship, attribute*, and *identifier*. Give an example, other than one in this text, of an E-R diagram. Define *maximum cardinality* and *minimum cardinality*. Give an example of three maximum cardinalities and two minimum cardinalities. Explain the notation in Figures 5-21 and 5-22.

Q6 How is a data model transformed into a database design?

Name the three components of a database design. Define *normalization* and explain why it is important. Define *data integrity problem* and describe its consequences. Give an example of a table with data integrity problems and show how it can be normalized into two or more tables that do not have such problems. Describe two steps in transforming a data model into a database design. Using an example not in this chapter, show how 1:N and N:M relationships are represented in a relational database.

Q7 What is the users' role in the development of databases?

Describe the users' role in the database development. Explain why it is easier and cheaper to change a data model than to change an existing database. Use the examples of Figures 5-26c and 5-27c in your answer. Describe two criteria for judging a data model. Explain why it is important to devote time to understanding a data model.

Q8 2024?

Describe the reasons for the creation of the relational model. Explain the comparison of the relational model to a parking garage. Describe factors that favor the continuation of the use of this model. Using AllRoad Parts, describe a storage need that does not fit into the natural structures of the relational model. Define *NoSQL data store* and give three examples. Define BigData and explain the elements of *vvv*. Explain two ways that knowledge of NoSQL databases is useful to you as a business professional. Explain what your posture should be with regard to relational databases and NoSQL databases if you are an MIS major or minor.

Using Your Knowledge with AllRoad Parts

Lucas is going to provide Addison with two tables of data. She will need to combine them using keys and foreign keys to create the report she wants. You will see how she does this in Chapter 9 and have a chance to do some of her work in Application Exercise 9-3. Explain how her knowledge gives her a competitive advantage. Describe one way you could use your knowledge of MongoDB at AllRoad Parts.

KEY TERMS AND CONCEPTS

MyMISLab

Go to **mymislab.com** to complete the problems marked with this icon .

USING YOUR KNOWLEDGE

5-1. Draw an entity-relationship diagram that shows the relationships among a database, database applications, and users.

5-2. Consider the relationship between *Adviser* and *Student* in Figure 5-21. Explain what it means if the maximum cardinality of this relationship is:
  a. N:1
  b. 1:1
  c. 5:1
  d. 1:5

5-3. Identify two entities in the data entry form in Figure 5-28. What attributes are shown for each? What do you think are the identifiers?

5-4. Visit *www.acxiom.com*. Navigate the site to answer the following questions.
  a. According to the Web site, what is Acxiom's privacy policy? Are you reassured by its policy? Why or why not?

  b. Make a list of 10 different products that Acxiom provides.
  c. Describe Acxiom's top customers.
  d. Examine your answers in parts b and c and describe, in general terms, the kinds of data that Acxiom must be collecting to be able to provide those products to those customers.
  e. What is the function of InfoBase?
  f. What is the function of PersonicX?
  g. In what ways might companies like Acxiom need to limit their marketing so as to avoid a privacy outcry from the public?
  h. Should there be laws that govern companies like Acxiom? Why or why not?
  i. Should there be laws that govern the types of data services that governmental agencies can buy from companies like Acxiom? Why or why not?

Figure 5-28
Sample Data Entry Form

COLLABORATION EXERCISE 5

Using the collaboration IS you built in Chapter 2 (pages 73-74), collaborate with a group of students to answer the following questions.

Figure 5-29 shows a spreadsheet that is used to track the assignment of sheet music to a choir—it could be a church choir or school or community choir. The type of choir does not matter because the problem is universal. Sheet music is expensive, choir members need to be able to take sheet music away for practice at home, and not all of the music gets back to the inventory. (Sheet music can be purchased or rented, but either way, lost music is an expense.)

Look closely at this data and you will see some data integrity problems—or at least some possible data integrity problems. For one, do Sandra Corning and Linda Duong really have the same copy of music checked out? Second,

did Mozart and J. S. Bach both write a Requiem, or in row 15 should J. S. Bach actually be Mozart? Also, there is a problem with Eleanor Dixon's phone number; several phone numbers are the same as well, which seems suspicious.

Additionally, this spreadsheet is confusing and hard to use. The column labeled *First Name* includes both people names and the names of choruses. *Email* has both email addresses and composer names, and *Phone* has both phone numbers and copy identifiers. Furthermore, to record a checkout of music, the user must first add a new row and then reenter the name of the work, the composer's name, and the copy to be checked out. Finally, consider what happens when the user wants to find all copies of a particular work: The user will have to examine the rows in each of four spreadsheets for the four voice parts.

	A	B	C	D	E	F
1	**Last Name**	**First Name**	**Email**	**Phone**	**Part**	
2	Ashley	Jane	JA@somewhere.com	703.555.1234	Soprano	
3	Davidson	Kaye	KD@somewhere.com	703.555.2236	Soprano	
4	Ching	Kam Hoong	KHC@overhere.com	703.555.2236	Soprano	
5	Menstell	Lori Lee	LLM@somewhere.com	703.555.1237	Soprano	
6	Corning	Sandra	SC2@overhere.com	703.555.1234	Soprano	
7		B-minor mass	J.S. Bach	Soprano Copy 7		
8		Requiem	Mozart	Soprano Copy 17		
9		9th Symphony Chorus	Beethoven	Soprano Copy 9		
10	Wei	Guang	GW1@somewhere.com	703.555.9936	Soprano	
11	Dixon	Eleanor	ED@thisplace.com	703.555.12379	Soprano	
12		B-minor mass	J.S. Bach	Soprano Copy 11		
13	Duong	Linda	LD2@overhere.com	703.555.8736	Soprano	
14		B-minor mass	J.S. Bach	Soprano Copy 7		
15		Requiem	J.S. Bach	Soprano Copy 19		
16	Lunden	Haley	HL@somewhere.com	703.555.0836	Soprano	
17	Utran	Diem Thi	DTU@somewhere.com	703.555.1089	Soprano	
18						
19						

Soprano | Alto | Tenor | Baritone&Bass

Figure 5-29
Spreadsheet Used for
Assignment of Sheet Music

In fact, a spreadsheet is ill suited for this application. A database would be a far better tool, and situations like this are obvious candidates for innovation.

a. Analyze the spreadsheet shown in Figure 5-29 and list all of the problems that occur when trying to track the assignment of sheet music using this spreadsheet.

b. Figure 5-30a shows a two-entity data model for the sheet-music-tracking problem.

    (1) Select identifiers for the *ChoirMember* and *Work* entities. Justify your selection.

    (2) This design does not eliminate the potential for data integrity problems that occur in the spreadsheet. Explain why not.

(3) Design a database for this data model. Specify key and foreign key columns.

c. Figure 5-30b shows a second alternative data model for the sheet-music-tracking problem. This alternative shows two variations on the *Work* entity. In the second variation, an attribute named *WorkID* has been added to *Work_Version3*. This attribute is a unique identifier for the work; the DBMS will assign a unique value to *WorkID* when a new row is added to the *Work* table.

    (1) Select identifiers for *ChoirMember, Work_Version2, Work_Version3,* and *Copy_Assignment.* Justify your selection.

Figure 5-30
Data-Model Alternatives for the Assignment of Sheet Music

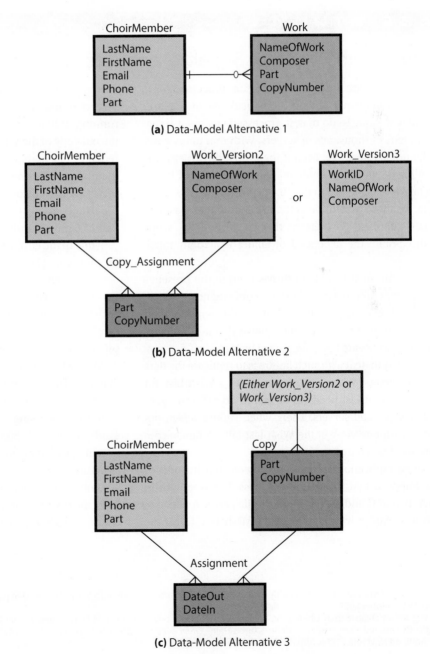

(a) Data-Model Alternative 1

(b) Data-Model Alternative 2

(c) Data-Model Alternative 3

(2) Does this design eliminate the potential for data integrity problems that occur in the spreadsheet? Why or why not?

(3) Design a database for the data model that uses *Work_Version2*. Specify key and foreign key columns.

(4) Design a database for the data models that uses *Work_Version3*. Specify key and foreign key columns.

(5) Is the design with *Work_Version2* better than the design for *Work_Version3*? Why or why not?

d. Figure 5-30c shows a third alternative data model for the sheet-music-tracking problem. In this data model, use either *Work_Version2* or *Work_Version3*, whichever you think is better.

(1) Select identifiers for each entity in your data model. Justify your selection.

(2) Summarize the differences between this data model and that in Figure 5-30b. Which data model is better? Why?

(3) Design a database for this data model. Specify key and foreign key columns.

e. Which of the three data models is the best? Justify your answer.

CASE STUDY 5

Fail Away with Dynamo, Bigtable, and Cassandra

As you learned in Case Study 1, Amazon.com processed more than 306 order items per second on its peak day of the 2012 holiday sales season. To do that, it processed customer transactions on tens of thousands of servers. With that many computers, failure is inevitable. Even if the probability of any one server failing is .0001, the likelihood that not one out of 10,000 of them fails is .9999 raised to the 10,000 power, which is about .37. Thus, for these assumptions the likelihood of at least one failure is 63 percent. For reasons that go beyond the scope of this discussion, the likelihood of failure is actually much greater.

Amazon.com must be able to thrive, even in the presence of such constant failure. Or, as Amazon.com engineers stated: "Customers should be able to view and add items to their shopping cart even if disks are failing, network routes are flapping, or data centers are being destroyed by tornados."[9]

The only way to deal with such failure is to replicate the data on multiple servers. When a customer stores a Wish List, for example, that Wish List needs to be stored on different, geographically separated servers. Then, when (notice *when*, not *if*) a server with one copy of the Wish List fails, Amazon.com applications obtain it from another server.

Such data replication solves one problem but introduces another. Suppose that the customer's Wish List is stored on servers A, B, and C and server A fails. While server A is down, server B or C can provide a copy of the Wish List, but if the customer changes it, that Wish List can only be rewritten to servers B and C. It cannot be written to A, because A is not running. When server A comes back into service, it will have the old copy of the Wish List. The next day, when the customer reopens his or her Wish List, two different versions exist: the most recent one on servers B and C and an older one on server A. The customer wants the most current one. How can Amazon.com ensure that it will be delivered? Keep in mind that 15.6 million orders are being shipped while this goes on.

None of the current relational DBMS products was designed for problems like this. Consequently, Amazon.com engineers developed Dynamo, a specialized data store for reliably processing massive amounts of data on tens of thousands of servers. Dynamo provides an always-open experience for Amazon.com's retail customers; Amazon.com also sells Dynamo store services to others via its S3 Web Services product offering.

Meanwhile, Google was encountering similar problems that could not be met by commercially available relational DBMS products. In response, Google created Bigtable, a data store for processing petabytes of data on hundreds of thousands of servers.[10] Bigtable supports a richer data model than Dynamo, which means that it can store a greater variety of data structures.

Both Dynamo and Bigtable are designed to be **elastic**; this term means that the number of servers can dynamically increase and decrease without disrupting performance.

---

[9]DeCandia, et al., "Dynamo: Amazon's Highly Available Key-Value Store," Proceedings of the 21st ACM Symposium on Operating Systems Principles, Stevenson, WA, October 2007.

[10]Fay Chang, Jeffrey Dean, Sanjay Ghemawat, Wilson C. Hsieh, Deborah A. Wallach, Mike Burrows, Tushar Chandra, Andrew Fikes, and Robert E. Gruber, "Bigtable: A Distributed Storage System for Structured Data," *OSDI 2006: Seventh Symposium on Operating System Design and Implementation*, Seattle, WA, last modified November 2006, *http://labs.google.com/papers/bigtable.html.*

In 2007, Facebook encountered similar data storage problems: Massive amounts of data, the need to be elastically scalable, tens of thousands of servers, and high volumes of traffic. In response to this need, Facebook began development on Cassandra, a data store that provides storage capabilities like Dynamo with a richer data model like Bigtable.[11,12] Initially, Facebook used Cassandra to power its Inbox Search. By 2008, Facebook realized that it had a bigger project on its hands than it wanted and gave the source code to the open source community. As of 2012, Cassandra is used by Facebook, Twitter, Digg, Reddit, Cisco, and many others.

Cassandra, by the way, is a fascinating name for a data store. In Greek mythology, Cassandra was so beautiful that Apollo fell in love with her and gave her the power to see the future. Alas, Apollo's love was unrequited and he cursed her so that no one would ever believe her predictions. The name was apparently a slam at Oracle.

Cassandra is elastic and fault-tolerant; it supports massive amounts of data on thousands of servers and provides **durability**, meaning that once data is committed to the data store, it won't be lost, even in the presence of failure. One of the most interesting characteristics of Cassandra is that clients (meaning the programs that run Facebook, Twitter, etc.) can select the level of consistency that they need. If a client requests that all servers always be current, Cassandra will ensure that that happens, but performance will be slow. At the other end of the trade-off spectrum, clients can require no consistency, whereby performance is maximized. In between, clients can require that a majority of the servers that store a data item be consistent.

Cassandra's performance is vastly superior to relational DBMS products. In one comparison, Cassandra was found to be 2,500 times faster than MySQL for write operations and 23 times faster for read operations[13] on massive amounts of data on hundreds of thousands of possibly failing computers!

QUESTIONS

5-5. Clearly, Dynamo, Bigtable, and Cassandra are critical technology to the companies that created them. Why did they allow their employees to publish academic papers about them? Why did they not keep them as proprietary secrets?

5-6. What do you think this movement means to the existing DBMS vendors? How serious is the NoSQL threat? Justify your answer. What responses by existing DBMS vendors would be sensible?

5-7. Is it a waste of your time to learn about the relational model and Microsoft Access? Why or why not?

5-8. Given what you know about AllRoad Parts, should it use a relational DBMS, such as Oracle Database or MySQL, or should it use Cassandra?

5-9. Suppose that AllRoad decides to use a NoSQL solution, but a battle emerges among the employees in the IT department. One faction wants to use Cassandra, but another faction wants to use a different NoSQL data store, named MongoDB (*www.mongodb.org*). Assume that you're Kelly, and Lucas asks for your opinion about how he should proceed. How do you respond?

---

[11]"Welcome to Apache Cassandra," The Apache Software Foundation, accessed June 2011, *http://cassandra.apache.org.*
[12]"The Cassandra Distributed Database," *Parleys*, accessed July 16, 2013, *http://www.parleys.com/#st=5&id=1866&sl=20.*
[13]"The Cassandra Distributed Database," Slide 21.

MyMISLab

Go to **mymislab.com** for Auto-graded writing questions as well as the following Assisted-graded writing questions:

5-10. Using your answer to question 5-3, draw an E-R diagram for the data entry form in Figure 5-28. Specify cardinalities. State your assumptions.

5-11. The partial E-R diagram in Figure 5-31 is for a sales order. Assume there is only one *Salesperson* per *SalesOrder*.
    a. Specify the maximum cardinalities for each relationship. State your assumptions, if necessary.
    b. Specify the minimum cardinalities for each relationship. State your assumptions, if necessary.

5-12. Mymislab Only – comprehensive writing assignment for this chapter.

Figure 5-31
Partial E-R Diagram for SalesOrder

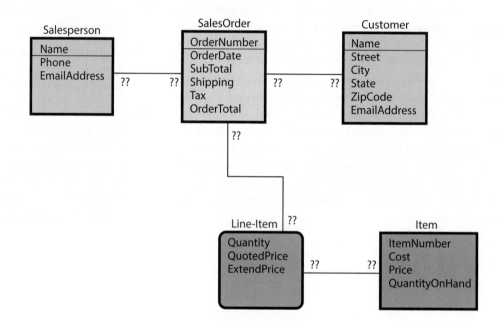

6

The Cloud

"What's your plan, Lucas?" Jason Green, CEO of AllRoad Parts, is meeting with Lucas Massey, IT director, and Kelly Summers, CFO, to discuss AllRoad Parts' Web hosting costs.

"Right now, Jason, we're fine. Our hosting service processes our transactions on time, and we've had no real outages, but…" Lucas trails off.

Kelly can't stand this. "Well, we're fine until you look at the bills we're running up. Our hosting costs have increased 350 percent *in a year*."

"Yes, Kelly, they have, but our volume's gone up 400 percent," Lucas replies.

"True enough, but…"

Jason has had enough and interrupts. "We've been over this before. No need to rehash it. We all agree that our hosting costs are too high. Lucas, I asked you to look into alternatives. What have you got?"

"The cloud."

"The *what?*" Kelly hopes he's not losing it.

"The cloud." Lucas repeats. "We move our Web servers and databases to the cloud."

Jason is curious. "OK, Lucas, I'll bite. What's the cloud?"

"It's a movement—I'd call it a fad, except I think it's here to stay."

"So how does it help us?" Jason asks.

"We lease server capability from a third party."

Kelly's confused. "But we're already doing that from our hosting vendor."

"Well, it's different," Lucas explains. "We can lease on very, very flexible, pay-as-you-go terms. If we have a run on a new popular item, like those hot new Fox suspensions, we can acquire more resources—they use the term *provision*—we can provision more resources."

"You mean each day? We can change the terms of our lease on a daily basis?" Kelly thinks that's not possible because she knows the terms of their contract with the current hosting vendor.

"No, I mean each hour. We can provision or release server resources by the hour." Lucas is enjoying this discussion.

Kelly is surprised. "No way. How do they do that? We have to give our hosting vendor at least a week's notice."

"Yeah, we do. But that's not how the cloud works."

Kelly persists. "I still don't get it."

"They use what's called *virtualization*. They don't actually provision new hardware; they provision new instances of servers on existing hardware."

"So one server is actually many?" Kelly's read about this somewhere.

"No, one server is virtually many." Lucas is having fun.

"Whatever." Kelly does *not* like to be corrected.

"The point is they can do this programmatically, no humans involved. We tell them we want a certain level of performance. They measure it, and when our workload increases, they give us another 50 or 100 servers; we use them for a few hours, until demand falls, and then they take them back." Lucas gets serious again.

"OK, so how much does it cost? This can't be cheap." Kelly is skeptical.

"How about a quarter an hour."

Jason's puzzled by that. "You mean a quarter of an hour? 15 minutes?"

"No, I mean 25 cents an hour…and probably less." Lucas grins as he says this.

"*What?*" Kelly's dumbfounded.

"No, I mean 25 cents an hour…and probably less."

"Yeah, that's it. That's for processing. For databases, we have to commit to a monthly charge. But I think that's less than 50 dollars a month for what we need." Lucas isn't quite sure because he's quoting preliminary prices. He thinks the actual costs could be less.

"Lucas, you've got to be kidding. We can knock thousands out of our hosting fees. This is *huge*." As Kelly says this, in the back of her mind she's thinking, "If it's true."

"Well, it's good; I don't know about huge," Lucas replies. "We still have development costs on our end. And we need to create the procedures, train people, the whole system thing…"

"Lucas, give me a plan. I want a plan." Jason is thinking about what these savings could mean to AllRoad's next two quarters…and beyond.

"I'll give you something next week," Lucas says.

"I want it by Friday, Lucas," Jason insists.

"OK."

STUDY QUESTIONS

Q1 Why is the cloud the future for most organizations?

Q2 What network technology supports the cloud?

Q3 How does the cloud work?

Q4 How do organizations use the cloud?

Q5 How can AllRoad Parts use the cloud?

Q6 How can organizations use cloud services securely?

Q7 2024?

CHAPTER PREVIEW

If you go into business for yourself, there's an excellent chance you'll have a problem just like AllRoad's. What is the best way to support your Web site or other information systems? Should you use the cloud? Most likely, the answer will be yes. So, then, which of your applications should use it and how? You need the knowledge of this chapter to participate in the conversations you'll have. Of course, you could just rely on outside experts, but that doesn't work in the twenty-first century. Many of your competitors will be able to ask and understand those questions—and use the money their knowledge saves them for other purposes, such as developing new business lines like selling 3D parts plans, as AllRoad Parts might do.

Or what if you work in product management for a large company? Does your product "talk" to some network? If not, could it? Should it? Will some cloud offering make sense? How will it connect to the cloud? How will you know without some knowledge of the cloud?

We begin this chapter with an overview of why the cloud is the future for most organizations. Then, in Q2 and Q3, we will discuss background technology that you need to know to better understand how the cloud works and what organizations can do with it. We'll discuss local area networks, the fundamentals of the Internet, how Web servers function, and the purpose of basic cloud technologies. Then we'll return to discussing how organizations can use the cloud, basic steps for setting up a cloud presence, and cloud security. We'll wrap up with the cloud in 2024.

Why Is the Cloud the Future for Most Organizations?

Until 2010 or so, most organizations constructed and maintained their own computing infrastructure. Organizations purchased or leased hardware, installed it on their premises, and used it to support organizational email, Web sites, e-commerce sites, and in-house applications such as accounting and operations systems (you'll learn about those in the next chapter). After about 2010, however, organizations began to move their computing infrastructure to the cloud, and it is likely that in the future all, or nearly all, computing infrastructure will be leased from the cloud. So, just what is the cloud, and why is it the future?

What Is the Cloud?

We define the **cloud** as the *elastic* leasing of *pooled* computer resources *over the Internet*. The term *cloud* is used because most early diagrams of three-tier and other Internet-based systems used a cloud symbol to represent the Internet (see Figure 5-13 for an example), and organizations came to view their infrastructure as being "somewhere in the cloud."

Elastic

Consider each of the italicized terms in the definition. The term **elastic**, which was first used this way by Amazon.com, means that the computing resources leased can be increased or decreased dynamically, programmatically, in a short span of time and that organizations pay for just the resources that they use.

Suppose that AllRoad Parts creates an ad to run during the Academy Awards. It believes it has a fantastic ad that will result in millions of hits on its Web site. However, it doesn't know, ahead of time, if there will be a thousand, or a million, or ten million, or even more site visits. Further, the ad may appeal more to one nationality than to another. Will 70 percent of those visits arise in the United States and the rest in Europe? Or will there be millions from Japan? Or Australia? Given this uncertainty, how does it prepare its computing infrastructure? AllRoad knows that if it cannot provide very short response time (say a fraction of a second) it will lose the benefit of an incredibly expensive ad. On the other hand, if the ad is a flop, preprovisioning of thousands of servers will add to the accumulation of wasted money.

Figure 6-1 shows an example of this situation, based on a real case supported by Amazon .com's CloudFront (see Q4). Suppose Figure 6-1 shows the processing on AllRoad Parts' Web site during the Academy Awards. Throughout the day, AllRoad is delivering less than 10 Gbps of its content to users. However, as soon as its ad runs (2 PM in this time zone), demand increases seven-fold and stays high for half an hour. After the announcement of Best Picture, when its ad runs again, demand again increases to 30 and 40 Gpbs for an hour and then returns to its base level.

Without an increase in servers, response time will be 3 or 5 seconds or more, which is far too long to maintain the attention of a charged-up Academy Awards viewer. However, AllRoad has contracted with its cloud vendor to add servers, wherever needed worldwide, to keep response time to less than 0.5 seconds. Using cloud technology, the cloud vendor will programmatically increase its servers to keep response time below the 0.5-second threshold. As demand falls after the ad runs a second time, it will release the excess servers and reallocate them at the end of the awards.

In this way, AllRoad need not build or contract for infrastructure that supports maximum demand. Had it done so, the vast majority of its servers would have been idle for most of the evening. And, as you'll learn, the cloud vendor can provision servers worldwide using the cloud; if a good portion of the excess demand is in Singapore, for example, it can provision extra servers in Asia and reduce wait time due to global transmission delays.

Pooled

The second key in the definition of cloud is *pooled*. Cloud resources are **pooled** because many different organizations use the same physical hardware; they share that hardware through virtualization. Cloud vendors dynamically allocate virtual machines to physical hardware as customer needs increase or decrease. Thus, servers that advertisers need for the Academy Awards can be reallocated to CPA firms that need them later that same day, to textbook publishers who need them for online student activity on Monday, or to the hotel industry that needs them later the next week.

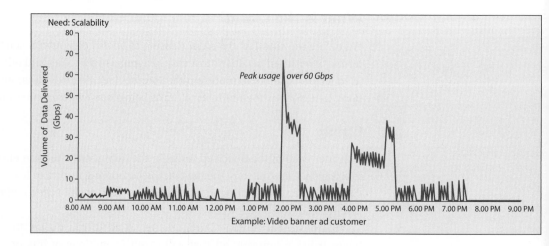

Figure 6-1
Example Video Banner
Ad Customer

An easy way to understand the essence of this development is to consider electrical power. In the very earliest days of electric power generation, organizations operated their own generators to create power for their company's needs. Over time, as the power grid expanded, it became possible to centralize power generation so that organizations could purchase just the electricity they needed from an electric utility.

Both cloud vendors and electrical utilities benefit from *economies of scale*. According to this principle, the average cost of production decreases as the size of the operation increases. Major cloud vendors operate enormous Web farms. Figure 6-2 shows the building that contains the computers in the Web farm that Apple constructed in 2011 to support its iCloud offering. This billion-dollar facility contains more than 500,000 square feet.[1] Amazon.com, IBM, Google, Microsoft, Oracle, and other large companies each operate several similar farms worldwide.

Over the Internet

Finally, the resources are accessed **over the Internet**. Big deal, you're saying. "I use the Internet all the time." Well, think about that for a minute. AllRoad Parts has contracted with the cloud vendor for a maximum response time; the cloud vendor adds servers as needed to meet that requirement. As stated, the cloud vendor may be provisioning, nearly instantaneously, servers all over the world. How does it do that? And not for just one customer, like AllRoad Parts, but for thousands?

In the old days, for such inter organizational processing to occur, developers from AllRoad Parts had to meet with developers from the cloud vendor and design an interface. "Our programs will do this, providing this data, and we want your programs to do that, in response, sending us this other data back." Such meetings took days and were expensive and error-prone. Given the design, the developers then returned home to write code to meet the agreed-on interface design, which may not have been understood in the same way by all parties.

Figure 6-2

Apple Data Center in Maiden, NC

Source: Google Earth.

---

[1]Patrick Thibodeau, "Apple, Google, Facebook Turn N.C. into Data Center Hub," *Computerworld*, June 3, 2011, *http://www.computerworld.com/s/article/9217259/Apple_Google_Facebook_turn_N.C._into_data_center_hub.*

It was a long, slow, expensive, and prone-to-failure process. If organizations had to do that today, cloud provisioning would be unaffordable and infeasible.

Instead, the computer industry settled on a set of standard ways of requesting and receiving services over the Internet. You will learn about some of these standards in Q3. For now, just realize those standards enable computers that have never "met" before to organize a dizzying, worldwide dance to deliver and process content to users on PCs, iPads, Google phones, Xboxes, and even exercise equipment in a tenth of second or less. It is absolutely fascinating and gorgeous technology! Unfortunately, you will only have the opportunity to learn a few basic terms in Q2 and Q3. Before we define and explain those terms, however, consider factors that make the cloud the future.

Why Is the Cloud Preferred to In-House Hosting?

Figure 6-3 compares and contrasts cloud-based and in-house hosting. As you can see, the positives are heavily tilted toward cloud-based computing. The cloud vendor Rackspace will lease you one medium server for less than a penny per hour. You can obtain and access that server

Figure 6-3
Comparison of Cloud and
In-House Alternatives

Cloud	In-House
Positive:	
Small capital requirements	Control of data location
Speedy development	In-depth visibility of security and disaster preparedness
Superior flexibility and adaptability to growing or fluctuating demand	
Known cost structure	
Possibly best-of-breed security/disaster preparedness	
No obsolescence	
Industry-wide economies of scale, hence cheaper	
Negative:	
Dependency on vendor	Significant capital required
Loss of control over data location	Significant development effort
Little visibility into true security and disaster preparedness capabilities	Annual maintenance costs
	Ongoing support costs
	Staff and train personnel
	Increased management requirements
	Difficult (impossible?) to accommodate fluctuating demand
	Cost uncertainties
	Obsolescence

today, actually within a few minutes. Tomorrow, if you need thousands of servers, you can readily scale up to obtain them. Furthermore, you know the cost structure; although you might have a surprise in regard to how many customers want to access your Web site, you won't have any surprises as to how much it will cost.

Another positive is that as long as you're dealing with large, reputable organizations, you'll be receiving best-of-breed security and disaster recovery (discussed in Chapter 12). In addition, you need not worry that you're investing in technology that will soon be obsolete; the cloud vendor is taking that risk. All of this is possible because the cloud vendor is gaining economies of scale by selling to an entire industry, not just to you.

The negatives of cloud computing involve loss of control. You're dependent on a vendor; changes in the vendor's management, policy, and prices are beyond your control. Further, you don't know where your data—which may be a large part of your organization's value—is located. Nor do you know how many copies of your data there are or even if they're located in the same country as you are. Finally, you have no visibility into the security and disaster preparedness that is actually in place. Your competition could be stealing your data and you won't know it.

The positives and negatives of in-house hosting are shown in the second column of Figure 6-3. For the most part, they are the opposite of those for cloud-based computing; note, however, the need for personnel and management. With in-house hosting, not only will you have to construct your own data center, you'll also need to acquire and train the personnel to run it and then manage those personnel and your facility.

Why Now?

A skeptic might respond to Figure 6-3 by saying, "If it's so great, why hasn't cloud hosting been used for years?" Why now?

In fact, cloud-based hosting (or a version of it under a different name) has been around since the 1960s. Long before the creation of the personal computer and networks, time-sharing vendors provided slices of computer time on a use-fee basis. However, the technology of that time, continuing up until the first decade of this century, did not favor the construction and use of enormous data centers, nor did the necessary Internet standards exist.

Companies can save a lot of money by using the cloud, and these savings translate into profit. This profit does not come without ethical concerns, however. The Ethics Guide on pages 204–205 examines these concerns.

Three factors have made cloud-based hosting advantageous today. First, processors, data communication, and data storage are so cheap that they are nearly free. At the scale of a Web farm of hundreds of thousands of processors, providing a virtual machine for an hour costs essentially nothing, as suggested by the 1.5 cent-per-hour price. Because data communication is so cheap, getting the data to and from that processor is also nearly free.

Second, virtualization technology enables the near instantaneous creation of a new virtual machine. The customer provides (or creates in the cloud) a disk image of the data and programs of the machine it wants to provision. Virtualization software takes it from there. Finally, as stated, Internet-based standards enable cloud-hosting vendors to provide processing capabilities in flexible yet standardized ways.

When Does the Cloud Not Make Sense?

Cloud-based hosting makes sense for most organizations. The only organizations for which it may not make sense are those that are required by law or by industry standard practice to have physical control over their data. Such organizations might be forced to create and maintain their own hosting infrastructure. A financial institution, for example, might be legally required to maintain physical control over its data. Even in this circumstance, however, it is possible to gain many of the benefits of cloud computing using private clouds and virtual private clouds, possibilities we consider in Q6.

Ethics Guide

CLOUDY PROFIT?

Alliance Partners (a fictitious name) is a data broker. You'll learn about data brokers in Chapter 9, but for now, just know that such companies acquire and buy consumer and other data from retailers, other data brokers, governmental agencies, and public sources and aggregate it into data profiles of individuals. Alliance specializes in acquiring and analyzing market, buyer, and seller data for real estate agents. Alliance sells an individual profile to qualified real estate agents for $100 to $1,500, depending on the amount of data and type of analysis requested.

Alliance is owned by three partners who started the business in 1999. They endured tough times during the dot-com collapse at the turn of the century, but crawled out of that hole and were doing well until they encountered severe revenue shortfalls in the 2008 real estate collapse. In late 2008, in order to reduce operational costs to survive the downturn, Alliance transitioned its data storage and processing from its own Web farm to the cloud. The elastic flexibility of the cloud enables Alliance to improve the speed and quality of its data services at a fraction of prior costs. Furthermore, using the cloud enabled it to reduce the in-house hardware support staff by 65 percent.

The partners meet twice a year to review their financial performance, evaluate strategy, and plan for both the next six months and the longer term. In 2008, in the midst of their revenue shortfalls, they met in a small suite in the local Hamilton Inn, ate stale doughnuts, and drank watery orange juice. This year, they've rented a facility in the British Virgin Islands in the Caribbean. The following conversation occurred between two of the partners at the onset of this year's meeting:

"Bart, what are we doing here?" Shelly, the partner in charge of sales and marketing, is challenging Bart Johnson, Alliance's managing partner.

"What do you mean, Shelly? Don't you like it here?"

"I *love* it here. So does my husband. But I also know we're paying $15,000 a night to rent this island!" Shelly rubs sunscreen on her hands as she talks.

"Well, we don't have the entire island." Bart sounds defensive.

"No, I guess not," she says. "They have to let some of the staff stay here. We're the only paying customers…the only nonlocals.

"But," Shelly continues, "that's not my point. My point is, how can we afford this level of expense? We'll pay nearly $200,000 for this meeting alone. Where are we meeting next? Some five-star resort on the moon?"

"Look, Shelly, as you're about to hear, our gross margin last year was 74 percent. We're a money machine! We're

swimming in profit! We can't spend money fast enough. One of the items on our agenda is whether we want to issue a $1 million, a $3 million, or a $5 million partners' distribution."

"No!" Shelly sounds stunned.

"Yup. Using the cloud, we've reduced our operational expense from 62 percent of our revenue to 9 percent. I'm plowing money back into R&D as fast as I can, but

there's only so much that Jacob and his crew can absorb. Meanwhile, order the lobster and wait until you taste tonight's wines."

"That's disgusting."

"OK," Bart says. "Don't drink the wine. You want your distribution?"

"No; I mean yes, but this is crazy. It can't last."

"Probably not. But it's what we've got right now."

DISCUSSION QUESTIONS

When answering the following questions, assume that Alliance has done nothing illegal, including paying all federal, state, and local taxes on a timely basis.

1. From the perspective of Kant's categorical imperative (pages 20–21), are Alliance's partners' meeting expenses and intended partner distribution unethical?

2. From the utilitarian perspective (pages 54–55), are Alliance's partners' meeting expenses and intended partner distribution unethical?

3. Milton Friedman, world-renowned economist at the University of Chicago, stated that corporate executives have a responsibility to make as much money as possible as long as they don't violate rules embodied in law and in ethical custom.[2]

   a. Do you agree with his statement? Why or why not?

   b. Friedman defined *ethical custom* narrowly to mean no *fraud* or *deception*. Using his definition, has Alliance acted ethically?

   c. Define, using your own words, *ethical custom*.

   d. Using your definition of *ethical custom,* has Alliance acted ethically?

4. Do you find any of the following excessive? Explain your answers:

   a. Spending nearly $200,000 on a five-day partners' meeting for three partners and their spouses?

   b. Earning a 74 percent gross profit?

   c. Paying a semiannual distribution of $1 million, $3 million, or $5 million? If so, which level is excessive to you?

5. Describe the primary driver in Alliance's current profitability.

6. From the data presented, what else might Alliance have done with its excess profits?

7. Do you think profitable companies, especially very profitable companies, have an ethical obligation to:

   a. Contribute to charity?

   b. Lower prices when it is possible to do so and continue to earn a reasonable profit?

   c. Contribute to environmental causes?

   d. When possible, pay large bonuses to all employees, not just senior management?

8. To most students, someone who earns $500,000 a year in income is rich. To someone who makes $500,000 a year, partners who pay themselves $1 million to $5 million every 6 months are rich. To someone making $2 million to $10 million a year, billionaires are rich. What do you think classifies someone as rich?

9. Do you think rich people have an ethical obligation to:

   a. Contribute to charity?

   b. Contribute to environmental causes?

   c. Forego governmental benefits to which they are entitled, e.g., not take Social Security that they don't need?

[2]Milton Friedman, "The Social Responsibility of Business Is to Increase Its Profits," *The New York Times Magazine,* September 13, 1970.

What Network Technology Supports the Cloud?

Many people use wireless networks at work or school assuming their information is protected. The Security Guide on pages 230–231 looks at why your information may not be as safe as you think.

A computer **network** is a collection of computers that communicate with one another over transmission lines or wirelessly. As shown in Figure 6-4, the three basic types of networks are local area networks, wide area networks, and internets.

A **local area network (LAN)** connects computers that reside in a single geographic location on the premises of the company that operates the LAN. The number of connected computers can range from two to several hundred. The distinguishing characteristic of a LAN is *a single location*. A **wide area network (WAN)** connects computers at different geographic locations. The computers in two separated company sites must be connected using a WAN. To illustrate, the computers for a college of business located on a single campus can be connected via a LAN. The computers for a college of business located on multiple campuses must be connected via a WAN.

The single- versus multiple-site distinction is important. With a LAN, an organization can place communications lines wherever it wants because all lines reside on its premises. The same is not true for a WAN. A company with offices in Chicago and Atlanta cannot run a wire down the freeway to connect computers in the two cities. Instead, the company contracts with a communications vendor that is licensed by the government and that already has lines or has the authority to run new lines between the two cities.

An **internet** is a network of networks. Internets connect LANs, WANs, and other internets. The most famous internet is "**the Internet**" (with an uppercase letter *I*), the collection of networks that you use when you send email or access a Web site. In addition to the Internet, private networks of networks, called *internets*, also exist. A private internet that is used exclusively within an organization is sometimes called an **intranet**.

The networks that comprise an internet use a large variety of communication methods and conventions, and data must flow seamlessly across them. To provide seamless flow, an elaborate scheme called a *layered protocol* is used. The details of protocols are beyond the scope of this text. Just understand that a **protocol** is a set of rules that programs on two communicating devices follow. There are many different protocols; some are used for LANs, some are used for WANs, some are used for internets and the Internet, and some are used for all of these. We will identify several common protocols in this chapter.

What Are the Components of a LAN?

Employers can and do monitor employees' online activities. What is the purpose of this monitoring and how is it done? Is there anything employees can do about it? The Guide on pages 232–233 considers these questions.

As stated, a LAN is a group of computers connected together on a single site. Usually the computers are located within a half-mile or so of each other. The key distinction, however, is that all of the computers are located on property controlled by the organization that operates the LAN. This means that the organization can run cables wherever needed to connect the computers.

Figure 6-5 shows a LAN that is typical of those in a **small office or a home office (SOHO)**. Typically, such LANs have fewer than a dozen or so computers and printers. Many businesses, of course, operate LANs that are much larger than this one. The principles are the same for a larger LAN, but the additional complexity is beyond the scope of this text.

The computers and printers in Figure 6-5 communicate via a mixture of wired and wireless connections. Computers 1 and 3 and printer 1 use wired connections; computers 2, 4, and 5 as

Type	Characteristic
Local area network (LAN)	Computers connected at a single physical site
Wide area network (WAN)	Computers connected between two or more separated sites
The Internet and internets	Networks of networks

Figure 6-4
Basic Network Types

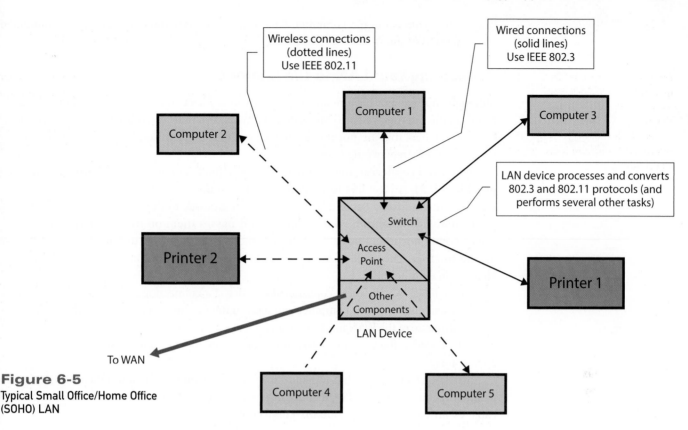

Figure 6-5
Typical Small Office/Home Office (SOHO) LAN

well as printer 2 use wireless connections. The devices and protocols used differ for wired and wireless connectivity.

The Institute for Electrical and Electronics Engineers (IEEE, pronounced "I triple E") sponsors committees that create and publish protocol and other standards. The committee that addresses LAN standards is called the *IEEE 802 Committee*. Thus, IEEE LAN protocols always start with the numbers 802.

The **IEEE 802.3 protocol** is used for wired LAN connections. This protocol standard, also called **Ethernet**, specifies hardware characteristics, such as which wire carries which signals. It also describes how messages are to be packaged and processed for wired transmission over the LAN.

Most personal computers today support what is called **10/100/1000 Ethernet**. These products conform to the 802.3 specification and allow for transmission at a rate of 10, 100, or 1,000 Mbps (megabits per second). Switches detect the speed that a given device can handle and communicate with it at that speed. If you check computer listings at Dell, Lenovo, and other manufacturers, you will see PCs advertised as having 10/100/1000 Ethernet. Today, speeds of up to 1 Gbps are possible on wired LANs.

By the way, the abbreviations used for communications speeds differ from those used for computer memory. For communications equipment, *k* stands for 1,000, not 1,024 as it does for memory. Similarly, *M* stands for 1,000,000, not 1,024 × 1,024; *G* stands for 1,000,000,000, not 1,024 × 1,024 × 1,024. Thus, 100 Mbps is 100,000,000 bits per second. Also, communications speeds are expressed in *bits*, whereas memory sizes are expressed in *bytes*.

Wireless LAN connections use the **IEEE 802.11 protocol**. Several versions of 802.11 exist, and as of 2013, the most current one is IEEE 802.11ac. The differences among these versions are beyond the scope of this discussion. Just note that the current standard, 802.11ac, allows speeds of up to 1.3 Gps, though few users have an Internet connection fast enough to take full advantage of that speed.

Bluetooth is another common wireless protocol. It is designed for transmitting data over short distances, replacing cables. Some devices, such as wireless mice and keyboards, use

Bluetooth to connect to the computer. Smartphones use Bluetooth to connect to automobile entertainment systems.

Connecting Your LAN to the Internet

Although you may not have realized it, when you connect your SOHO LAN, phone, iPad, or Kindle to the Internet, you are connecting to a WAN. You must do so because you are connecting to computers that are not physically located on your premises. You cannot start running wires down the street to plug in somewhere.

When you connect to the Internet, you are actually connecting to an **Internet service provider (ISP)**. An ISP has three important functions. First, it provides you with a legitimate Internet address. Second, it serves as your gateway to the Internet. The ISP receives the communications from your computer and passes them on to the Internet, and it receives communications from the Internet and passes them on to you. Finally, ISPs pay for the Internet. They collect money from their customers and pay access fees and other charges on your behalf.

Figure 6-6 shows the three common alternatives for connecting to the Internet. Notice that we are discussing how your computer connects to the Internet via a WAN; we are not discussing the structure of the WAN itself. WAN architectures and their protocols are beyond the scope of this text. Search the Web for "leased lines" or "PSDN" if you want to learn more about WAN architectures.

SOHO LANs (such as that in Figure 6-5) and individual home and office computers are commonly connected to an ISP in one of three ways: a special telephone line called a DSL line, a cable TV line, or a wireless-phone-like connection.

Digital Subscriber Line (DSL)

A **digital subscriber line (DSL)** operates on the same lines as voice telephones, but it operates so it does not interfere with voice telephone service. Because DSL signals do not interfere with telephone signals, DSL data transmission and telephone conversations can

Figure 6-6
Summary of LAN Networks

Type	Topology	Transmission Line	Transmission Speed	Equipment Used	Protocol Commonly Used	Remarks
Local area network	Local area network	UTP or optical fiber	Common: 10/100/1000 Mbps Possible: 1 Gbps	Switch NIC UTP or optical	IEEE 802.3 (Ethernet)	Switches connect devices, multiple switches on all but small LANs.
	Local area network with wireless	UTP or optical for nonwireless connections	Up to 600 Mbps	Wireless access point Wireless NIC	IEEE 802.11n, (802.11ac not yet common)	Access point transforms wired LAN (802.3) to wireless LAN (802.11).
Connections to the Internet	DSL modem to ISP	DSL telephone	Personal: Upstream to 1 Mbps, downstream to 40 Mbps (max 10 likely in most areas)	DSL modem DSL-capable telephone line	DSL	Can have computer and phone use simultaneously. Always connected.
	Cable modem to ISP	Cable TV lines to optical cable	Upstream to 1 Mbps Downstream 300 Kbps to 10 Mbps	Cable modem Cable TV cable	Cable	Capacity is shared with other sites; performance varies depending on others' use.
	WAN wireless	Wireless connection to WAN	500 Kbps to 1.7 Mbps	Wireless WAN modem	One of several wireless standards	Sophisticated protocols enables several devices to use the same wireless frequency.

occur simultaneously. A device at the telephone company separates the phone signals from the computer signals and sends the latter signal to the ISP. Digital subscriber lines use their own protocols for data transmission.

Cable Line

A cable line is the second type of WAN connection. **Cable lines** provide high-speed data transmission using cable television lines. The cable company installs a fast, high-capacity optical fiber cable to a distribution center in each neighborhood that it serves. At the distribution center, the optical fiber cable connects to regular cable-television cables that run to subscribers' homes or businesses. Cable signals do not interfere with TV signals.

Because up to 500 user sites can share these facilities, performance varies depending on how many other users are sending and receiving data. At the maximum, users can download data up to 50 Mbps and can upload data at 512 Kbps. Typically, performance is much lower than this. In most cases, the download speed of cable lines and DSL lines is about the same. Cable lines use their own protocols.

WAN Wireless Connection

A third way that you can connect your computer, mobile device, or other communicating device is via a **WAN wireless** connection. Amazon.com's Kindle, for example, uses a Sprint wireless network to provide wireless data connections. The iPhone uses a LAN-based wireless network if one is available and a WAN wireless network if not. The LAN-based network is preferred because performance is considerably higher. As of 2013, WAN wireless provides average performance of 500 Kbps, with peaks of up to 1.7 Mbps, as opposed to the typical 50 Mbps for LAN wireless.

How Does the Cloud Work?

Jason and Kelly are flabbergasted at the low cost of the cloud. They doubt that it's real. They would be less cautious if they understood how the cloud operates. This section will give you the basic understanding that they lack and enable you to be an effective consumer of cloud services.

The cloud resides in the Internet. So, in order to learn how the cloud works, you need a basic understanding of how the Internet works. With that background, you will learn how it is possible for a cloud vendor to provide dramatic elasticity to support the workload shown in Figure 6-1.

The technology that underlies the Internet and the additional technology that enables the cloud to work are complicated. Here we will stay at a high level and help you learn overarching concepts and basic definitions. We begin with a simple example.

An Internet Example

Figure 6-7 illustrates one use of the Internet. Suppose that you are sitting in snowbound Minneapolis, and you want to communicate with a hotel in sunny, tropical northern New Zealand. Maybe you are making a reservation using the hotel's Web site, or maybe you are sending an email to a reservations clerk inquiring about facilities or services.

To begin, note that this example is an internet because it is a network of networks. It consists of two LANs (yours and the hotel's) and four WANs. (In truth, the real Internet consists of tens of thousands of WANs and LANs, but to conserve paper, we don't show all of them.) A **hop** is the movement from one network to another. As drawn, in Figure 6-7, the shortest path from

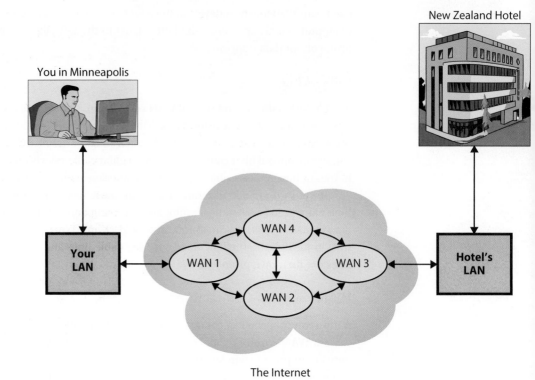

New Zealand Hotel

You in Minneapolis

Figure 6-7
Using the Internet for a Hotel
Reservation

The Internet

you to the hotel's LAN consists of four hops. This term is frequently used by cloud vendors when they discuss provisioning servers to minimize the number of hops.

Internet Addressing

As you can imagine, just like surface mail, every location on the Internet needs an address. For reasons that are beyond this discussion, an Internet address is called an **IP address**, which is a number that identifies a particular device. **Public IP addresses** identify a particular device on the public Internet. Because public IP addresses must be unique, worldwide, their assignment is controlled by a public agency known as **ICANN (Internet Corporation for Assigned Names and Numbers)**.

Private IP addresses identify a particular device on a private network, usually on a LAN. Their assignment is controlled within the LAN, usually by the LAN device shown in Figure 6-5. When you sign on to a LAN at a coffee shop, for example, the LAN device lends you a private IP address to use while you are connected to the LAN. When you leave the LAN, it reuses that address.

Use of Private IP Addresses

When your computer accesses a public site, say *www.pearsonhighered.com*, from within a LAN at, say, a coffee shop, your traffic uses your private IP address until it gets to the LAN device. At that point, the LAN device substitutes your private IP address with its public IP address and sends your traffic out onto the public Internet.

This private/public IP address scheme has two major benefits. First, public IP addresses are conserved. All of the computers on the LAN use only one public IP address. Second, by using private IP addresses, you need not register a public IP address for your computer with ICANN-approved agencies. Furthermore, if you had a public IP address for your computer, every time you moved it, say from home to school, the Internet would have to update its addressing mechanisms to route traffic to your new location. Such updating would be a massive burden.

Public IP Addresses and Domain Names

IP addresses have two formats. The most common form, called **IPv4**, has a four-decimal dotted notation such as 165.193.123.253; the second, called **IPv6**, has a longer format and will not concern us here. In your browser, if you enter *http://165.193.140.14*, your browser will connect with the device on the public Internet that has been assigned to this address.

Nobody wants to type IP addresses such as *http://165.193.140.14* to find a particular site. Instead, we want to enter names such as *www.pandora.com* or *www.woot.com* or *www.pearsonhighered.com*. To facilitate that desire, ICANN administers a system for assigning names to IP addresses. First, a **domain name** is a worldwide-unique name that is affiliated with a public IP address. When an organization or individual wants to register a domain name, it goes to a company that applies to an ICANN-approved agency to do so. Go Daddy (*www.godaddy.com*) is an example of such a company (Figure 6-8).

Go Daddy, or a similar agency, will first determine if the desired name is unique worldwide. If so, then it will apply to register that name to the applicant. Once the registration is completed, the applicant can affiliate a public IP address with the domain name. From that point onward, traffic for the new domain name will be routed to the affiliated IP address.

Note two important points: First, several (or many) domain names can point to the same IP address. Second, the affiliation of domain names with IP addresses is dynamic. The owner of the domain name can change the affiliated IP addresses at its discretion.

Before we leave addressing, you need to know one more term. A **URL (Uniform Resource Locator)** is an address on the Internet. Commonly, it consists of a protocol (such as http:// or ftp://) followed by a domain name or public IP address. A URL is actually quite a bit more complicated than this description, but that detailed knowledge is beyond the scope of this text, so we'll hurry along. The preferred pronunciation of URL is to say the letters U, R, L.

Processing on a Web Server

At this point, you know basic networking terms and have a high-level view of how the Internet works. To understand the value of the cloud, and how it works and how your organization can use it, you need to know a bit about the processing that occurs on a Web server. For this discussion, we will use the example of a Web storefront, which is a server on the Web from which you can buy products.

Figure 6-8
Go Daddy Screenshot
Source: © 2013 Go Daddy Operating Company, LLC. All rights reserved.

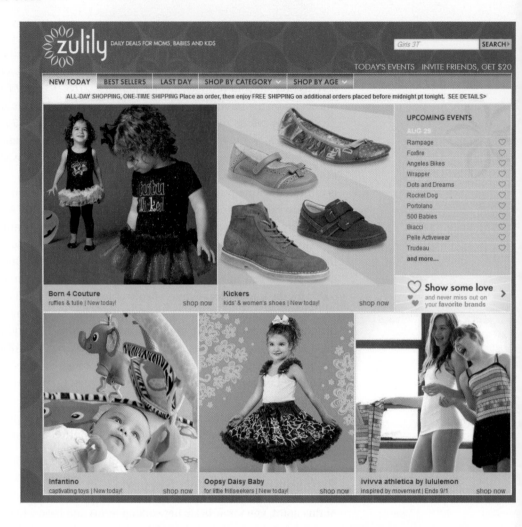

Figure 6-9
Sample of Commerce Server
Pages; Product Offer Pages

Source: Reprinted by permission of
Zulily. *www.zulily.com*

Suppose you want to buy an item from Zulily, a private buyer's site that sells clothing. To do so, you go to *www.zulily.com* and navigate to the product(s) that you want to buy (see Figure 6-9). When you find something you want, you add it to your shopping cart and keep shopping. At some point, you check out by supplying credit card data. But what happens when your order data arrives at the server?

Three-tier Architecture

Almost all Web applications use the **three-tier architecture**, which is a design of user computers and servers that consists of three categories, or tiers, as shown in Figure 6-10. The **user tier** consists of computers, phones, and other mobile devices that have browsers that request and process Web pages. The **server tier** consists of computers that run Web servers and process application programs. The **database tier** consists of computers that run a DBMS that processes requests to retrieve and store data. Figure 6-10 shows only one computer at the database tier. Some sites have multicomputer database tiers as well.

When you enter *www.zulily.com* in your browser, the browser sends a request that travels over the Internet to a computer in the server tier at the Zulily site. In response to your request, a server-tier computer sends back a **Web page**, which is a document that is coded in, usually, html (and, as discussed in Chapter 4, probably includes CSS, JavaScript, and other data).

Web servers are programs that run on a server-tier computer and manage traffic by sending and receiving Web pages to and from clients. A **commerce server** is an application program that runs on a server-tier computer. Typical commerce server functions are to obtain product data from a database, manage the items in a shopping cart, and coordinate the checkout

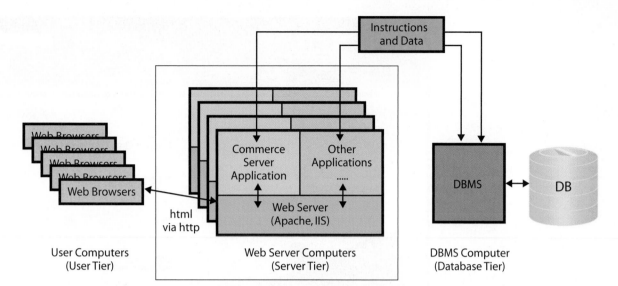

Figure 6-10
Three-tier Architecture

process. When a request comes to the server, the Web server examines it and sends it to the proper program for processing. Thus, the Web server passes e-commerce traffic to the commerce server. It passes requests for other applications to those applications. In Figure 6-10, the server-tier computers are running a Web server program, a commerce server application, and other applications having an unspecified purpose.

Watch the Three Tiers in Action!

Suppose the user of the Web page in Figure 6-9 clicks on shoes and then selects a particular shoe, say the Darkish Gray Dorine Mary Jane shoe. When the user clicks on that shoe, the commerce server requests that shoe's data from the DBMS, which reads it from the database and then returns the data (including pictures) to the commerce server. That server then formats the Web page with the data and sends the html version of that page to the user's computer. The result is the page shown in Figure 6-11.

Service-Oriented Architecture (SOA)

The cloud would be impossible without a design philosophy called the **service-oriented architecture (SOA)**. According to this philosophy, all interactions among computing devices are defined as services in a formal, standardized way. This philosophy enables all the pieces of the cloud to fit together, as you will see. However, understanding SOA (pronounced SO-ah) in depth requires you to learn more computer science than you need as a business professional. So, the best way for you to understand SOA is via a business analogy.

A SOA Analogy

Figure 6-12 shows a hypothetical arrangement of departments at AllRoad Parts. The Sales Department receives order requests and follows a process to have them approved for shipping. On request, the Credit Department verifies customer credit as needed to approve orders, and the Inventory Department verifies the availability of the inventory needed to fulfill an order.

In an informal, non-SOA-type organization, one salesperson would contact someone they know in Credit and ask something like, "Can you approve an allocation of $10,000 of credit to the ABC Bicycle Company?" In response the credit person might say, "Sure," and the salesperson might note the name of the person who approved the amount. Some days he or she might remember to record the date; other days, not so. Another salesperson might do something else, say contact a different person in Credit and ask something like, "I need $5,000 in credit for Order

Figure 6-11
Product Page

Source: Reprinted by permission of Zulily. *www.zulily.com*

12345," and that other person in Credit might say, "I don't know, send the order over, and if I can, I'll write 'Approved' on it." Other irregular, but similar, interactions could occur between the Sales and the Inventory departments.

Such operations are definitely *not* service-oriented. People are asking for credit verification in different ways and receiving responses in different ways. The process for approving an order varies from salesperson to salesperson, and possibly from day to day with the same salesperson. The records of approvals are inconsistent. Such an organization will have varying levels of process quality and inconsistent results, and should the company decide to open a facility in another city, these operations cannot be readily duplicated, nor should they be.

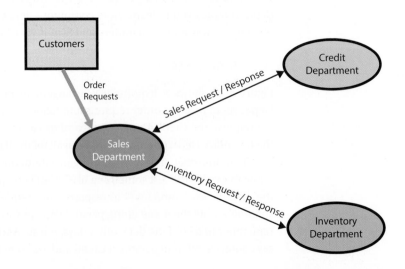

Figure 6-12
Approval Request Interactions
Among Three Departments

Using SOA principles, each department would formally define the services that it provides. Examples are:

For the Credit Department:

- CheckCustomerCredit
- ApproveCustomerCredit

For the Inventory Department

- VerifyInventoryAmount
- AllocateInventory
- ReleaseAllocatedInventory

Further, for each service, each department would formally state the data that it expects to receive with the request and the data that it promises to return in response. Every interaction is done exactly the same way. There is no personal contact between certain people in the departments; no salesperson need know who works in Credit or Inventory. Instead, requests are emailed to a generic email address in Credit or Inventory, and those departments decide who will process the request and how it will be processed. No department has or need have any knowledge of who works in another department nor how the department accomplishes its work. Each department is free to change personnel task assignments and to change the way it performs its services, and no other department needs to know that a change occurred. In SOA terms, we would say the work of the department is **encapsulated** in the department.

With this organization, if AllRoad wants to add another Inventory Department in another city, it can do so and no salesperson need change the way he or she sets up, submits, or receives responses to requests. Sales continues to send a VerifyInventoryAmount service request, formatted in the standard way, to the same email address.

With multiple sites, the Inventory function would change the way it implements service requests to first identify which of the several Inventory Departments should process the request. Sales would not know, nor need to know, this happened. AllRoad could dynamically create 1,000 Inventory Departments and the Sales Department need not change anything it does. Later, it could reduce those 1,000 Inventory Departments to three, and, again, sales need not make any change.

SOA for Three-tier Architecture

From this discussion, you can intuit how SOA is used to enable cloud processing. The description and advantages and disadvantages of this analogy for SOA are the same for the cloud. Consider Figure 6-13, which shows the three-tier architecture with SOA drawn in. In this case, the commerce server application formally defines services that browsers can request, the data they must provide with the request, and the data that each will receive in response to the request. Sample services are:

- ObtainPartData
- ObtainPartImages
- ObtainPartQuantityOnHand
- OrderPart

And so forth. Again, each service also documents the data it expects and the data it will return.

Now, JavaScript (or another language code) is written to invoke these services correctly. That JavaScript is included as part of the Web pages that the server sends to the browsers, and when users employ the browsers to purchase, the JavaScript behind the Web page invokes the services in the correct way.

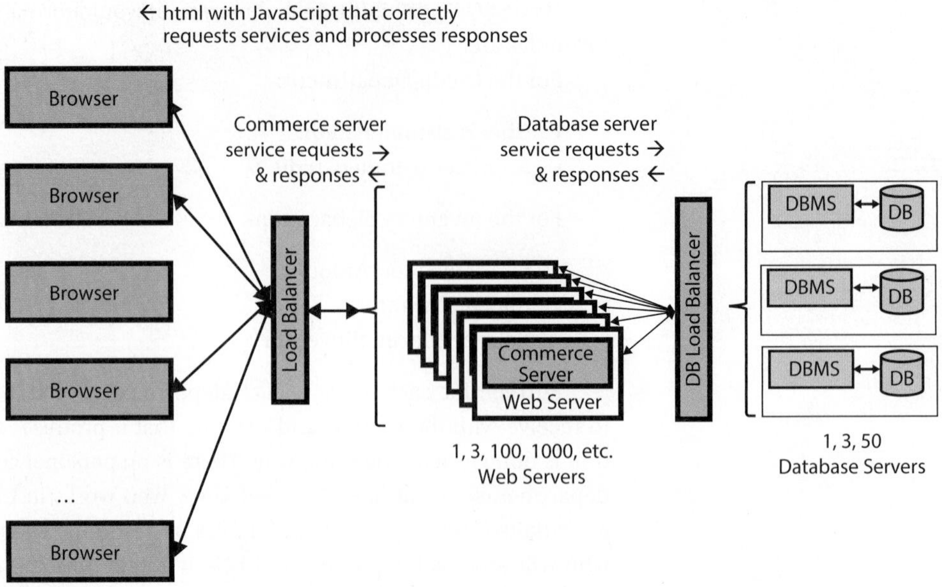

← html with JavaScript that correctly
requests services and processes responses

Figure 6-13
SOA Principles Applied to
Three-Tier Architecture

The server tier can consist of three servers at 3 AM, 3,000 servers at 11 AM, 6,000 servers at 6 PM, and 100 servers at 10 PM. Furthermore, those servers can move around the world; at one time of day, they can be all located in the United States, and at another time of day, they can all be located in Europe, and so on. Nothing, absolutely nothing, in the browsers need change as these servers are adjusted.

To take advantage of the multiple Web servers, a load-balancing program receives requests and sends them to an available server. The load-balancing program keeps data about the speed and health of all its assigned Web servers and allocates work to maximize throughput.

In addition, on the back end, SOA services are defined between the Web server and the database server. Accordingly, the database server need do nothing as the number and location of Web servers is adjusted. And that's a two-way street. Nothing in the Web servers need be changed if the number and location of database servers is adjusted. However, load balancing for database servers is considerably more complicated. See Case Study 5 (pages 194–195) to understand many of the factors involved.

Do not infer from this discussion that SOA services and the cloud are only used for three-tier processing. Such services and the cloud are used for multitudes of applications across the Internet. This three-tier application is just an example.

From this discussion, you can understand how cloud elasticity is possible. However, for many organizations to use the cloud and to be able to mix and match Web services, they need to agree on standard ways of formatting and processing service requests and data. That leads us to cloud standards and protocols. Again, we discuss these at a very high level.

Protocols Supporting Web Services

A protocol is a set of rules and data structures for organizing communication. Because the cloud's Web services use the Internet, the protocols that run the Internet also support cloud processing. We will start with them.

TCP/IP Protocol Architecture

The basic plumbing of the Internet is governed by protocols that are defined according to an arrangement called the **TCP/IP protocol architecture**. This architecture has five layers; one or more protocols are defined at each layer. Data communications and software vendors write computer programs that implement the rules of a particular protocol. (For protocols at the bottom layer, the physical layer, they build hardware devices that implement the protocol.)

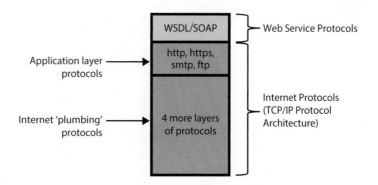

Figure 6-14
Protocols that Support
Web Services

Internet Protocols: http, https, smtp, and ftp

The only Internet protocols that you as a business professional are likely to encounter are those at the top, or the application layer of the TCP/IP architecture, shown in Figure 6-14. **Hypertext Transfer Protocol (http)** is the protocol used between browsers and Web servers. When you use a browser such as Internet Explorer, Safari, or Chrome, you are using a program that implements the http protocol. At the other end, at the New Zealand Hotel for example, there is a server that also processes http. Even though your browser and the server at the hotel have never "met" before, they can communicate with one another because they both follow the rules of http. Similarly, in Figure 6-13, the browsers send and receive service requests to and from the commerce server using http.

As you will learn in Chapter 12, there is a secure version of http called **https**. Whenever you see *https* in your browser's address bar, you have a secure transmission and you can safely send sensitive data like credit card numbers. When you are on the Internet, if you do not see *https*, then you should assume that all of your communication is open and could be published on the front page of your campus newspaper tomorrow morning. Hence, when you are using http, email, text messaging, chat, videoconferencing, or anything other than https, know that whatever you are typing or saying could be known by anyone else.

Two additional TCP/IP application-layer protocols are common. **smtp**, or **Simple Mail Transfer Protocol**, is used for email transmissions (along with other protocols). **ftp**, or **File Transfer Protocol**, is used to move files over the Internet. Google Grid and Microsoft SkyDrive use ftp behind the scenes to transmit files to and from their cloud servers to your computer.

WSDL, SOAP, XML, and JSON

To wrap up the discussion, we will briefly consider four standards that are used extensively for Web services and the cloud. Those standards and their purpose are as follows:

WSDL (Web Services Description Language)	A standard for describing the services, inputs and outputs, and other data supported by a Web service. Documents coded according to this standard are machine readable and can be used by developer tools for creating programs to access the service.
SOAP (no longer an acronym)	A protocol for requesting Web services and for sending responses to Web service requests.
XML (eXtensible Markup Language)	A markup language used for transmitting documents. Contains much metadata that can be used to validate the format and completeness of the document, but includes considerable overhead (see Figure 6-15a).
JSON (JavaScript Object Notation)	A markup language used for transmitting documents. Contains little metadata and is preferred for transmitting volumes of data between servers and browsers. While the notation is the format of JavaScript objects, JSON documents can be processed by any language (see Figure 6-15b).

```
<person>
    <firstName>Kelly</firstName>
    <lastName>Summers</lastName>
    <dob>12/28/1985</dob>
    <address>
        <streetAddress>309 Elm Avenue</streetAddress>
        <city>San Diego</city>
        <state>CA</state>
        <postalCode>98225</postalCode>
    </address>
    <phoneNumbers>
        <phoneNumber type="home">685 555-1234</phoneNumber>
        <phoneNumber type="cell">685 555-5678</phoneNumber>
    </phoneNumbers>
</person>
```

Figure 6-15a
Example XML Document

```
{
    "firstName": "Kelly",
    "lastName": "Summers",
    "dob": "12/28/1985",
    "address": {
        "streetAddress": "309 Elm Avenue",
        "city": "San Diego",
        "state": "CA",
        "postalCode": "98225"
    },
    "phoneNumber": [
        {
            "type": "home",
            "number": "685 555-1234"
        },
        {
            "type": "cell",
            "number": "685 555-5678"
        }
    ]
}
```

Figure 6-15b
Example JSON Document

Service authors (computer programmers) create WSDL documents to describe the services they provide and the inputs and outputs required. These WSDL documents are seldom read by humans. Instead, developer tools like Microsoft Visual Studio read the WSDL to configure the programming environment for programmers who write code to access that service.

As shown in Figure 6-14, SOAP, which is not an acronym though it looks like one, is a protocol that sits on top of http and the lower-level Internet protocols. *Sits on top of* means that it uses http to send and receive SOAP messages. (SOAP can also use smtp.) Programs that use Web services issue SOAP messages to request services; the Web service uses SOAP messages to return responses to service requests.

Finally, XML and JSON are ways of marking up documents so that both the service requestor and the service provider know what data they're processing. Figure 6-15 shows a simple example of both. As you can see, XML documents contain as much metadata as they do application data. These metadata are used to ensure that the document is complete and properly formatted. XML is used when relatively few messages are being transmitted and when ensuring a complete and correct document is crucial. Both WSDLs and SOAP messages are coded in XML.

As its name indicates, JSON uses the notation for JavaScript objects to format data. It has much less metadata and is preferred for the transmission of voluminous application data. Web servers use JSON as their primary way of sending application data to browsers.

With this technical background, you should no longer be skeptical that the benefits of the cloud are real. They are. However, this fact does not mean that every organization uses the cloud well. In the remainder of this chapter, we will describe generic ways that organizations can use the cloud, discuss how AllRoad Parts in particular can use the cloud, and finally, discuss an exceedingly important topic: cloud security.

 ## How Do Organizations Use the Cloud?

Organizations can use the cloud in several different ways. The first, and by far most popular, is to obtain cloud services from cloud service vendors.

Cloud Services from Cloud Vendors

In general, cloud-based service offerings can be organized into the three categories shown in Figure 6-16. An organization that provides **software as a service (SaaS)** provides not only hardware infrastructure, but also an operating system and application programs as well. For example, Salesforce.com provides hardware and programs for customer and sales tracking as a service. Similarly, Google provides Google Grid and Microsoft provides SkyDrive as a service. With Office 365, Exchange, Lync, and SharePoint applications are provided as a service "in the cloud."

You probably have heard of or have used Apple's iCloud, the cloud service that Apple uses to sync all of its customers' iOS devices. As of 2013, Apple provides 10 free applications in the iCloud. Calendar is a good example. When a customer enters an appointment in her iPhone, Apple automatically pushes that appointment into the calendars on all of that customer's iOS devices. Further, customers can share calendars with others that will be synchronized as well. Mail, pictures, applications, and other resources are also synched via iCloud.

An organization can move to SaaS simply by signing up and learning how to use it. In Apple's case, there's nothing to learn. To quote the late Steve Jobs, "It just works."

The second category of cloud hosting is **platform as a service (PaaS)**, whereby vendors provide hosted computers, an operating system, and possibly a DBMS. Microsoft Windows Azure, for example, provides servers installed with Windows Server. Customers of Windows Azure then add their own applications on top of the hosted platform. Microsoft SQL Azure provides a host with Windows Server and SQL Server. Oracle On Demand provides a hosted server with Oracle Database. Again, for PaaS, organizations add their own applications to the host. Amazon EC2 provides servers with Windows Server or Linux installed.

The most basic cloud offering is **infrastructure as a service (IaaS)**, which is the cloud hosting of a bare server computer or data storage. Rackspace provides hardware for customers

Cloud Category	Examples
SaaS (software as a service)	Salesforce.com iCloud Office 365
PaaS (platform as a service)	Microsoft Azure Oracle On Demand
IaaS (infrastructure as a service)	Amazon EC2 (Elastic Cloud 2) Amazon S3 (Simple Storage Service)

Figure 6-16
Three Fundamental Cloud Types

to load whatever operating system they want, and Amazon.com licenses S3 (Simple Storage Service), which provides unlimited, reliable data storage in the cloud.

Content Delivery Networks

A second major use of the cloud is to deliver content from servers placed around the world. A **content delivery network (CDN)** is a system of hardware and software that stores user data in many different geographical locations and makes those data available on demand. A CDN provides a specialized type of PaaS but is usually considered in its own category, as it is here.

Consider CDN applications: A news organization could use a CDN to store copies of its news articles. The CDN vendor replicates articles on servers, possibly worldwide, so as to speed response time. When a news reader accesses an article, the request is transmitted to a routing server that determines which CDN server is likely to deliver the article to the user the fastest. Because traffic changes rapidly, especially for popular sites, such calculations are made in real time. A request for content at one moment in time could be served by a computer in, say, San Diego, and a few moments later, that same request from that same user might be served by a computer in Salt Lake City. AllRoad would likely use a CDN to store Web site data during its Academy Awards ad, as discussed in Q1.

In addition to news articles, CDNs are often used to store and deliver content that seldom changes. For example, the company banner on an organization's Web page might be stored on many CDN servers. Various pieces of the Web page could be obtained from different servers on the CDN; all such decisions are made in real time to provide the fastest content delivery possible.

Figure 6-17 summarizes CDN benefits. The first two are self-explanatory. Reliability is increased because data are stored on many servers. If one server fails, any of a potentially large number of other servers can deliver the content. You will learn about denial-of-service (DOS) attacks in Chapter 12. For now, just understand that such security threats send so much data to a given server that the server's performance for legitimate traffic becomes unacceptable. By having multiple servers, CDNs help to protect against such attacks.

In some cases, CDNs reduce access costs for mobile users (those who do have a limited data account). By delivering the data faster, site connection charges can be reduced. Finally, many (but not all) CDN services are offered on a flexible, pay-as-you-go basis. Customers need not contract for fixed services and payments; they pay only for what they use, when they use it. Figure 6-18 shows an example of how CDN servers might be distributed. A number of vendors offer CDN.

Use Web Services Internally

The third way that organizations can use cloud technology is to build internal information systems using Web services. Strictly speaking, this is not using the cloud because it does not provide elasticity nor the advantages of pooled resources. It does advantageously use cloud standards, however, so we include it here.

Benefits of Content Delivery Networks

- Decreased, even guaranteed, load time
- Reduced load on origin server
- Increased reliability
- Protection form DOS attacks
- Reduce delivery costs for mobile users
- Pay-as-you-go

Figure 6-17
Benefits of Content Delivery Networks

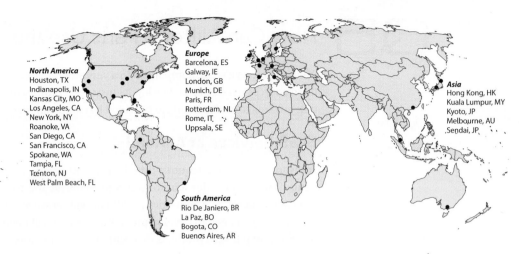

Figure 6-18
Servers Used in a Typical CDN Service

Figure 6-19 shows a Web services inventory application at AllRoad Parts. In this example, AllRoad is running its own servers on its own infrastructure. To do so, AllRoad sets up a private internet within the company, an internet that is generally not reachable from outside the company (you'll learn more about how this is done in Q6). AllRoad writes the applications for processing inventory using Web services standards; applications publish a WSDL; the Web services are accessed by other applications within the company using SOAP; and data are delivered using JSON. Application users access the inventory Web services using JavaScript that is sent down to the users' browsers.

Users of the inventory Web services include Sales, Shipping, Customer Service, Accounting, and other departments. Internal applications can use the inventory Web services like building blocks. They can use the services that they need—and no more. Because the Web services are encapsulated, the inventory system can be altered without affecting other applications. In this way, systems development is more flexible, and it will be faster and hence less costly.

As stated, however, this is not a cloud. In this example, AllRoad has a fixed number of servers; no attempt is made to make them elastic. Also, the servers are dedicated to inventory. During idle periods, they are not dynamically reused for other purposes. Some organizations remove this limit by creating a private cloud, as discussed in Q6.

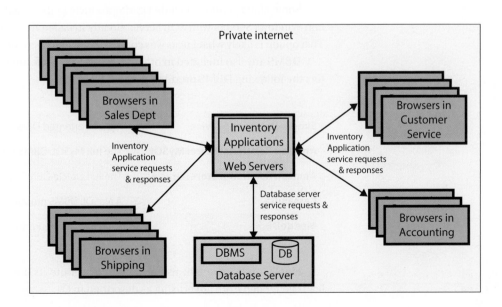

Figure 6-19
Web Services Principles Applied to Inventory Applications

How Can AllRoad Parts Use the Cloud?

AllRoad Parts is a small company with a very small IT Department. As such, it is unlikely to have the resources necessary to develop its own server infrastructure. Instead, it is far more likely to take advantage of cloud service provided by cloud vendors.

SaaS Services at AllRoad

Software as a service requires little investment in the hardware and software system components. The SaaS vendor administers and manages the cloud servers and makes the software available, usually as a thin-client. AllRoad will, however, need to transfer existing and create new data, it will need to develop procedures, and it will need to train users.

Some of the SaaS products that AllRoad could use are:

- Google Mail
- Google Drive
- Office 365
- Salesforce.com
- Microsoft CRM OnLine
- And many others…

You already know what the first four SaaS offerings are. Salesforce.com and Microsoft's CRM OnLine are customer relationship management systems, which you will learn about in Chapter 7.

PaaS Services at AllRoad

With PaaS, AllRoad leases hardware and operating systems in the cloud from the cloud vendor. For example, it can lease EC2 (Elastic Cloud 2, a PaaS product offered by Amazon.com), and Amazon.com will preinstall either Linux or Windows Server on the cloud hardware. Given that basic capability, AllRoad would then install its own software. For example, it could install its own, in-house developed applications, or it could install an e-commerce server product licensed from a software vendor. It could also license a DBMS, say SQL Server from Microsoft, and place it on an EC2 Windows Server instance. In the case of software licensed from others, AllRoad must purchase licenses that permit replication because Amazon.com will replicate it when it increases servers.

Some cloud vendors include DBMS products in their PaaS services. Thus, AllRoad could obtain Windows Servers with SQL Server already installed from the Microsoft Azure cloud offerings. That option is likely what Lucas was considering when he mentioned the $0.25 per hour per server.

DBMS are also included in other vendors' cloud offerings. As of June 2013, Amazon.com offers the following DBMS products with EC2:

Simple Database Service	A table-oriented DBMS with limited features
Amazon Relational Store: MySQL	The full MySQL DBMS product
Amazon Relational Store: Oracle	The full Oracle DBMS product
Cassandra	A NoSQL DBMS product (see Case Study 5, pages 194–195)
MongoDB	A NoSQL DBMS product that stores objects in JSON format

Finally, AllRoad might use a CDN to distribute its content worldwide and to respond to leads generated from advertising as described in Q1.

IaaS Services at AllRoad

As stated, IaaS provides basic hardware in the cloud. Some companies acquire servers this way and then load operating systems onto them. Doing so requires considerable technical expertise and management, and hence a small company like AllRoad is unlikely to do so.

AllRoad might, however, obtain data storage services in the cloud. Amazon.com, for example, offers data storage with its S3 product. Using it, organizations can place data in the cloud and even have that data be made elastically available. Again, however, a small organization like AllRoad would more likely use SaaS and PaaS because of the added value they provide.

How Can Organizations Use Cloud Services Securely?

The Internet and cloud services based on Internet infrastructure provide powerful processing and storage services at a fraction of the cost of private data centers. However, the Internet is a jungle of threats to data and computing infrastructure, as discussed in Chapter 12. How can organizations realize the benefits of cloud technology without succumbing to those threats?

The answer involves a combination of technologies that we will address, at a very high level, in this question. As you read, realize that no security story is ever over; threat creators constantly strive to find ways around security safeguards and occasionally they succeed. Thus, you can expect that cloud security will evolve beyond that described here throughout your career. We begin with a discussion of VPNs, a technology used to provide secure communication over the Internet.

Virtual Private Network (VPN)

A **virtual private network (VPN)** uses the Internet to create the appearance of private, secure connections. In the IT world, the term *virtual* means something that appears to exist but in fact does not. Here a VPN uses the public Internet to create the appearance of a private connection on a secure network.

A Typical VPN

Figure 6-20 shows one way to create a VPN to connect a remote computer, perhaps an employee working at a hotel in Miami, to a LAN at a Chicago site. The remote user is the VPN client. That client first establishes a public connection to the Internet. The connection can be obtained by accessing a local ISP, as shown in Figure 6-20, or, in some cases, the hotel itself provides a direct Internet connection.

In either case, once the Internet connection is made, VPN software on the remote user's computer establishes a connection with the VPN server in Chicago. The VPN client and VPN

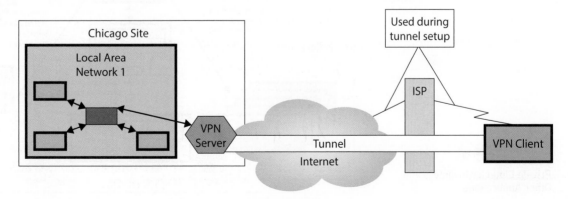

Figure 6-20
Remote Access Using
VPN: Actual Connections

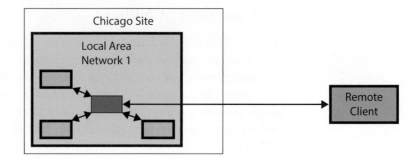

Figure 6-21
Remote Access Using VPN:
Apparent Connection

server then have a secure connection. That connection, called a **tunnel**, is a virtual, private pathway over a public or shared network from the VPN client to the VPN server. Figure 6-21 illustrates the connection as it appears to the remote user.

To secure VPN communications over the public Internet, the VPN client software *encrypts*, or codes (see Chapter 12, page 467), messages so their contents are protected from snooping. Then the VPN client appends the Internet address of the VPN server to the message and sends that package over the Internet to the VPN server. When the VPN server receives the message, it strips its address off the front of the message, *decrypts* the coded message, and sends the plain text message to the original address inside the LAN. In this way, secure private messages are delivered over the public Internet.

Using a Private Cloud

A **private cloud** is a cloud that is owned and operated by an organization for its own benefit. To create a private cloud, the organization creates a private internet and designs applications using Web services standards just as shown in Figure 6-17 (page 467). The organization then creates a farm of servers and manages those servers with elastic load balancing just as the cloud service vendors do. Because of the complexity of managing multiple database servers, most organizations choose not to replicate database servers. Figure 6-22 illustrates this possibility.

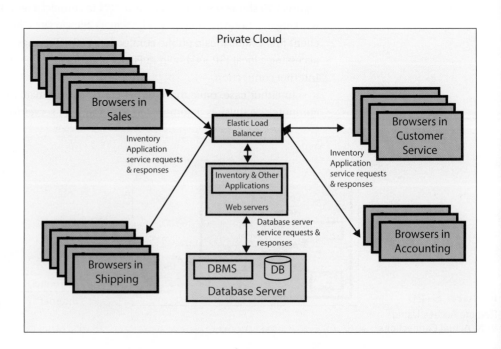

Figure 6-22
Private Cloud for Inventory and
Other Applications

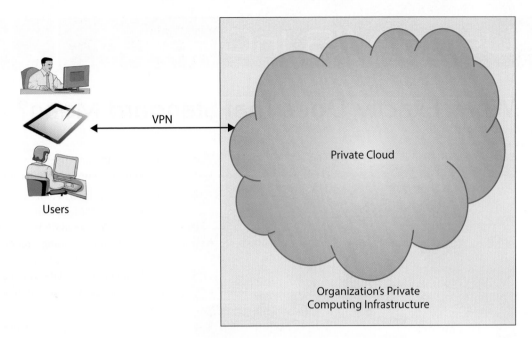

Figure 6-23
Accessing Private Cloud over a
Virtual Private Network

Private clouds provide security within the organizational infrastructure but do not provide secure access from outside that infrastructure. To provide such access, organizations set up a VPN and users employ it to securely access the private cloud as shown in Figure 6-23.

Private clouds provide the advantages of elasticity, but to questionable benefit. What can organizations do with their idle servers? Unlike the cloud vendors, they cannot repurpose them for use by other companies. Possibly a large conglomerate or major international company could balance processing loads across subsidiary business units and across different geographical regions. 3M, for example, might balance processing for its different product groups and on different continents, but it is difficult to imagine that, in doing so, it would save money or time. A small company like AllRoad Parts is very unlikely to develop a private cloud.

Microsoft, Amazon.com, Oracle, IBM, and other major cloud service vendors employ thousands of highly trained, very highly skilled personnel to create, manage, administer, and improve their cloud services. It is unimaginable that any noncloud company, even large ones like 3M, could build and operate a cloud service facility that competes. The only situation in which this might make sense is if the organization is required by law or business custom to maintain physical control over its stored data. Even in that case, however, the organization is unlikely to be required to maintain physical control over all data, so it might keep critically sensitive data on-premises and place the rest of the data and related applications into the facilities of a public cloud vendor. It might also use a virtual private cloud, which we consider next.

Using a Virtual Private Cloud

A **virtual private cloud (VPC)** is a subset of a public cloud that has highly restricted, secure access. An organization can build its own VPC on top of public cloud infrastructure like AWS or that provided by other cloud vendors. The means by which this is done are beyond the scope of this text, but think of it as VPN tunneling on steroids.

Using a VPC, an organization can store its most sensitive data on its own infrastructure and store the less sensitive data on the VPC. In this way, organizations that are required to have physical control over some of their data can place that data on their own servers and locate the

Using MIS InClass 6

What, Exactly, Does That Standard Mean?

Source: Lane Erickson/Fotolia

DATA AUDITOR

Most cloud users have no visibility into where their data are located and how they are managed. Their data might be managed using tight controls in highly secure facilities; on the other hand, they might be managed by teenagers in a trailer located in a flood-zone parking lot in Uzbekistan. Unless you are a very large client with the necessary security clearances, you just don't know.

Cloud vendors are understandably reluctant to reveal the locations of data, and they want (and need) the flexibility to move data where they can provide the best performance to their customers. So, what can users do to protect their data? They can contract with responsible, public companies like Amazon.com, Microsoft, IBM, Oracle, or others and hope. Or they can never use the cloud. But is there something else?

Working with a team as instructed by your professor, take a position on this issue by answering the following questions:

1. Search the Internet for "ISO 27001." Explain the purpose of this standard.

2. Does compliance with ISO 27001 mean that a data center is secure? Does it mean that no security threat against compliant data centers will be successful? What does it mean?

3. Search the Internet for evidence that Microsoft Azure complies with ISO 27001. Summarize your findings.

4. Search the Internet for evidence that Amazon's EC2 complies with ISO 27001. Summarize your findings.

   SAS 70 is an auditing standard that provides guidance for an auditor issuing a report about internal controls implemented by a cloud services provider. However, to assess the adequacy of data center controls, it is necessary to read and analyze the report that was prepared in accordance with SAS 70.

5. Search the Internet for evidence that Microsoft's auditors have issued a report in accordance with SAS 70. Summarize your findings.

6. Search the Internet for evidence that Amazon's auditors have issued a report in accordance with SAS 70. Summarize your findings.

7. Compare and contrast your answers to questions 3/4 and 5/6. Does your comparison cause you to believe that there are significant differences with regard to security and control between Azure and EC2?

8. Many small businesses operate with local servers running in storerooms, broom closets, and the like. Summarize the major risks of this situation. How can using a cloud vendor that scores well according to the standards discussed help such companies?

9. Suppose a publicly traded large organization operates its own Web farm and has certifications indicating that it has complied with ISO 27001 and has issued a statement of controls in accordance with SAS 70 that indicates controls are at least adequate. Is there any reason to believe that the organization's data assets on that Web farm are more or less secure than they would be if stored in Azure or EC2? Explain your answer.

10. Based on your answers to these questions, create a general statement as to the desirability, considering only data security, of storing data on Azure and EC2 as compared to storing it on servers managed in-house.

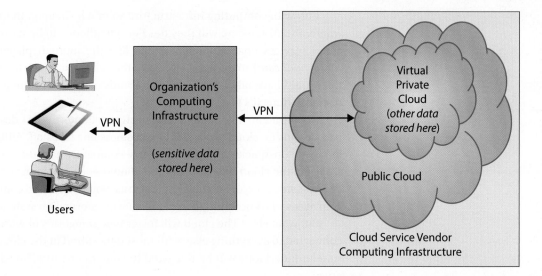

Figure 6-24
Using a Virtual Private Cloud (VPC)

rest of their data on the VPC as shown in Figure 6-24. By doing so, the organization gains the advantages of cloud storage and possibly cloud processing for that portion of its data that it need not physically control.

In some cases, organizations have obtained permission from regulating bodies to store even their very sensitive data on a VPC. For example, Case Study 6 (pages 236–238) discusses FinQloud, a VPC setup and managed by NASDAQ OMX, the owner of the NASDAQ and other financial exchanges.

Q7 2024?

So where does the cloud go in the next 10 years? Absent some unknown factor such as a federal tax on Internet traffic, cloud services will become faster, more secure, easier to use, and cheaper. Fewer and fewer organizations will set up their own computing infrastructure; instead they will benefit from the pooling of servers across organizations and from the economies of scale produced by cloud vendors.

But, looking a bit deeper, the cloud brings both good and bad news. The good news is that organizations can readily obtain elastic resources at very low cost. This trend will benefit everyone from individuals on the iCloud or Google Grid, to small groups using Office 365, to small companies like AllRoad Parts using PaaS, to huge organizations like NASDAQ OMS (Case Study 6) using IaaS.

So what's the bad news? That 500,000-square-foot Apple Web farm in Figure 6-2? Note the size of the parking lot. That tiny lot accommodates the entire operations staff. According to *Computerworld,* that building employs an operations staff of 50 people, which, spread over three shifts, 24/7, means that not many more than eight people will be running that center at any one time. Seems impossible, but is it? Again, look at the size of the parking lot.

And it's not just large companies like Apple. In 2013, every city of almost any size still supports small companies that install and maintain in-house email Exchange and other servers. If SaaS products like Google Grid or Office 365 replace those servers, what happens to those local jobs? They're gone! See Collaboration Exercise 6, page 236, for more on this topic.

But, with computing infrastructure so much cheaper, there have to be new jobs somewhere. By 2024, where will they be? For one, there will be more startups. Cheap and elastic cloud services enable small startups like the football player evaluation company Hudl (*www.hudl.com*) to access CDN and other cloud services for next to nothing, a capability that would have taken years and thousands of dollars in the past. Go to its site to check its response time; it's fast!

Organizations like AllRoad Parts can move into the 3D design sales business by storing part designs on cloud servers. If that business line takes off, AllRoad can elastically expand its infrastructure quickly and cheaply. Large companies gain the same advantages but on a larger scale. So, the cloud lifts all boats and should enable organizations to develop more information systems, cheaply and quickly, and thus (you knew it was coming!) increase the demand for employees who know how to use and manage information systems![3]

But what else? The cloud will foster new categories of work. By 2024, everything will be connected to everything else, with most data stored in the cloud. Mobile systems will be the standard; desktops will be relegated to content creators. So what new opportunities might arise?

Consider **remote action systems**, IS that provide computer-based activity or action at a distance. By enabling action at a distance, remote action systems save time and travel expense and make the skills and abilities of an expert available in places where he or she is not physically located. They also enable experts to scale their expertise. Consider a few examples.

Telediagnosis is a remote action system that healthcare professionals use to diagnose illness for rural or remote areas. **Telesurgery** uses telecommunications to link surgeons to robotic equipment at distant locations. In 2001, Dr. Jacques Marescaux, located in New York City, performed the first trans-Atlantic surgery when he successfully operated on a patient in Strasbourg, France. Such examples, which are still rare, have problems that must be overcome, but will become more common by 2024.[4]

Other uses for remote systems include **telelaw enforcement**, such as the RedFlex system that uses cameras and motion-sensing equipment to issue tickets for red-light and speeding violations. The RedFlex Group, headquartered in South Melbourne, Victoria, Australia, earns 87 percent of its revenue from traffic violations in the United States. It offers a turn-key traffic citation information system that includes all five components.[5]

Many remote systems are designed to provide services in dangerous locations, such as robots that clean nuclear reactors or biologically contaminated sites. Drones and other unoccupied military equipment are examples of remote systems used in war zones. And it's likely that drones will soon be used for private security as well. Look for them when you come back to visit campus in 2024.

But, even with these new opportunities, the news isn't all good. New York's Metropolitan Opera is arguably the finest opera company in the world. To see a live performance, you can drive to Manhattan, park your car, taxi to Lincoln Center, and pay $300 per seat. Or you can watch the same opera, remotely broadcast via Met Live, at a local movie theater, park your car for free, pay $30, and take a seat in the fourth row, where via the magic of digital broadcasting

---

[3]See, for example, *http://online.wsj.com/article/SB10001424127887323744604578470900844821388.html?mod =itp*, accessed May 2013.
[4]Injuries and deaths have increased from telesurgery as the procedures become more popular, spurring the FDA to look at the training programs used by doctors who participate. See *http://www.bloomberg.com/news/2013-03-05/robosurgery-suits-detail-injuries-as-death-reports-rise.html* for more information.
[5]Traffic citation information system is not a commonly accepted term, but providing all five components is essentially IS as a service, or ISaaS.

you can see details like the stitching on the singers' costumes. Details you just can't see from the $300 seats at the Met. And the sound quality is better. Wonderful, but now, who will go to a local opera performance?

Teleaction reduces the value of local mediocrity. The claim "Well, I'm not the best, but at least I'm here" loses value in a teleaction world. In 1990, when former Secretary of Labor Robert Reich wrote *The Work of Nations*,[6] he could sensibly claim that those who provide routine face-to-face services are exempt from the dangers of offshoring. That claim loses validity in the tele-action world.

By 2024, the value of the top-notch performers increases, possibly exponentially. Four million people watch the average Met Live broadcast; agents for the artists who perform at that venue will negotiate a sizable part of that $120 million gate. A famous surgeon or skating coach can reach a bigger market, faster and better, and be much better paid. So, if you can be the world's best at something, do it!

But what about the rest of us? If you're not the world's expert at something, then find a way to be indispensable to someone who is. Own the theaters that broadcast Met Live. Own the skating rink for the remote figure skating coach. Be the vendor of the food at some teleaction event.

Or become essential to the development, use, and management of information systems that support these new opportunities. A business background with IS expertise will serve you very well between now and 2024. The next six chapters discuss many existing and new IS applications. Keep reading!

---

[6]Robert Reich, *Work of Nations: Preparing Ourselves for Twenty-first Century Capitalism* (New York: Vintage Books, 1992), p. 176.

Security Guide

One of the questions in the Security Guide in Chapter 4 (page 147, question 6) has your professor installing spyware on your computer so she can obtain all your instant messages, email, and Web browser traffic. Actually, obtaining that data is quite a bit easier than using spyware.

All your professor, or you, has to do is to install a program called **packet analyzer**, also called a **packet sniffer**. The former term is used when the program is used for appropriate purposes and the latter term is used otherwise. We'll use *packet sniffer* here. Under either name, such programs read, record, and display all of the wireless packets that are in the airwaves around them.

Somewhere in your classroom there is a wireless device (like the LAN device in Figure 6-5) that is receiving and sending wireless packets to and from your computer, connecting you to the Internet, and performing other functions as discussed in this chapter. All of those wireless packets have to be broadcast in the open so they can reach the intended destination (when you send, that's the wireless device; when you receive, that's your computer or mobile device). So, all the packet sniffer does is capture all of the wireless packets floating around the room and format them in an easily accessible manner.

So, anyone in your classroom (and anyone *near* your classroom) can go to *www.wireshark.com* (or a similar site) and download and install a packet sniffer. Learning to use it isn't difficult, and the site provides video and other helpful documentation to speed the learning process. Once someone has done that, he or she can read nearly anything that anyone else in the room is sending or receiving over the LAN wireless network. That *anything* includes instant messages, most email, and any *http://* Web traffic.

Your professor is too professional to use a packet sniffer for such a violation of your privacy, but the guy sitting next to you may not be. It could be he who asks you, "Does Jennifer know you say such terrible things about her?" or "Did you enjoy looking at those models on VictoriasSecret .com in class?" or perhaps, "Why were you searching for the term 'DUI lawyer' in class today?"

What can you do? Well, for one, you can use *https://* instead of *http://*. If you do so, the packet sniffer will be able to tell that you went to a particular site, but it won't obtain data about what you did when you got there. For example, if you use *https://www.google.com*, the sniffer will be able to determine you went to *google.com*, but it won't be able to record what you searched for. However, for anything other than buying, few sites respond to both *http://* and *https://*. You can use

Source: Fotosearch/Getty Images

secure email, but almost no one else will, so that's not much help. Of course, if you never send anything that you wouldn't be proud to have published on the front page of the campus newspaper tomorrow, you won't have a problem with what *you* say. That doesn't help when flaky friends send you sensational material, however. The ultimate protection is not to use your computer or mobile device for any unauthorized purpose while in class.

 DISCUSSION QUESTIONS

1. Explain what packet sniffers do and describe the situation that enables them to succeed.
2. Besides your classroom, what other places do you visit for which packet sniffing might be a problem for you?
3. List five ways that you can protect yourself from packet sniffing intrusion.
4. List the evidence you have that your traffic has never been sniffed. You can answer this question with one word.
5. Is packet sniffing illegal? Is it unethical? Explain your answers.

6. If you use a mobile device, but connect with the cell tower wireless instead of the classroom's LAN, are you protected from packet sniffing? Why or why not?
7. Summarize your conclusions about your future behavior regarding wireless use in class.
8. [Optional for high achievers or sniffers in training] Go to *www.wireshark.com* and watch the introductory video. Explain how their packet sniffer formats wireless packets for easy consumption. List terms used in the video that you learned in this chapter.

Guide

IS IT SPYING OR JUST GOOD MANAGEMENT?

According to a 2003 survey by Bentley College, 92 percent of employers monitor employees' email, telephone, and Internet use.[7] That survey is 10 years old, and it is likely that, if anything, employer monitoring of employee activities has increased. A number of different techniques are used:

- **Key loggers.** As you learned in Chapter 4, a key logger is a program that records all of your keystrokes. Employers can install key loggers without a problem on any corporate computer. If you allow your employer to configure your personal mobile device as part of its BYOD policy, it can install a key logger on it as well.

  Key loggers do just what their name implies; they record *everything* you key: user IDs, passwords, text messages, emails, documents, and so forth. They are agnostic about what they record. If you check your personal banking account on an employer-owned computer, your employer (and its IT personnel) has everything it needs to manage your banking account. If you write a love letter to your spouse, the key logger will record it.

- **Log files.** Computer systems are indefatigable diarists. Your employer-provided computer or mobile device and any employer server that you connect to with a personal device keep extensive logs of your activity. Those logs show, in part, when you start work, when you end work, how long your computer is idle at work, and possibly, if the device has GPS, where your device has been. Logs also show what

files you process and much information about your activities over the employer-managed networks.

- **Packet sniffers.** A packet sniffer is a program that captures network traffic. Most operate on wireless networks, but they are readily installed to work on wired networks as well. The Security Guide on pages 230–231 explores how one might be used in your classroom. Packet sniffers obtain the text of unsecured email (most email), text messages, and Internet sites visited. They also can obtain voice traffic that is processed over the Internet. Any traffic that passes through the organization's networks, whether from your employer-provided device, your personal device, or your personal computer at home (if you're using the corporate network), can be sniffed.

Your employer could have video surveillance cameras, audio recorders, office spies, and numerous other ways of watching you, but let's leave those aside.

---

[7] W. Michael Hoffman, Laura P. Hartman, and Mark Rowe, "You've Got Mail and the Boss Knows," Center for Business Ethics, Bentley College, 2003, p. 1.

As you think about the amount of data that key logging files, log files, and packet sniffing files contain, you may feel secure that out of the millions of messages, your employer is unlikely to find your problematic ones. **Text mining** is the application of statistical techniques on text streams for locating particular words or patterns of particular words and even correlating word counts and patterns with personality profiles. The results can be used to find undesirable employees such as thieves, sexual predators, those engaged in an illicit romance, and any other profiles the employer creates (disgruntled employee?). So hiding in the company data pile is little protection.

Aha, you're thinking. What about the First Amendment? It protects me, no? Alas, no. The First Amendment preserves your free speech regarding laws Congress may enact, and while in some limited sense it does protect federal employees, it doesn't protect anyone else at work.

Well, you think, they can't fire me for just anything, can they? Alas, again, unless you have negotiated an employment contract, you are what the attorneys call *an employee at will.* That means the employer can fire you for any reason whatsoever.[8] The only exceptions are that you cannot be fired because of your race, gender, religion, or disability. You also cannot be fired for performing a public service such as jury duty. But, if you write an email on a computer at work that says your boss's spouse is a jerk, he or she can fire you (the boss, not the spouse).

 DISCUSSION QUESTIONS

1. List the types of data that you think it is appropriate for your employer to gather about you:
   a. On employer-provided devices.
   b. On personal devices used at work or at home on employer-provided networks.
2. As a manager, list the types of data that you would like to obtain on your employees.
3. If there are differences between your answers to questions 1 and 2, explain and justify the differences.
4. Under what circumstances do you think is it appropriate for your employer to install a key logger on your personal mobile device?
5. Suppose someone from your IT department informs you that the company has evidence that one of your married subordinates is conducting an affair with someone not his or her spouse:
   a. What would you do if the affair involves two people who work at your employer?
   b. What would you do if the affair involves someone not employed by your company?
   c. Do you think obtaining such knowledge is appropriate?
6. Given what you have learned regarding electronic surveillance at work, state your own personal guidelines for computer use.
7. Reread the definition of job security in Chapter 1. Using that definition as a foundation, state what you can do, as an employee at will, to avoid being fired for a frivolous reason.

[8]Lewis Maltby, *Can They Do That?* (New York: Penguin Group, 2009), pp. 60–62.

ACTIVE REVIEW

Use this Active Review to verify that you understand the ideas and concepts that answer the chapter's study questions.

Q1 Why is the cloud the future for most organizations?

Define *cloud* and explain the three key terms in your definition. Using Figure 6-3 as a guide, compare and contrast cloud-based and in-house hosting. Explain three factors that make cloud computing possible today. When does it not make sense to use a cloud-based infrastructure?

Q2 What network technology supports the cloud?

Define *computer network*. Explain the differences among LANs, WANs, intranet, internets, and the Internet. Describe protocol and explain the purpose of protocols. Explain the key distinction of a LAN. Describe the purpose of each component in Figure 6-5. Define *IEEE 802.3* and *802.11* and explain how they differ. List three ways of connecting a LAN or computer to the Internet. Explain the nature of each.

Q3 How does the cloud work?

Explain the statement, "The Internet is an internet." Define *IP address* and explain the different ways that public and private IP addresses are used. Describe the purpose of a domain name and explain how such names are associated with public IP addresses. Explain the role for agencies like Go Daddy. Define *URL*.

Define *three-tier architecture* and name and describe the role of each tier. Explain the role of each tier in Figure 6-10 as how the pages in Figures 6-9 and 6-11 are processed. Using the department analogy, define *SOA* and explain why departments are encapsulated. Summarize the advantages of using SOA in the three-tier architecture.

Define *TCP/IP protocol architecture* and explain, in general terms, the purpose of http, https, smtp, and ftp. Define the purpose and role of WSDL, SOAP, XML, and JSON. State a key difference between XML and JSON.

Q4 How do organizations use the cloud?

Define *SaaS, PaaS,* and *IaaS*. Provide an example of each. For each, describe the business situation in which it would be the

most appropriate option. Define *CDN* and explain the purpose and advantages of a CDN. Explain how Web services can be used internally.

Q5 How can AllRoad Parts use the cloud?

First, state why AllRoad is likely to use the cloud. Name and describe SaaS products that AllRoad could use. Explain several ways that AllRoad could use PaaS offerings. Summarize why it is unlikely that AllRoad would use IaaS.

Q6 How can organizations use cloud services securely?

Explain the purpose of a VPN and describe, in broad terms, how a VPN works. Define the term *virtual* and explain how it relates to VPN. Define *private cloud*. Summarize why the benefits of a private cloud are questionable. What kind of organization might benefit from such a cloud? Explain why it is unlikely that even very large organizations can create private clouds that compete with public cloud utilities. Under what circumstance might a private cloud make sense for an organization? Define *VPC* and explain how and why an organization might use one.

Q7 2024?

What is the likely future for the cloud? Summarize the good and bad news that the cloud brings. Explain why the photo in Figure 6-2 is disturbing. Explain the statement, "The cloud lifts all boats." Describe three categories of remote action systems. Explain how remote systems will increase the value of super-experts but diminish local mediocrity. What can other-than-super-experts do? Summarize how this 2024 discussion pertains to your career hopes.

Using Your Knowledge with AllRoad Parts

Name the principal advantage of the cloud to AllRoad Parts. For hosting its Web site, which cloud offering—SaaS, PaaS, or IaaS—makes the most sense, given the size and nature of AllRoad's business? Explain how AllRoad could use that offering. If AllRoad were larger and employed a more sophisticated IT staff, name another alternative that would make sense. Explain why.

KEY TERMS AND CONCEPTS

MyMISLab

Go to **mymislab.com** to complete the problems marked with this icon .

USING YOUR KNOWLEDGE

6-1. Define *cloud* and explain the three key terms in your definition. Using Figure 6-3 as a guide, compare and contrast cloud-based and in-house hosting. In your opinion, explain the three most important factors that make cloud-based hosting preferable to in-house hosting.

6-2. Apple invested more than $1 billion in the North Carolina data center shown in Figure 6-2. For Apple to spend such a sum, it must perceive the iCloud as being a key component of its future. Using the principles listed in Figure 3-12 (page 95), explain all the ways that you believe the iCloud will give Apple a competitive advantage over other mobile device vendors.

6-3. Suppose you manage a group of seven employees in a small business. Each of your employees wants to be connected to the Internet. Consider two alternatives:

Alternative A: Each employee has his or her own device and connects individually to the Internet.

Alternative B: The employees' computers are connected using a LAN, and the network uses a single device to connect to the Internet.

a. Sketch the equipment and lines required for each alternative.

b. Explain the actions you need to take to create each alternative.

c. Which of these two alternatives would you recommend?

6-4. Go to *http://aws.amazon.com* and search for AWS database offerings. Explain the differences among Simple Database Service, Amazon Relational Store, and MongoDB. Which of these three would you recommend for storing AllRoad Parts' 3D printing design files? (By the way, whenever you query the Internet for any AWS product, be sure to include the keyword *AWS* in your search. Otherwise, your search will result in Amazon's lists of books about the item you're searching for.)

6-5. Suppose Lucas wants AllRoad to set up a private internet, and he justifies this request on the basis of better security.

Explain why that is not a good decision, and rebut his claim about security by suggesting that AllRoad use a VPC. Justify your suggestion.

6-6. In five sentences or less, explain how the cloud will affect job prospects for you between now and 2024.

COLLABORATION EXERCISE 6

Using the collaboration IS you built in Chapter 2 (pages 73–74), collaborate with a group of students to answer the following questions.

The cloud is causing monumental changes in the information systems services industry. In every city, you will still see the trucks of local independent software vendors (ISVs) driving to their clients to set up and maintain local area networks, servers, and software. You'll know the trucks by the Microsoft, Oracle, and Cisco logos on their sides. For years, those small, local companies have survived, some very profitably, on their ability to set up and maintain LANs, connect user computers to the Internet, set up servers, sell Microsoft Exchange licenses, and install other software on both servers and user computers.

Once everything is installed, these companies continued to earn revenue by providing maintenance for problems that inevitably developed and support for new versions of software, connecting new user computers, and so forth. Their customers vary, but generally are smaller companies of, say, 3 to 50 employees—companies that are large enough to need email, Internet connections, and possibly some entry-level software applications such as QuickBooks.

1. Using the knowledge of this chapter and the intuition of the members of your team, summarize threats that cloud services present to such ISVs.

2. Suppose your team owns and manages one of these ISVs. You learn that more and more of your clients are choosing SaaS cloud services like Google for email, rather than setting up local email servers.
   a. What, if anything, can you do to prevent the encroachment of SaaS on your business?

   b. Given your answer to question 2a, identify three alternative ways you can respond.
   c. Which of the three responses identified in your answer to question 2b would you choose? Justify your choice.

3. Even if SaaS eliminates the need for email and other local servers, there will still remain viable services that you can provide. Name and describe those services.

4. Suppose instead of attempting to adapt an existing ISV to the threat of cloud services, you and your teammates decide to set up an entirely new business, one that will succeed in the presence of SaaS and other cloud services. Looking at businesses in and around your campus, identify and describe the IS needs those businesses will have in the cloud services world.

5. Describe the IS services that your new business could provide for the business needs you identified in your answer to question 4.

6. Given your answers to questions 1–5, would you rather be an existing ISV attempting to adapt to this new world or an entirely new company? Compare and contrast the advantages and disadvantages of each alternative.

7. Changing technology has, for centuries, eliminated the need for certain products and services and created the need for new products and services. What is new, today, however, is the rapid pace at which new technology is created and adapted. Using cloud services as an example, create a statement of the posture that business professionals should take with regard to technology in order to thrive in this fast-changing environment. Notice the verb in this assignment is *thrive*, and not just *survive*.

CASE STUDY 6

FinQloud Forever…Well, at Least for the Required Interval…

In 1937, the Securities and Exchange Commission (SEC) set out rules that stipulated records retention requirements for securities brokers and dealers. The SEC's concern was (and is) that records of financial transactions not be altered after the fact, that they be retained for a stipulated period of time,

and that indexes be created so that the records can be readily searched.

In 1937, the rules assumed that such records were recorded on paper media. With the rise of information systems storage, in 1997 the SEC updated the rules by stating that such records can be kept electronically, provided that the storage devices are write once, read many times (WORM) devices. This rule was readily accepted by the financial services industry because the first CDs and DVDs were WORM devices.

However, as technology developed, broker-dealers and other financial institutions wanted to store records using regular disk storage and petitioned the SEC for guidance on how they might do that. In May 2003, the SEC interpreted the rule to enable the storage of such records on read-write medium, provided that the storage mechanism included software that would prohibit data alternation:

> A broker-dealer would not violate the requirement in paragraph (f)(2)(ii)(A) of the rule if it used an electronic storage system that prevents the overwriting, erasing or otherwise altering of a record during its required retention period through the use of integrated hardware and software control codes. Rule 17a-4 requires broker-dealers to retain records for specified lengths of time. Therefore, it follows that the non-erasable and non-rewriteable aspect of their storage need not continue beyond that period.
>
> The Commission's interpretation does not include storage systems that only mitigate the risk a record will be overwritten or erased. Such systems—which may use software applications to protect electronic records, such as authentication and approval policies, passwords or other extrinsic security controls—do not maintain the records in a manner that is non-rewriteable and non-erasable. The external measures used by these other systems do not prevent a record from being changed or deleted. For example, they might limit access to records through the use of passwords. Additionally, they might create a "finger print" of the record based on its content. If the record is changed, the fingerprint will indicate that it was altered (but the original record would not be preserved). The ability to overwrite or erase records stored on these systems makes them non-compliant with Rule 17a-4(f).[9]

Notice the SEC specifically excludes extrinsic controls such as authentication, passwords, and manual procedures because it believes it would be possible for such systems to be readily misused to overwrite records. The SEC is striking a fine line in this ruling; if, for example, someone were to tamper with the storage systems' software, it would be possible to overwrite data. Apparently, the SEC assumes such tampering would be illegal and so rare as to not be a concern.

Given this ruling, organizations began to develop systems in compliance. The NASDAQ OMX Group, a multinational corporation that owns and operates the NASDAQ stock market as well as eight European exchanges, began to develop FinQloud, a cloud-based storage system that was developed to be compliant with the SEC's (and other regulating organizations') rulings. NASDAQ OMX operates in 70 different markets, in 50 countries worldwide, and claims that it processes one out of 10 stock transactions worldwide.[10]

Figure 6-25 shows the fundamental structure of the FinQloud system. On the back end, it uses Amazon's S3 product to provide scalable, elastic storage. When financial institutions submit records to FinQloud for storage, FinQloud processes the data in such a way that it cannot be updated, encrypts the data, and transmits the processed, encrypted data to AWS, where it is encrypted yet again and stored on S3 devices. Data is indexed on S3 and can be readily read by authorized users. NASDAQ OMX then claimed that FinQloud's processing and encryption is done is such a way that it meets the SEC requirement.

Of course, NASDAQ OMX knew that this statement would be perceived as self-serving, so it hired two independent companies to verify that claim: Jordan & Jordan, a securities industry consulting company, and Cohasset Associates, a document-processing consulting company. According to *The Wall Street Journal,* both organizations concluded that when properly configured, FinQloud meets the requirements of the SEC's rule (Rule 17a-3) as well as a similar rule set out by the Commodities Futures Trading Commission.[11]

Consequently, NASDAQ OMX customers can use FinQloud and as long as they can demonstrate that they have properly configured it, their auditors will find this system to be in compliance with the SEC rulings.

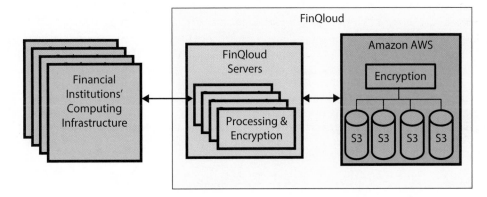

Figure 6-25
Components of the FinQloud System

[9]U.S. Securities and Exchange Commission, "SEC Interpretation: Electronic Storage of Broker-Dealer Records," last modified May 5, 2003, *http://www.sec.gov/rules/interp/34-47806.htm.*
[10]NASDAQ OMX, "NASDAQ OMX FinQloud," accessed May 2013, *http://www.nasdaqomx.com/technology/yourbusiness/finqloud/.*
[11]Greg MacSweeney, "Nasdaq OMX FinQloud R3 Meets SEC/CFTC Regulatory Requirements, Say Consultants," April 15, 2013, *http://www.wallstreetandtech.com/data-management/nasdaq-omx-finqloud-r3-meets-seccftc-reg/240152909.*

QUESTIONS

6-7. In your own words, summarize the dealer-broker record retention requirements.

6-8. Reread the SEC's 2003 interpretation. In your own words, explain the difference between "integrated hardware and software control codes" and software applications that use "authentication and approval policies, passwords, or other extrinsic controls." Give an example of each.

6-9. Clearly, in the view of the SEC, the likelihood of compromise of an integrated system of hardware and software is considerably less than the likelihood of compromise of a system of authentication, passwords, and procedures. Justify this view.

6-10. Do you agree with the view in question 6-9? Why or why not?

6-11. Investigate Jordan & Jordan (*www.jandj.com*) and Cohasset Associates (*www.cohasset.com*). If you were a consultant to a financial institution, to what extent would you rely on the statements of these organizations?

6-12. If you were a consultant to a financial institution, what else might you do to verify that FinQloud complies with the SEC ruling and its 2003 interpretation?

6-13. Explain how the knowledge that you have gained so far in this course helps you to understand the SEC's 2003 interpretation. Summarize how your knowledge would help you if you worked for a financial institution. Cast your answers to this question in a way that you could use in a job interview.

MyMISLab

Go to **mymislab.com** for Auto-graded writing questions as well as the following Assisted-graded writing questions:

6-14. Suppose that you work at AllRoad Parts and Kelly tells you that she doesn't believe that cheap, elastic provisioning of servers is possible. "There has to be a catch somewhere," she says. Write a one-page memo to her explaining how the cloud works. In your memo, include the role of standards for cloud processing.

6-15. Suppose you manage a sales department that uses the SaaS product Salesforce .com. One of your key salespeople refuses to put his data into that system. "I just don't believe that the competition can't steal my data, and I'm not taking that risk." How do you respond to him?

6-16. Mymislab Only – comprehensive writing assignment for this chapter.

Using IS for Competitive Advantage

In the previous six chapters, you gained a foundation of IS fundamentals. In Chapters 7–12, you will apply those fundamentals to learn how organizations use information systems to achieve their strategies. Part 3, Chapters 7–9, focuses on application of IS; Part 4, Chapters 10–12, focuses on management of IS.

Chapters 7–12 are introduced using a cloud-based, mobile application for the healthcare industry. To my knowledge, the system described here does not yet exist. However, it is entirely plausible, may be an excellent entrepreneurial opportunity, and features some of today's most exciting emerging technology in one of today's most important industries. Healthcare is much in the public debate because it is the source of great benefit, high costs, and many organizational and governmental funding problems. Many people see technology as one potential source of health cost reductions.

The figure on the next page shows the major actors involved in this system, which we will call Performance Recording, Integration, Delivery, and Evaluation (PRIDE). Using PRIDE, exercise workout data is collected from devices that conform to the ANT[1] protocol, which is a personal network communications protocol implemented by exercise equipment such as treadmills, stationary bikes, heart monitors, footpads, and the like. Using this protocol, data is transmitted from exercise devices to the Internet, either via a local area network or via a cell phone. That exercise data is then stored in a cloud database.

Once the data is stored in the cloud, individuals, healthcare professionals, health clubs, insurance companies, and employers can query and obtain exercise reports. Doctors can ensure that their patients are exercising neither too little nor too much; health clubs can integrate exercise class data with personal exercise

Hadoop

KM via SM

CRM Online

MapReduce

SOA / Mobile ERP

PRIDE

[1]See http://www.thisisant.com.

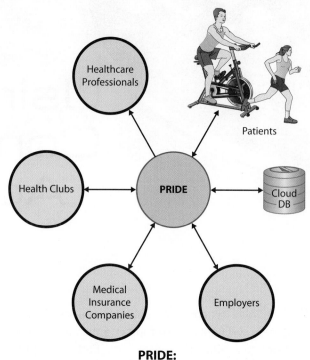

PRIDE:
Performance Recording, Integration, Display, and Evaluation

data; insurance companies can use that data to adjust policy rates for policy holders with healthy lifestyles, and employers can assess the effectiveness of investments they make into improving employee health.

Of course, privacy is crucial. The PRIDE system needs to be developed to give individuals complete control over the distribution of their data. We will consider this requirement in detail in Part 4.

As you are about to learn, a cardiac surgeon, Dr. Romero Flores, is driving his practice to develop a prototype of the healthcare and patient portion of the PRIDE system. He focuses on a prototype to learn whether patients will respond and whether his patients, and those of and his partners, achieve the health benefits they need. Once he has answers to these questions, he will determine how to proceed to an operational system that involves the other organizations shown in the figure above.

Does the PRIDE system generate sufficient value to be worth its cost? Can existing technology support this system? Is the PRIDE system a good investment? If you were a venture capitalist or an angel investor, would you invest in its development? You will have an opportunity to address these and other important questions on your own as you study the next six chapters. As a successful business professional, you will likely make similar assessments about this or other technology, in other industries, numerous times during your career.

Chapter 1 states that "future business professionals need to be able to assess, evaluate, and apply emerging information technology to business." We will use the PRIDE system to illustrate and allow you to practice that key skill.

Romero Flores, a cardiac surgeon, is calling the daughter of a recent cardiac bypass patient:

"Lindsey, this is Dr. Flores."

"Oh, no! Is Mom OK?" Lindsey panics as she hears Dr. Flores's voice.

"Everything's fine. She was just here, and she's doing fine. I have nothing urgent, but I do want to talk."

"Whew." Lindsey sits down on her desk and relaxes her grip on the phone. "What's wrong? Is Mom not taking her meds?"

"Well, in a way. Look, she's doing OK, but not great, and certainly not as well as she could be. She needs to be more active; she needs to start walking and exercising. She's not recovering the way we want her to. We need to get her moving."

"Dr. Flores, I know. But she lives alone. She's never been much of an exerciser. I've talked to her about it, and I will again, but I'm not sure it will do much good. I'd go over there every day, but I'm busy at work, I've got young kids that need me and..." Lindsey's voice trails off as she tries to imagine finding time to walk with her mom.

"I've got an idea that might help." Dr. Flores sounds optimistic.

"What's that?"

"We're starting a new program in our practice. Your mom would be one of the first. Does she have a treadmill at home?"

"Yes. Ted and I bought her one in February."

"Good. I know she has a cell phone, so the only other things she'll need are a heart rate monitor and an exercise watch to gather the data."

"How much do they cost?"

"I've got equipment she can borrow. We can try it. If this works like I hope, you can buy it...around $100. You think we can do this?"

"Maybe...though I'm not completely sure what you're proposing."

"OK. Here's the idea: Your mom wears a heart monitor and puts on the special watch. She gets on the treadmill and does

the exercises that I prescribe. Signals about her heart rate and her exercise activities go over the Internet to a database that we access here. Every morning I get a report about the exercise your mother's getting so I can see how she's doing. If she'll give permission, we can set it up so you get the report, too."

"Wow! That's interesting."

"We think so, too. That's why we're investing in this system. It is a trial, though; we're not sure how well it will work."

"It may not make her exercise, but at least we'll know sooner that she isn't."

"Right. And there might be some features we can implement that will help her motivation as well."

"So what do we do?"

"Make an appointment here with your mom. We'll explain everything and set up the equipment. You can try it at home, and if you need help, we'll send one of our staff members out to get everything working."

"I'll do it." Lindsey wonders how she'll talk her mom into this as she agrees with Dr. Flores.

"One other thing—we can evaluate her heart rate data and adjust her exercises if necessary. But we may need your help to ensure she understands that she needs to change her routine."

"You mean you can't program her treadmill from your office?"

"No. At least, not yet!"

"Every morning I get a report about the exercise your mother's getting so I can see how she's doing."

STUDY QUESTIONS

Q1 What are the basic types of processes?

Q2 How can information systems improve process quality?

Q3 How do information systems eliminate the problems of information silos?

Q4 How do CRM, ERP, and EAI support enterprise processes?

Q5 What are the elements of an ERP system?

Q6 What are the challenges of implementing and upgrading enterprise information systems?

Q7 How do inter-enterprise IS solve the problems of enterprise silos?

Q8 2024?

CHAPTER PREVIEW

This chapter explores processes and their supporting information systems within levels of an organization. We will extend the business process discussion from Chapter 3 to investigate three types of processes and the scope of information systems that they use. We will also investigate the concept of process quality and explain how information systems can be used to increase it. Then we will discuss how the use of information systems at one level of organization leads to information silos, explain the problems of such silos, and then show how those problems can be solved by information systems at the next level of organization. In particular, we'll discuss how enterprise systems such as CRM, ERP, and EAI (you'll learn the meaning of those terms) solve problems caused by workgroup information silos. ERP systems play a particularly important role, and we'll discuss their purpose and components and the major ERP vendors. Then we'll survey the major challenges that occur when implementing enterprise systems. We'll wrap up the chapter by showing how inter-enterprise IS can solve the problems of enterprise-level silos and finally, in 2024, discuss the implications of mobility and the cloud on future enterprise and inter-enterprise IS.

Q1 What Are the Basic Types of Processes?

As you learned in Chapter 3, a business process is a network of activities that generate value by transforming inputs into outputs. Activities are subparts of processes that receive inputs and produce outputs. Activities can be performed by humans only, by humans augmented by computer systems, and by computer systems only.

Figure 7-1 shows a simplified view of a three-activity process for approving customer orders. Each of these activities is, itself, a subprocess of this overall process. You can see that each step—check inventory, check credit, and approve special terms—receives inputs and transforms them into outputs. You will learn how to better diagram such processes in Chapter 10; for now, just view Figure 7-1 as showing the gist of a typical business process.

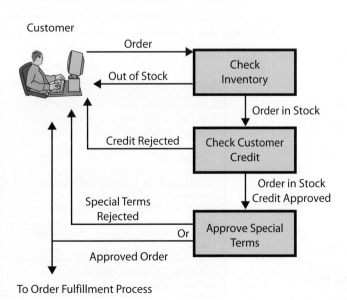

Figure 7-1
Business Process with Three Activities

How Do Structured Processes Differ from Dynamic Processes?

Businesses have dozens, hundreds, even thousands of different processes. Some processes are stable, almost fixed sequences of activities and data flows. For example, the process of a sales-clerk accepting a return at Nordstrom, or other quality retail stores, is fixed. If the customer has a receipt, take these steps...if the customer has no receipt, take these other steps. That process needs to be standardized so that customers are treated consistently and correctly, so that returned goods are accounted for appropriately, and so that sales commissions are reduced in a way that is fair to the sales staff.

Other processes are less structured, less rigid, and often creative. For example, how does Nordstrom's management decide what women's clothes to carry next spring? They can look at past sales, consider current economic conditions, and make assessments about women's acceptance of new styles at recent fashion shows, but the process for combining all those factors into orders of specific garments in specific quantities and colors is not nearly as structured as that for accepting returns.

In this text, we divide processes into two broad categories. **Structured processes** are formally defined, standardized processes that involve day-to-day operations: accepting a return, placing an order, purchasing raw materials, and so forth. They have the characteristics summarized in the left-hand column of Figure 7-2.

Dynamic processes are flexible, informal, and adaptive processes that normally involve strategic and less structured managerial decisions and activities. Deciding whether to open a new store location and how best to solve the problem of excessive product returns are examples, as is using Twitter to generate buzz about next season's product line. Dynamic processes usually require human judgment. The right-hand column of Figure 7-2 shows characteristics of dynamic processes.

We will discuss structured processes and information systems that support them in this chapter. We have already discussed one dynamic process, collaboration, in Chapter 2, and we will discuss another, social media, in Chapter 8. Some aspects of business intelligence, in Chapter 9, are also dynamic processes.

For the balance of this chapter, we will use the term *process* to mean *structured process*.

How Do Processes Vary by Organizational Scope?

Processes are used at three levels of organizational scope: workgroup, enterprise, and inter-enterprise. In general, the wider the scope of the process, the more challenging the process is to manage. For example, processes that support a single workgroup function, say accounts payable, are simpler and easier to manage than those that support a network of independent organizations, such as a supply chain. Consider processes at each of these three organizational scopes.

Structured	Dynamic
Support operational and structured managerial decisions and activities	Support strategic and less structured managerial decision and activities
Standardized	Less specific, fluid
Usually formally defined and documented	Usually informal
Exceptions rare and not (well) tolerated	Exceptions frequent and expected
Process structure changes slowly and with organizational agony	Adaptive processes that change structure rapidly and readily
Example: Customer returns, order entry, purchasing, payroll, etc.	**Example:** Collaboration, social networking, ill-defined, ambiguous situations

Figure 7-2
Structured Versus Dynamic Processes

Workgroup Processes

A **workgroup process** exists to enable workgroups to fulfill the charter, purpose, and goals of a particular group or department. A physicians' partnership, such as that of Dr. Flores, is a workgroup that follows processes to manage patient records, issue and update prescriptions, provide standardized postsurgery care, and so forth.

Figure 7-3 lists common workgroup processes. Notice that each of these processes is largely contained within a given department. These processes may receive inputs from other departments, and they may produce outputs that are used by other departments, but all, or at least the bulk of, the processes' activities lay within a single department.

A **workgroup information system** exists to support one or more processes within the workgroup. For example, an Operations department could implement an IS to support all three of the operations processes shown in Figure 7-3. Or an Accounting department might implement two or three different IS to support the accounting processes shown. Sometimes, workgroup information systems are called **functional information systems**. For example, an operations management system is a functional information system, as are a general ledger system and a cost accounting system. The program component of a functional information system is called a **functional application**.

General characteristics of workgroup information systems are summarized in the top row of Figure 7-4. Typical workgroup information systems support 10 to 100 users. Because the procedures for using them must be understood by all members of the group, those procedures are often formalized in documentation. Users generally receive formal training in the use of those procedures as well.

When problems occur, they almost always can be solved within the group. If accounts payable duplicates the record for a particular supplier, the accounts payable group can make the fix. If the Web storefront has the wrong number of items in the inventory database, that count can be fixed within the storefront group.

Workgroup	Workgroup Example Processes
Sales and marketing	• Lead generation • Lead tracking • Customer management • Sales forecasting • Product and brand management
Operations	• Order entry • Order management • Finished goods inventory management
Manufacturing	• Inventory (raw materials, goods-in-process) • Planning • Scheduling • Operations
Customer service	• Order tracking • Account tracking • Customer support
Human resources	• Recruiting • Compensation • Assessment • HR planning
Accounting	• General ledger • Financial reporting • Cost accounting • Accounts receivable • Accounts payable • Cash management • Budgeting • Treasury management

Figure 7-3
Common Workgroup Processes

Scope	Example	Characteristics
Workgroup	Doctor's Office/ Medical Practice	Support one or more workgroup processes. 10–100 users; procedures often formalized; problem solutions within group; workgroups can duplicate data; somewhat difficult to change
Enterprise	Hospital	Support one or more enterprise processes. 100–1,000s users; procedures formalized; problem solutions affect enterprise; eliminate workgroup data duplication; difficult to change
Inter-enterprise	PRIDE System	Support one or more inter-enterprise processes. 1,000s users; systems procedures formalized; problem solutions affect multiple organizations; can resolve problems of duplicated enterprise data; very difficult to change

Figure 7-4
Characteristics of Information Systems

(Notice, by the way, that the consequences of a problem are not isolated to the group. Because the workgroup information system exists to provide a service to the rest of the organization, its problems have consequences throughout the organization. The fix to the problem can usually be obtained within the group, however.)

Two or more departments within an organization can duplicate data, and such duplication can be very problematic to the organization, as we discuss in Q3. Finally, because workgroup information systems involve multiple users, changing them can be problematic. But, again, when problems do occur, they can be resolved within the workgroup.

Enterprise Processes

The Ethics Guide on pages 256–257 demonstrates how one person's actions can affect an entire company.

Enterprise processes span an organization and support activities in multiple departments. At a hospital, the process for discharging a patient supports activities in housekeeping, the pharmacy, the kitchen, nurses' stations, and other hospital departments.

Enterprise information systems support one or more enterprise processes. As shown in the second row of Figure 7-4, they typically have hundreds to thousands of users. Procedures are formalized and extensively documented; users always undergo formal procedure training. Sometimes enterprise systems include categories of procedures, and users are defined according to levels of expertise with the system as well as by level of authority.

The solutions to problems in an enterprise system involve more than one workgroup or department. As you will learn in this chapter, a major advantage of enterprise systems is that data duplication within the enterprise is either eliminated altogether or, if it is allowed to exist, changes to duplicated data are carefully managed to maintain consistency.

Because enterprise systems span many departments and involve potentially thousands of users, they are difficult to change. Changes must be carefully planned and cautiously implemented and users given considerable training. Sometimes users are given incentives and other inducements to motivate them to change.

CRM, ERP, and EAI are three enterprise information systems that we will define and discuss in Q4.

Inter-enterprise Processes

Inter-enterprise processes span two or more independent organizations. Considering the PRIDE system, the process for prescribing, tracking, and reporting patient exercise data spans the prescribing doctor, the patient, health clubs, insurance companies, and employers. Each of these organizations has activities to fulfill, all of which are governed by privacy settings maintained by patients.

Inter-enterprise information systems support one or more inter-enterprise processes. Such systems typically involve thousands of users, and solutions to problems require cooperation among different, usually independently owned, organizations. Problems are resolved by meeting, by contract, and sometimes by litigation.

Data are often duplicated among organizations; such duplication is either eliminated (as will be done with PRIDE) or carefully managed. Because of their wide span, complexity, and use by multiple companies, such systems can be exceedingly difficult to change. Supply chain management (discussed in the International Dimension, pages 489–505) is the classic example of an inter-enterprise information system. We will study inter-enterprise PRIDE examples throughout the remaining chapters of this text.

 # How Can Information Systems Improve Process Quality?

Processes are the fabric of organizations; they are the means by which people organize their activities to achieve the organization's goals. As such, process quality is an important, possibly the most important, determinant of organizational success.[2]

The two dimensions of process quality are efficiency and effectiveness. **Process efficiency** is a measure of the ratio of process outputs to inputs. If an alternative to the process in Figure 7-1 can produce the same order approvals/rejections (output) for less cost or produce more approvals/rejections for the same cost, it is more efficient.

Process effectiveness is a measure of how well a process achieves organizational strategy. If an organization differentiates itself on quality customer service, and if the process in Figure 7-1 requires 5 days to respond to an order request, then that process is ineffective. AllRoad Parts, which wants to differentiate itself based on the size of its inventory items, is investigating processes for helping customers use 3D printing to manufacture their own parts. The new processes are effective to the extent they help AllRoad expand its parts availability.

How Can Processes Be Improved?

Organizations can improve the quality (efficiency and/or effectiveness) of a process in one of three ways:

- Change the process structure.
- Change the process resources.
- Change both process structure and resources.

Change the Process Structure

In some cases, process quality can be changed just by reorganizing the process. The order approval process in Figure 7-1 might be made more efficient if customer credit was done first and inventory was checked second. This change might be more efficient because it would save the cost of checking inventory for customers whose credit will be denied. However, that change would also mean that the organization would pay for a credit check on customers for which it did not have appropriate inventory. We will investigate such changes further in Chapter 10. For now, just note that process structure has a strong bearing on process efficiency.

---

[2]The subject of this chapter is structured processes, and we will discuss process quality in terms of them. Note, however, that all of the concepts in this question pertain equally well to dynamic processes.

Changing process structure can also increase process effectiveness. If an organization chooses a cost-leader strategy, then that strategy might mean that no special terms should ever be approved. If the process in Figure 7-1 results in the authorization of orders with special terms, then eliminating the third activity will make it more effective (most likely it will save on operational costs as well).

Change Process Resources

Business process activities are accomplished by humans and information systems. One way to improve process quality is to change the allocation of those resources. For example, if the process in Figure 7-1 is not effective because it takes too long, one way to make it more effective is to identify the source of delays and then to add more resources. If delays are caused by the check customer credit activity, one way to increase process effectiveness is to add more people to that activity. Adding people should decrease delays, but it will also add cost, so the organization needs to find the appropriate balance between effectiveness and efficiency.

Another way to shorten the credit check process would be to use an information system to perform the customer credit checks. Depending on the development and operational costs of the new system, that change might also be less costly and therefore more efficient.

Change Both Process Structure and Process Resources

Of course, it is possible to improve process quality by changing both the process's structure and resources. In fact, unless a structure change is only a simple reordering of tasks, changing the structure of a process almost always involves a change in resources as well.

How Can Information Systems Improve Process Quality?

Information systems can be used to improve process quality by:

- Performing an activity.
- Augmenting a human who is performing an activity.
- Controlling data quality and process flow.

Performing an Activity

Information systems can perform the entirety of a process activity. In Figure 7-1, for example, the check credit activity could be entirely automated. When you purchase from Amazon.com or another major online retailer, information systems check your credit while your transaction is being processed. AllRoad Parts can sell its new 3D printing design products by automating the process of delivering purchased designs. Such a change will reduce operations and shipping costs and likely improve process efficiency.

Augmenting a Human Performing an Activity

A second way that information systems can improve process quality is by augmenting the actions of a human who is performing that activity. Consider the process of managing patient appointments. To schedule an appointment, patients call the doctor's office and talk with a receptionist who uses an appointment information system. That information system augments the appointment creation activity.

Controlling Data Quality Process Flow

A third way that information systems can improve process quality is by controlling data quality and process flow.

One of the major benefits of information systems is to control data quality. The IS can not only ensure that correct data values are being input, it can also ensure that data are complete before continuing process activities. The cheapest way to correct for data errors is at the source, and it avoids the problems that develop when process activities are begun with incomplete data.

Information systems also have a role in controlling process flow. Consider the order approval process in Figure 7-1. If this process is controlled manually, then someone, say a salesperson, will obtain the order data from the customer and take whatever actions are needed to push that order through the three steps in the order process. If the salesperson gets busy or is distracted or away from work for a few days, or if there are unexpected delays in one of the activities, it is possible for an order to be lost or the approval unnecessarily delayed.

If, however, an information system is controlling the order approval process, then it can ensure that steps are performed in accordance with an established schedule. The information system can also be relied upon to make correct process-routing decisions for processes that are more complicated than that in Figure 7-1. SharePoint workflows, discussed in the context of collaboration in Chapter 2, can be used to automate structured processes.

Q3 How Do Information Systems Eliminate the Problems of Information Silos?

An **information silo** is the condition that exists when data are isolated in separated information systems. For example, consider the six workgroups and their information systems in Figure 7-3. Reflect on these information systems for a moment and you'll realize that each one processes customer, sales, product, and other data, but each uses that data for its own purposes and will likely store slightly different data. Sales, for example, will store contact data for customers' purchasing agents, while Accounting will store contact data for customers' accounts payable personnel.

It's completely natural for workgroups to develop information systems solely for their own needs, but, over time, the existence of these separate systems will result in information silos that cause numerous problems.

What Are the Problems of Information Silos?

Figure 7-5 lists the major problems caused by information silos at the workgroup level, in this case, between the Sales and Marketing department and the Accounting department. First, data are duplicated. Sales and Marketing and Accounting applications maintain separate databases that store some of the same customer data. As you know, data storage is cheap, so the problem with duplication is not wasted disk storage. Rather, the problem is data inconsistency. Changes to customer data made in the Sales and Marketing application may take days or weeks to be made to the Accounting application's database. During that period, shipments will reach the customer without delay, but invoices will be sent to the wrong address. When an organization has inconsistent duplicated data, it is said to have a **data integrity** problem.

Additionally, when applications are isolated, business processes are disjointed. Suppose a business has a rule that credit orders over $15,000 must be preapproved by the Accounts Receivable department. If the supporting applications are separated, it will be difficult for the two activities to reconcile their data, and the approval will be slow to grant and possibly erroneous.

In the second row of Figure 7-5, Sales and Marketing wants to approve a $20,000 order with Ajax. According to the Sales and Marketing database, Ajax has a current balance of $17,800, so Sales and Marketing requests a total credit amount of $37,800. The Accounting database, however, shows Ajax with a balance of only $12,300 because the accounts receivable application has credited Ajax for a return of $5,500. According to Accounting's records, a total credit authorization of only $32,300 is needed in order to approve the $20,000 order, so that is all they grant.

Sales and Marketing doesn't understand what to do with a credit approval of $32,300. According to its database, Ajax already owes $17,800, so if the total credit authorization is only

Problem	Sales and Marketing		Accounting
Data duplication, data inconsistency	Ajax Construction Ship to: Reno, NV Bill to: Reno, NV		Ajax Construction Ship to: Reno, NV Bill to: Buffalo, NY
Disjointed processes	Get Credit Approval	Request $37,800 → ← Approve $32,300	Approve Customer Credit
Limited information and lack of integrated information	Order Data Is IndyMac a preferred customer?	??	Payment Data
Isolated decisions lead to organizational inefficiencies	Order Data Redouble sales efforts at IndyMac.		Payment Data OneWest has been slow to pay.
Increased expense	Sum of problems above.		

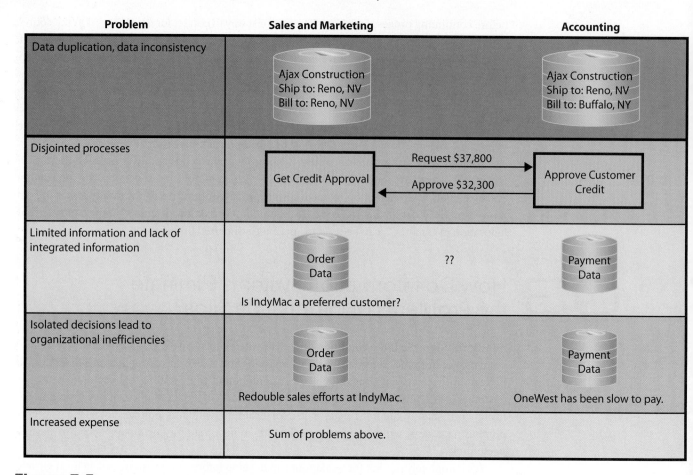

Figure 7-5
Problems Created by
Information Silos

$32,300, did Accounting approve only $14,500 of the new order? And why that amount? Both departments want to approve the order. It will take numerous emails and phone calls, however, to sort this out. These interacting business processes are disjointed.

A consequence of such disjointed activities is the lack of integrated enterprise information. For example, suppose Sales and Marketing wants to know if IndyMac is still a preferred customer. Suppose that determining whether this is so requires a comparison of order history and payment history data. However, with information silos, that data will reside in two different databases and, in one of them, IndyMac is known by the name of the company that acquired it, OneWest Bank. Data integration will be difficult. Making the determination will require manual processes and days, when it should be readily answered in seconds.

This leads to the fourth consequence: inefficiency. When using isolated functional applications, decisions are made in isolation. As shown in the fourth row of Figure 7-5, Sales and Marketing decided to redouble its sales effort with IndyMac. However, Accounting knows that IndyMac was foreclosed by the FDIC and sold to OneWest and has been slow to pay. There are far better prospects for increased sales attention. Without integration, the left hand of the organization doesn't know what the right hand of the organization is doing.

Finally, information silos can result in increased cost for the organization. Duplicated data, disjointed systems, limited information, and inefficiencies all mean higher costs.

How Do Organizations Solve the Problems of Information Silos?

As defined, an information silo occurs when data is stored in isolated systems. The obvious way to fix such a silo is to integrate the data into a single database and revise applications (and

Scope	Example	Example Information Silo	Enabling Technology
Workgroup	Doctor's Office/ Medical Practice	Physicians and hospitals store separated data about patients. Unnecessarily duplicate tests and procedures.	Functional applications.
		⬇	Enterprise applications (CRM, ERP, EAI) on enterprise networks.
Enterprise	Hospital	Hospital and local drug store pharmacy have different prescription data for the same patient.	
		⬇	Distributed systems using Web service technologies in the cloud.
Inter-enterprise	Inter-agency prescription application	No silo: Doctors, hospitals, pharmacies share patients' prescription and other data.	

Figure 7-6
Information Silos as Drivers

business processes) to use that database. If that is not possible or practical, another remedy is to allow the isolation, but to manage it to avoid problems.

The arrows in Figure 7-6 show this resolution at two levels of organization. First, isolated data created by workgroup information systems are integrated using enterprise-wide applications.

Second, today, isolated data created by information systems at the enterprise level are being integrated into inter-enterprise systems using distributed applications (such as PRIDE). These process data in a single cloud database or connect disparate, independent databases so that applications can process those databases as if they were one database. We will discuss inter-enterprise systems further in Q7.

For now, to better understand how isolated data problems can be resolved, consider an enterprise system at a hospital.

An Enterprise System for Patient Discharge

Figure 7-7 shows some of the hospital departments and a portion of the patient discharge process. A doctor initiates the process by issuing a discharge patient order. That order is delivered to the appropriate nursing staff, who initiates activities at the pharmacy, the patient's family, and kitchen. Some of those activities initiate activities back at the nursing staff. In Figure 7-7, the enterprise process (supported by the IS) is represented by a dotted red line.

Prior to the enterprise system, the hospital had developed procedures for using a paper-based system and informal messaging via the telephone. Each department kept its own records. When the new enterprise information system was implemented, not only was the data integrated into a database, but new computer-based forms and reports were created. The staff needed to transition from the paper-based system to the computer-based system. They also needed to stop making phone calls and let the new information system make notifications across departments. These measures involved substantial change, and most organizations experience considerable anguish when undergoing such transitions.

Eliminating information silos is not without security risk; for more information, see the Security Guide on pages 270–271.

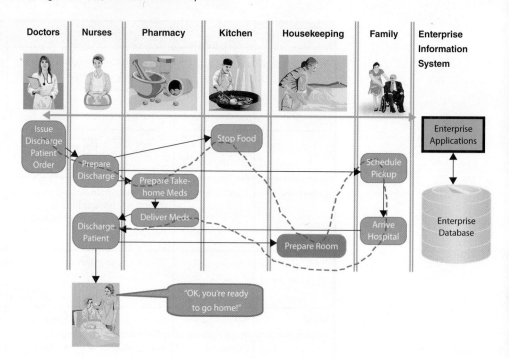

Figure 7-7
Example Enterprise Process
and Information System

 How Do CRM, ERP, and EAI Support Enterprise Processes?

Enterprise systems like the one in Figure 7-7 were not feasible until network, data communication, and database technologies reached a sufficient level of capability and maturity in the late 1980s and early 1990s. At that point, many organizations began to develop enterprise systems.

The Need for Business Process Engineering

As they did so, organizations realized that their existing business processes needed to change. In part, they needed to change to use the shared databases and to use new computer-based forms and reports. However, an even more important reason for changing business processes was that integrated data and enterprise systems offered the potential of substantial improvements in process quality. It became possible to do things that had been impossible before. Using Porter's language (Chapter 3, page 84), enterprise systems enabled the creation of stronger, faster, more effective *linkages* among value chains.

For example, when the hospital used a paper-based system, the kitchen would prepare meals for everyone who was a patient at the hospital as of midnight the night before. It was not possible to obtain data about discharges until the next midnight. Consequently, considerable food was wasted at substantial cost.

With the enterprise system, the kitchen can be notified about patient discharges as they occur throughout the day, resulting in substantial reductions in wasted food. But when should the kitchen be notified? Immediately? And what if the discharge is cancelled before completion? Notify the kitchen of the cancelled discharge? Many possibilities and alternatives exist. So, to design its new enterprise system, the hospital needed to determine how best to change its processes to take advantage of the new capability. Such projects came to be known as **business process reengineering**, which is the activity of altering existing and designing new business processes to take advantage of new information systems.

Unfortunately, business process reengineering is difficult, slow, and exceedingly expensive. Business analysts need to interview key personnel throughout the organization to determine how best to use the new technology. Because of the complexity involved, such projects require high-level, expensive skills and considerable time. Many early projects stalled when the enormity of the project became apparent. This left some organizations with partially implemented systems, which had disastrous consequences. Personnel didn't know if they were using the new system, the old system, or some hacked-up version of both.

The stage was set for the emergence of enterprise application solutions, which we discuss next.

Emergence of Enterprise Application Solutions

When the process quality benefits of enterprise-wide systems became apparent, most organizations were still developing their applications in-house. At the time, organizations perceived their needs as being "too unique" to be satisfied by off-the-shelf or altered applications. However, as applications became more and more complex, in-house development costs became infeasible. As stated in Chapter 4, systems built in-house are expensive not only because of their high initial development costs, but also because of the continuing need to adapt those systems to changing requirements.

In the early 1990s, as the costs of business process reengineering were coupled to the costs of in-house development, organizations began to look more favorably on the idea of licensing preexisting applications. "Maybe we're not so unique, after all."

Some of the vendors who took advantage of this change in attitude were PeopleSoft, which licensed payroll and limited-capability human resources systems; Siebel, which licensed a sales lead tracking and management system; and SAP, which licensed something new, a system called *enterprise resource management*.

These three companies, and ultimately dozens of others like them, offered not just software and database designs. They also offered standardized business processes. These **inherent processes**, which are predesigned procedures for using the software products, saved organizations from the expense, delays, and risks of business process reengineering. Instead, organizations could license the software and obtain, as part of the deal, prebuilt processes which the vendors assured them were based on "industry best practices."

Despite the clear benefits of inherent processes and ERP, there can be an unintended consequence. See the Guide on pages 272–273 and consider that risk.

Some parts of that deal were too good to be true because, as you'll learn in Q5, inherent processes are almost never a perfect fit. But the offer was too much for many organizations to resist. Over time, three categories of enterprise applications emerged: customer relationship management, enterprise resource planning, and enterprise application integration. Consider each.

Customer Relationship Management (CRM)

A **customer relationship management (CRM) system** is a suite of applications, a database, and a set of inherent processes for managing all the interactions with the customer, from lead generation to customer service. Every contact and transaction with the customer is recorded in the CRM database. Vendors of CRM systems claim that using their products makes the organization *customer-centric*. Though that term reeks of sales hyperbole, it does indicate the nature and intent of CRM packages.

Figure 7-8 shows four phases of the **customer life cycle**: marketing, customer acquisition, relationship management, and loss/churn. Marketing sends messages to the target market to attract customer prospects. When prospects order, they become customers who need to be supported. Additionally, relationship management processes increase the value of existing customers by selling them more product. Inevitably, over time the organization loses customers. When this occurs, win-back processes categorize customers according to value and attempt to win back high-value customers.

Figure 7-9 illustrates the major components of a CRM application. Notice that components exist for each stage of the customer life cycle. As shown, all applications process a common customer database. This design eliminates duplicated customer data and removes the possibility of inconsistent data. It also means that each department knows what has been happening with the customer at other departments. Customer support, for example, will know not to provide

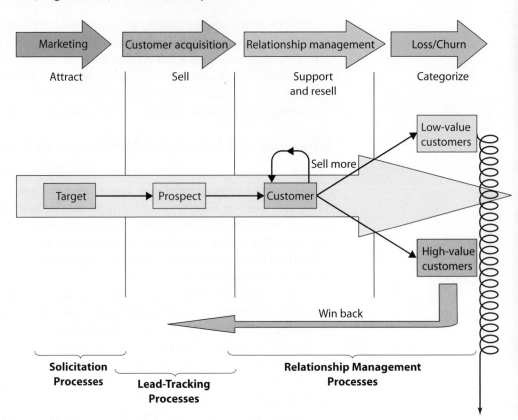

Figure 7-8

The Customer Life Cycle

Source: The Customer Life Cycle. Used with permission from Professor Douglas MacLachlan, Foster School of Business, University of Washington.

$1,000 worth of support labor to a customer that has generated $300 worth of business over time. However, they'll know to bend over backward for the customers that have generated hundreds of thousands of dollars of business. The result to the customers is that they feel like they are dealing with one entity, not many.

CRM systems vary in the degree of functionality they provide. One of the primary tasks when selecting a CRM package is to determine the features you need and to find a package that meets that set of needs. You might be involved in just such a project during your career. See the Using MIS InClass 7 on page 255.

Enterprise Resource Planning (ERP)

Enterprise resource planning (ERP) is a suite of applications called **modules**, a database, and a set of inherent processes for consolidating business operations into a single, consistent, computing platform. An **ERP system** is an information system based on ERP technology. As

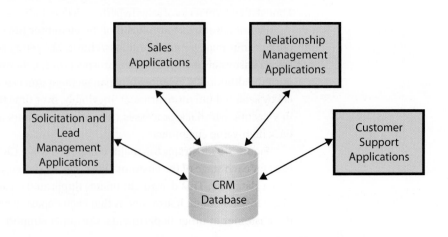

Figure 7-9

CRM Applications

Using MIS InClass 7

Choosing a CRM Product

Choosing a CRM product is complicated. Dozens of CRM products exist, and it's difficult to determine their different features and functions, let alone how easy they are to learn and use, how difficult they are to implement, and so forth. Choosing a CRM product requires knowledge of the organization's requirements, and often those requirements aren't fully known, or if they are known, they are changing as the organization grows.

This exercise is designed to give you a sense of the challenges involved when choosing a CRM product. Form a team of students, fire up your browsers, and answer the following questions:

1. Sage Act! and Goldmine are two lower-end CRM products. They began as sales lead tracking tools for individuals and small offices but have evolved since then.
   a. To learn about these products, visit *http://na.sage.com/ sage-act/* and *www.goldmine.com*.
   b. Classify these products as thin- versus thick-applications and PC and LAN versus cloud-based.

   c. It is difficult to compare the products based on the information just on those sites. To learn more, search the Web for "Act! versus Goldmine." Because these products change quickly, use only comparisons that have been done since 2013.
   d. Prepare a summary of your findings for a 2-minute presentation to the rest of the class. Include in your summary each product's intended market, costs, and relative strengths and weaknesses.

2. Salesforce.com and Sugar are CRM products that are intended for use by larger organizations than those that use Act! and Goldmine.
   a. To learn about those products, visit *www.salesforce.com* and *www.sugarcrm.com*.
   b. Classify these products as thin- versus thick-applications and PC and LAN versus cloud-based.
   c. To learn how others view these products, search the Web for "Salesforce versus Sugar CRM." Read several comparisons, but given the rapidly changing nature of these products, use only comparisons that have been done since 2013.
   d. Prepare a summary of your findings for a 2-minute presentation to the rest of the class. Include in your summary each product's intended market, costs, and relative strengths and weaknesses.

3. Given your answers to items 1–2 (and those of other teams if you have been presenting to each other), consider the desirability of CRM product offerings for a variety of businesses. Specifically, suppose you have been asked to recommend CRM products for further consideration. Choose three of the following five businesses and recommend two CRM products to each of the three. Justify your recommendations.
   a. An independent wedding planner who is working in her own business as a sole proprietor.
   b. An online vendor, such as *www.sephora.com*.
   c. A musical venue, such as *http://santafeopera.org*.
   d. A vacation cruise ship line, such as *www.hollandamerica .com*.
   e. A large manufacturer such as *www.ge.com*.

Prepare your findings for presentation to the rest of the class.

4. Summarize what you have learned from this exercise about choosing a CRM product. Formulate your summary as an answer to a job interviewer's question about the difficulties that organizations face when choosing software products.

Ethics Guide

DIALING FOR DOLLARS

Suppose you are a salesperson and your company's CRM forecasts that your quarterly sales will be substantially under quota. You call your best customers to increase sales, but no one is willing to buy more.

Your boss says that it has been a bad quarter for all of the salespeople. It's so bad, in fact, that the vice president of sales has authorized a 20 percent discount on new orders. The only stipulation is that customers must take delivery prior to the end of the quarter so that accounting can book the order. "Start dialing for dollars," she says, "and get what you can. Be creative."

Using your CRM, you identify your top customers and present the discount offer to them. The first customer balks at increasing her inventory: "I just don't think we can sell that much."

"Well," you respond, "how about if we agree to take back any inventory you don't sell next quarter?" (By doing this, you increase your current sales and commission, and you also help your company make its quarterly sales projections. The additional product is likely to be returned next quarter, but you think, "Hey, that's then and this is now.")

"OK," she says, "but I want you to stipulate the return option on the purchase order."

You know that you cannot write that on the purchase order because accounting won't book all of the order if you do. So you tell her that you'll send her an email with that stipulation. She increases her order, and accounting books the full amount.

With another customer, you try a second strategy. Instead of offering the discount, you offer the product at full price, but agree to pay a 20 percent credit in the next quarter. That way you can book the full price now. You pitch this offer as follows: "Our marketing department analyzed past sales using our fancy new computer system, and we know that increasing advertising will cause additional sales. So, if you order more product now, next quarter we'll give you 20 percent of the order back to pay for advertising."

In truth, you doubt the customer will spend the money on advertising. Instead, it will just take the credit and sit on a bigger inventory. That will kill your sales to the company next quarter, but you'll solve that problem then.

Even with these additional orders, you're still under quota. In desperation, you decide to sell product to a fictitious company that you say is owned by your brother-in-law. You set up a new account, and when accounting calls your brother-in-law for a credit check, he cooperates with your scheme. You then sell $40,000 of product

Source: © denis_romash/Fotolia

to the fictitious company and ship the product to your brother-in-law's garage. Accounting books the revenue in the quarter, and you have finally made quota. A week into the next quarter, your brother-in-law returns the merchandise.

Meanwhile, unknown to you, your company's ERP system is scheduling production. The program that creates the production schedule reads the sales from your activities (and those of the other salespeople) and finds a sharp increase in product demand. Accordingly, it generates a schedule that calls for substantial production increases and schedules workers for the production runs. The production system, in turn, schedules the material requirements with the inventory application, which increases raw materials purchases to meet the increased production schedule.

DISCUSSION QUESTIONS

1. Consider the email you write that agrees to take the product back.
   a. Is your action ethical according to the categorical imperative (pages 20–21) perspective?
   b. Is your action ethical according to the utilitarian perspective (pages 54–55)?
   c. If that email comes to light later, what do you think your boss will say?
2. Regarding your offer of the "advertising" discount:
   a. Is your action ethical according to the categorical imperative perspective?
   b. Is your action ethical according to the utilitarian perspective?

   c. What effect does that discount have on your company's balance sheet?
3. Regarding your shipping to the fictitious company:
   a. Is your action ethical according to the categorical imperative perspective?
   b. Is your action ethical according to the utilitarian perspective?
   c. Is your action legal?
4. Describe the effect of your activities on next quarter's inventories.
5. Setting aside ethical and legal issues, would you say the enterprise system is more of a help or a hindrance in this example?

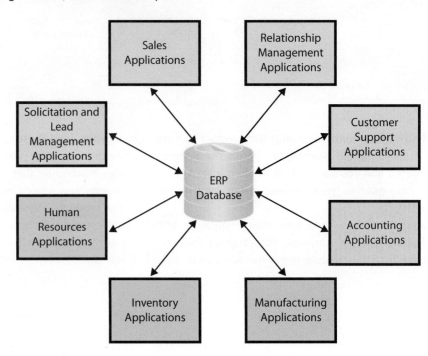

Figure 7-10
ERP Applications

shown in Figure 7-10, ERP systems include the functions of CRM systems, but also incorporate accounting, manufacturing, inventory, and human resources applications.

The primary purpose of an ERP system is integration; an ERP system allows the left hand of the organization to know what the right hand is doing. This integration allows real-time updates globally, whenever and wherever a transaction takes place. Critical business decisions can then be made on a timely basis using the latest data.

To understand the utility of this integration, consider the pre-ERP systems shown in Figure 7-11. This diagram represents the same processes used by a bicycle manufacturer that we discussed in Chapter 3. It includes five different databases, one each for vendors, raw materials, finished goods, manufacturing plan, and CRM. Consider the problems that appear with such separated data when the Sales department closes a large order, say, for 1,000 bicycles.

First, should the company take the order? Can it meet the schedule requirements for such a large order? Suppose one of the primary parts vendors recently lost capacity due to an earthquake, and the manufacturer cannot obtain parts for the order in time. If so, the order schedule ought not to be approved. However, with such separated systems this situation is unknown.

Even if parts can be obtained, until the order is entered into the finished goods database, purchasing is unaware of the need to buy new parts. The same comment applies to manufacturing. Until the new order is entered into the manufacturing plan, the Production department doesn't know that it needs to increase manufacturing. And, as with parts, does the company have sufficient machine and floor capacity to fill the order on a timely basis? Does it have sufficient personnel with the correct skill sets? Should it be hiring? Can production meet the order schedule? No one knows before the order is approved.

Figure 7-11 does not show accounting. We can assume, however, that the company has a separate accounting system that is similarly isolated. Eventually, records of business activity find their way to the Accounting department and will be posted into the general ledger. With such a pre-ERP system, financial statements are always outdated, available several weeks after the close of the quarter or other accounting period.

Contrast this situation with the ERP system in Figure 7-12. Here all activity is processed by ERP application programs (called *modules*) and consolidated data are stored in a centralized ERP database. When Sales is confronted with the opportunity to sell 1,000 bicycles, the information that it needs to confirm that the order, schedule, and terms are possible

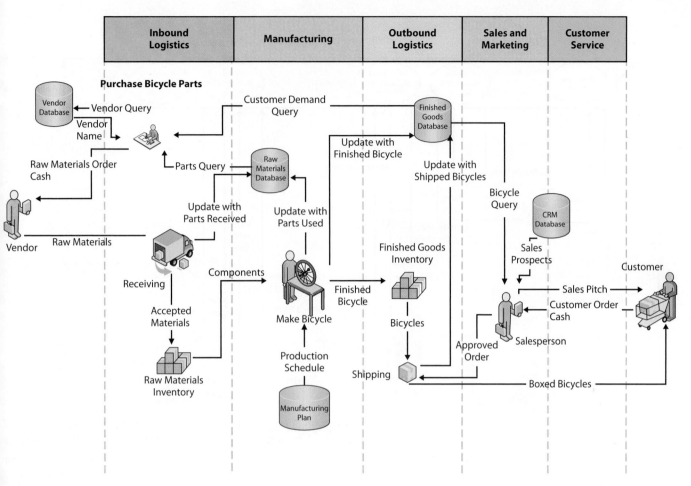

Figure 7-11
Pre-ERP Information Systems

can be obtained from the ERP system immediately. Once the order is accepted, all departments, including purchasing, manufacturing, human resources, and accounting, are notified. Further, transactions are posted to the ERP database as they occur; the result is that financial statements are available quickly. In most cases, correct financial statements can be produced in real time. With such integration, ERP systems can display the current status of critical business factors to managers and executives, as shown in the sales dashboard in Figure 7-13.

Of course, the devil is in the details. It's one thing to draw a rectangle on a chart, label it "ERP Applications," and assume that data integration takes all the problems away. It is far more difficult to write those application programs and to design the database to store that integrated data. Even more problematic, what procedures should employees and others use to process those application programs? Specifically, for example, what actions should salespeople take before they approve a large order? Here are some of the questions that need to be answered or resolved:

- How does the Sales department determine that an order is considered large? By dollars? By volume?
- Who approves customer credit (and how)?
- Who approves production capacity (and how)?
- Who approves schedule and terms (and how)?
- What actions need to be taken if the customer modifies the order?
- How does management obtain oversight on sales activity?

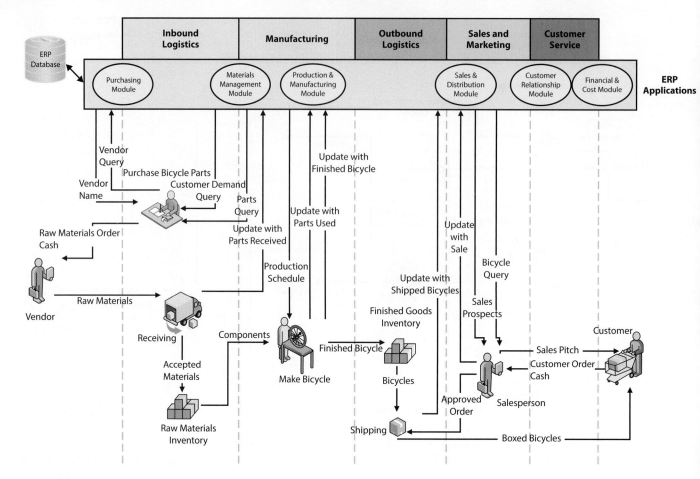

Figure 7-12
ERP Information Systems

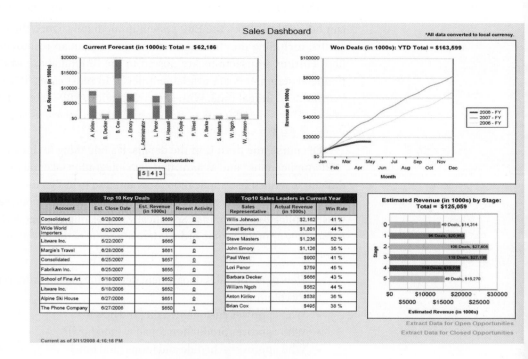

Figure 7-13
Sales Dashboard

Source: Microsoft Corporation

As you can imagine, many other questions must be answered as well. Because of its importance to organizations today, we will discuss ERP in further detail in Q5. Before we do so, however, consider the third type of enterprise system: EAI.

Enterprise Application Integration (EAI)

ERP systems are not for every organization. For example, some nonmanufacturing companies find the manufacturing orientation of ERP inappropriate. Even for manufacturing companies, some find the process of converting from their current system to an ERP system too daunting. Others are quite satisfied with their manufacturing application systems and do not wish to change them.

Companies for which ERP is inappropriate still have the problems associated with information silos, however, and some choose to use **enterprise application integration (EAI)** to solve those problems. EAI is a suite of software applications that integrates existing systems by providing layers of software that connect applications together. EAI does the following:

- It connects system "islands" via a new layer of software/system.
- It enables existing applications to communicate and share data.
- It provides integrated information.
- It leverages existing systems—leaving functional applications as is, but providing an integration layer over the top.
- It enables a gradual move to ERP.

The layers of EAI software shown in Figure 7-14 enable existing applications to communicate with each other and to share data. For example, EAI software can be configured to automatically carry out the data conversion required to make data compatible among different systems. When the CRM applications send data to the manufacturing application system, for example, the CRM system sends its data to an EAI software program. That EAI program makes the conversion and then sends the converted data to the ERP system. The reverse action is taken to send data back from the ERP to the CRM.

Although there is no centralized EAI database, the EAI software keeps files of metadata that describe data formats and locations. Users can access the EAI system to find the data they need. In some cases, the EAI system provides services that provide a "virtual integrated database" for the user to process.

The major benefit of EAI is that it enables organizations to use existing applications while eliminating many of the serious problems of isolated systems. Converting to an EAI system is not nearly as disruptive as converting to an ERP system, and it provides many of the benefits of ERP. Some organizations develop EAI applications as a stepping stone to complete ERP systems. Today many EAI systems use Web services standards to define the interactions among EAI components. Some or all of the processing for those components can be moved to the cloud as well.

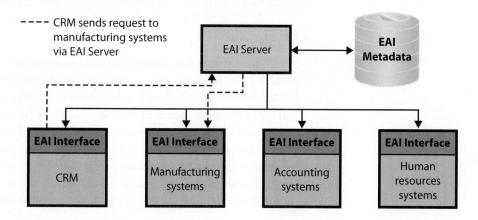

Figure 7-14
Design and Implementation for the Five Components

What Are the Elements of an ERP System?

Because of its importance to organizations today, we will consider ERP in more depth than CRM or EAI. To begin, the term *ERP* has been applied to a wide array of application solutions, in some cases erroneously. Some vendors attempted to catch the buzz for ERP by misapplying the term to applications that provided only one or two integrated functional applications.

The organization ERPsoftware360 publishes a wealth of information about ERP vendors, products, solutions, and applications. According to its Web site (*www.erpsoftware360.com/erp-101.htm*), for a product to be considered a true ERP product it must include applications that integrate:

- Supply chain (procurement, sales order processing, inventory management, supplier management, and related activities)
- Manufacturing (scheduling, capacity planning, quality control, bill of materials, and related activities)
- CRM (sales prospecting, customer management, marketing, customer support, call center support)
- Human resources (payroll, time and attendance, HR management, commission calculations, benefits administration, and related activities)
- Accounting (general ledger, accounts receivable, accounts payable, cash management, fixed asset accounting)

An ERP solution consists of application programs, databases, business process procedures, and training and consulting. We consider each in turn.

ERP Application Programs

ERP vendors design application programs to be configurable so that development teams can alter them to meet an organization's requirements without changing program code. Accordingly, during the ERP development process, the development team sets configuration parameters that specify how ERP application programs will operate. For example, an hourly payroll application is configured to specify the number of hours in the standard workweek, hourly wages for different job categories, wage adjustments for overtime and holiday work, and so forth. Deciding on the initial configuration values and adapting them to new requirements is a challenging collaboration activity. It is also one that you might be involved in as a business professional.

Of course, there are limits to how much configuration can be done. If a new ERP customer has requirements that cannot be met via program configuration, then it either needs to adapt its business to what the software can do or write (or pay another vendor to write) application code to meet its requirements. As stated in Chapter 4, such custom programming is expensive, both initially and in long-term maintenance costs. Thus, choosing an ERP solution that has applications that function close to the organization's requirements is critical to its successful implementation.

ERP Databases

An ERP solution includes a database design as well as initial configuration data. It does not, of course, contain the company's operational data. During development, the team must enter the initial values for that data as part of the development effort.

If your only experience with databases is creating a few tables in Microsoft Access, then you probably underestimate the value and importance of ERP database designs. SAP, the leading vendor of ERP solutions, provides ERP databases that contain more than 15,000 tables. The design includes the metadata for those tables, as well as their relationships to each other, and rules and constraints about how the data in some tables must relate to data in other tables. The ERP solution also contains tables filled with initial configuration data.

Reflect on the difficulty of creating and validating data models (as discussed in Chapter 5), and you will have some idea of the amount of intellectual capital invested in a database design of 15,000 tables. Also, consider the magnitude of the task of filling such a database with users' data!

Although we did not discuss this database feature in Chapter 5, large organizational databases contain two types of program code. The first, called a **trigger**, is a computer program stored within the database that runs to keep the database consistent when certain conditions arise. The second, called a **stored procedure**, is a computer program stored in the database that is used to enforce business rules. An example of such a rule would be never to sell certain items at a discount. Triggers and stored procedures are also part of the ERP solution. Developers and business users need to configure the operation of such code during the ERP implementation as well.

Business Process Procedures

The third component of an ERP solution is a set of inherent procedures that implement standard business processes. ERP vendors develop hundreds, or even thousands, of procedures that enable the ERP customer organization to accomplish its work using the applications provided by the vendor. Figure 7-15 shows a part of the SAP ordering business process; this process implements a portion of the inbound logistics activities. Some ERP vendors call the inherent processes that are defined in the ERP solution **process blueprints**.

Without delving into the details, you should be able to understand the flow of work outlined in this process. Every function (rounded rectangles in Figure 7-15) consists of a set of procedures for accomplishing that function. Typically, these procedures require an ERP user to use application menus, screens, and reports to accomplish the activity.

As with application programs, ERP users must either adapt to the predefined, inherent processes and procedures or design new ones. In the latter case, the design of new procedures may necessitate changes to application programs and to database structures as well. Perhaps you can begin to understand why organizations attempt to conform to vendor standards.

Training and Consulting

Because of the complexity and difficulty of implementing and using ERP solutions, ERP vendors have developed training curricula and numerous classes. SAP operates universities, in which customers and potential customers receive training both before and after the ERP implementation. In addition, ERP vendors typically conduct classes on site. To reduce expenses, the vendors sometimes train the organization's employees, called Super Users, to become in-house trainers in training sessions called **train the trainer**.

ERP training falls into two broad categories. The first category is training about how to implement the ERP solution. This training includes topics such as obtaining top-level management support, preparing the organization for change, and dealing with the inevitable resistance that develops when people are asked to perform work in new ways. The second category is training on how to use the ERP application software; this training includes specific steps for using the ERP applications to accomplish the activities in processes such as those in Figure 7-15.

ERP vendors also provide on-site consulting for implementing and using the ERP system. Additionally, an industry of third-party ERP consultants has developed to support new ERP customers and implementations. These consultants provide knowledge gained through numerous ERP implementations. Such knowledge is valued because most organizations only go through an ERP conversion once. Ironically, having done so, they now know how to do it. Consequently, some employees, seasoned by an ERP conversion with their employer, leave that company to become ERP consultants.

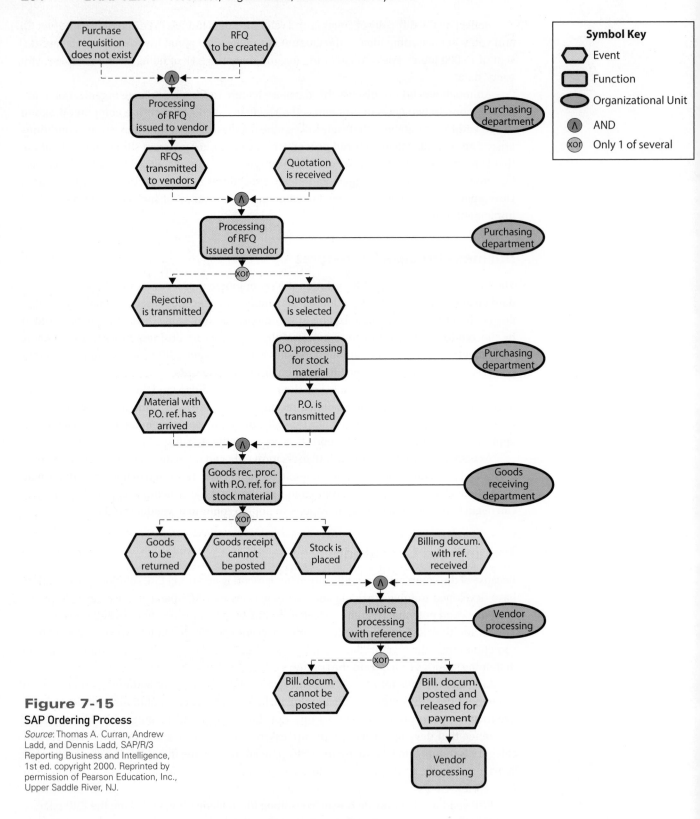

Figure 7-15

SAP Ordering Process

Source: Thomas A. Curran, Andrew Ladd, and Dennis Ladd, SAP/R/3 Reporting Business and Intelligence, 1st ed. copyright 2000. Reprinted by permission of Pearson Education, Inc., Upper Saddle River, NJ.

Industry-Specific Solutions

As you can tell, considerable work needs to be done to customize an ERP application to a particular customer. To reduce that work, ERP vendors provide starter kits for specific industries called **industry-specific solutions**. These solutions contain program and database configuration files as well as process blueprints that apply to ERP implementations in specific industries. Over time,

Company	ERP Market Rank	Remarks	Future
Epicor	5	Strong industry-specific solutions, especially retail.	Epicor 9 designed for flexibility (SOA). Highly configurable ERP. Lower cost.
Microsoft Dynamics	4	Four products acquired: AX, Nav, GP, and Solomon. AX and Nav more comprehensive. Solomon on the way out? Large VAR channel.	Products not well integrated with Office. Not integrated at all with Microsoft development languages. Product direction uncertain. Watch for Microsoft ERP announcement on the cloud (Azure).
Infor	3	Privately held corporation that has acquired an ERP product named Baan, along with more than 20 others.	Span larger small companies to smaller large companies. Offers many solutions.
Oracle	2	Combination of in-house and acquired (PeopleSoft, Siebel) products.	Intensely competitive company with strong technology base. Large customer base. Flexible SOA architecture. Expensive. Oracle CEO Ellison owns 70% of NetSuite.
SAP	1	Led ERP success. Largest vendor, most comprehensive solution. Largest customers.	Technology older. Expensive and seriously challenged by less expensive alternatives. Huge customer base. Future growth uncertain.

Figure 7-16
SAP Characteristics of Top ERP Vendors

SAP, which first provided such solutions, and other ERP vendors created dozens of such starter kits for manufacturing, sales and distribution, healthcare, and other major industries.

Which Companies Are the Major ERP Vendors?

Although more than 100 different companies advertise ERP products, not all of those products meet the minimal ERP criteria. Even of those that do, the bulk of the market is held by the five vendors shown in Figure 7-16. This figure shows market rank rather than market share because it is difficult to obtain comparable revenue numbers. Both Epicor and Infor are owned by private equity investors and do not publish financial data. Their rankings are based on what little sales data is publicly available. Microsoft's ERP revenue is combined with its CRM revenue, and its true ERP revenue is unknown. Similarly, Oracle and SAP combine ERP revenue with revenue from other products.

Q6 What Are the Challenges of Implementing and Upgrading Enterprise Information Systems?

Implementing new enterprise systems, whether CRM, ERP, or EAI, is challenging, difficult, expensive, and risky. It is not unusual for enterprise system projects to be well over budget and a year or more late. In addition to new ERP implementations, numerous organizations implemented ERP 15 or 20 years ago and now need to upgrade their ERP installation to meet new requirements. If you work in an organization that is already using enterprise systems, you may find yourself engaged in a significant upgrade effort. Whether from a new implementation or an upgrade, expense and risks arise from four primary factors (see Figure 7-17).

Collaborative Management

Unlike departmental systems in which a single department manager is in charge, enterprise systems have no clear boss. Examine the discharge process in Figure 7-7; there is no manager of discharge. The discharge process is a collaborative effort among many departments (and customers).

- Collaborative management

- Requirements gaps

- Transition problems

- Employee resistance

Figure 7-17
Four Primary Factors

With no single manager, who resolves the disputes that inevitably arise? All of these departments ultimately report to the CEO, so there is a single boss over all of them, but employees can't go to the CEO with a problem about, say, coordinating discharge activities between nursing and housekeeping. The CEO would throw them out of his or her office. Instead, the organization needs to develop some sort of collaborative management for resolving process issues.

Usually this means that the enterprise develops committees and steering groups for providing enterprise process management. Although this can be an effective solution, and in fact may be the *only* solution, the work of such groups is both slow and expensive.

Requirements Gaps

As stated in Q4, few organizations today create their own enterprise systems from scratch. Instead, they license an enterprise product that provides specific functions and features and that includes inherent procedures. But such licensed products are never a perfect fit. Almost always there are gaps between the organization's requirements and the application's capabilities.

The first challenge is identifying the gaps. To specify a gap, an organization must know both what it needs and what the new product does. However, it can be very difficult for an organization to determine what it needs; that difficulty is one reason organizations choose to license rather than to build. Further, the features and functions of complex products like CRM or ERP are not easy to identify. Thus, gap identification is a major task when implementing enterprise systems.

The second challenge is deciding what to do with gaps, once they are identified. Either the organization needs to change the way it does things to adapt to the new application, or the application must be altered to match what the organization does. Either choice is problematic. Employees will resist change, but paying for alterations is expensive, and, as noted in Chapter 4, the organization is committing to maintaining those alterations as the application is changed over time. Here organizations fill gaps by choosing their lesser regret.

Transition Problems

Transitioning to a new enterprise system is also difficult. The organization must somehow change from using isolated departmental systems to using the new enterprise system, while continuing to run the business. It's like having heart surgery while running a 100-yard dash.

Such transitions require careful planning and substantial training. Inevitably, problems will develop. Knowing this will occur, senior management needs to communicate the need for the change to the employees and then stand behind the new system as the kinks are worked out. It is an incredibly stressful time for all involved. We will discuss development techniques and implementation strategies further in Chapter 10.

Employee Resistance

People resist change. Change requires effort and it engenders fear. Considerable research and literature exists about the reasons for change resistance and how organizations can deal with it. Here we will summarize the major principles.

First, senior-level management needs to communicate the need for the change to the organization and reiterate this, as necessary, throughout the transition process. Second, employees fear change because it threatens **self-efficacy**, which is a person's belief that he or she can be successful at his or her job. To enhance confidence, employees need to be trained and coached on the successful use of the new system. Word-of-mouth is a very powerful factor, and in some cases key users are trained ahead of time to create positive buzz about the new system. Video demonstrations of employees successfully using the new system are also effective.

Third, in many ways, the primary benefits of a new ERP system are felt by the accounting and finance departments and the senior management. Many of the employees who are asked to change their activities to implement ERP will not receive any direct benefit from it. Therefore, employees may need to be given extra inducement to change to the new system. As one experienced change consultant said, "Nothing succeeds like praise or cash, especially cash." Straight-out pay for change is bribery, but contests with cash prizes among employees or groups can be very effective at inducing change.

Implementing new enterprise systems can solve many problems and bring great efficiency and cost savings to an organization, but it is not for the faint of heart.

How Do Inter-enterprise IS Solve the Problems of Enterprise Silos?

The discussion in Q4 illustrated the primary ways that enterprise systems solve the problems of workgroup information silos. In this question we will use the PRIDE example to show you how inter-enterprise systems can accomplish the same for enterprise silos. (The transition is shown by the lower arrow leading to the bottom row in Figure 7-6, page 251.)

Figure 7-18 shows the information silos that exist among healthcare providers, health clubs, and patients, the principal PRIDE users. Providers keep track of patient histories and maintain records of exercise recommendations, which are called exercise prescriptions in the PRIDE system. Health clubs maintain membership, class, personal trainer, and exercise performance data. At the club, the latter is gathered automatically from exercise equipment and member heart monitors and stored in a club database. At home, individuals generate exercise data on heart monitors and equipment; those data are recorded in mobile devices using exercise watches.

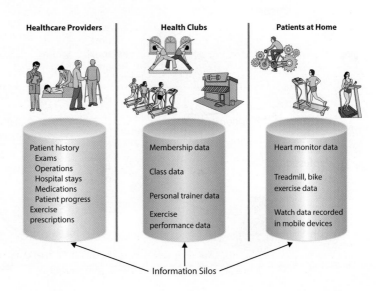

Figure 7-18
Information Silos Without PRIDE

The isolation of this exercise data causes problems. For example, doctors would like to have reports on exercise data that is stored in patient devices and in health clubs. Patients would like to have prescription data from their providers as well as exercise data from their time at health clubs. Health clubs would like to have exercise prescriptions and home workout data to integrate with the data they have. All three entities would like to produce reports from the integrated data.

Figure 7-19 shows the structure of an inter-enterprise system that meets the goals of the three types of participant. In this figure, the labeled rectangles inside the cloud represent mobile applications that could be native, thin-client, or both. Some of the application processing might be done on cloud servers as well as on the mobile devices. Those design decisions are not shown. As illustrated, this system assumes that all users receive reports on mobile devices, but, because of the large amount of keying involved, that healthcare providers submit and manage prescriptions using a personal computer.

As you can see, prescription and exercise data is integrated in the PRIDE database, which is a relational rather than a NoSQL database. (Case Study 7 shows the structure of major portions of that database.) The integrated data can be processed by a reporting application (Chapter 9) to create and distribute the reports as shown.

Systems like that shown in Figure 7-19 are referred to as **distributed systems** because applications processing is distributed across multiple computing devices. Standards such as http, https, html5, css3, JavaScript, and SOA using Web services enable programs to receive data from, and display data to, a variety of mobile and desktop devices.

PRIDE data is requested and delivered using the JSON.

Figure 7-19
Inter-enterprise PRIDE System

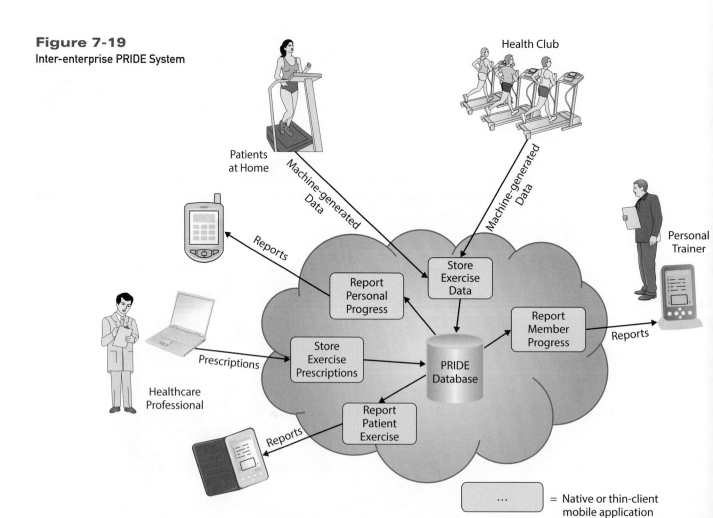

Q8 2024?

ERP vendors, like all software vendors today, are engaged in the development of new cloud-based products. To speed this process, you can expect many acquisitions by the major players such as Oracle and SAP. In fact, in 2012, Oracle and SAP seemed to be in a bidding war over companies that can add cloud-based products to their existing offerings. Search the Web for "Ariba" and "Vitrue acquisitions" to learn more.

The problem for all ERP vendors, but particularly for Oracle and SAP, is their past success. They have licensed and installed billions of dollars of client-server ERP software, and they cannot walk away from those products or the revenue of lucrative support contracts that they provide. Further, their customers face similar challenges. They want to move to the lower costs of the cloud, but they cannot plunge into new cloud-based solutions without causing considerable organizational turmoil, if not failure.

Thus, both ERP vendors and their customers seek application and systems migration strategies that will enable them to maintain quality service, while at the same time using the cloud as much as they can.

Mobile systems further complicate this situation. Not only do companies need to move their applications to the cloud, but they also need to provide both thin-client and native mobile applications. However, ERP systems contain business-critical and exceedingly confidential data; allowing access via mobile devices is potentially a serious security threat. See the BYOD policy discussion in Chapter 4.

In spite of the challenges, it doesn't take a great deal of imagination to realize that by 2024, workers in the warehouse, loading dock, and shipping department will all carry mobile devices that enable them to process ERP and other enterprise applications from wherever they happen to be. Managers, decision makers, and other knowledge workers will have similar applications on their own phones or other mobile devices, devices that they can access from work, other offices, the street, or at home. And (like PRIDE exercise equipment) machines, robots, and other forms of factory automation will generate and consume data.

Late-breaking news: In May 2013, SAP announced updates to a series of cloud-based SaaS applications that would enable organizations to keep their core SAP installation and data, while adding mobile-enabled cloud applications to that data.[3]

As of 2013, the story is just starting to be told. You can expect that it will evolve rapidly during the early years of your career. If you are interested in operations and information systems, mobile-cloud-CRM/ERP is a great opportunity for future employment.

---

[3]Chris Kanaracus, "SAP Updates Line-of-Business Cloud Apps," May 15, 2013, *http://www.infoworld.com/d/applications/sap-updates-line-of-business-cloud-apps-218649.*

Security Guide

ONE-STOP SHOPPING

In this chapter, you've learned how the problems of information silos shown in Figure 7-5 can be eliminated by increasing the scope of information systems: Workgroup-induced silos can be eliminated by developing enterprise IS, and enterprise-induced silos can be eliminated by developing inter-enterprise IS. Nowhere in this discussion, however, have we thought about security.

In fact, while removing information silos does have the advantages discussed, moving data into a single, centralized facility creates a potential security problem. Namely, fraudsters can find all the data they want in one convenient location. It's one-stop shopping. So, data integration can make organizations more vulnerable.

On the other hand, centralizing data in one location enables the organization to focus security measures on a single resource. The IS support staff need not manage security over several, possibly many, distributed databases, but rather can focus security management on a single database. So, assuming appropriate security management, the two factors counterbalance one another: Risk of loss is higher, but security against such loss can be focused and ultimately result in less actual risk.

However, inter-enterprise IS such as PRIDE have additional factors that make security more complicated. To start, for the purpose of this guide, let's assume that patient privacy is appropriately protected. Patients only share the data with each of the PRIDE entities (doctors, health clubs, insurance companies, and employers) that they want to.

Even with that assumption, however, there are significant privacy and security issues. First, consider the consequences for competing health clubs. Doctors, patients, and personal trainers need to see complete patient exercise data. A major portion of PRIDE's value results from all parties' ability to know *all* the exercise that the patient is doing. Neither doctors nor personal trainers can prescribe appropriately without complete data on all of a patient's exercise.

This means, however, that competing personal trainers (and health clubs) view data on their competitors' practices. Is this a problem? It's likely to be *perceived* as a problem even if there is no real danger, and that perception could limit PRIDE sales and use.

The degree of the actual problem depends on how much data control is lost via PRIDE reports. Is it possible to obtain all exercise data, for all patients? Can that data be downloaded and imported into other applications? Is there a competitive advantage in learning what other trainers and clubs are doing with their patients? And, how robust is PRIDE security? Once a trainer has access to some data, is it easy to gain access to the rest, either

Sources: © zentilia /Shutterstock and © andreiorlov/Fotolia

270

using reports and tools in PRIDE or using unauthorized access with techniques such as SQL injection (see Chapter 12)?

This example underlines some of the management problems of inter-enterprise IS. Unlike an enterprise system, where everyone works for the same employer and, except for inter-departmental rivalry, has the same incentive to protect data, an inter-enterprise system can connect competitors with different incentives and agendas. This fact not only increases security risk, it takes away one of the major ways of dealing with security flaws: procedures. In an enterprise system, it's possible for the organization to set up manual procedures that compensate for security weaknesses in programs or data controls. However, in an inter-enterprise system, if system users compete, they may have an incentive not to follow the compensating procedures.

PRIDE's use of the cloud brings up another important security concern, one that exists at both the enterprise and inter-enterprise levels. How secure is the cloud vendor? In the spring of 2012, LinkedIn lost the passwords for 6.5 million users to hackers because of what some security experts called defective security.[4] LinkedIn is not a cloud vendor, but that event at a large public data utility does cause one to wonder about the security of cloud storage. Most of the time, we don't even know the physical location of cloud data, let alone how well the data center is secured, who works there, what procedures and policies are in place, and so on. We will return to this question in Chapter 12; for now, understand that this issue exists.

DISCUSSION QUESTIONS

1. Summarize why security risk is higher for integrated databases than for information silos. Describe a factor that can compensate for this increased risk.

2. Using PRIDE as an example, explain how users' incentives to protect data differ between an enterprise system and an inter-enterprise system. How does the use of security procedures differ between the two types of system?

3. Suppose you are a health club owner and you are approached by a PRIDE salesperson who says, "The PRIDE database is located in a *xyz* cloud facility" where *xyz* is the name of a large, reputable company such as Amazon, Oracle, Microsoft, or IBM. You ask about data security and he says, "You and I don't know anything about their security, but it has to be better than the security you have on that server you're operating in the closet down the hallway." How do you respond?

4. If you were a personal trainer at a health club, explain the value to you of having competitors' data about patients you share. Explain the value to you of obtaining, if you can, data about competitors' PRIDE patients who you have never treated.

5. Suppose you are a personal trainer at a health club, and you are approached by a PRIDE salesperson who says, "Our system's security ensures that no one can see your patients' data." How do you respond?

6. Suppose the salesperson in question 5 says, "Only others who are treating the same patients as you can see your patient data." How can you verify the truth of this statement?

7. Suppose that a personal trainer at a health club uses a trivial password such as *dog*. One of that health club's members watches the personal trainer sign in, obtains that password, and later steals all of the data on the patients treated by that club.

   a. Who is responsible for the data theft?

   b. How do you respond if you are the personal trainer using the trivial password?

   c. If you are the club owner, how will you likely learn about this theft? How do you respond when you do learn of it?

   d. If you are a participating healthcare provider, how will you likely learn about this theft? How do you respond when you do learn of it?

   e. If you are a patient who is using this system, whom do you hold accountable, and why?

[4]Michael Hickins, "LinkedIn Password Breach Illustrates Endemic Security Issue," June 6, 2012, *http://blogs.wsj.com/cio/2012/06/06/ linkedin-password-breach-illustrates-endemic-security-issue.*

Guide

ERP AND THE STANDARD, STANDARD BLUEPRINT

Designing business processes is difficult, time consuming, and very expensive. Highly trained experts conduct seemingly countless interviews with users and domain experts to determine business requirements. Then even more experts join those people, and together this team invests thousands of labor hours to design, develop, and implement effective business processes that meet those requirements. All of this is a very high-risk activity, prone to failure. And it all must be done before IS development can even begin.

ERP vendors such as SAP have invested millions of labor hours into the business blueprints that underlie their ERP solutions. Those blueprints consist of hundreds or thousands of different business processes. Examples are processes for hiring employees, acquiring fixed assets, acquiring consumable goods, and custom "one-off" (a unique product with a unique design) manufacturing, to name just a few.

Additionally, ERP vendors have implemented their business processes in hundreds of organizations. In so doing, they have been forced to customize their standard blueprint for use in particular industries. For example, SAP has a distribution-business blueprint that is customized for the auto parts industry, for the electronics industry, and for the aircraft industry. Hundreds of other customized solutions exist as well.

Even better, the ERP vendors have developed software solutions that fit their business-process blueprints. In theory, no software development is required at all if the organization can adapt to the standard blueprint of the ERP vendor.

As described in this chapter, when an organization implements an ERP solution, it identifies any differences that exist between its business processes and the standard blueprint. Then the organization must remove that difference, which can be done in one of two ways: It changes business processes to fit the standard blueprint. Or, the ERP vendor or a consultant modifies the standard blueprint (and software solution that matches that blueprint) to fit the unique requirements.

In practice, such variations from the standard blueprint are rare. They are difficult and expensive to implement, and they require the using organization to maintain the variations from the standard as new versions of the ERP software are developed. Consequently, most organizations choose to *modify their processes* to meet the blueprint, rather than the other way around. Although such process changes are also difficult to implement, once the organization has converted to the standard blueprint, they need no longer support a "variation."

So, from a standpoint of cost, effort, risk, and avoidance of future problems, there is a huge incentive for organizations to adapt to the standard ERP blueprint.

Initially, SAP was the only true ERP vendor, but in the meantime other companies have developed and acquired ERP solutions as well. Because of competitive pressure across the software industry, all of these products are

Source: © Gilly Smith/Fotolia

beginning to have the same sets of features and functions. ERP solutions are becoming a commodity.

All of this is fine, as far as it goes, but it introduces a nagging question: If, over time, every organization tends to implement the standard ERP blueprint, and if, over time, every software company develops essentially the same ERP features and functions, then won't every business, worldwide, come to look just like every other business, worldwide? How will organizations gain a competitive advantage if they all use the same business processes?

If every auto parts distributor uses the same business processes, based on the same software, are they not all clones of one another? How will one distinguish itself? How will innovation occur? Even if one parts distributor does successfully innovate a business process that gives it a competitive advantage, will the ERP vendors be conduits to transfer that innovation to competitors? Does the use of "commoditized" standard blueprints mean that no company can sustain a competitive advantage?

 DISCUSSION QUESTIONS

1. Explain in your own words why an organization might choose to change its processes to fit the standard blueprint. What advantages accrue by doing so?
2. Explain how competitive pressure among software vendors will cause the ERP solutions to become commodities. What does this mean to the ERP software industry?
3. If two businesses use exactly the same processes and exactly the same software, can they be different in any way at all? Explain why or why not.

4. Explain the following statement: An ERP software vendor can be a conduit to transfer innovation. What are the consequences to the innovating company? To the software company? To the industry? To the economy?
5. In theory, such standardization might be possible, but worldwide, there are so many different business models, cultures, people, values, and competitive pressures, can any two businesses ever be exactly alike?

ACTIVE REVIEW

Use this Active Review to verify that you understand the ideas and concepts that answer the chapter's study questions.

Q1 What are the basic types of processes?

Define *structured* and *dynamic processes* and compare and contrast them. Define *workgroup processes, enterprise processes,* and *inter-enterprise processes* and explain their differences and challenges. Define those same levels of information systems. Define *functional systems* and *functional applications.*

Q2 How can information systems improve process quality?

Name, define, and give an example of two dimensions of process quality. Name and describe three ways that organizations can improve process quality. Name and describe three ways that information systems can be used to improve process quality.

Q3 How do information systems eliminate the problems of information silos?

Define *information silo,* and explain how such silos come into existence. When do such silos become a problem? Describe the two types of silos in Figure 7-6, and explain the meaning implied by the two arrows.

Q4 How do CRM, ERP, and EAI support enterprise processes?

Define *business process reengineering,* and explain why it is difficult and expensive. Explain two major reasons why developing enterprise information systems in-house is expensive. Explain the advantages of inherent processes. Define and differentiate among *CRM, ERP,* and *EAI.* Explain how the nature of CRM and ERP is more similar to each other than that of EAI.

Q5 What are the elements of an ERP system?

Describe the minimum capability of a true ERP product. Explain the nature of each of the following ERP solution components: programs, data, procedures, and training and consulting. For each, summarize the work that customers must perform. List the top five ERP vendors in decreasing order of market share.

Q6 What are the challenges of implementing and upgrading enterprise information systems?

Name and describe four sources of challenges when implementing enterprise systems. Describe why enterprise systems management must be collaborative. Explain two major tasks required to identify requirements gaps. Summarize the challenges of transitioning to an enterprise system. Explain why employees resist change, and describe three ways of responding to that resistance.

Q7 How do inter-enterprise IS solve the problems of enterprise silos?

Describe information silos that exist among healthcare providers, health clubs, and individuals with regard to patient exercise data. Describe problems that those silos create. Explain how the system shown in Figure 7-19 will solve the problems caused by those silos. Define *distributed systems,* and explain the benefits of SOA using Web services when implementing such systems.

Q8 2024?

State one reason for what seems to be an acquisition war between Oracle and SAP. Explain why these vendors' past success is a current hindrance. Summarize the complications of mobile ERP access. Describe how workers in 2024 might use mobile devices with ERP systems.

Using Your Knowledge with PRIDE

Knowledge of this chapter will help you understand the fundamental value offered by solutions like PRIDE; namely, the elimination of the problems of enterprise-level information silos. As you now know, silos that are caused by workgroup processes can be eliminated (or managed, in the case of EAI) with enterprise systems. Similarly, silos that are caused by enterprise processes can be eliminated with inter-enterprise systems like PRIDE. Also, the knowledge of this chapter prepares you to understand the difficulty of adapting and of managing inter-enterprise systems. Finally, Figure 7-19 helps you understand how mobile devices and a cloud database can be used to implement an inter-enterprise system.

KEY TERMS AND CONCEPTS

Business process reengineering   252
Customer life cycle   253
Customer relationship management
    (CRM) system   253
Data integrity   249
Distributed systems   268
Dynamic processes   244
Enterprise application integration
    (EAI)   261
Enterprise information system   246
Enterprise processes   246

Enterprise resource planning
    (ERP)   254
ERP system   254
Functional application   245
Functional information systems   245
Industry-specific solutions   264
Information silo   249
Inherent processes   253
Inter-enterprise processes   246
Inter-enterprise information
    systems   247

Modules   254
Process blueprints   263
Process effectiveness   247
Process efficiency   247
Self-efficacy   267
Stored procedure   263
Structured processes   244
Train the trainer   263
Trigger   263
Workgroup information system   245
Workgroup process   245

MyMISLab

Go to **mymislab.com** to complete the problems marked with this icon ⭐.

USING YOUR KNOWLEDGE

7-1. Using the example of your university, give examples of information systems for each of the three levels of scope shown in Figure 7-4. Describe three departmental information systems that are likely to duplicate data. Explain how the characteristics of information systems in Figure 7-4 relate to your examples.

7-2. In your answer to question 7-1, explain how the three workgroup information systems create information silos. Describe the kinds of problems that these silos are likely to cause. Use Figure 7-5 as a guide.

7-3. Using your answer to question 7-2, describe an enterprise information system that will eliminate the silos. Would the implementation of your system require business process reengineering? Explain why or why not.

7-4. Google or Bing each of the five vendors in Figure 7-16. In what ways have their product offerings changed since this text was written? Do these vendors have new products? Have they made important acquisitions? Have they been acquired? Have any new companies made important inroads into their market share? Update Figure 7-16 with any important late-breaking news.

7-5. Using the knowledge you gained from Chapters 4 and 6, how do you think mobile systems and the cloud will affect ERP solutions? Explain how mobile ERP might benefit the types of personnel shown in Figure 7-12.

COLLABORATION EXERCISE 7

Using the collaboration IS you built in Chapter 2 (pages 73–74), collaborate with a group of students to answer the following questions.

The county planning office issues building permits, septic system permits, and county road access permits for all building projects in a county in an eastern state. The planning office issues permits to homeowners and builders for the construction of new homes and buildings and for any remodeling projects that involve electrical, gas, plumbing, and other

utilities, as well as the conversion of unoccupied spaces, such as garages, into living or working space. The office also issues permits for new or upgraded septic systems and permits to provide driveway entrances to county roads.

Figure 7-20 shows the permit process that the county used for many years. Contractors and homeowners found this process slow and very frustrating. For one, they did not like its sequential nature. Only after a permit had been approved or rejected by the engineering review process would they find out

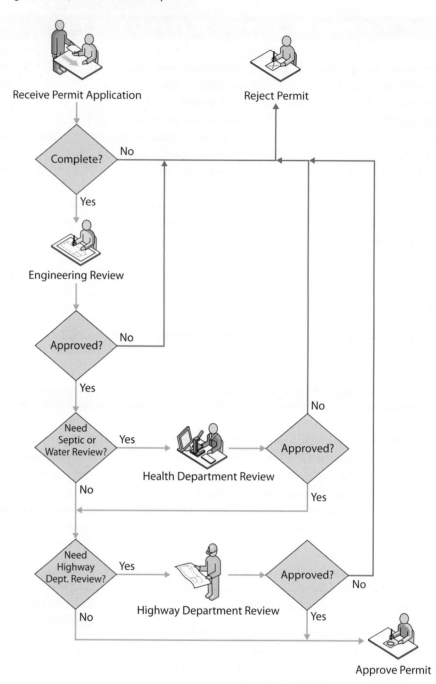

Figure 7-20
Building Permit Process, Old
Version

that a health or highway review was also needed. Because each
of these reviews could take 3 or 4 weeks, applicants requesting permits wanted the review processes to be concurrent
rather than serial. Also, both the permit applicants and county
personnel were frustrated because they never knew where a
particular application was in the permit process. A contractor
would call to ask how much longer, and it might take an hour
or longer just to find which desk the permits were on.

Accordingly, the county changed the permit process to
that shown in Figure 7-21. In this second process, the permit
office made three copies of the permit and distributed one to
each department. The departments reviewed the permits in

parallel; a clerk would analyze the results and, if there were no
rejections, approve the permit.

Unfortunately, this process had a number of problems,
too. For one, some of the permit applications were lengthy;
some included as many as 40 to 50 pages of large architec-
tural drawings. The labor and copy expense to the county was
considerable.

Second, in some cases departments reviewed documents unnecessarily. If, for example, the highway department rejected an
application, then neither the engineering nor health departments
needed to continue their reviews. At first, the county responded
to this problem by having the clerk who analyzed results cancel

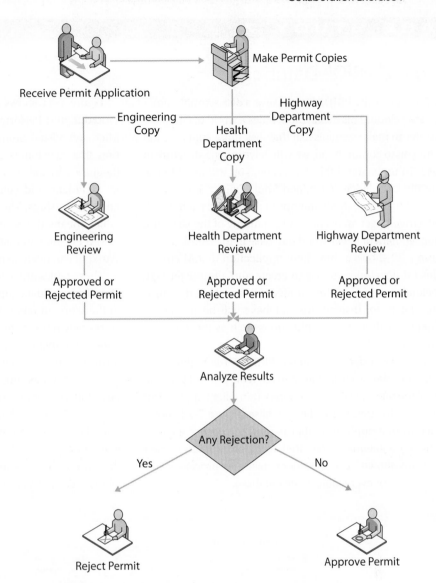

Figure 7-21
Building Permit Process,
Revised Version

Make Permit Copies

Receive Permit Application

Engineering
Copy

Health
Department
Copy

Highway
Department
Copy

Engineering
Review

Health Department
Review

Highway Department
Review

Approved or
Rejected Permit

Approved or
Rejected Permit

Approved or
Rejected Permit

Analyze Results

Any Rejection?

Yes

No

Reject Permit

Approve Permit

the reviews of other departments when a rejection was received. However, that policy was exceedingly unpopular with the permit applicants, because once the problem in a rejected application was corrected, the permit had to go back through the other departments. The permit would go to the end of the line and work its way back into the departments from which it had been pulled. Sometimes this resulted in a delay of 5 or 6 weeks.

Cancelling reviews was unpopular with the departments as well, because permit-review work had to be repeated. An application might have been nearly completed when it was cancelled due to a rejection in another department. When the application came through again, the partial work results from the earlier review were lost.

1. Explain why the processes in Figures 7-20 and 7-21 are classified as enterprise processes rather than departmental processes. Why are these processes not interorganizational processes?

2. Using Figure 7-8 as an example, redraw Figure 7-20 using an enterprise information system that processes a shared database. Explain the advantages of this system over the paper-based system in Figure 7-20.

3. Using Figure 7-10 as an example, redraw Figure 7-21 using an enterprise information system that processes a shared database. Explain the advantages of this system over the paper-based system in Figure 7-21.

4. Assuming that the county has just changed from the system in Figure 7-20 to the one in Figure 7-21, which of your answers in questions 2 and 3 do you think is better? Justify your answer.

5. Assume your team is in charge of the implementation of the system you recommend in your answer to question 4. Describe how each of the four challenges discussed in Q6 pertain to this implementation. Explain how your team will deal with those challenges.

CASE STUDY 7

Using the PRIDE Database

Figure 7-19 shows the PRIDE Database as a disk symbol, somewhere in the cloud. This disk symbol hides a world of complexity. In order to make symbols like that disk more concrete and easier for you to comprehend, we will delve into its structure in this case. To understand this discussion, you will need to use some of the knowledge you gained from Chapter 5. However, as you read this case, don't attempt to remember each detail. Instead, strive to get an overall understanding of the structure and management of a real-world database in the cloud.

Figure 7-22 shows a thin-client application that Microsoft provides for developers to use to create and administer SQL Azure cloud databases. This application is not used to process the database. Instead, the database will be processed using native or thin-client applications such as those shown in Figure 7-19.

In this figure, a database named PRIDE V1 is highlighted. When the developer clicks the Manage icon in the Database section of the menu, SQL Azure opens a thin-client application for working with that particular database. Figure 7-23 shows one page in that application that is used to process queries. Here the SQL statements required to define a table named Workout are shown. The developer needs to process statements like this for every table in the database.

Figure 7-24 shows three of the PRIDE V1 tables: Person, Workout, and Performance. These diagrams were created by Microsoft Visual Studio, which is a thick-client PC application that developers use to build applications and manage databases. Visual Studio accesses PRIDE V1 in the cloud, reads its metadata, and constructs these representations of tables and relationships. The 1...* notation on the lines between the tables means the relationship between them is 1:N. Thus, a row in Person can relate to many Workout rows, and a row in Workout can relate to many Performance rows.

These tables are used as follows: When a workout starts, the Store Exercise data application in Figure 7-19 stores a new row in the Workout table. As the workout proceeds, it periodically stores new rows in the Performance table that record exercise data so far, including Distance, Speed, Calories, Pulse, and so forth. It optionally records latitude and longitude for outside workouts such as runs and bike rides. A given workout might have 100 rows or more of Performance data.

Figure 7-25 shows the tables involved in prescribing workouts. Healthcare professionals create one or more standard workout profiles in the Profile table. A healthcare professional then prescribes that profile to a particular person, and this fact is recorded as a new row in the ProfilePrescription table.

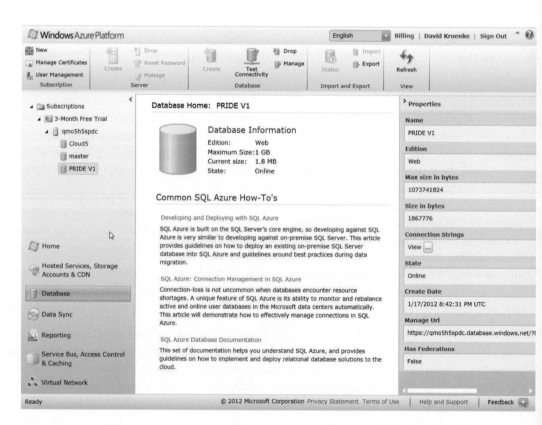

Figure 7-22

Thin-Client Application for Managing a Cloud Database

Source: Microsoft Corporation

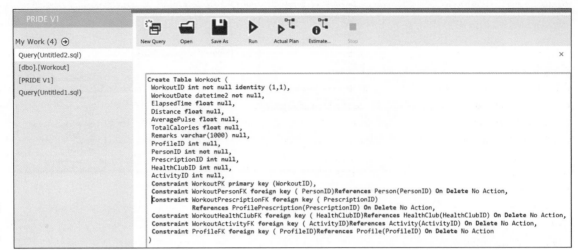

Figure 7-23
Defining the Workout Table with SQL
Source: © David Kroenke, 2012

Notice the relationships from Profile to ProfilePrescription and from Person to ProfilePrescription are 1:N. When a patient starts a workout according to that profile, a new row is created into Workout, and Performance data is also stored as just described (not shown). The notation 0..1 on the relationship line between Workout and Profile indicates that a Workout need not relate to any Profile. This rule is needed so that workout data can be stored even if a workout is not governed by a profile.

Figure 7-26 shows the names of all the tables in this database as well as their relationships. The tables with names preceded by the word *Terms_* contain data that PRIDE uses to determine how much, if any, of a person's data can be reported to a particular agency. For example, the table Terms_PersonHealthClub contains data that specifies how much of the person's data is to be shared with a particular health club. The *Terms_* table data is used by the three reporting applications in Figure 7-19 to limit data reported in accordance with each person's preferences.

QUESTIONS

7-6. Explain the advantages of locating the PRIDE database in the cloud. Dr. Flores and his partners could place it on one of their own servers in the practice. Give reasons why it would be unwise for them to do so.

7-7. Explain the origin of Figures 7-23 and 7-24. What application created each? Where did the data for constructing

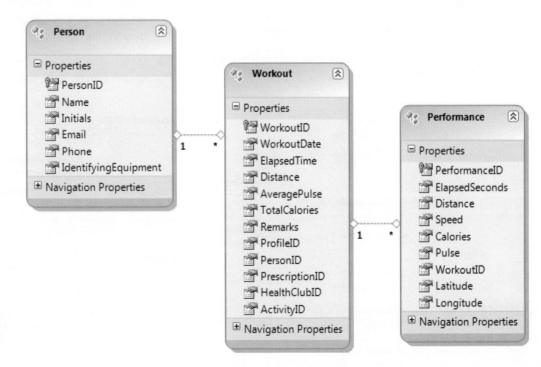

Figure 7-24
PRIDE: Person, Workout, and Performance Tables
Source: © David Kroenke, 2012

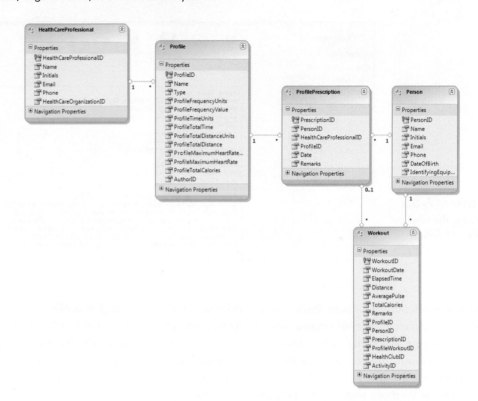

Figure 7-25
PRIDE: Tables Relating to
Exercise Prescriptions
Source: © David Kroenke, 2012

the tables in Figure 7-24 arise? Using your intuition and database knowledge, explain how the relationship between Person and Workout is defined in Figure 7-23. What coding in Figure 7-23 ensures that every row in Workout will correspond to some row in Person?

7-8. Explain how the Store Exercise Prescriptions application in Figure 7-19 will use the tables shown in Figure 7-25.

7-9. Explain how the Store Exercise Data application in Figure 7-19 will use the tables shown in Figure 7-25.

7-10. Explain how the Report Patient Exercise application in Figure 7-19 will use the tables shown in Figure 7-25.

7-11. Data in the Person table most likely duplicates data in health clubs' membership databases as well as data in healthcare providers' patient databases. Will this duplication create problems for the health clubs, healthcare providers, and PRIDE users? If not, say why not. If so, give two examples of problems and suggest ways that those problems can be solved.

7-12. Explain the ways in which the PRIDE database eliminates possible enterprise-level information silos. Explain ways that it might create another form of information silo.

7-13. Given what you know so far, do you think the PRIDE system is likely to be successful? Explain your answer.

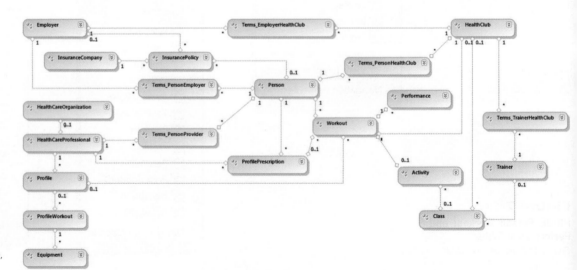

Figure 7-26
PRIDE: All Database
Tables
Source: © David Kroenke, 2012

MyMISLab

Go to **mymislab.com** for Auto-graded writing questions as well as the following Assisted-graded writing questions:

7-14. Using the patient discharge process in Figure 7-7, explain how the hospital benefits from an ERP solution. Describe why integration of patient records has advantages over separated databases. Explain the value of an industry-specific ERP solution to the hospital.

7-15. Consider the PRIDE system. Describe the information silos that exist prior to the implementation of PRIDE. Summarize problems caused by these silos. Explain how PRIDE eliminates information silos.

7-16. Mymislab Only – comprehensive writing assignment for this chapter.

Social Media Information Systems

Dr. Romero Flores is on the phone with Lindsey Garrett discussing the exercise activities of her mother, one of Dr. Flores's cardiac patients:

"Were you able to access your mother's exercise report?" Dr. Flores is referring to the browser report shown on the next page.

"Yes, I was, and it's not good, is it?"

"I'm afraid not. 94 calories in 11 treadmill sessions isn't the level of activity we want her to have."

"Yeah, I know, she's not doing anything. You know, it's a very strange thing, but she lied to me about this...my own mother, who *preached to me* that honesty's the best policy, flat out lied to me about her exercise..."

"I wouldn't go too far with that, Lindsey. She's going through quite a bit, and she's confused and frightened."

"Yeah, I know. But what do we do?"

"Well, first, let's be glad we've got the data and that we know what she's really doing...or not doing."

"Yeah, but where does that get us?"

"Well, we have a new PRIDE feature that involves social networking."

"Mom hates Facebook; I don't know why. Some weird fear or something."

"I don't mean Facebook. We're implementing virtual classes. Your mom signs up with a group and we have one of our staff members run group sessions where all the participants are using their own equipment, at home."

"I wonder if she'd do that."

"Go out to Endomondo.com— you'll see an example of how people are sharing their exercise data. We want to do something a little different, but with our own mobile app, or maybe a Facebook app, we haven't decided. Again, though, we're just getting started. Not sure this will work, but we'll provide staff to see if we can make it work."

"OK, I'll talk with her about it."

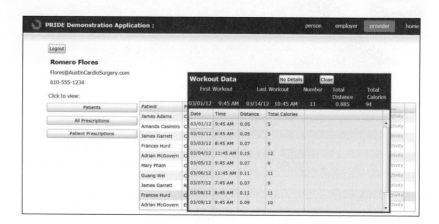

Later that day, Lindsey is on the phone with her mother. We hear just Lindsey's side of the conversation:

"Mom! I know what you think about Facebook. And it's Twitter, not Bitter. With a T!"

. . .

"Mother, nobody is going to see pictures of you in your PJs on your treadmill. We're not talking about any pictures."

. . .

"…nobody is going to see pictures of you in your PJs on your treadmill."

"Look, Mother. It's simple. You go to one session at Dr. Flores's office. You meet the other people that will be in your class…people just like you, your age, more or less, and all of whom have had heart surgery."

. . .

"Yes, I'll put an application on your cell phone. At the scheduled time, you sign in to the application…I'll show you how…and then you do your exercise, and your phone will show you how you're doing compared to the others. It will keep a record, too, so you can brag about it later."

. . .

STUDY QUESTIONS

Q1 What is a social media information system (SMIS)?

Q2 How do SMIS advance organizational strategy?

Q3 How do SMIS increase social capital?

Q4 What roles do SMIS play in the hyper-social organization?

Q5 How do (some) companies earn revenue from social media?

Q6 How can organizations manage the risks of social media?

Q7 2024?

"Don't tell me bragging's not nice, Little Ms. Mother who tried to deceive her doctor about her exercise..."

...

"Never mind. Anyway, there will be a little icon on the screen...a little picture-like thing. There won't be any pictures of you shown to anyone. Just a little icon with your first name. Or you can use a fake name, if you want. That doesn't matter."

...

"Look, I'll come over with the kids, and we'll set it up and show you how."

...

"No, don't bake anything. None of us need food. We need you to start doing your exercises. I'll see you tonight. OK?"

CHAPTER PREVIEW

Changes to social media are happening so rapidly that we all struggle to keep up with the latest developments. We revise this textbook every year, and even still, writing in August, I know that by the time you read this in January or later, a good portion of it will be obsolete. Unfortunately, I don't know which parts they will be.

In my experience, the best response to rapid technological change is to learn and understand underlying principles. Rather than show you Facebook or Google+ features that we know will change before the ink on this page is dry, let's instead focus on principles, conceptual frameworks, and models that will be useful when you address the opportunities and risks of social media systems in the early years of your professional career.

That knowledge will also help you avoid mistakes. Every day, you can hear businesspeople saying, "We're using Twitter." and "We've connected our Facebook page to our Web site." Or creating ads and news releases that say, "Follow us on Twitter." The important question is, for what? To be modern? To be hip? And do they have a social media policy?

We'll begin in Q1 by defining and describing the components of a social media information system, which will help you understand the commitment that organizations make when they use social media. As you've learned, the purpose of information systems is to help organizations achieve their strategy, and, in Q2, we'll consider how social media IS facilitate strategies. Next, in Q3 we will address how social media information systems increase social capital; Q4 will examine the role of social media information systems in creating the hyper-social organization. Q5 will address how some companies earn revenue from social media. We will then describe in Q6 how organizations can manage the risks of social media. We'll wrap up in Q7 with an odd analogy about the change in the relationship between individuals and organizations heading into 2024.

 What Is a Social Media Information System (SMIS)?

Social media (SM) is the use of information technology to support the sharing of content among networks of users. Social media enables people to form **communities**, **tribes**, or **hives**, all of which are synonyms that refer to a group of people related by a common interest. (The latter two terms are in vogue among business and technology writers.) A **social media information system (SMIS)** is an information system that supports the sharing of content among networks of users.

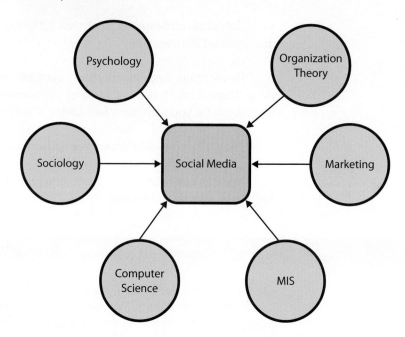

Figure 8-1
Social Media Is a Convergence
of Disciplines

As illustrated in Figure 8-1, social media is a convergence of many disciplines. In this book, we will focus on the MIS portion of Figure 8-1 by discussing SMIS and how they contribute to organizational strategy. If you decide to work in the SM field as a professional, you will need some knowledge of all these disciplines, except possibly computer science.

Three SMIS Roles

Before discussing the components of an SMIS, we need to clarify the roles played by the three organizational units shown in Figure 8-2:

- User communities
- Social media sponsors
- Social media application providers

User Communities

Forming communities is a natural human trait; anthropologists claim that the ability to form them is responsible for the progress of the human race. In the past, however, communities were based on family relationships or geographic location. Everyone in the village formed a community. The key difference of SM communities is that they are formed based on mutual interests and transcend familial, geographic, and organizational boundaries.

Because of this transcendence, most people belong to several, or even many, different user communities. Google+ recognized this fact when it created user circles that enable users

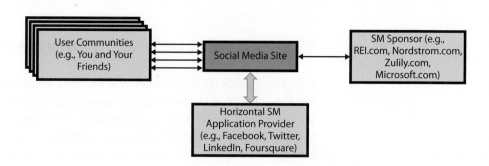

Figure 8-2
SMIS Organizational Roles

to allocate their connections (*people,* using Google+ terminology) to one or more community groups. Facebook and other SM application providers are adapting in similar ways.

Figure 8-3 expands on the community–SM site relationship in Figure 8-2. From the point of view of the SM site, Community A is a first-tier community that consists of users that have a direct relationship to that site. User 1, in turn, belongs to three communities: A, B, and C (these could be, say, classmates, professional contacts, and friends). From the point of view of the SM site, Communities B–E are second-tier communities because the relationships in those communities are intermediated by first-tier users. The number of second- and first-tier community members grows exponentially. If each community had, for example, 100 members, then the SM site would have 100×100, or 10,000, second-tier members and $100 \times 100 \times 100$ third-tier members. However, that statement is not quite true because communities overlap; in Figure 8-3, for example, user 7 belongs to Communities C and E. Thus, these calculations are the maximum number of users.

How the SM site chooses to relate to these communities depends on its goals. If the SM site is interested in pure publicity, it will want to relate to as many tiers of communities as it can. If so, it will create a **viral hook**, which is some inducement, such as a prize or other reward, for passing communications along through the tiers. If, however, the purpose of the SM site is to solve an embarrassing problem, say to fix a product defect, then the sponsors of the SM site would endeavor to constrain, as much as it can, the communications to Community A.

The exponential nature of relationships via community tiers offers sponsoring organizations both a blessing and a curse. An employee who is a member of Community A can share her sincere and legitimate pride in her organization's latest product or service with hundreds or thousands of people in her communities. However, she can also blast her disappointment

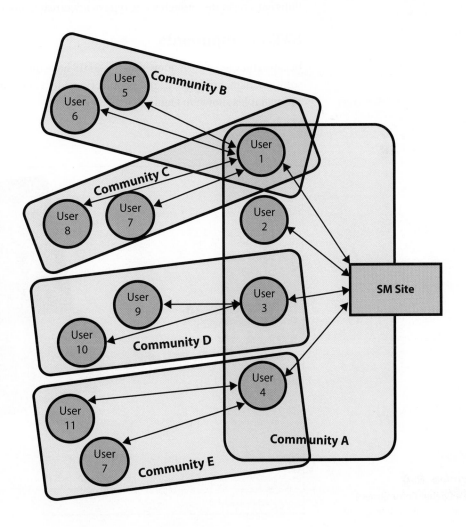

Figure 8-3
SM Communities

at some recent development to that same audience, or, worse, inadvertently share private and proprietary organizational data with someone in that audience who works for the competition.

Social media is a powerful tool, and to use it well, organizations must know their goals and plan accordingly, as you'll learn.

Social Media Sponsors

Social media sponsors are companies and other organizations that choose to support a presence on one or more SM sites. Figure 8-4 shows Microsoft's Surface page links to Facebook and Twitter in the bottom right corner of that page. When Microsoft places those icons on its promotional pages, it is making a commitment to invest considerable employee time and other costs to support social media. In particular, it needs to develop procedures and staff as well as train people to support that site, as you'll learn in the next section.

Social Media Application Providers

Social media application providers are the companies that operate the SM sites. Facebook, Twitter, LinkedIn, and Google are all SM application providers. These providers create the features and functions of the site, and they compete with one another for the attention of user communities and SM sponsors.

Social media has evolved in such a way that users expect to use SM applications without paying a license fee or other charge. Sponsors may or may not pay a fee, depending on the application and on what they do with it. On Facebook, for example, creating a company page is free, but Facebook charges a fee to advertise to communities that "Like" that page. Most SM applications earn revenue through some type of advertising model.

SMIS Components

Because they are information systems, SMIS have the same five components as all IS: hardware, software, data, procedures, and people. Consider each component for each of the three organizational roles shown in Figure 8-5.

Figure 8-4
Not a Casual Commitment
Source: Microsoft Corporation

Component	Role	Description
Hardware	User	Any user computing device
	SM sponsor	Any user computing device
	Application provider	Elastic, cloud-based servers
Software	User	Browser, iOS, Android, Windows 8, and other applications
	SM sponsor	Browser, application tools
	Application provider	Application, NoSQL or other DBMS
Data	User	User-generated content, connection data
	SM sponsor	Sponsor content
	Application provider	Content and connection data storage for rapid retrieval
Procedures	User	Informal, copy each other
	SM sponsor	Create, manage, remove content; extract value from content and connections; manage risk
	Application provider	Run and maintain application (beyond the scope of this text)
People	User	Adaptive, can be irrational
	SM sponsor	Key users
	Application provider	Staff to run and maintain application (beyond the scope of this text)

Figure 8-5
Five Components of SMIS

Hardware

Both community users and employees of SM sponsors process SM sites using desktops, laptops, and mobile devices. In most cases, SM application providers host the SM presence using elastic servers in the cloud.

Software

Users employ browsers and client applications, such as mobile applications, to read and submit data and to add and remove connections to communities and other users. SM sponsors contribute to the site via browsers or using specialized sponsor applications provided by the SM application provider. In some cases, like Facebook applications, SM sponsors create their own applications and interface those applications with the SM site.

SM application providers develop and operate their own custom, proprietary, social networking application software. As you learned in Chapter 4, supporting custom software is expensive over the long term; SM application vendors must do so because the features and functions of their applications are fundamental to their competitive strategy. They can do so because they spread the development costs over the revenue generated by millions of users.

As you learned in Case Study 5, many social networking vendors use a NoSQL database management system to process their data, although traditional relational DBMS products are used as well. Recall, too, that Facebook began development of Cassandra in-house (Case Study 5, pages 194–195), but donated it to the open-source community when it realized the expense and commitment of maintaining it.

Data

SM data falls into two categories: content and connections. **Content data** is data and responses to data that are contributed by users and SM sponsors. You provide the source content data for your Facebook site, and your friends provide response content when they write on your wall, make comments, tag you, or otherwise publish on your site.

Connection data is data about relationships. On Facebook, for example, the relationships to your friends are connection data. The fact that you've liked particular organizations is also connection data. Connection data differentiates SMIS from Web site applications. Both Web sites and social networking sites present user and responder content, but only social networking applications store and process connection data.

SM application providers store and retrieve SM data on behalf of sponsors and user communities. As explained in Case Study 5, they must do so in the presence of network and server failures, and they must do so rapidly. The problem is made somewhat easier, however, because SM content and connection data have a relatively simple structure.

Procedures

For social networking users, procedures are informal, evolving, and socially oriented. You do what your friends do. When the members of your tribe learn how to do something new and interesting, you copy them. Software is designed to be easy to learn and use.

Such informality makes using SMIS easy; it also means that unintended consequences are common. The most troubling examples concern user privacy. Many people have learned not to post pictures of themselves in front of their house numbers on the same publicly accessible site on which they're describing their new high-definition television. Many others, alas, have not.

For SM sponsors, social networking procedures cannot be so informal. Before initiating a social networking presence, organizations must develop procedures for creating content, managing user responses, removing obsolete or objectionable content, and extracting value from content. For an example of the latter, setting up an SMIS to gather data on product problems is a wasted expense unless procedures exist to extract knowledge from that social networking data. Organizations also need to develop procedures to manage SM risk, as described in Q6.

Procedures for operating and maintaining the SM application are beyond the scope of this text.

People

Users of social media do what they want to do depending on their goals and their personalities. They behave in certain ways and observe the consequences. They may or may not change their behavior. By the way, note that SM users aren't necessarily rational, at least not in purely monetary ways. See, for example, the study by Vernon Smith in which people walked away from free money because they thought someone else was getting more![1]

SM sponsors cannot be so casual. Anyone who contributes to an organization's SM site or who uses his or her position in a company to speak for an organization needs to be trained on both SMIS user procedures and the organization's social networking policy. We will discuss such procedures and policies in Q6.

Social media is creating new job titles, new responsibilities, and the need for new types of training. For example, what makes a good tweeter? What makes an effective wall writer? What type of person should be hired for such jobs? What education should they have? How does one evaluate candidates for such positions? All of these questions are being asked and answered today. Clearly it's a hot field, and because social media reinforces inherent human behavior, SM jobs are not likely to disappear anytime soon.

The staff to operate and maintain the SM application is beyond the scope of this text.

Not Free

How honest are people with social media? Reflect on ethical issues for social media in the Ethics Guide on pages 304–305.

Before we go on, you will sometimes read that SMIS are free. It is true that Facebook, Twitter, LinkedIn, and other sites do not charge for hardware, software, or data storage. However, unless

---

[1]Vernon Smith, *Rationality in Economics: Constructivist and Ecological Forms* (Cambridge, UK: Cambridge University Press, 2007), pp. 247–250.

the SM sponsor takes the foolish and irresponsible posture of letting its social networking presence do whatever it will, someone will need to develop, implement, and manage the social networking procedures just described. Furthermore, employees who contribute to and manage social networking sites generate direct labor costs.

How Do SMIS Advance Organizational Strategy?

In Chapter 3, Figure 3-1 (page 83), you learned the relationship of information systems to organizational strategy. In brief, strategy determines value chains, which determine business processes, which determine information systems. Insofar as value chains determine *structured* business processes, such as those discussed in Chapter 7, this chain is straightforward. However, social media is by its very nature *dynamic*; its flow cannot be designed or diagrammed, and, if it were, no sooner would the diagram be finished than the SM process would have changed.

Therefore, we need to back up a step and consider how value chains determine dynamic processes and thus set SMIS requirements. As you will see, social media fundamentally changes the balance of power among users, their communities, and organizations.

Before we consider each of the primary value chain activities, you need to know two important terms. Gossieaux and Moran, creators of the hyper-social organization theory, identify two kinds of communities that are important to commerce:[2]

- Defenders of belief
- Seekers of the truth

Defenders of belief share a common belief and form their hive around that belief. They seek conformity and want to convince others of the wisdom of their belief. A group that believes that Google+ is far superior to Facebook will engage in behaviors to convince others that this is true. When confronted with contrary evidence, they do not change their opinion, but become more firmly convinced of their belief.[3,4] Defenders-of-belief communities facilitate activities like sales and marketing. They are not effective for activities that involve innovation or problem solving. Such groups can form strong bonds and allegiance to an organization.

Seekers of the truth share a common desire to learn something, solve a problem, or make something happen. CFOs who want to learn how to manage the risk of placing financial data in the cloud seek "the truth." They share a common problem, but not a common solution to that problem. Not surprisingly, such tribes are incredible problem solvers and excel at innovation. They can be useful in customer service activity, as long as they don't conclude that the best way to solve a product problem is to use another company's product, something they might do because such groups seldom form a strong bond to an organization. The only organizational bond seekers of the truth are likely to form occurs when the organization demonstrates behavior that demonstrates that it, too, is committed to solving the community's shared problem.

Figure 8-6 summarizes how social media contributes to the five primary value chain activities and to the human resources support activity. Consider each row of this table.

Social Media and the Sales and Marketing Activity

In the past, organizations controlled their relationships with customers using structured processes and related information systems. In fact, the primary purpose of traditional CRM was to manage customer touches. Traditional CRM ensured that the organization spoke to customers

---

[2]Francois Gossieaux and Edward K. Moran, *The Hyper-Social Organization* (New York: McGraw-Hill, 2010), pp. 22, 23–25.

[3]Daniel Kahneman, Paul Slovic, and Amos Tversky, *Judgment Under Uncertainty: Heuristics and Biases* (Cambridge, UK: Cambridge University Press, 1982), p. 144.

[4]For a more modern treatment of this phenomenon than reference 3 and for fascinating research as to why such behavior occurs, see Jonathan Haidt, *The Righteous Mind: Why Good People Are Divided by Politics and Religion* (New York: Pantheon Books, 2012).

Activity	Community type	Focus	Dynamic process	Risks
Sales and marketing	Defender of belief	Outward to prospects	Social CRM Peer-to-peer sales	Loss of credibility Bad PR
Customer service	Seeker of the truth	Outward to customers	Peer-to-peer support	Loss of control
Inbound logistics	Seeker of the truth	Upstream supply chain providers	Problem solving	Privacy
Outbound logistics	Seeker of the truth	Downstream supply chain shippers	Problem solving	Privacy
Manufacturing and operations	Seeker of the truth	Outward for user design; Inward to operations and manufacturing	User-guided design Enterprise 2.0 Knowledge management	Efficiency/effectiveness
Human resources	Defender of belief	Employment candidates; Employee communications	Employee prospecting, recruiting, and evaluation SharePoint & Enterprise 2.0 for employee-to-employee communication	Error Loss of credibility

Figure 8-6
SM in Value Chain Activities

with one voice and that it controlled the messages, the offers, and even the support that customers received based on the value of a particular customer. In 1990, if you wanted to know something about an IBM product, you'd contact its local sales office; that office would classify you as a prospect and use that classification to control the literature, the documentation, and your access to IBM personnel.

Social CRM is a dynamic, SM-based CRM process. The relationships between organizations and customers emerge in a dynamic process as both parties create and process content. In addition to the traditional forms of promotion, employees in the organization create wikis, blogs, discussion lists, frequently asked questions, sites for user reviews and commentary, and other dynamic content. Customers search this content, contribute reviews and commentary, ask more questions, create user groups, and so forth. With social CRM, each customer crafts his or her own relationship with the company.

Social CRM flies in the face of the structured and controlled processes of traditional CRM. Because relationships emerge from joint activity, customers have as much control as companies. This characteristic is anathema to traditional sales managers who want structured processes for controlling what the customer reads, sees, and hears about the company and its products.

Further, traditional CRM is centered on lifetime value; customers that are likely to generate the most business get the most attention and have the most effect on the organization. However, with social CRM, the customer who spends 10 cents but who is an effective reviewer, commentator, or blogger can have more influence than the quiet customer who purchases $10 million a year. Such imbalance is incomprehensible to traditional sales managers.

However, traditional sales managers *are* happy to have defenders-of-belief groups sell their products using peer-to-peer recommendations. A quick look at products and their reviews on Amazon.com will show how frequently customers are willing to write long, thoughtful reviews of products they like or do not like. Amazon.com and other online retailers also allow readers to rate the helpfulness of reviews. In that way, substandard reviews are revealed for the wary.

Today, many organizations are struggling to make the transition from controlled, structured, traditional CRM processes to wide-open, adaptive, dynamic social CRM processes; this struggle represents a significant job opportunity for those interested in IS, sales, and social media.

Social Media and Customer Service

Product users are amazingly willing to help each other solve problems. Even more, they will do so without pay; in fact, payment can warp and ruin the support experience as customers fight with one another. SAP learned that it was better to reward its SAP Developer Network with donations on their behalf to charitable organizations than to give them personal rewards.[5]

Not surprisingly, organizations whose business strategy involves selling to or through developer networks have been the earliest and most successful at SM-based customer support. In addition to SAP, Microsoft has long sold through its network of partners. Its MVP (Most Valuable Professional) program is a classic example of giving praise and glory in exchange for customer-provided customer assistance (*http://mvp.support.microsoft.com*). Of course, the developers in their networks have a business incentive to participate because that activity helps them sell services to the communities in which they participate.

However, users with no financial incentive are also willing to help others. Amazon.com supports a program called Vine by which customers can be selected to give prerelease and new product reviews to the buyer community.[6] You'll need your psychology course to explain what drives people to strive for such recognition. MIS just provides the platform!

The primary risk of peer-to-peer support is loss of control. As stated, seekers of the truth will seek the truth, even if that means recommending another vendor's product over yours. We address that risk in Q6.

Social Media and Inbound and Outbound Logistics

Companies whose profitability depends on the efficiency of their supply chain have long used information systems to improve both the effectiveness and efficiency of structured supply chain processes. Because supply chains are tightly integrated into structured manufacturing processes, there is less tolerance for the unpredictability of dynamic, adaptive processes. Solving problems is an exception; social media can be used to provide numerous solution ideas and rapid evaluation of them. The Japanese earthquake in the spring of 2011 created havoc in the automotive supply chain when major Japanese manufacturers lacked power and, in some cases, facilities to operate. Social media was used to dispense news, allay fears of radioactive products, and address ever-changing needs and problems.

Seekers-of-the-truth communities provide better and faster problem solutions to complex supply chain problems. Social media is designed to foster content creation and feedback among networks of users, and that characteristic facilitates the iteration and feedback needed for problem solving, as described in Chapter 2.

Loss of privacy is, however, a significant risk. Problem solving requires the open discussion of problem definitions, causes, and solution constraints. Suppliers and shippers work with many companies; supply chain problem solving via social media is problem solving in front of your competitors.

Social Media and Manufacturing and Operations

Operations and manufacturing activities are dominated by structured processes. The flexibility and adaptive nature of social media would result in chaos if applied to the manufacturing line or to the warehouse. However, social media does play a role in product design as well as in employee knowledge sharing and management.

Crowdsourcing is the dynamic social media process of employing users to participate in product design or product redesign. eBay often solicits customers to provide feedback on their

---

[5]Francois Gossieaux and Edward K. Moran, *The Hyper-Social Organization* (New York: McGraw-Hill, 2010), pp. 8, 9.

[6] "About Customer Ratings," *Amazon.com*, accessed July 30, 2013, *http://www.amazon.com/gp/help/customer/display.html/ref=hp_200791020_vine?nodeId=200791020#vine*.

Enterprise 2.0 Component	Remarks
Search	People have more success searching than they do in finding from structured content.
Links	Links to enterprise resources (like on the Web).
Authoring	Create enterprise content via blogs, wikis, discussion groups, presentations, etc.
Tags	Flexible tagging (like Delicious) results in folksonomies of enterprise content.
Extensions	Using usage patterns to offer enterprise content via tag processing (like the style of Pandora).
Signals	Pushing enterprise content to users based on subscriptions and alerts.

Figure 8-7
McAfee's SLATES Enterprise 2.0 Model

eBay experience. As that site says, "There's no better group of advisors than our customers." User-guided design has been used to plan video games, shoes, and many other products.

Enterprise 2.0 is the application of social media to facilitate the cooperative work of people inside organizations. Enterprise 2.0 can be used in operations and manufacturing to enable users to share knowledge and problem-solving techniques.

Andrew McAfee, the originator of the term *Enterprise 2.0*, defined six characteristics that he refers to with the acronym **SLATES** (see Figure 8-7).[7] Workers want to be able to *search* for content inside the organization just like they do on the Web. Most workers find that searching is more effective than navigating content structures such as lists and tables of content. Workers want to access organizational content by *link*, just as they do on the Web. They also want to *author* organizational content using blogs, wikis, discussion groups, published presentations, and so on.

Enterprise 2.0 content is *tagged*, just like content on the Web, and tags are organized into structures, as is done on the Web at sites like Delicious (*www.delicious.com*). These structures organize tags as a taxonomy does, but, unlike taxonomies, they are not preplanned; they emerge. A **folksonomy** is content structure that has emerged from the processing of many user tags. Additionally, Enterprise 2.0 workers want applications to enable them to rate tagged content and to use the tags to predict content that will be of interest to them (as with Pandora), a process McAfee refers to as *extensions*. Finally, Enterprise 2.0 workers want relevant content pushed to them; they want to be *signaled* when something of interest to them happens in organizational content.

The potential problem with Enterprise 2.0 is the quality of its dynamic process. Because the benefits of Enterprise 2.0 result from emergence, there is no way to control for either effectiveness or efficiency. It's a messy process about which little can be predicted.

Social Media and Human Resources

The last row in Figure 8-6 concerns the use of social media and human resources. Social media is used for finding employee prospects, for recruiting candidates, and—in some organizations— for candidate evaluation.

Social media is also used for employee communications, using internal personnel sites such as MySite and MyProfile in SharePoint or other similar Enterprise 2.0 facilities. SharePoint provides a place for employees to post their expertise in the form of "Ask me about" questions. When employees are looking for an internal expert, they can search SharePoint for people who

---

[7]Andrew McAfee, "Enterprise 2.0: The Dawn of Emergent Collaboration," *MIT Sloan Management Review*, Spring 2006, accessed August 2001, *http://sloanreview.mit.edu/the-magazine/files/saleablepdfs/47306.pdf*.

have posted the desired expertise. SharePoint 2013 greatly extends support for social media beyond that in earlier SharePoint versions.

The risks of social media in human resources concern the possibility of error when using sites such as Facebook to form conclusions about employees. A second risk is that the SM site becomes too defensive as a defender of belief or is obviously promulgating an unpopular management message.

Study Figure 8-6 to understand the general framework by which organizations can accomplish their strategy via a dynamic process supported by SMIS. We will now turn to an economic perspective on the value and use of SMIS.

How Do SMIS Increase Social Capital?

Business literature defines three types of capital. Karl Marx defined **capital** as the investment of resources for future profit. This traditional definition refers to investments into resources such as factories, machines, manufacturing equipment, and the like. **Human capital** is the investment in human knowledge and skills for future profit. By taking this class, you are investing in your own human capital. You are investing your money and time to obtain knowledge that you hope will differentiate you from other workers and ultimately give you a wage premium in the workforce.

According to Nan Lin, **social capital** is the investment in social relations with the expectation of returns in the marketplace.[8] When you attend a business function for the purpose of meeting people and reinforcing relationships, you are investing in your social capital. Similarly, when you join LinkedIn or contribute to Facebook, you are (or can be) investing in your social capital.

What Is the Value of Social Capital?

According to Lin, social capital adds value in four ways:

- Information
- Influence
- Social credentials
- Personal reinforcement

Relationships in social networks can provide *information* about opportunities, alternatives, problems, and other factors important to business professionals. They also provide an opportunity to *influence* decision makers at one's employer or in other organizations who are critical to your success. Such influence cuts across formal organizational structures, such as reporting relationships. Third, being linked to a network of highly regarded contacts is a form of *social credential*. You can bask in the glory of those with whom you are related. Others will be more inclined to work with you if they believe critical personnel are standing with you and may provide resources to support you. Finally, being linked into social networks reinforces a professional's image and position in an organization or industry. It reinforces the way you define yourself to the world (and to yourself).

Social networks differ in value. The social network you maintain with your high school friends probably has less value than the network you have with your business associates, but not necessarily so. According to Henk Flap, the **value of social capital** is determined by the number of relationships in a social network, by the strength of those relationships, and by the resources controlled by those related.[9] If your high school friends happened to have been Mark Zuckerberg

---

[8]Nan Lin, *Social Capital: The Theory of Social Structure and Action* (Cambridge, UK: Cambridge University Press, 2002), Location 310 of the Kindle Edition.

[9]Henk D. Flap, "Social Capital in the Reproduction of Inequality," *Comparative Sociology of Family, Health, and Education,* Vol. 20 (1991), pp. 6179–6202. Cited in Nan Lin, *Social Capital: The Theory of Social Structure and Action* (Cambridge, UK: Cambridge University Press, 2002), Kindle location 345.

Using MIS InClass 8

Any Kayakers Here at the Grand Canyon?

Salesforce.com developed a social media platform named Chatter. Go to *www.salesforce.com/chatter* to learn its features, functions, and applications. As you'll see, Chatter can be used to connect employees and customers via social media. For example, it can connect salespeople with presale support personnel or customer service personnel with customers. The Chatter Web site illustrates these and numerous other example uses.

But a startling, and potentially groundbreaking, application is mentioned in a video of Beth Comstock, Chief Marketing Officer for General Electric: "We want to use Chatter to connect our employees, our customers, and our machines."

Did she mean that GE jet engines are going to be social media users? Will jet engines be friending the engines they met during testing? Will they be submitting reviews on mechanics, as in, "Don't accept maintenance from Charlie Smith, he's too rough with his tools"? Will jet engines be chatting with one another about the long flight to Hong Kong? During boring intervals on the long flight to Hong Kong?

Listen yourself: *www.youtube.com/embed/j3oLfn_nvUQ.* Comstock does indeed say, "And ultimately what is very exciting for us is how do we connect our customers, our employees, and our machines."

Foursquare for autos? While you're hiking in the Grand Canyon, will your car be finding other cars that also have kayaks on their roofs?

Form a team as directed by your professor and address the following questions:

1. Visit *www.salesforce.com/chatter* to learn Chatter's features and applications. Using what you learn, state one Chatter application for each of the value chain activities in Figure 8-6.

2. From the salesforce.com site, find three interesting Chatter applications other than General Electric's. Summarize those applications. Classify them in terms of Figure 8-6.

3. One obvious example for SM machines is for the machines to report operational status, say speed, temperature, fuel usage, and so on, depending on the type of machine, to a Chatter or other SM site. How can the organization use such reporting in the context of machine, customer, and employee social media?

4. Consider foursquare for machines. Besides cars with kayaks asking for the presence of other cars with kayaks, what other uses can your team envision? Consider machine-to-machine interactions as well as machine-to-human interactions.

5. Besides reporting operational status and foursquare for machines, what other applications for machine-employee-customer SM can you envision?

or Cameron and Tyler Winklevoss, and if you maintain strong relations with them via your high school network, then the value of that social network far exceeds any you'll have at work. For most of us, however, the network of our current professional contacts provides the most social capital.

So, when you use social networking professionally, consider those three factors. You gain social capital by adding more friends and by strengthening the relationships you have with existing friends. Further, you gain more social capital by adding friends and strengthening relationships with people who control resources that are important to you. Such calculations may seem cold, impersonal, and possibly even phony. When applied to the recreational use of social networking, they may be. But when you use social networking for professional purposes, keep them in mind.

Klout.com searches social media activity on Facebook, Twitter, and other sites, and creates what it calls a Klout Score, which is is a measure of individuals' social capital. Klout scores vary from 0 to 100; the more that others respond to your content, the higher your score. Also, responses from people who seldom respond are valued more than responses from those who respond frequently.[10]

How Do Social Networks Add Value to Businesses?

Organizations have social capital just as humans do. Historically, organizations created social capital via salespeople, customer support, and public relations. Endorsements by high-profile people are a traditional way of increasing social capital, but there are tigers in those woods.

Today, progressive organizations maintain a presence on Facebook, LinkedIn, Twitter, and possibly other sites. They include links to their social networking presence on their Web sites and make it easy for customers and interested parties to leave comments.

To understand how social networks add value to businesses, consider each of the elements of social capital: number of relationships, strength of relationships, and resources controlled by "friends."

Using Social Networking to Increase the Number of Relationships

In a traditional business relationship, a client (you) has some experience with a business, such as a restaurant or resort. Traditionally, you may express your opinions about that experience by word of mouth to your social network. However, such communication is unreliable and brief: You are more likely to say something to your friends if the experience was particularly good or bad; but, even then, you are likely only to say something to those friends whom you encounter while the experience is still recent. And once you have said something, that's it; your words don't live on for days or weeks.

Figure 8-8 shows the same relationships as shown in Figure 8-3 but cast into the framework of a restaurant that specializes in wedding receptions. Users 1–4 in this example have a direct relationship with the restaurant's SM site (Facebook or whatever is popular). Here, Communities B–D in Figure 8-3 have been replaced by weddings. (We'll assume that user 1 has two children who were married and held their receptions at the restaurant, not that user 1 is divorced and chose to have both of her wedding receptions at the same restaurant.)

Figure 8-8 indicates that weddings can potentially contribute more than just revenue. If the restaurant can find a way to induce members of the wedding party or wedding attendees to form a relationship with that restaurant, weddings will contribute substantially to the number of relationships in its social network and, depending on the strength and value of those connections, possibly contribute substantially to the restaurant's social capital.

Such relationship sales have been going on by word of mouth for centuries; the difference here is that SMIS allow such sales to scale to levels not possible in the past. SMIS also make those relationships visible and available for other purposes.

Using Social Networks to Increase the Strength of Relationships

To an organization, the **strength of a relationship** is the likelihood that the entity (person or other organization) in the relationship will do something that benefits the organization. An organization has a strong relationship with you if you buy its products, write positive reviews about it, post pictures of you using the organization's products or services, and so on.

---

[10]*http://klout.com/corp/how-it-works*, accessed August 2013.

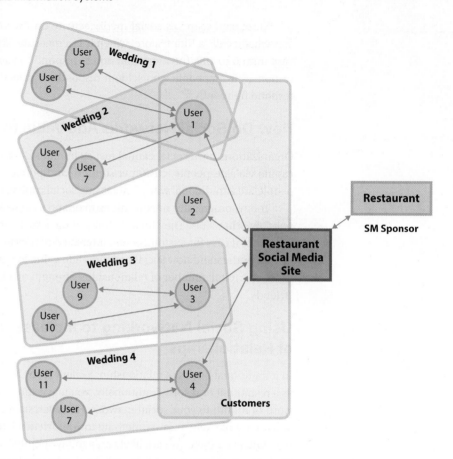

Figure 8-8
SM Communities

As stated earlier, social networks provide four forms of value: influence, information, social credentials, and reinforcement. If an organization can induce those in its relationships to provide more of any of those factors, it has strengthened that relationship.

In his autobiography, Benjamin Franklin provided a key insight.[11] He said that if you want to strengthen your relationship with someone in power, ask him to do you a favor. Before Franklin invented the public library, he would ask powerful strangers to lend him their expensive books. In that same sense, organizations have learned that they can strengthen their relationships with you by asking you to do them a favor. In Q4, we will discuss information systems that encourage the creation of user-generated content as a way of getting you to do them a favor. When you provide that favor, it strengthens your relationship with the organization.

Traditional capital depreciates. Machines wear out, factories get old, technology and computers become obsolete, and so forth. Does social capital also depreciate? Do relationships wear out from use? So far, the answer seems to be both yes and no.

Clearly, there are only so many favors you can ask of someone in power. And there are only so many times a company can ask you to review a product, post pictures, or provide connections to your friends. At some point, the relationship deteriorates due to overuse. So, yes, social capital does depreciate.

However, frequent interactions strengthen relationships and hence increase social capital. The more you interact with a company, the stronger your commitment and allegiance. But continued frequent interactions occur only when both parties see value in continuing the relationship. Thus, at some point, the organization must do something to make it worth your while to continue to do it a favor.

---

[11]Founding father of the United States. Author of *Poor Richard's Almanac.* Successful businessman; owner of a chain of print shops. Discoverer of groundbreaking principles in the theory of electricity. Inventor of bifocals, the potbelly stove, the lightning rod, and much more. Founder of the public library and the postal service. Darling of the French court and salons, and now, contributor to social network theory!

So, social capital does depreciate, but such depreciation can be ameliorated by adding something of value to the interaction. And continuing a successful relationship over time substantially increases relationship strength.

Connecting to Those with More Assets

Social media can have a positive impact on your personal brand. But what is a personal brand, and how does it help you craft authentic relationships with others? The Guide on pages 316–317 explores these questions.

The third measure of the value of social capital is the size of the assets controlled by those in the relationships. An organization's social capital is thus partly a function of the social capital of those to whom it relates. The most visible measure is the number of relationships. Someone with 1,000 loyal Twitter followers is usually more valuable than someone with 10. But the calculation is more subtle than that; if those 1,000 followers are college students and if the organization's product is adult diapers, the value of the relationship to the followers is low. A relationship with 10 Twitter followers who are in retirement homes would be more valuable.

There is no formula for computing social capital, but the three factors would seem to be more multiplicative than additive. Or, stated in other terms, the value of social capital is more in the form of

Social Capital = Number of Relationships × Relationship Strength × Entity Resources

than it is

Social Capital = Number of Relationships + Relationship Strength + Entity Resources

Again, do not take these equations literally; take them in the sense of the multiplicative interaction of the three factors.

This multiplicative nature of social capital means that a huge network of relationships to people who have few resources may be of less value than a smaller network with people with substantial resources. Furthermore, those resources must be relevant to the organization. Students with pocket change are relevant to Pizza Hut; they are irrelevant to a BMW dealership.

This discussion brings us to the brink of social networking practice. Most organizations today ignore the value of entity assets and simply try to connect to more people with stronger relationships. This area is ripe for innovation. Data aggregators such as ChoicePoint and Acxiom maintain detailed data about people worldwide. It would seem that such data could be used by information systems to calculate the potential value of a relationship to a particular individual. This possibility would enable organizations to better understand the value of their social networks as well as guide their behavior with regard to particular individuals.

Stay tuned; many possibilities exist, and some ideas, maybe yours, will be very successful.

Q4 What Roles Do SMIS Play in the Hyper-Social Organization?

Social media is increasingly used to evaluate potential employees. Read about the pitfalls and danger of this practice in the Security Guide on pages 314–315.

Social capital provides an economic perspective on social media. Another perspective is the sociological one developed by Gossieaux and Moran in a model they call the *hyper-social organization*. According to this model, using social media in an old-style, organization-centric manner is ineffective. The true value of social media can only be achieved when organizations use social media to interact with customers, employees, and partners in a more humane, relationship-oriented way. Rather than sending *messages* that attempt to manage, influence, and control, hyper-social organizations create *relationships* in which both parties perceive and gain value.

Thus, a **hyper-social organization** is an organization that uses social media to transform its interactions with customers, employees, and partners into mutually satisfying relationships with them and their communities. In particular, a hyper-social organization is one that has made the four transitions, called *pillars,* shown in Figure 8-9. The concepts and language of this model are marketing-oriented, but in this model, marketing is broadly conceived to pertain to employees and partners as well as customers. Consider each of the transitions in Figure 8-9.

Figure 8-9
Four Pillars of the Hyper-Social
Organization

> Consumers → Humans
> Market Segments → Tribes
> Channels → Networks
> Structure & Control → Messiness

Consumers Become Humans

According to recent studies, consumers are skeptical of organizational messages and no longer listen. A 2009 McKinsey study found that two-thirds of purchase-decision touch points involve SM-based reviews and recommendations outside the realm of organizational messaging.[12] Such skepticism may not be new; it could be that consumers have always held it, but until social media, advertising and PR were the consumers' only data source. New or not, that skepticism gives a competitive advantage to hyper-social organizations.

Today, customers want informed, useful interactions that help them solve particular problems and satisfy unique needs. Customers increasingly ignore prepackaged organizational messages that tout product benefits. An example of this new style is the sales force in Apple stores that has been trained to act as customer problem-solving consultants and not as sellers of products. (See Case Study 4, pages 153–155.) Organizations' SM sites need to mirror this behavior; otherwise, social media is nothing more than another channel for classic advertising.

Consider the social media groups that PRIDE will create to encourage patient exercise. Sending emails to members of those groups to promote exercise, or even to the tribes of those members, is using social media in a pre-hyper-social way. Patients, friends, and families are treated as entities to be influenced, and while such an email campaign is cheaper than printing and mailing instructions, it isn't more effective. However, if PRIDE creates an SM environment in which group members and families can share their successes and failures in an open and honest way, then PRIDE will be relating to the patients and their families as humans with complex personalities and difficult issues.

Market Segments Become Tribes

The second pillar of the hyper-social organization is the transformation of thinking from market segments to tribes. Market segments have key traits and characteristics; tribes, as we have seen, have relationships for defending beliefs or seeking the truth.

Using traditional market-segment thinking, AllRoad Parts, the company discussed in the first part of this book, would promote an upcoming bicycle motocross (BMX) event to a market segment of, say, 20- to 25-year-old men who work in retail and live in certain ZIP codes. Using tribal thinking, AllRoad would market to communities that defend the belief that BMX is a great sport or to communities that celebrated the inclusion of BMX in the Summer Olympics starting in 2008. Such tribal marketing would enable AllRoad to follow relationships beyond 25-year-old men to customers and markets that are ripe for sales, but of which AllRoad is ignorant. It might be, for example, that the community that celebrates BMX in the Olympics includes 65-year-old grandfathers who are predisposed to buy racing equipment for their grandsons. Relating to the community will bring those unknown customers into AllRoad's network.

A similar transformation is important within organizations. A company with an employee morale problem would, using market-segment thinking, find the categories of employees who are most discontented using the "market segment" of, say, job titles. They

---

[12]David Court, Dave Elzinga, Susan Mulder, and Ole Jorgen Vetvik, "The Consumer Decision Journey," *McKinsey Quarterly*, June 2009, *http://www.mckinseyquarterly.com/The_consumer_decision_journey_2373*.

might find a major source of discontent among customer support representatives who are working with customers frustrated by failures in a defective product. The traditional management response would be something like, "That's always a problem in customer support; give 'em a bonus." If, instead, the organization were to focus on the seeker-of-the-truth community inside the organization that wants the defective product fixed, it would engage engineers, parts purchasing agents, and manufacturing quality assurance employees, as well as customer support. By relating to and supporting a solution by that internal tribe, the company would not only improve morale but also solve the problem and increase internal social capital.

Channels Become Networks

According to the third pillar of the hyper-social organization, channels become networks. Prior to 1980, organizational communication was highly restricted to a few channels. The United States had three major national TV networks and no more than a half-dozen major national newspapers. Consumers got their news twice a day; in the morning paper and the evening news.

In that highly constrained environment, organizations could control messaging via paid advertising and public relations efforts to manipulate editors and writers. It was easy to get the consumers' attention because there were no alternatives. The Internet, Web sites, broadcast email, cable TV, and smartphones have blown those existing channels apart. Only old people watch the evening news, and they are notoriously poor consumers. With myriad communications channels available today, there is so much traffic that organizations find it nearly impossible to obtain attention in these channels.

As stated earlier, social media enables people to form communities based on common interests, and to obtain any of the consumers' attention organizations must today engage with networks in those communities, based on those interests. And the communities are bored with, even disdainful of, traditional product data.

According to Gossieaux and Moran, another key difference is that channels transmit *data,* whereas networks transmit *knowledge.* Actually, many consumers would disagree that ads, at least, carry data. They carry the subliminal message that if you, too, buy that car, or paint, or soap, you too will be handsome, admired, or clean and happy. In any case, that kind of "data" has no power in today's networks. Instead hyper-social organizations use channels to transmit messages valued by recipients. For example, doctors and staff can use PRIDE groups to communicate new exercise techniques that embody recent research on the relationship of exercise and postoperation health, on the latest developments in care, and so forth.

Structure and Control Become Messy

The final pillar of the hyper-social organization is, using our terms, a transition from a structured process to a dynamic one. Organizations and executives no longer plan and control organizational messaging. Such messaging emerges via a dynamic, SM-based process. That concept is anathema to traditional organizations and managers, and in the early years of your career, you are likely to be part of helping your organization overcome resistance to it.

To facilitate that transition, the hyper-social organization model defines a dynamic process, called **SEAMS**, with the five major activities shown in Figure 8-10. The theme that runs through all five of these activities is to engage with communities with authentic relationships that are important to them. Having done so, in the activate activity, connect your efforts to whatever value chain and process will achieve your organization's strategies. Make it easy to order your product, if sales are your goal, but not the obvious nor the immediate purpose of your relationship. Publish the successes of community members in ways that favor your organization, but that take a back seat to the community.

Activity	Description
Sense	Important communities. What they do, where they hang out, what they care about, how your organization can relate to them.
Engage	In relationships. Talk *with*, not to, community members (customers, employees, partners).
Activate	Connect communities to your internal value chains and processes (Figure 8-6).
Measure	Success in terms of social capital.
Story tell	Publicize community successes. Take a backseat role to the community.

Figure 8-10
SEAMS Dynamic Process
Activities

How Can SMIS Foster Hyper-Social Organizations?

SMIS play a key role for implementing the SEAMS process. Figure 8-11 summarizes important systems for each of the activities in Figure 8-10. Before discussing Figure 8-11, however, realize that all of these activities require the involvement of personnel in the hyper-social organization. Organizations need to staff and manage this activity, just as they did before for their media buying activity.

Sense

Sensing involves two functions: (1) determining what the communities you care about are saying about you and (2) identifying the structure, goals, and dynamic of communities with which you want to relate. For the first, many organizations hire reputation management services like those provided by Reputation.com and others. These services can be expensive because they must be staffed by human beings who read, comprehend, filter, and synthesize SM conversations about your organization. Of course, an organization can also do its own reputation management as well.

The second function is to identify communities with which you wish to engage and determine their type (defender of belief or seeker of truth), their structure, their key contributors, their goals and objectives, and their willingness to engage with organizations like yours. Given that data, you can then craft the best way of engaging those communities.

Engage

Once you have identified your important communities and have a plan, the next activity is to engage with those communities by creating relationships. Today, organizations use Facebook, Twitter, LinkedIn, and others for this purpose. They also support employee and partner blogs and other social media.

Activity	SMIS
Sense	Reputation management services (e.g., *www.reputation.com*); Twitter, Facebook, LinkedIn, blogs, other
Engage	Social media; Twitter, Facebook, LinkedIn, blogs, other
Activate	Integrate SM presence with CRM, ERP, other operational systems SOA useful
Measure	Social monitoring services (e.g., WebiMax); in-house metrics
Story tell	Blogs, videos, YouTube, white papers for benefit of SM communities

Figure 8-11
SEAMS Activities and SMIS

Personnel who perform these functions need to be trained in organizational policy and know the strategy and tactics to be used for the engagement. Many organizations have a few **key users** who are personnel trained to perform SM engagement tasks. Nonkey users submit ideas and responses to key users for publication in communities. In this way, the key users serve as a buffer and a filter for possible inappropriate content.

Activate

Although it is important that organizations engage in authentic relationships with the community and not attempt to use it as a pure advertising and sales channel, it is also important that the organization make it easy for community members to obtain sales-oriented materials and to purchase when they want to. Thus, hooks into the organization's CRM, ERP, and other operational systems need to be provided in a discreet and appropriate manner. By the way, designing applications according to SOA principles greatly facilitates this task.

Measure

As with the sensing activity, many organizations use outside social monitoring services such as WebiMax to assess the effectiveness of the organization's SM efforts. In addition, organizations also staff in-house measuring activities.

Measurements include not only the number of mentions in the target communities, but also the response to the organization's own SM presence. These measurements answer questions such as: How many commenters? How many reviewers? What is the traffic rate on the organization's SM sites, and how is it changing?

Gossieaux and Moran caution that such measurements are likely to overlook the **active lurker**, someone who reads, consumes, and observes activity in one social medium and then broadcasts it in some other medium. An example is someone who sees an interesting feature in a SM presence and sends a link to that feature to his or her friends. The sponsor of that SM presence will be able to measure the traffic generated from the shared link, but will not be able to determine which traffic is due to the active lurker.

Story Tell

Given relationships to important communities, the organization should then develop stories about its interaction with these places, or interaction within these places that involves it and publish those stories back to the community. A restaurant that specializes in wedding receptions might, for example, commission a video crew to "tell the story" of someone's wedding planning and then post that on an SM site that does this. YouTube is, of course, a common site for such videos. For more technical products, white papers on the appropriate use or solution to problems are also popular.

Storytelling must observe one limit, however. Stories must be authentic accounts of interactions that are important to the SM community. Thinly disguised advertisements will be ignored at best and ridiculed at worst.

 ## How Do (Some) Companies Earn Revenue from Social Media?

Free! Gmail is free! Facebook, Twitter, too. YouTube! Free!

As a business student, you know that nothing is free. Processing time, data communication, and data storage may be cheap, but they still cost something. And where does Web content come from? *Fortune* pays authors for the content that it offers for free. Who is paying those authors? And from what revenue? Even more important, with the dramatic transition from desktops to mobile devices, what happens to the existing revenue model?

Ethics Guide

SOCIAL MARKETING? OR LYING?

No one expects you to publish your ugliest picture on your Facebook page, but how far should you go to create a positive impression? If your hips and legs are not your best features, is it unethical to stand behind your sexy car in your photo? If you've been to one event with someone very popular in your crowd, is it unethical to publish photos that imply you meet as an everyday occurrence? Surely there is no obligation to publish pictures of yourself at boring events with unpopular people just to balance the scale for those photos in which you appear unrealistically attractive and overly popular.

As long as all of this occurs on a Facebook or Google+ account that you use for personal relationships, well, what goes around comes around. But in the following questions, consider the ethics of questionable social networking postings in the business arena:

Source: © Robert Michael/Corbis

DISCUSSION QUESTIONS

1. Suppose that a river rafting company starts a group on a social networking site for promoting rafting trips. Graham, a 15-year-old high school student who wants to appear more grown-up than he is, posts a picture of a handsome 22-year-old male as a picture of himself. He also writes witty and clever comments on the site photos and claims to play the guitar and be an accomplished masseur. Suppose someone decided to go on the rafting trip, in part because of Graham's postings, and was disappointed with the truth about Graham.

    a. Are Graham's actions ethical? Consider both the categorical imperative (pages 20–21) and utilitarian (pages 54–55) perspectives.

    b. According to either ethical perspective, does the rafting company have an ethical responsibility to refund that person's fees?

2. Suppose you own and manage the rafting company in question 1.

    a. Is it unethical for you to encourage your employees to write positive reviews about your company? Use both the categorical imperative and utilitarian perspectives.

    b. Does your assessment change if you ask your employees to use an email address other than the one they have at work? Use both the categorical imperative and utilitarian perspectives.

3. Suppose your rafting company has a Web site for customer reviews. In spite of your best efforts at camp cleanliness, on one trip (out of dozens) your staff accidentally served contaminated food and everyone became ill with food poisoning. One of those clients from that trip writes a poor review because of that experience. Is it ethical for you to delete that review from your site? Again, consider both the categorical and utilitarian perspectives.

4. Instead of being the owner, suppose you were at one time employed by this rafting company and you were, undeservedly you think, terminated. To get even, you use Facebook to spread rumors to your friends (many of whom are river guides) about the food quality of the company's trips.

    a. Are your actions legal?

    b. Are your actions unethical? Consider both the categorical imperative and utilitarian perspectives.

    c. Do you see any ethical distinctions between this situation and that in question 3?

5. Again, suppose that you were at one time employed by the rafting company and were undeservedly terminated. Using the company owner's name and other identifying data, you create a false Facebook account for her. You've known her for many years and have dozens of photos of her, some of which were taken at parties and are unflattering and revealing. You post those photos along with critical comments that she made about clients or employees. Most of the comments were made when she was tired or frustrated, and they are hurtful but, because of her wit, also humorous. You send friend invitations to people whom she knows, many of whom are the target of her biting and critical remarks. Are your actions unethical? Again, use both the categorical and utilitarian perspectives.

As you have seen in this chapter, companies vary widely in their SM use. Some companies use it only internally and make no attempt to earn revenue from it. Others offer it to the customers as a service—again without an attempt to gain direct SM revenue.

However, some companies, like Facebook, Google, and LinkedIn, do earn revenue from SM activities. In the case of LinkedIn, part of its revenue is earned the old-fashioned way, by selling upgrades to its standard SaaS product. As of May 2013, regular users access LinkedIn for free; businesses and individuals who want to use LinkedIn for recruiting can select one of three SaaS offerings at a monthly cost from $20 to $75. But selling SaaS is not the way that LinkedIn makes most of its money, and it's not the way that Facebook, Google, or most other revenue-earning companies earn SM revenue, either. Instead, they use a revenue model that came into existence around the turn of this century and was then referred to as Web 2.0. You'll still hear that term, although you'll see strong evidence in the next chapter that the term *Web 2.0* has become passé. But elements of Web 2.0 made the social media revenue model that we see today.

For our purposes, we can define **Web 2.0** as Web-delivered services and content that are paid for by advertising. Google led the way with search, later Gmail, and then YouTube. Today, it doesn't seem any great insight to realize that if someone is searching for *Oracle CRM* that he or she might be interested in Oracle ads or ads for CRM products from other vendors. Similarly, if someone sends an email indicating the possibility of purchasing an Audi A5 Cabriolet, it's not a great stretch to realize that person may be interested in ads from local Audi dealers, or BMW and Mercedes dealers as well. Or if someone is watching a soccer game on YouTube, maybe he or she likes soccer? While not mind-boggling to imagine, Google was the first to turn these interesting possibilities into substantial revenue and a substantial company.

Key Characteristics of Web 2.0

Several important characteristics lead to the success of Web 2.0. First, unlike traditional media such as newspapers, users can respond directly to Web ads by clicking on them. This characteristic is highly valued by advertisers. Run an ad in the print version of *The Wall Street Journal*, and you have no idea of who responds to that ad and how strongly. But place an ad for that same product in the online version, and you'll soon know the percentage of viewers who clicked that ad and what action they took next. This led to the **pay-per-click** revenue model in which advertisers display ads to potential customers for free and pay only when the customer clicks.

Obviously, the easiest way to gain more clicks is to have more viewers, so the competition was on to capture more and more users. Initially, two principal means were used to attract viewers: *free content* and *free software*. The desirability of free content wasn't initially obvious. Many traditional publishers attempted to sell Web subscriptions according to their traditional business models before realizing they could earn more revenue by giving the content away and selling ads. Over time, it became clear that interesting, free content was strongly attractive bait for viewers and hence ad clickers.

Thin-client browser applications and the cloud eased the delivery of free software. Companies such as Google were able to offer thin-client email such as Gmail for free as a service. The barrier to obtaining users was dramatically reduced by offering software that didn't need to be purchased or installed. Point your browser at it and "It just works!" to quote the late Steve Jobs.

Another way to grow ad revenue is to increase site value with user contributions. The term **use increases value** meant the more people used a site, the more value it had, and the more people would visit. Furthermore, the more value a site has, the more existing users will return. This phenomenon led to user comments and reviews, blogging, and, within a few years, social media. If you can get people to connect their tribe to a site, you will get more users, they will add more value, existing users will return more frequently, and, all things considered, the more ad clicks there will be.

Further, Web 2.0 encouraged **mashups**, which occur when the output from two or more Web sites is combined into a single user experience. Google's **My Maps** is an excellent mashup example. Google publishes Google Maps and provides tools for users to make custom modifications to those maps. Thus, users mash the Google Map product with their own knowledge. One user demonstrated the growth of gang activity to the local police by mapping new graffiti sites on Google Maps. Other users share their experiences or photos of hiking trips or other travel. See Figure 8-12 for another example.

In social media fashion, Google provides users a means for sharing their mashed-up map over the Internet and then indexes that map for Google search. If you publish a mashup of a Google map with your knowledge of a hiking trip on Mt. Pugh, anyone who performs a Google search for Mt. Pugh will find your map. Again, the more users who create My Maps, the greater the value of the My Maps site.

As stated, social media is the ultimate expression of use increasing value. The more tribes, the more people, and the more incentive people will have to come back again and again. So, social media would seem to be the next great revenue generator, except, possibly, for the movement from PCs to mobile devices.

Does Mobility Reduce Online Ad Revenue?

The ad click revenue model successfully emerged on PC devices where there is plenty of space for lots of ads. However, as users move from PCs to mobile devices, particularly small-screen smartphones, there is much less ad space. Does this mean a reduction in ad revenue?

On the surface, yes. According to Cowen analyst Jim Friedland, in 2012, Google generated $7 from each smartphone and about $30 from each desktop. However, growth in the number of mobile devices far exceeds PC growth; in 2012 alone the number of mobile devices worldwide is expected to grow from 509 million to 914 million.[13] According to Anne Frisbie of InMobi, the number of mobile devices is expected to reach 10 billion in the next five years,[14] which will

Figure 8-12
Mashup Example
Source: © Google

---

[13]Erick Schonfeld, "Cowen: Google's Mobile Ad Revenues Could Surge to $5.8 Billion in 2012," TechCrunch, last modified January 21, 2012, *http://techcrunch.com/2012/01/21/cowen-googles-mobile-ad-revenues-could-surge-to-5-8-billion-in-2012/*.
[14]Anne Frisbie, "The Global Mobile Advertising Revolution Has Arrived," *Forbes.com*, last modified May 3, 2012, *http://www.forbes.com/sites/ciocentral/2012/05/03/the-global-mobile-advertising-revolution-has-arrived/*.

exceed the world's population. Supporting this claim, Sarah Perez cites data from Cisco that predicts by 2016, 25 percent of the world's population will have two or more mobile devices.[15] So, even though the revenue per device may be lower for mobile devices than PCs, the sheer number of them may swamp the difference in revenue.

Furthermore, the number of devices is not the whole story. According to Peter Kafka, the average click-through rate of smartphones is 4.12 percent while that same rate on PCs is 2.39 percent.[16] So, mobile users click ads more often and hence generate more revenue. In June 2012, Marcus Moretti claimed, in fact, that for 1,000 ad impressions, Facebook earned $9.86 on mobile ads and $3.62 on Web ads.[17]

However, clicks aren't the final story, either. Because ads take up so much more space on mobile devices than they do on PCs, many of the mobile clicks could have been accidental. **Conversion rate** measures the frequency that someone who clicks on an ad makes a purchase, "Likes" a site, or takes some other action desired by the advertiser. According to Kafka, the conversion rate is more than twice as high on PCs as on smartphones, 5.2 percent to 2.0 percent, respectively. So, at least according to one study, PC ad clicks are more effective, on average, than mobile clicks.

Clickstream data is easy to gather, and as we have seen, analyses of it are widespread. It's possible, for example, to measure click and conversion rates by type of mobile device. According to Robert Hof, Android users are far more likely to click and convert on Facebook ads than iPhone users.[18] But why? Is it the device? Is it the way the ads are integrated into the user experience? Is it the user? Are Android users more curious (or hyper) than iPhone users? Or are iPhone users more discriminating? Or just older and less likely to buy things? We do not know.

What we can conclude from this morass of confusing data, however, is that mobile devices are most unlikely to spell the death of the Web/social media revenue model. The users are there, the interest is there, and what remains is a design problem: how best to configure the mobile experience to obtain legitimate clicks and conversions. The computer industry is superb at solving design problems; given the current dynamic evolution of mobile interfaces and USX, active, interesting, and compelling ways of presenting ads in iOS/Android/Window 8 environments are just around the corner.

Q6 How Can Organizations Manage the Risks of Social Media?

As you have seen, social media revolutionizes the ways that organizations communicate. Twenty years ago, most organizations managed all public and internal messaging with the highest degree of control. Every press conference, press release, public interview, presentation, and even academic paper needed to be preapproved by both the legal and marketing departments. Such approval could take weeks or months.

---

[15]Sarah Perez, "The Number of Mobile Devices Will Exceed World's Population by 2012 (& Other Shocking Figures)," TechCrunch, last modified February 14, 2012, *http://techcrunch.com/2012/02/14/the-number-of-mobile-devices-will-exceed-worlds-population-by-2012-other-shocking-figures/*.

[16]Peter Kafka, "When You Search on Your Phone, You Click on More Ads. On Purpose?," *All Things D*, last modified March 26, 2012, *http://allthingsd.com/20120326/when-you-search-on-your-phone-you-click-on-more-ads-on-purpose/*.

[17]Marcus Moretti, "It Turns Out Facebook's Mobile Ads Are Clicked on Much More Than Its Web Ads," *Business Insider*, last modified June 19, 2012, *http://www.businessinsider.com/so-it-turns-out-facebooks-mobile-ads-are-clicked-much-more-than-its-web-ads-2012-6#ixzz1zh2FTJfXC*.

[18]*http://www.forbes.com/sites/roberthof/2012/06/26/googles-android-kills-apples-ios-on-facebook-mobile-ad-performance/*.

Today, progressive hyper-social organizations have turned that model on its head. Employees are encouraged to engage with communities and, in most organizations, to identify themselves with their employer while doing so. All of this participation, all of this engagement, however, comes with risks. In this question, we will consider risks from employee communication and risks from nonemployee, user-generated content.

Managing the Risk of Employee Communication

The first step that any hyper-social organization should take is to develop and publicize a **social media policy**, which is a statement that delineates employees' rights and responsibilities. You can find an index to 100 different policies at the Social Media Today Web site.[19] In general, the more technical the organization, the more open and lenient the social policies. The U.S. military has, perhaps surprisingly, endorsed social media with enthusiasm, tempered by the need to protect classified data.

Intel Corporation has pioneered open and employee-trusting SM policies, policies that continue to evolve as they gain more experience with employee-written social media. The three key pillars of their policy in 2013 are:

- Disclose
- Protect
- Use Common Sense[20]

Those policies are further developed as shown in Figure 8-13. Visit *www.intel.com/ content/www/us/en/legal/intel-social-media-guidelines.html*. Read this policy carefully; it contains great advice and considerable wisdom.

Two elements in this list are particularly noteworthy. The first is the call for transparency and truth. As an experienced and wise business professional once told me, "Nothing is more serviceable than the truth." It may not be convenient, but it is serviceable, long term. Second, SM contributors and their employers should be open and above board. If you make a mistake, don't obfuscate; instead correct it, apologize, and make amends. The SM world is too open, too broad, and too powerful to fool.

When singer Amy Winehouse died in July 2011, both Microsoft and Apple tweeted messages about where to buy her music that the Twittersphere found distasteful and

Figure 8-13
Intel's Rules of Social Media Engagement
Source: Used with permission from Intel Corporation.

Disclose	Be transparent—use your real name and employer Be truthful—point out if you have a vested interest Be yourself—stick to your expertise and write what you know
Protect	Don't tell secrets Don't slam the competition Don't overshare
Use Common Sense	Add value—make your contribution worthwhile Keep it cool—don't inflame or respond to every criticism Admit mistakes—be upfront and quick with corrections

---

[19]"Social Media Employee Policy Examples from Over 100 Organizations," *Social Media Today*, http://socialmediatoday.com/ralphpaglia/141903/social-media-employee-policy-examples-over-100-companies-and-organizations.
[20]"Intel Social Media Guidelines," *Intel*, accessed July 2012, http://www.intel.com/content/www/us/en/legal/intel-social-media-guidelines.html.

objectionable.[21] After a loud outcry, both organizations were prompt with apologies and made amends to her family and friends, and the errors were forgotten by day's end. Had they done otherwise, we would still be hearing about them. See also Using Your Knowledge Question 8-5 on page 319.

Managing the Risk of User-Generated Content

User-generated content (UGC), which simply means content on your SM site that is contributed by nonemployee users, is the essence of SM relationships. As with any relationship, however, UGC comments can be inappropriate or excessively negative in tone or otherwise problematic. Organizations need to determine how they will deal with such content before engaging in social media.

Problem Sources

The major sources of UGC problems are:

- Junk and crackpot contributions
- Inappropriate content
- Unfavorable reviews
- Mutinous movements

When a business participates in a social network or opens its site to UGC, it opens itself to misguided people who post junk unrelated to the site's purpose. Crackpots may also use the network or UGC site as a way of expressing passionately held views about unrelated topics, such as UFOs, government cover-ups, fantastic conspiracy theories, and so forth. Because of the possibility of such content, SM sponsors should regularly monitor the site and remove objectionable material immediately. Monitoring can be done by employees, or companies such as Bazaarvoice that offer services not only to collect and manage ratings and reviews, but also to monitor the site for irrelevant content.

Unfavorable reviews are another risk. Research indicates that customers are sophisticated enough to know that few, if any, products are perfect. Most customers want to know the disadvantages of a product before purchasing it so they can determine if those disadvantages are important for their application. However, if every review is bad, if the product is rated 1 star out of 5, then the company is using social media to publish its problems. In this case, some action must be taken, as described next.

Mutinous movements are an extension of bad reviews. In January 2012, McDonald's opened a Twitter campaign to promote customer stories. Within a few hours, it was clear that disgruntled customers were hijacking the campaign. McDonald's pulled the Twitter hashtag and within a few hours, negative conversations stopped. To be able to respond promptly, McDonald's created a contingency plan for dealing with unwanted results in all of its social media marketing.[22]

---

[21]Sarah Kessler, "Microsoft Apologizes for 'Crass' Amy Winehouse Tweet," *CNN.com*, last modified July 26, 2011, *http://www.cnn.com/2011/TECH/social.media/07/25/apology.winehouse.tweet.mashable/index.html?iref=allsearch*.
[22]Marissa Brassfield, "McDonald's McDStories Twitter Promotion Sparks Huge Backlash," *Foodista*, last modified January 24, 2012, *http://www.foodista.com/blog/2012/01/24/mcdonalds-mcdstories-twitter-promotion-sparks-huge-backlash*.

Responding to Social Networking Problems

The first task in managing social networking risk is to know the sources of potential problems and to monitor sites for problematic content. Once such content is found, however, organizations must have a plan for creating the organization's response. Three possibilities are:

- Leave it
- Respond to it
- Delete it

If the problematic content represents reasonable criticism of the organization's products or services, the best response may be to leave it where it is. Such criticism indicates that the site is not just a shill for the organization, but contains legitimate user content. Such criticism also serves as a free source of product reviews, which can be useful for product development. For the criticism to be useful, the development team needs to know about it, so, as stated, processes to ensure that the criticism is found and communicated to the team are necessary.

A second alternative is to respond to the problematic content. However, this alternative is dangerous. If the response can be construed in any way as patronizing or insulting to the content contributor, it can enrage the community and generate a strong backlash. Also, if the response appears defensive, it can become a public relations negative.

In most cases, responses are best reserved for when the problematic content has caused the organization to do something positive as a result. For example, suppose a user publishes that he or she was required to hold for customer support for 45 minutes. If the organization has done something to reduce wait times, then an effective response to the criticism is to recognize it as valid and state, nondefensively, what has been done to reduce wait times.

If a reasoned, nondefensive response generates continued and unreasonable UGC from that same source, it is best for the organization to do nothing. Never wrestle with a pig; you'll get dirty and the pig will enjoy it. Instead, allow the community to constrain the user. It will.

Deleting content should be reserved for contributions that are inappropriate because they are contributed by crackpots, they have nothing to do with the site, or they contain obscene or otherwise inappropriate content. However, deleting legitimate negative comments can result in a strong user backlash. In the early days of social media, Nestlé created a PR nightmare on its Facebook account with its response to criticism it received about its use of palm oil. Someone altered the Nestlé logo, and in response Nestlé decided to delete all Facebook contributions that used that altered logo and did so in an arrogant, heavy-handed way. The result was a negative firestorm on Twitter.[23]

A sound principle in business is to never ask a question to which you do not want the answer. We can extend that principle to social networking; never set up a site that will generate content for which you have no effective response!

Q7 2024?

So much change is in the air: social media, hyper-social organizations, Web 2.0, Enterprise 2.0. Is there a hyper-hyper-social organization or an Enterprise 3.0 around the corner? We don't know. However, new mobile devices with innovative mobile-device USX, coupled with dynamic

---

[23]Bernhard Warner, "Nestlé's 'No Logo' Policy Triggers Facebook Revolt," *Social Media Influence*, March 19, 2010, *http://socialmediainfluence.com/2010/03/19/nestles-no-logo-policy-triggers-facebook-revolt/*.

and agile information systems based on cloud computing and dynamic virtualization, guarantee that monumental changes will continue to occur in between now and 2024.

If you haven't already, read the Using MIS InClass Exercise 8 on page 296. Watch Ms. Comstock's video. What does it mean to have machines participating in social media? She's no crackpot; she's the CMO of a billion-dollar company. Starbucks is concerned enough with SM change to have created a position of Chief Digital Officer (CDO), a position responsible for developing and managing innovative social media programs.[24]

Advance the clock 10 years. You're now the product marketing manager for an important new product series for your company . . . the latest in a line of, say, intelligent home appliances. How are you going to promote your products? Will your machines do SM with family members? Will your refrigerators publish what kids are eating after school on the family's social media site? And what even more creative idea will you need to have by then?

Think about your role as a manager in 2024. Your team has 10 people, 3 of whom report to you; 2 report to other managers; and 5 work for different companies. Your company uses OpenGizmo 2024 with integrated mobile video, augmented by Google/Facebook Whammo++ Star, all of which have many features that enable employees and teams to instantly publish their ideas in blogs, wikis, videos, and whatever other means have become available. Your employees no longer are assigned computers at work; a liberal, yet secure, BYOD policy enables them to use their own devices, often in their own, unique way. Of course, your employees have their own accounts on whatever Facebook, Twitter, LinkedIn, foursquare, and other social networking sites have become, and they regularly contribute to them.

How do you manage this team? If "management" means to plan, organize, and control, how can you accomplish any of these functions in this emergent network of employees? But, if you and your organization follow the lead of tech-savvy companies such as Intel, you'll know you cannot close the door on your employees' SM lives, nor will you want to. Instead, you'll harness the power of the social behavior of your employees and partners to advance your strategy.

In the context of CRM, hyper-social means that the vendor loses control of the customer relationship. Customers use all the vendor's touch points they can find to craft their own relationships. Emergence in the context of management means loss of control of employees. Employees craft their own relationships with their employers, whatever that might mean by 2024. Certainly it means a loss of control, one that is readily made public, to the world.

In the 1960s, when someone wanted to send a letter to Don Draper at Sterling Cooper, his or her secretary addressed the envelope to Sterling Cooper and down at the bottom added, "Attention: Don Draper." The letter was to Sterling Cooper, oh, by the way, also to Don Draper.

Email changed that. Today, someone would send an email to *DonDraper@SterlingCooper .com*, or even just to *Don@SterlingCooper.com*. That address is to a person and then to the company.

Social media changes addresses further. When Don Draper creates his own blog, people respond to Don's Blog, and only incidentally do they notice in the "About Don" section of the blog that Don works for Sterling Cooper. In short, the focus has moved in 50 years from organizations covering employee names to employees covering organization names.

Does this mean that organizations go away by 2024? Hardly. They are needed to raise and conserve capital and to organize vast groups of people and projects. No group of loosely affiliated people can envision, design, develop, manufacture, market, sell, and support an iPad. Organizations are required.

---

[24]Jennifer van Grove, "How Starbucks Is Turning Itself into a Tech Company," *VB/Social*, last modified June 12, 2012, *http://venturebeat.com/2012/06/12/starbucks-digital-strategy/*.

So what, then? Maybe we can take a lesson from biology. Crabs have an external exoskeleton. Deer, much later in the evolutionary chain, have an internal endoskeleton. When crabs grow, they must endure the laborious and biologically expensive process of shedding a small shell and growing a larger one. They are also vulnerable during the transition. When deer grow, the skeleton is inside and it grows with the deer. No need for vulnerable molting. And, considering agility, would you take a crab over a deer?

In the 1960s, organizations were the exoskeleton around employees. By 2024, they will be the endoskeleton, supporting the work of people on the exterior.

And we can extend this analogy even further. Think about PRIDE; based on a cloud database, it enables doctors and other healthcare professionals, patients, health clubs, trainers, insurance companies, employers, and possibly others to integrate patient postsurgery treatment, seamlessly, forming a new treatment entity. In terms of the biology analogy, these new possibilities require people to use their endoskeleton for interorganizational cooperative work and, in the process, form new super-organisms.

Mobility + cloud + social media mean fascinating opportunities for your nonroutine cognitive skills in the next 10 years!

Security Guide

SOCIAL RECRUITING

Social recruiting makes sense. Recruiting has always been a social process—prospecting for candidates, matching candidates' qualifications against job needs, interviewing employees to determine how they fit the organizational culture, background checks—all of these have a social component that can be enhanced with social media.

Today, some hyper-social organizations use in-house communities to locate prospects, using social media to ask employees to propose job candidates. In the recent downturn, some have created communities of "alumni" employees, meaning those who have been laid off, to keep track of them in case an opportunity to rehire good performers occurs.

In addition to in-house social media, employers also use candidates' SM sites, particularly LinkedIn, Facebook, and Twitter, to get a sense of the candidate as a person and to find any potential behavior or attitude problems. In fact, Reppler, a social networking image management company, reports that 91 percent of employers that it surveyed used social media to screen candidates. Furthermore, 69 percent of survey respondents reported that they had rejected candidates because of what they had on social media sites, but, on the positive side, 68 percent also reported that they had hired a candidate in part because of the content of that person's social networking site.[25]

In March 2012, Manuel Valdes and Shannon McFarland reported for the Associated Press that at least two employers had asked for Facebook login and password data so they could view private Facebook profile data.[26] In response, the Internet was aflame with outrage, but, the truth is, we don't know how prevalent that practice is. Most likely it's uncommon, but it could happen to you.

Meanwhile, LinkedIn is on track to earn $895 million from subscriptions, advertising, and licensing of software.[27] LinkedIn Recruiter, software that enables employers to dynamically search LinkedIn's 161 million members, sells for $8,000 per user, cheap when you consider that a traditional recruiter can earn $15,000 per employee hire and more. The bottom line for you: what you put in your LinkedIn profile matters.

Source: © Derren Nugent/Retna/Photoshot/Newscom

[25]*http://blog.reppler.com/2011/09/27/managing-your-online-image-across-social-networks/*.

[26]Manuel Valdes and Shannon McFarland, "Employers Asking Job Applicants for Facebook Passwords," *The Augusta Chronicle*, last modified March 20, 2012, *http://chronicle.augusta.com/latest-news/2012-03-20/employers-asking-job-applicants-facebook-passwords*.

[27]George Anders, "How LinkedIn Has Turned Your Resume into a Cash Machine," *Forbes*, last modified June 27, 2012, *http://www.forbes.com/sites/georgeanders/2012/06/27/how-linkedin-strategy/*.

And, by the way, LinkedIn recently lost 6.5 million passwords to hackers who posted them on a hacker Web site. According to Michael Hickins, editor of *CIO Journal*, security professionals assert that LinkedIn had not appropriately encrypted those passwords.[28] Adding even more fuel to the social recruiting security fire, many of those passwords were ridiculously simple: *god, 1234, the, job, work*, and, best of all for LinkedIn users, *link*.

So what guidelines can you take from these few paragraphs?

1. Stay on top of the latest security and privacy settings for sites like Facebook and Twitter. Use those settings to control who sees what.
2. Don't post questionable social media content. Remove questionable content posted or tagged by others.
3. Consider having two separate Facebook or other social media sites. Construct one "dummy" or "junker" site that has only the most acceptable content. If you're forced to divulge login and password, divulge those for your dummy site. Keep a second site for your personal use.

4. Pay attention to the content of your LinkedIn profile. Your profile will be searched by many besides your immediate connections.
5. Don't assume that organizations that require you to log in with passwords have strong security. Use different passwords for different sites so that you're still protected if one of the sites you use is hacked.
6. Create and use strong passwords: No words in any language; 10 to 12 characters; mixture of upper and lowercase, numbers, and special characters (see the Guide on pages 316–317).
7. Be proactive in protecting your online social reputation. Don't use foul language, post lewd pictures, or criticize colleagues or former employers. Apply the Intel social media guidelines (Figure 8-13) to your own social sites.
8. If you're in doubt about the content of your site, ask someone 20 years older than you to take a look. If you're embarrassed to do that, something is wrong.

DISCUSSION QUESTIONS

1. Grade yourself on the eight guidelines above. Be frank and honest. List changes you need to make in your social/ password behavior.
2. If you were in a job interview and the interviewer asked for your Facebook (or other) login and password, how would you respond?
3. Are you willing to create a second dummy Facebook (or other) site to reveal to employers if need be? Explain your answer.
4. Think of two organizations for which you would like to work. Assume both organizations review job candidates' SM data as part of their initial screening process.
   a. Name and describe three positive criteria that both companies could use to evaluate applicants. If you think the companies might use different criteria, explain the difference.
   b. Name and describe three indications of problematic issues that both companies could use to evaluate candidates. If you think the companies might use different criteria, explain the difference.

   c. If you were rejected because of a lack of social data supporting your criteria for item a or because of the presence of social data in the criteria for item b, would you know it?
5. Evaluate your own social data in light of your answer to question 4.
   a. Describe elements in your social data that support positive criteria.
   b. Describe elements in your social data that could indicate problematic issues.
6. Ask someone else to evaluate your social data in light of both sets of criteria in question 4. You can ask a friend, but you will likely obtain better information if you pick someone whom you do not know well. Most human resource screening personnel are in their 30s or 40s. Try to pick someone in that age group to evaluate your criteria, if you can.
7. Choose the most negative social data according to your answers to questions 5 and 6. Suppose you are in a job interview and you are asked about that problematic data. How will you respond?

[28]"LinkedIn Password Breach Illustrates Endemic Security Issue," *The Wall Street Journal*, last modified June 6, 2012, *http://blogs.wsj.com/cio/2012/06/06/linkedin-password-breach-illustrates-endemic-security-issue/*.

Guide

DEVELOPING YOUR PERSONAL BRAND

The Security Guide (on the previous two pages) discusses ways to avoid making mistakes with social media that will interfere with your ability to obtain a job. Follow that guide to minimize the long-term effect of the errors and indiscretions of your college years. Now consider the other side of that coin. Instead of attempting to minimize the bad, suppose we ask: How can you use social media to maximize the good?

Leading professionals use social media to build their personal brand. You may be too young, too inexperienced, and not yet unique enough to have a personal brand, but, then again, maybe not. And even if now isn't the right time to build a personal brand, you will need to have, build, and maintain your personal brand if you want to be a business leader.

So, what is it? It's not embarrassing self-promotion. It's not self-advertising, and it's not a resume of your recent experience. It is, instead, the means by which you conduct authentic relationships with the market for your talents and abilities. That market might be your professional colleagues, your employer, your fellow employees, your competition, or anyone who cares about what you care about.

Consider the principles in Figure 8-9, and apply them not to a hyper-social organization but to you as a hyper-social business professional. What does the first principle, Consumers → humans, mean to you personally? It means the people who consume your services are not just bosses and colleagues, but rather full-fledged human beings with the rich stew of complexity that all humans have. So how do you use social media to transform your relationships from a consumer-oriented nature to a human-oriented one?

Such a transformation is difficult. You don't want to share every detail of your personal life on your professional blog; few care about your vacation in the Bahamas. But they might want to know what you read while lying on the beach, why you read it, and what you learned from it. Or how disappointed you were about what you didn't learn. But your report has to be authentic. If you're reading Kierkegaard or Aristotle for the purpose of showing erudition on your personal blog, you missed the point. But if Kierkegaard has something interesting to say about the ethics of the latest business scandal that affects your professional interests, many who share those interests will want to know. And they will then have a way to approach you on a common interest. That common interest may lead to an exciting new job opportunity, or maybe it will lead to a fulfilling new relationship, or maybe it will go nowhere. You just don't know.

One caution, though: Maintaining a professional brand can become all consuming. Just like personal Facebook use can suck up most of your free time, so, too, maintaining your professional brand can become all consuming. Start modestly and work up from there.

Be guided by your personal strategy. Consider Figure 3-12 again, in light of your personal competitive strategy. What is your personal competitive advantage? Why would someone choose you, your expertise, your work products, over others? Then, with that knowledge, build your personal brand. But again, it's about authentic relationships and not about shameless advertising.

Realize, too, that a strong personal brand is essential to some careers. For example, if you want to be an independent consultant, say an expert on privacy and control for cloud data storage, you'll need to invest considerable time developing and maintaining your professional brand. But whether or not it's essential, having a strong personal brand is an asset in any field, in any job. And you can be sure that if you don't have one, one of your competitors will.

 DISCUSSION QUESTIONS

1. Using your own words, define and describe a personal brand.
2. Interpret each of the four principles in Figure 8-9 in the context of a personal brand. Indicate what each of the terms means in the context of personal branding, and describe the nature of the indicated transformation.
3. Pick a contemporary topic of interest in your major field of study. For example, if you're an operations major, pick something like *3D printing*. If you're an accounting major, choose something like *auditing in the cloud*. (Read question 4, however, before you pick.)
   a. Search the Web for opinions about the realities, contemporary uses, big issues and problems, or other interesting dimensions of your topic.
   b. Find two or three experts in that topic, and go to their professional brand sites. That brand might be a blog, a Web page, a collection of articles, an SM site on Facebook or LinkedIn, or some other public statement of their professionalism.
   c. Which of the sites is the best? Explain why you think so. In your answer, apply the principles of Figure 8-9.

4. Suppose you become an expert in the topic you used in your answer to question 3. Think about your experiences in the past year that relate to that topic. It could be experiences in class, out of class with fellow students, in conversations with roommates. It could be something that happened at your job at McDonald's. Whatever.
   a. Make a list of 10 experiences. Go back in time as far as necessary to identify 10 experiences.
   b. Describe how you could use social media, including blogs, to present five of the best of those 10 experiences in a way to build your professional brand.
   c. Using the principles of Figure 8-9, evaluate your description in item b.
5. Reflect on your answers to questions 1–4.
   a. Do you think having a personal brand is important for you? Explain why or why not. (The answer to this question may not be *yes*, and for good reasons.)
   b. What was the most difficult task for you when formulating your answers to question 4?
   c. Summarize what you have learned from this exercise about ways that you can get more value from your college experiences.

ACTIVE REVIEW

Use this Active Review to verify that you understand the ideas and concepts that answer this chapter's study questions.

Q1 What is a social media information system (SMIS)?

Define *social media, communities, tribes, hives,* and *social media information systems.* Name and describe three SMIS organizational roles. Explain the elements of Figure 8-3. Explain why placing a LinkedIn icon on a company Web site is not a casual decision. In your own words, explain the nature of the five components of SMIS for each of the three SMIS organizational roles.

Q2 How do SMIS advance organizational strategy?

Explain the terms *defenders of belief* and *seekers of the truth.* How do the goals of each type of community differ? Summarize how social media contributes to sales and marketing, customer support, inbound logistics, outbound logistics, manufacturing and operations, and human resources. Name SM risks for each activity. Define *social CRM, crowdsourcing,* and *Enterprise 2.0.* Explain each element in the SLATES model.

Q3 How do SMIS increase social capital?

Define *social capital* and explain four ways that social capital adds value. Name three factors that determine social capital and explain how "they are more multiplicative than additive."

Q4 What roles do SMIS play in the hyper-social organization?

Define *hyper-social organization.* Name the four pillars of hyper-social organization, explain each, and give an example of differences of each state in each transition. Explain how the term *messy* pertains to process types. Explain the nature of each SEAMS activity, and give an example of the user of SMIS for each.

Q5 How do (some) companies earn revenue from social media?

Describe three postures with regard to earning revenue from social media. Define *Web 2.0,* and describe the origins of the social media revenue model. Describe Web 2.0

characteristics. Explain the relationship of click, pay per click, click rate, and conversion rate. Summarize the PC vs. mobile click and conversion rate studies discussed here. Explain why concerns about mobile devices limiting ad revenue are overreactions.

Q6 How can organizations manage the risks of social media?

Name and describe two types of SM risk. Describe the purpose of an SM policy, and summarize Intel's six guiding principles. Describe an SM mistake, other than one in this text, and explain the wise response to it. Name four sources of problems of UGC; name three possible responses, and give the advantages and disadvantages of each.

Q7 2024?

Describe ways in which the use of social media is changing today. Summarize possible management challenges when controlling employees in 2024. Describe the text's suggested response. How does the change in forms of address since the 1960s indicate a change in the relationship of employees and organizations to the business world? Explain the relationship of the differences between crab and deer to this change.

Using Your Knowledge with PRIDE

This chapter has given you several important models for assessing the PRIDE system social media program. You can apply the components of SMIS to understand the commitment that Dr. Flores and his investors and developers must make. You can use organizational strategy and social capital models to assess the desirability of social media to companies that participate in PRIDE. You can also consider whether PRIDE might want to generate revenue via ads, at least for some PRIDE features. Finally, you are prepared to help Dr. Flores and his staff manage the risks of social media.

KEY TERMS AND CONCEPTS

MyMISLab

Go to **mymislab.com** to complete the problems marked with this icon ⭐.

USING YOUR KNOWLEDGE

8-1. Using the Facebook page of a company that you have ⭐ "Liked" (or would choose to), fill out the grid in Figure 8-5. Strive to replace the phrases in that grid with specific statements that pertain to Facebook, the company you like, and you and users whom you know. For example, if you and your friends access Facebook using an Android phone, enter that specific device.

8-2. Name a company for which you would like to work. Using Figure 8-6 as a guide, describe, as specifically as you can, how that company could use social media. Include community type, specific focus, processes involved, risks, and any other observations.
  a. Sales and marketing
  b. Customer service
  c. Inbound logistics
  d. Outbound logistics
  e. Manufacturing and operations
  f. Human resources

8-3. Visit *www.lie-nielsen.com* or *www.sephora.com*. On the site you chose, find links to social networking sites. In what ways are those sites sharing their social capital with you? In what ways are they attempting to cause you to share your social capital with them? Describe the business value of social networking to the business you chose.

8-4. Visit *www.intel.com/content/www/us/en/legal/intel-social-media-guidelines.html*. Using the four pillars that define a hyper-social organization, explain why Intel appears to be hyper-social.

8-5. Visit *http://socialmediatoday.com/ralphpaglia/141903/social-media-employee-policy-examples-over-100-companies-and-organizations*. Find an organization with a very restricted employee SM policy. Name the organization, and explain why you find that policy restrictive. Does that policy cause you to feel positive, negative, or neutral about that company? Explain.

COLLABORATION EXERCISE 8

Using the collaboration IS you built in Chapter 2 (pages 73–74), collaborate with a group of students to answer the following questions.

You most likely do not know much about the particular purposes and goals that Dr. Flores and his partners and staff have for the social media group they will create to motivate their cardiac patients to maintain their exercise programs. So, you can't realistically create a prototype social media site for that purpose. Instead, assume that you and your fellow students are going to create a social media group for maintaining motivation on an exercise program for getting and staying in shape for an intramural soccer or other sports team over the summer.

Or, if your group prefers, assume your goal is to maintain discipline for maintaining a diet, or some other program that requires discipline that can be assisted by a social group. Using iteration and feedback, answer the following questions:

1. State the particular goals of your group. Be as specific as possible.

2. Identify five different social media alternatives for helping your group to maintain discipline for the activity you selected. An obvious choice is a Facebook group, but find other alternatives as well. Visit *www.socialmediatoday.com* for ideas. Summarize each alternative.

3. Create a list of criteria for evaluating your alternatives. Use iteration and feedback to find creative criteria, if possible.

4. Evaluate your alternatives based on your criteria, and select one for implementation.

5. Implement a prototype of your site. If, for example, you chose a Facebook group, create a prototype page on Facebook.

6. Describe the five components of the SMIS you will create for your group. Be very specific with regard to the procedure and people components. Your goal should be to produce a result that could be implemented by any group of similarly motivated students on campus.

7. Assess your result. How likely is it to help your group members achieve the goals in item 1? If you see ways to improve it, describe them.

8. Write a two-paragraph summary of your work that group members could use in a job interview to demonstrate their knowledge of the use of social media for employee motivation.

CASE STUDY 8

Sedona Social

Sedona, Arizona, is a city of 10,000 people surrounded by Coconino National Forest. At an elevation of 4,500 feet, it is considerably higher than the valley cities of Phoenix and Tucson, but 2,000 feet below the altitude of Flagstaff. This middle elevation provides a moderate climate that is neither too hot in the summer nor too cold in the winter. Sedona is surrounded by gorgeous sandstone red/orange rocks and stunning red rock canyons as shown in Figure 8-14.

This beautiful city was the location for more than 60 movies, most of them westerns, between the 1930s and the 1950s. If you've ever watched an old black-and-white western, it was likely situated in Sedona. Among the well-known movies located in Sedona are *Stagecoach, Johnny Guitar, Angel and the Badman,* and *3:10 to Yuma.*

Many who visit Sedona believe there is something peaceful yet energizing about the area, especially in certain locations known as *vortices,* according to *VisitSedona.com.*

"Vortex sites are enhanced energy locations that facilitate prayer, meditation, mind/body healing, and exploring your relationship with your Soul and the divine. They are neither electric nor magnetic."[29]

Tests with scientific instruments have failed to identify any unusual readings of known energy types, and yet many people, of all religions and religious persuasions, believe there is something about Sedona that facilitates spiritual practice. For a city of its size, Sedona has many more churches than one

might expect, including the Catholic Chapel of the Holy Cross (shown in Figure 8-15), Protestant churches of many dominations, the Latter Day Saints (Mormon) church, the local synagogue, and the new-age Sedona Creative Life Center.

Because it is situated in the middle of a national forest, Sedona is surrounded by hundreds of miles of hiking trails; it is possible to hike every day for a year and not use all the trails. The area was home to Native Americans in the 12th and 13th centuries, and there are numerous cliff dwellings and other native sites nearby.

As a relatively young modern city, Sedona does not have the cultural history of Santa Fe or Taos, New Mexico. Nonetheless, there is a burgeoning arts community centered around Tlaquepaque, a 1980s-built shopping area modeled on a Mexican city of the same name.

As with many tourist destinations, there are tensions. Pink Jeep Tours runs daily trips of raucous tourists past vortices occupied by meditating spiritual practitioners. With its Hollywood past, Sedona is home to many Los Angeles expatriates, and at the local health food store it's possible to see 50-something blond women wearing tight pants and jewel-studded, fresh-from-Rodeo-Drive sandals fighting for the last pound of organic asparagus with aging male hippies shaking their white-gray ponytails off the shoulders of their tie-dyed shirts.

The emerging arts community wants to be serious; the uptown jeep-riding tourists (see Figure 8-16) want to have

---

[29]Sedona Chamber of Commerce, accessed July 30, 2013, *http://www.visitsedona.com/article/151.*

Figure 8-14
Sedona Red Rocks
Source: © David Kroenke

un with four-wheel thrills and margaritas (we hope in that sequence). Hikers want to visit petroglyphs, while nature preservers don't want the locations of those sites to be known. Those seeking spiritual guidance want enlightenment in silence, while the locals want to shut out everyone, just as long, that is, as their property values increase at a steady pace, year by year. Meanwhile, the Lear Jets and Citations fly in and out carrying who-knows-who Hollywood celebrity from her home behind the walls of Seven Canyons Resort. And businesses in town want to have reliable, year-round revenue and not too much competition.

Given all that, let's suppose that the Sedona Chamber of Commerce has just hired you as its first-ever manager of community social media. They want you to provide advice and assistance to local businesses in the development of their social media sites, and they want you to manage their own social media presence as well.

QUESTIONS

8-6. Search Facebook for *Sedona, Arizona*. Examine a variety of Sedona area pages that you find. Using the knowledge of this chapter and your personal social media experience, evaluate these pages and list several positive and negative features of each. Make suggestions on ways that they could be improved.

8-7. Repeat question 8-6 for another social media provider. As of this writing, possibilities are Twitter, LinkedIn, and Pinterest, but choose another social media provider if you wish.

Figure 8-15
Chapel of the Holy Cross
Source: © David Kroenke

Figure 8-16
Pink Jeep Tours
Source: © David Kroenke

8-8. The purpose of a Chamber of Commerce is to foster a healthy business climate for all of the businesses in the community. Given that purpose, your answers to questions 8-6 and 8-7, and the knowledge of this chapter, develop a set of 7 to 10 guidelines for local businesses to consider when developing their social media presence.

8-9. Sedona has quite a number of potentially conflicting community groups. Explain three ways that the Chamber of Commerce can use social media to help manage conflict so as to maintain a healthy business environment.

8-10. Examine Figure 8-6 and state how the focus of each of the primary value chain activities pertains to the Chamber of

Commerce. If one does not pertain, explain why. In your answer, be clear about who the Chamber's customers are.

8-11. Given your answer to question 8-10 and considering your responsibility to manage the Chamber's social media presences, state how each applicable row of Figure 8-6 guides the social media sites you will create.

8-12. Using your answers to these questions, write a job description for yourself.

8-13. Write a two-paragraph summary of this exercise that you could use to demonstrate your knowledge of the role of social media in commerce in a future job interview.

MyMISLab

Go to **mymislab.com** for Auto-graded writing questions as well as the following Assisted-graded writing questions:

8-14. According to Paul Greenberg, Amazon.com is the master of the 2-minute relationship, and Boeing is the master of the 10-year relationship.[30] Visit *www.boeing.com* and *www.amazon.com*. From Greenberg's statement and from the appearance of these Web sites, it appears that Boeing is committed to traditional CRM and Amazon.com to social CRM. Give evidence from each site that this might be true. Explain why the products and business environment of both companies cause this difference. Is there any justification for traditional CRM at Amazon.com? Why or why not? Is there any justification for social CRM at Boeing? Why or why not? Based on these companies, is it possible that a company might endorse Enterprise 2.0 but not endorse social CRM? Explain.

8-15. Google or Bing "Chloe" and search for sites that deal with Chloe fashion products. Identify companies that have purchased the Chloe AdWord. Follow three or four such links. Identify as many Web 2.0 features in the sites that you encounter as you can. Explain what you think the business rationale is for each site.

8-16. Mymislab Only – comprehensive writing assignment for this chapter.

---

[30]Paul Greenberg, *CRM at the Speed of Light,* 4th ed. (New York: McGraw-Hill, 2010), p. 105.

Business Intelligence Systems

Dr. Flores is talking with Maggie Jensen, one of the IS professionals who is developing the PRIDE system.

"Dr. Flores, check this out." Maggie is clearly excited to show him something.

"What is it?" Dr. Flores is busy, as always, but curious to see what she has.

"It's our new, well, I guess you'd call it a report, but it's more than that. It's a screenshot of my phone earlier today. I was on a stationary bike and competing against my last four exercises." Maggie hands him a printout from a phone (like that in the figure below).

"So the bicycle icons were moving?" Dr. Flores looks quickly at the phone.

"Exactly. The blue icons are my past workouts, and the green one was my workout this morning. I was spinning against myself," Maggie explains.

"So how could we use this?" Dr. Flores sounds a little skeptical.

Maggie was ready. "Well, for one, we could use it to motivate patients. They would compete against their past workout data."

"Yeah, although we might want to have some control over that. Some of our patients are excessively competitive. I'd hate to encourage them to go overboard." Dr. Flores nods at a very aggressive-looking 65-year-old walking out of an exam room.

"OK. Another option is to record the perfect workout for a given stage. Maybe have three or four versions of good workouts...and have the patients work out against those. We could put a red icon on the screen for the optimal workout...and reward them on the basis of how close they get to that optimal." Maggie's enthusiasm is infectious.

"I like that. Can you prototype it for me?"

"Sure." As she says this, she wonders how to get it done, but she knows it's possible.

"Meanwhile, I've got another question."

"What's that?" Maggie loves these dialogues.

"Well, the key word is *overboard*. We want our patients to exercise within a narrow range; too little effort and they don't get any benefit, and too much, they're endangering their health." From the expression on his face, Dr. Flores is clearly concerned.

"I understand."

"When they work out in a health facility, we control that. But here, we can't. To compensate, one of the docs or nurses checks each patient's previous day's workouts. We call or email if we see a problem."

Maggie is curious to know where this is heading. "That's what you wanted, I think."

"Right. But, as they say, 'Be careful what you ask for.' Now that the program is up and running, we're spending too many hours each day looking at patient workouts."

"Hmmm," Maggie pauses, "so you'd like an exception report?"

"Not sure what that is."

"Pretty much like it sounds. With each workout profile, we store bounds of performance, could be percentage under and over. Then, each morning, we create a report for any patients whose workouts are out of bounds. We send you reports about the exceptions to those bounds."

"I like the sound of that. But do we have to wait until morning? I mean, for the slackers, we can wait till morning. But if someone is overdoing it, I'd really like to know right away." Dr. Flores nods again at the patient exam room.

"You want to know in real time? As it's happening?"

"Is that possible?"

"Sure. It's just bits. We can produce any report you want, but you've got to pay for it."

"Ah, there's always that."

"There's always that," Maggie says with a chuckle.

"We can produce any report you want, but you've got to pay for it."

STUDY QUESTIONS

Q1 How do organizations use business intelligence (BI) systems?

Q2 What are the three primary activities in the BI process?

Q3 How do organizations use data warehouses and data marts to acquire data?

Q4 How do organizations use reporting applications?

Q5 How do organizations use data mining applications?

Q6 How do organizations use BigData applications?

Q7 What is the role of knowledge management systems?

Q8 What are the alternatives for publishing BI?

Q9 2024?

CHAPTER PREVIEW

The information systems described in Chapters 7 and 8 generate enormous amounts of data. The systems in Chapter 7 generate structured data that is used for operational purposes, such as tracking orders, inventories, payables, and so forth. This data has a potential windfall: It contains patterns, relationships, and clusters and can be used to classify, forecast, and predict. Social media data, from systems discussed in Chapter 8, is unstructured, but also provides that same windfall. However, there is so much social media data that it results in BigData collections, which need specialized processing.

This chapter considers business intelligence (BI) systems: information systems that can produce patterns, relationships, and other information from organizational structured and unstructured social data, as well as from external, purchased data. In addition to this data, another rich source of knowledge is employees themselves. Employees come to the organization with expertise, and as they gain experience in the organization they add to that expertise. Vast amounts of collective knowledge exist in every organization's employees. How can that knowledge be shared?

As a future business professional, business intelligence is a critical skill. According to Jim Goodnight, founder of SAS: "If you want to be successful in business, make sure you have some understanding of analytics and when to use them. People who can use analytics—such as data mining and forecasting—to turn raw data into better business decisions have never been in greater demand. With all the talk of 'Big Data,' organizations across industries need people who understand how to use analytics to make sense of it all. I encourage this year's graduates to learn about how and when analytics can support their decisions."[1]

This chapter begins by summarizing the ways organizations use business intelligence. It then describes the three basic activities in the BI process and illustrates those activities using the AllRoad Parts problem that was presented at the beginning of Chapter 5. We then discuss the role of data warehouses and data marts and next survey reporting, data mining, BigData, and knowledge management BI applications. After that, you'll learn alternatives for publishing the results of BI applications. We will wrap up the chapter with a 2024 observation that many people find frightening.

Q1 How Do Organizations Use Business Intelligence (BI) Systems?

Business intelligence (BI) systems are information systems that process operational, social, and other data to identify patterns, relationships, and trends for use by business professionals and other knowledge workers. These patterns, relationships, trends, and predictions are referred to as **business intelligence**. As information systems, BI systems have the five standard components: hardware, software, data, procedures, and people. The software component of a BI system is called a **BI application**.

In the context of their day-to-day operations, organizations generate enormous amounts of data. According to *Der Spiegel*, an estimated 2.8 zettabytes of data were created in 2012, with the expectation that this rate will grow to 40 zettabytes per year by 2020.[2] Business

---

[1]Eve Tahmincioglu, "CEO Advice for Grads: Travel, Learn, Follow Your Passion," *Today Money*, last modifed June 5, 2012, *http://lifeinc.today.msnbc.msn.com/_news/2012/06/05/12008767-ceo-advice-for-grads-travel-learn-follow-your-passion?lite*.

[2]Martin U. Müller, Marcel Rosenbach, and Thomas Schulz, "Living by the Numbers: Big Data Knows What Your Future Holds," *Der Spiegel*, accessed July 31, 2013, *http://www.spiegel.de/international/business/big-data-enables-companies-and-researchers-to-look-into-the-future-a-899964.html*.

intelligence is buried in that data, and the function of a BI system is to extract it and make it available to those who need it.

The boundaries of BI systems are blurry. In this text, we will take the broad view shown in Figure 9-1. Source data for a BI system can be the organization's own operational data, social media data, data that the organization purchases from data vendors, or employee knowledge. The BI application processes the data with reporting applications, data mining applications, BigData applications, and knowledge management applications to produce business intelligence for knowledge workers. Today such workers include not only analysts in the home office, but also operations and field personnel who use BI to approve loans, order goods, and decide where to police, to take a few examples.

How Do Organizations Use BI?

As shown in Figure 9-2, organizations use BI for all four of the collaborative tasks described in Chapter 2. Starting with the last row of Figure 9-2, business intelligence can be used just for informing. Medical staff can use PRIDE to learn how patients are using the new system. At the time of the analysis, the staff may not have any particular purpose in mind, but are just browsing the BI results for some future, unspecified purpose. At AllRoad Parts, the company we studied in Chapters 1–6, Kelly may just want to know how AllRoad's current sales compare to the forecast. She may have no particular purpose in mind; she just wants to know "how we're doing."

Moving up a row in Figure 9-2, some managers use BI systems for decision making. At the start of this chapter, Dr. Flores is concerned that some patients may be exercising too much; he can use BI to determine if anyone is and, if so, who they are. When planning items for future sales, AllRoad can use BI to help it decide which parts designs to sell for customers' 3D printing.

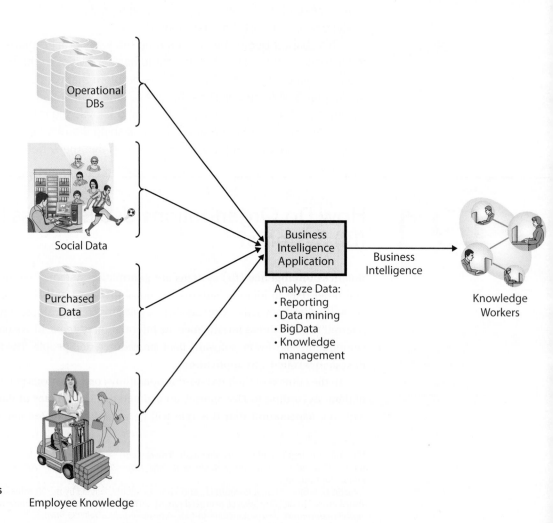

Figure 9-1
Components of a Business Intelligence System

Task	PRIDE Example	AllRoad Example
Project Management	Use PRIDE to reduce medical costs.	Create AllRoad Europe.
Problem Solving	How can we get our patients to follow exercise prescriptions better?	How can we reduce our inventory size but still have what our customers want?
Deciding	Which of our patients are exercising too much?	Which parts designs should we sell for customers to use for 3D printing?
Informing	In what ways are patients using the new system?	How do sales compare to our sales forecast?

Figure 9-2
Example Uses of Business Intelligence

(By the way, some authors define BI systems as supporting decision making only, in which case they use the older term **decision support systems** as a synonym for decision-making BI systems. We take the broader view here to include all four of the tasks in Figure 9-2 and will avoid the term *decision support systems*.)

Problem solving is the next category of business intelligence use. Again, a problem is a perceived difference between what is and what ought to be. Business intelligence can be used for both sides of that definition: determining *what is* as well as *what should be*. Dr. Flores and his partners may want to use BI to solve the problem of getting patients to exercise more faithfully according to their plan. AllRoad's competitive strategy is to maintain a huge inventory selection so it has the parts customers want. AllRoad might use BI to buy smarter, reducing its inventory but still maintaining its strategy.

Finally, business intelligence can be used during project management. PRIDE can be used to support a project to reduce medical costs reducing office visits. When AllRoad decides to open its European office, it can use business intelligence to determine which parts it should sell first and which vendors to contact to obtain those parts.

As you study Figure 9-2, recall the hierarchical nature of these tasks. Deciding requires informing; problem solving requires deciding (and informing); and project management requires problem solving (and deciding [and informing]).

What Are Typical BI Applications?

This section summarizes three BI applications that will give you a flavor of what is possible. Because *business intelligence* and the related term *BigData* are hot topics today, a Web search will produce dozens of similar examples. After you read this chapter, search for more applications that appeal to your particular interests.

Identifying *Changes* in Purchasing Patterns

Most students are aware that business intelligence is used to predict purchasing patterns. Amazon made the phrase "Customers who bought…also bought" famous; when we buy something today, we expect the e-commerce application to suggest what else we might want. Later in this chapter, you'll learn some of the techniques that are used to produce such recommendations.

More interesting, however, is identifying *changes* in purchasing patterns. Retailers know that important life events cause customers to change what they buy and, for a short interval, to form new loyalties to new store brands. Thus, when people start their first professional job, get married, have a baby, or retire, retailers want to know. Before BI, stores would watch the local newspapers for graduation, marriage, and baby announcements and send ads in response. That is a slow, labor-intensive, and expensive process.

Target wanted to get ahead of the newspapers and in 2002 began a project to use purchasing patterns to determine that someone was pregnant. By applying business intelligence techniques to its sales data, Target was able to identify a purchasing pattern of lotions, vitamins and other products that reliably predicts pregnancy. When Target observed that purchasing pattern, it sent ads for diapers and other baby-related products to those customers.

Its program worked—too well for one teenager who had told no one she was pregnant. When she began receiving ads for baby items, her father complained to the manager of the local Target store, who apologized. It was the father's turn to apologize when he learned that his daughter was, indeed, pregnant.[3]

BI for Entertainment

Amazon, Netflix, Pandora, Spotify, and other media-delivery organizations generate billions of bytes of data on consumer media preferences. Using that data, Amazon has begun to produce its own video and TV, basing plots and characters and selecting actors on the results of its BI analysis.[4]

Netflix decided to buy *House of Cards*, starring Kevin Spacey, based on its analysis of customers' viewing patterns. Similarly, Spotify processes data on customers' listening habits to determine locations where particular bands' songs are heard most often. Using that data, it then recommends the best cities for popular bands and other musical groups to perform.[5]

A popular adage among marketing professionals is that "buyers are liars," meaning they'll say they want one thing but purchase something else. That characteristic reduces the efficacy of marketing focus groups. BI produced from data on watching, listening, and rental habits, however, determines what people actually want, not what they say. Will this enable data miners like Amazon to become the new Hollywood? We will see.

Predictive Policing

Many police departments are facing severe budget constraints that force them to reduce on-duty police personnel and services. Given these budget cuts, police departments need to do more with less, which means, in part, finding better ways of utilizing their personnel.

In response to this challenge, the Los Angeles Police Department and Police Chief William J. Bratton used business intelligence, along with new business processes, to implement what they termed *predictive policing*.[6] Their program met with such success that it has been emulated by numerous police departments nationwide.

With **predictive policing**, police departments analyze data on past crimes, including location, date, time, day of week, type of crime, and related data, to predict where crimes are likely to occur. They then station police personnel in the best locations for preventing those crimes. According to the Los Angeles Police Department, "The analytic methods used in the predictive-policing model do not identify specific individuals. Rather, they surface particular times and locations predicted to be associated with an increased likelihood for crime."[7]

With the speed at which data is generated today and with the near-zero cost of processing, we can be certain that many even more innovative applications of BI will occur. Watch for them; they will present interesting career opportunities for you.

Given these examples, we next consider the process used to create business intelligence.

[3]Charles Duhigg, "How Companies Learn Your Secrets," *The New York Times,* last modified February 16, 2012, *http://www.nytimes.com/2012/02/19/magazine/shopping-habits.html?_r=2&hp=&pagewanted=all&.*
[4]Alistair Barr, "Crowdsourcing goes to Hollywood as Amazon makes movies," *Reuters,* last modified October 10, 2012, *http://www.reuters.com/article/2012/10/10/us-amazon-hollywood-crowd-idUSBRE8990JH20121010.*
[5]Martin U. Müller, Marcel Rosenbach, and Thomas Schulz, "Living by the Numbers: Big Data Knows What Your Future Holds," *Der Spiegel,* accessed July 31, 2013, *http://www.spiegel.de/international/business/big-data-enables-companies-and-researchers-to-look-into-the-future-a-899964.html.*
[6]Colleen McCue, *Data Mining and Predictive Analysis: Intelligence Gathering and Crime Analysis* (Burlington, Mass.: Butterworth-Heinemann, 2006).
[7]Charlie Beck and Colleen McCue, "Predictive Policing: What Can We Learn from Wal-Mart and Amazon about Fighting Crime in a Recession?," *Police Chief Magazine,* last modified November 2009, *http://www.policechiefmagazine.org/magazine/index.cfm?fuseaction=display_arch&article_id=1942&issue_id=112009.*

What Are the Three Primary Activities in the BI Process?

Figure 9-3 shows the three primary activities in the BI process: acquire data, perform analysis, and publish results. These activities directly correspond to the BI elements in Figure 9-1. **Data acquisition** is the process of obtaining, cleaning, organizing, relating, and cataloging source data. We will illustrate a simple data acquisition example for AllRoad Parts later in this question and discuss data acquisition in greater detail in Q3.

BI analysis is the process of creating business intelligence. The four fundamental categories of BI analysis are reporting, data mining, BigData, and knowledge management. We will illustrate a simple example of a reporting system for AllRoad later in this question and describe each of the categories of BI analysis in greater detail in Q4 through Q7, respectively.

Publish results is the process of delivering business intelligence to the knowledge workers who need it. **Push publishing** delivers business intelligence to users without any request from the users; the BI results are delivered according to a schedule or as a result of an event or particular data condition. **Pull publishing** requires the user to request BI results. Publishing media include print as well as online content delivered via Web servers, specialized Web servers known as *report servers*, and BI results that are sent via automation to other programs. We will discuss these publishing options further in Q8. For now, consider a simple example of the use of business intelligence at AllRoad.

Using Business Intelligence to Find Candidate Parts at AllRoad

At the start of Chapter 5, Drew and Addison asked Lucas, the director of IT services at AllRoad Parts, to provide an extract of AllRoad's sales and parts data. Drew was skeptical that they could do anything with it, but Addison was certain that she could use Access to find candidates for the sale of 3D parts designs from sales and parts data. Here we'll learn what she did.

To begin, Addison and Drew identified criteria for parts that customers might want to print with 3D. Their criteria and rationale were to find parts that were:

1. Provided by certain vendors (starting with just a few vendors that had already agreed to make part design files available for sale)
2. Purchased by larger customers (individuals and small companies would be unlikely to have 3D printers or the needed expertise to use them)
3. Frequently ordered (popular products)
4. Ordered in small quantities (3D printing is not suited for mass production)
5. Simple in design (easier to 3D print)

Addison knew that the fifth criterion would be difficult to evaluate because AllRoad doesn't store data on part complexity per se. After some discussion, she decided to use part weight

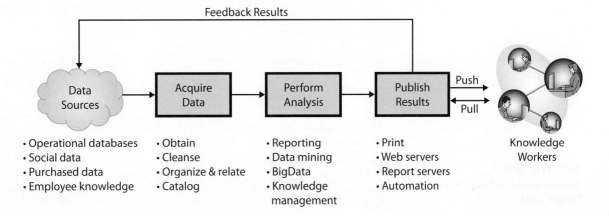

Figure 9-3
Three Primary Activities in the BI Process

and price as surrogates for simplicity. As Addison said, "If it doesn't weigh very much or cost very much, it probably isn't complex." At least, she decided to start that way and find out. Accordingly, she asked Lucas to include part weight in the part data extract.

Acquire Data

As shown in Figure 9-3, acquiring data is the first step in the BI process. In response to Addison and Drew's request for data, Lucas asked one of his employees to extract operational data to produce the following two tables:

> Sales (CustomerName, Contact, Title, Bill Year, Number Orders, Units, Revenue, Source, PartNumber)
> Part (PartNumber, Shipping Weight, Vendor)

Sample data for these two tables is shown in Figure 9-4. As Addison and Drew examined this data, they concluded they had what they needed and actually wouldn't need all of the data columns in the Sales table. They were surprised that the data was divided into different billing years, but because they planned to sum item sales over those years, that division wouldn't affect their analysis.

Analyze Data

Addison's first step was to combine the data in the two tables into a single table that contained both the sales and part data. Also, because she and Drew had already selected certain vendors to work with (those they knew would agree to release 3D parts design files), she set filtering criteria for those vendor names, as shown in Figure 9-5. In this Access query, the line between PartNumber in Order Extract and PartNumber in Part Data means that rows of the two tables are to be combined if they have matching values of PartNumber.

The result of this query is shown in Figure 9-6. Notice there are some missing and questionable values. Numerous rows have missing values of Contact and Title, and some of the rows

Order Extract

CustomerName	Contact	Title	Bill Year	Number Orders	Units	Revenue	Source	PartNumber
Island Biking	John Steel	Marketing Manager	2012	10	39	$195.22	AWS	200-227
Island Biking	John Steel	Marketing Manager	2011	14	59	$438.81	Internet	200-227
Island Biking	John Steel	Marketing Manager	2011	21	55	$255.96	AWS	200-227
Island Biking	John Steel	Marketing Manager	2012	4	11	$85.55	Internet	200-227
Kona Riders	Renate Messne	Sales Representative	2009	43	54	$349.27	Internet	200-203
Kona Riders	Renate Messne	Sales Representative	2010	30	53	$362.45	Internet	200-203
Kona Riders	Renate Messne	Sales Representative	2011	1	2	$14.34	Internet	200-203
Lone Pine Crafters	Jaime Yorres	Owner	2012	4	14	$108.89	Internet	200-203
Lone Pine Crafters	Jaime Yorres	Owner	2012	2	2	$15.56	Internet	200-203
Lone Pine Crafters	Jaime Yorres	Owner	2013	2	2	$15.56	Internet	200-203
Moab Mauraders	Carlos Gonzále	Accounting Manager	2012	2	4	$4,106.69	Internet	700-1680
Moab Mauraders	Carlos Gonzále	Accounting Manager	2012	3	7	$7,404.18	Internet	700-1680
Moab Mauraders	Carlos Gonzále	Accounting Manager	2012	2	6	$6,346.44	Internet	700-1680
Sedona Mountain Trails	Felipe Izquierc	Owner	2012	6	7	$73.46	Internet	300-1010
Sedona Mountain Trails	Felipe Izquierc	Owner	2012	3	7	$39.14	Phone	300-1010
Sedona Mountain Trails	Felipe Izquierc	Owner	2012	3	9	$74.59	Phone	300-1010
Sedona Mountain Trails	Felipe Izquierc	Owner	2011	5	20	$153.00	Phone	300-1010
Sedona Mountain Trails	Felipe Izquierc	Owner	2009	3	8	$37.14	Phone	300-1010
Sedona Mountain Trails	Felipe Izquierc	Owner	2010	1	0	$89.30	Internet	300-1010
Sedona Mountain Trails	Felipe Izquierc	Owner	2010	6	20	$73.13	Phone	300-1010
Sedona Mountain Trails	Felipe Izquierc	Owner	2009	4	8	$67.41	Internet	300-1010
Flat Iron Riders	Maria Anders	Sales Representative	2010	7	22	$11,734.25	Internet	500-2020
Flat Iron Riders	Maria Anders	Sales Representative	2012	2	1	$595.00	Internet	500-2020
Flat Iron Riders	Maria Anders	Sales Representative	2011	10	29	$16,392.25	Internet	500-2020
Flat Iron Riders	Maria Anders	Sales Representative	2012	20	32	$12,688.80	AWS	500-2020
Flat Iron Riders	Maria Anders	Sales Representative	2011	6	18	$6,701.40	AWS	500-2020
Flat Iron Riders	Maria Anders	Sales Representative	2010	6	24	$8,950.50	AWS	500-2020
Flat Iron Riders	Maria Anders	Sales Representative	2009	52	54	$27,272.25	Internet	500-2020
Flat Iron Riders	Maria Anders	Sales Representative	2011	2	3	$1,134.75	AWS	500-2020
Around the Horn	Ana Trujillo	Owner	2011	2	2	$14.13	Internet	200-217
Around the Horn	Ana Trujillo	Owner	2010	71	119	$1,034.83	AWS	300-1016
Around the Horn	Ana Trujillo	Owner	2009	12	50	$626.88	Internet	300-1016
Around the Horn	Ana Trujillo	Owner	2012	23	27	$403.67	Internet	300-1016
Around the Horn	Ana Trujillo	Owner	2011	11	35	$494.59	Internet	300-1016
Bon App Riding	Antonio Morer	Owner	2012	1	0	$158.30	Internet	300-1015
Bon App Riding	Antonio Morer	Owner	2011	1	0	$2,226.19	Internet	300-1015
Bottom-Dollar Bikes	Thomas Hardy	Sales Representative	2010	38	58	$31,824.00	Internet	500-2025
Bottom-Dollar Bikes	Thomas Hardy	Sales Representative	2012	11	21	$12,875.80	Internet	500-2025
Bottom-Dollar Bikes	Thomas Hardy	Sales Representative	2011	19	30	$16,719.50	Internet	500-2025

Figure 9-4a

Sample Extracted Data: Order Extract Table

Part Data				
ID ▾	PartNumber ▾	Shipping Weight ▾	Vendor	⤝ Click to Add ▾
9	200-219	7.28	DePARTures, Inc.	
22	200-225	3.61	DePARTures, Inc.	
23	200-227	5.14	DePARTures, Inc.	
11	200-207	9.23	DePARTures, Inc.	
28	200-205	4.11	DePARTures, Inc.	
29	200-211	4.57	DePARTures, Inc.	
10	200-213	1.09	DePARTures, Inc.	
37	200-223	3.61	DePARTures, Inc.	
45	200-217	1.98	DePARTures, Inc.	
2	200-209	10.41	DePARTures, Inc.	
3	200-215	1.55	DePARTures, Inc.	
47	200-221	10.85	DePARTures, Inc.	
42	200-203	3.20	DePARTures, Inc.	
17	300-1007	2.77	Desert Gear Supply	
13	300-1017	9.46	Desert Gear Supply	
50	300-1016	4.14	Desert Gear Supply	
27	300-1013	2.66	Desert Gear Supply	
8	300-1008	10.13	Desert Gear Supply	
30	300-1015	5.96	Desert Gear Supply	
15	300-1014	10.18	Desert Gear Supply	
7	300-1009	3.76	Desert Gear Supply	
6	300-1011	6.41	Desert Gear Supply	
43	300-1010	10.87	Desert Gear Supply	
31	300-1012	9.08	Desert Gear Supply	
1	500-2035	9.66	ExtremeGear	
41	500-2030	4.71	ExtremeGear	
40	500-2040	9.92	ExtremeGear	

Figure 9-4b
Sample Extracted Data: Part
Data Table

have a value of zero for Units. The missing contact data and title data isn't a problem; Lucas included it just in case Addison and Drew needed to contact a customer. Because they had their own contact data, they didn't need this data. But the values of zero units might be problematic. At some point, Addison and Drew might need to investigate what these values mean and possibly correct the data or remove those rows from the analysis. In the immediate term, however, they decided to proceed even with these incorrect values. You will learn in Q3 that, for a number of reasons, such problematic data is common in data extracts.

The data in Figure 9-6 has been filtered for their first criterion, to consider parts only from particular vendors. For their next criterion, they needed to decide how to identify large

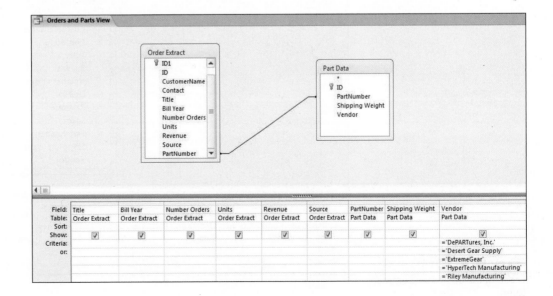

Figure 9-5
Joining *Order Extract* and
Filtered *Parts* Tables

Orders and Parts View

CustomerName	Contact	Title	Bill Year	Number Orders	Units	Revenue	Source	PartNumber	Shipping Weight	Vendor
Gordos Dirt Bikes	Sergio Gutiérrez	Sales Repres	2011	43	107	$26,234.12	Internet	100-108	3.32	Riley Manufacturing
Island Biking			2012	59	135	$25,890.62	Phone	500-2035	9.66	ExtremeGear
Big Bikes			2010	29	77	$25,696.00	AWS	700-1680	6.06	HyperTech Manufacturing
Lazy B Bikes			2009	19	30	$25,576.50	Internet	700-2280	2.70	HyperTech Manufacturing
Lone Pine Crafters	Carlos Hernández	Sales Repres	2012	1	0	$25,171.56	Internet	500-2030	4.71	ExtremeGear
Seven Lakes Riding	Peter Franken	Marketing M	2009	15	50	$25,075.00	Internet	500-2020	10.07	ExtremeGear
Big Bikes			2012	10	40	$24,888.00	Internet	500-2025	10.49	ExtremeGear
B' Bikes	Georg Pipps	Sales Manage	2012	14	23	$24,328.02	Internet	700-1680	6.06	HyperTech Manufacturing
Eastern Connection	Isabel de Castro	Sales Repres	2012	48	173	$24,296.17	AWS	100-105	10.73	Riley Manufacturing
Big Bikes	Carine Schmitt	Marketing M	2009	22	71	$23,877.48	AWS	500-2035	9.66	ExtremeGear
Island Biking	Manuel Pereira	Owner	2011	26	45	$23,588.86	Internet	500-2045	3.22	ExtremeGear
Mississippi Delta Riding	Rene Phillips	Sales Repres	2012	9	33	$23,550.25	Internet	700-2180	4.45	HyperTech Manufacturing
Uncle's Upgrades			2012	9	21	$22,212.54	Internet	700-1680	6.06	HyperTech Manufacturing
Big Bikes			2010	73	80	$22,063.92	Phone	700-1680	6.06	HyperTech Manufacturing
Island Biking			2012	18	59	$22,025.88	Internet	100-108	3.32	Riley Manufacturing
Uncle's Upgrades			2011	16	38	$21,802.50	Internet	500-2035	9.66	ExtremeGear
Hard Rock Machines			2012	42	57	$21,279.24	Internet	100-108	3.32	Riley Manufacturing
Kona Riders			2012	11	20	$21,154.80	Internet	700-1880	2.28	HyperTech Manufacturing
Moab Mauraders			2012	6	20	$21,154.80	Internet	700-2180	4.45	HyperTech Manufacturing
Lone Pine Crafters			2012	35	58	$21,016.59	Internet	100-106	6.23	Riley Manufacturing
Big Bikes	Carine Schmitt	Marketing M	2010	9	36	$20,655.00	Internet	500-2035	9.66	ExtremeGear
East/West Enterprises			2011	14	60	$20,349.00	Internet	100-104	5.80	Riley Manufacturing
Jeeps 'n More	Yvonne Moncada	Sales Agent	2012	47	50	$20,230.00	AWS	500-2030	4.71	ExtremeGear
East/West Enterprises			2009	14	60	$20,178.15	AWS	500-2035	9.66	ExtremeGear
Lone Pine Crafters			2012	20	54	$20,159.28	Internet	100-106	6.23	Riley Manufacturing
Lone Pine Crafters	Carlos Hernández	Sales Repres	2012	1	0	$20,137.27	Internet	500-2030	4.71	ExtremeGear
Lazy B Bikes			2012	21	29	$19,946.78	AWS	700-1580	7.50	HyperTech Manufacturing
Eastern Connection	Isabel de Castro	Sales Repres	2012	42	173	$19,907.06	Phone	100-105	10.73	Riley Manufacturing
Lazy B Bikes			2012	8	30	$19,724.25	AWS	700-1580	7.50	HyperTech Manufacturing

Figure 9-6

Sample *Orders* and *Parts View* Data

customers. To do so, Addison created the query in Figure 9-7, which sums the revenue, units, and average price for each customer. Looking at the query results in Figure 9-8, she and Drew decided to consider only customers having more than $200,000 in total revenue. Addison created a query having just those customers and named that query Big Customers.

Addison and Drew discussed what they meant by frequent purchase and decided to include items ordered an average of once a week or roughly 50 times per year. You can see that Addison set that criterion for Number Orders in the query in Figure 9-9. To select only parts that are ordered in small quantities, she first created a column that computes average order size (Units / [Number Orders]) and then set a criterion on that expression that the average must be less than 2.5. Their last two criteria were that the part be relatively inexpensive and that it be lightweight. They decided to select parts with a unit price (computed as Revenue / Units) less than 100 and a shipping weight less than 5 pounds.

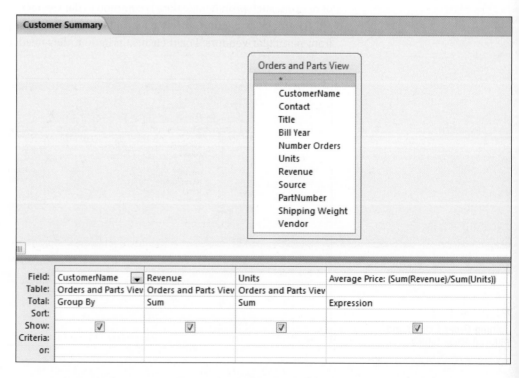

Figure 9-7

Creating the Customer Summary Query

Customer Summary			
CustomerName	SumOfRevenue	SumOfUnits	Average Price
Great Lakes Machines	$1,760.47	142	12.3976535211268
Seven Lakes Riding	$288,570.71	5848	49.3451963919289
Around the Horn	$16,669.48	273	61.0603611721612
Dewey Riding	$36,467.90	424	86.0092018867925
Moab Mauraders	$143,409.27	1344	106.7033234375
Gordos Dirt Bikes	$113,526.88	653	173.854335068913
Mountain Traders	$687,710.99	3332	206.395855432173
Hungry Rider Off-road	$108,602.32	492	220.736416056911
Eastern Connection	$275,092.28	1241	221.669848186946
Mississippi Delta Riding	$469,932.11	1898	247.593315542676
Island Biking	$612,072.64	2341	261.457770098249
Big Bikes	$1,385,867.98	4876	284.222310233798
Hard Rock Machines	$74,853.22	241	310.594267219917
Lone Pine Crafters	$732,990.33	1816	403.629038215859
Sedona Mountain Trails	$481,073.82	1104	435.755269474638
Flat Iron Riders	$85,469.20	183	467.044808743169
Bottom-Dollar Bikes	$72,460.85	154	470.52502012987
Uncle's Upgrades	$947,477.61	1999	473.975794047024
Ernst Handel Mechanics	$740,951.15	1427	519.236962438683
Kona Riders	$511,108.05	982	520.476624439919
Lazy B Bikes	$860,950.72	1594	540.119648619824
Jeeps 'n More	$404,540.62	678	596.667583185841
French Riding Masters	$1,037,386.76	1657	626.063224984912
B' Bikes	$113,427.06	159	713.377735849057
East/West Enterprises	$2,023,402.09	2457	823.525474074074
Bon App Riding	$65,848.90	60	1097.48160833333

Figure 9-8
Customer Summary

The results of this query are shown in Figure 9-10. Of all the parts that AllRoad sells, these 12 fit the criteria that Addison and Drew created.

Drew wondered what revenue potential these parts represent. Accordingly, Addison created a query that connected the selected parts with their past sales data. The results are shown in Figure 9-11.

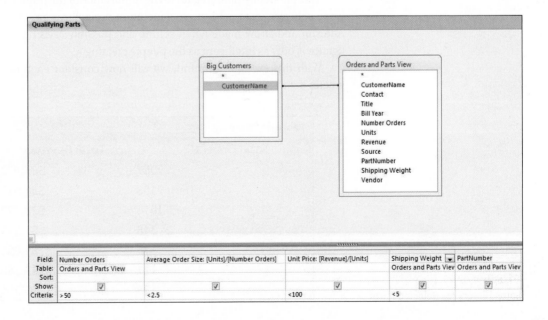

Figure 9-9
Qualifying Parts Query Design

Qualifying Parts				
Number Orders ▾	Average Order Size ▾	Unit Price ▾	Shipping Weight ▾	PartNumber ▾
275	1	9.14173854545455	4.14	300-1016
258	1.87596899224806	7.41284524793388	4.14	300-1016
110	1.18181818181818	6.46796923076923	4.11	200-205
176	1.66477272727273	12.5887211604096	4.14	300-1016
139	1.0431654676259	6.28248965517241	1.98	200-217
56	1.83928571428571	6.71141553398058	1.98	200-217
99	1.02020202020202	7.7775	3.20	200-203
76	2.17105263157895	12.0252206060606	2.66	300-1013
56	1.07142857142857	5.0575	4.57	200-211
73	1.15068493150685	5.0575	4.57	200-211
107	2.02803738317757	6.01096405529954	2.77	300-1007
111	2.07207207207207	6.01096434782609	2.77	300-1007

Figure 9-10

Qualifying Parts Query Results

Publish Results

Publish results is the last activity in the BI process shown in Figure 9-3. In some cases, this means placing BI results on servers for publication to knowledge workers over the Internet or other networks. In other cases, it means making the results available via a Web service for use by other applications. In still other cases, it means creating PDFs or PowerPoint presentations for communicating to colleagues or management.

In AllRoad's case, Addison and Drew communicated their results back to Jason and Kelly. Judging just by the results in Figure 9-11, there seems to be little revenue potential in selling designs for these parts. AllRoad earns minimal revenue from the parts themselves; the designs would have to be priced considerably lower, and that would mean almost no revenue.

In spite of the low revenue potential, AllRoad might still decide to offer 3D designs to customers. It might decide to give the designs away as a gesture of goodwill to its customers; this analysis indicates it will be sacrificing little revenue to do so. Or it might do it as a PR move intended to show that it's on top of the latest manufacturing technology. Or it might decide to postpone consideration of 3D printing because it doesn't see that many customers ordering the qualifying parts.

Of course, there is the possibility that Addison and Drew chose the wrong criteria. If they have time, it might be tempting for Addison and Drew to change their criteria and repeat the analysis. Such a course is a slippery slope, however. They might find themselves changing criteria until they obtain a result they want, which yields a very biased study.

This possibility points again to the importance of the human component of an IS. The hardware, software, data, and query-generation procedures are of little value if the decisions that Addison and Drew made when setting and possibly revising criteria are poor. Business intelligence is only as intelligent as the people creating it!

With this example in mind, we will now consider each of the activities in Figure 9-3 in greater detail.

Revenue Potential		
Total Orders ▾	Total Revenue ▾	PartNumber ▾
3987	$84,672.73	300-1016
2158	$30,912.19	200-211
1074	$23,773.53	200-217
548	$7,271.31	300-1007
375	$5,051.62	200-203
111	$3,160.86	300-1013
139	$1,204.50	200-205

Figure 9-11

Sales History for Selected Parts

Q3 How Do Organizations Use Data Warehouses and Data Marts to Acquire Data?

Although it is possible to create basic reports and perform simple analyses from operational data, this course is not usually recommended. For reasons of security and control, IS professionals do not want employees like Addison processing operational data. If Addison makes an error, that error could cause a serious disruption in AllRoad's operations. Also, operational data is structured for fast and reliable transaction processing. It is seldom structured in a way that readily supports BI analysis. Finally, BI analyses can require considerable processing; placing BI applications on operational servers can dramatically reduce system performance.

For these reasons, most organizations extract operational data for BI processing. For a small organization like AllRoad, the extraction may be as simple as an Access database. Larger organizations, however, typically create and staff a group of people who manage and run a **data warehouse**, which is a facility for managing an organization's BI data. The functions of a data warehouse are to:

- Obtain data
- Cleanse data
- Organize and relate data
- Catalog data

Collecting and selling data about consumer shopping habits is big business. But what information about you is being collected? And how is it being used? The Ethics Guide on pages 336-337 considers these questions.

Figure 9-12 shows the components of a data warehouse. Programs read operational and other data and extract, clean, and prepare that data for BI processing. The prepared data is stored in a data warehouse database using a data warehouse DBMS, which can be different from the organization's operational DBMS. For example, an organization might use Oracle for its operational processing, but use SQL Server for its data warehouse. Other organizations use SQL Server for operational processing, but use DBMSs from statistical package vendors such as SAS or SPSS in the data warehouse.

Data warehouses include data that is purchased from outside sources. The purchase of data about organizations is not unusual or particularly concerning from a privacy standpoint. However, some companies choose to buy personal consumer data (e.g., marital status) from data vendors

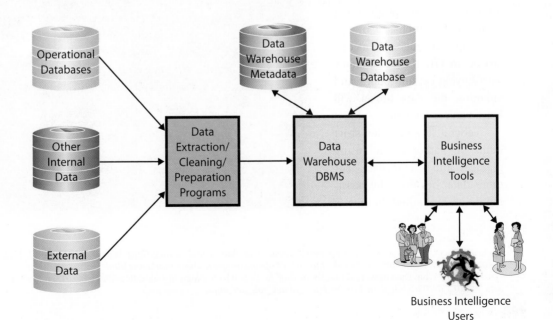

Figure 9-12
Components of a Data Warehouse

Business Intelligence Users

Ethics Guide

UNSEEN CYBERAZZI

A data broker or **data aggregator** is a company that acquires and purchases consumer and other data from public records, retailers, Internet cookie vendors, social media trackers, and other sources and uses it to create business intelligence that it sells to companies and the government. Two prominent data brokers are Datalogix and Acxiom Corporation.

Data brokers gather vast amounts of data. According to *The New York Times,* as of June 2012, Acxiom Corporation had used 23,000 servers to process data of 50 trillion transactions on 500 million consumers. It stores more than 15,000 data points on some consumers.[8]

So, what do data brokers do with all this data? If you buy pizza online on Friday nights only when you receive a substantial discount, a data broker (or the broker's customer) knows to send you a discount pizza coupon Friday morning. If you use a customer loyalty card at your local grocery store and regularly buy, say, large bags of potato chips, the data broker or its customer will send you coupons for more potato chips or for a second snack product that is frequently purchased by potato chip consumers. Or, as discussed in Q1, if you suddenly start buying certain lotions and vitamins, the data broker will know you're pregnant.

Federal law provides strict limits on gathering and using medical and credit data. For other data, however, the possibilities are unlimited. In theory,

data brokers enable you to view the data that is stored about you, but in practice it is difficult to learn how to request your data. Further, the process for doing so is torturous, and ultimately, the data that is released is limited to innocuous data such as your name, phone numbers, and current and former addresses.[9] Without an easy means for viewing all of your data, it is impossible to verify its accuracy.

Of even greater concern, however, is the unknown processing of such data. What business intelligence techniques are employed by these companies? What are the accuracy and reliability of those techniques? If the data broker errs in predicting that you'll buy a pizza on Friday night, who cares? But if the data broker errs in predicting that you're a terrorist, it matters. Data brokers are silent on these questions.

Source: Sergey Nivens/Shutterstock

---

[8]Natasha Singer, "Mapping, and Sharing, the Consumer Genome," *The New York Times,* last modified June 16, 2012, *http://www.nytimes.com/2012/06/17/technology/acxiom-the-quiet-giant-of-consumer-database-marketing.html.*

[9]Lois Beckett, "What Data Brokers Know About You," *RealClearTechnology,* last modified March 8, 2013, *http://www.realcleartechnology.com/articles/2013/03/08/what_data_brokers_know_about_you_326.html.*

DISCUSSION QUESTIONS

1. We've used Kant's categorical imperative as one criterion for assessing ethical behavior: *Act as if you would have your behavior be a universal law.* As a litmus test of this principle, we've said that if you're willing to publish your behavior in *The New York Times*, then your behavior conforms to the categorical imperative.

    a. Consider the inverse of that litmus test. Is it true that if you're not willing to publish your behavior in *The New York Times,* it is unethical? (You might find it easier to consider this question in a different but equivalent form: Your behavior is ethical *if and only if* you're willing to publish it in *The New York Times.*)

    b. Considering your answer to question a, if data brokers are unwilling to say what data they are collecting and how they are processing it, is it reasonable to conclude their behavior is unethical? Explain your answer.

2. Using business intelligence applied to consumer purchasing data for targeted marketing seems innocuous enough. However, is it? Using both the categorical imperative (pages 20–21) and utilitarian (pages 54–55) perspectives, assess the ethics of the following:

    a. Some people, whether from genetic factors, habit, lack of education, or other factors, are prone to overeating junk food. By focusing junk food sales offers at this market segment, data brokers or their customers are promoting obesity. Is their behavior ethical?

    b. Data brokers claim they can reliably infer ethnicity from consumer behavior data. Suppose they also determine that one ethnic group is more likely to attend college than others. Accordingly, they focus the marketing for college-prep materials, scholarships, and university admissions applications on this ethnic group. Over time, that group will be guided into positive (assuming you believe college is positive) decisions that other groups will not. Is this behavior different from ethnic profiling? Is it ethical?

3. Suppose a data broker correctly identifies that your grandmother is addicted to playing online hearts. From its business intelligence, it knows that frequent hearts players are strong prospects for online gambling. Accordingly, the data broker refers your grandmother's data to an online gambling vendor, one of its customers. Grandma gets hooked and loses all of her savings, including money earmarked for your college tuition.

    a. Is the data broker's behavior ethical?

    b. Assume the data broker says, "Look, it's not us, it's our customer, the online gambling vendor, that's causing the problem." Does the broker's posture absolve it of ethical considerations for Grandma's losses?

    c. Assume the online gambling vendor says, "Look, it's not us; it's Grandma. We provide fair and honest games. If Grandma likes to play games where the odds of winning are low, talk to Grandma." Assume in your answer that the gaming company has gone to great lengths to provide the elderly with an emotionally rewarding UX for games with low winning odds. Does the vendor's posture absolve it of any ethical considerations for Grandma's losses?

4. If all of your behavior is ethical, then, according to the categorical imperative, you are willing to have your life story printed in *The New York Times*. Thus, you needn't be concerned about the data and business intelligence created about you. However, consider the following:

    a. Suppose, as the most junior member of a club, you are required to purchase beer for your club's bimonthly beer fest. To obtain a substantial discount from the vendor, you use your customer loyalty card for these purchases. A data aggregator obtains your purchase history and classifies you as a heavy drinker. Unknown to you, the data aggregator informs your medical insurance company of its classification. Your insurance premiums increase, and you never know why. Using either the categorical imperative or utilitarianism, is there an ethical problem here?

    b. Do you think something should be done to reduce the likelihood of situations like that in question a? If so, what?

    c. Suppose you have a personal medical problem that you wish to keep private. Your condition requires you to purchase a particular set of off-the-shelf products from the pharmacy at your grocery store. A data aggregator observes your purchasing pattern, infers your problem, and sends you coupons and other promotional products that clearly identify your condition. Against your strongest wishes, your roommates become aware of your medical problem. Using either the categorical imperative or utilitarianism, is there an ethical problem here?

    d. Do you think something should be done to reduce the likelihood of situations like that in question c? If so, what?

5. According to the Privacy Act of 1974, the U.S. government is prohibited from storing many types of data about U.S. citizens. The act does not, however, prohibit it from purchasing business intelligence from data brokers. If the government purchases business intelligence that is based, in part, on data that it is prohibited from storing, is the government's behavior ethical? Use both the categorical imperative and utilitarian perspectives in your answer.

Figure 9-13
Examples of Consumer Data that Can Be Purchased

- Name, address, phone
- Age
- Gender
- Ethnicity
- Religion
- Income
- Education
- Voter registration
- Home ownership
- Vehicles
- Magazine subscriptions
- Hobbies
- Catalog orders
- Marital status, life stage
- Height, weight, hair and eye color
- Spouse name, birth date
- Children's names and birth dates

such as Acxiom Corporation. Figure 9-13 lists some of the consumer data that can be readily purchased. An amazing (and, from a privacy standpoint, frightening) amount of data is available.

Metadata concerning the data—its source, its format, its assumptions and constraints, and other facts about the data—is kept in a data warehouse metadata database. The data warehouse DBMS extracts and provides data to BI applications.

The term *business intelligence users* is different from *knowledge workers* in Figure 9-1. BI users are generally specialists in data analysis, whereas knowledge workers are often nonspecialist users of BI results. A loan approval officer at a bank is a knowledge worker, but not a BI user.

Problems with Operational Data

Most operational and purchased data has problems that inhibit its usefulness for business intelligence. Figure 9-14 lists the major problem categories. First, although data that is critical for successful operations must be complete and accurate, marginally necessary data need not be. For example, some systems gather demographic data in the ordering process. But, because such data is not needed to fill, ship, and bill orders, its quality suffers.

Security concerns about access to data are problematic. See the Security Guide on pages 362–363 for more information.

Problematic data is termed dirty data. Examples are a value of B for customer gender and of 213 for customer age. Other examples are a value of 999–999–9999 for a U.S. phone number, a part color of "gren," and an email address of *WhyMe@GuessWhoIAM.org*. The value of zero for Units in Figure 9-6 is dirty data. All of these values can be problematic for BI purposes.

Purchased data often contains missing elements. The contact data in Figure 9-6 is a typical example; orders can be shipped without contact data, so its quality is spotty and has many missing values. Most data vendors state the percentage of missing values for each attribute in the data they sell. An organization buys such data because for some uses, some data is better than no data at all. This is especially true for data items whose values are difficult to obtain, such as Number of Adults in Household, Household Income, Dwelling Type, and Education of Primary Income Earner. However, care is required here because for some BI applications a few missing or erroneous data points can seriously bias the analysis.

Inconsistent data, the third problem in Figure 9-14, is particularly common for data that has been gathered over time. When an area code changes, for example, the phone number for a given customer before the change will not match the customer's number afterward. Likewise, part codes can change, as can sales territories. Before such data can be used, it must be recoded for consistency over the period of the study.

- Dirty data
- Missing values
- Inconsistent data
- Data not integrated
- Wrong granularity
  - Too fine
  - Not fine enough
- Too much data
  - Too many attributes
  - Too many data points

Figure 9-14
Possible Problems with Source Data

Some data inconsistencies occur from the nature of the business activity. Consider a Web-based order-entry system used by customers worldwide. When the Web server records the time of order, which time zone does it use? The server's system clock time is irrelevant to an analysis of customer behavior. Coordinated Universal Time (formerly called Greenwich Mean Time) is also meaningless. Somehow, Web server time must be adjusted to the time zone of the customer.

Another problem is nonintegrated data. A particular BI analysis might require data from an ERP system, an e-commerce system, and a social networking application. Analysts may wish to integrate that organizational data with purchased consumer data. Such a data collection will likely have relationships that are not represented in primary key/foreign key relationships. It is the function of personnel in the data warehouse to integrate such data somehow.

Data can also have the wrong **granularity**, a term that refers to the level of detail represented by the data. Granularity can be too fine or too coarse. For the former, suppose we want to analyze the placement of graphics and controls on an order-entry Web page. It is possible to capture the customers' clicking behavior in what is termed *clickstream data*. Those data, however, include everything the customer does at the Web site. In the middle of the order stream are data for clicks on the news, email, instant chat, and a weather check. Although all of that data may be useful for a study of consumer browsing behavior, it will be overwhelming if all we want to know is how customers respond to an ad located differently on the screen. To proceed, the data analysts must throw away millions and millions of clicks.

Data can also be too coarse. For example, a file of regional sales totals cannot be used to investigate the sales in a particular store in a region, and total sales for a store cannot be used to determine the sales of particular items within a store. Instead, we need to obtain data that is fine enough for the lowest-level report we want to produce.

In general, it is better to have too fine a granularity than too coarse. If the granularity is too fine, the data can be made coarser by summing and combining. This is what Addison and Drew did with the sales data in Figure 9-6. Sales by Bill Year were too fine for their needs, so they summed sales data over those years. If the granularity is too coarse, however, there is no way to separate the data into constituent parts.

The final problem listed in Figure 9-14 is to have too much data. As shown in the figure, we can have either too many attributes or too many data points. Think back to the discussion of tables in Chapter 5. We can have too many columns or too many rows.

Consider the first problem: too many attributes. Suppose we want to know the factors that influence how customers respond to a promotion. If we combine internal customer data with purchased customer data, we will have more than a hundred different attributes to consider. How do we select among them? In Drew and Addison's case, they just ignored the columns they didn't need. But in more sophisticated data mining analyses, too many attributes can be problematic. Because of a phenomenon called the *curse of dimensionality*, the more attributes there are, the easier it is to build a model that fits the sample data but that is worthless as a predictor. There are other good reasons for reducing the number of attributes, and one of the major activities in data mining concerns efficient and effective ways of selecting attributes.

The second way to have an excess of data is to have too many data points—too many rows of data. Suppose we want to analyze clickstream data on CNN.com. How many clicks does that site receive per month? Millions upon millions! In order to meaningfully analyze such data we need to reduce the amount of data. One good solution to this problem is statistical sampling. Organizations should not be reluctant to sample data in such situations.

Data Warehouses Versus Data Marts

To understand the difference between data warehouses and data marts, think of a data warehouse as a distributor in a supply chain. The data warehouse takes data from the data manufacturers (operational systems and other sources), cleans and processes the data, and locates the data on the shelves, so to speak, of the data warehouse. The data analysts who work with a data

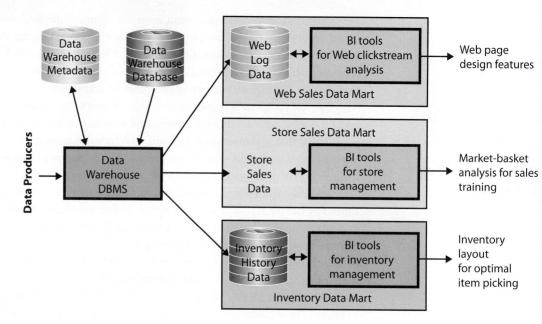

Figure 9-15
Data Mart Examples

warehouse are experts at data management, data cleaning, data transformation, data relationships, and the like. However, they are not usually experts in a given business function.

A **data mart** is a data collection, smaller than the data warehouse, that addresses the needs of a particular department or functional area of the business. If the data warehouse is the distributor in a supply chain, then a data mart is like a retail store in a supply chain. Users in the data mart obtain data that pertain to a particular business function from the data warehouse. Such users do not have the data management expertise that data warehouse employees have, but they are knowledgeable analysts for a given business function.

Figure 9-15 illustrates these relationships. In this example, the data warehouse takes data from the data producers and distributes the data to three data marts. One data mart is used to analyze clickstream data for the purpose of designing Web pages. A second analyzes store sales data and determines which products tend to be purchased together. This information is used to train salespeople on the best way to up-sell to customers. The third data mart is used to analyze customer order data for the purpose of reducing labor for item picking from the warehouse. A company like Amazon, for example, goes to great lengths to organize its warehouses to reduce picking expenses.

As you can imagine, it is expensive to create, staff, and operate data warehouses and data marts. Only large organizations with deep pockets can afford to operate a system like that shown in Figure 9-12. Smaller organizations like AllRoad operate subsets of this system, but they must find ways to solve the basic problems that data warehouses solve, even if those ways are informal.

Q4 How Do Organizations Use Reporting Applications?

A **reporting application** is a BI application that inputs data from one or more sources and applies reporting operations to that data to produce business intelligence. We will first summarize reporting operations and then illustrate two important reporting applications: RFM analysis and OLAP.

Basic Reporting Operations

Reporting applications produce business intelligence using five basic operations:

- Sorting
- Filtering
- Grouping
- Calculating
- Formatting

None of these operations is particularly sophisticated; they can all be accomplished using SQL and basic HTML or a simple report writing tool.

Addison at AllRoad used Access to apply all five of these operations. Examine, for example, Figure 9-11 (page 334). The results are *sorted* by Total Revenue, *filtered* for particular parts, sales are *grouped by* PartNumber, Total Orders and Total Revenue are *calculated*, and the calculations for Total Revenue are *formatted* correctly as dollar currency.

These simple operations can be used to produce complex and highly useful reports. Consider RFM analysis and Online Analytical Processing as two prime examples.

RFM Analysis

RFM analysis, a technique readily implemented with basic reporting operations, is used to analyze and rank customers according to their purchasing patterns.[10] RFM considers how *recently* (R) a customer has ordered, how *frequently* (F) a customer ordered, and how much *money* (M) the customer has spent.

To produce an RFM score, the RFM reporting tool first sorts customer purchase records by the date of their most recent (R) purchase. In a common form of this analysis, the tool then divides the customers into five groups and gives customers in each group a score of 1 to 5. The 20 percent of the customers having the most recent orders are given an R score of 1, the 20 percent of the customers having the next most recent orders are given an R score of 2, and so forth, down to the last 20 percent, who are given an R score of 5.

The tool then re-sorts the customers on the basis of how frequently they order. The 20 percent of the customers who order most frequently are given an F score of 1, the next 20 percent of most frequently ordering customers are given a score of 2, and so forth, down to the least frequently ordering customers, who are given an F score of 5.

Finally, the tool sorts the customers again according to the amount spent on their orders. The 20 percent who have ordered the most expensive items are given an M score of 1, the next 20 percent are given an M score of 2, and so forth, down to the 20 percent who spend the least, who are given an M score of 5.

Figure 9-16 shows sample RFM results. The first customer, Big 7 Sports, has ordered recently and orders frequently. Big 7 Sports' M score of 3 indicates, however, that it does not order the most

Customer	RFM Score		
Big 7 Sports	1	1	3
St. Louis Soccer Club	5	1	1
Miami Municipal	5	4	5
Central Colorado State	3	3	3

Figure 9-16
Example RFM Scores

---

[10]Arthur Middleton Hughes, "Boosting Response with RFM," *Marketing Tools*, May 1996. See also *http://dbmarketing.com*.

expensive goods. From these scores, the sales team can conclude that Big 7 Sports is a good, regular customer and that it should attempt to up-sell more expensive goods to Big 7 Sports.

The second customer in Figure 9-16 could represent a problem. St. Louis Soccer Club has not ordered in some time, but when it did order in the past, it ordered frequently, and its orders were of the highest monetary value. This data suggests that St. Louis Soccer Club might have taken its business to another vendor. Someone from the sales team should contact this customer immediately.

No one on the sales team should even think about the third customer, Miami Municipal. This company has not ordered for some time; it did not order frequently; and, when it did order, it bought the least expensive items, and not many of them. Let Miami Municipal go to the competition; the loss will be minimal.

The last customer, Central Colorado State, is right in the middle. Central Colorado State is an OK customer, but probably no one in sales should spend much time with it. Perhaps sales can set up an automated contact system or use the Central Colorado State account as a training exercise for an eager departmental assistant or intern.

Online Analytical Processing (OLAP)

Online analytical processing (OLAP), a second type of reporting application, is more generic than RFM. OLAP provides the ability to sum, count, average, and perform other simple arithmetic operations on groups of data. The defining characteristic of OLAP reports is that they are dynamic. The viewer of the report can change the report's format, hence the term *online*.

An OLAP report has measures and dimensions. A **measure** is the data item of interest. It is the item that is to be summed or averaged or otherwise processed in the OLAP report. Total sales, average sales, and average cost are examples of measures. A **dimension** is a characteristic of a measure. Purchase date, customer type, customer location, and sales region are all examples of dimensions.

Figure 9-17 shows a typical OLAP report. Here, the measure is *Store Sales Net*, and the dimensions are *Product Family* and *Store Type*. This report shows how net store sales vary by product family and store type. Stores of type *Supermarket* sold a net of $36,189 worth of nonconsumable goods, for example.

A presentation like that in Figure 9-17 is often called an **OLAP cube**, or sometimes simply a *cube*. The reason for this term is that some software products show these displays using three axes, like a cube in geometry. The origin of the term is unimportant here, however. Just know that an *OLAP cube* and an *OLAP report* are the same thing.

The OLAP report in Figure 9-17 was generated by Microsoft SQL Server Analysis Services and is displayed in an Excel pivot table. The data was taken from a sample instructional database, called Food Mart, that is provided with SQL Server.

It is possible to display OLAP cubes in many ways besides with Excel. Some third-party vendors provide more extensive graphical displays. For more information about such products, check for OLAP vendors and products at the Data Warehousing Review at *http://dwreview.com/OLAP/index.html*. For an example of a superb, easy-to-use OLAP tool, visit *www. TableauSoftware.com*. Tableau has a liberal student-use policy as well.

As stated earlier, the distinguishing characteristic of an OLAP report is that the user can alter the format of the report. Figure 9-18 shows such an alteration. Here, the user added another dimension, *Store Country* and *Store State*, to the horizontal display. Product-family sales

Figure 9-17

Example Grocery Sales OLAP Report

	A	B	C	D	E	F	G
1							
2							
3	Store Sales Net	Store Type ▼					
4	Product Family ▼	Deluxe Supermarket	Gourmet Supermarket	Mid-Size Grocery	Small Grocery	Supermarket	Grand Total
5	Drink	$8,119.05	$2,392.83	$1,409.50	$685.89	$16,751.71	$29,358.98
6	Food	$70,276.11	$20,026.18	$10,392.19	$6,109.72	$138,960.67	$245,764.87
7	Non-Consumable	$18,884.24	$5,064.79	$2,813.73	$1,534.90	$36,189.40	$64,487.05
8	Grand Total	$97,279.40	$27,483.80	$14,615.42	$8,330.51	$191,901.77	$339,610.90

	A	B	C	D	E	F	G	H	I
1									
2									
3	Store Sales Net			Store Type ▼					
4	Product Family ▼	Store Country ▼	Store State	Deluxe Superma	Gourmet Supermar	Mid-Size Groce	Small Grocery	Supermarket	Grand Total
5	Drink	USA	CA		$2,392.83		$227.38	$5,920.76	$8,540.97
6			OR	$4,438.49				$2,862.45	$7,300.94
7			WA	$3,680.56		$1,409.50	$458.51	$7,968.50	$13,517.07
8		USA Total		$8,119.05	$2,392.83	$1,409.50	$685.89	$16,751.71	$29,358.98
9	Drink Total			$8,119.05	$2,392.83	$1,409.50	$685.89	$16,751.71	$29,358.98
10	Food	USA	CA		$20,026.18		$1,960.53	$47,226.11	$69,212.82
11			OR	$37,778.35				$23,818.87	$61,597.22
12			WA	$32,497.76		$10,392.19	$4,149.19	$67,915.69	$114,954.83
13		USA Total		$70,276.11	$20,026.18	$10,392.19	$6,109.72	$138,960.67	$245,764.87
14	Food Total			$70,276.11	$20,026.18	$10,392.19	$6,109.72	$138,960.67	$245,764.87
15	Non-Consumable	USA	CA		$5,064.79		$474.35	$12,344.49	$17,883.63
16			OR	$10,177.89				$6,428.53	$16,606.41
17			WA	$8,706.36		$2,813.73	$1,060.54	$17,416.38	$29,997.01
18		USA Total		$18,884.24	$5,064.79	$2,813.73	$1,534.90	$36,189.40	$64,487.05
19	Non-Consumable Total			$18,884.24	$5,064.79	$2,813.73	$1,534.90	$36,189.40	$64,487.05
20	Grand Total			$97,279.40	$27,483.80	$14,615.42	$8,330.51	$191,901.77	$339,610.90

Figure 9-18
Example of Expanded Grocery Sales OLAP Report

are now broken out by store location. Observe that the sample data only includes stores in the United States, and only in the western states of California, Oregon, and Washington.

With an OLAP report, it is possible to **drill down** into the data. This term means to further divide the data into more detail. In Figure 9-19, for example, the user has drilled down into the stores located in California; the OLAP report now shows sales data for the four cities in California that have stores.

Notice another difference between Figures 9-18 and 9-19. The user has not only drilled down, she has also changed the order of the dimensions. Figure 9-18 shows *Product Family* and then store location within *Product Family*. Figure 9-19 shows store location and then *Product Family* within store location.

Both displays are valid and useful, depending on the user's perspective. A product manager might like to see product families first and then store location data. A sales manager might like to see store locations first and then product data. OLAP reports provide both perspectives, and the user can switch between them while viewing the report.

Unfortunately, all of this flexibility comes at a cost. If the database is large, doing the necessary calculating, grouping, and sorting for such dynamic displays will require substantial computing power. Although standard commercial DBMS products do have the features and functions required to create OLAP reports, they are not designed for such work. They are designed, instead, to provide rapid response to transaction-processing applications, such as order entry or manufacturing planning. Consequently, some organizations tune DBMS products on dedicated servers for this purpose. Today, many OLAP servers are being moved to the cloud.

How Do Organizations Use Data Mining Applications?

Data mining is the application of statistical techniques to find patterns and relationships among data for classification and prediction. As shown in Figure 9-20, data mining resulted from a convergence of disciplines. Data mining techniques emerged from statistics and mathematics and from artificial intelligence and machine-learning fields in computer science. As a result, data mining terminology is an odd blend of terms from these different disciplines. Sometimes people use the term *knowledge discovery in databases (KDD)* as a synonym for data mining.

Data mining and other business intelligence systems are useful, but they are not without their problems, as discussed in the Guide on pages 364–365.

Data mining techniques take advantage of developments in data management for processing the enormous databases that have emerged in the last 10 years. Of course, these data would not have been generated were it not for fast and cheap computers, and without such computers the new techniques would be impossible to compute.

Most data mining techniques are sophisticated, and many are difficult to use well. Such techniques are valuable to organizations, however, and some business professionals, especially those in finance and marketing, have become expert in their use. In fact, today there are many

				Store Type ▼					
Store Sales Net									
Store Country ▼	Store Sta	Store City	Product Family ▼	Deluxe Super	Gourmet Supermar	Mid-Size Groce	Small Grocery	Supermarket	Grand Total
USA	CA	Beverly Hills	Drink	$2,392.83					$2,392.83
			Food	$20,026.18					$20,026.18
			Non-Consumable	$5,064.79					$5,064.79
		Beverly Hills Total		$27,483.80					$27,483.80
		Los Angeles	Drink					$2,870.33	$2,870.33
			Food					$23,598.28	$23,598.28
			Non-Consumable					$6,305.14	$6,305.14
		Los Angeles Total						$32,773.74	$32,773.74
		San Diego	Drink					$3,050.43	$3,050.43
			Food					$23,627.83	$23,627.83
			Non-Consumable					$6,039.34	$6,039.34
		San Diego Total						$32,717.61	$32,717.61
		San Francisco	Drink				$227.38		$227.38
			Food				$1,960.53		$1,960.53
			Non-Consumable				$474.35		$474.35
		San Francisco Total					$2,662.26		$2,662.26
	CA Total			$27,483.80			$2,662.26	$65,491.35	$95,637.41
	OR		Drink	$4,438.49				$2,862.45	$7,300.94
			Food	$37,778.35				$23,818.87	$61,597.22
			Non-Consumable	$10,177.89				$6,428.53	$16,606.41
	OR Total			$52,394.72				$33,109.85	$85,504.57
	WA		Drink	$3,680.56		$1,409.50	$458.51	$7,968.50	$13,517.07
			Food	$32,497.76		$10,392.19	$4,149.19	$67,915.69	$114,954.83
			Non-Consumable	$8,706.36		$2,813.73	$1,060.54	$17,416.38	$29,997.01
	WA Total			$44,884.68		$14,615.42	$5,668.24	$93,300.57	$158,468.91
USA Total				$97,279.40		$14,615.42	$8,330.51	$191,901.77	$339,610.90
Grand Total				$97,279.40		$14,615.42	$8,330.51	$191,901.77	$339,610.90

Figure 9-19

Example of Drilling Down into Expanded Grocery Sales OLAP Report

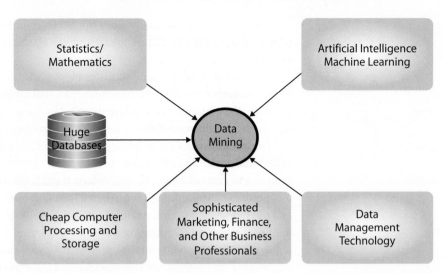

Figure 9-20
Source Disciplines of Data Mining

interesting and rewarding careers for business professionals who are knowledgeable about data mining techniques.

Data mining techniques fall into two broad categories: unsupervised and supervised. We explain both types in the following sections.

Unsupervised Data Mining

With **unsupervised data mining**, analysts do not create a model or hypothesis before running the analysis. Instead, they apply a data mining application to the data and observe the results. With this method, analysts create hypotheses *after the analysis*, in order to explain the patterns found.

One common unsupervised technique is **cluster analysis**. With it, statistical techniques identify groups of entities that have similar characteristics. A common use for cluster analysis is to find groups of similar customers from customer order and demographic data.

For example, suppose a cluster analysis finds two very different customer groups: One group has an average age of 33, owns three Android phones and two iPads, has an expensive home entertainment system, drives a Lexus SUV, and tends to buy expensive children's play equipment. The second group has an average age of 64, owns Arizona vacation property, plays golf, and buys expensive wines. Suppose the analysis also finds that both groups buy designer children's clothing.

These findings are obtained solely by data analysis. There is no prior model about the patterns and relationships that exist. It is up to the analyst to form hypotheses, after the fact, to explain why two such different groups are both buying designer children's clothes.

Supervised Data Mining

With **supervised data mining**, data miners develop a model *prior to the analysis* and apply statistical techniques to data to estimate parameters of the model. For example, suppose marketing experts in a communications company believe that cell phone usage on weekends is determined by the age of the customer and the number of months the customer has had the cell phone account. A data mining analyst would then run an analysis that estimates the effect of customer and account age.

One such analysis, which measures the effect of a set of variables on another variable, is called a **regression analysis**. A sample result for the cell phone example is:

$$CellphoneWeekendMinutes = 12 + (17\,period \times CustomerAge)$$
$$+ (23\,7 \times NumberMonthsOfAccount)$$

Using this equation, analysts can predict the number of minutes of weekend cell phone use by summing 12, plus 17.5 times the customer's age, plus 23.7 times the number of months of the account.

As you will learn in your statistics classes, considerable skill is required to interpret the quality of such a model. The regression tool will create an equation, such as the one shown. Whether that equation is a good predictor of future cell phone usage depends on statistical factors, such as *t* values, confidence intervals, and related statistical techniques.

Neural networks are another popular supervised data mining application used to predict values and make classifications such as "good prospect" or "poor prospect" customers. The term *neural networks* is deceiving because it connotes a biological process similar to that in animal brains. In fact, although the original *idea* of neural nets may have come from the anatomy and physiology of neurons, a neural network is nothing more than a complicated set of possibly nonlinear equations. Explaining the techniques used for neural networks is beyond the scope of this text. If you want to learn more, search *http://kdnuggets.com* for the term *neural network*.

In the next sections, we will describe and illustrate two typical data mining tools—market-basket analysis and decision trees—and show applications of those techniques. From this discussion, you can gain a sense of the nature of data mining. These examples should give you, a future manager, a sense of the possibilities of data mining techniques. You will need additional coursework in statistics, data management, marketing, and finance, however, before you will be able to perform such analyses yourself.

Market-Basket Analysis

Suppose you run a dive shop, and one day you realize that one of your salespeople is much better at up-selling to your customers. Any of your sales associates can fill a customer's order, but this one salesperson is especially good at selling customers items *in addition* to those for which they ask. One day, you ask him how he does it.

"It's simple," he says. "I just ask myself what is the next product they would want to buy. If someone buys a dive computer, I don't try to sell her fins. If she's buying a dive computer, she's already a diver and she already has fins. But these dive computer displays are hard to read. A better mask makes it easier to read the display and get the full benefit from the dive computer."

A **market-basket analysis** is an unsupervised data mining technique for determining sales patterns. A market-basket analysis shows the products that customers tend to buy together. In marketing transactions, the fact that customers who buy product X also buy product Y creates a **cross-selling** opportunity; that is, "If they're buying X, sell them Y" or "If they're buying Y, sell them X."

Figure 9-21 shows hypothetical sales data from 400 sales transactions at a dive shop. The number on the diagonal (shaded) in the first set of rows is the total number of times an item was sold. For example, the 270 on the diagonal cell for Masks means that 270 of the 400 transactions included masks. The 120 in the diagonal cell for Dive Computer means that 120 of the 400 transactions included dive computers.

We can use the number of times an item sold to estimate the probability that a customer will purchase an item. Because 270 of the 400 transactions were masks, we can estimate the probability that a customer will buy a mask to be 270/400, or .675. The probabilty of selling a dive computer is .3.

In market-basket terminology, **support** is the probability that two items will be purchased together. To estimate that probability, we examine sales transactions and count the number of times that two items occurred in the same transaction. For the data in Figure 9-21, fins and masks appeared together 250 times, and thus the support for fins and a mask is 250/400, or .625. Similarly, the support for fins and weights is 20/400, or .05.

These data are interesting by themselves, but we can refine the analysis by taking another step and considering additional probabilities. For example, what proportion of the customers

	Mask	Tank	Fins	Weights	Dive Computer
Mask	270	10	250	10	90
Tank	10	200	40	130	30
Fins	250	40	280	20	20
Weights	10	130	20	130	10
Dive Computer	90	30	20	10	120
	Support				
Num Trans	400				
Mask	0.675	0.025	0.625	0.025	0.225
Tank	0.025	0.5	0.1	0.325	0.075
Fins	0.625	0.1	0.7	0.05	0.05
Weights	0.025	0.325	0.05	0.325	0.025
Dive Computer	0.225	0.075	0.05	0.025	0.3
	Confidence				
Mask	1	0.05	0.892857143	0.076923077	0.75
Tank	0.037037037	1	0.142857143	1	0.25
Fins	0.925925926	0.2	1	0.153846154	0.166666667
Weights	0.037037037	0.65	0.071428571	1	0.083333333
Dive Computer	0.333333333	0.15	0.071428571	0.076923077	1
	Lift (Improvement)				
Mask		0.074074074	1.322751323	0.113960114	1.111111111
Tank	0.074074074		0.285714286	2	0.5
Fins	1.322751323	0.285714286		0.21978022	0.238095238
Weights	0.113960114	2	0.21978022		0.256410256
Dive Computer	1.111111111	0.5	0.238095238	0.256410256	

Figure 9-21
Market-Basket Analysis at a Dive Shop

who bought a mask also bought fins? Masks were purchased 270 times, and of those individuals who bought masks, 250 also bought fins. Thus, given that a customer bought a mask, we can estimate the probability that he or she will buy fins to be 250/270, or .926. In market-basket terminology, such a conditional probability estimate is called the **confidence**.

Reflect on the meaning of this confidence value. The likelihood of someone walking in the door and buying fins is 250/400, or .625. But the likelihood of someone buying fins, given that he or she bought a mask, is .926. Thus, if someone buys a mask, the likelihood that he or she will also buy fins increases substantially, from .625 to .926. Thus, all sales personnel should be trained to try to sell fins to anyone buying a mask.

Now consider dive computers and fins. Of the 400 transactions, fins were sold 280 times, so the probability that someone walks into the store and buys fins is .7. But of the 120 purchases of dive computers, only 20 appeared with fins. So the likelihood of someone buying fins, given he or she bought a dive computer, is 20/120, or .1666. Thus, when someone buys a dive computer, the likelihood that he or she will also buy fins falls from .625 to .1666.

The ratio of confidence to the base probability of buying an item is called **lift**. Lift shows how much the base probability increases or decreases when other products are purchased. The lift of fins and a mask is the confidence of fins given a mask, divided by the base probability of fins. In Figure 9-21, the lift of fins and a mask is .926/.7, or 1.32. Thus, the likelihood that people buy fins when they buy a mask increases by 32 percent. Surprisingly, it turns out that the lift of fins and a mask is the same as the lift of a mask and fins. Both are 1.32.

We need to be careful here, though, because this analysis only shows shopping carts with two items. We cannot say from this data what the likelihood is that customers, given that they bought a mask, will buy both weights and fins. To assess that probability, we need to analyze shopping carts with three items. This statement illustrates, once again, that we need to know what problem we're solving before we start to build the information system to mine the data.

The problem definition will help us decide if we need to analyze three-item, four-item, or some other sized shopping cart.

Many organizations are benefiting from market-basket analysis today. You can expect that this technique will become a standard CRM analysis during your career.

Decision Trees

A **decision tree** is a hierarchical arrangement of criteria that predict a classification or a value. Here we will consider decision trees that predict classifications. Decision tree analyses are an unsupervised data mining technique: The analyst sets up the computer program and provides the data to analyze, and the decision tree program produces the tree.

A common business application of decision trees is to classify loans by likelihood of default. Organizations analyze data from past loans to produce a decision tree that can be converted to loan-decision rules. A financial institution could use such a tree to assess the default risk on a new loan. Sometimes, too, financial institutions sell a group of loans (called a *loan portfolio*) to one another. An institution considering the purchase of a loan portfolio can use the results of a decision tree program to evaluate the risk of a given portfolio.

Figure 9-22 shows an example provided by Insightful Corporation, a vendor of BI tools. This example was generated using its Insightful Miner product. This tool examined data from 3,485 loans. Of those loans, 72 percent had no default and 28 percent did default. To perform the analysis, the decision tree tool examined six different loan characteristics.

In this example, the decision tree program determined that the percentage of the loan that is past due (*PercPastDue*) is the best first criterion. Reading Figure 9-22, you can see that of the 2,574 loans with a *PercPastDue* value of 0.5 or less (amount past due is less than half the loan amount), 94 percent were not in default. Reading down several lines in this tree, 911 loans had a value of *PercPastDue* greater than 0.5; of those loans, 89 percent were in default.

These two major categories are then further subdivided into three classifications. *CreditScore* is a creditworthiness score obtained from a credit agency; *MonthsPastDue* is the number of months since a payment; and *CurrentLTV* is the current ratio of outstanding balance of the loan to the value of the loan's collateral.

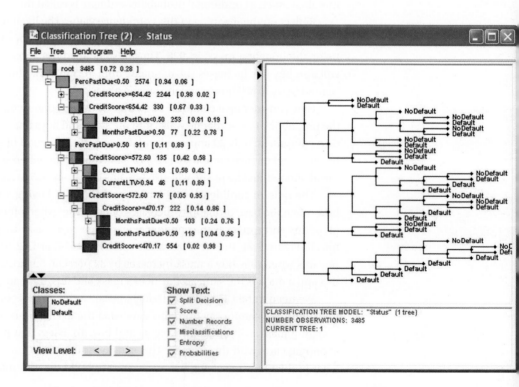

Figure 9-22

Credit Score Decision Tree

Source: Used with permission of Insightful Corporation. Copyright © 1999–2005 Insightful Corporation. All Rights Reserved.

With a decision tree like this, the financial institution can develop decision rules for accepting or rejecting the offer to purchase loans from another financial institution. For example:

- If percent past due is less than 50 percent, then accept the loan.
- If percent past due is greater than 50 percent *and*
- If *CreditScore* is greater than 572.6 *and*
- If *CurrentLTV* is less than .94, then accept the loan.
- Otherwise, reject the loan.

Of course, the financial institution will need to combine this risk data with an economic analysis of the value of each loan to determine which loans to take.

Decision trees are easy to understand and, even better, easy to implement using decision rules. They also can work with many types of variables, and they deal well with partial data. Organizations can use decision trees by themselves or combine them with other techniques. In some cases, organizations use decision trees to select variables that are then used by other types of data mining tools. For example, decision trees can be used to identify good predictor variables for neural networks.

 # How Do Organizations Use BigData Applications?

As stated in Chapter 5, BigData (also spelled Big Data) is a term used to describe data collections that are characterized by huge *volume*, rapid *velocity*, and great *variety*. To review:

- BigData data sets are at least a petabyte in size, and usually larger
- BigData is generated rapidly
- BigData has structured data, free-form text, log files, possibly graphics, audio, and video

MapReduce

Because BigData is huge, fast, and varied, it cannot be processed using traditional techniques. **MapReduce** is a technique for harnessing the power of thousands of computers working in parallel. The basic idea is that the BigData collection is broken into pieces, and hundreds or thousands of independent processors search these pieces for something of interest. That process is referred to as the *Map* phase. In Figure 9-23, for example, a data set having the logs of Google searches is broken into pieces, and each independent processor is instructed to search for and count search keywords. Figure 9-23, of course, shows just a small portion of the data; here you can see a portion of the keywords that begin with *H*.

As the processors finish, their results are combined in what is referred to as the *Reduce* phase. The result is a list of all the terms searched for on a given day and the count of each. The process is considerably more complex than described here, but this is the gist of the idea.

By the way, you can visit Google Trends to see an application of MapReduce. There you can obtain a trend line of the number of searches for a particular term or terms. Figure 9-24 shows the search trend for the term *Web 2.0*. The vertical axis is scaled; a value of 1.0 represents the average number of searches over that time period. This particular trend line, by the way, supports the contention that the term *Web 2.0* is fading from use. Go to *www.google.com/ trends* and enter the terms *Big Data, BigData*, and *Hadoop* to see why learning about them is a better use of your time!

Using MIS InClass 9

What Singularity Have We Wrought?

On May 18, 2012, Facebook went public at a valuation of $104 billion. On May 19, 2013, exactly a year after Facebook's problematic initial public offering (IPO), OLAP product provider Tableau Software raised $254 million in its IPO. The shares opened at $31 and closed $20 higher at $51. Marketo, a cloud-based marketing company, had its IPO that same day and its stock closed 78 percent above its opening price. Tech is hot.

What's next? What's the Next_Big_Thing? If you knew, you could identify the next Tableau or Marketo for investment or employment or perhaps start it yourself. Of course, no one knows for certain, but let's apply knowledge you already have as a guide.

Figure 1 casts the history of the computer industry into the frame of the five components of an information system. IBM led the hardware era. Hardware customers focused on writing their own software to accomplish some function; payroll and other accounting functions were common. Next came the software era that Microsoft led with Windows, but companies such as Oracle and SAP contributed to making software licensing a reality. The focus of software customers is creating data.

Data, really BigData, is the focus of the current era. Google, Facebook, and LinkedIn are data companies. As evidence, Facebook created Cassandra and Hadoop, *and gave them away to open-source*. Clearly, it perceives its value as data and not software. The focus of the data era is to influence behavior. And what era is next? What is the focus of the Procedures era? Answering that question is key to the Next_Big_Thing.

Note that at each stage, the customer focus pointed to the next component. Hardware customer focus was on software. Software focus was on data. Data focus is on behavior, or procedures. Will

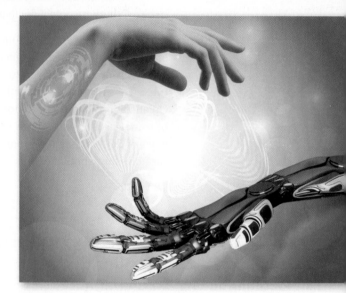

the procedure focus be on people? Form a team as directed by your professor and address the following questions:

1. Discuss the meaning of: "At each stage, the customer focus has pointed at the next component." Restate this phrase in the words of your own group.

2. Do you agree that the focus of the BigData era is to influence behavior? What other focus interpretations of today's era are possible?

3. Assume the next era computer industry will concern procedures and that the focus will be on people. One possible focus is to Eliminate Jobs. If that is the focus, what does it mean for business? For the economy? For you? Discuss your answers among your group and report your conclusions to the rest of the class.

4. Rather than Eliminate Jobs, another possible focus of the procedural component is to Enhance Human Life. Discuss ways in which that might happen. If it does, what opportunities will it create for you? Discuss your answers among your group and report your conclusions to the rest of the class.

5. Working with your group, identify two or three other procedural focus statements other than Eliminate Jobs or Enhance Human Life.

	Hardware	Software	(Big)Data	Procedures	People
Leaders	IBM	Microsoft Oracle SAP	Google Facebook LinkedIn	Next big leader	
Customer focus	Write software ⇒	Create data ⇒	Influence behavior ⇒	Something about people? ⇒	⇒ ?
Era	1955–1985 (30 years)	1985–2005 (20 years)	2005–2015??? (10 years?)		

Figure 1
Trends in the Computing Industry

6. Of all the focus statements you've considered, choose the one you think is most likely. Explain your choice. Using that statement, describe three business opportunities that could lead to the Next_Big_Thing.

7. One important question is what happens after the People-component-era? Where does the arrow on the far right go? Ray Kurzweil developed a concept he calls **the Singularity**,[11] which is the point at which computer systems become sophisticated enough that they can adapt and create their own software and hence adapt their behavior without human assistance. At that point, he claims that clouds of myriads of computers working 24/7 will accelerate away from humanity, and humans will become, well, what? Work with your team and state what you think the consequences of the singularity might be.

8. Given all of this, if there is a more exciting, important, and potentially rewarding field than MIS today, state what it is.

Hadoop

Hadoop is an open-source program supported by the Apache Foundation[12] that implements MapReduce on potentially thousands of computers. Hadoop could drive the process of finding and counting the Google search terms, but Google uses its own proprietary version of MapReduce to do so instead.

Hadoop began as part of Cassandra, but the Apache Foundation split it off to become its own product. Hadoop is written in Java and originally ran on Linux. Recently, Microsoft

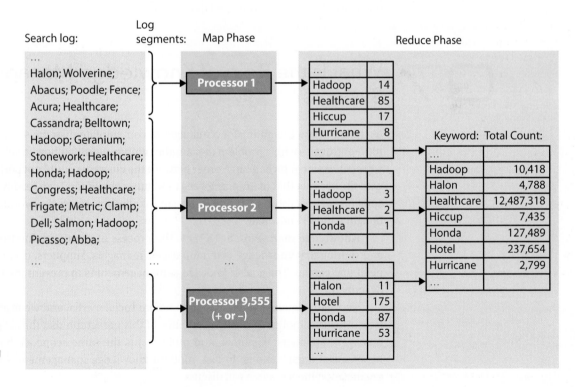

Figure 9-23
MapReduce Processing Summary

---

[11]*http://www.Singularity.com*
[12]A nonprofit corporation that supports open-source software projects, originally those for the Apache Web server, but today for a large number of additional major software projects.

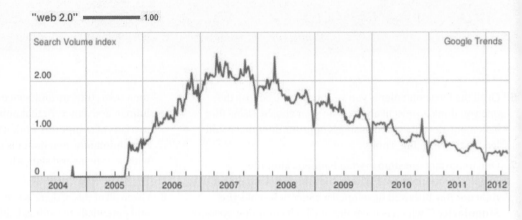

Figure 9-24
Google Trends on the Term
Web 2.0
Source: Google

announced a Hadoop product and service named HDInsight. Some companies implement Hadoop on server farms they manage themselves, and others run Hadoop in the cloud. Amazon.com supports Hadoop as part of its EC3 cloud offering. Hadoop includes a query language entitled **Pig**.

At present, deep technical skills are needed to run and use Hadoop. Judging by the development of other technologies over the years, it is likely that higher-level, easier-to-use query products will be implemented on top of Hadoop. For now, understand that experts are required to use it; you may be involved, however, in planning a BigData study or in interpreting results.

BigData analysis can involve both reporting and data mining techniques. The chief difference is, however, that BigData has volume, velocity, and variation characteristics that far exceed those of traditional reporting and data mining.

 What Is the Role of Knowledge Management Systems?

Nothing is more frustrating for a manager to contemplate than the situation in which one employee struggles with a problem that another employee knows how to solve easily. Or to learn of a customer who returns a large order because the customer could not perform a basic operation with the product that many employees (and other customers) can readily perform. Even worse, someone in the customer's organization may know how to use the product, but the people who bought it didn't know that.

Knowledge management (KM) is the process of creating value from intellectual capital and sharing that knowledge with employees, managers, suppliers, customers, and others who need that capital. The goal of knowledge management is to prevent the kinds of problems just described.

Knowledge management was done before social media, and we discuss two such KM systems. However, notice in the first sentence of this paragraph that the scope of KM (employees, managers, suppliers, customer, and others…) is the same scope as that of the use of SM in hyper-social organizations. In fact, modern knowledge management ascribes to hyper-social organization theory, as we will discuss.

Before we turn to those specific technologies, however, consider the overall goals and benefits of KM. KM benefits organizations in two fundamental ways:

- Improve process quality
- Increase team strength

As you know, process quality is measured by effectiveness and efficiency, and knowledge management can improve both. KM enables employees to share knowledge with each other and with customers and other partners. By doing so, it enables the employees in the organization to better achieve the organization's strategy. At the same time, sharing knowledge enables employees to solve problems more quickly and to otherwise accomplish work with less time and other resources, hence improving process efficiency.[13]

Additionally, recall from Chapter 2 that successful teams not only accomplish their assigned tasks, they also grow in capability, both as a team and as individuals. By sharing knowledge, team members learn from one another, avoid making repetitive mistakes, and grow as business professionals.

For example, consider the help desk at any organization, say, one that provides support for electronic components like iPhones. When a user has a problem with an iPhone, he or she might contact Apple support for help. The customer service department has, collectively, seen just about any problem that can ever occur with an iPhone. The organization, as a whole, knows how to solve the user's problem. However, that is no guarantee that a particular support representative knows how to solve that problem. The goal of KM is to enable employees to be able to use knowledge possessed collectively by people in the organization. By doing so, both process quality and team capability improve.

What Are Expert Systems?

The earliest KM systems, called expert systems, attempted to directly capture employee expertise. They existed long before social media, and in fact were in use long before the Internet.

Expert systems are rule-based systems that encode human knowledge in the form of **If/Then rules**. Such rules are statements that specify if a particular condition exists, then to take some action. Figure 9-25 shows an example of a few rules that could be part of a medical expert system for diagnosing heart disease. In this set of rules, the system examines various factors for heart disease and computes a *CardiacRiskFactor*. Depending on the value of that risk factor, other variables are given values.

The set of rules shown here may need to be processed many times because it is possible that *CardiacRiskFactor* is used on the If side of a rule occurring before these rules. Unlike this example, an operational expert system may consist of hundreds, if not thousands, of rules.

The programs that process a set of rules are called **expert systems shells**. Typically, the shell processes rules until no value changes. At that point, the values of all the variables are reported as results.

Figure 9-25
Example of If/Then Rules

```
Other rules here...

IF CardiacRiskFactor = 'Null' THEN Set CardiacRiskFactor = 0
IF PatientSex = 'Male' THEN Add 3 to CardiacRiskFactor
IF PatientAge >55 THEN Add 2 to CardiacRiskFactor
IF FamilyHeartHistory = 'True' THEN Add 5 to CardiacRiskFactor
IF CholesterolScore = 'Problematic' THEN Add 4 to CardiacRiskFactor
IF BloodPressure = 'Problematic' THEN Add 3 to CardiacRiskFactor
IF CardiacRiskFactor >15 THEN Set EchoCardiagramTest = 'Schedule'
...
Other rules here...
```

[13]Meridith Levinson. "Knowledge Management Definition and Solutions," *CIO Magazine*, accessed May 2012, *http://www.cio.com/article/40343/Knowledge_Management_Definition_and_Solutions?page=2.*

To create the system of rules, the expert system development team interviews human experts in the domain of interest. The rules in Figure 9-25 would have been obtained by interviewing cardiologists who are known to be particularly adept at diagnosing cardiac disease. Such a system encodes the knowledge of those highly skilled experts and makes it available to less-skilled or less-knowledgeable professionals.

Many expert systems were created in the late 1980s and early 1990s, but only a few have enjoyed success. They suffer from three major disadvantages. First, they are difficult and expensive to develop. They require many labor hours from both experts in the domain under study and designers of expert systems. This expense is compounded by the high opportunity cost of tying up domain experts. Such experts are normally some of the most sought-after employees in an organization.

Second, expert systems are difficult to maintain. Because of the nature of rule-based systems, the introduction of a new rule in the middle of hundreds of others can have unexpected consequences. A small change can cause very different outcomes. Unfortunately, such side effects cannot be predicted or eliminated. They are the nature of complex rule-based systems.

Finally, expert systems were unable to live up to the high expectations set by their name. Initially, proponents of expert systems hoped to be able to duplicate the performance of highly trained experts, like doctors. It turned out, however, that no expert system has the same diagnostic ability as knowledgeable, skilled, and experienced doctors. Even when expert systems were developed that came close in ability, changes in medical technology required constant changing of the expert system, and the problems caused by unexpected consequences made such changes very expensive.

The few expert systems that have been successful have addressed more restricted problems than duplicating a doctor's diagnostic ability. They address problems such as checking for harmful prescription drug interactions and configuring products to meet customer specifications. These systems require many fewer rules and are therefore more manageable to maintain. However, unless expert systems technology gets a boost from massively parallel computing (think MapReduce and Hadoop), their problems will cause them to fade from use.

What Are Content Management Systems?

Another form of knowledge management concerns knowledge that is encoded in documents. **Content management systems (CMS)** are information systems that support the management and delivery of documents including reports, Web pages, and other expressions of employee knowledge.

Typical users of content management systems are companies that sell complicated products and want to share their knowledge of those products with employees and customers. Someone at Toyota, for example, knows how to change the timing belt on the four-cylinder 2013 Toyota Camry. Toyota wants to share that knowledge with car owners, mechanics, and Toyota employees.

What Are the Challenges of Content Management?

Content management systems face serious challenges. First, most content databases are huge; some have thousands of individual documents, pages, and graphics. Second, CMS content is dynamic. Imagine the frequency of Web page changes at Apple or Google or Amazon that must occur each day!

Another complication for content management systems is that documents do not exist in isolation from each other. Documents refer to one another and when one changes, others must change as well. To manage these connections, content management systems must maintain linkages among documents so that content dependencies are known and used to maintain document consistency.

A fourth complication is that document contents are perishable. Documents become obsolete and need to be altered, removed, or replaced. Consider, for example, what happens

Figure 9-26

Microsoft.com Main Page Less than 2 Hours after Surface Announcement

Source: Microsoft Corporation

when a new product is announced. Figure 9-26 shows the main page for Microsoft.com less than 2 hours after its announcement of Surface. We can only wonder how many other pages on Microsoft.com needed to be changed within those 2 hours.

Finally, content is provided in many languages as demonstrated in Figure 9-27. 3M has tens of thousands of products, some of which are harmful when used improperly. 3M must publish product safety data for all such products in all the languages shown. Every document, in whatever language it was authored, must be translated into all languages before it can be published on 3M's site. And when one of them changes, all of the translated versions must change as well.

What Are Content Management Application Alternatives?

Three common alternatives for content management applications are:

- In-house custom
- Off-the-shelf
- Public search engine

Figure 9-27

Need for Many Languages of Content at 3M

Source: © 3M 2012. All Rights Reserved.

In the past, organizations developed their own *in-house content management applications*. A customer support department, for example, might develop in-house database applications to track customer problems and their resolution. Operations might develop an in-house system to track machine maintenance procedures. Like all custom applications, however, custom content management applications are expensive to develop and maintain. Unless the domain of the content management is crucial to the organization's strategy and no off-the-shelf solution is available, most organizations today choose not to support a custom CMS application.

Because of the expense of custom applications, many organizations today use *off-the-shelf* software. Horizontal market products like Microsoft SharePoint provide generalized facilities to manage documents and other content types. Some organizations choose vertical market off-the-shelf applications. An accounting firm, for example, may license a vertical market application to manage document flow for the processing of tax returns or the management of audit documents.

Such off-the-shelf products have considerably more functionality than most in-house systems, and they are far less expensive to maintain. Keep in mind, however, that organizations need to develop data structures and procedures for managing their content; they also need to train users.

Some organizations just rely on *Internet search engines*, such as Google or Bing, to manage their content. Because these engines search through all public sites of all organizations, they are usually the fastest and easiest way to find public documents, even within the organization. It may be easier, for example, for a General Motors employee to find a General Motors document using Google than using an in-house search engine.

This is content management on the cheap. Just put documents on a public server and let Google or Bing do the rest! However, documents that reside behind a corporate firewall are not publicly accessible and will not be reachable by Google or other search engines. Organizations must index their own proprietary documents and provide their own search capability for them.

How Do Hyper-Social Organizations Manage Knowledge?

In recent years, social media has changed the orientation of knowledge management. In the past, the focus was on structured systems such as expert systems and content management systems. These KM techniques relied on planned and prestructured content management and delivery methods. As you learned in the SLATES model in Chapter 8, social media fosters emergence. In the KM context, employees and others express their knowledge in a variety of modes and media, and the mechanisms for managing and delivering that knowledge emerge from usage.

Hyper-social knowledge management is the application of social media and related applications for the management and delivery of organizational knowledge resources. Progressive organizations encourage their employees to Tweet, post on Facebook or other social media sites, write blogs, and post videos on YouTube and any of the other sites. Of course, as discussed in Chapter 8, such organizations need to develop and publish an employee social media policy as well.

Hyper-organization theory provides a framework for understanding this new direction in KM. In this frame, the focus moves from the knowledge and content per se to the fostering of authentic relationships among the creators and the users of that knowledge.

Blogs provide an obvious example. An employee in customer support who writes a daily blog on current, common customer problems is expressing authentic opinions on the company's products, positive and possibly negative. If perceived as authentic, customers will comment upon blog entries and, in the process, teach others how they solved those problems themselves.

The open airing of product use issues may make traditional marketing personnel uncomfortable, but this KM technique does insert the company in the middle of customer conversations about possible product problems, and, while it does lose control, the organization is at least a party to those conversations. As stated in Chapter 8, hyper-social organizations move from controlled processes to messy ones.

Hyper-Social KM Alternative Media

Figure 9-28 lists common hyper-social KM alternative media, whether each medium is used for public, private, or either, and the best group type. Except for rich directories, you know what each of these is already, and we need not discuss them further.

A **rich directory** is an employee directory that includes not only the standard name, email, phone, and address, but also organizational structure and expertise. With a rich directory, it is possible to determine where in the organization someone works, who is the first common manager between two people, and what past projects and expertise an individual has. For international organizations, such directories also include languages spoken. Microsoft's product Active Directory is the most popular rich directory.

Rich directories are particularly useful in large organizations where people with particular expertise are unknown. For example, who at 3M knows which 3M product is the best to use to glue teak wood to fiberglass? Probably dozens, but who are they and who is the closest to a factory in Brazil? If no one is near Brazil, is there anyone who speaks Portuguese?

Resistance to Hyper-Social Knowledge Sharing

Two human factors inhibit knowledge sharing in hyper-social organizations. The first is that employees can be reluctant to exhibit their ignorance. Out of fear of appearing incompetent, employees may not submit entries to blogs or discussion groups. Such reluctance can sometimes be reduced by the attitude and posture of managers. One strategy for employees in this situation is to provide private media that can only be accessed by a smaller group of people who have an interest in a specific problem. Members of that smaller group can then discuss the issue in a less-inhibiting forum.

The other inhibiting human factor is employee competition. "Look," says the top salesperson. "I earn a substantial bonus from being the top salesperson. Why would I want to share

Media	Public or Private	Best for:
Blogs	Either	Defender of belief
Discussion groups (including FAQ)	Either	Problem solving
Wikis	Either	Either
Surveys	Either	Problem solving
Rich directories, (e.g., Active Directory)	Private	Problem solving
Standard SM (Facebook, Twitter, etc.)	Public	Defender of belief
YouTube	Public	Either

Figure 9-28
Hyper-Social KM Media

my sales techniques with others? I'd just be strengthening the competition." This understandable perspective may not be changeable. A hyper-social KM application may be ill-suited to a competitive group. Or the company may be able to restructure rewards and incentives to foster sharing of ideas among employees (e.g., giving a bonus to the group that develops the best idea).

If these two factors are limiting knowledge sharing, strong management endorsement can be effective, especially if that endorsement is followed by strong positive feedback. As we stated in Chapter 7, concerning employee resistance, "Nothing wrong with praise or cash...especially cash."

What Are the Alternatives for Publishing BI?

The previous discussions have illustrated the power and utility of reporting, data mining, and knowledge management BI applications. But, for BI to be actionable, it must be published to the right user at the right time. In this question, we will discuss the primary publishing alternatives and the functionality of BI servers, a special type of Web server.

Characteristics of BI Publishing Alternatives

Figure 9-29 lists four server alternatives for BI publishing. **Static reports** are BI documents that are fixed at the time of creation and do not change. A printed sales analysis is an example of a static report. In the BI context, most static reports are published as PDF documents.

Dynamic reports are BI documents that are updated at the time they are requested. A sales report that is current at the time the user accessed it on a Web server is a dynamic report. In almost all cases, publishing a dynamic report requires the BI application to access a database or other data source at the time the report is delivered to the user.

Pull options for each of the servers in Figure 9-29 are the same. The user goes to the site, clicks a link (or opens an email), and obtains the report. Because they're the same for all four server types, they are not shown in Figure 9-29.

Push options vary by server type. For email or collaboration tools, push is manual; someone, say a manager, an expert, or an administrator, creates an email with the report as an attachment (or URL to the collaboration tool) and sends it to the users known to be

Server	Report Type	Push Options	Skill Level Needed
Email or collaboration tool	Static	Manual	Low
Web server	Static/Dynamic	Alert/RSS	Low for static High for dynamic
SharePoint	Static/Dynamic	Alert/RSS Workflow	Low for static High for dynamic
BI server	Dynamic	Alert/RSS Subscription	High

Figure 9-29
BI Publishing Alternatives

interested in that report. For Web servers and SharePoint, users can create alerts and RSS feeds to have the server push content to them when the content is created or changed, with the expiration of a given amount of time, or at particular intervals. SharePoint workflows can also push content.

A BI server extends alert/RSS functionality to support user **subscriptions**, which are user requests for particular BI results on a particular schedule or in response to particular events. For example, a user can subscribe to a daily sales report, requesting that it be delivered each morning. Or the user might request that RFM analyses be delivered whenever a new result is posted on the server, or a sales manager might subscribe to receive a sales report whenever sales in his region exceed $1 million during the week. We explain the two major functions of a BI server in the next section.

The skills needed to create a publishing application are either low or high. For static content, little skill is needed. The BI author creates the content, and the publisher (usually the same person) attaches it to an email or puts it on the Web or a SharePoint site, and that's it. Publishing dynamic BI is more difficult; it requires the publisher to set up database access when documents are consumed. In the case of a Web server, the publisher will need to develop or have a programmer write code for this purpose. In the case of SharePoint and BI servers, program code is not necessarily needed, but dynamic data connections need to be created, and this task is not for the technically faint of heart. You'll need knowledge beyond the scope of this class to develop dynamic BI solutions. You should be able to do this, however, if you take a few more IS courses or major in IS.

What Are the Two Functions of a BI Server?

A **BI server** is a Web server application that is purpose-built for the publishing of business intelligence. The Microsoft SQL Server Report manager (part of Microsoft SQL Server Reporting Services) is the most popular such product today, but there are other products as well.

BI servers provide two major functions: management and delivery. The management function maintains metadata about the authorized allocation of BI results to users. The BI server tracks what results are available, what users are authorized to view those results, and the schedule upon which the results are provided to the authorized users. It adjusts allocations as available results change and users come and go.

As shown in Figure 9-30, all management data needed by any of the BI servers is stored in metadata. The amount and complexity of such data depends, of course, on the functionality of the BI server.

BI servers use metadata to determine what results to send to which users and, possibly, on which schedule. Today, the expectation is that BI results can be delivered to "any" device. In practice, *any* is interpreted to mean computers, smartphones, tablets, applications such as Microsoft Office, and SOA Web services.

BI systems truly add value. As described in the Guide on pages 364–365, not every system is a success, but simple ones like RFM and OLAP often are, and even complicated and expensive data mining applications can generate tremendous return if they are applied to appropriate problems and are well designed and implemented.

Figure 9-30

Elements of a BI System

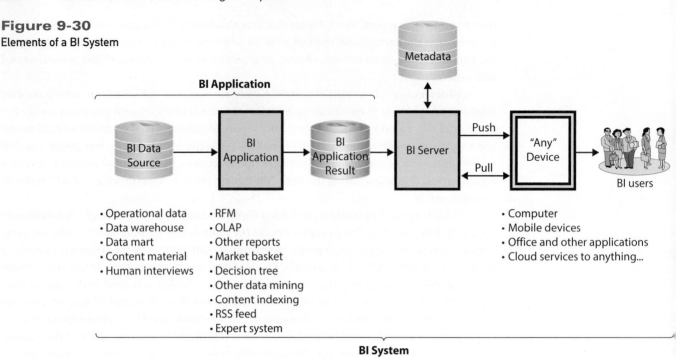

For example, suppose you never buy expensive jewelry on your credit card. If you travel to South America and attempt to buy a $5,000 diamond bracelet using that credit card, watch what happens! Especially if you make the attempt on a credit card other than the one for which you paid for the travel. A data mining application integrated into the credit card agency's purchase-approval process will detect the unusual pattern, on the spot, and require you to personally verify the purchase on the telephone or in some other way before it will accept the charge. Such applications are exceedingly accurate because they are well designed and implemented by some of the world's best data miners.

How will this change by 2024? We know that data storage is free, that CPU processors are becoming nearly so, that the world is generating and storing exponentially more information about customers, and that data mining techniques are only going to get better. I think it likely that by 2024 some companies will know more about your purchasing psyche than you, your mother, or your analyst.

In fact, it may be important to ask the question: How unsupervised do we want unsupervised data mining to be? Today, a data miner extracts a data set and inputs it into an unsupervised data mining application for analysis. The application finds patterns, trends, and other business intelligence and reports the results to the human analyst. The BI analyst examines the results and possibly iterates by finding more data and running more analyses.

But what happens when BI applications become sophisticated enough to replace the BI analyst? What happens when the unsupervised data mining application has features and functions to find its own data sets and to evaluate those data sets based on the results of a prior BI analysis? And then decides which BI analysis to perform next?

Machines work faster than humans and they work 24/7. At some point, will machines know so much about us that we are incapable of understanding the results? What happens when, because of complexity, such BI machines can only communicate with other BI machines?

Apply Kurzweil's singularity theory (Using MIS InClass 9, pages 350-351) to unsupervised data mining. What happens when machines can direct their own data mining activities? There will be an accelerating positive feedback loop among the BI machines. Then what will they know about us? Is it important that at that date we will lack the capacity to know what the machines will know?

This line of thinking exposes a future flaw that runs through this text. We've defined information as something possessed only by humans. If it's on a piece of paper or on a screen, it's data. If it's in the mind of a human, it is (or can be) information. When we're talking about simple reporting operations such as grouping and filtering, and so on, that's legitimate. But, in the day when unsupervised data mining truly is unsupervised, machines will possess and create information for themselves.

Do you know what your data mining application is doing tonight?

Security Guide

SEMANTIC SECURITY

Security is a very difficult problem—and risks grow larger every year. Not only do we have cheaper, faster computers (remember Moore's Law), we also have more data, more systems for reporting and querying that data, and easier, faster, and broader communication. We have organizational data in the cloud that is not physically under our control. All of these combine to increase the chances that private or proprietary information is inappropriately divulged.

Access security is hard enough: How do we know that the person (or program) who signs on as Megan Cho really is Megan Cho? We use passwords, but files of passwords can be stolen. Setting that issue aside, we need to know that Megan Cho's permissions are set appropriately. Suppose Megan works in the HR department, so she has access to personal and private data of other employees. We need to design the reporting system so that Megan can access all of the data she needs to do her job, and no more.

Also, the delivery system must be secure. A BI server is an obvious and juicy target for any would-be intruder. Someone can break in and change access permissions. Or a hacker could pose as someone else to obtain reports. Application servers help the authorized user, resulting in faster access to more information. But without proper security reporting, servers also ease the intrusion task for unauthorized users.

All of these issues relate to access security. Another dimension to security is equally serious and far more problematic: **semantic security**. Semantic security concerns the unintended release of protected information through the release of a combination of reports or documents that are independently not protected. The term **data triangulation** is also used for this same phenomenon.

Take an example from class. Suppose I assign a group project, and I post a list of groups and the names of students assigned to each group. Later, after the assignments have been completed and graded, I post a list of grades on the Web site. Because of university privacy policy, I cannot post the grades by student name or identifier, so instead I post the grades for each group. If you want to

SALARY INFORMATION

get the grades for each student, all you have to do is combine the list from Lecture 5 with the list from Lecture 10. You might say that the release of grades in this example does no real harm—after all, it is a list of grades from one assignment.

But go back to Megan Cho in HR. Suppose Megan evaluates the employee compensation program. The COO believes salary offers have been inconsistent over time and that they vary too widely by department. Accordingly, the COO authorizes Megan to receive a report that lists *SalaryOfferAmount* and *OfferDate* and a second report that lists *Department* and *AverageSalary*.

Those reports are relevant to her task and seem innocuous enough. But Megan realizes that she could use the information they contain to determine individual salaries—information she does not have and is not authorized to receive. She proceeds as follows.

Like all employees, Megan has access to the employee directory on the Web portal. Using the directory, she can obtain a list of employees in each department, and using the facilities of her ever-so-helpful report-authoring system she combines that list with the department and average-salary report. Now she has a list of the names of employees in a group and the average salary for that group.

Megan's employer likes to welcome new employees to the company. Accordingly, each week the company publishes an article about new employees who have been hired. The article makes pleasant comments about each person and encourages employees to meet and greet them.

Megan, however, has other ideas. Because the report is published on SharePoint, she can obtain an electronic copy of it. It's an Acrobat report, and using Acrobat's handy Search feature, she soon has a list of employees and the week they were hired.

She now examines the report she received for her study, the one that has *SalaryOfferAmount* and the offer date, and she does some interpretation. During the week of July 21, three offers were extended: one for $35,000, one for $53,000, and one for $110,000. She also notices from the "New Employees" report that a director of marketing programs, a product test engineer, and a receptionist were hired that same week. It's unlikely that they paid the receptionist $110,000; that sounds more like the director of marketing programs. So, she now "knows" (infers) that person's salary.

Next, going back to the department report and using the employee directory, she sees that the marketing director is in the marketing programs department. There are just three people in that department, and their average salary is $105,000. Doing the arithmetic, she now knows that the average salary for the other two people is $102,500. If she can find the hire week for one of those other two people, she can find out both the second and third person's salaries.

You get the idea. Megan was given just two reports to do her job. Yet she combined the information in those reports with publicly available information and was able to deduce salaries, for at least some employees. These salaries are much more than she is supposed to know. This is a semantic security problem.

 DISCUSSION QUESTIONS

1. In your own words, explain the difference between access security and semantic security.
2. Why do reporting systems increase the risk of semantic security problems?
3. What can an organization do to protect itself against accidental losses due to semantic security problems?
4. What legal responsibility does an organization have to protect against semantic security problems?
5. Suppose semantic security problems are inevitable. Do you see an opportunity for new products from insurance companies? If so, describe such an insurance product. If not, explain why not.

Guide

DATA MINING IN THE REAL WORLD

"I'm not really opposed to data mining. I believe in it. After all, it's my career. But data mining in the real world is a lot different from the way it's described in textbooks, for many reasons.

"One is that the data are always dirty, with missing values, values way out of the range of possibility, and time values that make no sense. Here's an example: Somebody sets the server system clock incorrectly and runs the server for a while with the wrong time. When they notice the mistake, they set the clock to the correct time. But all of the transactions that were running during that interval have an ending time before the starting time. When we run the data analysis, and compute elapsed time, the results are negative for those transactions.

"Missing values are a similar problem. Consider the records of just 10 purchases. Suppose that two of the records are missing the customer number, and one is missing the year part of the transaction date. So you throw out three records, which is 30 percent of the data. You then notice that two more records have dirty data, and so you throw them out, too. Now you've lost half your data.

"Another problem is that you know the least when you start the study. So you work for a few months and learn that if you had another variable—say the customer's ZIP code, or age, or something else—you could do a much better analysis. But those other data just aren't available. Or maybe they are available, but to get the data you have to reprocess millions of transactions, and you don't have the time or budget to do that.

"Overfitting is another problem, a huge one. I can build a model to fit any set of data you have. Give me 100 data points and in a few minutes, I can give you 100 different equations that will predict those 100 data points. With neural networks, you can create a model of any level of complexity you want, except that none of those equations will predict new cases with any accuracy at all. When using neural nets, you have to be very careful not to overfit the data.

"Then, too, data mining is about probabilities, not certainty. Bad luck happens. Say I build a model that predicts the probability that a customer will make a purchase. Using the model on new customer data, I find three customers who have a .7 probability of buying something. That's a good number, well over a 50–50 chance, but it's still possible that none of them will buy. In fact, the

Source: © io/Fotolia

probability that none of them will buy is .3 × .3 × .3, or .027, which is 2.7 percent.

"Now suppose I give the names of the three customers to a salesperson who calls on them, and sure enough, we have a stream of bad luck and none of them buys. This bad result doesn't mean the model is wrong. But what does the salesperson think? He thinks the model is worthless, and he can do better on his own. He tells his manager who tells her associate, who tells everyone in the Northeast Region, and sure enough, the model has a bad reputation all across the company.

"Another problem is seasonality. Say all your training data are from the summer. Will your model be valid for the winter? Maybe, but maybe not. You might even know that it won't be valid for predicting winter sales, but if you don't have winter data, what do you do?

"When you start a data mining project, you never know how it will turn out. I worked on one project for 6 months, and when we finished, I didn't think our model was any good. We had too many problems with data: wrong, dirty, and missing. There was no way we could know ahead of time that it would happen, but it did.

"When the time came to present the results to senior management, what could we do? How could we say we took 6 months of our time and substantial computer resources to create a bad model? We had a model, but I just didn't think it would make accurate predictions. I was a junior member of the team, and it wasn't for me to decide. I kept my mouth shut, but I never felt good about it. Fortunately, the project was cancelled later for other reasons.

"However, I'm only talking about my bad experiences. Some of my projects have been excellent. On many, we found interesting and important patterns and information, and a few times I've created very accurate predictive models. It's not easy, though, and you have to be very careful. Also, lucky!"

 DISCUSSION QUESTIONS

1. Summarize the concerns expressed by this data analyst.
2. Do you think the concerns raised here are sufficient to avoid data mining projects altogether?
3. If you were a junior member of a data mining team and you thought that the model that had been developed was ineffective, maybe even wrong, what would you do? If your boss disagrees with your beliefs, would you go higher in the organization? What are the risks of doing so? What else might you do?

ACTIVE REVIEW

Use this Active Review to verify that you understand the ideas and concepts that answer the chapter's study questions.

Q1 How do organizations use business intelligence (BI) systems?

Define *business intelligence* and *BI system*. Explain the components in Figure 9-1. Give an example, other than one in this text, of one way that an organization could use business intelligence for each of the four collaborative tasks in Figure 9-2. Describe one use of BI in retailing, entertainment, and law enforcement.

Q2 What are the three primary activities in the BI process?

Name and describe the three primary activities in the BI process. Using Figure 9-3 as a guide, describe the major tasks for each activity. Summarize how Addison and Drew used these activities to produce BI results for AllRoad. Explain the role of Figures 9-4 through 9-11.

Q3 How do organizations use data warehouses and data marts to acquire data?

Describe the need and functions of data warehouses and data marts. Name and describe the role of data warehouse components. List and explain the problems that can exist in data used for data mining and sophisticated reporting. Use the example of a supply chain to describe the differences between a data warehouse and data mart.

Q4 How do organizations use reporting applications?

Name and describe five basic reporting operations and summarize how Addison used them at AllRoad. Define *RFM analysis* and explain the actions that should be taken with customers who have the following scores: [1, 1, 1,], [5, 1, 1,], [1, 1, 3], and [1, 4, 1]. Explain OLAP and describe its unique characteristics. Explain the roles for measure and dimension in an OLAP cube. Illustrate an OLAP cube with a single measure and five dimensions, two dimensions on one axis and three on another. Show how drill down applies to your example.

Q5 How do organizations use data mining applications?

Define *data mining*, and explain how its use typically differs from reporting applications. Explain why data mining tools are difficult to use well. Describe the differences between unsupervised and supervised data mining. Use an example to illustrate cluster analysis and regression analysis. Define *neural networks*, and explain why the term is a misnomer. Define *support, confidence*, and *lift*, and describe these terms using the data in Figure 9-21. Describe a good application for market-basket analysis results. Describe the purpose of decision trees and explain how the data in Figure 9-22 is used to evaluate loans for possible purchase.

Q6 How do organizations use BigData applications?

Name and explain the three *v's* of BigData. Describe the general goal of MapReduce and explain, at a conceptual level, how it works. Explain the purpose of Hadoop and describe its origins. Define *Pig*.

Explain how Figure 9-24 could be produced by MapReduce. State one reason why Amazon offers Hadoop services as part of its EC3 offering.

Q7 What is the role of knowledge management systems?

Define *knowledge management*. Explain five key benefits of KM. Briefly describe three types of KM systems. Define *expert systems, If/Then rules*, and *expert system shell*. Explain how expert system rules are created. Differentiate expert system If/Then rules from decision tree If/Then rules. Summarize the three major disadvantages of expert systems and assess their future. Define *content management system (CMS)*. Describe five challenges organizations face for managing content. Name three CMS application alternatives and explain the use of each.

Explain how social media has changed the orientation of knowledge management. Define *hyper-social knowledge management*. Explain the hyper-social KM use of each medium in Figure 9-28. Explain the entries in the second and third columns of this figure. Define *rich directory* and explain three uses for it. Summarize possible employee resistance to hyper-social knowledge sharing, and name two management techniques for reducing it.

Q8 What are the alternatives for publishing BI?

Name four alternative types of server used for publishing business intelligence. Explain the difference between static and dynamic reports; explain the term *subscription*. Describe why dynamic reports are difficult to create.

Q9 2024?

Summarize the function of the credit card approval application. Explain how you think that application uses data. Summarize the way that unsupervised data mining could spiral out of the control of humans. In your opinion, is this a problem? Why or why not? Describe the singularity that could occur for data mining applications. Explain the information flaw that runs throughout this text.

Using Your Knowledge with PRIDE

From this chapter, you know the three phases of BI analysis, and you have learned common techniques for acquiring, processing, and publishing business intelligence. This knowledge will enable you to imagine innovative uses for data that your employer generates and also to know some of the constraints of such use. At PRIDE, the knowledge of this chapter will help you understand possible uses for the exercise data that is being generated. If PRIDE becomes a successful product, with millions of users, you know that BigData techniques can be used to analyze minute-by-minute exercise data.

KEY TERMS AND CONCEPTS

MyMISLab

Go to **mymislab.com** to complete the problems marked with this icon .

USING YOUR KNOWLEDGE

9-1. Explain in your own words how Addison used Access to implement each of the five criteria that she and Drew developed. Use Figures 9-5 through 9-10 in your answer.

9-2. Explain why the results in Figure 9-11 do not show promise for the selling of these part designs. In light of these results, should Addison and Drew look at changing their criteria? If so, how? If not, why not?

9-3. Given the results in Figure 9-11, list three actions that AllRoad can take. Recommend one of these actions and justify your recommendation.

9-4. Suppose you work at Costco or another major, national big-box store; you do a market-basket analysis and identify the 25 pairs of items in the store that have the highest lift and the 25 pairs that have the lowest lift. What would you do with this knowledge? Costco (or your big-box store) doesn't have salespeople, so up-selling is not an option. What else might you do with information about these items' lift? Consider advertising, pricing, item location in stores, and any other factor that you might adjust. Do you think the lift calculations are valid for all stores in the United States (or other country)?

Why or why not? Are the 50 pairs of products with the highest and lowest lift the best place to focus your attention? What other 50 pairs of products might you want to consider? Explain.

9-5. Describe a use for RFM analysis for AllRoad. Explain what you would do for customers who have the following scores: [1, 1, 1], [3, 1, 1], [1, 4, 1], [3, 3, 1], [1, 1, 3]. Is this analysis useful for AllRoad? Explain your answer.

9-6. Describe an application for market-basket analysis for AllRoad. Explain how you would use the knowledge that two items have a lift of 7. Explain how you would use the knowledge that two items have a lift of .003. If they have a lift of 1.03? If they have a lift of 2.1?

9-7. Considering all of the BI techniques in this chapter, which would be most likely to facilitate AllRoad's competitive strategy? Explain your answer.

9-8. Define the characteristics of BigData. Identify and describe three student-related applications at your university that meet BigData characteristics. Describe patterns and relationships that might be found within that data.

COLLABORATION EXERCISE 9

Using the collaboration IS you built in Chapter 2 (pages 73–74), collaborate with a group of students to answer the following questions.

Read Case Study 9 (pages 369–371) if you have not already done so. Undeniably, third-party cookies offer advantages to online sellers. They also increase the likelihood that consumers will receive online ads that are close to their interests; thus, third-party cookies can provide a consumer service as well. But at what cost to personal privacy? And what should be done about them? Working with your team, answer the following questions:

1. Summarize the ways that third-party cookies are created and processed. Even though cookies are not supposed to contain personally identifying data, explain how such data can readily be obtained. (See question 9-12, page 371.)

2. Numerous browser features, add-ins, and other tools exist for blocking third-party cookies. Search the Web for *block*

third-party cookies for xxx, and fill in the *xxx* with the name and version of your browser. Read the instructions, and summarize the procedures that you need to take to view the cookies issued from a given site.

3. In large measure, ads pay for the free use of Web content and even Web sites themselves. If, because of a fear of privacy, many people block third-party cookies, substantial ad revenue will be lost. Discuss with your group how such a movement would affect the valuation of Facebook and other ad-revenue-dependent companies. Discuss how it would affect the delivery of free online content such as that supplied by *Forbes* or other providers.

4. Many companies have a conflict of interest with regard to third-party cookies. On the one hand, such cookies help generate revenue and pay for Internet content. On the other hand, trespassing on users' privacy could turn out to be

a PR disaster. As you learned in your answer to question 2, browsers include options to block third-party cookies. However, in most cases, those options are turned off in the default browser installation. Discuss why that might be so. If sites were required to obtain your permission before installing third-party cookies, how would you determine whether to grant it? List criteria that your team thinks you would actually use (as opposed to what the team thinks you *should* do). Assess the effectiveness of such a policy.

5. The processing of third-party cookies is hidden; we don't know what is being done behind the scenes with the data about our own behavior. Because there is so much of it and so many parties involved, the possibilities are difficult to comprehend, even if the descriptions were available. And if your privacy is compromised by the interaction of seven different companies working independently, which is to be held accountable? Summarize consequences of these facts on consumers.

6. Summarize the benefits of third-party cookies to consumers.

7. Given all you have learned about third-party cookies, what does your team think should be done about them? Possible answers are: a) nothing; b) require Web sites to ask users before installing third-party cookies; c) require browsers to block third-party cookies; d) require browsers to block third-party cookies by default, but enable them at the users' option; e) something else. Discuss these alternatives among your team and recommend one. Justify your recommendation.

CASE STUDY 9

Hadoop the Cookie Cutter

A **cookie** is data that a Web site stores on your computer to record something about its interaction with you. The cookie might contain data such as the date you last visited, whether you are currently signed in, or something else about your interaction with that site. Cookies can also contain a key value to one or more tables in a database that the server company maintains about your past interactions. In that case, when you access a site, the server uses the value of the cookie to look up your history. Such data could include your past purchases, portions of incomplete transactions, or the data and appearance you want for your Web page. Most of the time cookies ease your interaction with Web sites.

Cookie data includes the URL of the Web site of the cookie's owner. Thus, for example, when you go to Amazon, it asks your browser to place a cookie on your computer that includes its name, *www.amazon.com*. Your browser will do so unless you have turned cookies off.

A **third-party cookie** is a cookie created by a site other than the one you visited. Such cookies are generated in several ways, but the most common occurs when a Web page includes content from multiple sources. For example, Amazon designs its pages so that one or more sections contain ads provided by the ad-servicing company, DoubleClick. When the browser constructs your Amazon page, it contacts DoubleClick to obtain the content for such sections (in this case, ads). When it responds with the content, DoubleClick instructs your browser to store a DoubleClick cookie. That cookie is a third-party cookie. In general, third-party cookies do not contain the name or any value that identifies a particular user. Instead, they include the IP address to which the content was delivered.

On its own servers, when it creates the cookie, DoubleClick records that data in a log, and if you click on the ad, it will add that fact of that click to the log. This logging is repeated every time DoubleClick shows an ad. Cookies have an expiration date, but that date is set by the cookie creator, and they can last many years. So, over time, DoubleClick and any other third-party cookie owner will have a history of what they've shown, what ads have been clicked, and the intervals between interactions.

But the opportunity is even greater. DoubleClick has agreements not only with Amazon, but also with many others, such as Facebook. If Facebook includes any DoubleClick content on its site, DoubleClick will place another cookie on your computer. This cookie is different from the one that it placed via Amazon, but both cookies have your IP address and other data sufficient to associate the second cookie as originating from the same source as the first. So, DoubleClick now has a record of your ad response data on two sites. Over time, the cookie log will contain data to show not only how you respond to ads, but also your pattern of visiting various Web sites on all those sites in which it places ads.

You might be surprised to learn how many third-party cookies you have. The browser Firefox has an optional feature called *Collusion* that tracks and graphs all the cookies on your computer. Figure 9-31 shows the cookies that were placed on my computer as I visited various Web sites. (After this display was generated, Collusion changed its user interface. If you install Collusion now, it just provides a list of third-party cookies.) As you can see, in Figure 9-31a, when I started my computer and browser, there were no cookies. The cookies on

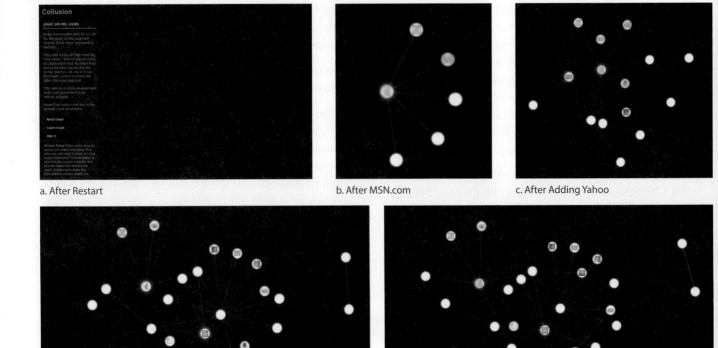

a. After Restart　　　　　　　　　b. After MSN.com　　　　　　　　　c. After Adding Yahoo

d. After Adding Seattle Times, LinkedIn, and Facebook　　　　e. After Closing All Browser Windows

Figure 9-31
Third-Party Cookie Growth
Source: © Mozilla

my computer after I visited *www.msn.com* are shown in Figure 9-31b. At this point, there are already five third-party cookies tracking my behavior. After I visited *www.yahoo.com* and *www. amazon.com* as well, I had 12 third-party cookies, as shown in Figure 9-31c. Finally, Figure 9-31d shows the too-many-to-count third-party cookies on my machine after I visited the *Seattle Times*, Facebook, and LinkedIn as well. All of that is disturbing and bothersome, so I closed all of my browser sessions. Figure 9-31e shows that even after closing I was still being watched by third-party cookies.

Who are these companies that are gathering my browser behavior data? You can find out using Ghostery®, another useful browser add-in feature (*www.ghostery.com*). Figure 9-32 shows the 10 third-party cookies installed by *www.zulily.com*, when I visited its site. If you click on the name of the third-party cookie owner, it will display the popup shown in this figure. Click on the *What is…* and you can find out who that company is and what it does.

Third-party cookies generate incredible volumes of log data. For example, suppose a company, such as DoubleClick,

shows 100 ads to a given computer in a day. If it is showing ads to 10 million computers (possible), that is a total of 1 billion log entries per day, or 365 billion a year. Truly this is BigData.

Storage is essentially free, but how can they possibly process all that data? How do they parse the log to find entries just for your computer? How do they integrate data from different cookies on the same IP address? How do they analyze those entries to determine which ads you clicked on? How do they then characterize differences in ads to determine which characteristics matter most to you? The answer, as you learned in Q6, is to use parallel processing. Using a MapReduce algorithm, they distribute the work to thousands of processors that work in parallel. They then aggregate the results of these independent processors and then, possibly, move to a second phase of analysis where they do it again. Hadoop, the open-source program that you learned about in Q6, is a favorite for this process. No wonder Amazon offers Hadoop MapReduce as part of EC3. It built it for itself, and now, given that it has it, why not lease it out?

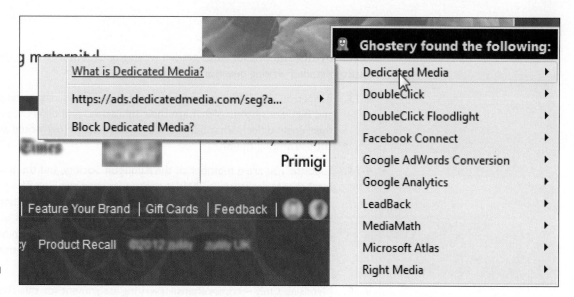

Figure 9-32
Ghostery® in Use

(See the collaboration exercise on pages 368–369 for a continuation of the discussion: third-party cookies—problem? Or opportunity?)

QUESTIONS

9-9. Using your own words, explain how third-party cookies are created.

9-10. Suppose you are an ad-serving company, and you maintain a log of cookie data for ads you serve to Web pages for a particular vendor (say Amazon).

    a. How can you use this data to determine which are the best ads?

    b. How can you use this data to determine which are the best ad formats?

    c. How could you use records of past ads and ad clicks to determine which ads to send to a given IP address?

    d. How could you use this data to determine how well the technique you used in your answer to question c was working?

    e. How could you use this data to determine that a given IP address is used by more than one person?

    f. How does having this data give you a competitive advantage vis-à-vis other ad-serving companies?

9-11. Suppose you are an ad-serving company, and you have a log of cookie data for ads served to Web pages of all your customers (Amazon, Facebook, etc.).

    a. Describe, in general terms, how you can process the cookie data to associate log entries for a particular IP address.

    b. Explain how your answers to question 9-10 change, given that you have this additional data.

    c. Describe how you can use this log data to determine users who consistently seek the lowest price.

    d. Describe how you can use this log data to determine users who consistently seek the latest fashion.

    e. Explain why uses like those in c and d above are only possible with MapReduce or a similar technique.

9-12. As stated, third-party cookies usually do not contain, in themselves, data that identifies you as a particular person. However, Amazon, Facebook, and other first-party cookie vendors know who you are because you signed in. Only one of them needs to reveal your identity to the ad-server, and your identity can then be correlated with your IP address. At that point, the ad-server and potentially all of its clients know who you are. Are you concerned about the invasion of your privacy that third-party cookies enable? Explain your answer.

MyMISLab

Go to **mymislab.com** for Auto-graded writing questions as well as the following Assisted-graded writing questions:

9-13. Reflect on the differences among reporting systems, data mining systems, and BigData systems. What are their similarities and differences? How do their costs differ? What benefits does each offer? How would an organization choose among them?

9-14. Suppose you are a member of the Audubon Society, and the board of the local chapter asks you to help it analyze its member data. The group wants to analyze the demographics of its membership against members' activity, including events attended, classes attended, volunteer activities, and donations. Describe two different reporting applications and one data mining application that they might develop. Be sure to include a specific description of the goals of each system.

9-15. Mymislab Only – comprehensive writing assignment for this chapter.

Information Systems Management

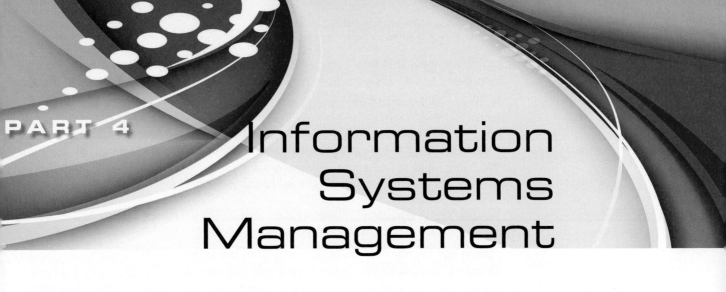

Part 4 addresses the management of development processes, of IS resources, and of IS security in Chapters 10, 11, and 12, respectively. Even if you are not an IS major, you need to know about these functions so that you can be a successful and effective consumer of IS professionals' services. Here's an example of why:

Dr. Romero Flores is meeting with Maggie Jensen, a business analyst who is part of the team developing the PRIDE system, and with Jason Weber, the office administrator.

"It's a mess. We really didn't know what we were doing." Jason sounds dejected and depressed.

Dr. Flores joins in, "Sunk by our own success. I would never have imagined."

"Hold it, guys. I wouldn't say *sunk*. We're a long way from *sunk*. But we do need to turn our attention to procedures and management." Maggie doesn't want this meeting to go too far downhill.

"I'll say. We've got patients calling for instructions on how to maintain their treadmills. OK, that's dumb. But a lot of patients have called about problems with the heart monitors. At least those devices have *heart* in their name. Many of them think we should know something about *heart* monitors, given that we're a cardiac surgery practice."

"OK. We started this project as a prototype; we wanted to know if it would work and if patients would respond to it. And now we know that it does and that many, not all, but many patients, more than three-fourths of them, in fact, will actively use PRIDE." Maggie summarizes the situation in an upbeat way.

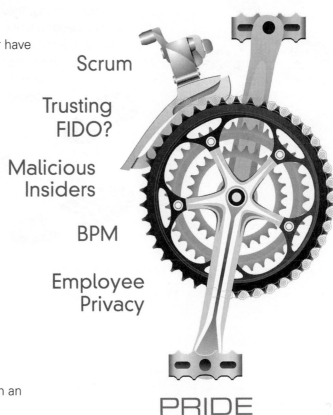

Scrum

Trusting FIDO?

Malicious Insiders

BPM

Employee Privacy

PRIDE

"Well, we know that they'll use it for a few months, anyway. We don't know how long they'll use it." It's clear from his voice that Jason wishes they'd never started this project.

"So, we have success with the prototype. Now we have to decide what to do next. Clearly, we need to look at our procedures and training and manage our users better. We might need to add some new players and resources. The help desk at equipment vendors, for example. Also, some local health clubs."

"Health clubs? Why?"

"Didn't you tell me that you're getting a lot of questions on what exercise to do next? Or how to get the same benefit from a different exercise? Now that spring is here, people want to exercise outside, some even to jog, rather than use their treadmills."

"There's another issue as well…" Dr. Flores enters the conversation with a heavy sigh, "We need to decide where we're going with this."

"What do you mean?"

"I need to meet with my medical partners and see what they want to do. We've demonstrated that it works with the prototype. Now, do we want this system to be just for our practice and our patients? Do we want to share it with others? Do we want to form a separate company and offer this service to more surgery practices? Maggie, I'm meeting with them next week at the end of the day. Probably around 6:30. I want you there."

Dr. Flores and his partners need to decide what to do with their new invention. Clearly, they need to know how better to use it in their practice, which means they need to finish the *system* of all five components, and not just the cloud, software, and database parts. We'll discuss that and more in Chapter 10. Beyond that, how are they going to support it, long-term? If they form a separate company, how does that company run the PRIDE infrastructure? We'll discuss IS management in Chapter 11. Finally, with a system like PRIDE, security and privacy are critical, and not just because patients ask for them. Medical practices have legal requirements to protect patient data. Chapter 12 wraps up IS management by discussing security.

As you can tell from the PRIDE example, this knowledge has value to you whether or not you are an IS major.

10

Development Processes

Following the meeting described on pages 373–374, Maggie, Dr. Flores, Dr. Christine Lomar, and Dr. Chris Vesper meet the next week. The three doctors are the partners and sole owners of Austin Cardiac Surgery. The purpose of the meeting is to determine what to do next.

Dr. Flores starts. "Our PRIDE prototype works, and patients are responding to it. The question is, what do we do next? It's not really finished, even for our use, and it may cost more than we want to pay to finish it. So?"

Dr. Vesper looks at Dr. Flores directly. "Romero, this has been your pet project, and I've gone along with you. I know you think it's fantastic, but I want to focus on surgery. This post-op care, techno stuff really doesn't interest me, and I don't think we should pay much attention to it."

"What are you saying, 'Drop it?'"

"Maybe. Or, if you want to keep playing around with it on your time and money, OK, but I don't really want the partners or the partnership to participate."

"OK, but I'm sorry to hear that. Christine, what do you think?"

"I'm in the middle between you two. I think there is value, and I appreciate treating patients more effectively in our post-op care. But we are a surgery practice, not a technology company. How much will it cost us to finish?"

"Maggie?"

"Dr. Flores asked me to put together a finished plan. At the minimum, we need to define the system procedures here at your practice and document them in some way. Then we need to train the staff. We may also need to involve some of our partners in this endeavor. I'd estimate that it's probably $25K for that, maybe more, but less than $50K."

"Ouch."

"Well, then there's another matter. Right now we're supporting the Garmin exercise watch and iPhones and iPads. To make this system more generally available, we need to support other watches and mobile devices and at least Android phones."

"We need to support other watches and mobile devices and at least Android phones."

"How much is that?" Dr. Lomar is being careful.

"Well, it depends on what devices..."

Dr. Vesper can't stand this discussion. "Look, I don't care what else there is. I don't even want to pay the minimum $25K! That's nuts. Let's get back to surgery."

Pandemonium breaks out among the three surgeons. Finally, Maggie breaks in.

"Here's a thought. Why don't we finish the PRIDE procedures here so that you all have a workable system for the devices we support currently? Then look for outside investors to take the system and technology and form a company around it. You all can take major ownership of the new company or license your system to it or something."

"What about the $25K?" Dr. Vesper isn't letting that slide.

"Well, you decide. If Drs. Flores and Lomar want to fund it, then they own more, or all, of the interest in the new company, or whatever. You all can figure that out."

"Maggie, thank you. I think we'll need to excuse you now while we sort this out among ourselves."

"I understand. I'll head on home, but call my cell phone if you have any questions."

"Thanks, Maggie." Both Dr. Lomar and Dr. Flores nod in agreement as Maggie leaves the room.

STUDY QUESTIONS

Q1 How are business processes, IS, and applications developed?

Q2 How do organizations use business process management (BPM)?

Q3 How is business process modeling notation (BPMN) used to model processes?

Q4 What are the phases in the systems development life cycle (SDLC)?

Q5 What are the keys for successful SDLC projects?

Q6 How can scrum overcome the problems of the SDLC?

Q7 2024?

As a future business professional, you will be involved in the development of new technology applications to your business. You may take the lead, as Dr. Flores has been doing in developing PRIDE, or you might be an office manager who implements procedures and trains people in the use of systems such as PRIDE. Or you might become a business analyst, like Maggie, and work as a liaison between users and technical staff. If nothing else, you may be asked to provide requirements and to test the system to ensure those requirements have been met. Whatever your role, it is important that you understand how processes and systems are developed and managed.

We begin in Q1 by clarifying what we're developing and introducing three different development processes. Then, in the next series of questions, we'll go into more detail for each. In Q2, we'll discuss business process management, and you'll learn how to interpret process diagrams that you may be called upon to evaluate during your career in Q3. Next, we'll discuss the stages of the systems development life cycle in Q4 and then in Q5 summarize the keys to successful SDLC project management. Q6 then presents a newer, possibly superior development process known as scrum, and we'll wrap up this chapter in Q7 with a discussion of how information systems careers are likely to change between now and 2024.

How Are Business Processes, IS, and Applications Developed?

Many business professionals become confused when discussing business processes, information systems, and applications. You can avoid this confusion by understanding that they are different, by knowing those differences, and by realizing how they relate to each other. That knowledge will make it easier for you to appreciate the ways that processes, systems, and applications are developed and, in turn, help you be more effective as a team member on development projects.

How Do Business Processes, Information Systems, and Applications Differ and Relate?

As you learned in Chapter 3, a business process consists of one or more activities. For example, Figure 10-1 shows activities in an ordering business process: A quotation is prepared and, assuming the customer accepts those terms, the order is processed. Inventory availability is verified, customer credit is checked, special terms, if any, are approved, and then the order is processed and shipped. Each of these activities includes many tasks, some of which involve processing exceptions (only part of the order is available, for example), but those exceptions are not shown.

The activities in a business process often involve information systems. In Figure 10-1, for example, all of the activities except Approve Special Terms use an information system. (For this example, we'll assume that special terms are rare and approved by having a salesperson walk down the hallway to the sales manager.) Each of these information systems has the five components that we've repeatedly discussed. The actors or participants in the business process are the users of the information systems. They employ IS procedures to use information systems to accomplish tasks in process activities.

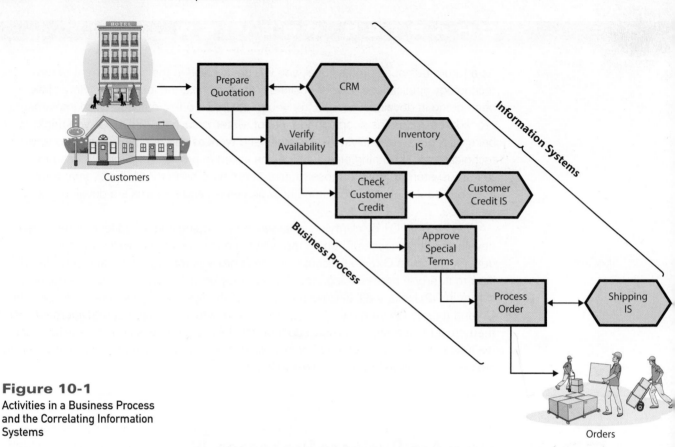

Figure 10-1
Activities in a Business Process
and the Correlating Information
Systems

Each of these information systems contains a software component. Developing software nearly always involves the data component and it often involves the specification and characteristics of hardware (e.g., mobile devices). Consequently, we define the term **application** to mean a combination of hardware, software, and data components that accomplishes a set of requirements. In Figure 10-1, the Customer Credit IS contains an application that processes a customer database to approve or reject credit requests.

As you can see from the example in Figure 10-1, this one business process uses four different IS. In general, we can say that a single business process relates to one or more information systems. However, notice that not all process activities use an IS; some require just manual tasks. In Figure 10-1, the Approve Special Terms activity uses no IS. Instead, as stated, salespeople walk down the hallway to ask their manager if terms are acceptable. In some cases (not in this example, however), it is possible for none of the activities to use an IS, in which case the entire business process is manual.

Now, consider any of the information systems in Figure 10-1, say the Inventory IS. In addition to providing features and functions to verify item availability, that IS has other features that support additional business processes. For example, the Inventory IS supports the item ordering process, the item stocking process, the item backorder process, and more. So, even though we cannot see it from Figure 10-1, we can correctly infer that IS supports many business processes. Further, every IS supports at least one business process; if it did not, it would have little utility to the organization that pays for it.

We can use the terminology of Chapter 5 to summarize these statements and state that the relationship of business processes and information systems is many-to-many. One business process can potentially use many IS, and a single IS can support potentially many business processes. Furthermore, a business process is not required to use an IS, but every IS supports at least one business process. Figure 10-2 shows the process/information system relationship using an entity-relationship diagram.

Figure 10-2
Relationship of Business
Processes and Information
Systems

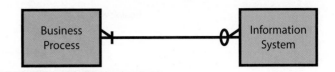

Every information system has at least one application because every IS includes a software component. We could further investigate the relationship between IS and applications, but that relationship is beyond the scope of this text.

So, to summarize:

1. Business processes, information systems, and applications have different characteristics and components.
2. The relationship of business processes to information systems is many-to-many, or N:M. A business process need not relate to any information system, but an information system relates to at least one business process.
3. Every IS has at least one application because every IS has a software component.

When you participate in development meetings, you'll sometimes hear people confuse these terms. They'll quickly switch back and forth among processes, systems, and applications without knowing that they've changed terms and contexts. With these understandings, you can add value to your team simply by clarifying these differences.

Which Development Processes Are Used for Which?

A fourth way to develop applications is to steal them. Read the Security Guide on pages 414–415 to learn more.

Over the years, many different processes have been tried for the development of processes, IS, and applications. In this chapter, we'll investigate three: business process management (BPM), systems development life cycle (SDLC), and scrum.

Business process management is a technique used to create new business processes and to manage changes to existing processes. Except for start-ups, organizations already have processes, in one form or another, in varying levels of quality. If they did not, they wouldn't be able to operate. Therefore, BPM is, in most cases, used to manage the evolution of existing business processes from one version to an improved version. We'll discuss BPM in Q2 and Q3.

As shown in Figure 10-3, the systems development life cycle (SDLC) is a process that can be used to develop both information systems and applications. The SDLC achieved prominence in the 1980s when the U.S. Department of Defense required that it be used on all software and systems development projects. It is common, well-known, and often used, but as you'll learn, frequently problematic. You need to know what it is and when and when not to use it. We'll discuss SDLC in Q4 and Q5.

Scrum is a new development process that was created, in part, to overcome the problems that occur when using the SDLC. Scrum is generic enough that it can be used for the development (and adaptation) of business processes, information systems, and applications. We'll discuss scrum in Q6.

		Development Processes		
		BPM	**SDLC**	**Scrum**
Scope	Business Processes	✓		✓
	Information Systems		✓	✓
	Applications		✓	✓

Figure 10-3
Scope of Development Processes

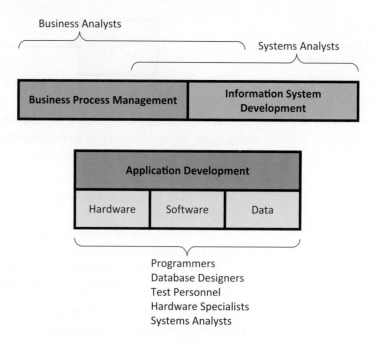

Figure 10-4
Role of Development Personnel

Personnel that take the most active and important role for each of these processes are shown in Figure 10-4. A **business analyst** is someone who is well versed in Porter's models (see Chapter 3) and in the organization's strategies and who focuses, primarily, on ensuring that business processes and information systems meet the organization's competitive strategies. As you would expect, the primary focus of a business analyst is business processes.

Systems analysts are IS professionals who understand both business and information technology. They focus primarily on IS development, but are involved with business analysts on the management of business processes as well. Systems analysts play a key role in moving development projects through the SDLC or scrum development process.

Applications are developed by technical personnel such as programmers, database designers, test personnel, hardware specialists, and other technical staff. Systems analysts play a key role in developing applications requirements and in facilitating the work of the programmers, testers, and users.

Because applications development involves technical details that are far from the scope of this introductory class, we will only be peripherally concerned with applications development here. If you have a technical bent, however, you should consider these jobs because they are absolutely fascinating and are in extremely high demand.

 ## How Do Organizations Use Business Process Management (BPM)?

For the purposes of this chapter, we will extend the definition of business processes that we used in Chapter 3. Here we will define a **business process** as a network of activities, repositories, roles, resources, and flows that interact to accomplish a business function. As stated in Chapter 3, *activities* are collections of related tasks that receive inputs and produce outputs. A *repository* is a collection of something; an inventory is a physical repository and a database is a data repository. The new terms in this definition are **roles**, which are collections of activities, and **resources**, which are people or computer applications that are assigned to roles. Finally, a flow is either a **control flow** that directs the order of activities or a **data flow** that shows the movement of data among activities and repositories.

To clarify these terms, think of roles as job titles. Example roles are *salesperson, credit manager, inventory supervisor*, and the like. Thus, an organization might assign three people (resources) to the salesperson role, or it might create an information system (resource) to perform the credit manager role.

Why Do Processes Need Management?

Business processes are not fixed in stone; they evolve for several reasons. To understand why, suppose you are a salesperson working at the company having the ordering process shown in Figure 10-1. When you joined the firm, they taught you to follow this process, and you've been using for it 2 years. It works fine as far as you know, so why does it need to be managed? Fundamentally, there are three reasons: to improve process quality, to adapt to changes in technology, and to adapt to changes in business fundamentals. Consider each.

Improve Process Quality

As you learned in Chapter 7, process quality has two dimensions: efficiency (use of resources) and effectiveness (accomplish strategy). The most obvious reason for changing a process is that it has efficiency or effectiveness problems. Consider a sales process. If the organization's goal is to provide high-quality service, then if the process takes too long or if it rejects credit inappropriately, it is ineffective and needs to be changed.

With regard to efficiency, the process may use its resources poorly. For example, according to Figure 10-1, salespeople verify product availability before checking customer credit. If checking availability means nothing more than querying an information system for inventory levels, that sequence makes sense. But suppose that checking availability means that someone in operations needs not only to verify inventory levels, but also to verify that the goods can be shipped to arrive on time. If the order delivery is complex, say the order is for a large number of products that have to be shipped from three different warehouses, an hour or two of labor may be required to verify shipping schedules.

After verifying shipping, the next step is to verify credit. If it turns out the customer has insufficient credit and the order is refused, the shipping-verification labor will have been wasted. So, it might make sense to check credit before checking availability.

Similarly, if the customer's request for special terms is disapproved, the cost of checking availability and credit is wasted. If the customer has requested special terms that are not normally approved, it might make sense to obtain approval of special terms before checking availability or credit. However, your boss might not appreciate being asked to consider special terms for orders in which the items are not available or for customers with bad credit.

As you can see, it's not easy to determine what process structure is best. The need to monitor process quality and adjust process design, as appropriate, is one reason that processes need to be managed.

Change in Technology

Changing technology is a second reason for managing processes. For example, suppose the equipment supplier who uses the business process in Figure 10-1 invests in a new information system that enables it to track the location of trucks in real time. Suppose that with this capability the company can provide next-day availability of goods to customers. That capability will be of limited value, however, if the existing credit-checking process requires 2 days. "I can get the goods to you tomorrow, but I can't verify your credit until next Monday" will not be satisfying to either customers or salespeople.

Thus, when new technology changes any of a process's activities in a significant way, the entire process needs to be evaluated. That evaluation is another reason for managing processes.

Change in Business Fundamentals

A third reason for managing business processes is a change in business fundamentals. A substantial change in any of the following factors might result in the need to modify business processes:

- Market (e.g., new customer category, change in customer characteristics)
- Product lines
- Supply chain
- Company policy
- Company organization (e.g., merger, acquisition)
- Internationalization
- Business environment

To understand the implications of such changes, consider just the sequence of verifying availability and checking credit in Figure 10-1. A new category of customers could mean that the credit-check process needs to be modified; perhaps a certain category of customers is too risky to be extended credit. All sales to such customers must be cash. A change in product lines might require different ways of checking availability. A change in the supply chain might mean that the company no longer stocks some items in inventory but ships directly from the manufacturer instead.

Or the company might make broad changes to its credit policy. It might, for example, decide to accept more risk and sell to companies with lower credit scores. In this case, approval of special terms becomes more critical than checking credit, and the sequence of those two activities might need to be changed.

Of course, a merger or acquisition will mean substantial change in the organization and its products and markets, as does moving portions of the business offshore or engaging in international commerce. Finally, a substantial change in the business environment, say, the onset of a recession, might mean that credit checking becomes vitally important and needs to be moved to first in this process.

What Are BPM Activities?

The factors just discussed will necessitate changes in business processes, whether the organization recognizes that need or not. Organizations can either plan to develop and modify business processes, or they can wait and let the need for change just happen to them. In the latter case, the business will continually be in crisis, dealing with one process emergency after another.

Figure 10-5 shows the basic activities in **business process management (BPM)**, a cyclical process for systematically creating, assessing, and altering business processes. This cycle begins by creating a model of the existing business process, called an **as-is model**. Then business users who are involved in the process (this could be you!) and business and systems analysts evaluate that model and make improvements. As you learned in Chapter 7, business processes can be improved by changing the structure of the process, by adding resources, or both. If the process structure is to be changed, a model of the changed process is constructed. Two common ways of adding resources to a process are to assign more people to process activities and to create or modify information systems.

The second activity in the BPM process is to create components. In this activity, the team designs changes to the business process at a depth sufficient for implementation. If the business process involves new information systems or changes to existing information systems then systems development projects are created and managed at this stage. Again, some activities involve IS, and some do not. For those that do, information systems procedures need to be created to enable users to accomplish their process tasks.

Implementing the new or changed process is the third activity in BPM. Here process actors are trained on the activities that they will perform and on the IS procedures that they will use.

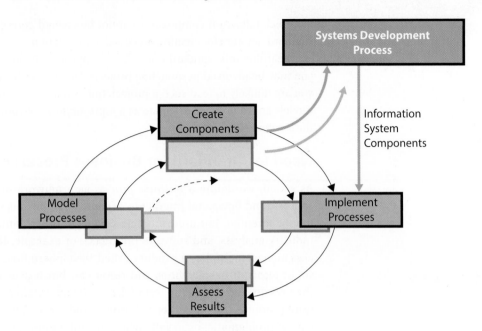

Figure 10-5
Four Stages of BPM

Converting from an existing process to a new or revised one usually meets with employee resistance, as you learned with regard to ERP implementations in Chapter 7. We will discuss four different conversion alternatives in Q4, when we discuss the SDLC. These four strategies pertain equally well to process implementation.

Once the process has been implemented, well-managed organizations don't stop there. Instead, they create policy, procedures, and committees to continually assess business process effectiveness. The Information Systems Audit and Control Association has created a set of standard practices called **COBIT (Control Objectives for Information and related Technology)** that are often used in the assessment stage of the BPM cycle. Explaining these standards is beyond the scope of this discussion, but you should know that they exist. See *www.isaca.org/cobit* for more information.

When the assessment process indicates that a significant need for change has arisen, the BPM cycle is repeated and adjusted. New process models are developed, and components are created, implemented, and assessed.

Effective BPM enables organizations to attain continuous process improvement. Like quality improvement, process improvement is never finished. Process effectiveness is constantly monitored, and processes are adjusted as and when required.

By the way, do not assume that business process management applies only to commercial, profit-making organizations. Nonprofit and government organizations have business processes just as commercial ones do, but most of these processes are service-oriented, rather than revenue-oriented. Your state's Department of Labor, for example, has a need to manage its processes, as does the Girl Scouts of America. BPM applies to all types of organizations.

How Is Business Process Modeling Notation (BPMN) Used to Model Processes?

One of the four stages of BPM, and arguably the most important stage, is to model business processes. Such models are the blueprint for understanding the current process and for designing new versions of processes. They also set the stage for the requirements for any information systems and applications that need to be created or adapted. If models are incomplete and incorrect, follow-on components cannot be created correctly. In this question, you will learn standard notation for creating process documentation.

Learning this standard notation is important to you because, as a business professional, you may be involved in modeling projects. Unless you become a business or systems analyst, you are unlikely to lead such a project, but as a user, you may be asked to review and approve models and you may participate as a representative of your department or area of expertise in the creation of new models.

Need for Standard for Business Processing Notation

As stated, we define a *business process* as a network of activities, repositories, roles, resources, and flows that interact to accomplish a business function. This definition is commonly accepted, but unfortunately dozens of other definitions are used by other authors, industry analysts, and software products. For example, IBM, a key leader in business process management, has a product called WebSphere Business Modeler that uses a different set of terms. It has activities and resources, but it uses the term *repository* more broadly than we do, and it uses the term *business item* for *data flow*. Other business-modeling software products use still other definitions and terms. These differences and inconsistencies can be problematic, especially when two different organizations with two different sets of definitions must work together.

Accordingly, a software-industry standards organization called the **Object Management Group (OMG)** created a standard set of terms and graphical notations for documenting business processes. That standard, called **Business Process Modeling Notation (BPMN)**, is documented at *www.bpmn.org*. A complete description of BPMN is beyond the scope of this text. However, the basic symbols are easy to understand, and they work naturally with our definition of business process. Hence, we will use the BPMN symbols in the illustrations in the chapter. All of the diagrams in this chapter were drawn using Microsoft Visio, which includes several BPMN symbol templates. Figure 10-6 summarizes the basic BPMN symbols.

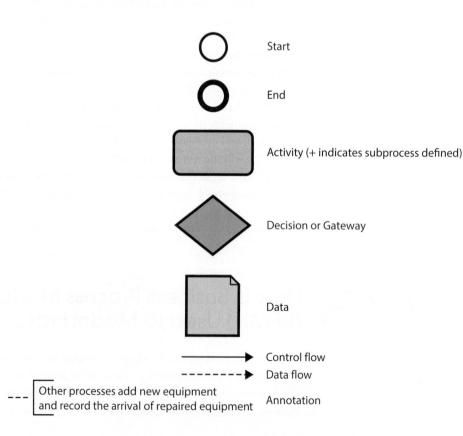

Figure 10-6
Business Process Management
Notation (BPMN) Symbols

Documenting the As-Is Business Order Process

Figure 10-7 shows the as-is, or existing, order process introduced in Figure 10-1. First, note that this process is a model, an abstraction that shows the essential elements of the process but omits many details. If it were not an abstraction, the model would be as large as the business itself. This diagram is shown in **swim-lane layout**. In this format, each role in the business process is given its own swim lane. In Figure 10-7, there are five roles, hence five swim lanes. All activities for a given role are shown in that role's swim lane. Swim-lane layout simplifies the process diagram and draws attention to interactions among components of the diagram.

Figure 10-7
Existing Order
Process

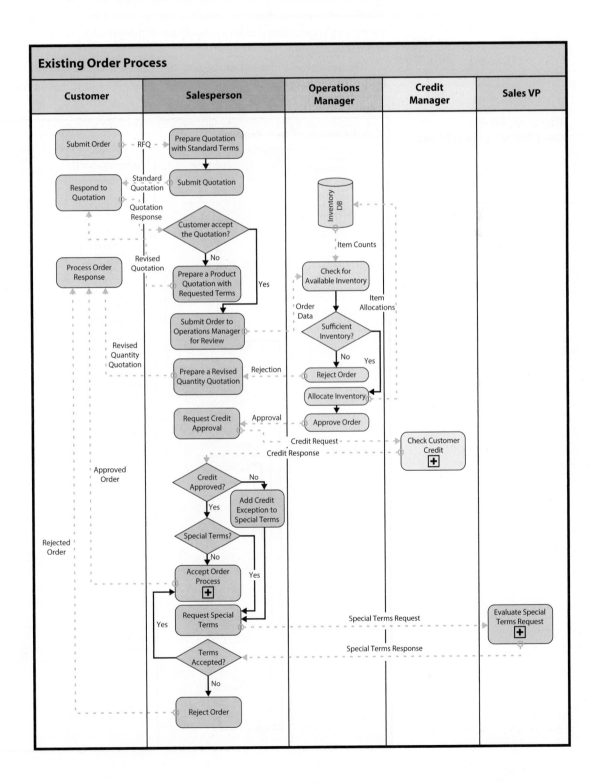

Two kinds of arrows are shown. Dotted arrows depict the flow of messages and data flows. Solid arrows depict the flow or sequence of the activities in the process. Some sequence flows have data associated with them as well. According to Figure 10-7, the customer sends an RFQ (request for quotation) to a salesperson (dotted arrow). That salesperson prepares a quotation in the first activity and then (solid arrow) submits the quotation back to the customer. You can follow the rest of the process in Figure 10-7. Allocate inventory means that if the items are available, they are allocated to the customer so that they will not be sold to someone else.

Diamonds represent decisions and usually contain a question that can be answered with yes or no. Process arrows labeled Yes and No exit two of the points of the diamond. Three of the activities in the as-is diagram contain a square with a plus (+) sign. This notation means that the activity is considered to be a subprocess of this process and that it is defined in greater detail in another diagram.

One of these three subprocesses, the Check Customer Credit subprocess, is shown in Figure 10-8. Note the role named *Customer Credit IS* in this subprocess. In fact, this role is

Figure 10-8
Check Customer Credit Process

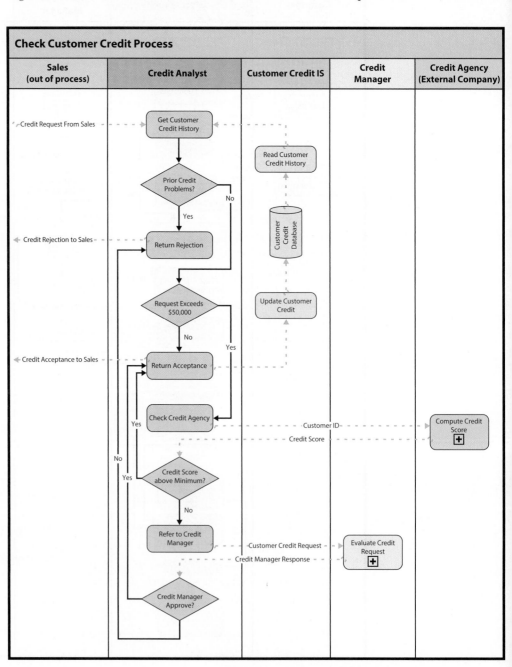

performed entirely by an information system, although we cannot determine that fact from this diagram. Again, each role is fulfilled by some set of resources, either people or information systems or both.

Once the as-is model has been documented, that model can then be analyzed for problems or for improvement opportunities. For example, the process shown in Figure 10-7 has a serious problem. Before you continue, examine these figures and see if you can determine what they are.

The problem involves allocations. The Operations Manager role allocates inventory to the orders as they are processed, and the Credit Manager role allocates credit to the customer of orders in process. These allocations are correct as long as the order is accepted. However, if the order is rejected, these allocations are not freed. Thus, inventory is allocated that will not be ordered, and credit is extended for orders that will not be processed.

One fix (several are possible) is to define an independent process for Reject Order (in Figure 10-7 that would mean placing a box with a + in the Reject Order activity) and then designing the Reject Order subprocess to free allocations. Creating such a diagram is left as exercise 3 in Using Your Knowledge (page 419).

Sometimes, BPMN diagrams are used to define process alternatives for discussion and evaluation. Another use is to document processes for employee training, and yet another use is to provide process requirements documentation for systems and application development. As a business professional, you may be asked to interpret and approve BPMN diagrams for any of these purposes.

What Are the Phases in the Systems Development Life Cycle (SDLC)?

The **systems development life cycle (SDLC)** is the traditional process used to develop information systems and applications. The IT industry developed the SDLC in the "school of hard knocks." Many early projects met with disaster, and companies and systems developers sifted through the ashes of those disasters to determine what went wrong. By the 1970s, most seasoned project managers agreed on the basic tasks that need to be performed to successfully build and maintain information systems. These basic tasks are combined into phases of systems development. As stated, SDLC rose to prominence when the U.S. Department of Defense required it on government contracts.

Different authors and organizations package the tasks into different numbers of phases. Some organizations use an eight-phase process, others use a seven-phase process, and still others use a five-phase process. In this book, we will use the following five-phase process:

1. Define System
2. Determine Requirements
3. Design System Components
4. Implement System
5. Maintain System

Figure 10-9 shows how these phases are related. Development begins when a business-planning process identifies a need for a new system. This need may come from a BPM design activity, or it might come from some other business planning process. For now, suppose that management has determined, in some way, that the organization can best accomplish its goals and objectives by constructing a new information system.

For the PRIDE system, Dr. Flores had the initial idea to connect his practice to patient exercise data in the cloud. With that idea, he hired Maggie Jensen, a business analyst, to manage the development of a prototype system to test the desirability of the system to his patients and his practice. At this point, he wants to start a systems development process to create that prototype.

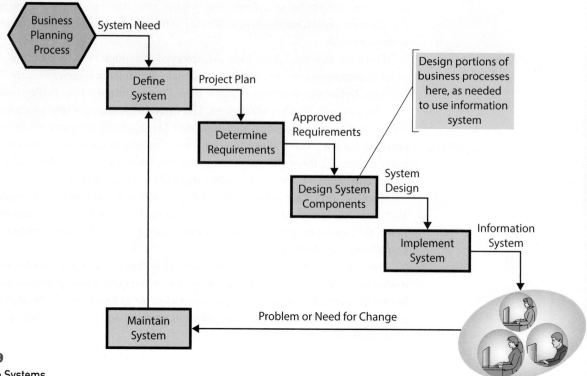

Figure 10-9
Five Phases of the Systems
Development Life Cycle (SDLC)

Developers in the first SDLC phase—system definition—use management's statement of the system needs in order to begin to define the new system (for PRIDE, this statement is based on experience with the prototype). The resulting project plan is the input to the second phase—**requirements analysis**. Here, developers identify the particular features and functions of the new system. The output of that phase is a set of approved user requirements, which become the primary input used to design system components. In phase 4, developers implement, test, and install the new system.

Over time, users will find errors, mistakes, and problems. They will also develop new requirements. The description of fixes and new requirements is input into a system maintenance phase. The maintenance phase starts the process all over again, which is why the process is considered a cycle.

In the following sections, we will consider each phase of the SDLC in more detail.

Define the System

In response to the need for the new system, the organization will assign a few employees, possibly on a part-time basis, to define the new system, assess its feasibility, and plan the project. In a large organization, someone from the IS department leads the initial team, but the members of that initial team are both users and IS professionals. For small organizations, and for startups like PRIDE, the team will be led by an outside consultant such as Maggie.

Define System Goals and Scope

As Figure 10-10 shows, the first step is to define the goals and scope of the new information system. Information systems exist to facilitate an organization's competitive strategy by supporting business processes or by improving decision making. At this step, the development team defines the goal and purpose of the new system in terms of these reasons.

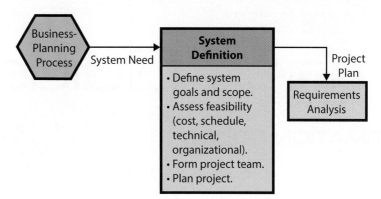

Figure 10-10
SDLC: System Definition Phase

Consider PRIDE. The goal of the system is to integrate patient exercise data and make it available in suitable reports to PRIDE participants. But who are they? In its ultimate form, Dr. Flores believes PRIDE can integrate activities of patients, healthcare professionals, health clubs, insurance companies, and employers. But how many of these organizations need to be involved in the first implementation? The team may choose to limit the scope just to patients and medical practices or perhaps to include health clubs as well.

In other systems, the scope might be defined by specifying the users, or the business processes, or the plants, offices, and factories that will be involved.

Assess Feasibility

Once we have defined the project's goals and scope, the next step is to assess feasibility. This step answers the question, "Does this project make sense?" The aim here is to eliminate obviously nonsensible projects before forming a project development team and investing significant labor.

Feasibility has four dimensions: *cost, schedule, technical*, and *organizational*. Because IS development projects are difficult to budget and schedule, cost and schedule feasibility can be only an approximate, back-of-the-envelope analysis. The purpose is to eliminate any obviously infeasible ideas as soon as possible.

Cost feasibility involves an assessment of the cost of the project. For PRIDE, this is a difficult assessment (see Case Study 10, pages 421–422). Clearly, it depends on the scope of the project. Even given an understanding of scope, however, as an inter-enterprise system, PRIDE involves numerous different parties with different goals and objectives. What requirements will they deem essential that Dr. Flores and Maggie don't yet know? Will they have a native application or a thin-client application? If the former, how many mobile devices will they need to support? How many users will there be, and how much data will they generate to be hosted in the cloud?

For a discussion of the ethical issues relating to cost estimates, see the Ethics Guide on pages 390–391.

At this point, all the team can do is to make rough estimates. Certainly, any potential investor will scrutinize these estimates, so Maggie will need to do more than guess. Still, at this point, the team doesn't need a precise total; they simply need a range of costs that are close.

Like cost feasibility, **schedule feasibility** is difficult to determine because it is hard to estimate the time it will take to build the system. However, if Maggie determines that it will take, say, no less than 6 months to develop the system and put it into operation, Dr. Flores and his partners can then decide if they can accept that minimum schedule. At this stage of the project, the organization should not rely on either cost or schedule estimates; the purpose of these estimates is simply to rule out any obviously unacceptable projects.

Technical feasibility refers to whether existing information technology is likely to be able to meet the needs of the new system. Because PRIDE uses new technology (the cloud) and innovative mobile devices (exercise equipment and other devices), Dr. Flores decided to build a prototype to test feasibility. As you learned at the start of this chapter, the results indicate that the system is technically feasible.

Ethics Guide

ESTIMATION ETHICS

A *buy-in* **occurs** when a company agrees to produce a system or product for less money than it knows the project will require. An example at PRIDE would be if Maggie agreed to build the system for, say, $50,000, when good estimating techniques indicate it would take $75,000. If the contract for the system or product is written for "time and materials," PRIDE's investors will ultimately pay the $75,000 for the finished system. Or the project will fail once the true cost is known. If the contract for the system or product is written for a fixed cost, then the developer will absorb the extra costs. Maggie would use the latter strategy if the contract opens up other business opportunities that are worth the $25,000 loss.

Buy-ins always involve deceit. Most would agree that buying-in on a time-and-materials project, planning to stick the customer with the full cost later, is wrong. Opinions on buying-in on a fixed-priced contract vary. You know you'll take a loss, but why? To build intellectual capital for sale elsewhere? For a favor down the road? Or for some other unethical reason?

What about in-house projects? Do the ethics change if an in-house development team is building a system for use in-house? If team members know there is only $50,000 in the budget, should they start the project if they believe that its true cost is $75,000? If they do start, at some point senior management will either have to admit a mistake and cancel the project with a loss or find the additional $25,000. Project sponsors can state all sorts of reasons for such buy-ins. For example, "I know the company needs this system. If management doesn't realize it and fund it appropriately, then we'll just force their hand."

These issues become even stickier if team members disagree about how much the project will cost. Suppose one faction of the team believes the project will cost $35,000, another faction estimates $50,000, and a third thinks $65,000. Can the project sponsors justify taking the average? Or should they describe the range of estimates?

Other buy-ins are more subtle. Suppose you are a project manager of an exciting new project that is possibly a career-maker for you. You are incredibly busy, working 6 days a week and long hours each day. Your team has developed an estimate for $50,000 for the project. A little voice in the back of your mind says that maybe not all costs for every aspect of the project are included in that estimate. You mean to follow up on that thought, but

Source: Olly/Fotolia

more pressing matters in your schedule take precedence. Soon you find yourself in front of management, presenting the $50,000 estimate. You probably should have found the time to investigate the estimate, but you didn't. Is there an ethical issue here?

Or suppose you approach a more senior manager with your dilemma. "I think there may be other costs, but I know that $50,000 is all we've got. What should I do?" Suppose the senior manager says something like, "Well, let's go forward. You don't know of anything else, and we can always find more budget elsewhere if we have to." How do you respond?

You can buy-in on schedule as well as cost. If the marketing department says, "We have to have the new product for the trade show," do you agree, even if you know it's highly unlikely that you'll make the deadline? What if marketing says, "If we don't have it by then, we should just cancel the project." Suppose it's not impossible to make that schedule; it's just highly unlikely. How do you respond?

 # DISCUSSION QUESTIONS

1. Assess the ethics of buying-in on a cost-and-materials project from both the perspective of the categorical imperative (pages 20–21) and utilitarianism (pages 54–55).
2. Are there circumstances in which buying-in on a cost-and-materials contract could be illegal? If so, state them.
3. Suppose you learn through the grapevine that your opponents in a competitive bid are buying-in on a time-and-materials contract. Does this change your answer to question 1?
4. Suppose you are a project manager who is preparing a request for a proposal on a cost-and-materials systems development project. What can you do to prevent buy-ins?
5. Under what circumstances do you think buying-in on a fixed-price contract is ethical? Use either the categorical imperative or utilitarian perspective or both. What are the dangers of this strategy?
6. Explain why in-house development projects are always time-and-materials projects.

7. Given your answer to question 5, assess the ethics of buying-in on an in-house project from the perspective of the categorical imperative and utilitarianism. Are there circumstances that will change your ethical assessment? If so, state what they are and why.
8. Suppose you ask a senior manager for advice as described in the guide. Does the manager's response absolve you of ethical responsibility? Suppose you ask the manager and then do not follow her guidance. What problems could result?
9. Explain how you can buy-in on schedule as well as costs.
10. For an in-house project, what is an ethical response to the marketing manager who says the project should be canceled if it will not be ready for the trade show? In your answer, suppose that you disagree with this opinion because you know the system has value regardless of whether it is done by the trade show.

Finally, **organizational feasibility** concerns whether the new system fits within the organization's customs, culture, charter, or legal requirements. For example, will doctors be willing to use PRIDE? Will they see it as an incursion into their practice? Even more, the PRIDE users who most need the system are sick, older people who may be technology-phobic. Dr. Flores needed the prototype to demonstrate that it would work with this audience.

Form a Project Team

If the defined project is determined to be feasible, the next step is to form the project team. Normally the team consists of both IS professionals and user representatives. The project manager and IS professionals can be in-house personnel or outside contractors. In Chapter 11, we will describe various means of obtaining IT personnel using outside sources and the benefits and risks of outsourcing.

Typical personnel on a development team are a manager (or managers for larger projects), business analysts, systems analysts, programmers, software testers, and users.

Systems analysts are closer to IT and are a bit more technical, though, as stated, there is considerable overlap in the duties and responsibilities of business and systems analysts. Both are active throughout the systems development process and play a key role in moving the project through it. Business analysts work more with managers and executives; systems analysts integrate the work of the programmers, testers, and users. Depending on the nature of the project, the team may also include hardware and communications specialists, database designers and administrators, and other IT specialists.

The team composition changes over time. During requirements definition, the team will be heavy with business and systems analysts. During design and implementation, it will be heavy with programmers, testers, and database designers. During integrated testing and conversion, the team will be augmented with testers and business users.

User involvement is critical throughout the system development process. Depending on the size and nature of the project, users are assigned to the project either full or part time. Sometimes users are assigned to review and oversight committees that meet periodically, especially at the completion of project phases and other milestones. Users are involved in many different ways. *The important point is for users to have active involvement and to take ownership of the project throughout the entire development process.*

The first major task for the assembled team is to plan the project. Team members specify tasks to be accomplished, assign personnel, determine task dependencies, and set schedules.

Determine Requirements

Determining the system's requirements is the most important phase in the systems development process. If the requirements are wrong, the system will be wrong. If the requirements are determined completely and correctly, then design and implementation will be easier and more likely to result in success.

Sources of Requirements

Examples of requirements are the contents and the format of Web pages and the functions of buttons on those pages, or the structure and content of a report, or the fields and menu choices in a data entry form. Requirements include not only what is to be produced, but also how frequently and how fast it is to be done. Some requirements specify the volume of data to be stored and processed.

If you take a course in systems analysis and design, you will spend weeks on techniques for determining requirements. Here we will just summarize that process. Typically, systems analysts interview users and record the results in some consistent manner. Good interviewing skills are crucial; users are notorious for being unable to describe what they want and need. Users also tend to focus on the tasks they are performing at the time of the interview. Tasks performed at the end of the quarter or end of the year are forgotten if the interview takes place mid-quarter. Seasoned and experienced systems analysts know how to conduct interviews to bring such requirements to light.

As listed in Figure 10-11, sources of requirements include existing systems as well as the Web pages, forms, reports, queries, and application features and functions desired in the new system. Security is another important category of requirements.

If the new system involves a new database or substantial changes to an existing database, then the development team will create a data model. As you learned in Chapter 5, that model must reflect the users' perspective on their business and business activities. Thus, the data model is constructed on the basis of user interviews and must be validated by those users.

Sometimes, the requirements determination is so focused on the software and data components that other components are forgotten. Experienced project managers ensure consideration of requirements for all five IS components, not just for software and data. Regarding hardware, the team might ask: Are there special needs or restrictions on hardware? Is there an organizational standard governing what kinds of hardware may or may not be used? Must the new system use existing hardware? What requirements are there for communications and network hardware?

Similarly, the team should consider requirements for procedures and personnel: Do accounting controls require procedures that separate duties and authorities? Are there restrictions that some actions can be taken only by certain departments or specific personnel? Are there policy requirements or union rules that restrict activities to certain categories of employees? Will the system need to interface with information systems from other companies and organizations? In short, requirements for all of the components of the new information system need to be considered.

These questions are examples of the kinds of questions that must be asked and answered during requirements analysis.

Role of a Prototype

Because requirements are difficult to specify, building a working prototype, as was done for the PRIDE system, can be quite beneficial. Whereas future systems users often struggle to understand and relate to requirements expressed as word descriptions and sketches, working with a prototype provides direct experience. As they work with a prototype, users will assess usability and remember features and functions they have forgotten to mention. Additionally, prototypes provide evidence to assess the system's technical and organizational feasibility. Further, prototypes create data that can be used to estimate both development and operational costs.

The Guide on pages 416–417 states the challenges and difficulties with project estimation in the real world.

To be useful, a prototype needs to work; mock-ups of forms and reports, while helpful, will not generate the benefits just described. The prototype needs to put the user into the experience of employing the system to do his or her tasks.

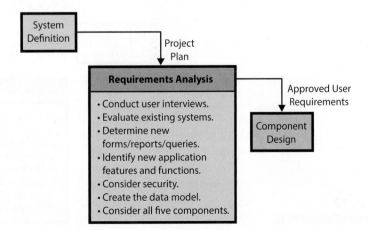

Figure 10-11

SDLC: Requirements Analysis Phase

Prototypes can be expensive to create; however, this expense is often justified not only for the greater clarity and completeness of requirements, but also because parts of the prototype can often be reused in the operational system. Much of the PRIDE code that generated the smartphone display at the start of Chapter 9 (page 323) will be reused in the operational system.

Unfortunately, systems developers face a dilemma when funding prototypes; the cost of the prototype occurs early in the process, sometimes well before full project funding is available. A common complaint is, "We need the prototype to get the funds, and we need the funds to get the prototype." Unfortunately, no uniform solution to this dilemma exists, except applying experience guided by intuition. Again we see the need for nonroutine problem-solving skills.

Approve Requirements

Once the requirements have been specified, the users must review and approve them before the project continues. The easiest and cheapest time to alter the information system is in the requirements phase. Changing a requirement at this stage is simply a matter of changing a description. Changing a requirement in the implementation phase may require weeks of reworking applications components and the database structure.

Design System Components

Each of the five components is designed in this stage. Typically, the team designs each component by developing alternatives, evaluating each of those alternatives against the requirements and then selecting from among those alternatives. Accurate requirements are critical here; if they are incomplete or wrong, then they will be poor guides for evaluation.

Figure 10-12 shows that design tasks pertain to each of the five IS components. For hardware, the team determines specifications for what the system will need. (The team is not designing hardware in the sense of building a CPU or a disk drive.) Program design depends on the source of the programs. For off-the-shelf software, the team must determine candidate products and evaluate them against the requirements. For off-the-shelf with alteration programs, the team identifies products to be acquired off-the-shelf and then determines the alterations required. For custom-developed programs, the team produces design documentation for writing program code.

If the project includes constructing a database, then during this phase database designers convert the data model to a database design using techniques such as those described in Chapter 5. If the project involves off-the-shelf programs, then little database design needs to be done; the programs will have been coded to work with a preexisting database design.

Procedure design differs, depending on whether the project is part of a BPM process or part of a systems development process. If the former, then business processes will already be designed, and all that is needed is to create procedures for using the application. If the latter, then

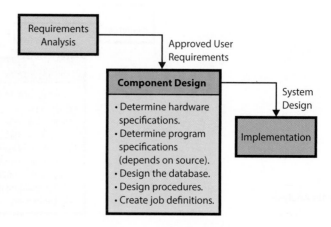

Figure 10-12
SDLC: Component Design Phase

procedures for using the system need to be developed, and it is possible that business processes that surround the system will be needed as well.

With regard to people, design involves developing job descriptions for the various roles. These descriptions will detail responsibilities, skills needed, training required, and so forth.

System Implementation

The term **implementation** has two meanings for us. It could mean to implement the information systems components only, or it could mean to implement the information system and the business processes that use the system. As you read the following task descriptions, keep in mind that the tasks can apply to both interpretations of implementation. Tasks in the implementation phase are to build and test system components and to convert users to the new system and possibly new business processes (see Figure 10-13).

Testing

Developers construct each of the components independently. They obtain, install, and test hardware. They license and install off-the-shelf programs; they write adaptations and custom programs as necessary. They construct a database and fill it with data. They document, review, and test procedures, and they create training programs. Finally, the organization hires and trains needed personnel. Once each component has been tested independently, the entire system is tested as an integrated whole.

Testing is important, time consuming, and expensive. A **test plan**, which is a formal description of the system's response to use and misuse scenarios, is written. Professional test engineers, called product quality assurance (PQA) test engineers, are hired for this task. Often, teams of these engineers are augmented by users as well.

System Conversion

Once the system has passed testing, the organization installs the new system. The term **system conversion** is often used for this activity because it implies the process of *converting* business activity from the old system to the new. Again, conversion can be to the new system only, or it can be to the new system, including new business processes.

Four types of conversion are possible: pilot, phased, parallel, and plunge. Any of the first three can be effective. In most cases, companies should avoid "taking the plunge"!

With **pilot installation**, the organization implements the entire system/business processes on a limited portion of the business. An example would be for PRIDE to use the new system for just a few patients. The advantage of pilot implementation is that if the system fails, the failure is contained within a limited boundary.

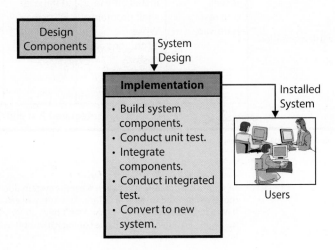

Figure 10-13
SDLC: Implementation Phase

As the name implies, with **phased installation** the new system/business processes are installed in phases across the organization(s). Once a given piece works, then the organization installs and tests another piece of the system, until the entire system has been installed. Some systems are so tightly integrated that they cannot be installed in phased pieces. Such systems must be installed using one of the other techniques.

With **parallel installation**, the new system/business processes run parallel with the old one until the new system is tested and fully operational. Parallel installation is expensive because the organization incurs the costs of running both the existing and the new system/business processes. Users must work double-time, if you will, to run both systems. Then considerable work is needed to reconcile the results of the new with the old.

The final style of conversion is **plunge installation** (sometimes called *direct installation*). With it, the organization shuts off the old system/business processes and starts the new one. If the new system/business processes fail, the organization is in trouble: Nothing can be done until either the new system/business processes are fixed or the old ones are reinstalled. Because of the risk, organizations should avoid this conversion style if possible. The one exception is if the new system is providing a new capability that will not disrupt the operation of the organization if it fails.

Figure 10-14 summarizes the tasks for each of the five components during the design and implementation phases. Use this figure to test your knowledge of the tasks in each phase.

Maintain System

With regard to information systems, **maintenance** is a misnomer; the work done during this phase is either to *fix* the system so that it works correctly or to *adapt* it to changes in requirements.

Figure 10-15 shows tasks during the maintenance phase. First, there needs to be a means for tracking both failures[1] and requests for enhancements to meet new requirements. For small

Figure 10-14
Design and Implementation
for the Five Components

	Hardware	Software	Data	Procedures	People	
Design	Determine hardware specifications.	Select off-the-shelf programs. Design alterations and custom programs as necessary.	Design database and related structures.	Design user and operations procedures.	Develop user and operations job descriptions.	
Implementation	Obtain, install, and test hardware.	License and install off-the-shelf programs. Write alterations and custom programs. Test programs.	Create database. Fill with data. Test data.	Document procedures. Create training programs. Review and test procedures.	Hire and train personnel.	**Unit test each component**
	Integrated Test and Conversion					

Note: Cells shaded brown represent software development.

---

[1]A *failure* is a difference between what the system does and what it is supposed to do. Sometimes you will hear the term *bug* used instead of failure. As a future user, call failures *failures* because that's what they are. Don't have a *bugs list*; have a *failures list*. Don't have an *unresolved bug*; have an *unresolved failure*. A few months of managing an organization that is coping with a serious failure will show you the importance of this difference in terms.

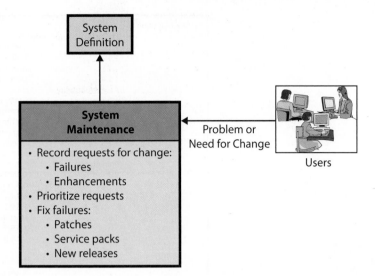

Figure 10-15
SDLC System Maintenance
Phase

systems, organizations can track failures and enhancements using word processing documents. As systems become larger, however, and as the number of failure and enhancement requests increases, many organizations find it necessary to develop a tracking database. Such a database contains a description of the failure or enhancement. It also records who reported the problem, who will make the fix or enhancement, what the status of that work is, and whether the fix or enhancement has been tested and verified by the originator.

Typically, IS personnel prioritize system problems according to their severity. They fix high-priority items as soon as possible, and they fix low-priority items as time and resources become available.

Because an enhancement is an adaptation to new requirements, developers usually prioritize enhancement requests separate from failures. The decision to make an enhancement includes a business decision that the enhancement will generate an acceptable rate of return.

Q5 What Are the Keys for Successful SDLC Projects?

SDLC projects are difficult to manage. In this question we will consider five keys to success:

- Create a work breakdown structure.
- Estimate time and costs.
- Create a project plan.
- Adjust the plan via trade-offs.
- Manage development challenges.

Create a Work Breakdown Structure

The key strategy for SDLC projects is to divide and conquer. Most such projects are too large, too complicated, and the duration too long to attempt to manage them as one piece. Instead, successful project managers break the project into smaller and smaller tasks until each task is small enough to estimate and to manage. Every task should culminate in one or more results called **deliverables**. Examples of deliverables are documents, designs, prototypes, data models, database designs, working data entry screens, and the like. Without a defined deliverable, it is impossible to know if the task was accomplished.

Tasks are interrelated, and to prevent them from becoming a confusing morass, project teams create a **work breakdown structure (WBS)**, which is a hierarchy of the tasks required

System definition			
1.1	Define goals and scope		
	1.1.1	Define goals	
	1.1.2	Define system boundaries	
	1.1.3	Review results	
	1.1.4	Document results	
1.2	Assess feasibility		
	1.2.1	Cost	
	1.2.2	Schedule	
	1.2.3	Technical	
	1.2.4	Organizational	
	1.2.5	Document feasibility	
	1.2.6	Management review and go/no-go decision	
1.3	Plan project		
	1.3.1	Establish milestones	
	1.3.2	Create WBS	
		1.3.2.1	Levels 1 and 2
		1.3.2.2	Levels 3+
	1.3.3	Document WBS	
		1.3.3.1	Create WBS baseline
		1.3.3.2	Input to Project
	1.3.4	Determine resource requirements	
		1.3.4.1	Personnel
		1.3.4.2	Computing
		1.3.4.3	Office space
		1.3.4.4	Travel and Meeting Expense
	1.3.5	Management review	
		1.3.5.1	Prepare presentation
		1.3.5.2	Prepare background documents
		1.3.5.3	Give presentation
		1.3.5.4	Incorporate feedback into plan
		1.3.5.5	Approve project
1.4	Form project team		
	1.4.1	Meet with HR	
	1.4.2	Meet with IT Director	
	1.4.3	Develop job descriptions	
	1.4.4	Meet with available personnel	
	1.4.5	Hire personnel	

Figure 10-16
Example Work Breakdown
Structure (WBS)

to complete a project. The WBS for a large project is huge; it might entail hundreds or even thousands of tasks. Figure 10-16 shows the WBS for the system definition phase for a typical IS project.

In Figure 10-16, the overall task, *System definition,* is divided into *Define goals and scope, Assess feasibility, Plan project,* and *Form project team.* Each of those tasks is broken into smaller tasks until the work has been divided into small tasks that can be managed and estimated.

Estimate Time and Costs

As stated, it is exceedingly difficult to determine duration and labor requirements for many development tasks. Fred Brooks[2] defined software as "logical poetry." Like poetry, software is not made of wood or metal or plastic; it is pure thought-stuff. Some years ago, when I pressed a seasoned software developer for a schedule, he responded by asking me, "What would Shakespeare have said if someone asked him how long it would take him to write *Hamlet*?" Another popular rejoinder is, "What would a fisherman say if you ask him how long it will take to catch three fish?" He doesn't know, and neither do I."

Organizations take a variety of approaches to this challenge. One is to avoid scheduling problems altogether and never develop systems and software in-house. Instead, they license packages, such as ERP systems, that include both business processes and information systems components. As stated in Chapter 7, even if the vendor provides workable processes, those processes will need to be integrated into the business. However, the schedule risk of integration activities is far less than those for developing processes, programs, databases, and other components.

---

[2]Fred Brooks was a successful executive at IBM in the 1960s. After retiring from IBM, he authored a classic book on IT project management called *The Mythical Man-Month.* Published by Addison-Wesley in 1975, the book is still pertinent today and should be read by every IS manager. It's informative and quite enjoyable to read as well.

But what if no suitable package exists? In this case, companies can admit the impossibility of scheduling a date for the completion of the entire system and take the best result they can get. Only the loosest commitments are made regarding the date of complete and final system functionality. Project sponsors dislike this approach because they feel like they are signing a blank check, and in fact, they are. But this approach doesn't treat fictional estimates and schedules as if they were real, which may be the only other alternative.

The third approach is to attempt to schedule the development project in spite of all the difficulties. Several different estimation techniques can be used. If the project is similar to a past project, the schedule data from that past project can be used for planning. When such similar past projects exist, this technique can produce quality schedule estimates. If there is no such past project, managers must make the best estimates they can. For computer coding, some managers estimate the number of lines of code that will need to be written and apply industry or company averages to estimate the time required. Other coding estimation techniques exist; visit *http://sunset.usc.edu/csse/research/COCOMOII/cocomo_main.html*. Of course, lines of code and other advanced techniques estimate schedules only for software components. The schedules for processes, procedures, databases, and the other components must be estimated using different methods.

Create a Project Plan

A project plan is a list of WBS tasks, arranged to account for task dependencies, with durations and resources applied. Some tasks cannot be started or finished until other tasks are completed. You can't, for example, put electrical wires in a house until you've built the walls. You can define task dependencies in planning software such as Microsoft Project, and it will arrange the plan accordingly.

Given dependencies, estimates for task duration and resource requirements are then applied to the WBS to form a project plan. Figure 10-17 shows the WBS as input to Microsoft Project, with task dependencies and durations defined. The display on the right, called a **Gantt chart**, shows tasks, dates, and dependencies.

The user has entered all of the tasks from the WBS and has assigned each task a duration. She has also specified task dependencies, although the means she used are beyond our

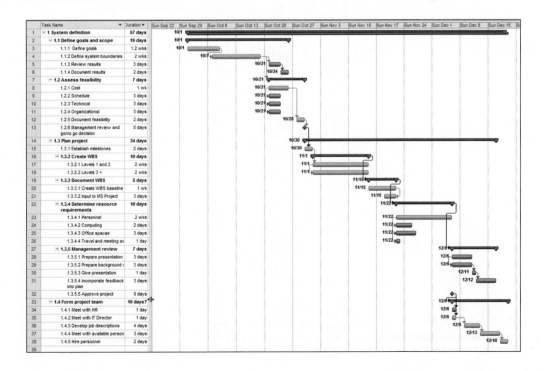

Figure 10-17
Gantt Chart of the WBS for the Definition Phase of a Project

discussion. The two red arrows emerging from task 4, *Define system boundaries,* indicate that neither the *Review results* task nor the *Assess feasibility* task can begin until *Define system boundaries* is completed. Other task dependencies are also shown; you can learn about them in a project management class.

The **critical path** is the sequence of activities that determine the earliest date by which the project can be completed. Reflect for a moment on that statement: The *earliest date* is the date determined by considering the *longest path* through the network of activities. Paying attention to task dependencies, the planner will compress the tasks as much as possible. Those tasks that cannot be further compressed lie on the critical path. Microsoft Project and other project-planning applications can readily identify critical path tasks.

Figure 10-17 shows the tasks on the critical path in red. Consider the first part of the WBS. The project planner specified that task 4 cannot begin until 2 days before task 3 ends. (That's the meaning of the red arrow emerging from task 3.) Neither task 5 nor task 8 can begin until task 4 is completed. Task 8 will take longer than tasks 5 and 6, and so task 8—not tasks 5 or 6—is on the critical path. Thus, the critical path to this point is tasks 3, 4, and 8. You can trace the critical path through the rest of the WBS by following the tasks shown in red, though the entire WBS and critical path are not shown.

Using Microsoft Project or a similar product, it is possible to assign personnel to tasks and to stipulate the percentage of time that each person devotes to a task. Figure 10-18 shows a Gantt chart for which this has been done. The notation means that Eleanore works only 25 percent of the time on task 3; Lynda and Richard work full time. Additionally, one can assign costs to personnel and compute a labor budget for each task and for the overall WBS. One can assign resources to tasks and use Microsoft Project to detect and prevent two tasks from using the same resources. Resource costs can be assigned and summed as well.

Managers can use the critical path to perform critical path analysis. First, note that if a task is on the critical path, and if that task runs late, the project will be late. Hence, tasks on the critical path cannot be allowed to run late if the project is to be delivered on time. Second, tasks not on the critical path can run late to the point at which they would become part of the critical path. Hence, up to a point, resources can be taken from noncritical path tasks to shorten tasks

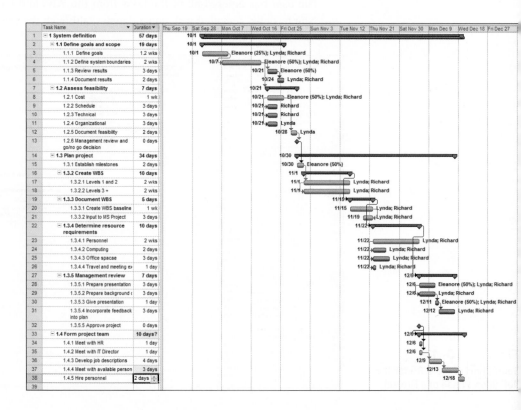

Figure 10-18

Gantt Chart with Resources (People) Assigned

on the critical path. **Critical path analysis** is the process by which project managers compress the schedule by moving resources, typically people, from noncritical path tasks onto critical path tasks.

Adjust Plan via Trade-offs

The project plan for the entire project results in a finish date and a total cost. During my career, I've been involved in about a dozen major development projects, and in every one the first response to a completed project plan has been, "Good heavens! No way! We can't wait that long or pay that much!" And my experience is not unusual.

Thus, the first response to a project plan is to attempt to reduce time and costs. Reductions can be made, but not out of thin air. An old adage in planning development projects is, "Believe your first number." Believe what you have estimated before your desires and wishes cloud your judgment.

So, how can schedules and costs be responsibly reduced? By considering trade-offs. A **trade-off** is a balancing of three critical factors: requirements, cost, and time. To understand this balancing challenge, consider the construction of something relatively simple—say, a piece of jewelry, such as a necklace, or the deck on the side of a house. The more elaborate the necklace or the deck, the more time it will take. The less elaborate, the less time it will take. Further, if we embellish the necklace with diamonds and precious gems, it will cost more. Similarly, if we construct the deck from old crates, it will be cheaper than if we construct it of clear-grained, prime Port Orford cedar.

We can summarize this situation as shown in Figure 10-19. We can *trade off* requirements against time and against cost. If we make the necklace simpler, it will take less time. If we eliminate the diamonds and gems, it will be cheaper. The same trade-offs exist in the construction of anything: houses, buildings, ships, furniture, *and* information systems.

The relationship between time and cost is more complicated. Normally, we can reduce time by increasing cost *only to a point.* For example, we can reduce the time it takes to produce a deck by hiring more laborers. At some point, however, there will be so many laborers working on the deck that they will get in one another's way, and the time to finish the deck

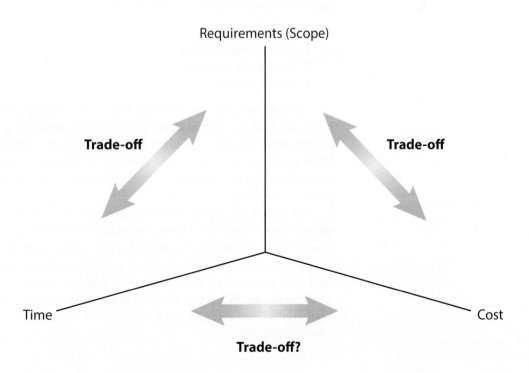

Figure 10-19
Primary Drivers of Systems
Development

will actually increase. At some point, adding more people creates **diseconomies of scale**, the situation that occurs when adding more resources creates inefficiencies. A famous adage in the software industry is **Brooks' Law** (named for the Fred Brooks discussed earlier), which states that adding more people to a late project makes it later. This occurs, in part, because new team members need to be trained by existing team members, who must be taken off productive tasks.

In some projects, we can reduce costs by increasing time. If, for example, we are required to pay laborers time-and-a-half for overtime, we can reduce costs by eliminating overtime. If finishing the deck—by, say, Friday—requires overtime, then it may be cheaper to avoid overtime by completing the deck sometime next week. This trade-off is not always true, however. Extending the project interval means that we need to pay labor and overhead for a longer period; thus, adding more time can also increase costs.

Consider how these trade-offs pertain to information systems. We specify a set of requirements for the new information system, and we schedule labor over a period of time. Suppose the initial schedule indicates the system will be finished in 3 years. If business requirements necessitate the project be finished in 2 years, we must shorten the schedule. We can proceed in two ways: reduce the requirements or add labor. For the former, we eliminate functions and features. For the latter, we hire more staff or contract with other vendors for development services. Deciding which course to take will be difficult and risky.

Using trade-offs, the WBS plan can be modified to shorten schedules or reduce costs. But they cannot be reduced by management fiat.

Manage Development Challenges

Given the project plan and management's endorsement and approval, the next stage is to do it. The final WBS plan is denoted as the **baseline WBS**. This baseline shows the planned tasks, dependencies, durations, and resource assignments. As the project proceeds, project managers can input actual dates, labor hours, and resource costs. At any point in time, planning applications can be used to determine whether the project is ahead of or behind schedule and how the actual project costs compare to baseline costs.

However, nothing ever goes according to plan, and the larger the project and the longer the development interval, the more things will violate the plan. Four critical factors need to be considered:

1. Coordination
2. Diseconomies of scale
3. Configuration control
4. Unexpected events

Development projects, especially large-scale projects, are usually organized into a variety of development groups that work independently. Coordinating the work of these independent groups can be difficult, particularly if the groups reside in different geographic locations or different countries. An accurate and complete WBS facilitates coordination, but no project ever proceeds exactly in accordance with the WBS. Delays occur, and unknown or unexpected dependencies develop among tasks.

The coordination problem is increased because software, as stated, is just thought-stuff. When constructing a new house, electricians install wiring in the walls as they exist; it is impossible to do otherwise. No electrician can install wiring in the wall as designed 6 months ago, before a change. In software, such physical constraints do not exist. It is entirely possible for a team to develop a set of application programs to process a database using an obsolete database design. When the database design was changed, all involved parties should have been notified, but this may not have occurred. Wasted hours, increased cost, and poor morale are the result.

Another problem is diseconomies of scale. The number of possible interactions among team members rises exponentially with the number of team members. Ultimately, no matter how well managed a project is, diseconomies of scale will set in.

As the project proceeds, controlling the configuration of the work product becomes difficult. Consider requirements, for example. The development team produces an initial statement of requirements. Meetings with users produce an adjusted set of requirements. Suppose an event then occurs that necessitates another version of requirements. After deliberation, assume the development team decides to ignore a large portion of the requirements changes resulting from the event. At this point, there are four different versions of the requirements. If the changes to requirements are not carefully managed, changes from the four versions will be mixed up, and confusion and disorder will result. No one will know which requirements are the correct, current ones.

Similar problems occur with designs, program code, database data, and other system components. The term **configuration control** refers to a set of management policies, practices, and tools that developers use to maintain control over the project's resources. Such resources include documents, schedules, designs, program code, test suites, and any other shared resource needed to complete the project. Configuration control is vital; a loss of control over a project's configuration is so expensive and disruptive that it can result in termination for senior project managers.

The last major challenge to large-scale project management is unexpected events. The larger and longer the project, the greater the chance of disruption due to an unanticipated event. Critical people can change companies; even whole teams have been known to pack up and join a competitor. A hurricane may destroy an office; the company may have a bad quarter and freeze hiring just as the project is staffing up; technology will change; competitors may do something that makes the project more (or less) important; or the company may be sold and new management may change requirements and priorities.

Because software is thought-stuff, team morale is crucial. I once managed two strong-headed software developers who engaged in a heated argument over the design of a program feature. The argument ended when one threw a chair at the other. The rest of the team divided its loyalties between the two developers, and work came to a standstill as subgroups sneered and argued with one another when they met in hallways or at the coffee pot. How do you schedule that event into your WBS? As a project manager, you never know what strange event is heading your way. Such unanticipated events make project management challenging, but also incredibly fascinating!

 How Can Scrum Overcome the Problems of the SDLC?

The systems development life cycle (SDLC) process is falling out of favor in the systems development community, primarily for two reasons. First, the nature of the SDLC denies what every experienced developer knows to be true: systems requirements are fuzzy and always changing. They change because they need to be corrected, or more is known, or users change their minds about what they want after they use part of the system, or business needs change, or technology offers other possibilities.

According to the SDLC, however, progress goes in a linear sequence from requirements to design to implementation. Sometimes this is called the **waterfall method** because the assumption is that once you've finished a phase, you never go back; you go over the waterfall into the pool of the next stage. Requirements are done. Then you do design. Design is done; then you implement. However, experience has shown that it just doesn't work that way.

Using MIS InClass 10 | A GROUP EXERCISE

Improving the Process of Making Paper Airplanes[3]

The purpose of this exercise is to demonstrate process concepts. In this exercise, students will form assembly lines to create paper airplanes. Each assembly line will have the same four activities, each called a Work Center (WC), as shown in Figure 10-20. Raw material is a stack of plain paper, finished goods are the folded airplanes, and WIP is "Work in Progress," which is the output of the WC prior to the next WC.

One student is assigned to each of the four WCs in the assembly line. Student 1, in WC 1, creates the first fold, as shown at the top of Figure 10-21. Student 2, at WC 2, folds the corners, also shown in Figure 10-21. The location and assembly instructions for Students 3 and 4 are also shown in Figure 10-21. In addition to the four students who fold the planes, seven other students observe, time, and record each assembly line, as listed below, using the three forms in Figure 10-22:

Observer 1: Use Form 1, record WC 1 task times.

Observer 2: Use Form 1, record WC 2 task times.

Observer 3: Use Form 1, record WC 3 task times.

Observer 4: Use Form 1, record WC 4 task times.

Observer 5: Use Form 2, record cycle time at the end of the line.

Observer 6: Use Form 3, record colored sheet throughput time.

Observer 7: Count WIP at the end of each run.

Each assembly line is run to construct 20 airplanes. Prior to beginning the process, each line will run a practice session of four or five planes. Then, clear the line, start the clock, and make the 20 airplanes. Each WC continues to work until the 20th plane is finished, which means that more than 20 will be started because there will be WIP when the 20th is finished. About halfway through the run, the instructor will insert a colored piece of paper as raw material. Each student assembler works at his or her own pace. As workers build planes, they should work at a comfortable pace and not speed. This is not a contest for maximum output, but for quality.

After the first run is completed, make a second run of 20 planes with all the same roles. However, each student can

work only when there is an airplane in the inbox (WIP) and no airplane in the outbox (WIP). Again, midway through the run the instructor will insert a colored sheet of paper.

After the runs:

1. Discuss the objectives of the assembly line. If you were in charge of an assembly line like this one, do you think your objectives would be efficiency or effectiveness? Specify the measures used to monitor progress toward your objective(s).

2. Assume that the WC folding is done by four machines. In that scenario, the second run uses different software from the first run. Does this new IS improve an activity, linkage, or control?

3. Are any data in an information silo on the first or second runs

4. Which measure changed most significantly from the first to the second run? Did you anticipate this? Are other processes with other measures just as subject to change with a similar minor change in information?

5. Were there any controls on the assembly process? Could an IS improve the process by improving control? On which measure(s) will this improvement appear?

Figure 10-20
Classroom Assembly Line Setup

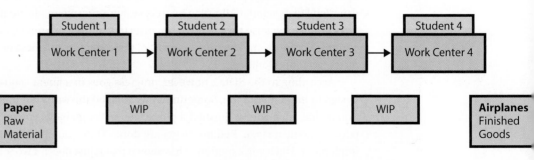

Student 1	Student 2	Student 3	Student 4
Work Center 1	Work Center 2	Work Center 3	Work Center 4

| **Paper** Raw Material | WIP | WIP | WIP | **Airplanes** Finished Goods |

---

[3]Based on "A Classroom Exercise to Illustrate Lean Manufacturing Pull Concepts," by Peter J. Billington, in *Decision Sciences Journal of Innovative Education,* 2(1), 2004, pp. 71–77.

Figure 10-21
Assembly (Folding) Instructions

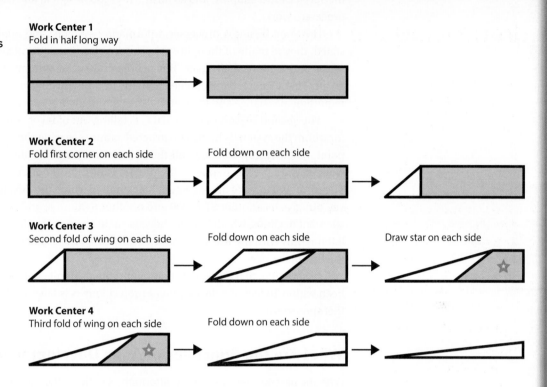

Work Center 1
Fold in half long way

Work Center 2
Fold first corner on each side   Fold down on each side

Work Center 3
Second fold of wing on each side   Fold down on each side   Draw star on each side

Work Center 4
Third fold of wing on each side   Fold down on each side

Figure 10-22
Airplane Folding
Recording Forms

Work Center _____ (1, 2, 3, or 4)

Unit	Run 1 (seconds)	Run 2 (seconds)
1		
2		
3		
4		
5		
6		
7		
8		
9		
10		
11		
12		
13		
14		
15		
16		
17		
18		
19		
20		
Sum		
Average		

Form 1: Airplane manufacturing task time. Observers 1, 2, 3, and 4 use this form to record assembly times for each Work Center.

System	Throughput Time for 20 Sheets Run 1	Throughput Time for 20 Sheets Run 2
Run 1		
Run 2		

Form 2: Airplane manufacturing cycle time for 20 airplanes. Observer 5 uses this form to record start and finish time for entire run of 20 planes.

System	Throughput Time for Colored Sheets Run 1	Throughput Time for Colored Sheets Run 2
Run 1		
Run 2		

Form 3: Paper airplane manufacturing color sheet throughput time. Observer 6 uses this form to record start and finish time for colored sheet.

In the beginning, systems developers thought the SDLC might work for IS and applications because processes like the SDLC work for building physical things. If you're going to build a runway, for example, you specify how long it needs to be, how much airplane weight the surface must support, and so forth. Then you design it, and then you build it. Here waterfall processes work.

However, business processes, information systems, and applications are not physical; as stated, they're made of thought-stuff. They're also social; they exist for people to inform themselves and achieve their goals. But people and social systems are incredibly malleable; they adapt. That characteristic enables humans to do many amazing things, but it also means that requirements change and the waterfall development process cannot work.

The second reason that the SDLC is falling out of favor is that it is very risky. The people for whom the system is being constructed cannot see what they have until the very end. At that point, if something is wrong, all the money and time has already been spent. Furthermore, what if, as frequently happens, the project runs out of money or time before it is completed? The result is a form of management blackmail in which the developers say, "Well, it's not done yet, but give us another $100,000 and another 6 months, and *then* we'll have it done." If management declines, which it might because at that point, the time and money are sunk, they are left not only with the loss but also with the unmet need that caused them to start the SDLC in the first place.

In short, the SDLC assumes that requirements don't change, which everyone who has ever been within 10 feet of a development project knows is false, and it's very risky for the business that sponsors it.

What Are the Principles of Agile Development Methodologies?

Over the past 40 years, numerous alternatives to the SDLC have been proposed, including *rapid application development,* the *unified process, extreme programming, scrum,* and others. All of these techniques addressed the problems of the SDLC, and by the turn of the last century, their philosophy had coalesced into what has come to be known as **agile development**, which means a development process that conforms to the principles in Figure 10-23. Scrum is an agile technique and conforms to these principles.

First, scrum and the other agile techniques expect and even welcome change. Given the nature of social systems, *expect* is not a surprise, but why *welcome*? Isn't welcoming requirements change a bit like welcoming a good case of the flu? No, because systems are created to help organizations and people achieve their strategies, and the more the requirements change, the closer they come to facilitating strategies. The result is better and more satisfying for both the users and the development team.

Second, scrum and other agile development processes are designed to frequently deliver a *working* version of some part of the product. Frequently means 1 to 8 weeks, not longer. This frequency means that management is at risk only for whatever costs and time have been consumed in that period. And, at the end of the period, they will have some usable product piece that has at least some value to the business.

Thus, unlike the SDLC, agile techniques deliver benefits early and often. The initial benefits might be small, but they are positive and increase throughout the process. With the SDLC, no value is generated until the very end. Considering the time value of money, this characteristic alone makes agile techniques more desirable.

The third principle in Figure 10-23 is that the development team will work closely with the customer until the project ends. Someone who knows the business requirements must be available to the development team and must be able and willing to clearly express, clarify, and elaborate on requirements. Also, customers need to be available to test the evolving work product and provide guidance on how well new features work.

- Expect, even welcome, changes in requirements
- Frequently deliver *working* version of the product
- Work closely with customer for the duration
- Design as you go
- Test as you go
- Team knows best how it's doing/how to change
- Can be used for business processes, information systems, and applications development

Figure 10-23
Principles of Agile (Scrum)
Development

The fourth principle is a tough one for many developers to accept. Rather than design the complete, overall system at the beginning, only those portions of the design that are needed to complete the current work are done. Sometimes this is called **just-in-time design**. Designing in this way means that the design is constantly changing, and existing designs may need to be revised, along with substantial revision to the work product produced so far. On the surface, it is inefficient. However, experience has shown that far too many teams have constructed elaborate, fanciful, and complete designs that turned out to be glamorous fiction as the requirements changed.

Test as you go, the next principle, is obvious if the team is going to be delivering working versions. Testing is initially conducted among members of the team but involves the business customer as well.

Development teams know how well they're doing. You could go into any development environment today and ask the team how it's doing and, once team members understood you were not about to inflict a new management program on them, you would find they know their strengths, weaknesses, bottlenecks, and process problems quite well. That principle is part of agile development methodologies. At the end of every deliverable or some other (short) milestone, the team meets to assess how it's doing and how it can improve.

Finally, agile development methodologies are generic. They can be applied to the creation of business processes, information systems, and applications. They are applicable to other team projects as well, but that subject is beyond the scope of this text.

What Is the Scrum Process?

Scrum is an agile development methodology developed by Jeff Sutherland, Jeff McKenna, and John Scumniotales for a project at the Easel Corporation[4] and extended by others over the past 15 years. *Scrum* is a rugby term and was first used for teamwork in a *Harvard Business Review* article written by Hirotaka Takeuchi and Ikujiro Nonaka.[5] In rugby, a *scrum* is a gathering of a team into a circle to restart play after a foul or other interruption. Think of it as a huddle in American football.

Scrum Essentials

As stated, scrum is an agile development process with the characteristics shown in Figure 10-24. First, the process is driven by a prioritized list of requirements that is created by the users and business sponsors of the new system. Scrum work periods can be as short as 1

---

[4]Chris Sims and Hillary Louise Johnson, *The Elements of Scrum* (Dymaxcon, 2011), pp. 65, 66.
[5]Hirotaka Takeuchi and Ikujiro Nonaka, "New New Product Development Game," *Harvard Business Review*, Jan. 1, 1986. Available for purchase at *http://hbr.org*.

- Requirements list drives process
- Each work period (1 to 4–8 weeks):
  - Select requirements to consider
  - Determine tasks to perform—select requirements to deliver
  - Team meets daily for 15 min (stand-up)
    - What I did yesterday
    - What I'm going to do today
    - What's blocking me
  - Test frequently
  - Paired work possible
  - Minimal documentation
  - Deliver (something) that works
  - Evaluate team's work process at end of period (and say thanks)
- Rinse and repeat until
  - Customer says we're done
  - Out of time
  - Out of money
- Three Principal roles
  - Product Owner (business professional)
  - Scrum Master
  - Team Members (7±2 people)

Figure 10-24
Scrum Essentials

week but, as with all agile processes, never longer than 8. Two to 4 weeks is recommended. Each work period, the team selects the top priority items that it will commit to delivering that period. Each workday begins with a **stand-up**, which is a 15-minute meeting in which each team member[6] states:

- What he or she has done in the past day
- What he or she will do in the coming day
- Any factors that are blocking his or her progress

The purpose of the stand-up is to achieve accountability for team members' progress and to give a public forum for blocking factors. Oftentimes one team member will have the expertise to help a blocked team member resolve the blocking issue.

Testing is done frequently, possibly many times per day. Sometimes the business owner of the project is involved in daily testing as well. In some cases, team members work in pairs; in **paired programming**, for example, two team members share the same computer and write a computer program together. Sometimes, one programmer will provide a test, and the other will either demonstrate that the code passes that test or alter the code so that it will. Then the two members switch roles. Other types of paired work are possible as well.

Minimal documentation is prepared. The result of the team's work is not design or other documents but, rather, a working version of the requirements that were selected at the start of the scrum period.

At the end of the scrum period, the working version of the product is delivered to the customer, who can, if desired, put it to use at that time, even in its not-fully-finished state. After the product is delivered, the team meets to evaluate its own process and to make changes as needed. Team members are given an opportunity to express thanks and receive recognition for superior work at these meetings. (Review the criteria for team success in Chapter 2, and you will see how scrum adheres to the principles of a successful team.)

Figure 10-25 summarizes the scrum process.

---

[6]Some scrum teams have the rule that only *pigs* can speak at stand-ups. The term comes from the joke about the difference between eggs and ham: the chicken is interested, but the pig is committed.

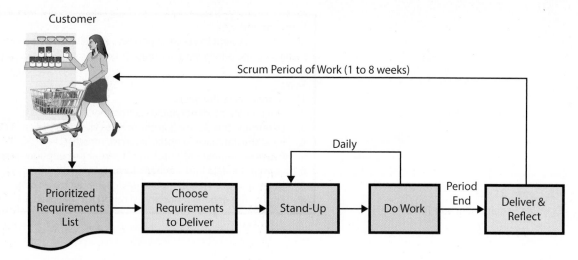

Figure 10-25
Scrum Process

When Are We Done?

Work continues in a repeating cycle of scrum periods until one of three conditions is met:

- The customer is satisfied with the product created and decides to accept the work product, even if some requirements are left unsatisfied.
- The project runs out of time.
- The project runs out of money.

Unlike the SDLC, if a scrum project terminates because of time or budget limitations, the customer will have some useful result for the time and money expended. It may not be the fully functioning version that was desired, but it is something that, assuming requirements are defined and prioritized correctly, can generate value for the project sponsors.

How Do Requirements Drive the Scrum Process?

Scrum is distinguished from other agile development methodologies, in part, by the way that it uses requirements to drive planning and scheduling. First, requirements are specified in a particular manner. One common format is to express requirements in terms of *who* does *what* and *why*.

For example, in the PRIDE system, a requirement could be expressed as:

"As a doctor, I want to view a patient's exercise records so I can make sure he is not doing too much."

Or,

"As a doctor, I want to view a patient's exercise records so I can make sure she is following her prescription."

Each of these requirements specifies who (the doctor) does what (view a patient's exercise data) and why (make sure she is following her prescription). It's not surprising that the requirement includes *who* and *what*, but the need for *why* may surprise you. The purpose of the why clause of the requirement is to set a context for the value that will be delivered by the requirement. Including it increases the likelihood that the product will deliver business value and not just blindly meet the requirement.

As stated, the product owner creates requirements and prioritizes them. For example, one of the two requirements above will be judged higher in importance than the other. All other things being equal, the team will satisfy the higher priority requirement first. This means, too, that if the project runs out of time or money, the highest priority requirements will have been completed first.

> Requirement:
> "As a doctor, I want to view the patient's exercise records so I can make sure she is following her prescription."
>
> Tasks:
> 1.   Authenticate the doctor.
> 2.   Obtain patient identifying data from doctor.
> 3.   Determine this doctor is authorized to view this patient's records.
> 4.   Read the database to obtain exercise records.
> 5.   Read the database to obtain most recent prescription record.
> 6.   Format the data into a generic format.
> 7.   Determine the type of mobile device the doctor is using.
> 8.   Format the generic report into a report for that mobile device.

Figure 10-26
Example Requirement and Tasks

Creating Requirements Tasks

Given a requirement, the team meets to create tasks that must be accomplished to meet that requirement. In Figure 10-25, this work is done in the *Choose requirements to deliver* activity.

Figure 10-26 shows eight tasks that need to be done to accomplish an example requirement. In the *Choose requirements to deliver* activity, tasks for additional requirements that might also be implemented in this scrum period are created.

Tasks are created in a team meeting because the team as a whole can iterate and allow members to give feedback. One team member will think of a task that needs to be done, of which other members are not aware. Or the team member will realize that a particular task is incomplete, or is doable in some other way, or doesn't really need to be done.

Scheduling Tasks

As described so far, scrum is a good idea, one of many agile processes that might be used. What makes scrum particularly innovative, however, is the way that tasks are scheduled.

Scrum methodology recognizes that developers are terrible, even wretched, at determining how long a task will take. However, developers are quite good at determining how long something will take in comparison to something else. So, while a developer may be poor at estimating the time required to do, say, Task 2 in Figure 10-26, he or she will likely be accurate when saying that Task 2 will take twice as long as Task 1, or some other ratio.

So, according to the scrum process, once the tasks are known for a given set of requirements, the next step is to assign each task a difficulty score, called *points*. The easiest task has a point score of 1. A task that will take five times longer is given a point score of 5, etc. For reasons that are beyond the scope of this discussion, points are expressed in values from a sequence of integers known as the Fibonacci sequence: {1, 2, 3, 5, 8, 13, 21, 34, 55, 89, 144, and?}. The question mark is used because any number larger than 144 is meaningless. Most likely 89 and 144 are meaningless as well. Tasks with such point scores need to be subdivided into multiple requirements. When all tasks have received points, the points are summed to a total for the requirement.

Scrum includes several different techniques for assigning points. Team estimation and planning poker are two. You can learn more about them in *The Elements of Scrum*.[7] The gist

---

[7]Chris Sims and Hillary Louise Johnson, *The Elements of Scrum* (Dymaxcon, 2011), pp. 125–133.

1. Team assigns 1 point to simplest task.
2. Times to deliver working tasks are compared to each other and assigned points (points are Fibonacci numbers). Use:
   a. Team estimation
   b. Planning poker
   c. Other
3. Using past experience, team computes its velocity… number of points it can accomplish per scrum period.
4. Working with product owner, team selects tasks for the upcoming scrum period, constrained by its velocity.

Figure 10-27
Summary of Scrum Estimation Techniques

of these techniques is to obtain team scores by applying the team's expertise in an iterative, feedback-generating process.

Committing to Finish Tasks

As teams work together, they will learn the total number of points of work they can accomplish each scrum period. That term is called the team's **velocity**. The team uses its velocity to determine how many requirements it can commit to accomplishing in the next scrum period. Of course, during the first period, the team will not know its velocity. In that case, senior members will need to make a guess. That guess may be far off, but it will get better as the team gains experience. Unlike the SDLC, there is at least well-founded hope that, over time, estimating will improve.

Suppose the five requirements on a team's prioritized requirements list total 125 points. If a team knows its velocity is 100 points per scrum period, they know they cannot do all five. However, if the top four total, say 80 points, they can commit to doing those four, plus something else. In this case, the team would go back to the product owner and ask if there is a requirement lower on the priority list that can be done for the available 20 points of capacity. This estimation technique is summarized in Figure 10-27.

Hocus-Pocus?

If you haven't participated in software or systems development, this process may sound like so much hocus-pocus. However, it has two very important characteristics that make it not so. First, scrum is a methodology that incorporates team iteration and feedback for scheduling and tasking, which, as you know by now, is a way for a team to create something together that exceeds what each member can do individually. Second, scrum provides a framework for process learning. As a team works more and more scrum periods together, it learns better and better how to assign points, and it learns more and more what its true velocity is.

However, as Don Nilson, a certified scrum master with years of experience at Microsoft and other companies says, "Scrum is a good technique. However, it is not magic. You cannot use it to obtain a $500,000 result for $150,000, nor can you use it to obtain a 24 person-year labor result for 12 person-years. You are, however, less likely to lose a lot of time or money than with the traditional SDLC."[8]

---

[8]Personal correspondence with the author, June 3, 2012.

Q7   2024?

Process and systems development will evolve in the next 10 years in four important ways. First, we will see a continuing focus on aligning business processes and information systems with business strategy, goals, and objectives. You and your classmates will be an important factor in that alignment. Unlike earlier generations of business professionals, you are truly computer literate. Although they might seem unimportant to you, your skills with Facebook, Twitter, foursquare, and so on have given you confidence in your ability to master computer-based systems. You also know that such systems can be easy or difficult to use, depending on their design.

Given this background, as future managers in accounting, finance, marketing, operations, and so forth you will be less willing, perhaps unwilling, to compromise. You know that information systems can be constructed to do what you want, and you'll be likely to insist on it.

Second, computer systems will be more easily changed and adapted in the future. Software vendors know that the key to their future growth is not having the single best solution, but rather on having a solution that is readily tailored to their customers' idiosyncrasies. When ERP was new, customers were willing to adapt their business processes to those of the vendors because there was no other choice. But, as indicated by the popularity of ERP industry-specific solution templates, ERP customers want more. They want to be able to do whatever it is they do to gain a competitive advantage, and adapting their business processes to the same processes used by everyone else isn't going to get them there. So, software vendors will find ways to make their solutions more agile using SOA and Web services, and, as a result, systems and processes will be more agile and better able to adapt to changing needs.

In the next 10 years, application development will become much faster. That will occur, in part, through the use of improved development processes such as scrum, but it will also occur because applications will become better at creating other applications. (See Using MIS InClass 9, pages 350–351). Whether or not we will reach Kurzweil's singularity before 2024, as he predicts, we do not know. We can depend, however, on applications that generate other applications far more effectively, and frequently, than they do now.

The third major change involves the cloud. Until very recently, when systems development teams wanted to build and test a new project, they would need to start a formal project and request funds to buy or lease development computers and communications infrastructure. Today, with elastic cloud computing, prototypes and even finished systems can be constructed in the cloud within very small hardware budgets. The result will be substantially more innovation, hard as that is to imagine!

Finally, between now and 2024, we will see the emergence of new software vendor business models. The Firm (*www.thefirmmpls.com*), a workout studio in Minneapolis, pays almost nothing in license fees for the full-service operations application that it obtains from the SaaS vendor MindBody, Inc. Instead, all of the credit card charges that The Firm customers make are processed by MindBody, Inc. This processing enables MindBody to earn a small amount on every customer transaction. MindBody supports more than 6,000 studios and trainers in the United States. Its software is a veritable money machine.

A key element of this new business model is the alignment between the goals of workout studios and MindBody. Both make more money when customers purchase. Therefore, MindBody's software includes features and functions that enable studio managers to determine which products, classes, trainers, and even ads and marketing campaigns are the most successful. Furthermore, MindBody has a window on the best practices in the industry. To motivate studios to adapt to new practices that will create more revenue, MindBody provides comparative statistics on any given studio's performance against that of similar companies in its region.

MindBody's business model is an example of a potentially monumental change in the way that business software is provided. Stay tuned!

Security Guide

PSST. THERE'S ANOTHER WAY, YOU KNOW...

"All this talk about BPM, and SDLC, and scrum is really un-necessary. There's another way, you know. We just download a copy of their source code, and we're in business. I have a friend who knows how to do that. We'd have the application in sec-onds, and it would save so much time and agony, no?"

Industrial espionage is as old as commerce. Infil-trating your competitors with spies and stealing whatever you can is nothing new. It's a way to save hundreds of labor years, maybe more. Of course, if you're so stupid as to steal the designs of an iPad, and next month bring your own iPad to market, the jig will be up. Apple, the FBI, and who knows who else will be upon you.

So, instead, you can just learn from the stolen designs and apply your new knowledge to build similar devices, doing it much faster than you could without the theft. Use what you learn from, say, iPad touch-screen design to build your own auto navigation touch screen.

Or choose a company less prominent than Apple. For example, find out where Dr. Flores and his team keep the PRIDE source code and take it. Then build your own PRIDE system in another country...say New Zealand or Singapore. How likely is it for Dr. Flores to know you're run-ning his code in New Zealand? Not likely, and, if he does learn of it, how much does he want to pay the one attorney in Austin, Texas, who knows New Zealand law and prosecu-tion? Plus, how would he prove you got the code from him?

Sound far-fetched? In June 2012, ESET, the antivirus software vendor based in Bratislava, Slovakia, detected a big spike in infections of a worm named ACAD/Medre.A.[9] Initially the spike was in Peru, but the malware soon spread. Investigation revealed that this worm copies itself into file folders containing drawings produced using AutoCAD, the world's most popular computer-based design software. Once there, it installs code to send copies of engineering drawings it finds on the host machine to one of several email servers in China. If Outlook is installed on the in-fected computer, it also sends copies of the computer's con-tact list and other email data.

ACAD/Medre.A was spread by unsuspecting engineers. An AutoCAD design consists of many files, and to transfer a design to a collaborator, engineers routinely compress the files in an AutoCAD design directory into a zip file and send it to legitimate recipients. Once the worm gets into a design directory, it's compressed with the legitimate files and rides along in the compressed file. When the recipient decom-presses the zip file, ACAD/Medre.A is decompressed as well. It then runs its payload to steal designs and email data.

Why Peru? Apparently, the original infection was on a server of a Peruvian manufacturer whose suppliers needed the manufacturer's engineering designs to create

Source: © Eliane SULLE/Alam

---
[9]*http://www.eset.com/fileadmin/Images/US/Docs/Business/white_Papers/ESET_ACAD_Medre_A_whitepaper.pdf.*

component parts. When suppliers copied the manufacturer's drawings, they copied the worm as well. Soon the worm was on its way around the world.

Was it serious? According to the ESET, tens of thousands of engineering drawings were leaked. ESET says, however, that when it notified the providers of those email servers in China, the providers shut those server sites down, so the damage is supposed to be stopped. Autodesk, the vendor of AutoCAD, took corrective and protective action as well.

DISCUSSION QUESTIONS

1. If, in your absence, your roommate opens your desk and eats the top layer of your 2-pound box of chocolates, you'll know it; at least you'll know they're gone. But, if in your absence, your roommate uses your computer to copy your MIS term project onto his flash drive, do you know? If so, how? If not, why not?

2. Of course *your* roommate wouldn't steal your term project. So, instead, suppose the person across the hall obtains the name of your computer and your logon name (the name you enter when your computer starts). She could surreptitiously watch you enter your password and learn it, too. But let's say instead that she notices the 75 pictures of your family basset hound, Fido, taped to your desk and correctly guesses that your password is *Fido*. With that data and a little knowledge, she uses your dorm's network to access shared folders on your computer, *from her computer*. (Search the Internet for *How to share a folder in Windows (or Mac)* if you don't know what shared folders are.) When she finds your MIS term paper in one of your shared folders and copies it to her computer, do you know? Why or why not?

3. How does the situation in question 2 differ from packet sniffing? (Reread the packet sniffing Security Guide in Chapter 6, pages 230–231 if necessary). What's required for her to steal your paper from a shared folder? What's required to steal that paper using packet sniffing? Which is easier?

4. As a student, you're unlikely to share many folders, but once you start work, you're likely to do so. Is the scenario in question 2 possible at work? Does it matter if your employer has strong network security? What is the one thing you can do to protect yourself from the person in the cubicle down the hallway accessing your shared folders?

5. Now consider the suppliers in this guide who had their designs stolen. Will they know their designs were stolen? How will they find out? How will they know which designs were taken? How can they assess their damages?

6. It's possible for companies to configure their network so that email can only be sent to their own Internet service provider. Such a configuration would thwart the ACAD/Medre.A worm, and indeed it did, for all the companies that had such security. Companies with large, knowledgeable IS departments (see Chapter 11) most likely will, but in this case hundreds did not. If you're the owner of a small business, what can you do?

7. Search the Internet for the term *industrial espionage*. Find one example of espionage that has been conducted using malware. Summarize the problem and the damages. What could the companies involved have done to avoid losses?

Guide

THE REAL ESTIMATION PROCESS

"I'm a software developer. I write programs in an object-oriented language called C# (pronounced 'C-sharp'). I'm a skilled object-oriented designer, too. I should be—I've been at it 12 years and worked on major projects for several software companies. For the last 4 years, I've been a team leader. I lived through the heyday of the dot-com era and now work in the development group at a Windows RT application vendor.

"All of this estimating theory is just that—theory. It's not really the way things work. Sure, I've been on projects in which we tried different estimation techniques. But here's what really happens: You develop an estimate using whatever technique you want. Your estimate goes in with the estimates of all the other team leaders. The project manager sums all those estimates together and produces an overall estimate for the project.

"By the way, in my projects, time has been a much bigger factor than money. At one software company I worked for, you could be 300 percent over your dollar budget and get no more than a slap on the wrist. Be 2 weeks late, however, and you were finished.

"Anyway, the project managers take the project schedule to senior management for approval, and what happens? Senior management thinks they are negotiating. 'Oh, no,' they say, 'that's way too long. You can surely take a month off that schedule. We'll approve the project, but we want it done by February 1 instead of March 1.'

"Now, what's their justification? They think that tight schedules make for efficient work. You know that everyone will work extra hard to meet the tighter time frame. They know Parkinson's Law—'Work expands so as to fill the time available for its completion.' So, fearing the possibility of wasting time because of too-lenient schedules, they lop a month off our estimate.

"Estimates are what they are; you can't knock off a month or two without some problem, somewhere. What does happen is that projects get behind, and then management expects us to work longer and longer hours.

"Not that our estimation techniques are all that great, either. Most software developers are optimists. They schedule things as if everything will go as planned, but things seldom do. Also, schedulers usually don't allow for vacations, sick days, trips to the dentist, training on new technology, peer reviews, and all the other things we do in addition to writing software.

416

"So we start with optimistic schedules on our end, then management negotiates a month or two off, and voilà, we have a late project. After a while, management has been burned by late projects so much that they mentally add the month or even more back onto the official schedule. Then both sides work in a fantasy world, where no one believes the schedule, but everyone pretends they do.

"I like my job. I like software development. Management here is no better or worse than in other places. As long as I have interesting work to do, I'll stay here. But I'm not working myself silly to meet these fantasy deadlines."

 DISCUSSION QUESTIONS

1. What do you think of this developer's attitude? Do you think he's unduly pessimistic or do you think there's merit to what he says?

2. What do you think of his idea that management thinks they're negotiating? Should management negotiate schedules? Why or why not?

3. Suppose a project actually requires 12 months to complete. Which do you think is likely to cost more: (a) having an official schedule of 11 months with at least a 1-month overrun or (b) having an official schedule of 13 months and, following Parkinson's Law, having the project take 13 months?

4. Suppose you are a business manager, and an information system is being developed for your use. You review the scheduling documents and see that little time has been allowed for vacations, sick leave, miscellaneous other work, and so forth. What do you do?

5. Describe the intangible costs of having an organizational belief that schedules are always unreasonable.

6. If this developer worked for you, how would you deal with his attitude about scheduling?

7. Do you think there is something different when scheduling information systems development projects than when scheduling other types of projects? What characteristics might make such projects unique? In what ways are they the same as other projects?

8. What do you think managers should do in light of your answer to question 7?

9. This guide assumes an SDLC process. How would the situation be different if the developer had been using scrum?

ACTIVE REVIEW

Use this Active Review to verify that you understand the ideas and concepts that answer the chapter's study questions.

Q1 How are business processes, IS, and applications developed?

Using your own words, explain the differences among business processes, information systems, and applications. State the components of each. Using the terminology from Chapter 5, describe the relationship of business processes and IS. Name three development processes and state which processes are used for the development of business processes, information systems, and applications. Explain the primary roles of business and systems analysts.

Q2 How do organizations use business process management (BPM)?

State the definition of business process used in this chapter and define *roles, resources,* and *data flows.* Explain three reasons why business processes need to be managed. Describe the need for BPM, and explain why it is a cycle. Name the four stages of the BPM process, and summarize the activities in each. Define *as-is model.* Explain the role of COBIT.

Q3 How is business process modeling notation (BPMN) used to model processes?

Explain the need for a process documentation standard. Describe swim-lane layout. Explain each of the symbols in Figures 10-7 and 10-8 and describe the relationship of these two diagrams. Describe the problems in the process in Figure 10-7 and suggest one solution. Name three uses for BPMN diagrams.

Q4 What are the phases in the systems development life cycle (SDLC)?

Describe the origins of the SDLC and how it came to prominence. Name five basic systems development activities. Describe tasks required for the definition, requirements, and design steps. Explain the tasks required to implement a system, and describe four types of system conversion. State specific activities for each of the five components during the design and implementation stages. Explain why the term *maintenance* is a misnomer when applied to information systems; state tasks performed during systems maintenance.

Q5 What are the keys for successful SDLC projects?

Name five keys for successful development projects. Explain the purpose of a work breakdown structure. Summarize the difficulties of development estimation, and describe three ways of addressing it. Explain the elements in the Gantt chart in Figure 10-17. Define *critical path,* and explain critical path analysis. Summarize requirements, cost, and schedule trade-offs. List and explain four critical factors for development project management.

Q6 How can scrum overcome the problems of the SDLC?

Explain two reasons that the SDLC is falling out of favor. In your own words, explain the meaning and importance of each of the principles in Figure 10-23. Explain how each of the scrum essential items in Figure 10-24 is implemented in the scrum process shown in Figure 10-25. Name three elements in a scrum requirement. Describe what is unique about the way that scrum determines the time required to accomplish a task. Define *velocity,* and explain how it is used in scheduling. Explain how scrum provides a framework for process learning.

Q7 2024?

Name four ways that process and systems development will evolve in the next 10 years. Explain how the computer literacy of you and your classmates contributes to process and systems alignment. Summarize the key to growth for software vendors and explain how that contributes to process and system agility. Describe how the elastic cloud will foster innovation. Using the example of MindBody, explain how new business models will enable software to be delivered to customers in innovative ways.

Using Your Knowledge with PRIDE

Dr. Flores, his partners, and potential investors need to know the basics of development processes, which to use for what and the advantages of using the SDLC and scrum. Before accepting investments, they need to understand the difficulties and risks of developing processes, IS, and applications, particularly inter-enterprise systems, such as PRIDE.

At some point in your career, you will need this knowledge as well.

KEY TERMS AND CONCEPTS

MyMISLab

Go to **mymislab.com** to complete the problems marked with this icon .

USING YOUR KNOWLEDGE

10-1. Search Google or Bing for the phrase *what is a business* *analyst*. Investigate several of the links that you find and answer the following questions:
  a. What are the primary job responsibilities of a business analyst?
  b. What knowledge do business analysts need?
  c. What skills/personal traits do business analysts need?

10-2. Search Google or Bing for the phrase *what is a systems analyst*. Investigate several of the links that you find and answer the following questions:
  a. What are the primary job responsibilities of a systems analyst?
  b. What knowledge do systems analysts need?
  c. What skills/personal traits do systems analysts need?
  d. Would a career as a systems analyst be interesting to you? Explain why or why not.
  e. Using your answers to this question and to question 10-1, compare and contrast the jobs of business and systems analyst.

10-3. Using your own experience and knowledge, create a process diagram for a Reject Order activity that would fix the allocation problem in Figure 10-7. Use Figure 10-8 as an example. Use Visio 2010 and the standard BPMN shapes, if possible. Explain how your process fixes the allocation problem.

10-4. Choose an important project type in a business discipline of interest to you. In accounting it could be an audit; in marketing it could be a plan for using social media; in operations, it could be a project of opening a new warehouse. Choose a major activity that is important and that you find interesting. Compare and contrast the use of a process such as the SDLC to using a process such as scrum for your project. Which process would you recommend? Justify your recommendation.

10-5. Jump to the next chapter (Chapter 11) and read the opening vignette. Explain how Dr. Flores and Maggie could use a scrum process for managing Ajit. Describe how doing so would reduce the risk of failure.

COLLABORATION EXERCISE 10

Using the collaboration IS you built in Chapter 2 (pages 73–74), collaborate with a group of students to answer the following questions.

Wilma Baker, Jerry Barker, and Chris Bickel met in June 2012 at a convention of resort owners and tourism operators. They sat next to each other by chance while waiting for a presentation; after introducing themselves and laughing at the odd sound of their three names, they were surprised to learn that they managed similar businesses. Wilma Baker lives in Santa Fe, New Mexico, and specializes in renting homes and apartments to visitors to Santa Fe. Jerry Barker lives in Whistler Village, British Columbia, and specializes in renting condos to skiers and other visitors to the Whistler/Blackcomb Resort. Chris Bickel lives in Chatham, Massachusetts, and specializes in renting homes and condos to vacationers to Cape Cod.

The three agreed to have lunch after the presentation. During lunch, they shared frustrations about the difficulty of obtaining new customers, especially in the current economic downturn. Barker was especially concerned about finding customers to fill the facilities that had been constructed to host the Olympics in the prior year.

As the conversation developed, they began to wonder if there was some way to combine forces (i.e., they were seeking a competitive advantage from an alliance). So, they decided to skip one of the next day's presentations and meet to discuss ways to form an alliance. Ideas they wanted to discuss further were sharing customer data, developing a joint reservation service, and exchanging property listings.

As they talked, it became clear they had no interest in merging their businesses; each wanted to stay independent. They also discovered that each was very concerned, even paranoid, about protecting their existing customer base from poaching. Still, the conflict was not as bad as it first seemed. Barker's business was primarily the ski trade, and winter was his busiest season; Bickel's business was mostly Cape Cod vacations, and she was busiest during the summer. Baker's high season was the summer and fall. So, it seemed there was enough difference in their high seasons that they would not necessarily cannibalize their businesses by selling the others' offerings to their own customers.

The question then became how to proceed. Given their desire to protect their own customers, they did not want to develop a common customer database. The best idea seemed to be to share data about properties. That way they could keep control of their customers but still have an opportunity to sell time at the others' properties.

They discussed several alternatives. Each could develop her or his own property database, and the three could then share those databases over the Internet. Or they could develop a centralized property database that they would all use. Or they could find some other way to share property listings.

Because we do not know Baker, Barker, and Bickel's detailed requirements, you cannot develop a plan for a specific system. In general, however, they first need to decide how elaborate an information system they want to construct. Consider the following two alternatives:

a. They could build a simple system centered on email. With it, each company sends property descriptions to the others via email. Each independent company then forwards these descriptions to its own customers, also using email. When a customer makes a reservation for a property, that request is then forwarded back to the property manager via email.

b. They could construct a more complex system using a Web-based, shared database that contains data on all their properties and reservations. Because reservations tracking is a common business task, it is likely that they can license an existing application with this capability.

In your answers to 1 and 2, use Microsoft Visio and BPMN templates to construct your diagram. If you don't have those templates, use the cross-functional and basic flowchart templates. If you do not have access to Visio, use PowerPoint instead.

1. Create a process diagram for alternative a, using Figure 10-8 as a guide. Each company will need to have a role for determining its available properties and sending emails to the other companies that describe them. They will also need to have a role for receiving emails and a role for renting properties to customers. Assume the companies have from three to five agents who can fulfill these roles. Create a role for the email system if you think it is appropriate. Specify roles, activities, repositories, and data flows.

2. Create a process diagram for alternative b, using Figure 10-8 as a guide. Each company will need to have a role for determining its available properties and adding them to the reservation database. They will also need a role for renting properties that accesses the shared database. Assume the companies have from three to five agents who can fulfill these roles. Create a role for the property database application. Specify roles, activities, repositories, and data flows.

3. Compare and contrast your answers in questions 1 and 2. Which is likely to be more effective in generating rental income? Which is likely to be more expensive to develop? Which is likely to be more expensive to operate?

4. If you were a consultant to Baker, Barker, and Bickel, which alternative would you recommend? Justify your recommendation.

The Cost of PRIDE?

If Dr. Flores, his partners, and outside investors are to continue the PRIDE project, they need to assess its investment potential. Dr. Flores might be willing to take some loss for the sake of professional service to his patients, but from the dialog in the opening of this chapter, it doesn't sound likely that his partners would. And no successful investor would consider putting money into a losing proposition.

To assess PRIDE's investment potential, we need to know the revenue potential as well as the costs of developing and operating it. We don't know the PRIDE business model, so we cannot assess the revenue aspect of this investment. Such an assessment belongs in an entrepreneurship text and not in an MIS text, in any case.

However, it is appropriate for us to discuss what a system such as PRIDE will cost. By now, you should have sufficient knowledge to at least be able to determine the important cost factors, even though you don't know the particular values.

Figure 10-28 lists potential development and operational cost sources for each of the five components of the PRIDE system. Most of these cost sources are obvious from the discussion of the SDLC in this chapter. A few, however, may be unexpected. For one, notice the hardware and software developer infrastructure costs. Developers need computers on which to write and test code, and they need development software such as Microsoft Visual Studio. There are likely network, server, and cloud-services costs for developers as well. Finally, developers will need mobile devices of the type for which they are developing. A full panoply of iOS devices, Android devices, and Windows RT devices will be needed if all of those operations systems are to be supported.

In the case of PRIDE, software is all custom-developed, so appreciable software development costs should be anticipated. Estimating those costs will be difficult. We will discuss PRIDE security in Chapter 12; for now, realize that applications will need to be developed to enable users to enter and update their security settings. All software will need to be designed to limit access to that prescribed by users' security settings.

Sources of data development costs are self-explanatory. As stated in the chapter, there is normally considerable uncertainty about the time required for data modeling and database design. Because of the PRIDE prototype, this uncertainty will be less.

Procedures for all users must be designed and documented. These tasks are often more expensive than anticipated because those who develop the system may believe it will be easier to use than it is. Procedures need to be more detailed and better documented than they believe. Finally, operational jobs need to be defined, job descriptions written for operations and support personnel, and possibly for development personnel if ongoing development is anticipated. Personnel need to be hired and trained.

As you learned in this chapter, test plans need to be written and integrated system testing conducted. This activity may necessitate full-time product quality assurance (PQA) personnel as well.

Figure 10-28
Sources of PRIDE Costs

	Hardware	Software	Data	Procedures	People

Development	• Developer hardware infrastructure
	• Development cloud-servers
		• Developer software infrastructure
		• Prescription entry application
		• Exercise equipment application
		• Performance reporting application for:
		  Healthcare providers
		  Patients
		  Health clubs
		• Security/privacy applications
			• Data modeling
			• Database design
			• Test data entry
			• Setup data for operational
			• Development cloud storage costs
				• Design and document procedures for:
				  Healthcare providers
				  Patients
				  Health clubs
					• Create staff job descriptions
					• Hire operations and support personnel
					• Train personnel

	Integration and Testing Costs				
Operational	• PRIDE servers • Maintenance developer hardware • Maintenance & testing cloud-servers	• Software maintenance expenses	• Operational cloud storage costs • Backup and recovery costs	• Customer support expense	• Salaries • Contractor fees • New employee training • Ongoing training

The major sources of non-maintenance, operational expense will be cloud hardware, staff salaries, and contractor fees. Depending on how popular and how difficult PRIDE is to use, there may be considerable customer support expense as well. Of course, operational expenses depend upon the number of users and the frequency of their use. The staff will need to estimate usage data and, if possible, develop an operational cost model that is driven by the number of active users.

Maintenance costs are an unknown. They depend upon the quality of the initial software and how much rework is needed once the system becomes operational. They also depend upon how much the PRIDE environment changes. Competitors may force the development of new features and functions, and changes in medical practice payment, insurance policies, and governmental regulations may force changes that will not be known until they occur.

QUESTIONS

Suppose that you have been hired by a potential investor to assess the adequacy of the cost forecasts that the PRIDE team developed. Assume the team has used a model of cost sources like that in Figure 10-28.

The potential investor has asked you to address the following questions, in particular:

10-6. Which development expenses are likely to be
   a. The largest
   b. The most difficult to estimate
   c. Not included in Figure 10-28

10-7. Which operational expenses are likely to be
   a. The largest
   b. The most difficult to estimate
   c. Not included in Figure 10-28

10-8. Considering operational expenses,
   a. Which operational costs depend upon the number of doctors and the frequency of their use, and which do not?
   b. Which operational costs depend upon the number of patients and the frequency of their use, and which do not?
   c. Which operational costs depend upon the number of health club users and the frequency of their use, and which do not?
   d. How would a potential investor use answers to questions 10-8 a–c for assessing the long-run costs if PRIDE is successful?

10-9. Suppose Dr. Flores has told your investor that he is willing to hire Maggie and other experts as needed to fully investigate any two sources of costs.
   a. Of the cost sources in Figure 10-28, which two would you choose? Justify your choice.
   b. List and describe criteria you would use for assessing the completeness and accuracy of the response.

10-10. Suppose you decide, using data that we do not yet have, that the PRIDE upside potential is large enough to justify the investment risk, if the cost estimates are accurate. They might be quite accurate, but then again, they could be low by a factor of 3 or even 5. How would you advise the investor who hired you?

10-11. Suppose the investor who hired you tells you that you haven't done your job if you can't get closer than a factor of 3 to 5 in your assessment of their cost assessment. How do you respond?

10-12. Assume that some of the costs are simply not knowable, by anyone, however skilled they are, at the time of the analysis. A good example is the cost of adapting PRIDE software to changes in healthcare law. Did you include any such costs in your answer to question 10-9? If so, are you wasting Maggie's time and Dr. Flores' money by asking questions about them? How would you advise your investor to consider such costs?

MyMISLab

Go to **mymislab.com** for Auto-graded writing questions as well as the following Assisted-graded writing questions:

10-13. At the start of this chapter, the PRIDE prototype has been successful. Use the five steps of the SDLC to summarize, in one page, the work that remains to be done to transform PRIDE into an operational system. Consider just healthcare providers, patients, and health clubs.

10-14. Read the criteria for team success in Chapter 2. Explain scrum characteristics that support achieving team success.

10-15. Mymislab Only – comprehensive writing assignment for this chapter.

Information Systems Management

"I've worked with him before, but not on a JavaScript project." Maggie Jensen is discussing the pros and cons of outsourcing PRIDE development to India with Dr. Romero Flores.

"But it was a phone application?" Dr. Flores has just finished a 3-hour heart surgery, and he's struggling to move from the world of surgery to that of high tech.

"Yes, but native iOS..." Maggie can't tell if he knows what iOS means. "It's an iPad/iPhone application."

"Well, why don't we do that?" Dr. Flores is still distracted.

"We can. But then we have to develop native applications for Android and Windows 8, if we go there. So, we have to do a lot of rewriting."

"And we don't have to do that if we use JavaScript?" Dr. Flores is getting into the flow of the conversation.

"Nope."

"Why doesn't everyone do that?" he asks.

"Well, it's newer and today's browsers implement html5 differently, so we still have to do a bit of customizing." Maggie is hoping this isn't too much geek speak.

"You mean it's different with IE than with Chrome?" Dr. Flores shows he's understanding her.

"Yes, and different from Safari and Opera, and different on different phones..."

"Why don't they all do it the same way?"

"Wish I knew. It's frustrating to all of us. Actually, the problem is the way they implement css3 more than it is html5..." As she says this, she realizes she's gone too far....

"Stop! That's enough! I thought heart surgery was complicated...So tell me about this guy."

"His name is Ajit Barid. At least that's the name of his company." Maggie looks a little sheepish.

"That's not his name?"

"I don't know. Maybe. You know what Ajit Barid means?" She starts to smile...

"No. What?"

"Invincible cloud."

"Ummm...probably not the name his mother gave him...or she was prophetic. Maggie, this makes me nervous. I don't know anything about doing business in India. The guy takes our money and runs, what do we do?" Dr. Flores is down to business now.

"Well, we don't pay him till he delivers...or at least not much. But I've had a positive experience with him, and his references are good."

"What if he gives our code to somebody else? Or our ideas? What if we find some horrible bug in his code, and we can't find him to fix it? What if he just disappears? What if he gets two-thirds done and then loses interest...or goes to work on someone else's project?" Dr. Flores is on a roll.

"All are risks, I agree. But it will cost you four to six times as much to develop over here." She starts to list risks on the whiteboard.

"Well, it's been my experience that you get what you pay for in this life..."

"You want me to find you some local developers?" Maggie thinks local development is a poor choice but wants him to feel comfortable with the decision.

"Yes, no, I mean no. I don't think so. How'd you meet him?"

"At a conference when he was working for Microsoft in their Hyderabad facility. He was programming SharePoint cloud features. When the iPad took off, he left Microsoft and started his own company. That's when I hired him to build the iOS app."

"That worked out OK?" Dr. Flores wants to be convinced.

"Yes, but it was one of his first jobs...he had to get it right for us."

"What do you think? What would you do?"

Maggie is taken aback by the question...it's not what she expects from a successful heart surgeon. "Well, I think the biggest risk is his success. You know, the restaurant that gets the great reviews and then is buried in new customers and the kitchen falls apart."

"Doesn't he have more employees now?"

"Yes, he does, and I know he's a good developer, but I don't know whether he's a good manager."

"OK, what else?" Dr. Flores is all business.

"I don't know anything about doing business in India."

STUDY QUESTIONS

Q1 What are the functions and organization of the IS department?

Q2 How do organizations plan the use of IS?

Q3 What are the advantages and disadvantages of outsourcing?

Q4 What are your user rights and responsibilities?

Q5 2024?

"Well, JavaScript and css3 are different than Objective-C, which is what he used for the iPad. But they can be easier, too. On the other hand, css can be tricky. I guess I'd say inexperience with this dev environment would be another risk factor."

"What about money?"

"Well, like I said, we structure the agreement so we don't pay much until we know it all works."

"So what else do you worry about?" Again, he's appealing to her expertise.

"Loss of time. Maybe he gets distracted, doesn't finish the app, or hires someone else to do it, and they can't. And September rolls around and we find that, while we're not out any real money, we've lost most of a year of time."

"I don't like the sound of that."

"Neither do I," Maggie responds while she adds schedule risk to her list.

"You think maybe we should bite the bullet and hire our own programmers?"

"Good heavens, no! No way! That would be incredibly expensive, we couldn't keep them busy, and you don't know anything about managing software people. That would be a disaster." Maggie is certain here, and she tries to make that obvious as she speaks.

"But what about long term?"

"Long term, we'll need a small operations staff. One that keeps everything running, answers customer questions, deals with security problems, and so forth. But I think you'll be outsourcing development for a very long time." Again, she speaks with an authoritative tone.

"So?" Dr. Flores's tone shows he wants to wrap up this conversation.

Maggie summarizes, "Let me finish the requirements document and then get a proposal and bid from Ajit as well as a local, domestic developer. We'll look at the proposals and bids and then make a decision. One problem, though..."

"What's that?"

"The local developer may outsource it anyway."

"You mean we pay the local developer to hire Ajit or his cousin?" Dr. Flores shakes his head.

"Something like that."

Dr. Flores gets up from the table. "That's crazy."

"Maybe not. Let's see what we get."

CHAPTER PREVIEW

Information systems are critical to organizational success and, like all critical assets, need to be managed responsibly. In this chapter, we will survey the management of IS and IT resources. We begin by discussing the major functions and the organization of the IS department. Then we will consider planning the use of IT/IS. Outsourcing is the process of hiring outside vendors to provide business services and related products. For our purposes, outsourcing refers to hiring outside vendors to provide information systems, products, and applications. We will examine the pros and cons of outsourcing and describe some of its risks. Finally, we will conclude this chapter by discussing the relationship of users to the IS department. In this last section, you will learn both your own and the IS department's rights and responsibilities. We continue this discussion in 2024 with a new challenge: mobile devices at work.

What Are the Functions and Organization of the IS Department?

The major functions of the information systems department[1] are as follows:

- Plan the use of IS to accomplish organizational goals and strategy.
- Manage outsourcing relationships.
- Protect information assets.
- Develop, operate, and maintain the organization's computing infrastructure.
- Develop, operate, and maintain applications.

We will consider the first two functions in Q2 and Q3 of this chapter. The protection function is the topic of Chapter 12. The last two functions are important for IS majors, but less so for other business professionals; therefore, we will not consider them in this text. To set the stage, consider the organization of the IS department.

How Is the IS Department Organized?

Figure 11-1 shows typical top-level reporting relationships. As you will learn in your management classes, organizational structure varies depending on the organization's size, culture, competitive environment, industry, and other factors. Larger organizations with independent divisions will have a group of senior executives such as those shown here for each division. Smaller companies may combine some of these departments. Consider the structure in Figure 11-1 as typical.

The title of the principal manager of the IS department varies from organization to organization. A common title is **chief information officer, or CIO**. Other common titles are *vice president of information services, director of information services*, and, less commonly, *director of computer services*.

In Figure 11-1, the CIO, like other senior executives, reports to the *chief executive officer* (CEO), though sometimes these executives report to the *chief operating officer* (COO), who, in turn, reports

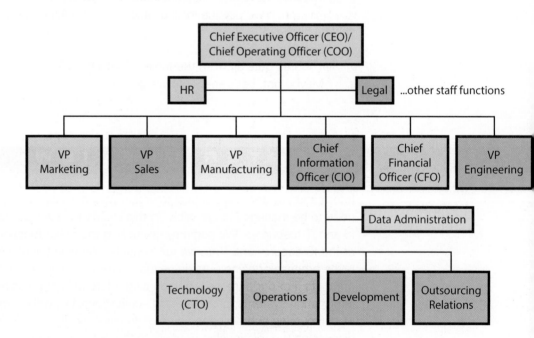

Figure 11-1
Typical Senior-Level
Reporting Relationships

---

[1]Often, the department we are calling the *IS department* is known in organizations as the *IT department*. That name is a misnomer, however, because the IT department manages systems as well as technology. If you hear the term *IT department* in industry, don't assume that the scope of that department is limited to technology.

to the CEO. In some companies, the CIO reports to the *chief financial officer* (CFO). That reporting arrangement might make sense if the primary information systems support only accounting and finance activities. In organizations such as manufacturers that operate significant nonaccounting information systems, the arrangement shown in Figure 11-1 is more common and effective.

The structure of the IS department also varies among organizations. Figure 11-1 shows a typical IS department with four groups and a data administration staff function.

Most IS departments include a *technology* office that investigates new information systems technologies and determines how the organization can benefit from them. For example, today many organizations are investigating social media and elastic cloud opportunities and planning how they can use those capabilities to better accomplish their goals and objectives. An individual called the **chief technology officer, or CTO**, often heads the technology group. The CTO evaluates new technologies, new ideas, and new capabilities and identifies those that are most relevant to the organization. The CTO's job requires deep knowledge of information technology and the ability to envision and innovate applications for the organization.

The next group in Figure 11-1, *Operations,* manages the computing infrastructure, including individual computers, in-house server farms, networks, and communications media. This group includes system and network administrators. As you will learn, an important function for this group is to monitor the user experience and respond to user problems.

The third group in the IS department in Figure 11-1 is *Development.* This group manages the process of creating new information systems as well as maintaining existing ones. (Recall from Chapter 10 that in the context of information systems *maintenance* means either fixing problems or adapting existing information systems to support new features and functions.)

The size and structure of the development group depend on whether programs are developed in-house. If not, this department will be staffed primarily by business and systems analysts who work with users, operations, and vendors to acquire and install licensed software and to set up the system components around that software. If the organization develops programs in-house, then this department will include programmers, test engineers, technical writers, and other development personnel.

The last IS department group in Figure 11-1 is *Outsourcing Relations*. This group exists in organizations that have negotiated outsourcing agreements with other companies to provide equipment, applications, or other services. You will learn more about outsourcing later in this chapter.

Figure 11-1 also includes a *Data Administration* staff function. The purpose of this group is to protect data and information assets by establishing data standards and data management practices and policies.

There are many variations on the structure of the IS department shown in Figure 11-1. In larger organizations, the operations group may itself consist of several different departments. Sometimes, there is a separate group for data warehousing and data marts.

As you examine Figure 11-1, keep the distinction between IS and IT in mind. *Information systems (IS)* exist to help the organization achieve its goals and objectives. Information systems have the five components we have discussed throughout this text. *Information technology (IT)* is simply technology. It concerns the products, techniques, procedures, and designs of computer-based technology. IT must be placed into the structure of an IS before an organization can use it.

What IS-Related Job Positions Exist?

IS departments provide a wide range of interesting and well-paying jobs. Many students enter the MIS class thinking that the IS departments consist only of programmers and computer technicians. If you reflect on the five components of an information system, you can understand why this cannot be true. The data, procedures, and people components of an information system require professionals with highly developed interpersonal communications skills.

Figure 11-2 summarizes the major job positions in the IS industry. With the exception of computer technician and possibly PQA test engineer, all of these positions require a 4-year

Figure 11-2

Job Positions in the
Information Systems
Industry

Title	Responsibilities	Knowledge, Skill, and Characteristics Requirements	United States 2013 Salary Range (USD)
Business analyst	Work with business leaders and planners to develop processes and systems that implement business strategy and goals.	Knowledge of business planning, strategy, process management, and technology. Can deal with complexity. See big picture but work with details. Strong interpersonal and communications skills needed.	$75,000–$125,000
System analyst	Work with users to determine system requirements, design and develop job descriptions and procedures, help determine system test plans.	Strong interpersonal and communications skills. Knowledge of both business and technology. Adaptable.	$65,000–$125,000
Programmer	Design and write computer programs.	Logical thinking and design skills, knowledge of one or more programming languages.	$50,000–$150,000
PQA test engineer	Develop test plans, design and write automated test scripts, perform testing.	Logical thinking, basic programming, superb organizational skills, eye for detail.	$40,000–$95,000
Technical writer	Write program documentation, help-text, procedures, job descriptions, training materials.	Quick learner, clear writing skills, high verbal communications skills.	$40,000–$95,000
User support representative	Help users solve problems, provide training.	Communications and people skills. Product knowledge. Patience.	$40,000–$75,000
Computer technician	Install software, repair computer equipment and networks.	Associate degree, diagnostic skills.	$30,000–$65,000
Network administrator	Monitor, maintain, fix, and tune computer networks.	Diagnostic skills, in-depth knowledge of communications technologies and products.	$75,000–$200,000+
Consultant	Wide range of activities: programming, testing, database design, communications and networks, project management, security and risk management, social media, strategic planning.	Quick learner, entrepreneurial attitude, communications and people skills. Respond well to pressure. Particular knowledge depends on work.	From $35 per hour for a contract tester to more than $500 per hour for strategic consulting to executive group.
Salesperson	Sell software, network, communications, and consulting services.	Quick learner, knowledge of product, superb professional sales skills.	$65,000–$200,000+
Small-scale project manager	Initiate, plan, manage, monitor, and close down projects.	Management and people skills, technology knowledge. Highly organized.	$75,000–$150,000
Large-scale project manager	Initiate, plan, monitor, and close down complex projects.	Executive and management skills. Deep project management knowledge.	$150,000–$250,000+
Database administrator	Manage and protect database.	Diplomatic skills, database technology knowledge.	$75,000–$250,000
Chief technology officer (CTO)	Advise CIO, executive group, and project managers on emerging technologies.	Quick learner, good communications skills, business background, deep knowledge of IT.	$125,000–$300,000+
Chief information officer (CIO)	Manage IT department, communicate with executive staff on IT- and IS-related matters. Member of the executive group.	Superb management skills, deep knowledge of business and technology, and good business judgment. Good communicator. Balanced and unflappable.	$150,000–$500,000, plus executive benefits and privileges.

degree. Furthermore, with the exception of programmer and PQA test engineer, they all require business knowledge. In most cases, successful professionals have a degree in business. Note, too, that most positions require good verbal and written communications skills. Business, including information systems, is a social activity.

Many of the positions in Figure 11-2 have a wide salary range. Lower salaries are for professionals with limited experience or for those who work in smaller companies or on small projects. The higher salaries are for those with deep knowledge and experience who work for large companies on large projects. Do not expect to begin your career at the high end of these ranges. As noted, all salaries are for positions in the United States and are shown in U.S. dollars.

(By the way, for all but the most technical positions, knowledge of a business specialty can add to your marketability. If you have the time, a dual major can be an excellent choice. Popular and successful dual majors are accounting and information systems, marketing and information systems, and management and information systems.)

How Do Organizations Plan the Use of IS?

We begin our discussion of IS functions with planning. Figure 11-3 lists the major IS planning functions.

Align Information Systems with Organizational Strategy

The purpose of an information system is to help the organization accomplish its goals and objectives. In order to do so, all information systems must be aligned with the organization's competitive strategy.

Recall the four competitive strategies from Chapter 3. The first two strategies are that an organization can be a cost leader either across an industry or within an industry segment. Alternatively, for the second two strategies, an organization can differentiate its products or services either across the industry or within a segment. Whatever the organizational strategy, the CIO and the IS department must constantly be vigilant to align IS with it.

Maintaining alignment between IS direction and organizational strategy is a continuing process. As strategies change, as the organization merges with other organizations, as divisions are sold, IS must evolve along with the organization. As you learned in Chapter 10, maintaining that alignment is an important role for BPM and for COBIT, in particular.

Unfortunately, however, adapting IS to new versions of business processes is neither easy nor quick. For example, switching from in-house hosting to cloud hosting requires time and resources. Such a change must also be made without losing the organization's computing infrastructure. The difficulty of adapting IS is often not appreciated in the executive suite. Without a persuasive CIO, IS can be perceived as a drag on the organization's opportunities.

Communicate IS Issues to the Executive Group

This last observation leads to the second IS planning function in Figure 11-3. The CIO is the representative for IS and IT issues within the executive staff. The CIO provides the IS perspective during discussions of problem solutions, proposals, and new initiatives.

- Align information systems with organizational strategy; maintain alignment as organization changes.
- Communicate IS/IT issues to executive group.
- Develop/enforce IS priorities within the IS department.
- Sponsor steering committee.

Figure 11-3
Planning the Use of IS/IT

Using MIS InClass 11 | A GROUP EXERCISE

Setting Up the PRIDE Systems IS Department

Let's suppose that Dr. Flores was able to obtain investment funds sufficient to implement PRIDE for medical practices, patients, and health clubs. Assume that he and his investors elected to wait until they had that portion of the business operating before they included insurance companies and employers.

Clearly, it makes no sense to attempt to integrate the new company with his surgical practice. Assume that, instead, the investment group formed a new entity entitled PRIDE Systems. PRIDE Systems will employ the managers, sales and marketing, and customer support personnel to take PRIDE to a broad market. Additionally, through a combination of in-house personnel and outsourcing, they will also staff an IS department.

Suppose you are asked to help plan that new department. Form a team as directed by your professor and address the following questions:

1. State the major functions of this new IS department. Explain how each of the functions defined in this chapter pertain to PRIDE.

2. Assume that the experience of hiring Ajit Barid worked well and that PRIDE Systems plans to continue application development with him. Describe factors that may make the investors nervous about this decision. Explain how you would respond to each of those factors.

3. Assume that PRIDE Systems will hire a cloud vendor to provide PaaS functionality. Explain what this means in general and what it means in particular for PRIDE.

4. Given your answers to questions 2 and 3,
   a. What will be the function and goals of the Operations group (see Figure 11-1)?
   b. What will be the function and goals of the Development group? What job descriptions will this group need to staff?
   c. What will be the function and goals of the Outsourcing Relations group?
   d. Will PRIDE Systems need a CTO? Justify your answer.

Source: Golden Pixels/SuperFusion/SuperStock

5. Understanding that PRIDE Systems is a small startup company that needs to conserve its investment dollars, would you recommend outsourcing any of the following functions? If so, explain the risks of doing so. If not, explain how you would justify the costs associated with staffing that function with employees.
   a. CTO
   b. Operations
   c. Outsourcing relations

6. Using Drucker's analogy, is IS Management in the front room or the back room for PRIDE Systems?

7. Summarize what you have learned in this exercise in a one-minute statement that you could use in a job interview with a small company.

For example, when considering a merger, it is important that the company consider integration of information systems in the merged entities. This consideration needs to be addressed during the evaluation of the merger opportunity. Too often, such issues are not considered until after the deal has been signed. Such delayed consideration is a mistake; the costs of the integration need to be factored into the economics of the purchase. Involving the CIO in high-level discussions is the best way to avoid such problems.

Develop Priorities and Enforce Them Within the IS Department

The next IS planning function in Figure 11-3 concerns priorities. The CIO must ensure that priorities consistent with the overall organizational strategy are developed and then communicated to the IS department. At the same time, the CIO must also ensure that the department evaluates proposals and projects for using new technology in light of those communicated priorities.

Technology is seductive, particularly to IS professionals. The CTO may enthusiastically claim, "By moving all our reporting services to the cloud, we can do this and this and this…" Although true, the question that the CIO must continually ask is whether those new possibilities are consistent with the organization's strategy and direction.

Thus, the CIO must not only establish and communicate such priorities, but enforce them as well. The department must evaluate every proposal, at the earliest stage possible, as to whether it is consistent with the organization's goals and aligned with its strategy.

Furthermore, no organization can afford to implement every good idea. Even projects that are aligned with the organization's strategy must be prioritized. The objective of everyone in the IS department must be to develop the most appropriate systems possible, given constraints on time and money. Well-thought-out and clearly communicated priorities are essential.

Sponsor the Steering Committee

The final planning function in Figure 11-3 is to sponsor the steering committee. A **steering committee** is a group of senior managers from the major business functions that works with the CIO to set the IS priorities and decide among major IS projects and alternatives.

The steering committee serves an important communication function between IS and the users. In the steering committee, information systems personnel can discuss potential IS initiatives and directions with the user community. At the same time, the steering committee provides a forum for users to express their needs, frustrations, and other issues they have with the IS department.

One other task related to planning the use of IT is establishing the organization's computer-use policy. For more on computer-use issues, read the Ethics Guide on pages 432–433.

Typically, the IS department sets up the steering committee's schedule and agenda and conducts the meetings. The CEO and other members of the executive staff determine the membership of the steering committee.

What Are the Advantages and Disadvantages of Outsourcing?

Outsourcing is the process of hiring another organization to perform a service. Outsourcing is done to save costs, to gain expertise, and to free management time.

The father of modern management, Peter Drucker, is reputed to have said, "Your back room is someone else's front room." For instance, in most companies, running the cafeteria is not an essential function for business success; thus, the employee cafeteria is a "back room." Google wants to be the worldwide leader in search and mobile computing hardware and applications, all supported by ever-increasing ad revenue. It does not want to be known for how well it runs cafeterias. Using Drucker's sentiment, Google is better off hiring another company, one that specializes in food services, to run its cafeterias.

Because food service is some company's "front room," that company will be better able to provide a quality product at a fair price. Outsourcing to a food vendor will also free Google's management from attention on the cafeteria. Food quality, chef scheduling, plastic fork acquisition, waste disposal, and so on will all be another company's concern. Google can focus on search, mobile computing, and advertising-revenue growth.

Ethics Guide

USING THE CORPORATE COMPUTER

Suppose you work at a company that has the following computer-use policy:

Computers, email, social networking, and the Internet are to be used primarily for official company business. Small amounts of personal email can be exchanged with friends and family, and occasional usage of the Internet is permitted, but such usage should be limited and never interfere with your work.

Suppose you are a manager and you learn that one of your employees has been engaged in the following activities:

1. Playing computer games during work hours
2. Playing computer games on the company computer before and after work hours
3. Responding to emails from an ill parent
4. Watching DVDs during lunch and other breaks
5. Sending emails to plan a party that involves mostly people from work
6. Sending emails to plan a party that involves no one from work
7. Searching the Web for a new car
8. Reading the news on *CNN.com*
9. Checking the stock market over the Internet
10. Bidding on items for personal use on eBay
11. Selling personal items on eBay
12. Paying personal bills online
13. Paying personal bills online when traveling on company business
14. Buying an airplane ticket for an ill parent over the Internet
15. Changing the content of a personal Facebook page
16. Changing the content of a personal business Web site
17. Buying an airplane ticket for a personal vacation over the Internet
18. Sending personal Twitter messages

DISCUSSION QUESTIONS

1. Using the categorical imperative (pages 20–21) and utilitarian (pages 54–55) perspectives, assess the ethics of each situation above.

2. Suppose someone from the IS department notifies you that one of your employees is spending 3 hours a day writing Twitter messages. How do you respond?

3. For question 2, suppose you ask how the IS department knows about your employee, and you are told, "We secretly monitor computer usage." Do you object to such monitoring? Why or why not?

4. Suppose someone from the IS department notifies you that one of your employees is sending dozens of personal emails every day. When you ask how he or she knows the emails are personal, you are told that IS measures account activity and when suspicious email usage is suspected the IS department reads employees' email.

Do you think such reading is legal? Using the categorical imperative and utilitarianism, assess the ethics of secretly reading employees' email. How do you respond about your employee?

5. As an employee, if you know that your company occasionally reads employees' email, does that change your behavior? If so, does that justify the company reading your email? Do the ethics of this situation differ from having someone read your personal postal mail that happens to be delivered to you at work? Why or why not?

6. Write what you think is the best corporate policy for personal computer usage at work. Specifically address Facebook, Pinterest, Twitter, and other personal social networking sites. Justify your policy using either the categorical imperative or utilitarianism.

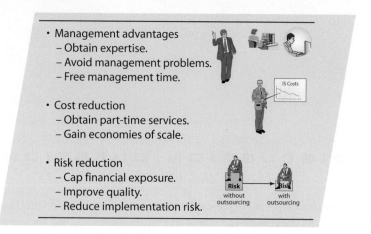

Figure 11-4
Popular Reasons for Outsourcing
IS Services

Outsourcing Information Systems

Many companies today have chosen to outsource portions of their information systems activities. Figure 11-4 lists popular reasons for doing so. Consider each major group of reasons.

Management Advantages

First, outsourcing can be an easy way to gain expertise. Neither Maggie nor Dr. Flores knows how to build either an iOS or a JavaScript application. Maggie could learn to do so, but it is not the direction in which she wants to go with her business and her career. Similarly, neither one knows how to create and manage a cloud-based report server for PRIDE reporting. Outsourcing the development of these applications is one way to obtain that expertise.

Another reason for outsourcing is to avoid management problems. As Maggie indicates, hiring their own programmers and test personnel would be a disaster for Dr. Flores and PRIDE. Maggie wants to be a business analyst and consultant; Dr. Flores wants to continue surgery. Neither knows how to manage development personnel, and neither wants to. Outsourcing the development function saves them from needing this expertise.

Similarly, some companies choose to outsource to save management time and attention. Lucas at AllRoad Parts has the skills to manage a new software development project, but he may choose to not invest the time.

Note, too, that it's not just Lucas's time. It is also time from more senior managers who approve the purchase and hiring requisitions for that activity. And those senior managers, like Kelly, will need to devote the time necessary to learn enough about server infrastructure to approve or reject the requisitions. Outsourcing saves both direct and indirect management time.

Cost Reduction

Other common reasons for choosing to outsource concern cost reductions. With outsourcing, organizations can obtain part-time services. Another benefit of outsourcing is to gain economies of scale. If 25 organizations develop their own payroll applications in-house, then when the tax law changes 25 different groups will have to learn the new law, change their software to meet the law, test the changes, and write the documentation explaining the changes. However, if those same 25 organizations outsource to the same payroll vendor, then that vendor can make all of the adjustments once, and the cost of the change can be amortized over all of them (thus lowering the cost that the vendor must charge).

Risk Reduction

Another reason for outsourcing is to reduce risk. First, outsourcing can cap financial risk. In a typical outsourcing contract, the outsource vendor will agree to a fixed price contract for services. This occurs, for example, when companies outsource their hardware to cloud vendors. Another way to cap financial risk is as Maggie recommends: delay paying the bulk of the fee until the work is completed and the software (or other component) is working. In the first case, it reduces risk by capping the total due; in the second, it ensures that little money need be spent until the job is done.

Second, outsourcing can reduce risk by ensuring a certain level of quality or avoiding the risk of having substandard quality. A company that specializes in food service knows what to do to provide a certain level of quality. It has the expertise to ensure, for example, that only healthy food is served. So, too, a company that specializes in, say, cloud-server hosting knows what to do to provide a certain level of reliability for a given workload.

Note that there is no guarantee that outsourcing will provide a certain level of quality or quality better than could be achieved in-house. If it doesn't outsource the cafeteria, Google might get lucky and hire only great chefs. Maggie might get lucky and hire the world's best software developer. But, in general, a professional outsourcing firm knows how to avoid giving everyone food poisoning or how to develop new mobile applications. And, if that minimum level of quality is not provided, it is easier to hire another vendor than it is to fire and rehire internal staff.

Finally, organizations choose to outsource IS in order to reduce implementation risk. Hiring an outside cloud vendor reduces the risk of picking the wrong brand of hardware or the wrong virtualization software or implementing tax law changes incorrectly. Outsourcing gathers all of these risks into the risk of choosing the right vendor. Once the company has chosen the vendor, further risk management is up to that vendor.

International Outsourcing

Choosing to use an outsourcing developer in India is not unique to PRIDE. Many firms headquartered in the United States have chosen to outsource overseas. Microsoft and Dell, for example, have outsourced major portions of their customer support activities to companies outside the United States. India is a popular source because it has a large, well-educated, English-speaking population that will work for 20 to 30 percent of the labor cost in the United States. China and other countries are used as well. In fact, with modern telephone technology and Internet-enabled service databases, a single service call can be initiated in the United States, partially processed in India, then Singapore, and finalized by an employee in England. The customer knows only that he has been put on hold for brief periods of time.

International outsourcing is particularly advantageous for customer support and other functions that must be operational 24/7. Amazon.com, for example, operates customer service centers in the United States, India, and Ireland. During the evening hours in the United States, customer service reps in India, where it is daytime, handle the calls. When night falls in India, customer service reps in Ireland handle the early morning calls from the east coast of the United States. In this way, companies can provide 24/7 service without requiring employees to work night shifts.

By the way, as you learned in Chapter 1, the key protection for your job is to become someone who excels at nonroutine symbolic analysis. Someone with the ability to find innovative applications of new technology is also unlikely to lose his or her job to overseas workers.

What Are the Outsourcing Alternatives?

Organizations have found hundreds of different ways to outsource information systems and portions of information systems. Figure 11-5 organizes the major categories of alternatives according to information systems components.

Some organizations outsource the acquisition and operation of computer hardware. Electronic Data Systems (EDS) has been successful for more than 30 years as an outsource vendor of hardware infrastructure. Figure 11-5 shows another alternative, outsourcing the computers in the cloud via IaaS.

Acquiring licensed software, as discussed in Chapters 4 and 10, is a form of outsourcing. Rather than develop the software in-house, an organization licenses it from another vendor.

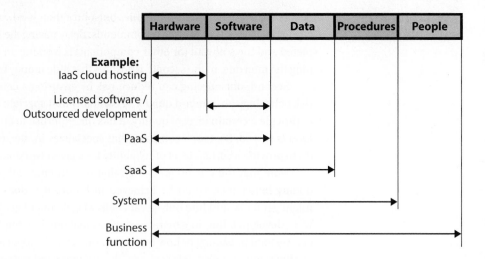

Figure 11-5
IS/IT Outsourcing Alternatives

Such licensing allows the software vendor to amortize the cost of software maintenance over all of the users, thus reducing that cost for all who use it. Another option is Platform as a Service (PaaS), which is the leasing of hardware with preinstalled operating systems as well as possibly DBMS systems. Microsoft's Azure is one such PaaS offering.

Some organizations choose to outsource the development of software. Such outsourcing might be for an entire application, as with PRIDE, or it could also be for making customizations to licensed software, as is frequently done with ERP implementations.

Yet another alternative is Software as a Service (SaaS), in which hardware and both operating system and application software are leased. Salesforce.com is a typical example of a company that offers SaaS.

It is also possible to outsource an entire system. PeopleSoft (now owned by Oracle) attained prominence by providing the entire payroll function as an outsourced service. In such a solution, as the arrow in Figure 11-5 implies, the vendor provides hardware, software, data, and some procedures. The company need provide only employee and work information; the payroll outsource vendor does the rest.

Finally, some organizations choose to outsource an entire business function. For years, many companies have outsourced to travel agencies the function of arranging for employee travel. Some of these outsource vendors even operate offices within the company facilities. Such agreements are much broader than outsourcing IS, but information systems are key components of the applications that are outsourced.

What Are the Risks of Outsourcing?

Not everyone agrees on the desirability of outsourcing. For potential pitfalls, read the example in the Guide on pages 444–445.

With so many advantages of outsourcing and so many different outsourcing alternatives, you might wonder why any company has in-house IS/IT functions. In fact, outsourcing presents significant risks, as listed in Figure 11-6.

Loss of Control

The first risk of outsourcing is a loss of control. For PRIDE, once Dr. Flores contracts with Ajit, Ajit is in control. At least for several weeks or months. If he makes PRIDE a priority project and devotes his attention and that of his employees as needed, all can work out well. On the other hand, if he obtains a larger, more lucrative contract soon after he starts PRIDE, schedule and quality problems can develop. Neither Dr. Flores nor Maggie has any control over this eventuality. If they pay at the end, they may not lose money, but they can lose time.

For service-oriented outsourcing, say the outsourcing of IT infrastructure, the vendor is in the driver's seat. Each outsource vendor has methods and procedures for its service. The

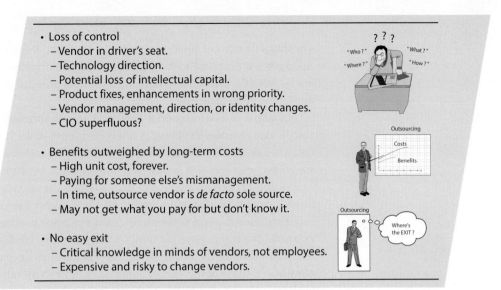

- Loss of control
  - Vendor in driver's seat.
  - Technology direction.
  - Potential loss of intellectual capital.
  - Product fixes, enhancements in wrong priority.
  - Vendor management, direction, or identity changes.
  - CIO superfluous?

- Benefits outweighed by long-term costs
  - High unit cost, forever.
  - Paying for someone else's mismanagement.
  - In time, outsource vendor is *de facto* sole source.
  - May not get what you pay for but don't know it.

- No easy exit
  - Critical knowledge in minds of vendors, not employees.
  - Expensive and risky to change vendors.

Figure 11-6
Outsourcing Risks

organization and its employees will have to conform to those procedures. For example, a hardware infrastructure vendor will have standard forms and procedures for requesting a computer, for recording and processing a computer problem, or for providing routine maintenance on computers. Once the vendor is in charge, employees must conform.

When outsourcing the cafeteria, employees have only those food choices that the vendor provides. Similarly, when obtaining computer hardware and services, the employees will need to take what the vendor supports. Employees who want equipment that is not on the vendor's list will be out of luck.

Unless the contract requires otherwise, the outsource vendor can choose the technology that it wants to implement. If the vendor, for some reason, is slow to pick up on a significant new technology, then the hiring organization will be slow to attain benefits from that technology. An organization can find itself at a competitive disadvantage because it cannot offer the same IS services as its competitors.

Another concern is a potential loss of intellectual capital. The company may need to reveal proprietary trade secrets, methods, or procedures to the outsource vendor's employees. As part of its normal operations, that vendor may move employees to competing organizations, and the company may lose intellectual capital as that happens. The loss need not be intellectual theft; it could simply be that the vendor's employees learned to work in a new and better way at your company, and then they take that learning to your competitor.

Similarly, all software has failures and problems. Quality vendors track those failures and problems and fix them according to a set of priorities. When a company outsources a system, it no longer has control over prioritizing those fixes. Such control belongs to the vendor. A fix that might be critical to your organization might be of low priority to the outsource vendor.

Other problems are that the outsource vendor may change management, adopt a different strategic direction, or be acquired. When any of those changes occur, priorities may change, and an outsource vendor that was a good choice at one time might be a bad fit after it changes direction. It can be difficult and expensive to change an outsource vendor when this occurs.

The final loss-of-control risk is that the company's CIO can become superfluous. When users need a critical service that is outsourced, the CIO must turn to the vendor for a response. In time, users learn that it is quicker to deal directly with the outsource vendor, and soon the CIO is out of the communication loop. At that point, the vendor has essentially replaced the CIO, who has become a figurehead. However, employees of the outsource vendor work for a different company, with a bias toward their employer. Critical managers will thus not share the same goals and objectives as the rest of the management team. Biased, bad decisions can result.

Benefits Outweighed by Long-Term Costs

The initial benefits of outsourcing can appear huge. A cap on financial exposure, a reduction of management time and attention, and the release of many management and staffing problems are all possible. (Most likely, outsource vendors promise these very benefits.) Outsourcing can appear too good to be true.

In fact, it *can be* too good to be true. For one, although a fixed cost does indeed cap exposure, it also removes the benefits of economies of scale. If PRIDE demand takes off, and suddenly needs 200 servers instead of 20, the using organization will pay 200 times the fixed cost of supporting one server. It is possible, however, that because of economies of scale, the costs of supporting 200 servers are far less than 10 times the costs of supporting 20 servers. If they were hosting those servers in-house, they and not the vendor would be the beneficiary.

Also, the outsource vendor may change its pricing strategy over time. Initially, an organization obtains a competitive bid from several outsource vendors. However, as the winning vendor learns more about the business, and as relationships develop between the organization's employees and those of the vendor, it becomes difficult for other firms to compete for subsequent contracts. The vendor becomes the *de facto* sole source and, with little competitive pressure, might increase its prices.

Another problem is that an organization can find itself paying for another organization's mismanagement, with little knowledge that that is the case. If PRIDE outsources its servers, it is difficult for it to know if the vendor is well managed. The PRIDE investors may be paying for poor management; even worse, PRIDE may suffer the consequences of poor management, such as lost data. It will be very difficult for PRIDE to learn about such mismanagement.

No Easy Exit

The final category of outsourcing risk concerns ending the agreement. There is no easy exit. For one, the outsource vendor's employees have gained significant knowledge of the company. They know the server requirements in customer support, they know the patterns of usage, and they know the best procedures for downloading operational data into the data warehouse. Consequently, lack of knowledge will make it difficult to bring the outsourced service back in-house.

Also, because the vendor has become so tightly integrated into the business, parting company can be exceedingly risky. Closing down the employee cafeteria for a few weeks while finding another food vendor would be unpopular, but employees would survive. Shutting down the enterprise network for a few weeks would be impossible; the business would not survive. Because of such risk, the company must invest considerable work, duplication of effort, management time, and expense to change to another vendor. In truth, choosing an outsource vendor can be a one-way street.

At PRIDE, if, after the initial application development, the team decides to change development vendors, it may be very difficult to do. The new vendor will not know the application code as well as the current one who created it. It may become infeasible in terms of time and money to consider moving to another, better, lower-cost vendor.

Choosing to outsource is a difficult decision. In fact, the correct decision might not be clear, but time and events could force the company to decide.

What Are Your User Rights and Responsibilities?

As a future user of information systems, you have both rights and responsibilities in your relationship with the IS department. The items in Figure 11-7 list what you are entitled to receive and indicate what you are expected to contribute.

You have a right to:
- Computer hardware and programs that allow you to perform your job proficiently
- Reliable network and Internet connections
- A secure computing environment
- Protection from viruses, worms, and other threats
- Contribute to requirements for new system features and functions
- Reliable systems development and maintenance
- Prompt attention to problems, concerns, and complaints
- Properly prioritized problem fixes and resolutions
- Effective training

You have a responsibility to:
- Learn basic computer skills
- Learn standard techniques and procedures for the applications you use
- Follow security and backup procedures
- Protect your password(s)
- Use computers and mobile devices according to your employer's computer-use policy
- Make no unauthorized hardware modifications
- Install only authorized programs
- Apply software patches and fixes when directed to do so
- When asked, devote the time required to respond carefully and completely to requests for requirements for new system features and functions
- Avoid reporting trivial problems

Figure 11-7
User Information Systems
Rights and Responsibilities

Your User Rights

You have a right to have the computing resources you need to perform your work as proficiently as you want. You have a right to the computer hardware and programs that you need. If you process huge files for data-mining applications, you have a right to the huge disks and the fast processor that you need. However, if you merely receive email and consult the corporate Web portal, then your right is for more modest requirements (leaving the more powerful resources for those in the organization who require them).

You have a right to reliable network and Internet services. *Reliable* means that you can process without problems almost all of the time. It means that you never go to work wondering, "Will the network be available today?" Network problems should be a rare occurrence.

You also have a right to a secure computing environment. The organization should protect your computer and its files, and you should not normally even need to think about security. From time to time, the organization might ask you to take particular actions to protect your computer and files, and you should take those actions. But such requests should be rare and related to specific outside threats.

You have a right to participate in requirements meetings for new applications that you will use and for major changes to applications that you currently use. You may choose to delegate this right to others, or your department may delegate that right for you, but if so, you have a right to contribute your thoughts through that delegate.

You have a right to reliable systems development and maintenance. Although schedule slippages of a month or two are common in many development projects, you should not have to endure schedule slippages of 6 months or more. Such slippages are evidence of incompetent systems development.

Additionally, you have a right to receive prompt attention to your problems, concerns, and complaints about information services. You have a right to have a means to report problems and to know that your problem has been received and at least registered with the IS department. You have a right to have your problem resolved, consistent with established priorities. This means that an annoying problem that allows you to conduct your work will be prioritized below another's problem that interferes with his ability to do his job.

Finally, you have a right to effective training. It should be training that you can understand and that enables you to use systems to perform your particular job. The organization should provide training in a format and on a schedule that is convenient to you.

Your User Responsibilities

With the popularity of mobile devices, you must also follow your organization's policy on the use of mobile devices at work. See the Security Guide on pages 442–443.

You also have responsibilities toward the IS department and your organization. Specifically, yo have a responsibility to learn basic computer skills and to learn the techniques and procedure for the applications you use. You should not expect hand-holding for basic operations. No should you expect to receive repetitive training and support for the same issue.

You have a responsibility to follow security and backup procedures. This is especially im portant because actions that you fail to take might cause problems for your fellow employee and your organization as well as for you. In particular, you are responsible for protecting you password(s). In the next chapter, you will learn that this is important not only to protect you computer but, because of intersystem authentication, also to protect your organization's net works and databases as well.

You have a responsibility for using your computer resources in a manner that is consisten with your employer's policy. Many employers allow limited email for critical family matter while at work, but discourage frequent and long casual email. You have a responsibility to kno your employer's policy and to follow it. Further, if your employer has a policy concerning use c personal mobile devices at work, you are responsible for following it.

You also have a responsibility to make no unauthorized hardware modifications to you computer and to install only authorized programs. One reason for this policy is that you IS department constructs automated maintenance programs for upgrading your compute Unauthorized hardware and programs might interfere with these programs. Additionally, th installation of unauthorized hardware or programs can cause you problems that the IS depart ment will have to fix.

You have a responsibility to install computer updates and fixes when asked to do so. Thi is particularly important for patches that concern security and backup and recovery. Whe asked for input to requirements for new and adapted systems, you have a responsibility to tak the time necessary to provide thoughtful, complete responses. If you do not have that time, yo should delegate your input to someone else.

Finally, you have a responsibility to treat information systems professionals professionally Everyone works for the same company, everyone wants to succeed, and professionalism an courtesy will go a long way on all sides. One form of professional behavior is to learn basic com puter skills so that you avoid reporting trivial problems.

 ## 2024?

Many changes and developments will have a major effect on the organizational management o IS and IT resources in the next 10 years. Most organizations will move their internal hardwar infrastructure into the cloud. Sure, some companies will be concerned enough about securit that they'll keep some data on their own, privately controlled servers, but vast amounts of hard ware infrastructure will migrate to the cloud. Running a computer center for anyone other tha a cloud vendor is not a promising career.

We will most certainly see the rise in the use of mobile devices at work. Mobile devices wi become cheaper, more powerful, with dynamic, maybe even game-like user experiences. The will be ubiquitous.

Organizations will develop BYOD policies that meet their needs and strategies, and man will encourage employees to bring their own devices to work. At some point, that might eve become a requirement. "What mobile device do you use?" could become a standard interviev question.

By 2024, organizations will use social media inside the organization in true Enterpris 2.0 style. Organizational knowledge management will be done using social media, and mos projects will have a social media component, or perhaps that has it backward. Social media sites will have a project component.

I suspect that by 2024, the SDLC will be a thing of the past, at least as far as we know it today. New systems will be developed using some variation of agile technologies, and changes to existing systems will be accomplished with a mixture of classic SDLC phases and agile techniques.

Meanwhile, organizations will continue to lose control, as summarized in the Security Guide on pages 442–443, while mobile devices are becoming even more popular. When employees come to work with their own computing devices that are more powerful than any computer they have at work, and when those devices access networks that are paid for by the employees, how will the IS department maintain control?

For a few years, organizations may be able to maintain some semblance of control with restrictive BYOD policies. That policy will work for a while, but ultimately it's doomed. For one, at some point that policy will put employees at a competitive disadvantage. Employees will want to access the network using whatever hardware they have, wherever they happen to be. If they can't, their competitors will.

But there's a second reason that limiting access to the corporate network won't work. Employees will move off the network! "Ah, we can't access SharePoint from our iPads, so let's use my Google Drive instead of the corporate SharePoint site. I'll share my folder with the whole team, and then we can get to it using our own mobile devices. Here, I'll copy the data from the computer at work onto my Drive, and we can take it from there." Or, "Let's create a Google+ circle." Or…

Now, all the corporate data are out on someone's Google Grid or Google+ account or somewhere else and has been shared with, well, who knows? Employee Jones made a mistake; instead of sharing her Google+ circle with her teammates at work, she shared it on a public circle. Now, anyone, or any crawler, that stumbles over that data has access to it.

There doesn't seem to be an answer for managing the risk of data loss. Maybe buy insurance? All of this sets the stage for Chapter 12…on security.

Security Guide

ARE WE PROTECTING THEM FROM ME OR ME FROM THEM?

I'm Justin, I work in operations. My boss asked me to join a committee the IS department just created. The purpose of the committee is to determine our company's BYOD[2] policy. Well, that's not quite right. The IS department will determine the policy, but they want to hear from active mobile users before they do so. This committee may be a waste of time. I don't know. But I do meet some interesting people from around the company.

It's strange how fast things change. My grandfather worked for IBM in the 1960s. I saw him last weekend, and when I told him about this committee, he laughed. He said when he was working at IBM, he wanted to take an adding machine home once. I guess all it did was to add and subtract; it didn't even multiply. Anyway, he wanted to take it home for the weekend to work on budgets, but to get it past security on the way out of the building, he had to have a permission slip signed by his boss and by the facilities department head. I guess the thing weighed 40 pounds. He said there was no way he could take a computer home then; it weighed a couple of tons and needed special power and an air-conditioned room.

"BYOD!" he said, "They want you to bring your own computer to work? Crazy. I couldn't even take an adding machine out, and they want you to bring your computer in?" Then he asked, "What keeps you from taking all their secret data?"

"That's one of the things we talk about."

"I'll bet you do."

Fifty years: that's how long it's been since he carried that 40-pound adding machine home.

His story got me wondering when the data security problem started. Long before mobile devices, I think. Twenty years ago, you could copy data onto a CD and take it out of the office. Later you could use a thumb drive or take it home on your laptop and, if you wanted to steal it, copy it onto one of your home computers. Now, we can take data on our own mobile devices if we want. So, mobile devices aren't a new data security threat.

Now that I think about it, maybe it isn't what I'm taking *out* that's a threat; maybe it's what I'm bringing *in*. The

---

[2]Bring Your Own Device. From Chapter 4, pp. 142–143.

IS department doesn't know what programs I've got on my mobile device. That must be why they want to "configure" it. They want to see that I don't have malware that could damage the corporate network? But I know they add programs of their own to it as well.

That part makes me nervous. I heard that one company installs *key loggers*, you know, a program that records all the user's keystrokes into a file. The IS department regularly checks what owners are doing with *their own devices*. Plus, on the committee, I've learned one plan is to install a program that IS can use to remotely wipe all the programs off mobile devices, at their command. They say they need it in case we lose our devices. OK, I get that. But

what if someone makes a mistake? Wipes out my device by accident? Or what if I quit? Or they fire me? Will they wipe all the programs off my mobile device then? Will they take my own programs?

Right now, I'm at a standstill with my employer. They don't trust the programs I put on my mobile device, and I don't trust them to install programs on it, either. Maybe this BYOD thing isn't such a good idea, after all. Maybe they should just buy me the computers they want me to use at work. I'll still bring my mobile device to work, but I'll use my own wireless network, not theirs, and I won't do work with it. Is that why my boss wants me on this committee?

DISCUSSION QUESTIONS

1. The obvious reason for the IS department to sponsor a user committee to help set up BYOD policy is to learn what users do and don't want. What other reasons might the department have for setting up this committee?

2. Justin has to work (unpaid) overtime to make up his regular work when he attends the BYOD meetings. He says he meets interesting people. What are other benefits that he receives by attending these meetings?

3. Rather than in-person committee meetings, the IS department could set up a social media presence to gather user feedback. Name the facilities (wiki, survey, etc.) that you think such a presence should have. Summarize the advantages and disadvantages of in-person versus social media for this purpose.

4. Clearly, over the past 50 years, organizations have lost considerable control over their data. What are the potential consequences of this loss? Which of those potential consequences do you see as real?

5. In your opinion, which is the greater threat of mobile devices at work: the data the employees take *out* or the programs they bring *in*? Explain your answer.

6. Summarize the reasons that Justin is at a standstill with his employer regarding their configuration of his mobile

device. How can a BYOD policy break this standstill? If you think it's impossible, say why.

7. Using approximate but realistic numbers, estimate the cost of hardware and software for a company of 450 employees. Assume computers last three years, and that the annual cost of supporting users is 40 percent of the hardware and software costs. Assume half of the employees can do their work with mobile devices and, of that 50 percent, assume that 80 percent will do so. Finally, assume the cost of supporting a mobile user is $350 per year.

   a. What is the total annual cost for hardware, software, and support assuming no mobile devices are used?

   b. What is the total annual cost for hardware, software, and support assuming mobile devices are used as indicated in the question?

   c. Are the savings of allowing employees to use their mobile devices worth the data security, network, and other risks?

   d. What other benefits accrue to organizations and employees when mobile devices are used?

   e. Formulate your own statement on the desirability of employees using their own mobile devices at work.

Guide

IS OUTSOURCING FOOL'S GOLD?

"**People are kidding** themselves. It sounds so good—just pay a fixed, known amount to some vendor for your computer infrastructure, and all your problems go away. Everyone has the computers they need, the network never goes down, and you never have to endure another horrible meeting about network protocols, https, and the latest worm. You're off into information systems nirvana....

"Except it doesn't work that way. You trade one set of problems for another. Consider the outsourcing of computer infrastructure. What's the first thing the outsource vendor does? It hires all of the employees who were doing the work for you. Remember that lazy, incompetent network administrator the company had—the one who never seemed to get anything done? Well, he's baaaaack, as an employee of your outsource company. Only this time he has an excuse, 'Company policy won't allow me to do it that way.'

"So the outsourcers get their first-level employees by hiring the ones you had. Of course, the outsourcer says it will provide management oversight, and if the employees don't work out, they'll be gone. What you're really outsourcing is middle-level management of the same IT personnel you had. But there's no way of knowing whether the managers they supply are any better than the ones you had.

"Also, you think you had bureaucratic problems before? Every vendor has a set of forms, procedures, committees, reports, and other management 'tools.' They will tell you that you have to do things according to the standard blueprint. They have to say that because if they allowed every company to be different, they'd never be able to gain any leverage themselves, and they'd never be profitable.

"So now you're paying a premium for the services of your former employees, who are now managed by strangers who are paid by the outsource vendor, who evaluates those managers on how well they follow the outsource vendor's profit-generating procedures. How quickly can they turn your operation into a clone of all their other clients? Do you really want to do that?

"Suppose you figure all this out and decide to get out of it. Now what? How do you undo an outsource agreement? All the critical knowledge is in the minds of the outsource vendor's employees, who have no incentive to work for you. In fact, their employment contract probably prohibits it. So now you have to take an existing operation within your own

Source: © lapas77/Fotolia

444

company, hire employees to staff that function, and relearn everything you ought to have learned in the first place.

"Gimme a break. Outsourcing is fool's gold, an expensive leap away from responsibility. It's like saying, 'We can't figure out how to manage an important function in our company, so you do it!' You can't get away from IS problems by hiring someone else to manage them for you. At least you care about *your* bottom line."

 DISCUSSION QUESTIONS

1. Hiring an organization's existing IS staff is common practice when starting a new outsourcing arrangement. What are the advantages of this practice to the outsource vendor? What are the advantages to the organization?

2. Suppose you work for an outsource vendor. How do you respond to the charge that your managers care only about how they appear to their employer (the outsource vendor), not how they actually perform for the organization?

3. Consider the statement, "We can't figure out how to manage an important function in our company, so you do it!" Do you agree with the sentiment of this statement? If this is true, is it necessarily bad? Why or why not?

4. Explain how it is possible for an outsource vendor to achieve economies of scale that are not possible for the hiring organization. Does this phenomenon justify outsourcing? Why or why not?

5. In what ways is outsourcing IS infrastructure like outsourcing the company cafeteria? In what ways is it different? What general conclusions can you make about infrastructure outsourcing?

6. This guide assumes that the outsourcing agreement is for the organization's computing infrastructure. Outsourcing for software development, as PRIDE is doing, involves less direct involvement with the contractor. Explain how your answers to questions 1–5 would be different for software outsourcing.

7. How do your answers to questions 1–5 differ if the outsourcing agreement is just for PaaS resources?

ACTIVE REVIEW

Use this Active Review to verify that you understand the ideas and concepts that answer the chapter's study questions.

Q1 What are the functions and organization of the IS department?

List the five primary functions of the IS department. Define *CIO* and explain the CIO's typical reporting relationships. Name the four groups found in a typical IS department, and explain the major responsibilities of each. Define *CTO,* and explain typical CTO responsibilities. Explain the purpose of the data administration function.

Q2 How do organizations plan the use of IS?

Explain the importance of strategic alignment as it pertains to IS planning. Explain why maintaining alignment can be difficult. Describe the CIO's relationship to the rest of the executive staff. Describe the CIO's responsibilities with regard to priorities. Explain challenges to this task. Define *steering committee* and explain the CIO's role with regard to it.

Q3 What are the advantages and disadvantages of outsourcing?

Define *outsourcing*. Explain how Drucker's statement, "Your back room is someone else's front room" pertains to outsourcing. Summarize the management advantages, cost advantages, and risks of outsourcing. Differentiate among IaaS, PaaS, and SaaS, and give an example of each. Explain why international outsourcing can be particularly advantageous. Describe skills you can develop that will protect you from having your job outsourced. Summarize the outsourcing risks concerning control, long-term costs, and exit strategy.

Q4 What are your user rights and responsibilities?

Explain in your own words the meaning of each of your user rights as listed in Figure 11-7. Explain in your own words the meaning of each of your user responsibilities in Figure 11-7.

Q5 2024?

List the changes and developments that will have an effect on an organization's management of IS and IT. Summarize the predictions for scrum and Enterprise 2.0. Explain what is predicted to happen for development processes. Explain why loss of data control is inevitable, and discuss why restrictive BYOD policies are not viable. Describe how employees may move off that network, and discuss the security threat that occurs. Name one solution for managing the risk of data loss.

Using Your Knowledge with PRIDE

You now know the primary responsibilities of the IS department and can understand why it may implement the standards and policies that it does. You know the planning functions of IS and how they relate to the rest of your organization. You also know the reasons for outsourcing IS services, the most common and popular outsource alternatives, and the risks of outsourcing. Finally, you know your rights and responsibilities with regard to services provided by your IS department.

As described in Using MIS InClass 10, the new entity PRIDE Systems needs to set up an IS department. The knowledge of this chapter will help you understand what needs to be done, whether you work for PRIDE Systems, are a potential investor in PRIDE Systems, or are an advisor to a potential investor.

KEY TERMS AND CONCEPTS

Chief information officer (CIO) 426	Green computing 447	Steering committee 431
Chief technology officer (CTO) 427	Outsourcing 431	

MyMISLab

Go to **mymislab.com** to complete the problems marked with this icon .

USING YOUR KNOWLEDGE

11-1. According to this chapter, information systems, products, and technology are not malleable; they are difficult to change, alter, or bend. How do you think senior executives other than the CIO view this lack of malleability? For example, how do you think IS appears during a corporate merger?

11-2. Suppose you represent an investor group that is acquiring hospitals across the nation and integrating them into a unified system. List five potential problems and risks concerning information systems. How do you think IS-related risks compare to other risks in such an acquisition program?

11-3. What happens to IS when corporate direction changes rapidly? How will IS appear to other departments? What happens to IS when the corporate strategy changes frequently? Do you think such frequent changes are a greater problem to IS than to other business functions? Why or why not?

COLLABORATION EXERCISE 11

Using the collaboration IS you built in Chapter 2 (pages 73–74), collaborate with a group of students to answer the following questions.

Green computing is environmentally conscious computing consisting of three major components: power management, virtualization, and e-waste management. In this exercise, we focus on power.

You know, of course, that computers (and related equipment, such as printers) consume electricity. That burden is light for any single computer or printer. But consider all the computers and printers in the United States that will be running tonight, with no one in the office. Proponents of green computing encourage companies and employees to reduce power and water consumption by turning off devices when not in use.

Is this issue important? Is it just a concession to environmentalists to make computing professionals appear virtuous? Form a team and develop your own, informed opinion by considering computer use at your campus.

1. Search the Internet to determine the power requirements for typical computing and office equipment. Consider laptop computers, desktop computers, CRT monitors, LCD monitors, and printers. For this exercise, ignore server computers. As you search, be aware that a *watt* is a measure of electrical power. It is *watts* that the green computing movement wants to reduce.

2. Estimate the number of each type of device in use on your campus. Use your university's Web site to determine the number of colleges, departments, faculty, staff, and students. Make assumptions about the number of computers, copiers, and other types of equipment used by each.

3. Using the data from items 1 and 2, estimate the total power used by computing and related devices on your campus.

4. A computer that is in screensaver mode uses the same amount of power as one in regular mode. Computers that are in sleep mode, however, use much less power, say 6 watts per hour. Reflect on computer use on your campus and estimate the amount of time that computing devices are in sleep versus screensaver or use mode. Compute the savings in power that result from sleep mode.

5. Computers that are automatically updated by the IS department with software upgrades and patches cannot be allowed to go into sleep mode because if they are sleeping they will not be able to receive the upgrade. Hence, some universities prohibit sleep mode on university computers (sleep mode is never used on servers, by the way). Determine the cost, in watts, of such a policy.

6. Calculate the monthly cost, in watts, if:
   a. All user computers run full time night and day.
   b. All user computers run full time during work hours and in sleep mode during off-hours.
   c. All user computers are shut off during nonwork hours.

7. Given your answers to items 1–6, is computer power management during off-hours a significant concern? In comparison to the other costs of running a university, does this issue really matter? Discuss this question among your group and explain your answer.

CASE STUDY 11

iApp$$$$ 4 U

Let's suppose that you have a great idea for an iOS application. It doesn't matter what it is; it could be something to make life easier for college students or your parents or something to track healthcare expenses and payments for your grandparents. Whatever it is, let's assume that the idea is a great one.

First, what is the value of that idea? According to Raven Zachary, writing on the O'Reilly blog, it is zero.[3]

Nada. According to Zachary, no professional iPhone developer (he wrote this in 2008 about iPhone apps) will take equity or the promise of future revenue sharing in exchange for cash. There is too much cash-paying work. And ideas are only as good as their implementation, a fact that is true for every business project, not just iOS applications.

So, how can you go about getting your iOS application developed? According to *OS X Daily*, in 2010 iOS developers in the United States and countries in the European Union were charging $50 to $250 per hour, and a typical, smaller application required 4 to 6 weeks to create.[4] TechCrunch polled 124 developers and found that the average cost of creating an iPhone app was $6,453,[5] but that number included projects that were programmed using cheaper, offshore developers.

These costs are incomplete. They include programming time, but not time to specify requirements nor to design the user interface, both of which are time-consuming tasks. Also, it is not clear that these costs include testing time nor the time needed to marshal the app through the Apple review process before it can appear in the App Store.

So, what are your options? First, do as much work as you can. Reread the stages in the systems development life cycle in Chapter 10 (pages 387–397). Determine how many of those stages you can do yourself. Unless you are already a skilled object-oriented programmer and comfortable writing in Objective-C, you cannot do the coding yourself. You might, however, be able to reduce development costs if you design the user interface and specify the ways that your users will employ it. You can also develop at least the skeleton of a test plan. You might also perform some of the testing tasks yourself.

If you have, let's round up, say $10,000 that you're willing to invest, then you could outsource the development to a developer in the United States. If not, you have two other possible choices: outsource offshore or hire a computer science student. Elance is a clearinghouse for iOS development experts;

it lists developers, their locations, typical costs, and ratings provided by previous customers.[6] As you can see, you can hire developers in India, Russia, the Ukraine, Romania, and other countries. Costs tend to be in the $2,000 range for a simple app, but again, that estimate probably does not include all the costs you will incur getting your application into the App Store.

What about hiring a local computer science student? The price might be right, certainly far less than a professional developer, but this alternative is fraught with problems. First, good students are in high demand, and, second, good students are, well, students. They need to study and don't have as much time to devote to your app. And, hard as it is to believe, some students are flakes. However, if you have a friend whom you trust, you might make this option work.

One other option is to divide and conquer. Break your really great idea up into smaller apps. Pick one that is sure to be a hit and sell it cheaply, say for $.99. Use the money that you earn from that application to fund the next application, one that you might sell for more.

QUESTIONS

11-4. What characteristics make a mobile application great? Describe at least five characteristics that compel you to buy applications. What characteristics would make an application easy and cheap to develop? Difficult and expensive?

11-5. Visit *http://techcrunch.com/2013/06/24/it-device-sales-to-rise-6-to-2-4b-in-2013-driven-by-android-tablets-smartphones-pcs-continue-decline* (or a more recent survey than this June 2013 survey). Summarize how the market for mobile application development is changing.

11-6. Reread pages 387–397 of Chapter 10 about the SDLC process. List tasks to perform and assess whether you could perform each task. If you cannot perform that task, describe how you could outsource that task and estimate how much you think it would cost for a simple application.

11-7. Visit *www.elance.com* and identify five potential outsource vendors that you could use to develop your app. Describe criteria you would use for selecting one of these vendors.

---

[3]Raven Zachary, "Turning Ideas into iPhone Applications," *O'Reilly Media*, last modified November 21, 2008, *http://blogs.oreilly.com/iphone/2008/11/turning-ideas-into-application.html*.

[4]"iPhone Development Costs," *OSXDaily*, last modified September 7, 2010, *http://osxdaily.com/2010/09/07/iphone-development-costs/*.

[5]Alex Ahlund, "iPhone App Sales, Exposed," TechCrunch, last modified May 16, 2010, *http://techcrunch.com/2010/05/16/iphone-app-sales-exposed/*.

[6]"iPhone Development Experts Group," Elance, accessed August 6, 2013, *http://www.elance.com/groups/iPhone_Development_Experts*.

1-8. Explain how you think Google's purchase of Motorola Mobility changes the opportunity for iOS apps. In theory, does this purchase cause you to believe it would be wiser for you to develop on the Android or on the Windows 8 phone?

1-9. Search the Web for "Android developers" and related terms. Does it appear that the process of creating an Android app is easier, cheaper, or more desirable than creating an iOS app?

11-10. This case assumes that you have made the decision to develop an iOS application. Take an opposing view that developing a thin-client browser application would be a better decision. Explain how you would justify a thin-client app as a better decision.

11-11. Prepare a 1-minute summary of your experience with this exercise that you could use in a job interview to demonstrate innovative thinking. Give your summary to the rest of your class.

MyMISLab

Go to **mymislab.com** for Auto-graded writing questions as well as the following Assisted-graded writing questions:

11-12. Consider the following statement: "In many ways, choosing an outsource vendor is a one-way street." Explain what this statement means. Do you agree with it? Why or why not? Does your answer change depending on what systems components are being outsourced? Why or why not?

11-13. Using the dialogue that opened this chapter, as well as Figures 11-4 and 11-6, list the advantages and disadvantages of outsourcing PRIDE application development. Briefly describe each.

11-14. Mymislab Only – comprehensive writing assignment for this chapter.

Information Security Management

"We have to *design* it for privacy…and security." Ajit Barid is videoconferencing with Dr. Romero Flores and Maggie Jensen. Ajit is in his company offices in Hyderabad, India; Dr. Flores is in his office in Austin, Texas; and Maggie is in her office in Denver, Colorado.

"That sounds expensive. What do you mean, Ajit?" Dr. Flores is still getting comfortable with his outsourcing vendor.

"Well, to do this right, we need to design it so that the patient has control over the dissemination of the data." Ajit's voice comes in clearly, even though he is 11,000 miles away.

"Yes, I think we had that in our requirements statement."

"Dr. Flores," Maggie jumps into the conversation, "because we'll have, we hope, thousands and thousands of users, we need to store their privacy settings in a database."

"OK. I get that."

"That's the way to do it, but it also means that we need to have proper security over that database," Ajit continues.

"All right. I get that, too. So we just have people sign into the privacy database with their name and password?"

"Yes, we do, but we have to be careful to avoid problems like SQL injection attacks." Ajit doesn't know how much to explain.

"*Injection*? Now we're speaking my language. But what is SQL?"

Maggie doesn't want the conversation to get technical. She knows they're going to get bogged down as Dr. Flores tries to understand. He's a very bright man, and he won't be able to let anything go. She doesn't want to use their time tutoring him on SQL.

"How about this, Dr. Flores…" Maggie says cautiously, "rather than use your time for these details, why don't you let us work through the issues? There are a number of well-known attacks and issues that we need to design for, and we'll do that."

"OK, but I was starting to enjoy this. Injections. You guys have sutures, too?"

"No, but we talk about Band-Aids over bugs…"

"Ajit!" Maggie interrupts, "Let's let Dr. Flores get back to his practice.

MyMISLab™

Visit **mymislab.com** for simulations, tutorials, and end-of-chapter problems.

"We have to design it for privacy…and security."

You and I can talk about this offline." Maggie is determined to cut this conversation off before it's out of control.

Ajit and Maggie videoconference an hour later:

"OK, Maggie, I'm sorry. I just couldn't resist. I wanted to get his reaction to *viruses* and *worms*, too…"

"I'm so glad you didn't." Maggie is relieved he sees her point. "What have you got?"

"The relationships between people and healthcare professionals, employers, insurance companies, and health clubs are all many-to-many."

"Right. I understand that, Ajit, but what does it have to do with privacy?"

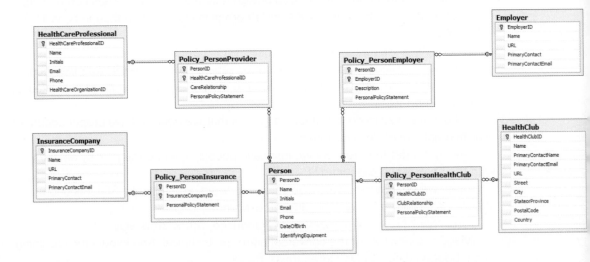

STUDY QUESTIONS

Q1 What is the goal of information systems security?

Q2 How big is the computer security problem?

Q3 How should you respond to security threats?

Q4 How should organizations respond to security threats?

Q5 How can technical safeguards protect against security threats?

Q6 How can data safeguards protect against security threats?

Q7 How can human safeguards protect against security threats?

Q8 How should organizations respond to security incidents?

Q9 2024?

"Well, we can use the intersection table for each to store the patient's privacy settings. And we only let the patients have access to forms having this data." (See above.)

"Makes sense. I like it…a clean design."

"Privacy settings are carried in the PersonalPolicyStatement attribute. Possible values are 'No access,' 'Non-identifying,' 'Summary,' and 'Full Access.' The last two include patient identity."

"OK, but don't hard-code them. We may have others."

"Would I do that? If we showed this to Dr. Flores, he'd see what we mean by *design for security*."

"Ajit, don't go there."

"OK."

CHAPTER PREVIEW

This chapter provides an overview of the major components of information systems security. We begin in Q1 by defining the goals of IS security and then, in Q2, discuss the size of the computer security problem. Next, in Q3, we address how you, both as a student today and as a business professional in the future, should respond to security threats. Then, in Q4, we ask what organizations need to do to respond to security threats. After that, Q5 through Q7 address security safeguards. Q5 discusses technical safeguards that involve hardware and software components, Q6 addresses data safeguards, and Q7 discusses human safeguards that involve procedure and people components. Q8 then summarizes what organizations need to do when they incur a security incident, and we wrap up the chapter with a preview of IS security in 2024.

Unfortunately, threats to data and information systems are increasing and becoming more complex. In fact, the U.S. Bureau of Labor Statistics estimates that demand for security specialists will increase by more than 50 percent between 2008 and 2018.[1] If you find this topic attractive, majoring in information systems with a security specialty would open the door to many interesting jobs.

 # What Is the Goal of Information Systems Security?

Information systems security involves a trade-off between cost and risk. To understand the nature of this trade-off, we begin with a description of the security threat/loss scenario and then discuss the sources of security threats. Following that, we'll state the goal of information systems security.

The IS Security Threat/Loss Scenario

Figure 12-1 illustrates the major elements of the security problem that individuals and organizations confront today. A **threat** is a person or organization that seeks to obtain or alter data or other IS assets illegally, without the owner's permission and often without the owner's

---

[1]U.S. Bureau of Labor Statistics, *Occupational Outlook Handbook, 2010–2011 Edition*, last modified March 29, 2012, *http://www.bls.gov/oco/ocos305.htm#outlook*. The information security specialty is included in the network systems and data communications category.

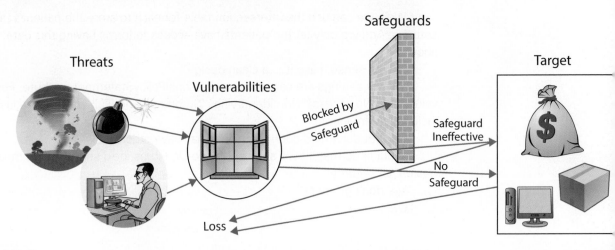

Figure 12-1
Threat/Loss Scenario

knowledge. A **vulnerability** is an opportunity for threats to gain access to individual or organizational assets. For example, when you buy something online, you provide your credit card data; when that data is transmitted over the Internet, it is vulnerable to threats. A **safeguard** is some measure that individuals or organizations take to block the threat from obtaining the asset. Notice in Figure 12-1 that safeguards are not always effective; some threats achieve their goal despite safeguards. Finally, the **target** is the asset that is desired by the threat.

Figure 12-2 shows examples of threats/targets, vulnerabilities, safeguards, and results. In the first two rows, an Xbox gamer (the threat) wants your credit card data (the target) to buy more games using your account. As stated previously, when you provide your credit card data for an online transaction, that data is vulnerable to the threat as it travels over the Internet. However, if, as shown in the first row of Figure 12-2, you conduct your transaction using https rather than http (discussed in Q5), you will be using an effective safeguard, and you will successfully counter the threat.

If, however, as described in the second row of Figure 12-2, you send your credit card data to a friend via email, you will, in most cases, have no safeguard at all. That data is open to any threat that happens to sniff your traffic on the Internet. In this case, you may soon be paying for hours and hours of Xbox games for a person you do not even know.

The bottom row of Figure 12-2 shows another situation. Here an employee at work obtains sensitive data and posts it on what he thinks is a work-only Google+ group. However, the employee errs and instead posts it to a public group. The target is the sensitive data, and the vulnerability is public access to the group. In this case, there are several safeguards that should have prevented this loss; the employee needed passwords to obtain the sensitive data and to join the private work-only group. The employer has procedures that state employees are not to post confidential data to any public site, such as Google+, but these procedures were either unknown or ignored.

Threat/Target	Vulnerability	Safeguard	Result	Explanation
Xbox Live gamer wants your credit card data	You use your credit card to buy online	Buy only using https	No loss	Effective safeguard
	You send credit card data to friend in email	None	Loss of credit card data	No safeguard
Employee posts sensitive data to public Google+ group	Public access to not-secure group	Passwords Procedures Employee training	Loss of sensitive data	Ineffective safeguard

Figure 12-2
Examples of Threat/Loss

A third safeguard is the training that all employees are given. Because the employee ignores the procedures, though, all of those safeguards are ineffective and the data is exposed to the public.

What Are the Sources of Threats?

Figure 12-3 summarizes the sources of security threats. The type of threat is shown in the columns, and the type of loss is shown in the rows.

Human Error

Human errors and mistakes include accidental problems caused by both employees and non-employees. An example is an employee who misunderstands operating procedures and accidentally deletes customer records. Another example is an employee who, in the course of backing up a database, inadvertently installs an old database on top of the current one. This category also includes poorly written application programs and poorly designed procedures. Finally, human errors and mistakes include physical accidents, such as driving a forklift through the wall of a computer room.

Computer Crime

The second threat type is *computer crime*. This threat type includes employees and former employees who intentionally destroy data or other system components. It also includes hackers who break into a system and virus and worm writers who infect computer systems. Computer crime also includes terrorists and those who break into a system to steal for financial gain.

Natural Events and Disasters

Natural events and disasters are the third type of security threat. This category includes fires, floods, hurricanes, earthquakes, tsunamis, avalanches, and other acts of nature. Problems in this category include not only the initial loss of capability and service, but also losses stemming from actions to recover from the initial problem.

| | | Threat | | |
		Human Error	**Computer Crime**	**Natural Disasters**
Loss	**Unauthorized data disclosure**	Procedural mistakes	Pretexting Phishing Spoofing Sniffing Hacking	Disclosure during recovery
	Incorrect data modification	Procedural mistakes Incorrect procedures Ineffective accounting controls System errors	Hacking	Incorrect data recovery
	Faulty service	Procedural mistakes Development and installation errors	Usurpation	Service improperly restored
	Denial of service (DOS)	Accidents	DOS attacks	Service interruption
	Loss of infrastructure	Accidents	Theft Terrorist activity	Property loss

Figure 12-3
Security Problems and Sources

What Types of Security Loss Exist?

Five types of security loss exist: unauthorized data disclosure, incorrect data modification, faulty service, denial of service, and loss of infrastructure. Consider each.

Unauthorized Data Disclosure

Unauthorized data disclosure occurs when a threat obtains data that is supposed to be protected. It can occur by human error when someone inadvertently releases data in violation of policy. An example at a university is a department administrator who posts student names, identification numbers, and grades in a public place, when the releasing of names and grades violates state law. Another example is employees who unknowingly or carelessly release proprietary data to competitors or to the media. WikiLeaks is a famous example of unauthorized disclosure; the situation described in the third row of Figure 12-2 is another example.

The popularity and efficacy of search engines has created another source of inadvertent disclosure. Employees who place restricted data on Web sites that can be reached by search engines might mistakenly publish proprietary or restricted data over the Web.

Of course, proprietary and personal data can also be released and obtained maliciously. **Pretexting** occurs when someone deceives by pretending to be someone else. A common scam involves a telephone caller who pretends to be from a credit card company and claims to be checking the validity of credit card numbers: "I'm checking your MasterCard number; it begins with 5491. Can you verify the rest of the number?" Thousands of MasterCard numbers start with 5491; the caller is attempting to steal a valid number.

Phishing is a similar technique for obtaining unauthorized data that uses pretexting via email. The **phisher** pretends to be a legitimate company and sends an email requesting confidential data, such as account numbers, Social Security numbers, account passwords, and so forth. Phishing compromises legitimate brands and trademarks. See Using MIS InClass 1 (page 462) for more.

Spoofing is another term for someone pretending to be someone else. If you pretend to be your professor, you are spoofing your professor. **IP spoofing** occurs when an intruder uses another site's IP address to masquerade as that other site. **Email spoofing** is a synonym for phishing.

Sniffing is a technique for intercepting computer communications. With wired networks, sniffing requires a physical connection to the network. With wireless networks, no such connection is required: **Drive-by sniffers** simply take computers with wireless connections through an area and search for unprotected wireless networks. They can monitor and intercept wireless traffic at will. Even protected wireless networks are vulnerable, as you will learn. Spyware and adware are two other sniffing techniques discussed later in this chapter.

Other forms of computer crime include **hacking**, which is breaking into computers, servers, or networks to steal data such as customer lists, product inventory data, employee data, and other proprietary and confidential data.

Finally, people might inadvertently disclose data during recovery from a natural disaster. During a recovery, everyone is so focused on restoring system capability that they might ignore normal security safeguards. A request such as "I need a copy of the customer database backup" will receive far less scrutiny during disaster recovery than at other times.

Incorrect Data Modification

The second type of security loss in Figure 12-3 is *incorrect data modification*. Examples include incorrectly increasing a customer's discount or incorrectly modifying an employee's salary, earned days of vacation, or annual bonus. Other examples include placing incorrect information, such as incorrect price changes, on a company's Web site or company portal.

Incorrect data modification can occur through human error when employees follow procedures incorrectly or when procedures have been designed incorrectly. For proper internal control on systems that process financial data or control inventories of assets, such as products and equipment, companies should ensure separation of duties and authorities and have multiple checks and balances in place.

A final type of incorrect data modification caused by human error includes *system errors*. An example is the lost-update problem discussed in Chapter 5 (page 174).

Computer criminals can make unauthorized data modifications by hacking into a computer system. For example, hackers could hack into a system and transfer people's account balances or place orders to ship goods to unauthorized locations and customers.

Finally, faulty recovery actions after a disaster can result in incorrect data changes. The faulty actions can be unintentional or malicious.

Faulty Service

The third type of security loss, *faulty service*, includes problems that result because of incorrect system operation. Faulty service could include incorrect data modification, as just described. It also could include systems that work incorrectly by sending the wrong goods to a customer or the ordered goods to the wrong customer, inaccurately billing customers, or sending the wrong information to employees. Humans can inadvertently cause faulty service by making procedural mistakes. System developers can write programs incorrectly or make errors during the installation of hardware, software programs, and data.

Usurpation occurs when computer criminals invade a computer system and replace legitimate programs with their own, unauthorized ones that shut down legitimate applications and substitute their own processing to spy, steal and manipulate data, or achieve other purposes. Faulty service can also result when service is improperly restored during recovery from natural disasters.

Denial of Service

Human error in following procedures or a lack of procedures can result in **denial of service (DOS)**, the fourth type of loss. For example, humans can inadvertently shut down a Web server or corporate gateway router by starting a computationally intensive application. An OLAP application that uses the operational DBMS can consume so many DBMS resources that order-entry transactions cannot get through.

Computer criminals can launch denial-of-service attacks in which a malicious hacker floods a Web server, for example, with millions of bogus service requests that so occupy the server that it cannot service legitimate requests. Also, computer worms can infiltrate a network with so much artificial traffic that legitimate traffic cannot get through. Finally, natural disasters may cause systems to fail, resulting in denial of service.

Loss of Infrastructure

Many times, human accidents cause loss of infrastructure, the last loss type. Examples are a bulldozer cutting a conduit of fiber-optic cables and a floor buffer crashing into a rack of Web servers.

Theft and terrorist events also cause loss of infrastructure. For instance, a disgruntled, terminated employee might walk off with corporate data servers, routers, or other crucial equipment. Terrorist events also can cause the loss of physical plants and equipment.

Natural disasters present the largest risk for infrastructure loss. A fire, flood, earthquake, or similar event can destroy data centers and all they contain.

You may be wondering why Figure 12-3 does not include terms such as viruses, worms, and Trojan horses. The answer is that viruses, worms, and Trojan horses are techniques for causing some of the problems in the figure. They can cause a denial-of-service attack, or they can be used to cause malicious, unauthorized data access or data loss.

Finally, a new threat term has come into recent use. An **Advanced Persistent Threat (APT)** is a sophisticated, possibly long-running computer hack that is perpetrated by large, well-funded organizations such as governments. APTs are a means to engage in cyberwarfare. Examples of APT are *Stuxnet* and *Flame*. Stuxnet is reputed to have been used to set back the Iranian nuclear program by causing Iranian centrifuges to malfunction. Flame is a large, complex computer program that is reputed to have hacked into computers and is said to operate as a cyberspy, capturing screen images, email, and text messages and even searching nearby smartphones using Bluetooth communication. Search the Internet for these terms to learn more. If you work in the military or for intelligence agencies, you will certainly be concerned, if not involved, with APTs. We return to this topic in Q9.

Goal of Information Systems Security

As shown in Figure 12-1, threats can be stopped, or if not stopped, the costs of loss can be reduced by creating appropriate safeguards. Safeguards are, however, expensive to create and maintain. They also reduce work efficiency by making common tasks more difficult, adding additional labor expense. The goal of information security is to find an appropriate trade-off between the risk of loss and the cost of implementing safeguards.

Business professionals need to consider that trade-off carefully. In your personal life, you should certainly employ antivirus software. You should probably implement other safeguards that you'll learn about in Q3. Some safeguards, such as deleting browser cookies, will make using your computer more difficult. Are such safeguards worth it? You need to assess the risks and benefits for yourself.

Similar comments pertain to organizations, though they need to go about it more systematically. The bottom line is not to let the future unfold without careful analysis and action as indicated by that analysis. Get in front of the security problem by making the appropriate trade-off for your life and your business.

How Big Is the Computer Security Problem?

We do not know the full extent of the financial and data losses due to computer security threats. Certainly, the losses due to human error are enormous, but few organizations compute those losses and even fewer publish them. Losses due to natural disasters are also enormous and impossible to compute. The 2011 earthquake in Japan, for example, shut down Japanese manufacturing, and losses rippled through the supply chain from the Far East to Europe and the United States. One can only imagine the enormous expense for Japanese companies as they restored their information systems.

Furthermore, no one knows the cost of computer crime. For one, there are no standards for tallying crime costs. Does the cost of a denial-of-service attack include lost employee time, lost revenue, or long-term revenue losses due to lost customers? Or, if an employee loses a $2,000 laptop, does the cost include the value of the data that was on it? Does it include the cost of the time of replacing it and reinstalling software? Or, if someone steals next year's financial plan, how is the cost of the value that competitors glean determined?

Second, all the studies on the cost of computer crime are based on surveys. Different respondents interpret terms differently, some organizations don't report all their losses, and some won't report computer crime losses at all. Absent standard definitions and a more accurate way of gathering crime data, we cannot rely on the accuracy of any particular estimate. The most we can do is look for trends by comparing year-to-year data, assuming the same methodology is used by the various types of survey respondents.

Figure 12-4 shows the results of a survey done over three years.[2] It was commissioned by Hewlett-Packard and performed by the Ponemon Institute, a consulting group that specializes

---

[2]Ponemon Institute, *2012 Cost of Cyber Crime Study: United States.* October 2012.

Figure 12-4

Computer Crime Costs per
Organizational Respondent
Worldwide, in Millions of U.S.
Dollars)

Source: Ponemon Institute. *2012 Cost
of Cyber Crime Study: United States,*
October 2012, p. 6.

	2012	2011	2010
Maximum	$46.0	$36.5	$51.9
Median	$6.2	$5.9	$3.8
Minimum	$1.4	$1.5	$1.0

in computer crime. As shown, the study estimated the median loss per organization in 2012 to be $6.2 million, nearly double that in 2010. The range over these three years, however, remained more or less the same. From this we can conclude that the cost of crime for most organizations is increasing, but within bounds. Computer criminals aren't taking more per incident, but they're taking more from more organizations.

By the way, this data underlines the problems of tallying crime data from surveys. In 2012, no organization reported less than $1.2 million in loss. Clearly, the survey did not include small companies that incurred small losses. Given the large number of small companies, those unknown losses could be substantial.

Figure 12-5, from the same Ponemon study, shows the average cost and percent of total incidents of the five most expensive types of attack. Without tests of significance, it's difficult to determine if the differences shown are random; they could be. But, taking the data at face value, it appears the source of most of the increase in computer crime costs is malicious insiders. The number of attacks of this type is slightly decreasing, but the average cost of such attacks is increasing, possibly dramatically. Apparently, insiders are getting better at stealing more. The study, by the way, defined an insider as an employee, temporary employee, contractor, or business partner. The average costs of the remaining categories are slightly decreasing.

In addition to this data, Ponemon also surveyed losses by type of asset compromised. It found that data loss was the single most expensive consequence of computer crime, accounting for 44 percent of costs in 2012. Business disruption was the second highest cost, at 30 percent in 2012. Equipment losses and damages were only 5 percent of the lost value. Clearly, value lies in data and not in hardware!

Looking to the future, in a separate study,[3] Ponemon reported that 80 percent of its respondents believe that the data on mobile devices poses significant risks to their organizations and 73 percent reported that this threat was greater in 2012 than it was in 2011. The second most worrisome concern was advanced persistent threats.

Figure 12-5

Average Computer Crime Cost
and Percent of Attacks by Type
5 Most Expensive Types)

Source: Ponemon Institute. *2012 Cost
of Cyber Crime Study: United States,*
October 2012, p. 13.

	2012	2011	2010
Denial of Services	$172,238 (20%)	$187,506 (17%)	No data
Malicious Insiders	$166,251 (8%)	$105,352 (9%)	$100,300 (11%)
Web-based Attacks	$125,795 (12%)	$141,647 (13%)	$143,209 (15%)
Malicious Code	$109,533 (26%)	$126,787 (23%)	$124,083 (26%)
Stolen Devices	$23,541 (12%)	$24,968 (13%)	$25,663 (15%)

---

[3]Ponemon Institute, *2013 State of the EndPoint,* December 2012.

The *2012 Cost of Computer Crime Study* includes an in-depth analysis of the effect of different security policies on the savings in computer crime. The bottom line is that organizations that spend more to create the safeguards discussed in Q4–Q7 (later in this chapter) experience less computer crime and suffer smaller losses when they do. Security safeguards do work!

If you search for the term *computer crime statistics* on the Web, you will find numerous similar studies. Many are based on dubious sampling techniques, and some seem to be written to promote a particular safeguard product or point of view. Be aware of such bias as you read.

Using the Ponemon study, the bottom line, as of 2012, is:

- The median average cost of computer crime is increasing.
- Malicious insiders are an increasingly serious security threat.
- Data loss is the principal cost of computer crime.
- Survey respondents believe mobile device data is a significant security threat.
- Security safeguards work.

How Should You Respond to Security Threats?

As stated at the end of Q1, your personal IS security goal should be to find an effective trade-off between the risk of loss and the cost of safeguards. However, few individuals take security as seriously as they should, and most fail to implement even low-cost safeguards.

Figure 12-6 lists recommended personal security safeguards. The first safeguard is to take security seriously. You cannot see the attempts that are being made, right now, to compromise your computer. However, they are there.

Unfortunately, the first sign you will receive that your security has been compromised will be bogus charges on your credit card or messages from friends complaining about the disgusting email they just received from your email account. Professor Randy Boyle of Longwood University, author of *Applied Information Security* and *Corporate Computer and Network Security*, studies threats using intrusion detection systems. An **intrusion detection system (IDS)** is a computer program that senses when another computer is attempting to scan the disk or otherwise access a computer. According to Boyle, "When I run an IDS on a computer on the public Internet, some nights I get more than 1,000 attempts, mostly from foreign countries. There is nothing you can do about it except use reasonable safeguards."[4]

If you decide to take computer security seriously, the single most important safeguard you can implement is to create and use strong passwords. We discussed ways of doing this in Chapter

---

- Take security seriously
- Create strong passwords
- Use multiple passwords
- Send no valuable data via email or IM
- Use https at trusted, reputable vendors
- Remove high-value assets from computers
- Clear browsing history, temporary files, and cookies (CCleaner or equivalent)
- Regularly update antivirus software
- Demonstrate security concern to your fellow workers
- Follow organizational security directives and guidelines
- Consider security for all business initiatives

Figure 12-6
Personal Security Safeguards

---

[4]Private correspondence with the author, August 20, 2011.

(pages 24–25). To summarize, do not use any word, in any language, as part of your password. Use passwords with a mixture of upper- and lowercase letters and numbers and special characters.

Such nonword passwords are still vulnerable to a **brute force attack** in which the password cracker tries every possible combination of characters. John Pozadzides estimates that a brute force attack can crack a six-character password of either upper- or lowercase letters in about 5 minutes. However, brute force requires 8.5 days to crack that length password having a mixture of upper- and lowercase letters, numbers, and special characters. A 10-digit password of only upper- and lower-case letters takes 4.5 years to crack, but one using a mix of letters, numbers, and special characters requires nearly 2 million years. A 12-digit, letter-only password requires 3 million years, and a 12-digit mixed password will take many, many millions of years.[5] All of these estimates assume, of course, that the password contains no word in any language. The bottom line is this: Use long passwords with no words, 10 or more characters, and a mix of letters, numbers, and special characters.

In addition to using long, complex passwords, you should also use different passwords for different sites. That way, if one of your passwords is compromised, you do not lose control of all of your accounts.

Never send passwords, credit card data, or any other valuable data in email or IM. As stated numerous times in this text, most email and IM is not protected by encryption (see Q5), and you should assume that anything you write in email or IM could find its way to the front page of *The New York Times* tomorrow.

Buy only from reputable vendors, and when buying online, use only https. If the vendor does not support https in its transactions (look for *https://* in the address line of your browser), do not buy from that vendor.

You can reduce your vulnerability to loss by removing high-value assets from your computers. Now, and especially later as a business professional, make it your practice not to travel out of your office with a laptop or other device that contains any data that you do not need. In general, store proprietary data on servers or removable devices that do not travel with you. (Office 365, by the way, uses https to transfer data to and from SharePoint. You can use it or a similar application for processing documents from public locations such as airports while you are traveling.)

Your browser automatically stores a history of your browsing activities and temporary files that contain sensitive data about where you've visited, what you've purchased, what your account names and passwords are, and so forth. It also creates **cookies**, which are small files that your browser stores on your computer when you visit Web sites (see Case Study 9, pages 369–371). Cookies enable you to access Web sites without having to sign in every time, and they speed up processing of some sites. Unfortunately, some cookies also contain sensitive security data. The best safeguard is to remove your browsing history, temporary files, and cookies from your computer and to set your browser to disable history and cookies.

CCleaner is a free, open source product that will do a more thorough job of removing all such data (*http://download.cnet.com/ccleaner/*) than browsers do. You should make a backup of your computer before using CCleaner, however.

Removing and disabling cookies presents an excellent example of the trade-off between improved security and cost. Your security will be substantially improved, but your computer will be more difficult to use. You decide, but make a conscious decision; do not let ignorance of the vulnerability of such data make the decision for you.

We will address the use of antivirus software in Q5. The last three items in Figure 12-6 apply once you become a business professional. With your coworkers, and especially with those whom you manage, you should demonstrate a concern and respect for security. You should also follow all organizational security directives and guidelines. Finally, like Maggie and Ajit at the start of this chapter, consider security in all of your business initiatives.

Management sets security policies to ensure compliance with security law, as discussed in the Ethics Guide on pages 464–465.

---

[5]John Pozadzides, "How I'd Hack Your Weak Passwords." *One Man's Blog*, last modified March 26, 2007, *http://onemansblog.com/2007/03/26/how-id-hack-your-weak-passwords/*. When Pozadzides wrote this in 2007, it was for a personal computer. Using 2013 technology, these times would be half or less. Using a cloud-based network of servers for password cracking would cut these times by 90 percent or more.

Using MIS InClass 12 | A GROUP EXERCISE

Phishing for Credit Cards, Identifying Numbers, Bank Accounts

A phisher is an individual or organization that spoofs legitimate companies in an attempt to illegally capture personal data such as credit card numbers, email accounts, and driver's license numbers. Some phishers install malicious program code on users' computers as well.

Phishing is usually initiated via email. Phishers steal legitimate logos and trademarks and use official-sounding words in an attempt to fool users into revealing personal data or clicking a link. Phishers do not bother with laws about trademark use. They place names and logos like Visa, MasterCard, Discover, and American Express on their Web pages and use them as bait. In some cases, phishers copy the entire look and feel of a legitimate company's Web site.

In this exercise, you and a group of your fellow students will be asked to investigate phishing attacks. If you search the Web for *phishing*, be aware that your search may bring the attention of an active phisher. Therefore, do not give any data to any site that you visit as part of this exercise!

1. To learn the fundamentals of phishing, visit the following site: *www.microsoft.com/protect/fraud/phishing/symptoms .aspx*. To see recent examples of phishing attacks, visit *www .fraudwatchinternational.com/phishing/*.
   a. Using examples from these Web sites, describe how phishing works.
   b. Explain why a link that appears to be legitimate, such as *www .microsoft.mysite.com* may, in fact, be a link to a phisher's site.
   c. List five indicators of a phishing attack.
   d. Write an email that you could send to a friend or relative who is not well versed in technical matters that explains what phishing is and how that person can avoid it.

2. Suppose you received the email in Figure 1 and mistakenly clicked *See more details here*. When you did so, you were taken

to the Web page shown in Figure 2. List every phishing symptom that you find in these two figures and explain why it is a symptom.

3. Suppose you work for an organization that is being phished.
   a. How would you learn that your organization is being attacked?
   b. What steps should your organization take in response to the attack?
   c. What liability, if any, do you think your organization has for damages to customers that result from a phishing attack that carries your brand and trademarks?

4. Summarize why phishing is a serious problem to commerce today.

5. Describe actions that industry organizations, companies, governments, or individuals can take to help reduce phishing.

Your Order ID: "17152492"
Order Date: "09/07/12"
Product Purchased: "Two First Class Tickets to Cozumel"
Your card type: "CREDIT"
Total Price: "$349.00"

Hello, when you purchased your tickets you provided an incorrect mailing address.
See more details here
Please follow the link and modify your mailing address or cancel your order. If you have questions, feel free to contact us account@usefulbill.com

Figure 1
Fake Phishing Email

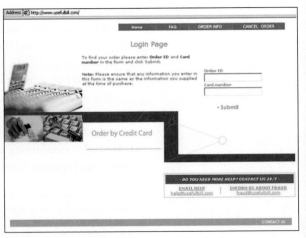

Figure 2
Fake Phishing Screen

Q4 How Should Organizations Respond to Security Threats?

Q3 discussed ways that you as an individual should respond to security threats. In the case of organizations, a broader and more systematic approach needs to be taken. To begin, senior management needs to address two critical security functions: security policy and risk management.

Considering the first, senior management must establish a company-wide security policy that states the organization's posture regarding data that it gathers about its customers, suppliers, partners, and employees. At a minimum, the policy should stipulate:

- What sensitive data the organization will store
- How it will process that data
- Whether data will be shared with other organizations
- How employees and others can obtain copies of data stored about them
- How employees and others can request changes to inaccurate data
- What employees can do with their own mobile devices at work

Specific policy depends on whether the organization is governmental or nongovernmental, on whether it is publically held or private, on the organization's industry, on the relationship of management to employees, and on other factors. As a new hire, seek out your employer's security policy if it is not discussed with you in new-employee training.

The second senior management security function is to manage risk. Risk cannot be eliminated, so *manage risk* means to proactively balance the trade-off between risk and cost. This trade-off varies from industry to industry and from organization to organization. Financial institutions are obvious targets for theft and must invest heavily in security safeguards. On the other hand, a bowling alley is unlikely to be much of a target, unless, of course, it stores credit card data on computers or mobile devices (a decision that would be part of its security policy and that would seem unwise, not only for a bowling alley but also for most small businesses).

To make trade-off decisions, organizations need to create an inventory of the data they store and the threats to which that data is subject. Figure 12-3 is a good source for understanding categories and frequencies of threat. Given this inventory, the organization needs to decide how much risk it wishes to take or, stated differently, which security safeguards it wishes to implement.

An easy way to remember information systems safeguards is to arrange them according to the five components of an information system, as shown in Figure 12-7. Some of the safeguards involve computer hardware and software. Some involve data; others involve procedures and people. We will consider technical, data, and human safeguards in the next three questions.

Hardware	Software	Data	Procedures	People

Technical Safeguards	**Data Safeguards**	**Human Safeguards**
Identification and authorization	Data rights and responsibilities	Hiring
Encryption	Passwords	Training
Firewalls	Encryption	Education
Malware protection	Backup and recovery	Procedure design
Application design	Physical security	Administration
		Assessment
		Compliance
		Accountability

Figure 12-7
Security Safeguards as They Relate to the Five Components

Ethics Guide

SECURING PRIVACY

Some organizations have legal requirements to protect the customer data they collect and store, but the laws may be more limited than you think. The **Gramm-Leach-Bliley (GLB) Act**, passed by Congress in 1999, protects consumer financial data stored by financial institutions, which are defined as banks, securities firms, insurance companies, and organizations that supply financial advice, prepare tax returns, and provide similar financial services.

The **Privacy Act of 1974** provides protections to individuals regarding records maintained by the U.S. government, and the privacy provisions of the **Health Insurance Portability and Accountability Act (HIPAA)** of 1996 give individuals the right to access health data created by doctors and other healthcare providers. HIPAA also sets rules and limits on who can read and receive your health information.

The law is stronger in other countries. In Australia, for example, the Privacy Principles of the Australian Privacy Act of 1988 govern not only government and healthcare data, but also records maintained by businesses with revenues in excess of AU$3 million.

Most consumers would say, however, that online retailers have an ethical requirement to protect a customer's credit card and other data, and most online retailers would agree. Or at least the retailers would agree that they have a strong business reason to protect that data. A substantial loss of credit card data by any large online retailer would have detrimental effects on both sales and brand reputation.

Data aggregators like Acxiom Corporation further complicate the risk to individuals because they develop a complete profile of households and individuals. And no federal law prohibits the U.S. government from buying information products from the data accumulators.

But let's bring the discussion closer to home. What requirements does your university have on the data it maintains about you? State law or university policy may govern those records, but no federal law does. Most universities consider it their responsibility to provide public access to graduation records. Anyone can determine when you graduated, your degree, and your major. (Keep this service in mind when you write your resume.)

Most professors endeavor to publish grades by student number and not by name, and there may be state law that requires that separation. But what about your work? What about the papers you write, the answers you give on exams? What about the emails you send to your professor? The data are not protected by federal law, and they are probably not protected by state law. If your professor chooses to cite your

work in research, she will be subject to copyright law, but not privacy law. What you write is no longer your personal property; it belongs to the academic community. You can ask your professor what she intends to do with your coursework, emails, and office conversations, but none of these data are protected by law.

The bottom line is this: Be careful where you put your personal data. Large, reputable organizations are likely to endorse ethical privacy policy and to have strong and effective safeguards to effectuate that policy. But individuals and small organizations might not. If in doubt, don't give the data.

DISCUSSION QUESTIONS

1. As stated in the case, when you order from an online retailer, the data you provide is not protected by U.S. privacy law. Does this fact cause you to reconsider setting up an account with a stored credit card number? What is the advantage of storing the credit card number? Do you think the advantage is worth the risk? Are you more willing to take the risk with some companies than with others? If so, state the criteria you use for choosing to take the risk.

2. Suppose you are the treasurer of a student club and you store records of club members' payments in a database. In the past, members have disputed payment amounts; therefore, when you receive a payment, you scan an image of the check or credit card invoice and store the scanned image in a database. Unfortunately, you have placed that database into a shared folder. (See the Security Guide in Chapter 10, pages 414–415.)

   One day, you are using your computer in a local coffee shop. A malicious student watches you sign in. Your name is visible, and your password is very short so it's easy for that student to see what it is. While you're enjoying your coffee, the malicious student learns the name of your computer from the coffee shop's wireless device, uses your login and password to connect to your shared folder, and then copies the club database. You know nothing about this until the next day, when a club member complains that a popular student Web site has published the names, bank names, and bank account numbers for everyone who has given you a check.

   What liability do you have in this matter? Could you be classified as a financial institution because you are taking students' money? (You can find the GLB at *www .ftc.gov/privacy/privacyinitiatives/glbact.html*.) If so, what liability do you have? If not, do you have any other liability? Does the coffee shop have liability?

   Even if you have no legal liability, was your behavior ethical? Explain your answer. In this and in questions 3, 4, and 5, use either the categorical imperative or utilitarianism in your answer.

3. Suppose you are asked to fill out a study questionnaire that requires you to enter identifying data, as well as answers to personal questions. You hesitate to provide the data, but the top part of the questionnaire states, "All responses will be strictly confidential." So, you fill out the questionnaire.

   Unfortunately, the person who is managing the study visits that same wireless coffee shop that you visited (in question 2), but this time the malicious student is sniffing packets to see what might turn up.

   The study manager joins the coffee shop's wireless network and starts her email. Her first message is from a small online Web store at which she has just opened an account. The email says, in part, "Welcome! Your account name is *Emily100* and your password is Jd5478IaE$%$55."

   "Eureka!" says the packet-sniffing, malicious student to himself as the packets carrying that email appear on his screen. "That looks like a pretty good password. Well, Emily100, I'll bet you use it on other accounts, like maybe your email?" The malicious student signs into email using Emily100 and password Jd5478IaE$%$55 and, sure enough, he's in. First thing he reads are emails to the study monitors, emails that contain attachments containing all of the study results. The next day, your name and all of your "confidential" responses appear on the public student Web site.

   Did the person conducting the study violate a law? Did she do anything unethical? What mistake(s) did she make?

4. In question 3, does the online Web site that sent the email have any legal liability for this loss? Did it do anything unethical?

5. In question 2, did the malicious student do anything illegal? Unethical? In question 3, did the malicious student do anything illegal? Unethical?

6. Given these two scenarios, describe good practice for computer use at public wireless facilities.

7. Considering your answers to the above questions, state three to five general principles to guide your actions as you disseminate and store data.

Q5 How Can Technical Safeguards Protect Against Security Threats?

Technical safeguards involve the hardware and software components of an information system. Figure 12-8 lists primary technical safeguards. Consider each.

Identification and Authentication

Every information system today should require users to sign on with a user name and password. The user name *identifies* the user (the process of **identification**), and the password *authenticates* that user (the process of **authentication**).

Passwords have important weaknesses. In spite of repeated warnings (don't let this happen to you!), users often share their passwords, and many people choose ineffective, simple passwords. In fact, a 2011 Verizon report states, "Absent, weak, and stolen credentials are careening out of control."[6] Because of these problems, some organizations choose to use smart cards and biometric authentication in addition to passwords.

Smart Cards

A **smart card** is a plastic card similar to a credit card. Unlike credit, debit, and ATM cards, which have a magnetic strip, smart cards have a microchip. The microchip, which holds far more data than a magnetic strip, is loaded with identifying data. Users of smart cards are required to enter a **personal identification number (PIN)** to be authenticated.

Biometric Authentication

Biometric authentication uses personal physical characteristics such as fingerprints, facial features, and retinal scans to authenticate users. Biometric authentication provides strong authentication, but the required equipment is expensive. Often, too, users resist biometric identification because they feel it is invasive.

Biometric authentication is in the early stages of adoption. Because of its strength, it likely will see increased usage in the future. It is also likely that legislators will pass laws governing the use, storage, and protection requirements for biometric data. For more on biometrics, search for *biometrics* at *http://searchsecurity.techtarget.com*.

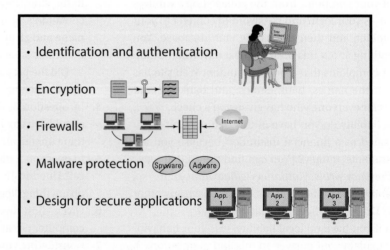

Figure 12-8
Technical Safeguards

- Identification and authentication
- Encryption
- Firewalls
- Malware protection
- Design for secure applications

---

[6]*Verizon 2011 Data Breach Investigations Report*, accessed June 2012, *http://www.verizonbusiness.com/resources/reports/rp_data-breach-investigations-report-2011_en_xg.pdf*.

Note that authentication methods fall into three categories: what you know (password or PIN), what you have (smart card), and what you are (biometric).

Single Sign-on for Multiple Systems

Information systems often require multiple sources of authentication. For example, when you sign on to your personal computer, you need to be authenticated. When you access the LAN in your department, you need to be authenticated again. When you traverse your organization's WAN, you will need to be authenticated to even more networks. Also, if your request requires database data, the DBMS server that manages that database will authenticate you yet again.

It would be annoying to enter a name and password for every one of these resources. You might have to use and remember five or six different passwords just to access the data you need to perform your job. It would be equally undesirable to send your password across all of these networks. The further your password travels, the greater the risk it can be compromised.

Instead, today's operating systems have the capability to authenticate you to networks and other servers. You sign on to your local computer and provide authentication data; from that point on your operating system authenticates you to another network or server, which can authenticate you to yet another network and server, and so forth. Because this is so, your identity and passwords open many doors beyond those on your local computer; remember this when you choose your passwords!

Authentication for the Internet is moving, in the future, beyond passwords. You'll learn more about this in Case Study 12: Will You Trust FIDO?

Encryption

Encryption is the process of transforming clear text into coded, unintelligible text for secure storage or communication. Considerable research has gone into developing **encryption algorithms** (procedures for encrypting data) that are difficult to break. Commonly used methods are DES, 3DES, and AES; search the Web for these terms if you want to know more about them.

A **key** is a number used to encrypt the data. It is called a *key* because it unlocks a message, but it is a number used with an encryption algorithm and not a physical thing like the key to your apartment.

To encode a message, a computer program uses the encryption method with the key to convert a noncoded message into a coded message. The resulting coded message looks like gibberish. Decoding (decrypting) a message is similar; a key is applied to the coded message to recover the original text. With **symmetric encryption**, the same key (again, a number) is used to encode and to decode. With **asymmetric encryption**, two keys are used; one key encodes the message, and the other key decodes the message. Symmetric encryption is simpler and much faster than asymmetric encryption.

A special version of asymmetric encryption, **public key/private key**, is used on the Internet. With this method, each site has a public key for encoding messages and a private key for decoding them. Before we explain how that works, consider the following analogy.

Suppose you send a friend an open combination lock (like you have on your gym locker). Suppose you are the only one who knows the combination to that lock. Now, suppose your friend puts something in a box and locks the lock. Now, neither your friend nor anyone else can open that box. They send the locked box to you, and you apply the combination to open the box.

A public key is like the combination lock, and the private key is like the combination. Your friend uses the public key to code the message (lock the box), and you use the private key to decode the message (use the combination to open the lock).

Now, suppose we have two generic computers, A and B. Suppose B wants to send an encrypted message to A. To do so, A sends B its public key (in our analogy, A sends B an open combination lock). Now B applies A's public key to the message and sends the resulting coded message back to A. At that point, neither B nor anyone other than A can decode that message. It

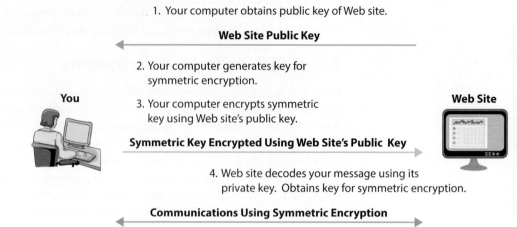

1. Your computer obtains public key of Web site.

Web Site Public Key

2. Your computer generates key for symmetric encryption.

You

3. Your computer encrypts symmetric key using Web site's public key.

Symmetric Key Encrypted Using Web Site's Public Key

Web Site

4. Web site decodes your message using its private key. Obtains key for symmetric encryption.

Communications Using Symmetric Encryption

5. All communications between you and Web site use symmetric encryption.

Figure 12-9
The Essence of https
(SSL or TLS)

is like the box with a locked combination lock. When A receives the coded message, A applies its private key (the combination in our analogy) to unlock or decrypt the message.

Again, public keys are like open combination locks. Computer A will send a lock to anyone who asks for one. But A never sends its private key (the combination) to anyone. Private keys stay private.

Most secure communication over the Internet uses a protocol called **https**. With https, data are encrypted using a protocol called the **Secure Sockets Layer (SSL)**, which is also known as **Transport Layer Security (TLS)**. SSL/TLS uses a combination of public key/private key and symmetric encryption.

The basic idea is this: Symmetric encryption is fast and is preferred. But the two parties (say you and a Web site) don't share a symmetric key. So, the two of you use public/private encryption to share the same symmetric key. Once you both have that key, you use symmetric encryption.

Figure 12-9 summarizes how SSL/TLS works when you communicate securely with a Web site.

1. Your computer obtains the public key of the Web site to which it will connect.
2. Your computer generates a key for symmetric encryption.
3. Your computer encodes that key using the Web site's public key. It sends the encrypted symmetric key to the Web site.
4. The Web site then decodes the symmetric key using its private key.
5. From that point forward, your computer and the Web site communicate using symmetric encryption.

At the end of the session, your computer and the secure site discard the keys. Using this strategy, the bulk of the secure communication occurs using the faster symmetric encryption. Also, because keys are used for short intervals, there is less likelihood they can be discovered.

Use of SSL/TLS makes it safe to send sensitive data such as credit card numbers and bank balances. Just be certain that you see *https://* in your browser and not just *http://*.

Firewalls

A **firewall** is a computing device that prevents unauthorized network access. A firewall can be a special-purpose computer, or it can be a program on a general-purpose computer or on a router.

Organizations normally use multiple firewalls. A **perimeter firewall** sits outside the organizational network; it is the first device that Internet traffic encounters. In addition to perimeter firewalls, some organizations employ **internal firewalls** inside the organizational network. Figure 12-10 shows the use of a perimeter firewall that protects all of an organization's computers and a second internal firewall that protects a LAN.

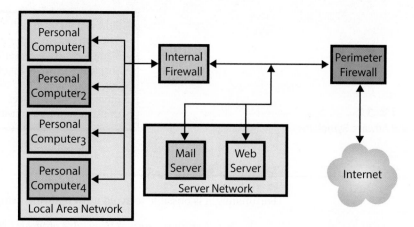

Figure 12-10
Use of Multiple Firewalls

A **packet-filtering firewall** examines each part of a message and determines whether to let that part pass. To make this decision, it examines the source address, the destination address(es), and other data.

Packet-filtering firewalls can prohibit outsiders from starting a session with any user behind the firewall. They can also disallow traffic from particular sites, such as known hacker addresses. They can prohibit traffic from legitimate, but unwanted, addresses, such as competitors' computers, and filter outbound traffic as well. They can keep employees from accessing specific sites, such as competitors' sites, sites with pornographic material, or popular news sites. As a future manager, if you have particular sites with which you do not want your employees to communicate, you can ask your IS department to enforce that limit via the firewall.

Packet-filtering firewalls are the simplest type of firewall. Other firewalls filter on a more sophisticated basis. If you take a data communications class, you will learn about them. For now, just understand that firewalls help to protect organizational computers from unauthorized network access.

No computer should connect to the Internet without firewall protection. Many ISPs provide firewalls for their customers. By nature, these firewalls are generic. Large organizations supplement such generic firewalls with their own. Most home routers include firewalls, and Microsoft Windows has a built-in firewall as well. Third parties also license firewall products.

Malware Protection

The next technical safeguard in our list in Figure 12-8 concerns malware. We defined the important terms in Chapter 4. To review, **malware** is viruses, Trojan horses, worms, spyware, and adware.

- A **virus** is a computer program that replicates itself. The program code that causes unwanted or harmful activity is called the **payload**.
  - **Trojan horses** are viruses that masquerade as useful programs or files.
  - A **worm** is a virus that propagates using the Internet or other computer networks.
- **Spyware** programs are installed on the user's computer without the user's knowledge or permission.
- **Adware** is similar to spyware but it watches user activity and produces pop-up ads.

Figure 12-11 lists some of the symptoms of adware and spyware. Sometimes these symptoms develop slowly over time as more malware components are installed. Should these symptoms occur on your computer, remove the spyware or adware using antimalware programs.

- Slow system startup
- Sluggish system performance
- Many pop-up advertisements
- Suspicious browser homepage changes
- Suspicious changes to the taskbar and other system interfaces
- Unusual hard-disk activity

Figure 12-11
Spyware and Adware Symptoms

Malware Safeguards

Fortunately, it is possible to avoid most malware using the following malware safeguards:

1. *Install antivirus and antispyware programs on your computer.* Your IS department will have a list of recommended (perhaps required) programs for this purpose. If you choose a program for yourself, choose one from a reputable vendor. Check reviews of antimalware software on the Web before purchasing.

2. *Set up your antimalware programs to scan your computer frequently.* You should scan your computer at least once a week and possibly more often. When you detect malware code, use the antimalware software to remove it. If the code cannot be removed, contact your IS department or antimalware vendor.

3. *Update malware definitions.* **Malware definitions**—patterns that exist in malware code—should be downloaded frequently. Antimalware vendors update these definitions continuously, and you should install these updates as they become available.

4. *Open email attachments only from known sources.* Also, even when opening attachments from known sources, do so with great care. With a properly configured firewall, email is the only outside-initiated traffic that can reach user computers.

   Most antimalware programs check email attachments for malware code. However, all users should form the habit of *never* opening an email attachment from an unknown source. Also, if you receive an unexpected email from a known source or an email from a known source that has a suspicious subject, odd spelling, or poor grammar, do not open the attachment without first verifying with the known source that the attachment is legitimate.

5. *Promptly install software updates from legitimate sources.* Unfortunately, all programs are chock full of security holes; vendors are fixing them as rapidly as they are discovered, but the practice is inexact. Install patches to the operating system and application programs promptly.

6. *Browse only in reputable Internet neighborhoods.* It is possible for some malware to install itself when you do nothing more than open a Web page. Don't go there!

Design for Secure Applications

The final technical safeguard in Figure 12-8 concerns the design of applications. As you learned in the opening vignette, Ajit and Maggie are designing PRIDE with security in mind; PRIDE will store users' privacy settings in a database, and they will develop all applications to first read the privacy settings before revealing any data in exercise reports. Most likely, they will design their programs so that privacy data is processed by programs on servers; that design means that such data need be transmitted over the Internet only when it is created or modified.

By the way, the term **SQL injection attack**, mentioned in the opening vignette, occurs when users enter a SQL statement into a form in which they are supposed to enter a name or other data. If the program is improperly designed, it will accept this code and make it part of the database command that it issues. Improper data disclosure and data damage and loss are possible consequences. A well-designed application will make such injections ineffective.

As a future IS user, you will not design programs yourself. However, you should ensure that any information system developed for you and your department includes security as one of the application requirements.

Q6 How Can Data Safeguards Protect Against Security Threats?

Data safeguards protect databases and other organizational data. Two organizational units are responsible for data safeguards. **Data administration** refers to an organization-wide function that is in charge of developing data policies and enforcing data standards. Data administration is a staff function to the CIO, as discussed in Chapter 11.

Database administration refers to a function that pertains to a particular database. ERP, CRM, and MRP databases each have a database administration function. Database administration develops procedures and practices to ensure efficient and orderly multiuser processing of the database, to control changes to the database structure, and to protect the database. Database administration was summarized in Chapter 5.

Both data and database administration are involved in establishing the data safeguards in Figure 12-12. First, data administration should define data policies such as "We will not share identifying customer data with any other organization" and the like. Then data administration and database administration(s) work together to specify user data rights and responsibilities. Third, those rights should be enforced by user accounts that are authenticated at least by passwords.

The organization should protect sensitive data by storing it in encrypted form. Such encryption uses one or more keys in ways similar to that described for data communication encryption. One potential problem with stored data, however, is that the key might be lost or that disgruntled or terminated employees might destroy it. Because of this possibility, when data are encrypted, a trusted party should have a copy of the encryption key. This safety procedure is sometimes called **key escrow**.

Another data safeguard is to periodically create backup copies of database contents. The organization should store at least some of these backups off premises, possibly in a remote location. Additionally, IT personnel should periodically practice recovery to ensure that the backups are valid and that effective recovery procedures exist. Do not assume that just because a backup is made that the database is protected.

Physical security is another data safeguard. The computers that run the DBMS and all devices that store database data should reside in locked, controlled-access facilities. If not, they are subject not only to theft, but also to damage. For better security, the organization should keep a log showing who entered the facility, when, and for what purpose.

When organizations store databases in the cloud, all of the safeguards in Figure 12-12 should be part of the cloud service contract.

Figure 12-12
Data Safeguards

- Define data policies
- Data rights and responsibilities
- Rights enforced by user accounts authenticated by passwords
- Data encryption
- Backup and recovery procedures
- Physical security

Q7 How Can Human Safeguards Protect Against Security Threats?

Read more about how to secure the security system in the Security Guide on pages 480–481.

Human safeguards involve the people and procedure components of information systems. In general, human safeguards result when authorized users follow appropriate procedures for system use and recovery. Restricting access to authorized users requires effective authentication methods and careful user account management. In addition, appropriate security procedures must be designed as part of every information system, and users should be trained on the importance and use of those procedures. In this section, we will consider the development of human safeguards for employees. According to the survey of computer crime discussed in Q2, crime from malicious insiders is increasing in frequency and cost. This fact makes safeguards even more important.

Human Safeguards for Employees

Figure 12-13 lists security considerations for employees. Consider each.

Position Definitions

Effective human safeguards begin with definitions of job tasks and responsibilities. In general, job descriptions should provide a separation of duties and authorities. For example, no single individual should be allowed to both approve expenses and write checks. Instead, one person should approve expenses, another pay them, and a third should account for the payment. Similarly, in inventory, no single person should be allowed to authorize an inventory withdrawal and also to remove the items from inventory.

- Position definition
  - Separate duties and authorities
  - Determine least privilege
  - Document position sensitivity

- Hiring and screening

- Dissemination and enforcement
  - Responsibility
  - Accountability
  - Compliance

- Termination
  - Friendly

  - Unfriendly

Figure 12-13
Security Policy for In-House Staff

Given appropriate job descriptions, user accounts should be defined to give users the *least possible privilege* needed to perform their jobs. For example, users whose job description does not include modifying data should be given accounts with read-only privileges. Similarly, user accounts should prohibit users from accessing data their job description does not require. Because of the problem of semantic security, even access to seemingly innocuous data may need to be limited.

Finally, the security sensitivity should be documented for each position. Some jobs involve highly sensitive data (e.g., employee compensation, salesperson quotas, and proprietary marketing or technical data). Other positions involve no sensitive data. Documenting *position sensitivity* enables security personnel to prioritize their activities in accordance with the possible risk and loss.

Hiring and Screening

Security considerations should be part of the hiring process. Of course, if the position involves no sensitive data and no access to information systems, then screening for information systems security purposes will be minimal. When hiring for high-sensitivity positions, however, extensive interviews, references, and background investigations are appropriate. Note, too, that security screening applies not only to new employees, but also to employees who are promoted into sensitive positions.

Dissemination and Enforcement

Employees cannot be expected to follow security policies and procedures that they do not know about. Therefore, employees need to be made aware of the security policies, procedures, and responsibilities they will have.

Employee security training begins during new-employee training, with the explanation of general security policies and procedures. That general training must be amplified in accordance with the position's sensitivity and responsibilities. Promoted employees should receive security training that is appropriate to their new positions. The company should not provide user accounts and passwords until employees have completed required security training.

Enforcement consists of three interdependent factors: responsibility, accountability, and compliance. First, the company should clearly define the security *responsibilities* of each position. The design of the security program should be such that employees can be held *accountable* for security violations. Procedures should exist so that when critical data are lost, it is possible to determine how the loss occurred and who is accountable. Finally, the security program should encourage security *compliance*. Employee activities should regularly be monitored for compliance, and management should specify the disciplinary action to be taken in light of noncompliance.

Management attitude is crucial: Employee compliance is greater when management demonstrates, both in word and deed, a serious concern for security. If managers write passwords on staff bulletin boards, shout passwords down hallways, or ignore physical security procedures, then employee security attitudes and employee security compliance will suffer. Note, too, that effective security is a continuing management responsibility. Regular reminders about security are essential.

Termination

Companies also must establish security policies and procedures for the termination of employees. Many employee terminations are friendly and occur as the result of promotion, retirement, or when the employee resigns to take another position. Standard human resources policies should ensure that system administrators receive notification in advance of the employee's last day, so that they can remove accounts and passwords. The need to recover keys for encrypted data and any other special security requirements should be part of the employee's out-processing.

Unfriendly termination is more difficult because employees may be tempted to take malicious or harmful actions. In such a case, system administrators may need to remove user accounts and passwords prior to notifying the employee of his or her termination. Other actions may be needed to protect the company's data assets. A terminated sales employee, for example, may attempt to take the company's confidential customer and sales-prospect data for future use at another company. The terminating employer should take steps to protect those data prior to the termination.

The human resources department should be aware of the importance of giving IS administrators early notification of employee termination. No blanket policy exists; the information systems department must assess each case on an individual basis.

Human Safeguards for Nonemployee Personnel

Business requirements may necessitate opening information systems to nonemployee personnel—temporary personnel, vendors, partner personnel (employees of business partners), and the public. Although temporary personnel can be screened, to reduce costs the screening will be abbreviated from that for employees. In most cases, companies cannot screen either vendor or partner personnel. Of course, public users cannot be screened at all. Similar limitations pertain to security training and compliance testing.

In the case of temporary, vendor, and partner personnel, the contracts that govern the activity should call for security measures appropriate to the sensitivity of the data and the IS resources involved. Companies should require vendors and partners to perform appropriate screening and security training. The contract also should mention specific security responsibilities that are particular to the work to be performed. Companies should provide accounts and passwords with the least privilege and remove those accounts as soon as possible.

The situation differs with public users of Web sites and other openly accessible information systems. It is exceedingly difficult and expensive to hold public users accountable for security violations. In general, the best safeguard from threats from public users is to *harden* the Web site or other facility against attack as much as possible. **Hardening** a site means to take extraordinary measures to reduce a system's vulnerability. Hardened sites use special versions of the operating system, and they lock down or eliminate operating systems features and functions that are not required by the application. Hardening is actually a technical safeguard, but we mention it here as the most important safeguard against public users.

Finally, note that the business relationship with the public, and with some partners, differs from that with temporary personnel and vendors. The public and some partners use the information system to receive a benefit. Consequently, safeguards need to protect such users from internal company security problems. A disgruntled employee who maliciously changes prices on a Web site potentially damages both public users and business partners. As one IT manager put it, "Rather than protecting ourselves from them, we need to protect them from us." This is an extension of the fifth guideline in Figure 12-7.

Account Administration

The administration of user accounts, passwords, and help-desk policies and procedures is another important human safeguard.

Account Management

Account management concerns the creation of new user accounts, the modification of existing account permissions, and the removal of unneeded accounts. Information system administrators perform all of these tasks, but account users have the responsibility to notify the administrators of the need for these actions. The IS department should create standard procedures for this purpose. As a future user, you can improve your relationship with IS personnel by providing early and timely notification of the need for account changes.

The existence of accounts that are no longer necessary is a serious security threat. IS administrators cannot know when an account should be removed; it is up to users and managers to give such notification.

Password Management

Passwords are the primary means of authentication. They are important not just for access to the user's computer, but also for authentication to other networks and servers to which the user may have access. Because of the importance of passwords, the National Institute of Standards and Technology (NIST) recommends that employees be required to sign statements similar to those shown in Figure 12-14.

When an account is created, users should immediately change the password they are given to one of their own. In fact, well-constructed systems require the user to change the password on first use.

Additionally, users should change passwords frequently thereafter. Some systems will require a password change every 3 months or perhaps more frequently. Users grumble at the nuisance of making such changes, but frequent password changes reduce not only the risk of password loss, but also the extent of damage if an existing password is compromised.

Some users create two passwords and switch back and forth between those two. This strategy results in poor security, and some password systems do not allow the user to reuse recently used passwords. Again, users may view this policy as a nuisance, but it is important.

Help-Desk Policies

In the past, help desks have been a serious security risk. A user who had forgotten his password would call the help desk and plead for the help-desk representative to tell him his password or to reset the password to something else. "I can't get this report out without it!" was (and is) a common lament.

The problem for help-desk representatives is, of course, that they have no way of determining that they are talking with the true user and not someone spoofing a true user. But they are in a bind: If they do not help in some way, the help desk is perceived to be the "unhelpful desk."

To resolve such problems, many systems give the help-desk representative a means of authenticating the user. Typically, the help-desk information system has answers to questions that only the true user would know, such as the user's birthplace, mother's maiden name, or last four digits of an important account number. Usually, when a password is changed, notification of that change is sent to the user in an email. Email, as you learned, is sent as plaintext, however, so the new password itself ought not to be emailed. If you ever receive notification that your password was reset when you did not request such a reset, immediately contact IT security. Someone has compromised your account.

All such help-desk measures reduce the strength of the security system, and, if the employee's position is sufficiently sensitive, they may create too large a vulnerability. In such a case, the user may just be out of luck. The account will be deleted, and the user must repeat the account-application process.

Figure 12-14
Sample Account
Acknowledgment Form
Source: National Institute of Standards
and Technology, Introduction to
Computer Security: The NIST Handbook,
Publication 800–812

> I hereby acknowledge personal receipt of the system password(s) associated with the user IDs listed below. I understand that I am responsible for protecting the password(s), will comply with all applicable system security standards, and will not divulge my password(s) to any person. I further understand that I must report to the Information Systems Security Officer any problem I encounter in the use of the password(s) or when I have reason to believe that the private nature of my password(s) has been compromised.

Systems Procedures

Figure 12-15 shows a grid of procedure types—normal operation, backup, and recovery Procedures of each type should exist for each information system. For example, the order-entry system will have procedures of each of these types, as will the Web storefront, the inventory system, and so forth. The definition and use of standardized procedures reduces the likelihood of computer crime and other malicious activity by insiders. It also ensures that the system's security policy is enforced.

Procedures exist for both users and operations personnel. For each type of user, the company should develop procedures for normal, backup, and recovery operations. As a future user you will be primarily concerned with user procedures. Normal-use procedures should provide safeguards appropriate to the sensitivity of the information system.

Backup procedures concern the creation of backup data to be used in the event of failure. Whereas operations personnel have the responsibility for backing up system databases and other systems data, departmental personnel have the need to back up data on their own computers. Good questions to ponder are, "What would happen if I lost my computer or mobile device tomorrow?" "What would happen if someone dropped my computer during an airport security inspection?" "What would happen if my computer was stolen?" Employees should ensure that they back up critical business data on their computers. The IS department may help in this effort by designing backup procedures and making backup facilities available.

Finally, systems analysts should develop procedures for system recovery. First, how will the department manage its affairs when a critical system is unavailable? Customers will want to order and manufacturing will want to remove items from inventory even though a critical information system is unavailable. How will the department respond? Once the system is returned to service, how will records of business activities during the outage be entered into the system? How will service be resumed? The system developers should ask and answer these questions and others like them and develop procedures accordingly.

Security Monitoring

Security monitoring is the last of the human safeguards we will consider. Important monitoring functions are activity log analyses, security testing, and investigating and learning from security incidents.

Many information system programs produce *activity logs*. Firewalls produce logs of their activities, including lists of all dropped packets, infiltration attempts, and unauthorized access attempts from within the firewall. DBMS products produce logs of successful and failed log-ins. Web servers produce voluminous logs of Web activities. The operating systems in personal computers can produce logs of log-ins and firewall activities.

	System Users	**Operations Personnel**
Normal operation	Use the system to perform job tasks, with security appropriate to sensitivity.	Operate data center equipment, manage networks, run Web servers, and do related operational tasks.
Backup	Prepare for loss of system functionality.	Back up Web site resources, databases, administrative data, account and password data, and other data.
Recovery	Accomplish job tasks during failure. Know tasks to do during system recovery.	Recover systems from backed up data. Perform role of help desk during recovery.

Figure 12-15
Systems Procedures

None of these logs adds any value to an organization unless someone looks at them. Accordingly, an important security function is to analyze these logs for threat patterns, successful and unsuccessful attacks, and evidence of security vulnerabilities.

Today, most large organizations actively investigate their security vulnerabilities. They may employ utilities such as Nessus or AppScan to assess their vulnerabilities. Many companies create **honeypots**, which are false targets for computer criminals to attack. To an intruder, a honeypot looks like a particularly valuable resource, such as an unprotected Web site, but in actuality the only site content is a program that determines the attacker's IP address. Organizations then use IP traceback programs, such as Sam Spade, to determine who has attacked them.[7] If you are technically minded, detail-oriented, and curious, a career as a security specialist in this field is almost as exciting as it appears on *CSI*. To learn more, check out Sam Spade, HotBot, or AppScan. See also *Applied Information Security*.[8]

Another important monitoring function is to investigate security incidents. How did the problem occur? Have safeguards been created to prevent a recurrence of such problems? Does the incident indicate vulnerabilities in other portions of the security system? What else can be learned from the incident?

Security systems reside in a dynamic environment. Organization structures change. Companies are acquired or sold; mergers occur. New systems require new security measures. New technology changes the security landscape, and new threats arise. Security personnel must constantly monitor the situation and determine if the existing security policy and safeguards are adequate. If changes are needed, security personnel need to take appropriate action.

Security, like quality, is an ongoing process. There is no final state that represents a secure system or company. Instead, companies must monitor security on a continuing basis.

Q8 How Should Organizations Respond to Security Incidents?

The last component of a security plan that we will consider is incident response. Figure 12-16 lists the major factors. First, every organization should have an incident-response plan as part of the security program. No organization should wait until some asset has been lost or compromised before deciding what to do. The plan should include how employees are to respond to security problems, whom they should contact, the reports they should make, and steps they can take to reduce further loss.

Consider, for example, a virus. An incident-response plan will stipulate what an employee should do when he notices the virus. It should specify whom to contact and what to do. It may stipulate that the employee should turn off his computer and physically disconnect from the network. The plan should also indicate what users with wireless computers should do.

> - Have plan in place
> - Centralized reporting
> - Specific responses
>   – Speed
>   – Preparation pays
>   – Don't make problem worse
> - Practice

Figure 12-16
Factors in Incident Response

---

[7]For this reason, do *not* attempt to scan servers for fun. It won't take the organization very long to find you, and it will not be amused!

[8]Randall Boyle, *Applied Information Security* (Upper Saddle River, NJ: Pearson Education, 2010).

The plan should provide centralized reporting of all security incidents. Such reporting will enable an organization to determine if it is under systematic attack or whether an incident is isolated. Centralized reporting also allows the organization to learn about security threats, take consistent actions in response, and apply specialized expertise to all security problems.

When an incident does occur, speed is of the essence. The longer the incident goes on, the greater the cost. Viruses and worms can spread very quickly across an organization's networks, and a fast response will help to mitigate the consequences. Because of the need for speed, preparation pays. The incident-response plan should identify critical personnel and their off-hours contact information. These personnel should be trained on where to go and what to do when they get there. Without adequate preparation, there is substantial risk that the actions of well-meaning people will make the problem worse. Also, the rumor mill will be alive with all sorts of nutty ideas about what to do. A cadre of well-informed, trained personnel will serve to dampen such rumors.

Finally, organizations should periodically practice incident response. Without such practice, personnel will be poorly informed on the response plan, and the plan itself may have flaws that only become apparent during a drill.

 # 2024?

What will be the status of information security by 2024? Will we have found a magic bullet to eliminate security problems? No. Human error is a constant; well-managed organizations will plan better for it and know how to respond better when it does occur, but as long as we have humans, we'll have error. Natural disasters are similar. The horrific events surrounding Hurricane Katrina in 2005 and the Japanese tsunami in 2011, as well as Hurricane Sandy in 2012, have alerted the world that we need to be better prepared, and more companies will set up hot or cold sites and put more data in well-prepared clouds. So, we'll be better prepared, but natural disasters are natural, after all.

Unfortunately, it is likely that sometime in the next 10 years some new, major incidents of cyberwarfare will have occurred. APTs will become more common, if indeed, they are not already common but we don't know it. It would appear that both Stuxnet and Flame have been in operation for 2 or 3 years. Will those who were damaged by them retaliate? It seems likely they will, at least, try. Will some new nation or group enter the cyberwar picture? That also seems likely. Unless you're in the security and intelligence business, there isn't much you can do about it. But don't be surprised if some serious damage is inflicted somewhere in the world due to APTs.

As of June 2013, many U.S. citizens are concerned with PRISM, the intelligence program by which the National Security Agency (NSA) requested and received data about Internet activities from major Internet providers. After the initial hullabaloo, it appears that Internet providers did not allow the government direct access to their servers, but rather delivered only data about specific individuals, as legally requested according to security laws enacted after 9/11. If so, then PRISM represents a legal governmental request for data, different only in scale from a governmental request for banking data about an organized crime figure. As of June 2013, Edward Snowden, the man who exposed the PRISM program, appears to be not an advocate for Internet freedom and privacy but rather a traitor who sold government secrets to China and Russia for private gain. However, the episode does raise the question of what governmental intrusion should be allowed into private data. We can hope the revelation of the existence of PRISM will spark a public conversation on the balance of national security and data privacy.

What about computer crime? It is a game of cat and mouse. Computer criminals find a vulnerability to exploit, and they exploit it. Computer security experts discover that vulnerability and create safeguards to thwart it. Computer criminals find a new vulnerability to exploit, computer security forces thwart it, and so it goes. The next major challenges will likely be those affecting mobile devices. But security on these devices will be improved as threats emerge that exploit their vulnerabilities. This cat-and-mouse game is likely to continue for at least the next 10 years. No super-safeguard will be devised to prevent computer crime, nor will any particular computer crime be impossible to thwart. However, the skill level of this cat-and-mouse activity is likely to increase, and substantially so. Because of increased security in operating systems and other software, and because of improved security procedures and employee training, it will become harder and harder for the lone hacker to find some vulnerability to exploit. Not impossible, but vastly more difficult.

So, what will happen? Cloud vendors and major organizations will continue to invest in safeguards; they'll hire more people (maybe you), train them well, and become ever more difficult to infiltrate. Although some criminals will continue to attack these fortresses, most will turn their attention to less protected, more vulnerable, midsized and smaller organizations and to individuals. You can steal $50 million from one company or $50 from a million people with the same cash result. And, in the next 10 years, because of improved security at large organizations, the difficulty and cost of stealing that $50 million will be much higher than stealing $50 a million times. Take another look at Figure 12-6—and not for the purpose of the exam!

Part of the problem is porous national borders. As Professor Boyle states:

> People can freely enter the U.S. electronically without a passport. They can commit numerous crimes with few repercussions. There are no real electronic IDs. There are very few lawmen that know anything about electronic crimes beyond what they read in the news. Gangs, well organized and motivated by money, commit most of the crime. Electronic lawlessness is the order of the day.[9]

If someone in Romania steals from Google or Apple or Microsoft or Boeing or AirBus and then disappears into a cloud of networks in Uzbekistan, those large organizations have the expertise to know how to proceed and to decide whether it will be worth it. They also have the needed financial resources. But if that same criminal steals from you in Nashville, what do the local law enforcement authorities know to do? Or even the Tennessee state authorities? And, if your portion of the crime is for $50, how many calls to Uzbekistan do they want to make?

Again, according to Professor Boyle:

> At the federal level, finances and politics take precedence over electronic security. The situation will likely be solved as it was in the past. Strong local "electronic" sheriffs will take control of the electronic border and enforce existing laws. It will take a couple decades (at least). Technology is moving faster than either the public or elected officials can educate themselves.[10]

Take yet another look at Figure 12-6. Send a copy to your loved ones.

That's it! You've reached the end of this text. Take a moment to consider how you will use what you learned, as described in the Guide on pages 482–483.

---

[9]Private correspondence with the author, August 24, 2011.
[10]Private correspondence with the author, August 24, 2011.

Security Guide

METASECURITY

Recall from Chapter 5 that metadata is data about data. In a similar vein, metasecurity is security about security. In other words, it asks the question, "How do we secure the security system?"

Consider an obvious problem: What is a secure way to store a file of accounts and passwords? Such files must exist; otherwise operating systems would be unable to authenticate users. But how should one store such a file? It cannot be stored as plain text because anyone who reads the file gains unlimited access to the computer, the network, and other assets. So, it must be stored in encrypted form, but how? And who should know the encryption key? (As stated in the Security Guide in Chapter 8, pages 314–315, LinkedIn lost the passwords for 6.5 million users. The primary reason, according to Gary McGraw, was that LinkedIn had not encrypted those passwords in its security database.[11])

Consider another problem. Suppose you work at the help desk at Vanguard Funds, and part of your job is to reset user passwords when users forget them. Clearly, this is an essential job that needs to be done, but what keeps you from resetting the passwords of accounts held by elderly people who never look at their statements? What keeps you from accessing those accounts with your reset password and moving funds to the accounts of your friends?

The accounting profession has dealt with some of these problems for decades and has developed a set of procedures and standards known as *accounting controls.* In general, these controls involve procedures that provide checks and balances, independent reviews of activity logs, control of critical assets, and so forth. Properly designed and implemented, such controls will catch the help-desk representative performing unauthorized account transfers. But many computer network threats are new, proper safeguards are under development, and some threats are not yet known.

The safeguards for some problems have unexpected consequences. For example, suppose you give one of your employees the task of finding security flaws in your network and financial applications (an activity called *white-hat hacking*). Assume that your employee finds ways to crack

---

[11]Gary McGraw, as quoted in Michael Hickins, "LinkedIn Password Breach Illustrates Endemic Security Issue," *Wall Street Journal*, June 6, 2012, *http://blogs.wsj.com/cio/2012/06/06/linkedin-password-breach-illustrates-endemic-security-issue/*.

into your system and, say, schedule undetectable, unauthorized shipments of goods from inventory to any address he wants. Your employee reports the flaws, and you fix them. Except, how do you know she reported all the flaws she found?

Further, when she's finished, what do you do with your white-hat hacker? You are afraid to fire her because you have no idea what she'll do with the information she has. But what job can she safely perform now that she knows the holes in your security system? Do you want her, ever again, to have an account and password in your corporate computer network? Even if you fix all the problems she reports, which is doubtful, you suspect that she can always find more.

Or consider Microsoft's problem. If you were a computer criminal, where is the ultimate place to lodge a Trojan horse or trapdoor? In Windows code. Microsoft hires hundreds of people to write its operating system: people who work all over the world. Of course, Microsoft performs background screening on everyone it can, but did it get a complete and accurate background report on every Windows programmer in India, France, Ireland, China, and so on? Microsoft uses careful procedures for controlling what code gets into its products, but even still, somebody at Microsoft must lose sleep over the possibilities.

Ironically, the answers for many metasecurity problems lie in openness. Encryption experts generally agree that any encryption algorithm that relies on secrecy is ultimately doomed because the secret will get out. Secrecy with encryption must lie only with the (temporary) keys that are used and not with a secret method. Thus, encryption algorithms are published openly, and anyone with a mathematical bent is encouraged to find (and report) flaws. An algorithm is safe to deploy only when thousands of people have tested and retested it. One very common wireless security protocol, Wired Equivalency Protocol, or WEP, was unwisely deployed before it was tested, and thousands upon thousands of wireless networks are vulnerable as a result.

Clearly, hardware and software are only part of the problem. Metasecurity extends to the data, procedures, and people components as well. It's a fascinating field, one that is continually developing, and one of great importance. It would make an interesting career choice—but be careful what you learn!

DISCUSSION QUESTIONS

1. Explain the term *metasecurity*. Describe two metasecurity problems not mentioned in this guide.
2. Explain the control problem that exists when personnel can reset customer passwords. Describe a way to reduce this threat using an audit log and at least two independent employees.
3. Describe the dilemma posed by an in-house hacker. Describe the problem of using an outside company for hacking. If you were asked to manage a project to test your computer network security, would you use in-house or outsourced personnel? Why?

4. A typical corporate computer has software from Microsoft, SAP, Siebel, Oracle, and possibly dozens of smaller vendors. How do users know that none of the software from these companies contains a Trojan horse?
5. Explain why part of the security solution lies in openness. Describe how openness applies to accounting controls such as the one you designed in your answer to question 2. Explain the danger of procedural controls that rely on secrecy.

Guide

THE FINAL, FINAL WORD

Congratulations! You've made it through the entire book. With this knowledge, you are well prepared to be an effective user of information systems. And with work and imagination, you can be much more than that. Many interesting opportunities are available to those who can apply information in innovative ways. Your professor has done what she can do, and the rest, as they say, is up to you.

So what's next? In Chapter 1, we claimed that Introduction to MIS is the most important course in the business curriculum today. That claim was based on the organization's innovative use of nearly free data communications and data storage. By now, you've learned many of the ways that businesses and organizations use these resources and information systems based upon those resources. You've also seen how businesses like AllRoad Parts use information systems to solve problems and further their competitive strategies. With PRIDE, you've investigated the use of mobile and cloud technology for an inter-enterprise system.

How can you use that knowledge? Chapter 1 claimed that future business professionals must be able "to assess, evaluate, and apply emerging information technology to business." Have you learned how to do that? At least, are you better able to do that than you were before this class? You probably know the meaning of many more terms than you did when you started, and such knowledge is important. But even more important is the ability to use that knowledge to apply MIS to your business interests.

Chapter 1 also reviewed the work of the RAND Corporation and that of Robert Reich on what professional workers in the 21st century need to know. Those sources state that such workers need to know how to innovate the use of technology and how to "collaborate, reason abstractly, think in terms of systems, and experiment." Have you learned those behaviors? Or, at least, are you better at them than you were when you started this course?

As of May 2013, the official national unemployment rate was about 7.6 percent, with the real unemployment rate, which includes those who have stopped looking for work, much higher. Under these circumstances, good jobs will be difficult to obtain. You need to apply every asset you have. One of those assets is the knowledge you've gained in this class. Take the time to do the exercises at the end of this guide, and then use the answers in your job interviews!

Look for the job you truly want to do, get that job, and work hard. In the movie *Glass: A Portrait of Philip in Twelve Parts,* the composer Philip Glass claimed he knew the secret

Source: © Radius Images/Corbis

to success. It was, he said, "Get up early and work hard all day." That quotation seems obvious and hardly worth stating, except that it has the ring of truth. And, if you can find a job you truly love, it isn't even hard. Actually, it's fun, most of the time. So, use what you've learned in this class to obtain the job you really want!

DISCUSSION QUESTIONS

1. Reflect on what you have learned from this course. Write two paragraphs about how the knowledge you have gained will help you to "assess, evaluate, and apply emerging information technology to business." Shape your writing around the kind of job that you want to obtain upon graduation.

2. Write two paragraphs about how the knowledge and experiences you've had in this class will help you "collaborate, reason abstractly, think in terms of systems, and experiment." Again, shape your writing around the kind of job you wish to obtain.

3. Using your answer to question 1, extract three or four sentences about yourself that you could use in a job interview.

4. Using your answer to question 2, extract three or four sentences about yourself that you could use in a job interview.

5. Practice using your answers to questions 3 and 4 in a job interview with a classmate, roommate, or friend.

ACTIVE REVIEW

Use this Active Review to verify that you understand the ideas and concepts that answer the chapter's study questions.

Q1 What is the goal of information systems security?

Define *threat, vulnerability, safeguard,* and *target.* Give an example of each. List three types of threats and five types of security losses. Give different examples for the three rows of Figure 12-2. Summarize each of the elements in the cells of Figure 12-3. Explain why it is difficult to know the true cost of computer crime. Explain the goal of IS security.

Q2 How big is the computer security problem?

Explain why it is difficult to know the true size of the computer security problem in general and of computer crime in particular. List the takeways in this question and explain the meaning of each.

Q3 How should you respond to security threats?

Explain each of the elements in Figure 12-6. Define *IDS,* and explain why the use of an IDS program is sobering, to say the least. Define *brute force attack.* Summarize the characteristics of a strong password. Explain how your identity and password do more than just open doors on your computer. Define *cookie* and explain why using a program like CCleaner is a good example of the computer security trade-off.

Q4 How should organizations respond to security threats?

Name and describe two security functions that senior management should address. Summarize the contents of a security policy. Explain what it means to manage risk. Summarize the steps that organizations should take when balancing risk and cost.

Q5 How can technical safeguards protect against security threats?

List five technical safeguards. Define *identification* and *authentication.* Describe three types of authentication. Explain how SSL/TLS works. Define *firewall,* and explain its purpose.

Define *malware,* and name five types of malware. Describe six ways to protect against malware. Summarize why malware is a serious problem. Explain how PRIDE is designed for security.

Q6 How can data safeguards protect against security threats?

Define *data administration* and *database administration,* and explain their difference. List data safeguards.

Q7 How can human safeguards protect against security threats?

Summarize human safeguards for each activity in Figure 12-12. Summarize safeguards that pertain to nonemployee personnel. Describe three dimensions of safeguards for account administration. Explain how system procedures can serve as human safeguards. Describe security monitoring techniques.

Q8 How should organizations respond to security incidents?

Summarize the actions that an organization should take when dealing with a security incident.

Q9 2024?

What, in the opinion of the author, is likely to happen regarding cyberwarfare in the next 10 years? Explain how the phrase *cat and mouse* pertains to the evolution of computer crime. Describe the types of security problems that are likely to occur in the next 10 years. Explain how the focus of computer criminals will likely change in the next 10 years. Explain how this is likely to impact smaller organizations, and you.

Using Your Knowledge with PRIDE

As an employee, investor, or advisor to PRIDE Systems, you can use the knowledge of this chapter to understand the security threats to which any business is subject. You know the need to trade off cost vs. risk. You also know three categories of safeguards, and the major types of safeguards for each. And, unlike Dr. Flores, you know what it means to design for security. You can also help ensure that PRIDE Systems employees and PRIDE users create and use strong passwords.

KEY TERMS AND CONCEPTS

Advanced Persistent Threat
  (APT)   457
Adware   469
Asymmetric encryption   467
Authentication   466
Biometric authentication   466
Brute force attack   461
Cookies   461
Data administration   471
Data safeguards   471
Database administration   471
Denial of service (DOS)   457
Drive-by sniffer   456
Email spoofing   456
Encryption   467
Encryption algorithms   467
FIDO   487
Firewall   468
Gramm-Leach-Bliley (GLB) Act   464
Hacking   456
Hardening   474

Health Insurance Portability and
  Accountability Act (HIPAA)   464
Honeypots   477
https   468
Human safeguards   472
Identification   466
Internal firewalls   468
Intrusion detection system
  (IDS)   460
IP spoofing   456
Key   467
Key escrow   471
Malware   469
Malware definitions   470
Packet-filtering firewall   469
Payload   469
Perimeter firewall   468
Personal identification number
  (PIN)   466
Phisher   456
Phishing   456

Pretexting   456
Privacy Act of 1974   464
Public key/private key   467
Safeguard   454
Secure Sockets Layer (SSL)   468
Smart cards   466
Sniffing   456
Spoofing   456
Spyware   469
SQL injection attack   470
Symmetric encryption   467
Target   454
Technical safeguards   466
Threat   453
Transport Layer Security
  (TLS)   468
Trojan horses   469
Usurpation   457
Virus   469
Vulnerability   454
Worm   469

MyMISLab

Go to **mymislab.com** to complete the problems marked with this icon ⭐.

USING YOUR KNOWLEDGE

12-1. Credit reporting agencies are required to provide you with a free credit report each year. Most such reports do not include your credit score, but they do provide the details on which your credit score is based. Use one of the following companies to obtain your free report: *www.equifax.com*, *www.experion.com*, and *www.transunion.com*.

   a. You should review your credit report for obvious errors. However, other checks are appropriate. Search the Web for guidance on how best to review your credit records. Summarize what you learn.

   b. What actions can you take if you find errors in your credit report?

   c. Define *identity theft*. Search the Web and determine the best course of action if someone thinks he or she has been the victim of identity theft.

12-2. Suppose you lose your company laptop at an airport. What should you do? Does it matter what data are stored on your disk drive? If the computer contained sensitive or proprietary data, are you necessarily in trouble? Under what circumstances should you now focus on updating your resume for your new employer?

 12-3. Suppose you alert your boss to the security threats in Figure 12-3 and to the safeguards in Figure 12-7. Suppose he says, "Very interesting. Tell me more." In preparing for the meeting, you decide to create a list of talking points.

   a. Write a brief explanation of each threat in Figure 12-3.

   b. Explain how the five components relate to safeguards.

   c. Describe two to three technical, two to three data, and two to three human safeguards.

   d. Write a brief description about the safeguards in Figure 12-12.

   e. List security procedures that pertain to you, a temporary employee.

   f. List procedures that your department should have with regard to disaster planning.

COLLABORATION EXERCISE 12

Using the collaboration IS you built in Chapter 2 (pages 73–74), collaborate with a group of students to answer the following questions.

The purpose of this activity is to assess the current state of computer crime.

1. Search the Web for the term *computer crime* and any related terms. Identify what you and your teammates think are the five most serious recent examples. Consider no crime that occurred more than 6 months ago. For each crime, summarize the loss that occurred and the circumstances surrounding the loss, and identify safeguards that were not in place or were ineffective in preventing the crime.

2. Search the Web for the term *computer crime statistics* and find two sources other than the Ponemon surveys cited in Q2.
   a. For each source, explain the methodology used and explain strengths and weaknesses of that methodology.
   b. Compare the data in the two new sources to that in Q2 and describe differences.
   c. Using your knowledge and intuition, describe why you think those differences occurred.

3. Go to *www.ponemon.org/local/upload/file/2012_US_Cost_ of_Cyber_Crime_Study_FINAL6%20.pdf* and download the 2012 report (or a more recent report if one is available).
   a. Summarize the survey with regard to safeguards and other measures that organizations use.
   b. Summarize the study's conclusions with regard to the efficacy of organizational security measures.
   c. Does your team agree with the conclusions in the study? Explain your answer.

4. Suppose that you are asked by your boss for a summary of what your organization should do with regard to computer security. Using the knowledge of this chapter and your answer to questions 1–3 above, create a PowerPoint presentation for your summary. Your presentation should include, but not be limited to:
   a. Definition of key terms
   b. Summary of threats
   c. Summary of safeguards
   d. Current trends in computer crime
   e. What senior managers should do about computer security
   f. What managers at all levels should do about computer security

CASE STUDY 12

Will You Trust FIDO?

This text has stressed that the best protection users can provide themselves is strong passwords. The problem is that such passwords are easy to forget, no matter how clever the mnemonic for recalling them. Plus, some sites require users to regularly change their passwords, and people forget which password is current, especially for sites they seldom visit. As stated by David O'Connell, senior analyst at Nucleus Research, "Passwords are inconvenient, and people are careless with them. In a recent survey we conducted with enterprise users, we found that one-third of all people record passwords somewhere, whether on a sticky note or in a computer file."[12]

Of course, when malicious code infects a computer, one of the first things it does is search for files that include the word *password* or some variant. And, once the code has downloaded the password file, all of the user's sites and accounts are open. Even worse, because many users don't know their computer has been infiltrated until long after the attack, they don't know to change their passwords until it is too late.

Users sometimes avoid having multiple passwords by using one identity for multiple sites. Many Web sites, for example, offer to authenticate you using your Facebook or other common credentials. The site accepts your name and password and passes it over to Facebook for authentication. However tempting this might be, you should never do it because you have no way of telling what else that site is doing with your Facebook credentials. It could be doing only what it says. Or it could be saving your credentials in a database, which may or may not be secure, or it could be selling your credentials to a criminal in Nigeria. You have no way of knowing what it's doing. In general, use your credentials only at the site for which they were created.

As of 2013, numerous alternatives to password authentication are under development. Some are biometric such as

---

[12]Jeff Vance, "Beyond passwords: 5 new ways to authenticate users," *NetworkWorld,* last modified May 30, 2007, *http://www.networkworld.com/ research/2007/060407-multifactor-authentication.html?page=3.*

fingerprints or retinal scans; some rely on user behavior such as keystroke rhythm. It turns out that all of us have idiosyncrasies in the way we type that can be used to identify us. Voice can also be used to identify individuals; visit *www.porticusinc.com* to see one example.

Other alternatives to passwords include the picture password in Windows 8 in which the user makes three gestures over a photo. Still other options include naming the people in a group photo or providing facts about people in photos that only the user would know.

These authentication methods make fewer demands on users' memories, but they all suffer one defect: If the user's authentication is compromised once, it is compromised for all of the sites on which that authentication method is used.

To correct this defect, in 2012, Lenovo, PayPal, and other sponsoring organizations began development of a set of open standards and protocols known as **FIDO** or Fast Identity OnLine.[13] Since then, Google and other major organizations have joined the effort.

The standards are still under development, but the basic schematic, as of this writing, is shown in Figure 12-17. Users purchase an authenticating device, either as part of their mobile device or PC or as a separate USB device. The security of those devices can be improved by backing them up with a password or PIN. The user and the FIDO device are associated by the vendor of the device, shown as a Token Vendor in Figure 12-17. That vendor provides a secret value, like a private key, once to the device and once to an independent third-party called a FIDO Repository. The plan calls for many such repositories to exist; their purpose is to provide FIDO authenticating data to Web servers.

After a user has been authenticated, a plug-in to the user's browser will use the private key data to generate a one-time password (OTP; this means the password is used just for one session with a Web site) and send it to the Web site. There the Web server will pass the OTP to another FIDO application, the Validation Cache. The cache will, the first time it encounters an OTP from a user, contact a FIDO repository to obtain the user's private key data. It uses this data to validate the OTP. This contact with the FIDO repository need only be done once per user per Web site.

FIDO does not eliminate the need to send private data over the Internet, but it substantially reduces it. The private key data must be sent once to the user, once to each FIDO Repository, and once to each Web site the user visits. After that, only temporary OTPs are exchanged between the user and the Web site. Furthermore, the user's authentication data never leaves the user's device. Your password or PIN, for example, is never sent over a network.

Will you trust FIDO? Probably. The consortium is doing security business the right way: forming open standards and asking the community to find holes and problems long before the standard is implemented. It also has the support of major, well-funded organizations. Unless some fatal, nonfixable flaw is found in the FIDO scheme, you most likely will be using it within a few years.

QUESTIONS

12-4. Summarize the problems associated with passwords.

12-5. Explain why you should not use your Facebook credentials to authenticate yourself to non-Facebook Web sites.

12-6. Describe three authentication methods other than passwords.

12-7. Explain the advantages of FIDO to users and to Web sites.

12-8. Briefly describe how FIDO works.

12-9. Describe factors that will determine whether FIDO becomes an industry standard.

12-10. Is FIDO gaining popularity with users and vendors? Search the Web to find out.

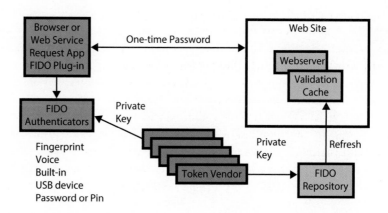

Figure 12-17
FIDO Schematic
Source: Based on *http://www fidoalliance.org/how-it-works.html,* accessed May, 2013.

[13]"How Fido Works," *Fido Alliance,* accessed August 12, 2013, *http://www.fidoalliance.org/how-it-works.html.*

MyMISLab

Go to **mymislab.com** for Auto-graded writing questions as well as the following Assisted-graded writing questions:

12-11. Suppose you need to terminate an employee who works in your department. Summarize security protections you must take. How would you behave differently if this termination were a friendly one?

12-12. Read about MapReduce and Hadoop on pages 349–352 of Chapter 9 if you have not already done so. Is MapReduce suitable for password cracking? Explain your answer. Assume that it is. If it takes 4.5 years for one computer to crack a password, how long will it take 10,000 computers to crack one using Hadoop? If it takes 2 million years to crack a password, how long will it take 10,000 computers to crack one? What does this tell you about password construction?

12-13. Mymislab Only – comprehensive writing assignment for this chapter.

The International Dimension

INTERNATIONAL MIS

Q1 How Does the Global Economy Affect Organizations and Processes?

Today's businesses compete in a global market. International business has been sharply increasing since the middle of the 20th century. After World War II, the Japanese and other Asian economies exploded when those countries began to manufacture and sell goods to the West. The rise of the Japanese auto industry and the semiconductor industry in southeastern Asia greatly expanded international trade. At the same time, the economies of North America and Europe became more closely integrated.

Since then, a number of other factors have caused international business to mushroom. The fall of the Soviet Union opened the economies of Russia and Eastern Europe to the world market. Even more important, the telecommunications boom during the dot-com heyday caused the world to be encircled many times over by optical fiber that can be used for data and voice communications.

After the dot-com bust, optical fiber was largely underused and could be purchased for pennies on the dollar. Plentiful, cheap telecommunications enabled people worldwide to participate in the global economy. Before the advent of the Internet, if a young Indian professional wished to participate in the Western economy, he or she had to migrate to the West—a process that was politicized and limited. Today, that same young Indian professional can sell his or her goods or services over the Internet without leaving home. The Chinese economy has also benefitted from plentiful, cheap telecommunications and has become more open to the world.

All of these developments led columnist and author Thomas Friedman to claim, now famously, that "the world is flat," implying seamless integration among the world's economies. That claim and the popular book[1] of the same name fit with the business press's biases and preconceptions, and it seemed to make intuitive sense. A general sense that the world's economies were integrated came to pervade most business thinking.

However, Harvard professor Pankaj Ghemawat decided to look deeper, and the data he found prompted him to write a *Foreign Policy* article titled "Why the World Isn't Flat.[2]" His

---

[1]Thomas L. Friedman, *The World Is Flat 3.0: A Brief History of the Twenty-First Century* (New York: Farrar, Strauss and Giroux, 2007).

[2]"Pankaj Ghemawat, "Why the World Isn't Flat," *Foreign Policy*, March 2007, *http://www.foreignpolicy.com/articles/2007/02/14/why_the_world_isnt_flat*.

article was published in 2007; the fact that it took such solid research and more than 6 years to gain widespread attention is a testament to the power of bias and preconception.

Some of Ghemawat's data is summarized in Figure ID-1. Including cross-border telecommunications Internet and voice that averages less than 7 percent. Even international commerce, which most people think is a large factor in all economies, is less than 20 percent, when corrected for double-counting.[3]

Figure ID-1

Percent of Cross-Border Commerce

Source: Pankaj Ghemawat, *www.ted .com/talks/pankaj_Ghemawat_actually_ the_world_isn_t_flat.html*

Commerce Type	Cross-Border Percent
Telecommunication	Voice: 2 percent Internet and Voice: 7 percent
Immigration	3 percent immigrants
Investment	10 percent direct investment
Exports	20 percent commerce

Does this mean that international business is not important to you? No, it does not. What it does mean, as Ghemawat points out, is that most of the opportunity of international commerce is ahead of us. The world is not (yet) flat. While information systems have already played a key role in international commerce, their effect in the future is likely to be larger. As Web services become more widespread, it becomes easier to link information systems together. As mobile devices continue their exploding growth in developing countries, even more users will enter the world economy via the Internet. And as collaboration tools become more powerful, it becomes possible to provide services as well products on the international stage. Opportunity abounds.

How Does the Global Economy Change the Competitive Environment?

To understand the effect of globalization, consider each of the elements in Figure ID-2.

The enlarging Internet-supported world economy has altered every one of the five competitive forces. Suppliers have to reach a wider range of customers, and customers have to consider a wider range of vendors. Suppliers and customers benefit not just from the greater size of the economy, but from the ease with which businesses can learn about each other using tools such as Google and Bing and, in China, Baibu.com.

Because of the data available on the Internet, customers can also learn of substitutions more easily. The Internet has made it substantially easier for new market entrants, although not in all cases. Amazon.com, Apple, and Google, for example, have garnered such a large market

---

[3]"Pankaj Ghemawat: Actually, the World Isn't Flat," *TED,* last updated October 2012, *http://www.ted.com/talks/ pankaj_ghemawat_actually_the_world_isn_t_flat.html.*

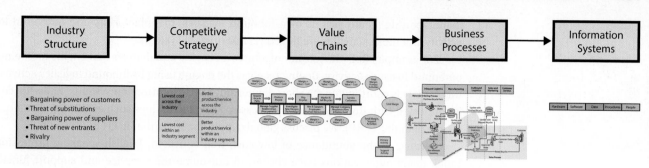

Figure ID-2
Organizational Strategy
Determines Information Systems

share that it would be difficult for any new entrant to challenge them. Still, in other industries, the global economy facilitates new entrants. Finally, the global economy has intensified rivalry by increasing product and vendor choices and by accelerating the flow of information about price, product, availability, and service.

How Does the Emerging Global Economy Change Competitive Strategy?

The emerging global economy changes thinking about competitive strategies in two major ways: product localization and product differentiation. First, the sheer size and complexity of the global economy means that any organization that chooses a strategy allowing it to compete industry-wide is taking a very big bite! Competing in many different countries, with products localized to the language and culture of those countries, is an enormous and expensive task.

For example, to promote Windows worldwide, Microsoft must produce versions of Windows in dozens of different languages. Even in English, Microsoft produces a U.K. version, a U.S. version, an Australian version, and so forth. The problem for Microsoft is even greater because different countries use different character sets. In some languages, writing flows from left to right. In other languages, it flows from right to left. When Microsoft set out to sell Windows worldwide, it embarked on an enormous project.

The second major way today's world economy changes competitive strategies is that its size, combined with the Internet, enables unprecedented product differentiation. If you choose to produce the world's highest quality and most exotic oatmeal—and if your production costs require you to sell that oatmeal for $350 a pound—your target market might contain only 200 people worldwide. The Internet allows you to find them—and them to find you.

The decision involving a global competitive strategy requires the consideration of these two changing factors.

How Does the Global Economy Change Value Chains and Business Processes?

Because of information systems, any or all of the value chain activities in Figure ID-2 can be performed anywhere in the world. An international company can conduct sales and marketing efforts locally, for every market in which it sells. 3M divisions, for example, sell in the United States with a U.S. sales force, in France with a French sales force, and in Argentina with an Argentinean sales force. Depending on local laws and customs, those sales offices may be owned by 3M, or they may be locally owned entities with which 3M contracts for sales and marketing services. 3M can coordinate all of the sales efforts of these entities using the same CRM system. When 3M managers need to roll up sales totals for a sales projection, they can do so using an integrated, worldwide system.

Manufacturing of a final product is frequently distributed throughout the world. Components of the Boeing 787 are manufactured in Italy, China, England, and numerous other countries and delivered to Washington and South Carolina for final assembly. Each manufacturing facility has its own inbound logistics, manufacturing, and outbound logistics activity, but those activities are linked via information systems.

For example, Rolls-Royce manufactures an engine and delivers that engine to Boeing via its outbound logistics activity. Boeing receives the engine using its inbound logistics activity. All of this activity is coordinated via shared, inter-enterprise information systems. Rolls-Royce's CRM is connected with Boeing's supply processes, using techniques such as CRM and enterprise resource planning (ERP). We discuss global supply chains further in Q4.

Because of the abundance of low-cost, well-educated, English-speaking professionals in India, many organizations have chosen to outsource their service and support functions to India. Some accounting functions are outsourced to India as well.

World time differences enable global virtual companies to operate 24/7. Boeing engineers in Los Angeles can develop a design for an engine support strut and send that design to Rolls-Royce in England at the end of their day. The design will be waiting for Rolls-Royce engineers at the start of their day. They review the design, make needed adjustments, and send it back to Boeing in Los Angeles, where the reviewed, adjusted design arrives at the start of the workday in Los Angeles. The ability to work around the clock by moving work into other time zones increases productivity.

What Are the Characteristics of International IS Components?

To understand the effect of internationalization on information systems, consider the five components. Computer hardware is sold worldwide, and most vendors provide documentation in at least the major languages; so, it has always been possible to obtain local hardware and set up local networks. Today, however, the emergence of the international cloud makes it even easier for any company, anywhere in the world, to obtain the latest in server technology. It does need to know how to do so, however, pointing to a possible future role for you as an international IS major.

Regarding software, consider the user interface for an international information system. Does it include a local-language version of Windows? What about the software application itself? Does an inventory system used worldwide by Boeing suppose that each user speaks English? If so, at what level of proficiency? If not, what languages must the user interface support?

Next, consider the data component. Suppose that the inventory database has a table for parts data, and that table contains a column named Remarks. Further suppose Boeing needs to integrate parts data from three different vendors: one in China, one in India, and one in England. What language is to be used for recording remarks? Does someone need to translate all of the remarks into one language? Into three languages?

The human components—procedures and people—are obviously affected by language and culture. As with business processes, information systems procedures need to reflect local cultural values and norms. For systems users, job descriptions and reporting relationships must be appropriate for the setting in which the system is used. We will say more about this in Q5.

What's Required to Localize Software?

The process of making a computer program work in a second language is called **localizing** software. It turns out to be surprisingly hard to do. To localize a document or the content of a Web page, all you need to do is hire a translator to convert your document or page from one language to another. The situation is much more difficult for a computer program, however.

Consider a program you use frequently—say, Microsoft Word—and ask what would need to be done to translate it to a different language. The entire user interface needs to be translated. The menu bar and the commands on it will need to be translated. It is possible that some of the icons will need to be changed because some graphic symbols that are harmless in one culture are confusing or offensive in another.

What about an application program such as CRM that includes forms, reports, and queries? The labels on each of these will require translation. Of course, not all labels translate into words of the same length, and so the forms and reports may need to be redesigned. The questions and prompts for queries, such as "Enter part number for back order," must also be translated.

All of the documentation will need to be translated. That should be just a matter of hiring a translator, except that all of the illustrations in the documentation will need to be redrawn in the second language.

Think, too, about error messages. When someone attempts to order more items than there are in inventory, the application produces an error message. All of those messages will need to be translated. There are other issues as well. Sorting order is one. Spanish uses accents on certain letters, and it turns out that an accented *ó* will sort after *z* when you use the computer's default sort ordering. Figure ID-3 summarizes the factors to address when localizing software.

Programming techniques can be used to simplify and reduce the cost of localization. However, those techniques must be used in design, long before any code is written. For example, suppose that when a certain condition occurs, the program is to display the message "Insufficient quantity in stock." If the programmer codes all such messages into the computer program, then, to localize that program, the programmer will have to find every such message in the code and then ask a translator to change that code. A preferred technique is to give every error message a unique identifier and to create a separate error file that contains a list of identifiers and their associated text. Then, when an error occurs, program code uses the identifier to obtain the text of the message to be displayed from the error file. During localization, translators simply translate the file of error messages into the second language.

The bottom line for you, as a future manager, is to understand two points: (1) Localizing computer programs is much more difficult, expensive, and time consuming than translating documents. (2) If a computer program is likely to be localized, then plan for that localization from the beginning, during design. In addition, when considering the acquisition of a company in a foreign country, be sure to budget time and expense for the localization of information systems.

What Are the Problems and Issues of Global Databases?

When we discussed CRM and ERP in Chapter 7, you learned the advantage of having all data stored in a single database. In brief, a single database reduces data integrity problems and makes it possible to have an integrated view of the customer or the operations of the organization.

International companies that have a single database must, however, declare a single language for the company. Every Remark or Comment or other text field needs to be in a single language. If not, the advantages of a single database disappear. This is not a problem for companies that commit to a single company language. For example, Thomas Keidel, former CEO of the Mahr Company (*www.mahr.com*), states, "We standardized on English as the official company language; we use English in our meetings, in our emails, and in other correspondence. We have

- Translate the user interface, including menu bars and commands.
- Translate, and possibly redesign, labels in forms, reports, and query prompts.
- Translate all documentation and help text.
- Redraw and translate diagrams and examples in help text.
- Translate all error messages.
- Translate text in all message boxes.
- Adjust sorting order for different character set.
- Fix special problems in Asian character sets and in languages that read and write from right to left.

Figure ID-3
Factors to Address When Localizing a Computer Program

to do this because we have factories and offices in 20 countries, and it would be impossible to make any decision otherwise. We chose English because it is a language that most business professionals have in common."[4] For companies like this, standardizing on a language for database contents is not a problem.

A single database is not possible, however, for companies that use multiple languages. Such companies often decide to give up on the benefits of a single database to let divisions in different countries use different databases, with data in local languages. For example, an international manufacturer might allow a component manufacturing division in South Korea to have a database in Korean and a final assembly division in Brazil to have a different database in Portuguese. In this scenario, the company needs applications to export and import data among the separate databases.

Besides language, performance is a second issue that confronts global databases. When using a single database, data transmission speeds are often too slow to process data from a single geographic location. If so, companies sometimes distribute their database to locations around the world.

Distributed database processing refers to the processing of a single database that resides in multiple locations. If the distributed database contains copies of the same data items, it is called a **replicated database**. If the distributed database does not contain copies of the same data, but rather divides the database into nonoverlapping segments, it is called a **partitioned database**. In most cases, querying either type of distributed database can improve performance without too much development work. However, updating a replicated database so that changes are correctly made to all copies of the data is full of challenges that require highly skilled personnel to solve. Still, companies like Amazon.com, which operates call centers in the United States, India, and Ireland, have invested in applications that are able to successfully update distributed databases worldwide. Given this infrastructure, Amazon.com then made this distributed database technology available via its Web services, as you learned in Chapters 5 and 6. The cloud has made the international distribution of data much easier.

Q3 What Are the Challenges of International Enterprise Applications?

As you learned in Chapter 7, workgroup business processes and functional applications support particular activities within a single department or business activity. Because the systems operate independently, the organization suffers from islands of automation. Sales and marketing data, for example, are not integrated with operations or manufacturing data.

You learned that many organizations eliminate the problems of information silos by creating enterprise systems. With international IS, however, such systems may not be worthwhile.

Advantages of Functional Systems

Lack of integration is disadvantageous in many situations, but it has *advantages* for international organizations and international systems. For example, if an order-processing functional system located in the United States is independent from the manufacturing systems located in Taiwan, it becomes unnecessary to accommodate language, business, and cultural differences within a single system. U.S. order-processing systems can operate in English and reflect the practices and culture of the United States. Taiwanese manufacturing information systems can operate in Chinese and reflect the business practices and culture of Taiwan. As long as there is an adequate data interface between the two systems, they can operate independently, sharing data when necessary.

---

[4]Private correspondence with the author, August 2011.

Enterprise systems, such as ERP, solve the problems of data isolation by integrating data into a database that provides a comprehensive and organization-wide view. However, as discussed in Q2, that advantage requires that the company standardize on a single language and, most likely, place that database in a single location. Otherwise, separated, functional databases are needed.

Problems of Inherent Processes

Processes inherent in ERP and other applications are even more problematic. Each software product assumes that the software will be used by people filling particular roles and performing their actions in a certain way. ERP vendors justify this standardization by saying that their procedures are based on industry-wide best practices and that the organization will benefit by following these standard processes. That statement may be true, but some inherent processes may conflict with cultural norms. If they do, it will be very difficult for management to convince the employees to follow those processes. Or at least it will be difficult in some cultures to do so.

Differences in language, culture, norms, and expectations compound the difficulties of international process management. Just creating an accurate as-is model is difficult and expensive; developing alternative international processes and evaluating them can be incredibly challenging. With cultural differences, it can be difficult just to determine what criteria should be used for evaluating the alternatives, let alone performing the evaluation.

Because of these challenges, in the future it is likely that international business processes will be developed more like inter-enterprise business processes. A high-level process will be defined to document the service responsibilities of each international unit. Then Web services will be used to connect those services into an integrated, enterprise, international system. Because of encapsulation, the only obligation of an international unit will be to deliver its defined service. One service can be delivered using procedures based on autocratic management policies, and another can be delivered using procedures based on collaborative management policies. The differences will not matter in a Web service-based enterprise system.

Q4 How Do Inter-enterprise IS Facilitate Global Supply Chain Management?

A **supply chain** is a network of organizations and facilities that transforms raw materials into products delivered to customers. Figure ID-4 shows a generic supply chain. Customers order from retailers, who in turn order from distributors, who order from manufacturers, who order from suppliers. In addition to the organizations shown here, the supply chain also includes transportation companies, warehouses, and inventories and some means for transmitting messages and information among the organizations involved.

Because of disintermediation, not every supply chain has all of these organizations. Some companies sell directly to the customer. Both the distributor and retailer organizations are omitted from their supply chains. In other supply chains, manufacturers sell directly to retailers and omit the distribution level.

The term *chain* is misleading. *Chain* implies that each organization is connected to just one company up the chain (toward the supplier) and down the chain (toward the customer). That is not the case. Instead, at each level an organization can work with many organizations both up and down the supply chain. Thus, a supply chain is a *network*.

To appreciate the international dimension of a supply chain, consider Figure ID-5. Suppose you decide to take up cross-country skiing. You go to REI (either by visiting one of its stores or its Web site) and purchase skis, bindings, boots, and poles. To fill your order, REI removes those items from its inventory of goods. Those goods have been purchased, in turn, from distributor/importers.

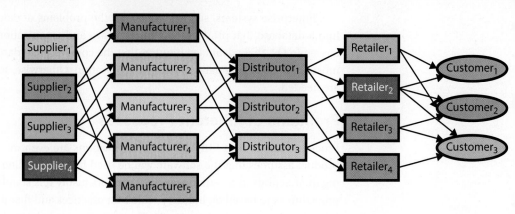

Figure ID-4
Supply Chain Relationships

According to Figure ID-5, REI purchases the skis, bindings, and poles from one distributor/importe
and the boots from a second. The distributor/importers, in turn, purchase the required items from
the manufacturers, which, in turn, buy raw materials from their suppliers.

In Figure ID-5, notice the national flags on the suppliers and manufacturers. For example
the pole manufacturer is located in Brazil and imports plastic from China, aluminum from
Canada, and fittings from Italy. The poles are then imported to REI in the United States by the
Importer/Distributor$_1$.

The only source of revenue in a supply chain is the customer. In the REI example, you spend
your money on the ski equipment. From that point all the way back up the supply chain to the
raw materials suppliers, there is no further injection of cash into the system. The money you
spend on the ski equipment is passed back up the supply chain as payments for goods or raw
materials. Again, the customer is the only source of revenue.

The Importance of Information in the Supply Chain

Since the global economic recession that began with the financial crisis of 2008, the focus of
many businesses, worldwide, has been to reduce costs. Supply chain costs are a primary target
for such reductions, especially among companies that have a global supply chain. Figure ID-6
illustrates how Walmart overhauled its supply chain to eliminate distributors and other inter
mediaries, enabling it to buy directly from manufacturers. Walmart's goal is to increase sales
and revenues from its private-label goods. At the same time, it also has consolidated purchasing

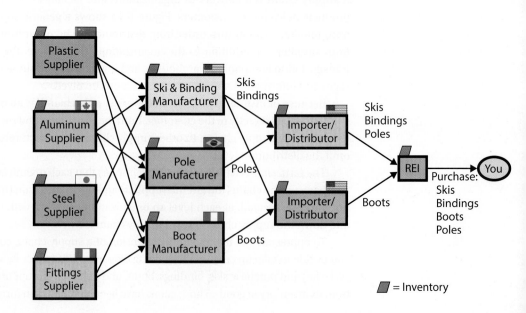

Figure ID-5
Supply Chain Example

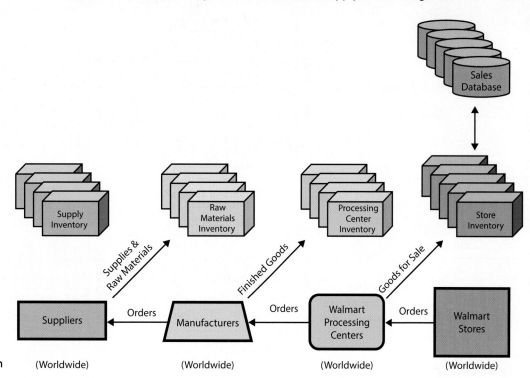

Figure ID-6
Example Walmart Supply Chain

and warehousing into four global merchandising centers, such as the one near Mexico City that processes goods for emerging markets.[5]

As you'll learn in your production and supply chain courses, many different factors determine the cost and performance of a supply chain. However, information is one of the most important. Consider, for example, inventory management at each of the companies in Figure ID-6. How do those companies decide when and how much to purchase? How does the new Walmart processing center in Mexico City determine how many pairs of jeans, ice chests, or bottles of vitamin C to order? How large should the orders be? How frequently should orders be placed? How are those orders tracked? What happens when a shipment disappears? Information is a major factor in making each of those decisions, along with dozens of others. To provide insight into the importance of information, consider just one example, the bullwhip effect.

How Can Information Relieve the Bullwhip Effect?

The **bullwhip effect** is a phenomenon in which the variability in the size and timing of orders increases at each stage up the supply chain, from customer to supplier. Figure ID-7 depicts the situation. In a famous study, the bullwhip effect was observed in Procter & Gamble's supply chain for diapers.[6]

Except for random variation, diaper demand is constant. Diaper use is not seasonal; the requirement for diapers does not change with fashion or anything else. The number of babies determines diaper demand, and that number is constant or possibly slowly changing.

Retailers do not order from the distributor with the sale of every diaper package. The retailer waits until the diaper inventory falls below a certain level, called the *reorder quantity*. Then the retailer orders a supply of diapers, perhaps ordering a few more than it expects to sell to ensure that it does not have an outage.

---

[5]Jim Jubak, "China Feels Global Market Pain," *Jubak's Journal*, last updated August 12, 2010, *http://articles. moneycentral.msn.com/Investing/JubaksJournal/global-markets-pain-moves-to-china.aspx.*
[6]Hau L. Lee, V. Padmanabhan, and S. Whang, "The Bullwhip Effect in Supply Chains," *Sloan Management Review,* Spring 1997, pp. 93–102.

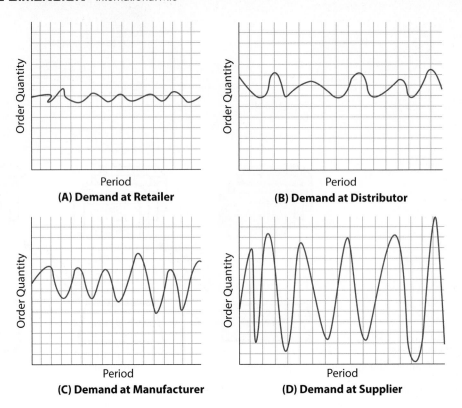

Figure ID-7
The Bullwhip Effect

The distributor receives the retailer's order and follows the same process. It waits until it supply falls below the reorder quantity, and then it reorders from the manufacturer, with per haps an increased amount to prevent outages. The manufacturer, in turn, uses a similar proces with the raw-materials suppliers.

Because of the nature of this process, small changes in demand at the retailer are amplifie at each stage of the supply chain. As shown in Figure ID-7, those small changes become quit large variations on the supplier end.

The bullwhip effect is a natural dynamic that occurs because of the multistage nature of th supply chain. It is not related to erratic consumer demand, as the study of diapers indicated You may have seen a similar effect while driving on the freeway. One car slows down, the car jus behind it slows down a bit more abruptly, which causes the third car in line to slow down eve more abruptly, and so forth, until the thirtieth car or so is slamming on its brakes.

The large fluctuations of the bullwhip effect force distributors, manufacturers, and sup pliers to carry larger inventories than should be necessary to meet the real consumer demand Thus, the bullwhip effect reduces the overall profitability of the supply chain. Eliminating o at least reducing the bullwhip effect is particularly important for international supply chain where logistics costs are high and shipping times are long.

One way to eliminate the bullwhip effect is to give all participants in the supply chain acces to consumer-demand information from the retailer. Each organization can thus plan its inventor or manufacturing based on the true demand (the demand from the only party that introduce money into the system) and not on the observed demand from the next organization up the sup ply chain. Of course, an *inter-enterprise information system* is necessary to share such data.

Consider the Walmart example in Figure ID-8. Along the bottom, each entity orders from th entity up the supply chain (the entity to its left in Figure ID-8). Thus, for example, the Walmart pro cessing centers order finished goods from manufacturers. Without knowledge of the true deman this supply chain is vulnerable to bullwhip effects. However, if each entity can, via an informatio system, obtain data about the true demand—that is, the demand from the retail customers who ar the source of funds for this chain—then each can anticipate orders. The data about true deman will enable each entity to meet order requirements, while maintaining a smaller inventory.

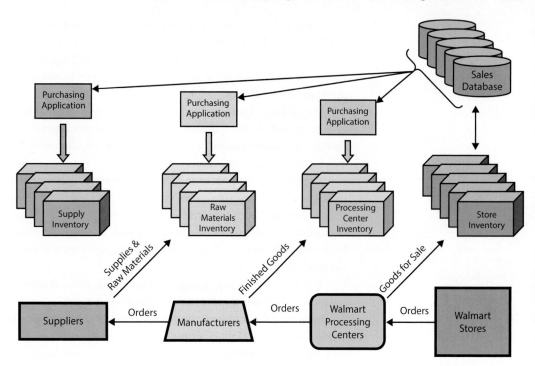

 # Q5

What Are the Challenges of International IS Management?

Size and complexity make international IS management challenging. The components of international information systems are larger and more complex. Projects to develop them are larger and more complicated to manage. International IS departments are bigger and composed of people from many cultures with many different native languages. International organizations have more IS and IT assets, and those assets are exposed to more risk and greater uncertainty. Because of the complexity of international law, security incidents are more complicated to investigate.

Why Is International IS Development More Challenging?

The factors that affect international information systems development are more challenging than those that affect international software development. If the *system* is truly international, if many people from many different countries will be using the system, then the development project is exceedingly complicated.

To see why, consider the five components. Running hardware in different countries is not a problem, especially using the cloud, and localizing software is manageable, assuming programs were designed to be localized. Databases pose more difficulties. First, is a single database to be used, and if so, is it to be distributed? If so, how will updates be processed? Also, what language, currency, and units of measure will be used to store data? If multiple databases are to be used, how are data going to be transported among them? Some of these problems are difficult, but they are solvable, and cloud-based databases make them more so.

The same cannot be said for the procedure and people components. An international system is used by people who live and work in cultures that are vastly different from one another. The way customers are treated in Japan differs substantially from the way customers are treated in Spain, which differs substantially from the way they are treated in the United States. Therefore, the procedures for using a CRM will be correspondingly different.

Consider the relationship of business processes and information systems as discusse in Chapter 10. Information systems are supposed to facilitate the organization's competitiv strategy and support business processes. But what if the underlying business processes diffe Customer support in Japan and customer support in Spain may involve completely differer processes and activities.

Even if the purpose and scope can be defined in some unified way, how are requirements t be determined? Again, if the underlying business processes differ, then the specific requiremen for the information system will differ. Managing requirements for a system in one culture is diff cult, but managing requirements for international systems can be many times more difficult.

There are two responses to such challenges: (1) either define a set of standard business prc cesses or (2) develop alternative versions of the system that support different processes in di ferent countries. Both responses are problematic. The first response requires conversion of th organization to different work processes, and, as you learned in Chapter 7, such conversion ca be exceedingly difficult. People resist change, and they will do so with vehemence if the chang violates cultural norms.

The second response is easier to implement, but it creates system design challenges. It als means that, in truth, there is not one system, but many.

In spite of the problems, both responses are used. For example, SAP, Oracle, and other ER vendors define standard business processes via the inherent procedures in their software prod ucts. Many organizations attempt to enforce those standard procedures. When it becomes orga nizationally infeasible to do so, organizations develop exceptions to those inherent procedure and develop programs to handle the exceptions. This choice means high maintenance expens

What Are the Challenges of International Project Management?

Managing a global IS development project is difficult because of project size and complexit Requirements are complex, many resources are required, and numerous people are involve Team members speak different languages, live in different cultures, work in different time zone and seldom meet face to face.

One way to understand how these factors affect global project management is to cor sider each of the project management knowledge areas as set out by the International Proje Management Institute's document, the *PMBOK® Guide* (*www.pmi.org/PMBOK-Guide-anc Standards.aspx*). Figure ID-9 summarizes challenges for each knowledge area. Project ii tegration is more difficult because international development projects require the comple integration of results from distributed work groups. Also, task dependencies can span team working in different countries, increasing the difficulty of task management.

The scope and requirements definition for international IS is more difficult, as just dis cussed. Time management is more difficult because teams in different cultures and countrie work at different rates. Some cultures have a 35-hour workweek, and some have a 60-hou workweek. Some cultures expect 6-week vacations, and some expect 2 weeks. Some culture thrive on efficiency of labor, and others thrive on considerate working relationships. There is n standard rate of development for an international project.

In terms of cost, different countries and cultures pay vastly different labor rates. Usin critical path analysis, managers may choose to move a task from one team to another. Doin so, however, may substantially increase costs. Thus, management may choose to accept a dela rather than move work to an available (but more expensive) team. The complex trade-offs tha exist between time and cost become even more complex for international projects.

Quality and human resources are also more complicated for international projects. Qualit standards vary among countries. The IT industry in some nations, such as India, has investe heavily in development techniques that increase program quality. Other countries, such as th United States, have been less willing to invest in quality. In any case, the integration of progran of varying quality results in an inconsistent system.

Knowledge Areas	Challenge
Project integration	Complex integration of results from distributed work groups. Management of dependencies of tasks from physically and culturally different work groups.
Requirements (scope)	Need to support multiple versions of underlying business processes. Possibly substantial differences in requirements and procedures.
Time	Development rates vary among cultures and countries.
Cost	Cost of development varies widely among countries. Two members performing the same work in different countries may be paid substantially different rates. Moving work among teams may dramatically change costs.
Quality	Quality standards vary among cultures. Different expectations of quality may result in an inconsistent system.
Human resources	Worker expectations differ. Compensation, rewards, work conditions vary widely.
Communications	Geographic, language, and cultural distance among team members impedes effective communication.
Risk	Development risk is higher. Easy to lose control.
Procurement	Complications of international trade.

Figure ID-9
Challenges for International IS Project Management

Worker expectations vary among cultures and nations. Compensation, rewards, and worker conditions vary, and these differences can lead to misunderstandings, poor morale, and project delays.

Because of these factors, effective team communication is exceedingly important for international projects, but because of language and culture differences and geographic separation, such communication is difficult. Effective communication is also more expensive. Consider, for example, just the additional expense of maintaining a team portal in three or four languages.

If you consider all of the factors in Figure ID-9, it is easy to understand why project risk is high for international IS development projects. So many things can go wrong. Project integration is complex; requirements are difficult to determine; cost, time, and quality are difficult to manage; worker conditions vary widely; and communication is difficult. Finally, project procurement is complicated by the normal challenges of international commerce.

What Are the Challenges of International IS Management?

Chapter 11 defined the four primary responsibilities of the IS department: plan, operate, develop, and protect information systems and supporting infrastructure. Each of these responsibilities becomes more challenging for international IS organizations.

Regarding planning, the principal task is to align IT and IS resources with the organization's competitive strategy. The task does not change character for international companies; it just becomes more complex and difficult. Multinational organizations and operations are complicated; thus, the business processes that support their competitive strategies also tend to be complicated. Furthermore, changes in global economic factors can mean dramatic changes in processes and necessitate changes in IS and IT support. Technology adoption can also cause remarkable change. The increasing use of cell phones in developing countries, for example, changes the requirements for local information systems. The price of oil and energy can change international business processes. For these reasons, planning tasks for international IS are larger and more complex.

Three factors create challenges for international IS operations. First, conducting operations in different countries, cultures, and languages adds complexity. Go to the Web site of any multinational corporation, say *www.3m.com* or *www.dell.com*, and you'll be asked to click on the country in which you reside. When you click, you are likely to be directed to a Web server running in some other country. Those Web servers need to be managed consistently, even though they are operated by people living in different cultures and speaking various languages.

The second operational challenge of international IS is the integration of similar, but different, systems. Consider inventory. A multinational corporation might have dozens of different inventory systems in use throughout the world. To enable the movement of goods, many of these systems need to be coordinated and integrated.

Or consider customer support that operates from three different support centers in three different countries. Each center may have its own information system, but the data among those systems will need to be exported or otherwise shared. If not, then a customer who contacts one center will be unknown to the others.

The third complication for operations is outsourcing. Many organizations have chosen to outsource customer support, training, logistics, and other backroom activities. International outsourcing is particularly advantageous for customer support and other functions that must be operational 24/7. Many companies outsource logistics to UPS because doing so offers comprehensive, worldwide shipping and logistical support. The organization's information systems usually need to be integrated with outsource vendors' information systems, and this may need to be done for different systems, all over the world.

The fourth IS department responsibility is protecting IS and IT infrastructure. We consider that function next.

How Does the International Dimension Affect Computer Security Risk Management?

Computer security risk management is more difficult and complicated for international information systems. First, IT assets are subject to more threats. Infrastructure will be located at sites all over the world, and those sites differ in the threats to which they are exposed. Some will be subject to political threats, others to the threat of civil unrest, others to terrorists, and still others to threats of natural disasters of every conceivable type. Place your data center in Kansas and it's subject to tornados. Place your data center internationally, and it's potentially subject to typhoons/hurricanes, earthquakes, floods, volcanic eruption, or mudslides. And don't forget epidemics that will affect the data center employees.

Second, the likelihood of a threat is more difficult to estimate for international systems. What is the likelihood civil unrest in Egypt will threaten your data center in Cairo? How does an organization assess that risk? What is the likelihood that a computer programmer in India will insert a Trojan horse into code that she writes on an outsourcing contract?

In addition to risk, international information systems are subject to far greater uncertainty. Uncertainty reflects the likelihood that something that "we don't know that we don't know" will cause an adverse outcome. Because of the multitudinous cultures, religions, nations, beliefs, political views, and crazy people in the world, uncertainty about risks to IS and IT infrastructure is high. Again, if you place your data center in Kansas, you have some idea of the magnitude of the uncertainty to which you are exposed, even if you don't know exactly what it is. Place a server in a country on every continent of the world, and you have no idea of the potential risks to which they are exposed.

Regarding safeguards, technical and data safeguards do not change for international information systems. Because of greater complexity, more safeguards or more complex safeguards may be needed, but the technical and data safeguards described in Chapter 12 all work for international systems. Human safeguards are another matter. For example, can an organization depend on the control of separation of duties and authorities in a culture for which graft is an accepted norm? Or what is the utility of a personal reference in a culture in which it is considered exceedingly rude to talk about someone when they are not present? Because of these differences, human safeguards need to be chosen and evaluated on a culture-by-culture basis.

In short, risk management for both international information systems and IT infrastructure is more complicated, more difficult, and subject to greater uncertainty.

Setting Up Information Systems in Foreign Offices

To illustrate the challenges of international IS management, suppose that AllRoad Parts decides to open an office in Europe. How might it go about developing information systems for that office?

Before answering that question, consider the experience of Thomas Keidel, chairman of the Mahr Group, a midsized, multinational firm headquartered in Germany:

> For all of our foreign offices, we obtain hardware and networking equipment from the local economy. Once we have purchased or leased a facility, local vendors supply and set up hardware, a local area network, and access to the Internet in accordance with our specifications. Then, we bring in our own IT professionals from Germany to install software. As much as possible, we use the same software worldwide. We use the same accounting software and chart of accounts, and we use the same business processes, worldwide. Twice a year we conduct internal audits to verify compliance.
>
> One difference we do allow, however, is to conduct transactions in local currency. We assume the risk of currency fluctuations at headquarters, and if there is any currency hedging to do, we do it at headquarters. We want our foreign offices focused on sales and manufacturing and not on currency valuation opportunities and risks.[7]

Because it is a manufacturer, Mahr operates an ERP system, for which it maintains a centralized database in Germany that is accessed via its own leased communication lines worldwide. It also requires that the same computer-assisted-design (CAD) software be used worldwide. As Keidel notes, "That way we can exchange designs among all of our facilities without problems."

ACTIVE REVIEW

Use this Active Review to verify that you understand the ideas and concepts that answer the study questions.

Q1 How does the global economy affect organizations and processes?

Describe how the global economy has changed since the mid-20th century. Explain how the dot-com bust influenced the global economy and changed the number of workers worldwide. Summarize why the idea that the world is flat gained momentum and why that notion is incorrect. State how the lack of a "flat" world presents business opportunities. Summarize the ways in which today's global economy influences the five competitive forces. Explain how the global economy changes the way organizations assess industry structure. How does the global economy change competitive strategy? How do global information systems benefit the value chain? Using Figure 3-6 (page 89) as a guide, explain how each primary value chain activity can be performed anywhere in the world.

Q2 What are the characteristics of international IS components?

Explain how internationalization affects the five components of an IS. What does it mean to localize software? Summarize the work required to localize a computer program. In your own words, explain why it is better to design a program to be

Private correspondence with the author, August 2011.

localized rather than attempt to adapt an existing single-language program to a second language. Explain the problems of having a single database for an international IS. Define *distributed database, replicated database,* and *partitioned database.* State a source of problems for processing replicated databases.

Q3 What are the challenges of international enterprise applications?

Summarize the advantages of functional systems for international companies. Summarize the issues of inherent processes for multinational ERP. Explain how SOA services could be used to address the problems of international enterprise applications.

Q4 How do inter-enterprise IS facilitate global supply chain management?

Define *supply chain,* and explain why the term *chain* is misleading. Under what circumstances are not all of the organizations in Figure ID-5 part of the supply chain? Name the only source of revenue in a supply chain. Explain how Walmart is attempting to reduce supply costs. Describe the bullwhip

effect and explain why it adds costs to a supply chain. Explain how the system shown in Figure ID-8 can eliminate the bullwhip effect.

Q5 What are the challenges of international IS management?

State the two characteristics that make international IS management challenging.

Explain the difference between international systems development and international software development. Using the five-component framework, explain why international system development is more difficult. Give an example of one complication for each knowledge area in Figure ID-9. State the four responsibilities for IS departments. Explain how each of these responsibilities is more challenging for international IS organizations. Describe three factors that create challenges for international IS operations. Explain why international IT assets are subject to more threats. Give three examples. Explain why the likelihood of international threats is more difficult to determine. Describe uncertainty and explain why it is higher for international IS organizations. Summarize the strategy that Mahr uses when creating IS infrastructure in foreign offices.

KEY TERMS AND CONCEPTS

Bullwhip effect 497	Localizing 492	Replicated database 494
Distributed database processing 494	Partitioned database 494	Supply chain 495

MyMISLab

Go to **mymislab.com** to complete the problems marked with this icon .

USING YOUR KNOWLEDGE

ID-1. Suppose that you are about to have a job interview with a multinational company, such as 3M, Starbucks, or Coca-Cola. Further suppose that you wish to demonstrate an awareness of the changes for international commerce that the Internet and modern information technology have made. Using the information in Q1, create a list of three questions that you could ask the interviewer regarding the company's use of IT in its international business.

ID-2. Suppose you work for a business that has $100 million in annual sales that is contemplating acquiring a company in Mexico. Assume you are a junior member of a team that is analyzing the desirability of this acquisition. Your boss, who is not technically savvy, has asked you to prepare a summary of the issues that she should be aware in the merging of information systems of the two companies. She wants your summary to include a list of questions that she should ask of both your IS department and the IS department personnel in the prospective acquisition. Prepare that summary.

D-3. Using the data in this module as well as in Chapter 7, summarize the strengths and weaknesses of functional systems, CRM, and ERP. How do the advantages and disadvantages of each change in an international setting? For your answer, create a table with strength and weakness columns and with one row for each of the four systems types.

MyMISLab

Go to **mymislab.com** for Auto-graded writing questions as well as the following Assisted-graded writing questions:

ID-4. Suppose that you are a junior member of a newly formed, international team that will meet regularly for the next year. You have team members in Europe, North and South America, Japan, Hong Kong, Singapore, Australia, and India. All of your team meetings will be virtual; some will be synchronous, but many will be asynchronous. The team leader has asked you to help prepare the environment for these meetings. In particular, he asked you to summarize the challenges that will occur in conducting these team meetings. He also wants you to assess the strengths and weaknesses of the following collaboration tools: email, Google Drive, Google+, Windows SkyDrive, Microsoft SharePoint, WebEx, and Microsoft Office 365. Use Figure ID-9, the discussion in Q5, and information in Chapter 2 to prepare your assessment.

ID-5. Assume you are Lucas at AllRoad. Using your knowledge from Q5, write a one-page memo to Kelly explaining what needs to be done to set up information systems in a new European office. State and justify any assumptions you make.

ID-6. Mymislab Only – comprehensive writing assignment for this chapter.

Application Exercises

All exercise files can be found on the following Web site: *www.pearsonhighered.com/kroenke*.

Chapter 1

1-1. The spreadsheet in Microsoft Excel file **Ch01Ex01_U7e.xlsx** contains records c employee activity on special projects. Open this workbook and examine the dat that you find in the three spreadsheets it contains. Assess the accuracy, relevancy, an sufficiency of this data to the following people and problems.

  a. You manage the Denver plant, and you want to know how much time your employee are spending on special projects.

  b. You manage the Reno plant, and you want to know how much time your employee are spending on special projects.

  c. You manage the Quota Computation project in Chicago, and you want to know hov much time your employees have spent on that project.

  d. You manage the Quota Computation project for all three plants, and you want t know the total time employees have spent on your project.

  e. You manage the Quota Computation project for all three plants, and you want t know the total labor cost for all employees on your project.

  f. You manage the Quota Computation project for all three plants, and you want t know how the labor-hour total for your project compares to the labor-hour totals fc the other special projects.

  g. What conclusions can you make from this exercise?

1-2. The database in the Microsoft Access file **Ch01Ex02_U7e.accdb** contains th same records of employee activity on special projects as in Applicatio Exercise 1-1. Before proceeding, open that database and view the records in the Employe Hours table.

  a. Eight queries have been created that process this data in different ways. Using th criteria of accuracy, relevancy, and sufficiency, select the single query that is most af propriate for the information requirements in Application Exercise 1-1, parts a–f. If n query meets the need, explain why.

  b. What conclusions can you make from this exercise?

  c. Comparing your experiences on these two projects, what are the advantages and dis advantages of spreadsheets and databases?

Chapter 2

2-1. Suppose that you have been asked to assist in the managerial decision about hov much to increase pay in the next year. Assume you are given a list of the depar ments in your company, along with the average salary for employees in each departmer for major companies in your industry. Additionally, you are given the names and salarie of 10 people in each of three departments in your company.

Assume you have been asked to create a spreadsheet that shows the names of the I employees in each department, their current salary, the difference between their currer salary and the industry average salary for their department, and the percent their salar would need to be increased to meet the industry average. Your spreadsheet should als compute the average increase needed to meet the industry average for each departmer and the average increase, company-wide, to meet industry averages.

    a. Use the data in the file **Ch02Ex01_U7e.docx** and create the spreadsheet.

    b. How can you use this analysis to contribute to the employee salary decision? Based on this data, what conclusions can you make?

    c. Suppose other team members want to use your spreadsheet. Name three ways you can share it with them and describe the advantages and disadvantages of each.

2-2. Suppose that you have been asked to assist in the managerial decision about how much to increase pay in the next year. Specifically, you are tasked to determine if there are significant salary differences among departments in your company.

    You are given an Access database with a table of employee data with the following structure:

      EMPLOYEE (Name, Department, Specialty, Salary)

    where *Name* is the name of an employee who works in a department, *Department* is the department name, *Specialty* is the name of the employee's primary skill, and *Salary* is the employee's current salary. Assume that no two employees have the same name. You have been asked to answer the following queries:

    (1) List the names, department, and salary of all employees earning more than $100,000.

    (2) List the names and specialties of all employees in the Marketing department.

    (3) Compute the average, maximum, and minimum salary of employees in your company.

    (4) Compute the average, minimum, and maximum salary of employees in the Marketing department.

    (5) Compute the average, minimum, and maximum salary of employees in the Information Systems department.

    (6) *Extra credit:* Compute the average salary for employees in every department. Use *Group By*.

    a. Design and run Access queries to obtain the answers to these questions, using the data in the file **Ch02Ex02_U7e.accdb**.

    b. Explain how the data in your answer contributes to the salary increase decision.

    c. Suppose other team members want to use your Access application. Name three ways you can share it with them, and describe the advantages and disadvantages of each.

Chapter 3

3-1. Figure AE-1 shows an Excel spreadsheet that the resort bicycle rental business uses to value and analyze its bicycle inventory. Examine this figure to understand the meaning of the data. Now use Excel to create a similar spreadsheet. Note the following:

- The top heading is in 20-point Calibri font. It is centered in the spreadsheet. Cells A1 through H1 have been merged.
- The second heading, Bicycle Inventory Valuation, is in 18-point Calibri, italics. It is centered in cells A2 through H2, which have been merged.
- The column headings are set in 11-point Calibri, bold. They are centered in their cells, and the text wraps in the cells.

    a. Make the first two rows of your spreadsheet similar to that in Figure AE-1. Choose your own colors for background and type, however.

    b. Place the current date so that it is centered in cells C3, C4, and C5, which must be merged.

    c. Outline the cells as shown in Figure AE-1.

	A	B	C	D	E	F	G	H
1				Resort Bicycle Rental				
2				Bicycle Inventory Valuation				
3				Saturday, May 31, 2014				
4	Make of Bike	Bike Cost	Number on Hand	Cost of Current Inventory	Number of Rentals	Total Rental Revenue	Revenue per Bike	Revenue as Percent of Cost of Inventory
5	Wonder Bike	$325	12	$3,900	85	$6,375	$531	163.5%
6	Wonder Bike II	$385	4	$1,540	34	$4,570	$1,143	296.8%
7	Wonder Bike Supreme	$475	8	$3,800	44	$5,200	$650	136.8%
8	LiteLift Pro	$655	8	$5,240	25	$2,480	$310	47.3%
9	LiteLift Ladies	$655	4	$2,620	40	$6,710	$1,678	256.1%
10	LiteLift Racer	$795	3	$2,385	37	$5,900	$1,967	247.4%

Figure AE-1
Excel Spreadsheet

d. Figure AE-1 uses the following formulas:

Cost of Current Inventory = Bike Cost × Number on Hand
Revenue per Bike = Rental Revenue × Number on Hand
Revenue as a Percent of Cost of Inventory = Total Rental Revenue × Cost of Current Inventory

Use these formulas in your spreadsheet, as shown in Figure AE-1.

e. Format the cells in the columns, as shown.

f. Give three examples of decisions that management of the bike rental agency might make from this data.

g. What other calculation could you make from this data that would be useful to the bike rental management? Create a second version of this spreadsheet in your worksheet document that has this calculation.

3-2. In this exercise, you will learn how to create a query based on data that a user enters and how to use that query to create a data entry form.

a. Download the Microsoft Access file **Ch03Ex02_U7e.accdb**. Open the file and familiarize yourself with the data in the Customer table.

b. Click *Create* in the Access ribbon. Click the icon labeled *Query Design*. Select the Customer table as the basis for the query by double-clicking on *Customer*. Close the Show Table dialog. Drag CustomerName, CustomerEmail, DateOfLastRental, BikeLastRented, TotalNumberOfRentals, and TotalRentalRevenue into the columns of the query results pane (the table at the bottom of the query design window).

c. In the CustomerName column, in the row labeled Criteria, place the following text:

[Enter Name of Customer:]

Type this exactly as shown, including the square brackets. This notation tells Access to ask you for a customer name to query.

d. In the ribbon, click the red exclamation mark labeled *Run*. Access will display a dialog box with the text "Enter Name of Customer:" (the text you entered in the query Criteria row). Enter the value *Maple, Rex* and click OK.

e. Save your query with the name *Parameter Query*.

f. Click the Home tab on the ribbon and click the Design View (upper left-hand button on the Home ribbon). Replace the text in the Criteria column of the CustomerName column with the following text. Type it exactly as shown:

Like "*" & [Enter part of Customer Name to search by:] & "*"

g. Run the query by clicking Run on the ribbon. Enter *Maple* when prompted *Enter part of Customer Name to search by*. Notice that the two customers who have the name Maple are displayed. If you have any problems, ensure that you have typed the phrase above *exactly* as shown into the Criteria row of the CustomerName column of your query.

h. Save your query again under the name *Parameter Query*. Close the query window.

i. Click *Create* on the Access ribbon. Under the Forms group, choose *Form Wizard*. In the dialog that opens, in the Tables/Queries box, click the down arrow. Select *Query: Parameter Query*. Click the double chevron << symbol and all of the columns in the query will move to the Selected Fields area.

j. Click *Next* two times. In the box under *What title do you want for your form?* enter *Customer Query Form* and click *Finish*.

k. Enter *Maple* in the dialog box that appears. Access will open a form with the values for Maple, Rex. At the bottom of the form, click the right-facing arrow and the data for Maple, Nichole will appear.

l. Close the form. Select *Object Type* and *Forms* in the Access Navigation Pane. Double-click the Customer Query Form and enter the value *Amanda*. Access will display data for all four customers having the value Amanda in their name.

Chapter 4

4-1. Sometimes you will have data in one Office application and want to move it to another Office application without rekeying it. Often this occurs when data was created for one purpose but then is used for a second purpose. For example, Figure AE-2 presents a portion of an Excel spreadsheet that shows the assignment of computers to employees. Lucas, an employee at AllRoad Parts, might use such a spreadsheet to track who has what equipment.

Suppose that you (or Lucas) want to use this data to help you assess how to upgrade computers. Let's say, for example, that you want to upgrade all of the computers' operating systems to Windows 8. Furthermore, you want to first upgrade the computers that most need upgrading, but suppose you have a limited budget. To address this situation, you would like to query the data in Figure AE-2, find all computers that do not have Windows 8, and then select those with slower CPUs or smaller memory as candidates for upgrading. To do this, you need to move the data from Excel into Access.

Once you have analyzed the data and determined the computers to upgrade, you want to produce a report. In that case, you may want to move the data from Access back to Excel, or perhaps into Word. In this exercise, you will learn how to perform these tasks.

	A	B	C	D	E	F	G	H
1	EmpLastName	EmpFirstName	Plant	Computer Brand	CPU (GHz)	Memory (	Disk (GB)	OS
2	Ashley	Linda	Denver	Dell	3	4	400	Windows 7
3	Davidson	Victor	Denver	Dell	2	3	250	Windows 7
4	Ching	Diem Thi	Denver	HP	2	3	100	Windows 7
5	Collins	James	Denver	Dell	1	1	120	Vista
6	Corning	Haley	Denver	HP	1.2	1	120	Windows 7
7	Scott	Richard	Denver	HP	1.8	2	100	Vista
8	Corovic	Anna	Denver	Dell	3	2	250	Windows 8
9	Lane	Kathy	Denver	Lenovo	2	1.512	250	Vista
10	Wei	James	Denver	IBM	2	1	120	Windows 7
11	Dixon	Mary	Denver	IBM	1	1.512	120	Vista
12	Lee	Matthew	Denver	Dell	0.5	1	80	XP
13	Duong	Steven	Denver	Dell	0.5	0.512	40	XP
14	Bosa	William	Denver	HP	1	2	150	Windows 7
15	Drew	Tony	Denver	HP	1	3	100	Windows 7
16	Adams	Mark	Denver	HP	1	1	80	XP
17	Lunden	Nicole	Denver	Lenovo	2	2	200	Windows 8
18	Utran	Bryan	Denver	Dell	2	1	120	Windows 7
19								
20		Primary Contact:	Kaye Davidson					

Figure AE-2
Sample Excel Data for Import

a. To begin, download the Excel file **Ch04Ex01_U7e.xlsx** into one of your directories. We will import the data in this file into Access, but before we do so, familiarize yourself with the data by opening it in Excel. Notice that there are three worksheets in this workbook. Close the Excel file.

b. Create a blank Access database. Name the database Ch04Ex02_Answer. Place it in some directory; it may be the same directory into which you have placed the Excel file, but it need not be. Close the default table that Access creates and delete it.

c. Now, we will import the data from the three worksheets in the Excel file **Ch04Ex01_U7e.xlsx** into a single table in your Access database. On the ribbon, select *External Data* and in the Import & Link section, click *Excel*. Start the import. For the first worksheet (Denver), you should select *Import the source data into a new table in the current database*. Ignore the warning about the first row by clicking OK. Be sure to click *First Row Contains Column Headings* when Access presents your data. You can use the default Field types and let Access add the primary key. Name your table *Employee* and click *Finish*. There is no need to save your import script.

For the Miami and Boston worksheets, again click *External Data, Import Excel*, but this time select *Append a copy of the records to the table Employees*. Select the Miami worksheet and click *Finish*. Repeat to import the Boston office employees.

d. Open the *Employee* table and examine the data. Notice that Access has erroneously imported a blank line and the *Primary Contact* data into rows at the end of each data set. This data is not part of the employee records, and you should delete it (in three places—once for each worksheet). The *Employee* table should have a total of 40 records.

e. Create a parameterized query on this data. Place all of the columns except *ID* into the query. In the *OS* column, set the criteria to select rows for which the value is not *Windows 8*. In the *CPU* (GHz) column, enter the criterion: <=*[Enter cutoff value for CPU]* and in the *Memory* (GB) column, enter the criterion: <=*[Enter cutoff value for Memory]*. Test your query. For example, run your query and enter a value of *2* for both CPU and memory. Verify that the correct rows are produced.

f. Use your query to find values of CPU and memory that give you as close to a maximum of 15 computers to upgrade as possible.

g. When you have found values of CPU and memory that give you 15, or nearly 15, computers to upgrade, leave your query open. Now, click *External data, Word*, and create a Word document that contains the results of your query. Adjust the column widths of the created table so that it fits on the page. Write a memo around this table explaining that these are the computers that you believe should be upgraded.

4-2. Assume you have been asked to create a spreadsheet to help make a buy-versus-lease decision about the servers for your organization. Assume that you are considering the servers for a 5-year period, but you do not know exactly how many servers you will need. Initially, you know you will need five servers, but you might need as many as 50, depending on the success of your organization's e-commerce activity. (By the way, many organizations are still making these calculations. However, those that have moved to the cloud no longer need to do so!)

a. For the buy-alternative calculations, set up your spreadsheet so that you can enter the base price of the server hardware, the price of all software, and a maintenance expense that is some percentage of the hardware price. Assume that the percent you enter covers both hardware and software maintenance. Also assume that each server has a 3-year life, after which it has no value. Assume straight-line depreciation for computers used less than 3 years, and that at the end of the 5 years you can sell the computers you have used for less than 3 years for their depreciated value. Also assume that your organization pays 2 percent interest on capital expenses. Assume th servers cost $5,000 each, and the needed software costs $750. Assume that the maintenance expense varies from 2 to 7 percent.

b. For the lease-alternative calculations, assume that the leasing vendor will lease the same computer hardware you can purchase. The lease includes all the software you need as well as all maintenance. Set up your spreadsheet so that you can enter various lease costs, which vary according to the number of years of the lease (1, 2, or 3). Assume the cost of a 3-year lease is $285 per machine per month, a 2-year lease is $335 per machine per month, and a 1-year lease is $415 per machine per month. Also, the lessor offers a 5 percent discount if you lease from 20 to 30 computers and a 10 percent discount if you lease from 31 to 50 computers.

c. Using your spreadsheet, compare the costs of buy versus lease under the following situations. (Assume you either buy or lease. You cannot lease some and buy some.) Make assumptions as necessary and state those assumptions.

(1) Your organization requires 20 servers for 5 years.

(2) Your organization requires 20 servers for the first 2 years and 40 servers for the next 3 years.

(3) Your organization requires 20 servers for the first 2 years, 40 servers for the next 2 years, and 50 servers for the last year.

(4) Your organization requires 10 servers the first year, 20 servers the second year, 30 servers the third year, 40 servers the fourth year, and 50 servers the last year.

(5) For the previous case, does the cheaper alternative change if the cost of the servers is $4,000? If it is $8,000?

Chapter 5

5-1. In some cases, users want to use Access and Excel together. They process relational data with Access, import some of the data into Excel, and use Excel's tools for creating professional-looking charts and graphs. You will do exactly that in this exercise.

Download the Access file **Ch05Ex01_U7e.accdb**. Open the database and select *DATABASE TOOLS/Relationships*. As you can see, there are three tables: *Product*, *VendorProductInventory*, and *Vendor*. Open each table individually to familiarize yourself with the data.

For this problem, we will define *InventoryCost* as the product of *IndustryStandardCost* and *QuantityOnHand*. The query *InventoryCost* computes these values for every item in inventory for every vendor. Open that query and view the data to be certain you understand this computation. Open the other queries as well so that you understand the data they produce.

a. Sum this data by vendor and display it in a pie chart like that shown in Figure AE-3 (your totals will be different from those shown). Proceed as follows:

(1) Open Excel and create a new spreadsheet.

(2) Click *DATA* on the ribbon and select *From Access* in the *Get External Data* ribbon category.

(3) Navigate to the location in which you have stored the Access file **Ch05Ex01_U7e.accdb**.

(4) Select the query that contains the data you need for this pie chart.

(5) Import the data into a worksheet.

(6) Format the appropriate data as currency.

(7) Select the range that contains the data, press the Function key, and proceed from there to create the pie chart. Name the data and pie chart worksheets appropriately.

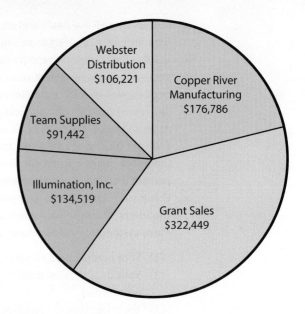

Figure AE-3
Data Displayed in Pie-Chart
Format

b. Follow a similar procedure to create the bar chart shown in Figure AE-4. Place the
data and the chart in separate worksheets and name them appropriately.

5-2. Reread the Guide on pages 186–187. Suppose you are given the task of con
verting the salesperson's data into a database. Because his data is so poorly
structured, it will be a challenge, as you will see.

a. Download the Excel file named **Ch05Ex02_U7e.xlsx**. This spreadsheet contains data that
fits the salesperson's description in the Guide. Open the spreadsheet and view the data.

b. Download the Access file with the same name, **Ch05Ex02_U7e.accdb**. Open the data
base, select *DATABASE TOOLS*, and click *Relationships*. Examine the four tables and
their relationships.

c. Somehow, you have to transform the data in the spreadsheet into the table structure
in the database. Because so little discipline was shown when creating the spreadsheet
this will be a labor-intensive task. To begin, import the spreadsheet data into a new
table in the database; call that table *Sheet1* or some other name.

d. Copy the *Name* data in *Sheet1* onto the clipboard. Then, open the *Customer* table and
paste the column of name data into that table.

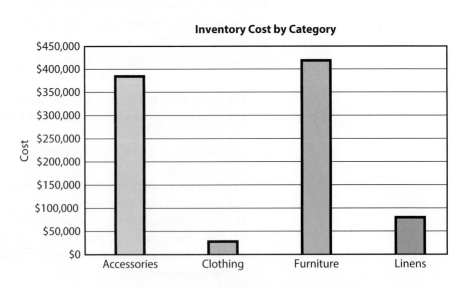

Figure AE-4
Data Displayed in Bar-Chart
Format

e. Unfortunately, the task becomes messy at this point. You can copy the *Car Interests* column into *Make or Model of Auto*, but then you will need to straighten out the values by hand. Phone numbers will need to be copied one at a time.

f. Open the *Customer* form and manually add any remaining data from the spreadsheet into each customer record. Connect the customer to his or her auto interests.

g. The data in the finished database has much more structure than that in the spreadsheet. Explain why that is both an advantage and a disadvantage. Under what circumstances is the database more appropriate? Less appropriate?

5-3. In this exercise, you will create a two-table database, define relationships, create a form and a report, and use them to enter data and view results.

a. Download the Excel file **Ch05Ex03_U7e.xlsx**. Open the spreadsheet and review the data in the *Employee* and *Computer* worksheets.

b. Create a new Access database with the name *Ch05Ex03_Solution*. Close the table that Access automatically creates and delete it.

c. Import the data from the Excel spreadsheet into your database. Import the *Employee* worksheet into a table named *Employee*. Be sure to check *First Row Contains Column Headings*. Select *Choose my own primary key* and use the ID field as that key.

d. Import the *Computer* worksheet into a table named *Computer*. Check *First Row Contains Column Headings*, but let Access create the primary key.

e. Open the relationships window and add both *Employee* and *Computer* to the design space. Drag ID from *Employee* and drop it on *EmployeeID* in *Computer*. Check *Enforce Referential Integrity* and the two checkmarks below. Ensure you know what these actions mean.

f. Open the Form Wizard dialog box (under *Create, More Forms*) and add all of the columns for each of your tables to your form. Select *View your data by Employee*. Title your form *Employee* and your subform *Computer*.

g. Open the *Computer* subform and delete *EmployeeID* and *ComputerID*. These values are maintained by Access, and it is just a distraction to keep them. Your form should appear like the one shown in Figure AE-5.

h. Use your form to add two new computers to *Amanda Ashley*. Both computers are Dells, and both use Vista; one costs $750, and the other costs $1,400.

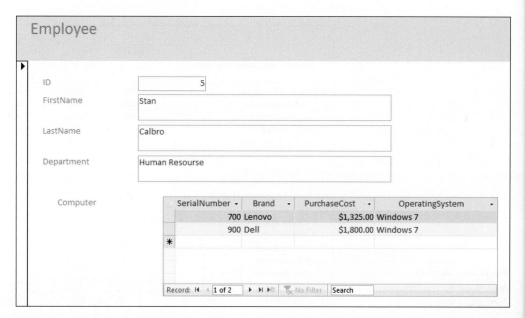

Figure AE-5
Employee Computer Assignment Form

i. Delete the Lenovo computer for Stan Calbro.

j. Use the Report Wizard (under *Create*) to create a report having all data from both the *Employee* and *Computer* tables. Adjust the report design until you find a design you like. Correct the label alignment if you need to.

Chapter 6

6-1. Numerous Web sites are available that will test your Internet data communication speed. You can find one good example at *www.speakeasy.net/speedtest/*. (If that site is no longer active, Google or Bing "What is my Internet speed?" to find another speed-testing site. Use it.)

a. While connected to your university's network, go to Speakeasy and test your speed against servers in Seattle, New York City, and Atlanta. Compute your average upload and download speeds.

b. Go home, or to a public wireless site, and run the Speakeasy test again. Compute your average upload and download speeds. If you are performing this test at home, are you getting the performance you are paying for?

c. Contact a friend or relative in another state. Ask him or her to run the Speakeasy test against those same three cities.

d. Compare the results in parts a–c. What conclusion, if any, can you draw from these tests?

6-2. Assume you have been asked to create an Office application to estimate cloud computing costs. You decide to create a spreadsheet into which your customers can provide their cloud computing needs and which you can then import into an Access database and use queries to compute cloud computing costs.

Figure AE-6 shows the structure of the spreadsheet into which your customers will input their requirements. You can download this spreadsheet in the Excel file **Ch06Ex02_U7e. xlsx**. Figure AE-7 shows an Access table that has costs corresponding to the requirements in Figure AE-6. You can download this database in the Access file **Ch06Ex02_U7e.accdb**.

a. Import the spreadsheet data into the Access database.

b. Write queries to compute the cost of each resource.

Figure AE-6
Worksheet for Inputting Cloud Computing Requirements

	A	B	C	D	E	F	G
1		Jan-13	Feb-13	Mar-13	Apr-13	May-13	Jun-13
2	**Compute requirements (hours):**						
3							
4	Extra Small Instance	1800	1800	1800	1800	1800	1800
5	Small Instance	2000	2000	2400	2400	0	0
6	Medium Instance	900	1800	2700	3600	3600	3600
7	Large Instance	0	500	1000	1500	2000	2000
8	Extra Large Instance	0	0	0	1000	1200	1500
9							
10	Storage requirements:						
11	Storage Required (GB)	30	35	40	45	50	55
12	Storage Transactions (1000s)	30	30	35	35	40	40
13							
14	Database requirements (number of instances)						
15	10GB Database	2	2	2	2	2	2
16	20GB Database	0	3	3	3	3	3
17	30GB Database		4	4	4	4	4
18	40GB Database	0	0	0	3	3	3
19	50GB Database	0	0	2	2	3	0

ID	Resource Name	Units	Cost
1	Extra Small Instance	Hours	$0.05
2	Small Instance	Hours	$0.12
3	Medium Instance	Hours	$0.24
4	Large Instance	Hours	$0.48
5	Extra Large Instance	Hours	$0.96
6	StorageRequired	GB / month	$0.15
7	StorageTransactions	10,000	$0.01
8	10GB Database	Each	$9.99
9	20GB Database	Each	$199.98
10	30GB Database	Each	$299.97
11	40GB Database	Each	$399.96
12	50GB Database	Each	$499.95

Figure AE-7
Cloud Computing Costs

c. Create a report that shows the cost for each type of resource for each month. Show the total costs for the 6-month period for each resource as well. Include a grand total of all the costs.

d. Create a pie chart that breaks out the total costs by resource. *Hint:* You can import the query data back into Excel.

e. Create a pie chart that breaks out the total costs by month. *Hint:* You can import the query data back into Excel.

f. Assume that processing costs increase by 10 percent across the board. Repeat parts c, d, and e for the changed costs.

Chapter 7

7-1. Suppose your manager asks you to create a spreadsheet to compute a production schedule. Your schedule should stipulate a production quantity for seven products that is based on sales projections made by three regional managers at your company's three sales regions.

a. Create a separate worksheet for each sales region. Use the data in the Word file **Ch07Ex01_U7e.docx**. This file contains each manager's monthly sales projections for the past year, actual sales results for those same months, and projections for sales for each month in the coming quarter.

b. Create a separate worksheet for each manager's data. Import the data from Word into Excel.

c. On each of the worksheets, use the data from the prior four quarters to compute the discrepancy between the actual sales and the sale projections. This discrepancy can be computed in several ways: You could calculate an overall average, or you could calculate an average per quarter or per month. You could also weight recent discrepancies more heavily than earlier ones. Choose a method that you think is most appropriate. Explain why you chose the method you did.

d. Modify your worksheets to use the discrepancy factors to compute an adjusted forecast for the coming quarter. Thus, each of your spreadsheets will show the raw forecast and the adjusted forecast for each month in the coming quarter.

e. Create a fourth worksheet that totals sales projections for all of the regions. Show both the unadjusted forecast and the adjusted forecast for each region and for the company overall. Show month and quarter totals.

f. Create a bar graph showing total monthly production. Display the unadjusted an adjusted forecasts using different colored bars.

7-2. *A* Figure AE-8 is a sample bill of materials, a form that shows the components an parts used to construct a product. In this example, the product is a child's wagor Such bills of materials are an essential part of manufacturing functional applications a well as ERP applications.

This particular example is a form produced using Microsoft Access. Creating suc a form is a bit tricky, so this exercise will guide you through the steps required. You ca then apply what you learn to produce a similar report. You can also use Access to experi ment on extensions of this form.

a. Create a table named *PART* with columns *PartNumber, Level, Description QuantityRequired*, and *PartOf. Description* and *Level* should be text, *PartNumbe* should be AutoNumber, and *QuantityRequired* and *PartOf* should be numeri long integer. Add the *PART* data shown in Figure AE-8 to your table.

b. Create a query that has all columns of *PART*. Restrict the view to rows having a valu of 1 for *Level*. Name your query *Level1*.

c. Create two more queries that are restricted to rows having values of 2 or 3 for *Leve* Name your queries *Level2* and *Level3*, respectively.

d. Create a form that contains *PartNumber, Level,* and *Description* from *Level1*. You ca use a wizard for this if you want. Name the form *Bill of Materials*.

e. Select the Subform/Subreport tool in the Controls section of the DESIGN ribbon an create a subform in your form in part d. Set the data on this form to be all of the co umns of *Level2*. After you have created the subform, ensure that the Link Child Field

Ajax Toy Manufacturing
Bill of Materials

PartNumber	Level		Description			
1	1		Deluxe Wagon III			

Parts Contained

PartNumber ▾	Level ▾	Description ▾	QuantityRequired ▾	PartOf ▾
2	2	Handle Bar	1	1

PartNumber ▾	Level ▾	Descrption ▾	QuantityRequir ▾	PartOf ▾
3	3	Bar Grip	2	2
4	3	Bar Tang	1	2
14	3	Bar Stock	1	2
* (New)			0	2

PartNumber ▾	Level ▾	Description ▾	QuantityRequired ▾	PartOf ▾
5	2	Wagon Body, Metal	1	1

PartNumber ▾	Level ▾	Descrption ▾	QuantityRequir ▾	PartOf ▾
* (New)			0	5

PartNumber ▾	Level ▾	Description ▾	QuantityRequired ▾	PartOf ▾
6	2	Front Wheel Assembly	1	1

PartNumber ▾	Level ▾	Descrption ▾	QuantityRequir ▾	PartOf ▾
7	3	Front Wheels	2	6
8	3	Axle	1	6
9	3	Wheel retainer	2	6
* (New)			0	6

PartNumber ▾	Level ▾	Description ▾	QuantityRequired ▾	PartOf ▾
10	2	Rear Wheel Assembly	1	1

PartNumber ▾	Level ▾	Descrption ▾	QuantityRequir ▾	PartOf ▾
11	3	Rear Wheels	2	10
12	3	Axle	1	10
13	3	Wheel retainer	2	10
* (New)			0	10

| * (New) | | | 0 | 1 |

Record: I◄ ◄ 1 of 4 ► ►I ►⊞ 🔻 No Filter   Search

Figure AE-8
Bill of Materials Example

property is set to *PartOf* and that the Link Master Fields property is set to *PartNumber*. Close the *Bill of Materials* form.

 f. Open the subform created in part e and create a subform on it using the Subform/ Subreport control. Set the data on this subform to be all of the columns of *Level3*. After you have created the subform, ensure that the Link Child Fields property is set to *PartOf* and that the Link Master Fields property is set to *PartNumber*. Close the *Bill of Materials* form.

 g. Open the *Bill of Materials* form. It should appear as in Figure AE-8. Open and close the form and add new data. Using this form, add sample BOM data for a product of your own choosing.

 h. Following the process similar to that just described, create a *Bill of Materials Report* that lists the data for all of your products.

 i. (**Optional, challenging extension**) Each part in the BOM in Figure AE-8 can be used in at most one assembly (there is space to show just one *PartOf* value). You can change your design to allow a part to be used in more than one assembly as follows: First, remove *PartOf* from PART. Next, create a second table that has two columns: *AssemblyPartNumber* and *ComponentPartNumber*. The first contains a part number of an assembly, and the second contains a part number of a component. Every component of a part will have a row in this table. Extend the views described above to use this second table and to produce a display similar to Figure AE-8.

Chapter 8

8-1. Suppose you are the manager of social media policy for an organization having 1,000 employees with seven different offices throughout North America. Further suppose that the CEO has requested a report showing a list of all of the employees' blogs, the employees' job titles and departments, and the purpose and URL of each blog. She doesn't want to control employees; she just wants to know where they are.

 a. Explain the conditions under which using a spreadsheet to track this data would be appropriate.

 b. Suppose that employees can have more than one blog, but that a blog is only supported by a single employee. Further suppose that you decide that you need to track the dates on which a blog was first created and the date of the last posting, if the blog is no longer active. Design a database for these requirements.

 c. Fill your database with the sample data in the Word document **Ch08Ex01_U7e.docx**. EmployeeID is a unique identifier; a null value for EndDate means the blog is still active. Do not retype this data; import it instead. You can either import it several times, each time to a different table, or you can import it once and use queries to fill the tables.

 d. Create a report that you believe is suitable for the CEO's needs. Justify the content and structure of your report.

8-2. Assume that you have been given the task of compiling evaluations that your company's purchasing agents make of their vendors. Each month, every purchasing agent evaluates all of the vendors that he or she has ordered from in the past month on three factors: price, quality, and responsiveness. Assume the ratings are from 1 to 5, with 5 being the best. Because your company has hundreds of vendors and dozens of purchasing agents, you decide to use Access to compile the results.

 a. Create a database with three tables: VENDOR (*VendorNumber, Name, Contact*), PURCHASER (*EmpNumber, Name, Email*), and RATING (*EmpNumber, VendorNumber, Month, Year, Price Rating, QualityRating, ResponsivenessRating*). Assume that

VendorNumber and *EmpNumber* are the keys of VENDOR and PURCHASER, respectively. Decide what you think is the appropriate key for RATING.

   b. Create appropriate relationships.

   c. Import the data in the Excel file **Ch08Ex02_U7e.xlsx**. Note that data for Vendor
Purchaser, and Rating are stored in three separate worksheets.

   d. Create a query that shows the names of all vendors and their average scores.

   e. Create a query that shows the names of all employees and their average scores
Hint: In this and in part f, you will need to use the *Group By* function in your query

   f. Create a parameterized query that you can use to obtain the minimum, maximum
and average ratings on each criterion for a particular vendor. Assume you will ente
VendorName as the parameter.

   g. Using the data created by your queries, what conclusions can you make about vendors or purchasers?

Chapter 9

9-1.   OLAP cubes are very similar to Microsoft Excel pivot tables. For this exercise, as
sume that your organization's purchasing agents rate vendors similar to the situa
tion described in Application Exercise 8-2.

   a. Open the Excel file **Ch09Ex01_U7e.xlsx**. The spreadsheet has the following column
names: *VendorName, EmployeeName, Date, Year,* and *Rating.*

   b. Under the *INSERT* ribbon in Excel, click *Pivot Table.*

   c. When asked to provide a data range, drag your mouse over the column names and
data values so as to select all of the data. Excel will fill in the range values in the ope
dialog box. Place your pivot table in a new worksheet. Click OK.

   d. Excel will create a field list on the right-hand side of your spreadsheet. Underneath it
a grid labeled Drag fields between areas below: should appear. Drag and drop the field
named *VendorName* into the area named ROWS. Observe what happens in the pivo
table to the left (in column A). Now drag and drop *EmployeeName* on to COLUMNS
and *Rating* on to VALUES. Again observe the effect of these actions in the pivot table
to the left. Voilà! You have a pivot table.

   e. To see how the pivot table works, drag and drop more fields onto the grid in the
bottom right hand side of your screen. For example, drop *Year* just underneath
EmployeeName. Then move *Year* above *Employee.* Now move *Year* below *Vendor.* A
of this action is just like an OLAP cube, and, in fact, OLAP cubes are readily displayee
in Excel pivot tables. The major difference is that OLAP cubes are usually based or
thousands or more rows of data.

9-2.   It is surprisingly easy to create a market-basket report using table data in Access
To do so, however, you will need to enter SQL expressions into the Access quer
builder. Here, you can just copy SQL statements to type them in. If you take a database
class, you will learn how to code SQL statements like those you will use here.

   a. Create an Access database with a table named *Order_Data* having column
OrderNumber, ItemName, and *Quantity,* with data types Number (*LongInteger*), Shor
Text (50), and Number (*LongInteger*), respectively. Define the key as the composit
(*OrderNumber, ItemName*). (You can do this in the table designer by highlighting both
columns and clicking the Primary Key icon.)

   b. Import the data from the Excel file **Ch09Ex02_U7e.xlsx** into the *Order_Data* table.

   c. Now, to perform the market-basket analysis, you will need to enter several SQI
statements into Access. To do so, click *CREATE/Query Design.* Click Close when the

Show Table dialog box appears. Right-click in the gray section above the grid in the window. Select SQL View. Enter the following expression exactly as it appears here:

```
SELECT    T1.ItemName as FirstItem,
          T2.ItemName as SecondItem
FROM      Order_Data T1, Order_Data T2
WHERE     T1.OrderNumber =
          T2.OrderNumber
AND       T1.ItemName <> T2.ItemName;
```

Click the red exclamation point in the toolbar to run the query. Correct any typing mistakes and, once it works, save the query using the name TwoItem Basket.

d. Now enter a second SQL statement. Again, click *CREATE/Query Design*. Click Close when the Show Table dialog box appears. Right-click in the gray section above the grid in the window. Select SQL View. Enter the following expression exactly as it appears here:

```
SELECT    TwoItemBasket.FirstItem,
          TwoItemBasket.SecondItem,
          Count(*) AS SupportCount
FROM      TwoItemBasket
GROUP BY  TwoItemBasket.FirstItem,
          TwoItemBasket.SecondItem;
```

Correct any typing mistakes and, once it works, save the query using the name SupportCount.

e. Examine the results of the second query and verify that the two query statements have correctly calculated the number of times that two items have appeared together. Explain further calculations you need to make to compute support.

f. Explain the calculations you need to make to compute lift. Although you can make those calculations using SQL, you need more SQL knowledge to do it, and we will skip that here.

g. Explain, in your own words, what the query in part c seems to be doing. What does the query in part d seem to be doing? Again, you will need to take a database class to learn how to code such expressions, but this exercise should give you a sense of the kinds of calculations that are possible with SQL.

9-3. Suppose you are Addison at AllRoad Parts. Download the Access file **Ch09Ex03_U7e.acccdb**, which contains the data extract that Addison and Drew used in Chapter 9.

1. Suppose ExtremeGear decides not to release its 3D design files at any price. Remove parts provided by it from consideration and repeat the data analysis in Chapter 9.

2. Addison and Drew decide, in light of the absence of ExtremeGear's part designs, to repeat their analysis with different criteria as follows:
   - Large customers are those who have ordered more than 900 parts.
   - Frequent purchases occur at least 25 times per year.
   - Small quantities have an average order size of 3 or less.
   - Inexpensive parts cost less than $75.
   - Shipping weight is less than 4 pounds.
   Repeat the data analysis in Chapter 9.

3. How does the second set of criteria change the results?

4. What recommendations would you make to Kelly and Jason in light of your analysis?

Chapter 10

10-1. In this exercise, you will use Visio to create process diagrams in BPMN notation.

    a. Download the Visio file **Ch10Ex01_U7e.vsd** from this text's support site. Open the file and familiarize yourself with this diagram, which is a copy of Figure 10-7.

    b. Notice that Visio includes the BPMN shapes. Go to the Shape organizer to see other types of flowchart shapes that Visio supports.

    c. Create a new Visio diagram. Add BPMN shapes that you may want to use.

    d. Model the customer process Respond to Quotation. Make sure your process accepts the inputs shown in **Ch10Ex01_U7e.vsd** and produces the outputs shown in that figure. Create your process so that your company checks prices and delivery dates, and requests changes, if appropriate. Include other logic, if necessary.

    e. Show your work by saving your document as a PDF file.

10-2. Suppose you are given the task of comparing labor costs of meetings for systems development projects to budgets. Download the Word file **Ch10Ex02_U7e.doc** and the Excel file with the same name. The Word file has records of meeting dates, times, and attendees. The document was created from informal notes taken at the meetings. The Excel file has the project budgets as well as labor costs for different categories of employees.

Assume your company uses the traditional systems-first process illustrated in Figure 10-12. Further assume that each SDLC step requires two types of meetings. *Working meetings* involve users, business analysts, systems analysts, programmers, and PQA test engineers. *Review meetings* involve all of those people, plus level-1 and level-2 managers of both user departments and the IS department.

    a. Using either Access or Excel, whichever you think is better suited to the task, import the Word data to a work file and compute the total labor for each type of employee for each meeting.

    b. Using the file you created in part a, compute the total labor for each type of employee for each phase of the project.

    c. Combine your answer in part b with the data in the Excel file **Ch10Ex02_U7e.xlsx** to compute the total cost of meetings of each phase of the project.

    d. Use a graphic chart of the type you think best to show the differences between meeting cost and budget.

    e. Comment on your choice of Excel or Access for your work file. If you were to do this exercise over, would you use that same tool again? Why or why not?

10-3. Use Access to develop a failure-tracking database application. Use the sample data in the Excel file **Ch10Ex03_U7e.xlsx** for this exercise. The data includes columns for the following:

> *FailureNumber*
> *DateReported*
> *FailureDescription*
> *ReportedBy (the name of the PQA engineer reporting the failure)*
> *ReportedBy_email (the email address of the PQA engineer reporting the failure)*
> *FixedBy (the name of the programmer who is assigned to fix the failure)*
> *FixedBy_email (the email address of the programmer assigned to fix the failure)*
> *DateFailureFixed*
> *FixDescription*

DateFixVerified

VerifiedBy (the name of the PQA engineer verifying the fix)

VerifiedBy_email (the email address of the PQA engineer verifying the fix)

a. The data in the spreadsheet are not normalized. Normalize the data by creating a *Failure* table, a *PQA Engineer* table, and a *Developer* table. Assume problems are reported and verified by PQA engineers and problems are fixed by developers. Add other appropriate columns to each table. Create appropriate relationships.

b. Create one or more forms that can be used to report a failure, to report a failure fix, and to report a failure verification. Create the form(s) so that the user can use a combo box to pull down the name of a PQA engineer or developer from the appropriate table to fill in the *ReportedBy, FixedBy,* and *VerifiedBy* fields.

c. Construct a report that shows all failures sorted by reporting PQA engineer and then by *Date Reported.*

d. Construct a report that shows only fixed and verified failures.

e. Construct a report that shows only fixed but unverified failures.

Chapter 11

11-1. Suppose you have just been appointed manager of a help desk with an IS department. You have been there for just a week, and you are amazed to find only limited data to help you manage your employees. In fact, the only data kept concerns the processing of particular issues, called *Tickets*. The following data are kept: *Ticket#, Date_Submitted, Date_Opened, Date_Closed, Type (new or repeat), Reporting_ Employee_ Name, Reporting_Employee_Division, Technician_Name_Problem_System,* and *Problem_ Description.* You can find sample Ticket data in the Excel file **Ch11Ex01_U7e.xlsx**.

As a manager, you need information that will help you manage. Specifically, you need information that will help you learn who are your best- and worst-performing technicians, how different systems compare in terms of number of problems reported and the time required to fix those problems, how different divisions compare in terms of problems reported and the time required to fix them, which technicians are the best and worst at solving problems with particular systems, and which technicians are best and worst at solving problems from particular divisions.

a. Use either Access or Excel, or a combination of the two, to produce the information you need using the data in the Excel file **Ch11Ex01_U7e.xlsx**. In your answer, you may use queries, formulas, reports, forms, graphs, pivot tables, pivot charts, or any other type of Access or Excel display. Choose the best display for the type of information you are producing.

b. Explain how you would use these different types of information to manage your department.

c. Specify any additional information that you would like to have produced from this data to help you manage your department.

d. Use either Access or Excel, or a combination, to produce the information in part c.

Chapter 12

12-1. Deceit as practiced by phishers is amazingly simple to implement. To see how simple, perform the following tasks:

a. Open any html editor, such as Dreamweaver or Expression Web.

b. Create a Web page with the title "Phishing Examples" and the subtitle "Go to These Sites."

c. Under the subtitle, create a hyperlink that will display the text "*www.msn.com.* However, set the target of this link to be *www.yahoo.com*.

d. Create a second hyperlink that will display the text "*www.google.com.*" However, se the target of this link to *www.bing.com*.

e. Test your Web page. Click each link and observe where your browser goes.

f. Explain how this exercise pertains to phishing.

12-2. Develop a spreadsheet model of the cost of a virus attack at an organization tha has three types of computers: employee workstations, data servers, and Web serv ers. Assume that the number of computers affected by the virus depends on the severity of the virus. For the purposes of your model, assume that there are three levels of viru: severity: *Low-severity* incidents affect fewer than 30 percent of the user workstations and none of the data or Web servers. *Medium-severity* incidents affect up to 70 percent of the user workstations, up to half of the Web servers, and none of the data servers. *High severity* incidents can affect all organizational computers.

a. Assume 40 percent of the incidents are low severity, 35 percent are medium severity and 25 percent are high severity.

b. Assume employees can remove viruses from workstations themselves, but that spe cially trained technicians are required to repair the servers. The time to eliminate a vi rus from an infected computer depends on the computer type. Let the time to remove the virus from each type be an input into your model. Assume that when users elimi nate the virus themselves, they are unproductive for twice the time required for the removal. Let the average employee hourly labor cost be an input to your model. Le the average cost of a technician also be an input into your model. Finally, let the tota number of user computers, data servers, and Web servers be inputs into your model.

c. Run your simulation 10 times. Use the same inputs for each run, but draw a random number (assume a uniform distribution for all random numbers) to determine the severity type. Then, draw random numbers to determine the percentage of comput ers of each type affected, using the constraints detailed earlier. For example, if the attack is of medium severity, draw a random number between 0 and 70 to indicate the percentage of infected user workstations and a random number between 0 and 50 to indicate the percentage of infected Web servers.

d. For each run, calculate the total of lost employee hours, the total dollar cost of los employee labor hours, the total hours of technician labor needed to fix the servers and the total cost of technician labor. Finally, compute the total overall cost. Show the results of each run. Show the average costs and hours for the 10 runs.

Glossary

10/100/1000 Ethernet   A type of Ethernet that conforms to the IEEE 802.3 protocol and allows for transmission at a rate of 10, 100, or 1,000 Mbps (megabits per second). 207

3D printing (additive manufacturing)   The process of creating three-dimensional objects by fusing two-dimensional layers of plastic, metal, and other substances on top of one another. 2

Abstract reasoning   The ability to make and manipulate models. 8

Access   A popular personal and small workgroup DBMS product from Microsoft. 166

Active lurker   Someone who reads, consumes, and observes activity in one social medium and then broadcasts it in another medium. 303

Activity   A business function that receives inputs and produces outputs. An activity can be performed by a human, by a computer system, or by both. 90

Advanced Persistent Threat (APT)   A sophisticated, possibly long-running, computer hack that is perpetrated by large, well-funded organizations like governments. APTs are a means to engage in cyberwarfare. 457

Adware   Programs installed on the user's computer without the user's knowledge or permission that reside in the background and, unknown to the user, observe the user's actions and keystrokes, modify computer activity, and report the user's activities to sponsoring organizations. Most adware is benign in that it does not perform malicious acts or steal data. It does, however, watch user activity and produce pop-up ads. 147, 469

Agile development   An adaptive project management process based on the principles listed in Figure 10-23. Can be used for the management of many types of projects; in this text it applies to the development of information systems. 406

Android   A mobile operating system that is a version of Linux. Android runs on the Google Nexus 7, the Amazon Kindle Fire, as well as many other mobile devices. 119

Application   Synonym for application software. 378

Application software   Programs that perform a business function. Some application programs are general purpose, such as Excel or Word. Other application programs are specific to a business function, such as accounts payable. 122

ARM   A computer architecture and instruction set that is designed for portable devices such as smartphones and tablets. 120

As-is model   A model that represents the current situation and processes. 382

Asymmetric encryption   An encryption method whereby different keys are used to encode and to decode the message; one key encodes the message, and the other key decodes the message. Asymmetric encryption is slower and more complicated than symmetric encryption. 467

Asynchronous communication   Information exchange that occurs when all members of a work team do not meet at the same time, such as those who work different shifts or in different locations. 48

Attributes   Characteristics of an entity. Example attributes of *Order* would be *OrderNumber, OrderDate, SubTotal, Tax, Total*, and so forth. Example attributes of *Salesperson* would be *SalespersonName, Email, Phone*, and so forth. 175

Authentication   The process whereby an information system verifies (validates) a user. 466

Baseline WBS   The final work-breakdown structure that shows the planned tasks, dependencies, durations, and resource assignments. 402

BI analysis   The process of creating business intelligence. The four fundamental categories of BI analysis are reporting, data mining, BigData, and knowledge management. 329

BI application   The software component of a BI system. 325

BI server   A Web server application that is purpose-built for the publishing of business intelligence. 359

BigData   A term used to describe data collections that are characterized by huge volume, rapid velocity, and great variety. 185

Bigtable   A nonrelational data store developed by Google. 184

Binary digits   The means by which computers represent data; also called *bits*. A binary digit is either a zero or a one. 115

Biometric authentication   The use of personal physical characteristics, such as fingerprints, facial features, and retinal scans, to authenticate users. 466

Bits   The means by which computers represent data; also called *binary digits*. A bit is either a zero or a one. 115

BlackBerry OS   One of the most successful early mobile operating systems; was primarily used by business users on BlackBerry devices. 119

Bluetooth   A common wireless protocol designed for transmitting data over short distances, replacing cables. 207

Bring your own device (BYOD) policy   An official organizational policy that states employees' permissions and responsibilities when using personal mobile devices for organizational business. 142

Brooks' Law   The famous adage that states: *Adding more people to a late project makes the project later*. Brooks' Law is true not only because a larger staff requires increased coordination, but also because new people need to be trained. The only people who can train the new employees are the existing team members, who are thus taken off productive tasks. The costs of training new people can overwhelm the benefit of their contributions. 402

Brute force attack   A password-cracking program that tries every possible combination of characters. 461

Bullwhip effect   A phenomenon in which the variability in the size and timing of orders increases at each stage up the supply chain, from customer to supplier. 497

Business analyst   (1) A person who understands business strategies, goals, and objectives and who helps businesses develop and manage business processes and information systems. (2) Someone who is well versed in Porter's models, organizational strategy, and systems alignment theory, like COBIT, and who also understands the proper role for technology. 380

Business intelligence (BI)   The processing of operational and other data to create information that exposes patterns, relationships, and trends of importance to the organization. 325

Business intelligence (BI) systems   Information systems that process operational and other source data to identify patterns, relationships, and trends and to make predictions. 325

Business process   (1) A network of activities, repositories, roles, resources, and flows that interact to achieve some business function; sometimes called a *business system*. (2) A network of activities that generate value by transforming inputs into outputs. 90, 380

Business process management (BPM)   A cyclical process for systematically creating, assessing, and altering business processes. 91, 382

Business Process Modeling Notation (BPMN)   Standard set of terms and graphical notations for documenting business processes. 384

Business process reengineering   The activity of altering existing and designing new business processes to take advantage of new information systems technology. 252

Bytes   (1) Eight-bit chunks of data. (2) Characters of data. 115, 160

Cable line   Cable television lines that provide high-speed data transmission. 209

Capital   Resources that are invested with the expectation of future gain. 295

Cassandra   A durable, nonrelational data store that operates over hundreds or thousands of servers. Originally developed by Facebook but later turned over to the open-source community; has become an Apache Top-Level Project. 184

Central processing unit (CPU)   The portion of a computer that selects instructions, processes them, performs arithmetic and logical comparisons, and stores results of operations in memory. 114

Charms   In Windows 8 applications, icons that slides in from the right of the display. 138

Chief information officer (CIO)   The title of the principal manager of the IS department. Other common titles are *vice president of information services, director of information services*, and, less commonly, *director of computer services*. 426

Chief technology officer (CTO)   The head of the technology group. The CTO filters new ideas and products to identify those that are most relevant to the organization. The CTO's job requires deep knowledge of information technology and the ability to envision how new IT could affect an organization over time. 427

Chrome   A term that refers to visual overhead such as menus, status bars, and scroll bars, in a computer display. 137

Client   PCs, tablets, and smartphones that access servers via the cloud. 115

Closed source   Source code that is highly protected and only available to trusted employees and carefully vetted contractors. 127

Cloud   A term that refers to elastic leasing of pooled computer resources over the Internet. 199

Cluster analysis   An unsupervised data mining technique whereby statistical techniques are used to identify groups of entities that have similar characteristics. A common use for cluster analysis is to find groups of similar customers in data about customer orders and customer demographics. 345

COBIT (Control Objectives for Information and related Technology)   A set of standard practices, created by the Information Systems Audit and Control Association, that are used in the assessment stage of the BPM cycle to determine how well an information system complies with an organization's strategy. 383

Collaboration   The activity of two or more people working together to achieve a common goal via a process of feedback and iteration. 8, 37

Collaboration information system   An information system that supports collaboration. See also *collaboration system*. 46

Collaboration system   An information system that supports collaboration. See also *collaboration information system*. 46

Columns   Also called *fields*, or groups of bytes. A database table has multiple columns that are used to represent the attributes of an entity. Examples are *PartNumber*, *EmployeeName*, and *SalesDate*. 160

Commerce server   An application program that runs on a server tier computer. A typical commerce server obtains product data from a database, manages items in users' shopping carts, and coordinates the checkout process. 212

Communities   Groups of people related by a common interest. 285

Competitive strategy   The strategy an organization chooses as the way it will succeed in its industry. According to Porter, there are four fundamental competitive strategies: cost leadership across an industry or within a particular industry segment and product differentiation across an industry or within a particular industry segment. 85

Computer hardware   Electronic components and related gadgetry that input, process, output, store, and communicate data according to be instructions encoded in computer programs or software. One of the five fundamental components of an information system. 11

Computer-based information system   An information system that includes a computer. 11

Confidence   In market-basket terminology, the probability estimate that two items will be purchased together. 347

Configuration control   A set of management policies, practices, and tools that developers use to maintain control over the project's resources. 403

Connection data   In social media systems, data about relationships. 290

Content data   In social media systems, data and responses to data that are contributed by users and SM sponsors. 289

Content delivery network (CDN)   An information system that serves content to Web pages over the Internet. To reduce wait time, data is typically stored and served from many geographic locations. 220

Content management systems (CMS)   Information systems that support the management and delivery of documentation including reports, Web pages, and other expressions of employee knowledge. 354

Context-sensitive chrome   Chrome that pops up in the display only when needed and appropriate. 137

Control flow   A BPMN symbol that documents the flow of activity in a business process. 380

Conversion rate   Measures the frequency that someone who clicks on an ad makes a purchase, "likes" a site, or takes some other action desired by the advertiser. 308

Cookie   A small file that is stored on the user's computer by a browser. Cookies can be used for authentication, for storing shopping cart contents and user preferences, and for other legitimate purposes. Cookies can also be used to implement spyware. 369, 461

Cooperation   The process by which a group of people having the same skills work in parallel to shorten the time required to accomplish a job, e.g., four painters each painting one wall of a room. 37

Cost   The cost of a business process is equal to the cost of the inputs plus the cost of activities. 90

Cost feasibility   An assessment of the cost of an information system development project that compares estimated costs to the available budget. Can also refer to development plus operational costs vs. value delivered. 389

Critical path   The sequence of activities that determine the earliest date by which the project can be completed. 400

Critical path analysis   The process by which project managers compress a schedule by moving resources, typically people, from noncritical path tasks to critical path tasks. 401

Cross-selling   The sale of related products to customers based on salesperson knowledge, market-basket analysis, or both. 346

Crowdsourcing   The dynamic social media process of employing users to participate in product design or redesign. 293

Crow's feet   Lines on an entity-relationship diagram that indicate a 1:N relationship between two entities. 177

Crow's-foot diagram   A type of entity-relationship diagram that uses a crow's foot symbol to designate a 1:N relationship. 177

Custom-developed software   Software that is tailor-made for a particular organization's requirements. 122

Customer life cycle   Taken as a whole, the processes of marketing, customer acquisition, relationship management, and loss/churn that must be managed by CRM systems. 253

Customer relationship management (CRM) system   A suite of applications, a database, and a set of inherent processes for managing all the interactions with the customer, from lead generation to customer service. 253

Data   Recorded facts or figures. One of the five fundamental components of an information system. 11

Data acquisition   In business intelligence systems, the process of obtaining, cleaning, organizing, relating, and cataloging source data. 329

Data administration   An organization-wide function that develops and enforces data policies and standards. 471

Data aggregator   See *data broker*. 336

Database A self-describing collection of integrated records. 160

Database administration A person or department that develops procedures and practices to ensure efficient and orderly multiuser processing of the database, to control changes to database structure, and to protect the database. 168, 471

Database application A collection of forms, reports, queries, and application programs that facilitates users' processing of a database. A database can be processed by many different database applications. 168

Database management system (DBMS) A program for creating, processing, and administering a database. A DBMS is a large and complex program that is licensed like an operating system. Microsoft Access and Oracle Database are example DBMS products. 166

Database tier In the three-tier architecture, the tier that runs the DBMS and receives and processes requests to retrieve and store data. 212

Data broker A company that acquires and purchases consumer and other data from public records, retailers, Internet cookie vendors, social media trackers, and other sources and uses it to create business intelligence that it sells to companies and the government. 336

Data flow A BPMN symbol that documents the movement of data among activities and repositories in a business process. 380

Data integrity In a database or a collection of databases, the condition that exists when data values are consistent and in agreement with one another. 249

Data integrity problem In a database, the situation that exists when data items disagree with one another. An example is two different names for the same customer. 179

Data mart A data collection, smaller than a data warehouse, that addresses the needs of a particular department or functional area of a business. 340

Data mining The application of statistical techniques to find patterns and relationships among data for classification and prediction. 343

Data model A logical representation of the data in a database that describes the data and relationships that will be stored in the database. Akin to a blueprint. 175

Data safeguards Measures used to protect databases and other data assets from threats. Includes data rights and responsibilities, encryptions, backup and recovery, and physical security. 471

Data triangulation See *semantic security*. 362

Data warehouse A facility for managing an organization's BI data. 335

DB2 A popular, enterprise-class DBMS product from IBM. 166

Decision support systems Some authors define business intelligence (BI) systems as supporting decision making only, in which case they use this older term as a synonym for decision-making BI systems. 327

Decision tree A hierarchical arrangement of criteria that predict a classification or a value. 348

Defenders of belief In social media, a community that shares a common strongly held belief; such groups seek conformity and want to convince others of the wisdom of their belief. 291

Deliverables Tasks that are measurable or observable steps in a development project. 397

Denial of service (DOS) Security problem in which users are not able to access an information system; can be caused by human errors, natural disaster, or malicious activity. 457

Desktop virtualization Also called *client virtualization* and *PC virtualization*. The process of storing a user's desktop on a remote server. It enables users to run their desktop from many different client computers. 120

Digital subscriber line (DSL) A communications line that operates on the same lines as voice telephones, but do so in such a manner that their signals to not interfere with voice telephone service. 208

Dimension A characteristic of an OLAP measure. Purchase date, customer type, customer location, and sales region are examples of dimensions. 342

Direct interaction Driving application behavior by implementing obvious actions on user content; for example clicking on an album to open the album's contents. 137

Discussion forums Forms of asynchronous communication in which one group member posts an entry and other group members respond. A better form of group communication than email, because it is more difficult for one person to monopolize the discussion or for the discussion to go off track. 50

Diseconomies of scale A principle that states as development teams become larger, the average contribution per worker decreases. 402

Distributed database processing The processing of a single database that resides in multiple locations. 494

Distributed systems Systems in which application processing is distributed across multiple computing devices. 268

Domain name A worldwide unique name that is registered in the domain name system (DNS) and is affiliated with a public IP address. 211

Drill down With an OLAP report, to further divide the data into more detail. 343

Drive-by sniffer   A person who takes a computer with a wireless connection through an area and searches for unprotected wireless networks in an attempt to gain free Internet access or to gather unauthorized data. 456

Dual processor   A computer with two CPUs. 114

Durability   A condition of a data store in which, once data is committed to the data store, it won't be lost, even in the presence of computer or network failure. 195

Dynamic processes   Flexible, informal, and adaptive processes that normally involve strategic and less specific managerial decisions and activities. 244

Dynamic reports   Business intelligence documents that are updated at the time they are requested. 358

Dynamo   A nonreational data store developed by Amazon .com 184

Elastic   In cloud computing, the situation that exists when the amount of resource leased can be dynamically increased or decreased, programmatically, in a short span of time, and organizations pay for just the resource that they use. This term was first used in this way by Amazon.com. 194, 199

Email   A form of asynchronous communication in which participants send comments and attachments electronically. As a form of group communication, it can be disorganized, disconnected, and easy to hide from. 50

Email spoofing   A synonym for *phishing*. A technique for obtaining unauthorized data that uses pretexting via email. The *phisher* pretends to be a legitimate company and sends email requests for confidential data, such as account numbers, Social Security numbers, account passwords, and so forth. Phishers direct traffic to their sites under the guise of a legitimate business. 456

Encapsulated   A characteristic of systems design in which the details of a process are hidden from users of that process. A formal interface is defined for the process that specifies how the process is to be accessed, what data it requires, and the data that it will produce. The means by which that process creates those results are never exposed, nor do they need to be. 215

Encryption   The process of transforming clear text into coded, unintelligible text for secure storage or communication. 467

Encryption algorithms   Algorithms used to transform clear text into coded, unintelligible text for secure storage or communication. 467

Enterprise 2.0   The application of social media to facilitate the cooperative work of people inside organizations. 294

Enterprise application integration (EAI)   A suite of software applications that integrates existing systems by providing layers of software that connect applications together. 261

Enterprise information system   Information systems that support cross-functional processes and activities in multiple departments. 246

Enterprise processes   Processes that span an organization and support activities in multiple departments. 246

Enterprise resource planning (ERP)   A suite of applications called modules, a database, and a set of inherent processes for consolidating business operations into a single, consistent, computing platform. 254

Entity   In the E-R data model, a representation of some thing that users want to track. Some entities represent a physical object; others represent a logical construct or transaction. 175

Entity-relationship (E-R) data model   A tool for constructing data models that defines the entities stored in a database and the relationships between those entities. 175

Entity-relationship (E-R) diagrams   A type of diagram used by database designers to document entities and their relationships to each other. 177

ERP system   An information system based upon ERP technology. 254

Ethernet   Another name for the IEEE 802.3 protocol, Ethernet is a communications standard that specifies how messages are to be packaged, processed, and transmitted for wired transmission over a LAN. 207

Exabyte (EB)   1,024 PB. 116

Experimentation   A careful and reasoned analysis of an opportunity, envisioning potential products or solutions or applications of technology, and then developing those ideas that seem to have the most promise, consistent with the resources you have. 9

Expert systems   Rule-based systems that encode human knowledge in the form of if/then rules. 353

Expert systems shells   A program in an expert system that processes a set of rules, typically many times, until the values of the variables no longer change, at which point the system reports the results. 353

FIDO   Fast Identity OnLine. A set of open standards and protocols under development as an alternative to password authentication. 487

Fields   Also called *columns*; groups of bytes in a database table. A database table has multiple columns that are used to represent the attributes of an entity. Examples are *PartNumber*, *EmployeeName*, and *SalesDate*. 160

File   A group of similar rows or records. In a database, sometimes called a *table*. 160

File server   A networked computer that stores files. 53

File Transfer Protocol (ftp)   An applications-layer protocol used to transfer files over the Internet. 217

Firewall   Computing devices located between public and private networks that prevent unauthorized access to or from the internal network. A firewall can be a special-purpose computer or it can be a program on a general-purpose computer or on a router. 468

Firmware   Computer software that is installed into devices such as printers, print services, and various types of communication devices. The software is coded just like other software, but it is installed into special, programmable memory of the printer or other device. 123

Five-component framework   The five fundamental components of an information system—computer hardware, software, data, procedures, and people—that are present in every information system, from the simplest to the most complex. 11

Five forces model   Model, proposed by Michael Porter, that assesses industry characteristics and profitability by means of five competitive forces—bargaining power of suppliers, threat of substitution, bargaining power of customers, rivalry among firms, and threat of new entrants. 84

Folksonomy   A structure of content that emerges from the activity and processing of many users. 294

Foreign keys   A column or group of columns used to represent relationships. Values of the foreign key match values of the primary key in a different (foreign) table. 163

Functional application   Software that provides features and functions necessary to support a particular business activity (function). 245

Functional information systems   Workgroup information systems that support a particular business function. 245

Gantt chart   A chart that shows tasks, dates, dependencies, and possibly resources. 399

Gigabyte (GB)   1,024 MB. 116

GNU   A set of tools for creating and managing open source software. Originally created to develop an open source Unix-like operating system. 123

GNU general public license (GPL) agreement   One of the standard license agreements for open source software. 123

Google Drive   A free thin-client application for sharing documents, spreadsheets, presentations, drawings, and other types of data. Includes version tracking. Formerly known as Google Docs. 53

Gramm-Leach-Bliley (GLB) Act   Passed by Congress in 1999, this act protects consumer financial data stored by financial institutions, which are defined as banks, securities firms, insurance companies, and organizations that provide financial advice, prepare tax returns, and provide similar financial services. 464

Granularity   The level of detail in data. Customer name and account balance is large granularity data. Customer name, balance, and the order details and payment history of every customer order is smaller granularity. 339

Graphical queries   Queries in which criteria are created when the user clicks on a graphic. 172

Green computing   Environmentally conscious computing consisting of three major components: power management, virtualization, and e-waste management. 447

Hacking   A form of computer crime in which a person gains unauthorized access to a computer system. Although some people hack for the sheer joy of doing it, other hackers invade systems for the malicious purpose of stealing or modifying data. 456

Hadoop   An open-source program supported by the Apache Foundation that manages thousands of computers and which implements MapReduce. 351

Hardening   A term used to describe server operating systems that have been modified to make them especially difficult for them to be infiltrated by malware. 474

Health Insurance Portability and Accountability Act (HIPAA)   The privacy provisions of this 1996 act give individuals the right to access health data created by doctors and other health-care providers. HIPAA also sets rules and limits on who can read and receive a person's health information. 464

Hives   In social media, a group of people related by a common interest. 285

Honeypots   False targets for computer criminals to attack. To an intruder, a honeypot looks like a particularly valuable resource, such as an unprotected Web site, but in actuality the only site content is a program that determines the attacker's IP address. 477

Hop   In an internet, the movement from one network to another. 209

Horizontal-market application   Software that provides capabilities common across all organizations and industries; examples include word processors, graphics programs, spreadsheets, and presentation programs. 122

Host operating system   In virtualization, the operating system that hosts the virtual operating systems. 120

https   An indication that a Web browser is using the SSL/TLS protocol to provide secure communication. 217, 468

Human capital   The investment in human knowledge and skills with the expectation of future gain. 295

Human safeguards   Steps taken to protect against security threats by establishing appropriate procedures for users to following during system use. 472

Hyper-social knowledge management The application of social media and related applications for the management and delivery of organizational knowledge resources. 356

Hyper-social organization An organization that uses social media to transform its interactions with customers, employees, and partners into mutually satisfying relationships with them and their communities. 299

Hypertext Transfer Protocol (http) An application-layer protocol used between browsers and Web servers. 217

ICANN (Internet Corporation for Assigned Names and Numbers) The organization responsible for managing the assignment of public IP addresses and domain names for use on the Internet. Each public IP address is unique across all computers on the Internet. 210

Identification The process whereby an information system identifies a user by requiring the user to sign on with a user name and password. 466

Identifier An attribute (or group of attributes) whose value is associated with one and only one entity instance. 175

IEEE 802.3 protocol A standard for packaging and managing traffic on wired local area networks. 207

IEEE 802.11 protocol A standard for packaging and managing traffic on wireless local area networks. 207

If/Then rules Statements that specify that if a particular condition exists, then a particular action should be taken. Used for both expert systems and decision trees. 353

Implementation In the context of the systems development life cycle, the phase following the design phase consisting of tasks to build, test, and convert users to the new system. 395

Industry-specific solutions An ERP template that is designed to serve the needs of companies or organizations in specific industries. Such solutions save time and lower risk. The development of industry-specific solutions spurred ERP growth. 264

Information (1) Knowledge derived from data, where *data* is defined as recorded facts or figures; (2) data presented in a meaningful context; (3) data processed by summing, ordering, averaging, grouping, comparing, or other similar operations; (4) a difference that makes a difference. 16

Information silo A condition that exists when data are isolated in separated information systems. 249

Information system (IS) A group of hardware, software, data, procedure, and people components that interact to produce information. 11

Information technology (IT) The products, methods, inventions, and standards that are used for the purpose of producing information. 15

Infrastructure as a service (IaaS) The cloud hosting of a bare server computer or data storage. 219

Inherent processes The procedures that must be followed to effectively use licensed software. For example, the processes inherent in ERP systems assume that certain users will take specified actions in a particular order. In most cases, the organization must conform to the processes inherent in the software. 253

Inter-enterprise information systems Information systems that support one or more inter-enterprise processes. 247

Inter-enterprise processes Processes that span two or more independent organizations. 246

Internal firewalls Firewalls that sit inside the organizational network. 468

Internet When spelled with a small *i*, as in *internet*, a private network of networks. When spelled with a capital *I*, as in *Internet*, the public internet known as the Internet. 206

Internet service provider (ISP) An ISP provides users with Internet access. An ISP provides a user with a legitimate Internet address; it serves as the user's gateway to the Internet; and it passes communications back and forth between the user and the Internet. ISPs also pay for the Interent. They collect money from their customers and pay access fees and other charges on the users' behalf. 208

Intranet A private internet (note small *i*) used within a corporation or other organization. 206

Intrusion detection system (IDS) A computer program that senses when another computer is attempting to scan the disk or otherwise access a computer. 460

iOS The operating system used on the iPhone, iPod Touch, and iPad. 119

IP address A series of dotted decimals in a format like 192.168.2.28 that identifies a unique device on a network or internet. 210

IP spoofing A type of spoofing whereby an intruder uses another site's IP address as if it were that other site. 456

IPv4 The most commonly used Internet layer protocol; has a four-decimal dotted notation, such as 165.193.123.253. 211

IPv6 An Internet layer protocol that uses 128-bit addresses and is gradually replacing IPv4. 211

Just-in-time data Data delivered to the user at the time it is needed. 136

Just-in-time design Rather than design the complete, overall system at the beginning, only those portions of the design that are neede to complete the current work are done. Common for agile development techniques such as scrum. 407

Key (1) A column or group of columns that identifies a unique row in a table. Also referred to as a Primary Key.

(2) A number used to encrypt data. The encryption algorithm applies the key to the original message to produce the coded message. Decoding (decrypting) a message is similar; a key is applied to the coded message to recover the original text. 162, 467

Key escrow A control procedure whereby a trusted party is given a copy of a key used to encrypt database data. 471

Key loggers Malicious spyware that captures keystrokes without the user's knowledge. Used to steal user names, passwords, account numbers, and other sensitive data. 146

Key users Users trained to perform social media (SM) engagement and management tasks. 303

Kilobyte (K) 1,024 bytes. 116

Knowledge management (KM) The process of creating value from intellectual capital and sharing that knowledge with employees, managers, suppliers, customers, and others who need it. 352

Libraries In version-control collaboration systems, shared directories that allow access to various documents by means of permissions. 57

License A contract that stipulates how a program can be used. Most specify the number of computers on which the program can be installed, some specify the number of users that can connect to and use the program remotely. Such agreements also stipulate limitations on the liability of the software vendor for the consequences of errors in the software. 121

Lift In market-basket terminology, the ratio of confidence to the base probability of buying an item. Lift shows how much the base probability changes when other products are purchased. If the lift is greater than 1, the change is positive; if it is less than 1, the change is negative. 347

Linkages In Porter's model of business activities, interactions across value chain activities. 90

Linux A version of Unix that was developed by the open-source community. The open-source community owns Linux, and there is no fee to use it. Linux is a popular operating system for Web servers. 119

Local area network (LAN) A network that connects computers that reside in a single geographic location on the premises of the company that operates the LAN. The number of connected computers can range from two to several hundred. 206

Localizing The process of making a computer program work in more than one human language. 492

Lost-update problem A problem that exists in database applications in which two users update the same data item, but only one of those changes is recorded in the data. Can be resolved using locking. 174

Mac OS An operating system developed by Apple Computer Inc., for the Macintosh. The current version is Mac OS X Initially, Macintosh computers were used primarily by graphic artists and workers in the arts community, but today Macs are used more widely. 118

Machine code Code that has been compiled from source code and is ready to be processed by a computer. Cannot be understood by humans. 126

Main memory Memory that works in conjunction with the CPU. Stores data and instructions read by the CPU and stores the results of the CPU's computations. 114

Maintenance In the context of information systems, (1) to fix the system to do what it was supposed to do in the first place or (2) to adapt the system to a change in requirements. 396

Malware Viruses, worms, Trojan horses, spyware, and adware. 469

Malware definitions Patterns that exist in malware code. Antimalware vendors update these definitions continuously and incorporate them into their products in order to better fight against malware. 470

Management information systems (MIS) The development and use of information systems that help organizations achieve their strategy. 10

Managerial decisions Decisions that concern the allocation and use of resources. 42

Many-to-many (N:M) relationships Relationships involving two entity types in which an instance of one type can relate to many instances of the second type, and an instance of the second type can relate to many instances of the first. For example, the relationship between Student and Class is N:M. One student may enroll in many classes, and one class may have many students. Contrast with *one-to-many relationships*. 177

MapReduce A two-phase technique for harnessing the power of thousands of computers working in parallel. During the first phase, the Map phase, computers work on a task in parallel; during the second phase, the Reduce phase, the work of separate computers in combined, eventually obtaining a single result. 349

Margin The difference between the value that an activity generates and the cost of the activity. 88

Market-basket analysis A data mining technique for determining sales patterns. A market-basket analysis shows the products that customers tend to buy together. 346

Mashup The combining of output from two or more Web sites into a single user experience. 306

Maximum cardinality The maximum number of entities that can be involved in a relationship. Common examples of maximum cardinality are 1:N, N:M, and 1:1. 178

Measure The data item of interest on an OLAP report. It is the item that is to be summed, averaged, or otherwise processed in the OLAP cube. Total sales, average sales, and average cost are examples of measures. 342

Megabyte (MB) 1,024 KB. 116

Metadata Data that describe data. 163

Microsoft Windows The most popular nonmobile client operating system. Also refers to Windows Server, a popular server operating system that competes with Linux. 117

Minimum cardinality The minimum number of entities that must be involved on one side of a relationship, typically zero or one. 178

Mobile device A small, lightweight, power-conserving, computing device that is capable of wireless access. 131

Mobile device management (MDM) software Products that install and update mobile-device software, backup and restore mobile devices, wipe software and data from devices in the event the device is lost or the employee leaves the company. Such products also report usage and provide other mobile device management data. 143

Mobile systems Information systems that support users in motion. 131

Modern-style applications Windows applications that are touch-screen oriented and provide context-sensitive, pop-up menus. 118

Modules A suite of applications in an ERP system. 254

MongoDB An open-source, document-oriented, non-relational DBMS. 184

Moore's Law A law, created by Gordon Moore, stating that the number of transistors per square inch on an integrated chip doubles every 18 months. Moore's prediction has proved generally accurate in the 40 years since it was made. Sometimes this law is stated that the performance of a computer doubles every 18 months. Although not strictly true, this version gives the gist of the idea. 5

Multi-user processing When multiple users process the database at the same time. 174

My Maps A browser-based mapping system provided by Google that enables users to mash up their content with content provided by others as well as with maps provided by Google. 306

MySQL A popular open source DBMS product that is license-free for most applications. 166

Native application A thick-client application that is designed to work with a particular operating system, and sometimes further limited to work only with a particular mobile device that runs that operating system. 117

Network A collection of computers that communicate with one another over transmission lines. 206

Neural networks A popular supervised data mining technique used to predict values and make classifications, such as "good prospect" or "poor prospect." 346

Nonvolatile Memory that preserves data contents even when not powered (e.g., magnetic and optical disks). With such devices, you can turn the computer off and back on, and the contents will be unchanged. 116

Normal forms Forms of tables that remove duplicated data and other problems. 180

Normalization The process of converting poorly structured tables into two or more better-structured tables. 178

NoSQL databases Nonrelational databases that support very high transaction rates processing relatively simple data structures, replicated on many servers in the cloud. 184

Object Management Group (OMG) A software industry standards organization that created a standard set of terms and graphical notations for documenting business processes. 384

Object-oriented When referring to languages, ones that can be used to create difficult, complex applications, and, if used properly, will result in high-performance code that is easy to alter when requirements change 127

Off-the-shelf software Software that is used without making any changes. 122

Off-the-shelf with alterations software Software bought off-the-shelf but altered to fit an organization's specific needs. 122

OLAP cube A presentation of an OLAP measure with associated dimensions. The reason for this term is that some products show these displays using three axes, like a cube in geometry. Same as *OLAP report*. 342

One-of-a-kind application Software that is developed for a specific, unique need, usually for a single company's requirements. 122

One-to-many (1:N) relationships Relationships involving two entity types in which an instance of one type can relate to many instances of the second type, but an instance of the second type can relate to at most one instance of the first. For example, the relationship between *Department* and *Employee* is 1:N. A department may relate to many employees, but an employee relates to at most one department. 177

Online analytical processing (OLAP) A dynamic type of reporting system that provides the ability to sum, count, average, and perform other simple arithmetic operations on groups of data. Such reports are dynamic because users can change the format of the reports while viewing them. 342

Open source   1) Source code that is available for a community to access; 2) A collaborative effort by which software developers create a product such as Linux; the developers often volunteer their time. In most cases, the jointly-developed product can be used without paying a license fee. 126

Operating system (OS)   A computer program that controls the computer's resources: It manages the contents of main memory, processes keystrokes and mouse movements, sends signals to the display monitor, reads and writes disk files, and controls the processing of other programs. 117

Operational decisions   Decisions that concern the day-to-day activities of an organization. 42

Oracle Database   A popular, enterprise-class DBMS product from Oracle Corporation. 166

Organizational feasibility   Whether an information system fits within an organization's customer, culture, and legal requirements. 392

Outsourcing   The process of hiring another organization to perform a service. Outsourcing is done to save costs, to gain expertise, and to free up management time. 431

Over the Internet   When applied to cloud computing, the provisioning of world-wide servers over the Internet. 201

Packet analyzer   Program used for appropriate purposes to read, record, and display all of the wireless packets that are broadcast in the vicinity of the computer running the analyzer. 230

Packet-filtering firewall   A firewall that examines each packet and determines whether to let the packet pass. To make this decision, it examines the source address, the destination addresses, and other data. 469

Packet sniffers   Program used for inappropriate purposes to read, record, and display all of the wireless packets that are broadcast in the vicinity of the computer running the sniffer. 230

Paired programming   The situation in which two computer programmers share the same computer and develop a computer program together. 408

Parallel installation   A type of system conversion in which the new system runs in parallel with the old one and the results of the two are reconciled for consistency. Parallel installation is expensive because the organization incurs the costs of running both systems, but it is the safest form of installation. 396

Partitioned database   A distributed database that divides the database into nonoverlapping segments. 494

Payload   The program codes of a virus that causes unwanted or hurtful actions, such as deleting programs or data, or even worse, modifying data in ways that are undetected by the user. 146, 469

Pay per click   Revenue model in which advertisers display ads to potential customers for free and pay only when the customer clicks. 306

PC virtualization   Synonym for *desktop virtualization*. 120

People   As part of the five-component framework, one of the five fundamental components of an information system; includes those who operate and service the computers, those who maintain the data, those who support the networks, and those who use the system. 11

Perimeter firewall   A firewall that sits outside the organizational network; it is the first device that Internet traffic encounters. 468

Personal identification number (PIN)   A form of authentication whereby the user supplies a number that only he or she knows. 466

Petabyte (PB)   1,024 TB 116

Phased installation   A type of system conversion in which the new system is installed in pieces across the organization(s). Once a given piece works, then the organization installs and tests another piece of the system, until the entire system has been installed. 396

Phisher   An individual or organization that spoofs legitimate companies in an attempt to illegally capture personal data, such as credit card numbers, email accounts, and driver's license numbers. 456

Phishing   A technique for obtaining unauthorized data that uses pretexting via email. The *phisher* pretends to be a legitimate company and sends an email requesting confidential data, such as account numbers, Social Security numbers, account passwords, and so forth. 456

Pig   Query language used with Hadoop. 352

Pilot installation   A type of system conversion in which the organization implements the entire system on a limited portion of the business. The advantage of pilot implementation is that if the system fails, the failure is contained within a limited boundary. This reduces exposure of the business and also protects the new system from developing a negative reputation throughout the organization(s). 395

PixelSense   The Microsoft product formerly known as Surface. It allows many users to process the same table-top touch interface. Primarily used in hotels and entertainment centers. 152

Platform as a service (PaaS)   Vendors provide hosted computers, an operating system, and possibly a DBMS. 219

Plunge installation   A type of system conversion in which the organization shuts off the old system and starts the new system. If the new system fails, the organization is in trouble: Nothing can be done until either the new system is fixed or the old system is reinstalled. Because of the risk, organizations should avoid this conversion style if possible. Sometimes called *direct installation.* 396

Pooled The situation in which many different organizations use the same physical hardware. 200

Power curve A graph that shows the relationship of the power (the utility that one gains from a software product) as a function of the time using that product. 65

Predictive policing Using data on past crimes to predict where future crimes are likely to occur. 328

Pretexting Deceiving someone over the Internet by pretending to be another person or organization. 456

Primary activities Activities that contribute directly to the production, sale, or service of a product. 88

Primary key One or more columns in a relation whose values identify a unique row of that relation. Also known as a key. 162

Privacy Act of 1974 Federal law that provides protections to individuals regarding records maintained by the U.S. government. 464

Private cloud In-house hosting, delivered via Web service standards, which can be dynamically configured. 224

Private IP address A type of IP address used within private networks and internets. Private IP addresses are assigned and managed by the company that operates the private network or internet. 210

Problem A *perceived* difference between what is and what ought to be. 44

Procedures Instructions for humans. One of the five fundamental components of an information system. 11

Process blueprints In an ERP application, comprehensive sets of inherent processes for all organizational activities, each of which is documented with diagrams that use a set of standardized symbols. 263

Process effectiveness A measure of how well a process achieves organizational strategy. 247

Process efficiency A measure of the ratio of process outputs to inputs. 247

Project data Data that is part of a collaboration's work product. 46

Project metadata Data that is used to manage a project. Schedules, tasks, budgets, and other managerial data are examples. 46

Protocol A set of rules for packaging and processing traffic on a network. 206

Public IP Address An IP address used to identify a particular device on the Internet. Such IP addresses are assigned to major institutions in blocks by the Internet Corporation for Assigned Names and Numbers (ICANN). Each IP address is unique across all computers on the Internet. 210

Public key/private key A special version of asymmetric encryption that is popular on the Internet. With this method, each site has a public key for encoding messages and a private key for decoding them. 467

Publish results The process of delivering business intelligence to the knowledge workers who need it. 329

Pull data Data that mobile or other computing devices request from the server. 141

Pull publishing In business intelligence (BI) systems, the mode whereby users must request BI results. 329

Push data Data that the server sends to or pushes onto mobile or other computing devices. 141

Push publishing In business intelligence (BI) systems, the mode whereby the BI system delivers business intelligence to users without any request from the users, according to a schedule, or as a result of an event or particular data condition. 329

Quad processor A computer with four CPUs. 114

Quick Launch A menu with links to important content on a SharePoint site. 75

RAM Random Access Memory. Another name for a computer's main memory. 114

Records Also called *rows*, groups of columns in a database table. 160

Regression analysis A type of supervised data mining that estimates the values of parameters in a linear equation. Used to determine the relative influence of variables on an outcome and also to predict future values of that outcome. 345

Relation The more formal name for a database table. 163

Relational databases Databases that store data in the form of relations (tables with certain restrictions) and that represents record relationships using foreign keys. 163

Relationships Associations among entities or entity instances in an E-R model or an association among rows of a table in a relational database. 176

Remote action system An information system that provides action at a distance, such as telesurgery or telelaw enforcement. 228

Replicated database A distributed database that contains copies of the same data items. 494

Reporting application A business intelligence application that inputs data from one or more sources and applies reporting operations to that data to produce business intelligence. 340

Repository In a business process model, a collection of something; for example, a database is a repository of data. 90

Requirements analysis   The second phase in the SDLC, in which developers conduct user interviews; evaluate existing systems; determine new forms/reports/queries; identify new features and functions, including security; and create the data model. 388

Resources   People or information system applications that are assigned to roles in business processes. 380

RFM analysis   A technique readily implemented with basic reporting operations to analyze and rank customers according to their purchasing patterns. 341

Rich directory   An employee directory that includes not only the standard name, email, phone, and address, but also expertise, organizational relationships, and other employee data. 357

Roaming   Occurs when users move their activities, especially long-running transactions, across devices. 140

Roles   In a business process, collections of activities. 380

Rows   Also called *records*, groups of columns in a database table. 160

Safeguard   Any action, device, procedure, technique, or other measure that reduces a system's vulnerability to a threat. 454

Schedule feasibility   Whether an information system will be able to be developed on the timetable needed. 389

Screen-sharing applications   Applications that offer users the ability to view the same whiteboard, application, or other display over a network. 48

SEAMS   In social media, a process for transitioning organizational messaging from a structured to a dynamic process. 301

Secure Sockets Layer (SSL)   A protocol that uses both asymmetric and symmetric encryption. When SSL is in use, the browser address will begin with https://. The most recent version of SSL is called TLS. 468

Seekers of the truth   In social media, a community that shares to learn something, solve a problem, or make something happen. 291

Self-efficacy   A person's belief that he or she can successfully perform the tasks required in his or her job. 267

Semantic security   Concerns the unintended release of protected data through the release of a combination of reports or documents that are not protected independently. 362

Server   A computer that provides some type of service, such as hosting a database, running a blog, publishing a Web site, or selling goods. Server computers are faster, larger, and more powerful than client computers. 114

Server farm   A large collection of server computers that is organized to share work and compensate for one another's failures. 114

Server tier   In the three-tier architecture, the tier that consists of computers that run Web servers for generating Web pages and responding to requests from browsers. Web servers also process application programs. 212

Server virtualization   The process of running two or more operating system instances on the same server. The host operating system runs virtual operating system instances as applications. 120

Service-oriented architecture (SOA)   A design philosophy that dictates that all interactions among computing devices are defined as services in a formal, standardized way. SOA makes the cloud possible. 213

Showrooming   The practice of visiting a brick-and-mortar store to examine and evaluate products with the intention of later buying those products on the Internet. 132

Simple Mail Transfer Protocol (smtp)   The protocol used for email transmission. 217

Site license   A license purchased by an organization to equip all the computers on a site with certain software. 121

Slates   Synonym for a tablet device, increasingly obsolete. 114

SLATES   Acronym developed by Andrew McAfee that summarizes key characteristics of Enterprise 2.0: search, links, author, tagged, extensions, signaled. 294

Small office/home office (SOHO)   A business office with usually fewer than 10 employees often located in the business professional's home. 206

Smart cards   Plastic cards similar to credit cards that have microchips. The microchip, which holds much more data than a magnetic strip, is loaded with identifying data. Normally requires a PIN. 466

Sniffing   A technique for intercepting computer communications. With wired networks, sniffing requires a physical connection to the network. With wireless networks, no such connection is required. 456

Social capital   The investment in social relations with expectation of future returns in the marketplace. 295

Social CRM   CRM that includes social networking elements and gives the customer much more power and control in the customer/vendor relationship. 292

Social media (SM)   The use of information technology to support the sharing of content among networks of users. 285

Social media application providers   Companies that operate social media sites. Facebook, Twitter, LinkedIn, and Google are all social media application providers. 288

Social media information system (SMIS)   An information system that supports the sharing of content among networks of users. 285

Social media policy   A statement that delineates employees' rights and responsibilities when generating social media content. 309

Social media sponsors   Companies and other organizations that choose to support a presence on one or more social media sites. 288

Software   Instructions for computers. One of the five fundamental components of an information system. 11

Software as a service (SaaS)   Leasing hardware infrastructure, operating systems, and application programs to another organization. 219

Source code   Computer code as written by humans and that is understandable by humans. Source code must be translated into machine code before it can be processed. 126

Spoofing   When someone pretends to be someone else with the intent of obtaining unauthorized data. If you pretend to be your professor, you are spoofing your professor. 456

Spyware   Programs installed on the user's computer without the user's knowledge or permission that reside in the background and, unknown to the user, observe the user's actions and keystrokes, modify computer activity, and report the user's activities to sponsoring organizations. Malicious spyware captures keystrokes to obtain user names, passwords, account numbers, and other sensitive information. Other spyware is used for marketing analyses, observing what users do, Web sites visited, products examined and purchased, and so forth. 146, 469

SQL injection attack   The situation that occurs when a user obtains unauthorized access to data by entering a SQL statement into a form in which they are supposed to enter a name or other data. If the program is improperly designed, it will accept this statement and make it part of the SQL command that it issues to the DBMS. 470

SQL Server   A popular enterprise-class DBMS product licensed by Microsoft. 166

Stand-up   In scrum, a 15-minute meeting in which each team member states what he/she has done in the past day, what he/she will do in the coming day, and any factors that are blocking his/her progress. 408

Static reports   Business intelligence documents that are fixed at the time of creation and do not change. 358

Steering committee   A group of senior managers from a company's major business functions that works with the CIO to set the IS priorities and decide among major IS projects and alternatives. 431

Storage hardware   Hardware that saves data and programs. Magnetic disks are by far the most common storage device, although optical disks, such as CDs and DVDs, also are popular. 114

Stored procedure   A computer program stored in the database that is used to enforce business rules. 263

Strategic decisions   Decisions that concern broad-scope, organizational issues. 42

Strength of a relationship   In social media, the likelihood that a person or other organization in a relationship will do something that will benefit the organization. 297

Strong password   A password with the following characteristics: at least 10 characters; does not contain the user's user name, real name, or company name; does not contain a complete dictionary word, in any language; is different from the user's previous passwords; and contains both upper- and lowercase letters, numbers, and special characters. 24

Structured decision   A type of decision for which there is a formalized and accepted method for making the decision. 43

Structured processes   Formally defined, standardized processes that involve day-to-day operations: accepting a return, placing an order and purchasing raw materials are common examples. 244

Structured Query Language (SQL)   An international standard language for processing database data. 168

Subscriptions   User requests for particular business intelligence results on a stated schedule or in response to particular events. 359

Supervised data mining   A form of data mining in which data miners develop a model prior to the analysis and apply statistical techniques to data to estimate values of the parameters of the model. 345

Supply chain   A network for organizations and facilities that transforms raw materials into products delivered to customers. 495

Support   In market-basket terminology, the probability that two items will be purchased together. 346

Support activities   In Porter's value chain model, the activities that contribute indirectly to value creation: procurement, technology, human resources, and the firm's infrastructure. 88

Surface   a) Until 2012, a Microsoft hardware–software product that enabled people to interact with data on the surface of a table. Renamed PixelSense. b) After 2012, the name of Microsoft's tablet computing device. 124

Swim-lane layout   A process diagram layout similar to swim lanes in a swimming pool; each role in the process is shown in its own horizontal rectangle, or lane. 385

Switching costs   Business strategy of locking in customers by making it difficult or expensive to change to another product or supplier. 95

Symbian   A mobile client operating system that is popular on phones in Europe and the Far East, but less so in North America. 119

Symmetric encryption   An encryption method whereby the same key is used to encode and to decode the message. 467

Synchronous communication Information exchange that occurs when all members of a work team meet at the same time, such as face-to-face meetings or conference calls. 48

System A group of components that interact to achieve some purpose. 11

System conversion The process of converting business activity from the old system to the new. 395

Systems analyst IS professionals who understand both business and technology. They are active throughout the systems development process and play a key role in moving the project from conception to conversion and, ultimately, maintenance. Systems analysts integrate the work of the programmers, testers, and users. 380

Systems development life cycle (SDLC) The classical process used to develop information systems. The basic tasks of systems development are combined into the following phases: system definition, requirements analysis, component design, implementation, and system maintenance (fix or enhance). 387

Systems thinking The mental activity of making one or more models of the components of a system and connecting the inputs and outputs among those components into a sensible whole, one that explains the phenomenon observed. 8

Table Also called *files*, groups of similar rows or records in a database. 160

Target The asset that is desired by a security threat. 454

TCP/IP protocol architecture A protocol architecture having five layers and one or more protocols defined at each layer. Programs are written to implement the rules of a particular protocol. 216

Team surveys Forms of asynchronous communication in which one team member creates a list of questions and other team members respond. Microsoft SharePoint has built-in survey capability. 50

Technical feasibility Whether existing information technology will be able to meet the needs of a new information system. 389

Technical safeguards Security safeguards that involve the hardware and software components of an information system. 466

Telediagnosis A remote access system used by health care professionals to provide expertise in rural or remote areas. 228

Telelaw enforcement A remote access system that provides law enforcement capability. 228

Telesurgery A remote access system that links surgeons to robotic equipment and patients at a distance. 228

Terabyte (TB) 1,024 GB. 116

Test plan Groups of action and usage sequences for validating the capability of new using software. 395

Text mining The application of statistical techniques on text streams for locating particular words, patterns of particular words, and even correlating those word counts and patterns with personality profiles. 233

The Internet The public collection of networks used for transmitting data, worldwide. 206

The Singularity The point at which computer systems become sophisticated enough that they can create and adapt their own software and hence adapt their behavior without human assistance. 351

Thick-client application A software application that requires programs other than just the browser on a user's computer; that is, that requires code on both client and server computers. See also *native application*. 117

Thin-client application A software application that requires nothing more than a browser. 117

Third-party cookie A cookie created by a site other than the one visited. 369

Threat A person or organization that seeks to obtain or alter data or other IS assets illegally, without the owner's permission and often without the owner's knowledge. 453

Three-tier architecture Architecture used by most e-commerce server applications. The tiers refer to three different classes of computers. The user tier consists of users' computers that have browsers that request and process Web pages. The server tier consists of computers that run Web servers and in the process generate Web pages and other data in response to requests from browsers. Web servers also process application programs. The third tier is the database tier, which runs the DBMS that processes the database. 212

Trade-off In project management, a balancing of three critical factors: requirements, cost, and time. 401

Train the trainer Training sessions in which vendors train the organization's employees, called Super Users, to become in-house trainers in order to improve training quality and reduce training expenses. 263

Transport Layer Security (TLS) The new name for a later version of Secure Sockets Layer (SSL). 468

Tribes In social media, groups of people related by a common interest. 285

Trigger A computer program stored within the database that is executed when certain conditions arise. Primarily used to maintain database consistency. 263

Trojan horses Viruses that masquerade as useful programs or files. A typical Trojan horse appears to be a computer game, an MP3 music file, or some other useful, innocuous program. 146, 469

Tunnel A virtual, private pathway over a public or shared network from the VPN client to the VPN server. 224

Unified Modeling Language (UML) A series of diagramming techniques that facilitates OOP development. UML has dozens of different diagrams for all phases of system development. UML does not require or promote any particular development process. Generally less popular that the E-R model. 175

Unix An operating system developed at Bell Labs in the 1970s. It has been the workhorse of the scientific and engineering communities since then. 119

Unstructured decision A type of decision for which there is no agreed-on decision-making method. 43

Unsupervised data mining A form of data mining whereby the analysts do not create a model or hypothesis before running the analysis. Instead, they apply the data mining technique to the data and observe the results. With this method, analysts create hypotheses after the analysis to explain the patterns found. 345

URL (Uniform Resource Locator) An address on the Internet. Consists of a protocol followed by a domain name or public IP address. 211

Use increases value The concept that the more people use a site, the more value it has, and the more people will visit. Furthermore, the more value a site has, the more existing users will return. 306

User experience (UX) A term that refers not only to the user interface (UI), but also to the way the application affects the user's emotions and motivation to continue to use the interface. 137

User-generated content (UGC) Content on an organization's social media presence that is contributed by nonemployee users. 310

User interface (UI) The presentation format of an application that consists of windows, menus, icons, dialog boxes, toolbars, etc., as well as user content. 137

User tier In the three-tier architecture, the tier that consists of computers, phones, and other mobile devices that have browsers and request or process Web pages and other services. 212

Usurpation Occurs when unauthorized programs invade a computer system and replace legitimate programs. Such unauthorized programs typically shut down the legitimate system and substitute their own processing to spy, steal and manipulate data, or achieve other purposes. 457

Value As defined by Porter, the amount of money that a customer is willing to pay for a resource, product, or service. 88

Value chain A network of value-creating activities. 88

Value of social capital Value of social network that is determined by the number of relationships in a social network, by the strength of those relationships, and by the resources controlled by those related. 295

Velocity In scrum, the total number of points of work that a team can accomplish in each scrum period. 411

Version control The process that occurs when the collaboration tool limits and sometimes even directs user activity. 57

Version management Tracking of changes to documents by means of features and functions that accommodate concurrent work. 53

Vertical-market application Software that serves the needs of a specific industry. Examples of such programs are those used by dental offices to schedule appointments and bill patients, those used by auto mechanics to keep track of customer data and customers' automobile repairs, and those used by parts warehouses to track inventory, purchases, and sales. 122

Videoconferencing Communication technology that enables online conferencing using video. 49

Viral hook An inducement that causes someone to share an ad, link, file, picture, movie, or other resource with friends and associates over the Internet. 287

Virtualization The process whereby multiple operating systems run as clients on a single host operating system. Gives the appearance of many computers running on a single computer. 120

Virtual machines (vm) Computer programs that present the appearance of an independent operating system within a second host operating system. The host can support multiple virtual machines, possibly running different operating system programs (Windows, Linux), each of which is assigned assets such as disk space, devices, network connections, over which it has control. 120

Virtual meetings Meetings in which participants do not meet in the same place and possibly not at the same time. 48

Virtual private cloud (VPC) A subset of a public cloud that has highly restricted, secure access. 225

Virtual private network (VPN) A WAN connection alternative that uses the Internet or a private internet to create the appearance of private point-to-point connections. In the IT world, the term *virtual* means something that appears to exist that does not exist in fact. Here, a VPN uses the public Internet to create the appearance of a private connection. 223

Virus A computer program that replicates itself. 146, 469

Volatile Data that will be lost when the computer or device is not powered. 116

Vulnerability An opportunity for threats to gain access to individual or organizational assets. Some vulnerabilities exist because there are no safeguards or because the existing safeguards are ineffective. 454

WAN wireless A communications system that provides wireless connectivity to a wide area network. 209

Waterfall method The assumption that one phase of the SDLC can be completed in its entirety and the project can progress, without any backtracking, to the next phase of the SDLC. Projects seldom are that simple; backtracking is normally required. 403

Web 2.0 Web-delivered services and content that are paid for by advertising. 306

Webinar A virtual meeting in which attendees can view a common presentation on one of the attendee's computer screen for formal and organized presentations. 49

Web page Document encoded in HTML that is created, transmitted, and consumed using the World Wide Web. 212

Web servers programs that run on a server-tier computer and that manage HTTP traffic by sending and receiving Web pages to and from clients and by processing client requests. 212

Wide area network (WAN) A network that connects computers at different geographic locations. 206

Windows RT A version of Windows 8 that is specifically designed to provide a touch-based interface for devices that use ARM architecture, including phones, tablets, and some computers. 120

Windows Server A version of Windows that has been specifically designed and configured for server use. It has much more stringent and restrictive security procedures than other versions of Windows and is popular on servers in organizations that have made a strong commitment to Microsoft. 120

Work breakdown structure (WBS) A hierarchy of the tasks required to complete a project; for a large project, it might involve hundreds or thousands of tasks. 397

Workflow control Collaboration tool feature in which software manages the flow of documents, approvals, rejections, and other characteristics among a collaborating team. 58

Workgroup information system An information system that supports a particular department or workgroup. 245

Workgroup process A process that exists to enable work groups to fulfill the charter, purpose, and goals of a particular group or department. 245

Worm A virus that propagates itself using the Internet or some other computer network. Worm code is written specifically to infect another computer as quickly as possible. 146, 469